The Personal Writings of Joseph Smith

The Personal Writings of Joseph Smith

Compiled and Edited by Dean C. Jessee

Deseret Book

Salt Lake City, Utah

To my wife, June

©1984 Deseret Book Company
All rights reserved
Printed in the United States of America

No part of this book may be reproduced in any
form or by any means without permission in writing
from the publisher, Deseret Book Company,
P.O. Box 30178, Salt Lake City, Utah 84130

First printing February 1984
Second printing April 1984
Third printing March 1985

Library of Congress Cataloging in Publication Data

Smith, Joseph, 1805-1844.
    The personal writings of Joseph Smith.

    Includes index.
    1. Smith, Joseph, 1805-1844. 2. Mormons—Biography.
I. Jessee, Dean C. II. Title
BX8695.S6A362 1983   289.3'092'4   [B]83-18937
ISBN 0-87747-974-7

Contents

Maps

Photographs

Preface

In general, it matters very little whether or not a person writes his own diaries, letters, and speeches or delegates others to write for him, because, as H. C. Hockett has pointed out, if the one whose name appears on a work is the responsible source of the ideas set forth, he is the real author even if the writing is that of another.[1] There are instances, however, when the question of authorship is of more than passing importance—as in historical studies in which an individual's personality is observable primarily through his own writings. Ernest R. May has noted that no one can pretend to read a person's innermost thoughts or feelings in what someone else wrote for him,[2] and Edward H. Carr adds that biography cannot be written unless the biographer can achieve some kind of special contact with the mind of the person about whose life he is writing.[3] Medievalists have found that in spite of the existence of countless documents bearing the name of Philip the Fair (1268-1314), his contemporaries have written practically nothing that describes his personality, nor have students of that period been able to identify with certainty a single word that could be said to have been written or dictated by him. And although some of the royal papers reveal a unique style, there is no way to know whether the French king may have written or dictated any of them. "We therefore resign ourselves," concludes Charles-Victor Langlois, "we will never know who Philip the Fair was."[4]

The problem of understanding who Joseph Smith was, what his personality was like, is not so hopeless, but nevertheless real. For while the Mormon prophet produced a sizable collection of papers, the question remains as to how clearly they reflect his own thoughts and personality. The answer lies in the documents themselves and becomes particularly clear when we note that the sources are not the *past* but only the raw materials whence we form our *conception* of the past, and in using them we inherit the limitations that produced them—the lack of personal writing, the wide use of clerks taking dictation or even being assigned to write for him, and the editorial reworking of reports of what he did and said. For example, Howard Coray, employed with E. D. Woolley in 1840 to work on the Prophet's *History*, relates that Joseph furnished all the material and that "our business, was not only to combine, and arrange in chronological order, but to spread out or amplify not a little, in as good historical style as may be."[5]

When Joseph Smith began his record-keeping career in the early 1830s, he tenaciously sought to preserve records of personal and public value and to hand down to posterity an accurate picture of his life and the work in which he was engaged. The history he produced is of monumental importance. But limitations inherent in record keeping and history writing have had a screening effect upon our understanding of the Prophet. The very sources that inform also tend to obscure.

One reason for this devolves from Joseph Smith's dependence upon others to write for him. Considering his background and the trying conditions in which he lived, it is doubtful that he would have kept records at all had he not been directed by the Lord to do so. He wrote that because indigent circumstances required the exertions of his father's entire family to sustain themselves, he had been deprived of the benefit of an education, being instructed merely in "reading writing and the ground rules of Arithmatic," which constituted his "whole literary acquirements."⁶

Although Joseph's writing compares favorably with his contemporaries', he seldom used the pen himself, dictating or delegating most of his writing to clerks. A complicated life and feelings of literary inadequacy explain this dependence. He lamented his "lack of fluency in address," his "writing imperfections," and his "inability" to convey his ideas in writing. Communication seemed to him to present an insurmountable barrier. He wrote of the almost "total darkness of paper pen and ink," and the "crooked broken scattered and imperfect language." Toward the end of his life, he rejoiced that for three years he had been able to keep several clerks in constant employ to accompany him "everywhere" and record what he said and did.⁷ But however efficient they may have been, they were unable to fully preserve one essential ingredient in their work that would have been in Joseph's own writings—his own personality. One notes, for example, a marked shift in style between two entries in his "Diary," the first written by the Prophet himself and the other written by his clerk Willard Richards:

September 23 [1835] This day Joseph Smith, Jr. was at home writing blessings for my most beloved brotheren. I have been hindered by a multitude of visitors but the Lord has blessed our souls this day. May God grant to continue his mercies unto my house, this night for Christ sake. This day my Soul has desired the salvation of Brother Ezra Thayr. Also Brother Noah Packard came to my house and let the Chappel Committee have one thousand dollers, by loan, for the building the house of the Lord. Oh may God bless him with an hundred fold, even the things of the earth, for this ritious act. My heart is full of desire to day, to be blessed of the God of Abraham with prosperity, until I will be able to pay all my debts; for it is the delight of my soul to be honest. O Lord that thou knowest right well! Help me and I will give to the poor.

April 17 [1843] Monday. Green grass begins to be seen. Walked out in the city with Clayton. Called on brother Taylor. Handed him the letter purporting to be from the Attorney Gen. of the U. States and gave him instruction about it. Looked at several lots. Called at Samuel Bennets to make arrangements to leave the house above the old burying ground. Returned home. Had conversation with Erastus Snow. Received 50 gold sovereigns of P. P. Pratt for the temple.

Although both entries accurately report Joseph Smith's activities for the days indicated, the reader comes away with very different perceptions of his personality. But because editorial procedures in his day did not require the precise definition of authorship, the distinction was lost when his diaries were incorporated into his *History.*

Another point where Joseph Smith's personality is obscured in writings attributed to him derives from the editorial practice, common even in our own time, of inserting ghostwritten material—writings of other eyewitnesses that have been changed from indirect to direct discourse to give the impression that Joseph wrote them.[8]

This is illustrated in the account of Zion's Camp as recorded in the *History of the Church.* In the absence of a Joseph Smith journal for that period, the compilers used the journal of another participant, Heber C. Kimball, changing his third-person narrative to maintain the first-person format of the *History.* On June 21, 1834, Heber C. Kimball reported the visit of men from Ray County, Missouri, to the Camp to determine its purpose. He noted that as the visitors listened to the Prophet speak, they "melted into compassion . . . arose and offered him their hands, and said they would use their influence to allay the excitement which everywhere prevailed." As reported by Brother Kimball, Joseph Smith comes across as natural and unassuming, but when the dialogue is shifted to first-person narrative to give the impression that Joseph himself is writing ("when I had closed a lengthy speech, the spirit of which melted them into compassion . . ."), there emerges a sense of pride, an almost egotistic image, that may not accurately represent Joseph Smith at all.

The sources indicate that the greatest distortion occurs at points where other personalities have intruded themselves between Joseph and the reader. Even in the preservation of his speeches, one finds a somewhat clouded view because short-hand skills were not sufficiently developed or mastered among Joseph Smith's clerks to allow verbatim reports of what he said, and the procedures for publishing them were also not exact.

While most of the Prophet's discourses have been preserved essentially as reported, one finds an occasional instance where the hand of the editor has been particularly heavy. For example, Willard Richards reported a segment of the Prophet's May 21, 1843, address merely with the words "rough stone rolling down hill." But those who later prepared the discourse for publication fleshed out the notation to read:

I am like a huge, rough stone rolling down from a high mountain; and the only polishing I get is when some corner gets rubbed off by coming in contact with some-thing else, striking with accelerated force against religious bigotry, priestcraft, lawyer-craft, lying editors, suborned judges and jurors, and the authority of perjured executives, backed by mobs, blasphemers, licentious and corrupt men and women—all hell knocking off a corner here and a corner there. Thus I will become a smooth and polished shaft in the quiver of the Almighty, who will give me dominion over all and every one of them, when their refuge of lies shall fail, and their hiding place shall be destroyed, while these smooth-polished stones with which I come in contact be-come marred.

While there is no doubt that the general content of this statement is accurate, the style and hence the impressions of Joseph Smith given here probably reflect the personality of the editor more than they do Joseph's.

If the image of the Prophet that emerges from his writings appears inconsistent or contradictory, the problem may be one of understanding the sources. Like an ancient mummy, all wrapped up for preservation, the detailed outlines of Joseph Smith lie hidden or deformed behind the efforts of numerous clerks, editors, and ghostwriters. To use his letters, diaries, and speeches to understand his personality is confusing unless we can separate his own writings from what others wrote for him. While the writings of those who helped Joseph keep his history are usually accurate in their presentation of subject matter and events, the deeper manifestations of thought and personality may at best be secondhand.

None of Joseph Smith's clerks realized that their methods of preserving what he said and did would, to a certain extent, blur the very individuality they sought to portray. And yet, whatever their literary or editorial shortcomings, the value of their contribution in preserving the records of Joseph's life and times is monumental.

The real importance of Joseph Smith's holograph writings (the writings he produced with his own hand) lies in their being his expression of his own thoughts and attitudes, his own contemplations and reflections. They not only reveal idiosyncrasies of his education and literary orientation but also clearly reflect his inner makeup and state of mind—his moods and feelings. Furthermore, they provide a framework for judging his religious claims.

In 1839 Joseph wrote from the jail at Liberty, Missouri, that "the things of God are of deep import; and time, and experience, and careful and ponderous and solemn thoughts can only find them out."[9] He spent his life defending his claim to a special dispensation of religious knowledge, noting that "the envy and wrath of man" had been his common lot and that "deep water" was what he was wont to swim in.[10] Such was his experience that a little more than a year before his death he told an audience in Nauvoo, "If I had not actually got into this work and been called of God, I would back out. But I cannot back out: I have no doubt of the truth."[11]

The underlying issue facing the student of Joseph Smith is the credibility of Joseph's religious experience. Beginning in his own lifetime, his enemies charged him with deception and fraud, and critics of a later time have argued that the image of Joseph in the pages of his *History* was fashioned by an editorial reworking of the historical sources. Recognizing that final answers to the question of Joseph Smith's religious claims do not lie within the framework of the historical record, I contend that it *is* within that framework that we can evaluate the content of the sources and their use or misuse. If the process of preserving a record of the life of the founder and leader of The Church of Jesus Christ of Latter-day Saints erects a barrier to understanding his motives and personality, the unraveling of that process can serve as a means of identifying him and as a yardstick for comparing the public Joseph with the private one to see how he looks with the editorial props removed. Here then, in these pages, is Joseph Smith presented as clearly as his own writings will allow.

Acknowledgments

To produce a book like this one requires the help of many individuals and institutions. I have benefited from the encouragement of long-suffering friends and the expertise of scores of people with specialized skills and knowledge. Conspicuous for their help during the various stages in the preparation of this work were: my colleagues in the Joseph Fielding Smith Institute for Church History at Brigham Young University, particularly Leonard Arrington, under whose direction the project was conceived; Richard L. Anderson and Charles Tate of Brigham Young University; Noel Barton at the LDS Genealogy Department; James L. Kimball and Jeffery Johnson of the LDS Church Archives; Debbie Lilenquist, formerly with the Church Historical Department; and Ronald A. Millett, Eleanor Knowles, Jack Lyon, Ralph Reynolds, Richard Tice, Karen Morales, Susan Conard, Sylvia Voigt, and Sherie Johnson of Deseret Book Company.

The documents presented here, many in facsimile form, have been obtained from a number of sources including libraries, archives, historical societies, and private collectors of manuscripts. The Church of Jesus Christ of Latter-day Saints holds the largest collection of Joseph Smith papers, and Don Schmidt, the Church archivist, and his staff have rendered assistance without which this work would not have been possible. I thank Richard Howard, historian of the Reorganized

Church of Jesus Christ of Latter Day Saints, and the staff of the RLDS Church Archives at Independence, Missouri, for the use of their valuable holdings on Joseph Smith. Other institutions that have generously cooperated in providing source material are: Yale University Library; the Chicago Historical Society; Illinois State Historical Society; the Historical Society of Pennsylvania; the Henry E. Huntington Library and Art Gallery; the University of Utah Library; and private collectors Brent Ashworth of Provo, Utah; Steven Barnett of Provo, Utah; Dr. J. C. Hayward of Logan, Utah; Mark Hofmann of Salt Lake City; and Richard Marks of Phoenix, Arizona.

In making these acknowledgments I nevertheless assume sole responsibility for defects and errors that inevitably creep into a book of this kind.

Introduction

The papers of Joseph Smith consist of a sizable collection housed mainly in the archives of The Church of Jesus Christ of Latter-day Saints in Salt Lake City, Utah, but significant materials are located at a number of other depositories in the United States. These papers can be listed under five general headings:

1. Sacred writings, which include the Book of Mormon, Book of Moses, Book of Abraham, a revision of the King James Version of the Bible, and numerous separate revelations, most of which have been published in the Doctrine and Covenants. Practically all of these writings have been canonized as scripture by followers of Joseph Smith.

2. Ten diaries or volumes containing diary material covering the time period between November 27, 1832 and June 22, 1844, but with extensive gaps and periods of sketchy information.

3. Manuscript reports of speeches and sermons.

4. Approximately four hundred letters and other documents.

5. A six-volume twenty-three-hundred-page history spanning his lifetime, written between June 1838 and August 1856. This work, begun under the Prophet's direction, draws heavily from the materials in the previous categories.

While the Joseph Smith papers are a substantial expression of his life and times, they are not totally the product of his own mind. The purpose of this book is to present the core of material that most accurately reflects his thought and personality. This includes writings from four specific categories:

1. All of the known holograph writings of Joseph Smith except a revelation copied into a record book, a page from the Kirtland Egyptian papers, and a few brief notes ("Br. Sloane give an order of six dollers and sixty cents for some lime which will be explained, Joseph Smith Mayor"; "Brother Woodworth Please let the bearer have some Lumber &c., Joseph Smith" etc.).

2. A number of documents that were undoubtedly originally holographs but are now available only from handwritten or published copies.

3. A number of items in the handwriting of clerks which state specifically that Joseph is dictating.

4. Materials that are not holographs and are not designated as having been dictated but because of style[1] and content appear to have been dictated—documents that seem to have required his personal attention. From this category, I have not presumed to include everything, but I feel that the writings presented here are highly representative.

The revelations or documents contained in the canon of LDS scripture are not included in this book, except as an occasional one may have been part of a letter or diary.

Editorial Method

To preserve the characteristics of someone's writing is to preserve evidence of personality, literary orientation, training, temperament, and mood. Since a major hindrance to understanding Joseph Smith has been the editorial barrier that arises between him and those who learn about him through reading his writings, I have made an effort to keep editorial intrusion to a minimum. By identifying the holograph and dictated material and presenting these writings as he and his clerks wrote them, I hope to illuminate characteristics of his personality, his educational attainment, and the culture of his age. Letting him speak for himself allows us to see the impact of particular situations upon his expression, the development of his writing ability, the spontaneity and onrush of ideas that characterized his thought, and to see him in much the same light that those who received his letters or read the original documents saw him. In essence, we observe Joseph through a first draft, unimproved by the usual reworking. If this procedure helps define his personality, it also suggests caution in comparing his writings with other works that are not original drafts, for even professional writers are not exempt from refining their prose. James A. Michener has noted that he writes almost everything three times, "and would not even dare to send out the first draft of an important letter." He regarded himself as "not a good writer first time around," but as "one of the world's great rewriters."[2] And Ernest Hemingway confessed that he reworked the ending of *Farewell to Arms* thirty-nine times in order to "[get] the words right."[3]

The following rules have governed the publication of this book:

1. **Everything in Joseph Smith's handwriting is printed in this typeface.**

2. All spelling, punctuation, and capitalization have been retained as they appear in the originals. Where the exact spelling is not clear, current usage is given. Spacing between daily diary entries and some paragraphing have been added.

3. Missing or unintelligible words are indicated by dots and dashes within brackets—dots [..] representing the approximate number of missing letters, and dashes [— —] the approximate number of missing words.

4. Conjectural reading of a missing or unintelligible word is placed within brackets: [absolute].

5. Editorial insertions are italicized and enclosed in brack-

ets [*sentence unfinished*], but expanded initials or textual clarifications are not italicized: W[illiam], ritious [righteous]. Underlined words in the original are italicized.

6. Handwriting other than Joseph Smith's follows a slash mark and note identifying the writer: /[15] The termination of the writer's hand is followed by another slash or by the boldface type indicating Joseph Smith's own handwriting.

7. Line-end hyphenated words in the original are indicated by a double dash at the point of the hyphen: instruc=ted.

8. Superior letters have been lowered: J^r to Jr.

9. Page numbers in brackets designate the end of the page in the original: [p. 1].

10. Occasional smudges of ink are not designated, but where they delete a word or letter they are treated as a strike-through.

11. Above-the-line insertions are enclosed in angle brackets at the point designated in the original manuscript: ‹ ›. If no point of insertion was indicated, the placement of the insertion has been determined by the context.

12. Where a word or letter has been written over, the corrected reading is used; if the change corrects more than a slip of the pen, the original reading is given in a note.

Place names are located on maps in the appendix.

Photographic reproductions of Joseph Smith holographs and samples of clerical handwriting follow the pertinent documents.

Descriptive Symbols

The following symbols have been used to identify and describe the sources used as copy texts.

ADS   *Autograph Document Signed*
       A document written and signed by its author.

ALS   *Autograph Letter Signed*
       A letter written and signed by its author.

Dft   *Draft*
       A preliminary version of a letter of document, usually bearing alterations.

DS   *Document Signed*
       A document written by someone other than its author, but signed by him.

Ds   *Document signed*
       A document written and signed by someone other than its author.

LS   *Letter Signed*
       A letter written by someone other than its author, but signed by him.

Ls   *Letter signed*
       A letter written and signed by someone other than its author.

Ms   *Manuscript*
       A handwritten text.

P   *Published text*
           A letter or document available only in
           published form.
RC   *Retained Copy*
           A retained copy of a letter or document, on
           loose sheets or copied in a letterbook,
           written by someone other than its author,
           but signed by him.
Rc   *Retained copy*
           A retained copy of a letter or document, on
           loose sheets or copied in a letterbook,
           neither written nor signed by its author.
[S]   *Signature excised*
           Used with other symbols to indicate that an
           autograph signature has been cut from the
           document.
Tr   *Transcript*
           A typed or handwritten copy of a document
           made at a substantially later time than the
           original writing.

Part 1
Diaries
and
Histories

History, 1832

The opening words of the revelation given to the newly organized Church of Christ on April 6, 1830 ("Behold, there shall be a record kept among you"), not only marked the beginning of the Mormon record-keeping tradition, but also Joseph Smith's personal writing career.[1] As the work began, the Book of Mormon scribe Oliver Cowdery was assigned to write the Church history;[2] but in March 1831, after Cowdery had been sent to Missouri on other business, John Whitmer was appointed historian in his place.[3] Five months later, Whitmer was assigned, along with the Church printer, William W. Phelps, and the recently returned Oliver Cowdery, to prepare Church revelations and oversee their publication in Missouri. In addition, Whitmer was instructed to "continue in . . . making a history of all the important things which he shall observe" concerning the Church.[4] However, when Joseph Smith visited Missouri in the summer of 1832, he came away with misgivings about the history and subsequently cautioned Whitmer to "remember the commandment to keep a history of the church" and to "show himself approved" in the responsibility of his calling.[5]

The following manuscript, produced in this setting of Joseph Smith's concern about the writing of a Church history, marks his initial personal attempt to record his experience. Written between 20 July and 27 November 1832,[6] and intended as a record of his own life and a history of "the rise of the church," this document is one of several beginnings of a history made during the 1830s as Joseph and his associates struggled to produce a satisfactory record.

A History of the life of Joseph Smith Jr. an account of his marvilous experience and of all the mighty acts which he doeth in the name of Jesus Ch[r]ist the son of the living God of whom he beareth record and also an account of the rise of the church of Christ in the eve of time according as the Lord brough ‹t› forth and established by his hand ‹ firstly› he receiving the testamony from on high seccondly the min=istering of Angels thirdly the reception of the holy Priesthood by the ministring of Aangels to adminster the letter of the Gospel—‹—the Law and commandments as they were given unto him—›and the ordinencs, forthly a confirmation and reception of the high Priesthood after the holy order of the son of the living God pow=er and ordinence from on high to preach the Gospel in the administration and demonstra=tion of the spirit the Kees of the Kingdom of God confered upon him and the continuation of the blessings of God to him &c————I was born in the town of Charon in the ‹State› of Vermont North America on the twenty third day of December AD 1805 of goodly Parents who spared no pains to instructing me in ‹the› christian religion at the age of about ten years my Father Joseph Smith Siegnior moved to Palmyra Ontario County in the State of New York and being in indigent circumstances were obliged to labour hard for the support of a large Family having nine chilldren[7] and as it require=d the exertions of all that were able to render any assistance for the support of the Family therefore we were deprived of the bennifit of an education suffice it to say I was mearly instruc=tid in reading and writing and the ground ‹rules› of Arithmatic which constuted my whole lite=rary acquirements. At about the age of twelve years my mind become seriously imprest [p. 1] with regard to the all important concerns for the well=fare of my immortal Soul which led me to search=ing the

scriptures believeing as I was taught, that they contained the
word of God thus applying myself to them and my intimate
acquaintance with those of different denominations led me to
marvel excedingly for I discovered that ‹they did not ~~adorn~~›
~~instead~~ of adorning their profession by a holy walk and God=ly
conversation agreeable to what I found contain=ed in that sacred
depository this was a grief to my Soul thus from the age of twelve
years to fifteen I pondered many things in my heart concerning
the sittuation of the world of mankind the contentions and
divi[si]ons the wicke[d]ness and abominations and the darkness
which pervaded the ~~of the~~ minds of mankind my mind become
excedingly distressed for I become convicted of my sins and by
searching the scriptures I found that ~~mand~~ ‹mankind› did not
come unto the Lord but that they had apostatised from the true
and liveing faith and there was no society or denomination that
built upon the gospel of Jesus Christ as recorded in the new
testament and I felt to mourn for my own sins and for the sins of
the world for I learned in the scriptures that God was the same
yesterday to day and forever that he was no respecter to persons
for he was God for I looked upon the sun the glorious luminary of
the earth and also the moon rolling in their magesty through the
heavens and also the stars shining in their courses and the earth
also upon whic=h I stood and the beast of the field and the fowls
of heaven and the fish of the waters and also man walking forth
upon the face of the earth in magesty and in the strength of
beauty whose power and intiligence in governing the things
which are so exceding great and [p. 2] marvilous even in
the likeness of him who created ~~him~~ ‹them› and when I
considered upon these things my heart exclai=med well hath the
wise man said ~~the~~ ‹it is a› fool ‹that› saith in his heart there is no
God my heart exclaimed all all these bear testimony and bespeak
an omnipotant and omnipreasant power a being who makith Laws
and decreeeth and bindeth all things in their bounds who filleth
Eternity who was and is and will be from all Eternity to Eternity
and when I considered all these things and that ‹that› being
seeketh such to worship him as wors=hip him in spirit and in

- For other early accounts of the First Vision, see:
  (2) pp. 75, 76 herein. [1835]
  (3) pp. 199, 200 " . [1838]
  6 (4) p. 213 " . [1842]

truth therefore I cried unto the Lord for mercy for there was
none else to whom I could go and ~~to~~ obtain mercy and the Lord
heard my cry in the wilderne=ss and while in ‹the› attitude of
calling upon the Lord ‹in the 16th year of my age› a piller of ~~fire~~
light above the brightness of the sun at noon day come down from
above and rested upon me and I was filled with the spirit of god
and the ‹Lord› opened the heavens upon me and I saw the Lord
and he spake unto me saying Joseph ‹my son› thy sins are
forgiven thee. go thy ‹way› walk in my statutes and keep my
commandments behold I am the Lord of glory I was crucifyed for
the world that all those who believe on my name may have
Eternal life ‹behold› the world lieth in sin ~~and~~ at this time and
none doeth good no not one they have turned asside from the
gospel and keep not ‹my› commandments they draw near to me
with their lips while their hearts are far from me and mine anger
is kindling against the inhabitants of the earth to visit them
acording to th[e]ir ungodliness and to bring to pass that which
‹hath› been spoken by the mouth of the prophe=ts and
Ap[o]stles behold and lo I come quickly as it [is] wr=itten of me
in the cloud ‹clothed› in the glory of my Father and my soul was
filled with love and for many days I could rejoice with great Joy
and the Lord was with me but [I] could find none that would
believe the hevnly vision nevertheless I pondered these things in
my heart ~~about that time my mother and~~ but after many days
[p. 3] I fell into transgression and sinned in many things which
brought a wound upon my soul and there were many things which
transpired that cannot be writen and my Fathers family have
suffered many persicutions and afflictions and it came to pass when
I was seventeen years of age I called again upon the Lord and he
shewed unto me a heavenly vision for behold an angel of the Lord
came and stood before me and it was by night and he called me by
name and he said the Lord had forgiven me my sins and he revealed
unto me that in the Town of Manchester Ontario County N.Y.
there was plates of gold upon which there was engravings which
was engraven by Maroni & his fathers the servants of the living
God in ancient days and deposited by the commandments of God

and kept by the power thereof and that I should go and get them
and he revealed unto me many things concerning the inhabitants
of of the earth which since have been revealed in com=mandments
& revelations and it was on the 22d day of Sept. AD 1822 and thus
he appeared unto me three times in one night and once on the next
day and then I immediately went to the place and found where the
plates was deposited as the angel of the Lord had commanded me
and straightway made three attempts to get them and then being
excedingly frightened I supposed it had been a dreem of Vision but
when I considred I knew that it was not therefore I cried unto the
Lord in the agony of my soul why can I not obtain them behold the
angel appeared unto me again and said unto me you have not kept
the commandments of the Lord which I gave unto you therefore
you cannot now obtain them for the time is not yet fulfilled
therefore thou wast left unto temptation that thou mightest be
made acquainted with the power of the advisary therefore repent
and call on the Lord thou shalt be forgiven and in his own due time
thou shalt obtain them [p. 4] for now I had been tempted of the
advisary and saught the Plates to obtain riches and kept not the
commandment that I should have an eye single to the glory of God
therefore I was chastened and saught diligently to obtain the plates
and obtained them not untill I was twenty one years of age and in
this year I was married to Emma Hale[8] Daughter of Isaach Hale[9]
who lived in Harmony Susquehana County Pensylvania on the
18th [of] January AD. 1827, on the 22d day of Sept of this same
year I ob=tained the plates and ~~the~~ in December following we
mooved to Susquehana by the assistence of a man by the name of
Martin Haris[10] who became convinced of the visions and gave me
fifty Dollars to bare my expences and because of his faith and this
rightheous deed the Lord appeared unto him in a vision and shewed
unto him his marvilous work which he was about to do and ‹he›
imediately came to Su[s]quehanna and said the Lord had shown
him that he must go to new York City with some of the
c‹h›aracters so we proceeded to coppy some of them and he took
his Journy to the Eastern Cittys[11] and to the Learned ‹saying›
read this I pray thee and the learned said I cannot but if he

wo=uld bring the plates they would read it but the Lord had
fo‹r›bid it and he returned to me and gave them to ‹me to›
translate and I said I said [I] cannot for I am not learned but the
Lord had prepared speettieke spectacles for to read the Book
therefore I commenced translating the char=acters and thus the
Prop[h]icy of Is‹ia›ah was fulfilled which is writen in the 29
chapter concerning the book and it came to pass that after we had
translated 116 pages that he desired to carry them to read to his
friends that peradventure he might convince them of the truth
therefore I inquired of the Lord and the Lord said unto me that he
must not take them and I spoke unto him (Martin) the word of the
Lord [p. 5] and he said inquire again and I inquired again and also
the third time and the Lord said unto me let him go with them only
he shall covenant with me that he will not shew them to only but
four persons and he covenented withe Lord that he would do
according to the word of the Lord therefore he took them and took
his journey unto his friends to Palmira Wayne County & State of N
York and he brake the covenent which he made before the Lord
and the Lord suffered the writings to fall into the hands of wicked
men and Martin was chastened for his transgression and I also was
chastened also for my transgression for asking the Lord the third
time[12] wherefore the Plates was taken from me by the power of God
and I was not able to obtain them for a season and it came to pass
after much humility and affliction of soul I obtained them again
when [the] Lord appeared unto a young man by the name of Oliver
Cowdry and shewed unto him the plates in a vision and also the
truth of the work and what the Lord was about to do through me
his unworthy servant therefore he was desirous to come and write
for me and translate[13] now my wife had writen some for me to
translate and also my Brother Samuel H Smith[14] but we had be
come reduced in property and my wives father was about to turn me
out of doors & I had not where to go and I cried unto the Lord that
he would provide for me to accom=plish the work whereunto he
had comman=ded me

A History of the life of Joseph Smith Jr an account
of his marvilous experience and of all the mighty acts
which he doeth in the name of Jesus Christ the son
of the living God of whom he beareth record
and also an account of the rise of the church of
Christ in the eve of time according as the Lord brought
forth and established by his hand firstly he receiving
the testamony from on high secondly the ministr-
istering of Angels thirdly the reception of
the holy Priesthood by the ministring of —
Aangels to administer the letter of the Gospel—
—the Law and commandments as they were given unto him—
and the ordinencs, forthly a confirmation
and reception of the high Priesthood after
the holy order of the son of the living God pow-
-er and ordinenc from on high to preach
the Gospel in the administration and demonstra-
-tion of the spirit the Kees of the Kingdom of God
confered upon him and the continuation of the
blessings of God to him &c ————
I was born in the town of Charon in the State of Vermont
North America on the twenty third day of December
AD 1805 of goodly Parents who spared no pains
to instruct me in the christian religion at the age of
about ten years my Father Joseph Smith Siegnior
moved to Palmyra Ontario county in the State of
New York and being in indigent circumstances were
obliged to labour hard for the support of a large
Family having nine children and as it requir-
=ed the exertions of all that were able to render
any assistance for the support of the Family
therefore we were deprived of the benefit of an
education suffice it to say I was merely instru-
-tied in reading and writing and the ground rules
of Arithmatic which constuted my whole literary acquirements. At about the age of twelve
years my mind become seriously imprest

History, 1832, Joseph Smith Letterbook 1, p. 1. Handwriting of Frederick G. Williams and Joseph Smith. See text, p. 4. (LDS Church Archives.)

2

with regard to the all important concerns for the welfare of my immortal soul which led me to searching the scriptures believing as I was taught, that they contained the word of god thus applying myself to them and my intimate acquaintance with those of different denominations led me to marvel exceedingly for I discovered that they did not adorn their profession by a holy walk and godly conversation agreeable to what I found contained in that sacred depository this was a grief to my soul thus from the age of twelve years to fifteen I pondered many things in my heart concerning the situation of the world of mankind the contentions and divisions the wickeness and abominations and the darkness which pervaded the minds of mankind my mind become exceedingly distressed for I become convicted of my sins and by searching the scriptures I found that mankind did not come unto the Lord but that they had apostatised from the true and living faith and there was no society or denomination that built upon the gospel of Jesus Christ as recorded in the new testament and I felt to mourn for my own sins and for the sins of the world for I learned in the scriptures that God was the same yesterday to day and forever that he was no respecter to persons for he was God for I looked upon the sun the glorious luminary of the earth and also the moon rolling in their majesty through the heavens and also the stars shining in their courses and the earth also upon which I stood and the beast of the field and the fowls of heaven and the fish of the waters and also man walking forth upon the face of the earth in majesty and in the strength of beauty whose power and intelligence in governing the things which are so exceeding great and

History, 1832, Joseph Smith Letterbook 1, p. 2. Handwriting of Joseph Smith. See text, pp. 4-5. (LDS Church Archives.)

marvilous even in the likeness of him who created them and when I considered upon these things my heart exclaimed well hath the wise man said it is a fool that saith in his heart there is no God my heart exclaimed all all these bear testimony and bespeak an omnipotant and omnipresant power a being who makith Laws and decreeeth and bindeth all things in their bounds who filleth Eternity who was and is and will be from all Eternity to Eternity and when I considered all these things and that that being seeketh such to worship him as worship him in spirit and in truth therefore I cried unto the Lord for mercy for there was none else to whom I could go and to obtain mercy and the Lord heard my cry in the wilderness and while in the attitude of calling upon the Lord in the 16th year of my age a pillar of fire light above the brightness of the sun at noon day come down from above and rested upon me and I was filled with the spirit of god and the Lord opened the heavens upon me and I saw the Lord and he spake unto me saying Joseph my son thy sins are forgiven thee. go thy way walk in my statutes and keep my commandments behold I am the Lord of glory I was crucifyed for the world that all those who believe on my name may have Eternal life behold the world lieth in sin at this time and none doeth good no not one they have turned asside from the gospel and keep not my commandments they draw near to me with their lips while their hearts are far from me and mine anger is kindling against the inhabitants of the earth to visit them according to their ungodliness and to bring to pass that which hath been spoken by the mouth of the prophets and apostles behold and lo I come quickly as it was written of me in the cloud clothed in the glory of my Father and my soul was filled with love and for many days I could rejoice with great joy and the Lord was with me but could find none that would believe the heavenly vision nevertheless I pondered these things in my heart but after many days

History, 1832, Joseph Smith Letterbook 1, p. 3. Handwriting of Joseph Smith. See text, pp. 5-6. (LDS Church Archives.)

I fell into transgression and sinned in many things which brought a wound upon my soul and there were many things which transpired that cannot be written and my Father's family have suffered many persecutions and afflictions and it came to pass when I was seventeen years of age I called again upon the Lord and he shewed unto me a heavenly vision for behold an angel of the Lord came and stood before me and it was by night and he called me by name and he said the Lord had forgiven me my sins and he revealed unto me that in the Town of Manchester Ontario County N.Y. there was plates of gold upon which there was engravings which was engraven by Maroni & his fathers the servant of the living God in ancient days and deposited by the commandments of God and kept by the power thereof and that I should go and get them and he revealed unto me many things concerning the inhabitants of the earth which since have been revealed in commandments & revelations and it was on the 22d day of Sept. AD 1822 and thus he appeared unto me three times in one night and once on the next day and then I immediately went to the place and found where the plates was deposited as the angel of the Lord had commanded me and straightway made three attempts to get them and then being exceedingly frightened I supposed it had been a dream of vision but when I considered I knew that it was not therefore I cried unto the Lord in the agony of my soul why can I not obtain them behold the angel appeared unto me again and said unto me you have not kept the commandments of the Lord which I gave unto you therefore you cannot now obtain them for the time is not yet fulfilled therefore thou wast left unto temptation that thou mightest be made acquainted with the power of the advisary therefore repent and call on the Lord thou shalt be forgiven and in his own due time thou shalt obtain them

History, 1832, Joseph Smith Letterbook 1, p. 4. Handwriting of Frederick G. Williams. See text, pp. 6-7. (LDS Church Archives.)

for now I had been tempted of the advorsary and saught [?]
the Plates to obtain riches and kept not the commandment
that I should have an eye single to the glory of God
therefore I was chastened and saught diligently to obtain the
plates and obtained them not until I was twenty one
years of age and in this year I was married to Emma
Hale Daughter of Isaac Hale who lived in Harmony
Susquehana County Pennsylvania on the 18th January
AD 1827, on the 22d day of Sept of this same year I obtained the plates and the in December following we
moved to Susquehana by the assistance of a man by the
name of Martin Harris who became convinced of th[e]
vision and gave me fifty Dollars to bare my expences
and because of his faith and this righteous deed the
Lord appeared unto him in a vision and shewed unto
him his marvilous work which he was about to do
and immediately came to Susquehannah and said the Lord
had shown him that he must go to new york City
with some of the Caracters so we proceeded to copy some
of them and he took his Journey to the Eastern
Cittys and to the Learned saying read this I pray thee
and the learned said I cannot but if he would bring the plates they would read it but
the Lord had forbid it and he returned to me
and gave them to me to translate and I said I
cannot for I am not learned but the Lord
had prepared spectacles for to read
the Book therefore I commenced translating the characters and thus the Prophesy of Isaiah was fulfilled which
is writen in the 29 chap concerning the book and
it came to pass that after we had translated 116
pages that he desired to carry them to read to his
friends that peradventure he might convince them
of the truth therefore I inquired of the Lord and th[e]
Lord said unto me that he must not take them
and I spake unto him (Martin) the word of the Lor[d]

History, 1832, Joseph Smith Letterbook 1, p. 5. Handwriting of Frederick G. Williams and Joseph Smith. See text, pp. 7-8. (LDS Church Archives.)

and he should enquire again and I enquired again
and also the third time and the Lord said unto
me let him go with them only he shall covenant
with me that he will not shew them to only but
four persons and he covenanted with the Lord that he
would do according to the word of the Lord therefore
he took them and took his journey unto his friend
to Palmira Wayn county & State of New York and he
brake the covenent which he made before the
Lord and the Lord suffered the writings to
fall into the hands of wicked men and Martin
was chastened for his transgression and I also was
chastened also for my transgression for asking
the Lord the third time wherefore the Plates was
taken from me by the power of God and
I was not able to obtain them for a season
and it came to pass after much humility and
affliction of Soul I obtained them again when
Lord appeared unto a young man by the name
of Oliver Cowdry and shewed unto him the
plates in a vision and also the truth of the
work and what the Lord was about to do through
me his unworthy servant therefore he was desirous
to come and write for me to translate now my
wife had writen some for me to translate and
also my Brother Samuel H Smith but we
had become reduced in property and my wives
father was about to turn me out of doors &
I had not where to go and I cried unto the
Lord that he would provide for me to accom-
-plish the work whereunto he had command-
-ed me

History, 1832, Joseph Smith Letterbook 1, p. 6. Handwriting of Frederick G. Williams. See text, p. 8. (LDS Church Archives.)

Diaries, 1832-1834, 1835-1836

In November 1832, as Joseph Smith struggled to define his record-keeping responsibility, he discontinued the personal history he had begun writing earlier that year in favor of a more comprehensive approach. On November 27 he had his clerk Frederick G. Williams begin recording letters and documents of value to himself and to the Church in the book containing the discontinued personal history, and on the same day he started writing a personal diary in another book. This letter-book-diary format continued intermittently throughout the rest of his life and provided most of the source material from which his *History of the Church* was eventually compiled.

The Joseph Smith diaries presented here are his first two, written between 1832 and 1836. Unlike the later volumes of his diary, which were mostly produced by secretaries from their observations of his activity, these two early journals were largely in his own handwriting or were dictated, and therefore more clearly represent his personality.

Diary, 1832-1834

Joseph Smith Jr-
Record Book Baught for to note all the minute circumstances
that comes under my observation

Joseph Smith Jrs Book for Record Baught on the 27th of
November 1832 for the purpose to keep a minute acount of all
things that come under my obse[r]vation &c– –

Oh may God grant that I may be directed in all my thaughts Oh
bless thy Servent Amen [p. 1]

November 28th [1832] this day I have [spent] in reading and
wr=iting this Evening my mind is calm and serene for which I
thank the Lord———

November 29th [1832] this day road from Kirtland[1] to Chardon
to see my Sister Sop[h]ronia[2] and also ca[lled?] to see my Sister
Catherine[3] [and fou?]nd them [well?]
this Evening Brother Fr=ederic[4] Prophecyed that next spring I
should go to the city of Pitts=Burg to establish a Bis=hopwrick
and within one year I should go to the City of New York the Lord
spare the life of thy servent Amen [p. 2]

November 30th 1830 [i.e., 1832] this day retu[r]ned home to
Kirtla=nd found all well to the Joy and satisfaction of my soul on
my return home stopped at Mr Kings[5] bore testmony to him and
Family &c–

December 1th [1832] ‹bore testimony to Mr Gilmore[6]› wrote–
and cor=rected revelations & c——

December 2th [1832] the sabath went ~~to went~~ to meeting &c

December 3d [1832] ordaind Brother Packherd[7] with my own
hand also Brother umfiry [Humphery][8] came to see me from the
East & braught news from Brother Lyman Johnson[9] and Orson
Pratt[10] &c. also held a conference in the Evening Br Jese and

Mogan [Morgan?] and William Mclelen was excommunicated[11] from the church &c— [p. 3]

December 4th [1832] this day I been unwell done but litle been at home all day regulated some things this Evening feel better in my mind then I have for a few days back Oh Lord deliver ~~out~~ thy servent out of temtations and fill his heart with wisdom and understanding

December 5th [1832] this day ~~wr=ote leters~~ copying letters and translating and in evening held a council to advise with Brother Solomon Humphry it was ordered by the council that he should be a comp=anion with Brother Noah packard in the work of the ministry———

December 6th [1832] translating and received a revelation explaining the Parable the wheat and the tears[12] &c— [p. 4]

October 4th [1833] makeing prep=eration to go East with Freeman Nickerson[13] A request of Brother Da=vid Elliott[14] to call on his Brother in Law Peter Warrin St. kathrine up=per Cannada———
Coburg Richard Lyman request of Uncle John—

[October] 5th [1833] this day started and Journy to the East came to Ashtibuly [Ashtabula, Ohio] <stayed> Lambs tavern

[October] 6th [1833] arrived at Springfield [Erie County, Pennsylvania] <on the Sabbath> found the Brotheren in mee=ting Brother Sidney[15] spoke to the people &c— and in the [p. 5] <Evening> held a meeting at Brother Ruds[16] had a great congre=gation paid good attention Oh God Seal our te[s]timony—to their hearts Amen——/ [17]Continued at springfield untill tuesday the 8th [October 1833] Journeyed that day to br. Roundays[18] at Elk creek [Erie County, Pennsylvania] taried there over night came the next day to a tavern the next day thursday the

10th [October 1833] we ar[i]ved at Br Job Lewises[19] at Westfield the breatheren by a previous appointment met there for meeting we spoke to them as the spirite gave [p. 6] utterence they were greatly grati=fyed they appeared to be strong in the faith left there friday the 11 [October 1833] and came to the house of an infi=del by the Name of Nash[20] reasond with him but to no effect came Saturday the 12th [October 1833 to] the house of of father Nicke[r]son[21] **I feel very well in my mind the Lord is with us but have much anxiety about my family &c;——**[22]

Sunday the 13th [October 1833] held a meeti=ng at freeman Nicker=son['s] had a large congregation Brother Sidney preached & I bear record to the people the Lord gave his spirit in [a] [p. 7] marvilous maner for which I am thankful to the God of Ab[r]aham Lord bless my family and preserve them

Monday 14th [October 1833] at the same pla=ce this day expect to start for Canada Lord be with us on our Journy Amen &c—— / [23]Monday evening arived at Lodi [Cattaraugus County, New York] had an appointment preached to a small congre=gation made an appointment for tuesday at 10 oclock the 15th [October 1833] the meeting was appointed to be held in the Presbetarian meeting house [p. 8] but when the hour arived the man who kept the key of the house refused to open the door the meeting was thus prevented we came immedeately away and left the people in great confusion journeyed till ~~satter day~~ friday 17 [i.e., October 18, 1833][24] Arived at Freeman Nickerson's[25] in upper Canada having after we came into Cana=da passed through a very fine Country and well cultivated and had many peculiar feelings in relation to both the country and people we were kindly received at freeman Nickerso=ns [p. 9]

On Sunday the 19th [i.e., October 20, 1833] held meeting at brantford[26] on Sunday at 10 o clock to a very attentive congre=gation at candle lighting the same evening held m=eeting at mount plesent[27] where freeman Nickerson lived to a very large congre=gation which gave good heed to the things which were spoken what may be the result we cannot tell but the p[r]ospect is flatte=ring this morning Monday the 20 [i.e., October 21, 1833] enjoy pretty good [p. 10] health with good prospects of doing good calculate to stay in Canada till the Mon=day of next week then the Lord willing will start for home. left Mount plesent tuesday [October 22, 1833] and arived at the village of Coulburn[28] held meeting at candle lighting the evening was very bad snowing vehemently we were publickly opposed by a Wesleyen Methodist he was very tumultious but destitute of reason or knowledge he would not [p. 11] give us an oppertunity to reply this was on the 22nd [October 1833] we find that conviction is res=ting on the minds of some we hope that great good may yet be done in Canada which O Lord grant for thy names sake during our stay at mount plesent we [had] an inter=view with a Mr Wilkeson of the methodist order being a leader in that sect he could not stand against our words whether he will receive the truth the Lord only knows he seemed to [be] honest [p. 12] Written at Coulburn wednesday morning the 23 [October 1833] at the house of a Mr Bemer left Mr Be=mers on thursday 24 [October 1833] came to watterford [Norfolk District, Ontario] held meeting at 1 o clock to spoke to a small congregation being a very wet day after meeting returned to mount plesent and held meeting at at candle lighting to a large congregati=on one man [Eleazer] Freeman Nick=erson declared his full belief in the truth of the work is with his wife who is also convinced to be baptised on sunday great excitement [p. 13] prevailes in every place where we have been the result we leave in the hand of God. written at the house of Free=man Nickerson in mount plesent on friday morning the 24th [i.e., October 25, 1833] **this afternoon at Mr Pattricks exp=ect to hold a Meeting this Evening &c— peop=le very superstitious Oh God esta[b]lish thy word among this people held a meeting this even=ing had an attentive con=ngregation the spirit gave utterance [p. 14]**

Saterday 25th [i.e., October 26, 1833] held a mee=ting at Mount Plasant the people very tender

/ [29] Sunday 26 [i.e., October 27, 1833] held a meeting in Mount plesent to a large congregation twelve came forward and was

baptized and many more were deeply impress=ed appointed a
meeting for this day monday the 27 [i.e., October 28, 1833] at the
request of some who desires to be baptized at candle lig=hting held
a meeting for con=firmation we broke bread laid on hands for the
gift of the holy spirit had a good [p. 15] meeting the spirit was given
in great ~~to~~ power to some and the rest had great ~~pease~~ peace may
God carry on his work in this place till all shall know him Amen.
Held meet=ing yesterday at 10 o clock after meeting two came
forward and were baptized confirmed them at the watters edge held
meeting last evening ordained br E[leazer] F[reeman] Nick=erson to
the office of Elder had a good meeting one of the sisters got the [p.
16] gift of toungues which made the saints rejoice may God increse
the gifts among them for his sons sake this morning we bend our
course for home may the Lord prosper our journey Amen

Tuesday the 29th [October 1833] **left Mountpleasant for home**

30th [October 1833] continued on our Journy Wensday and on

Thirsday 31th [October 1833] arrived at Buffalo

~~**Friday 32th Started from Buffalo**~~ **[p. 17]**

/[30]Friday, November 1 [1833]<Nove-> Left Buffalo, N.Y. at 8
o'clock A.M. and arrived at home Monday, the 4th [November
1833] at 10, A.M. found my family all well according to the
promise of the Lord, for which blessing I feel to thank his holy
name; Amen.

**November 13th [1833] nothing of note transpired from the 4th
of Nove[m]ber u[n]til this day in the morning at 4 Oh clock I was
awoke by Brother Davis[31] knocking at <my> door saying Brother
Joseph [p. 18] come git <up> and see the signs in the heavens and
I arrose and beheld to my great Joy the stars fall from heaven[32]
yea they fell like hail stones a litteral fullfillment of the word of
God as recorded in the holy scriptures and a sure sign that the**

coming of Christ is clost at hand Oh how marvellous are thy
works Oh Lord and I thank thee for thy me[r]cy u‹n›to me thy
servent Oh Lord save me in thy kingdom for Christ sake Amen
[p. 19]

November 19th ‹AD 1833› from the 13th u[n]till this date
nothing of note has transpired since the great sign in the heavins
this day my ‹h[ea]rt› is somewhat sorrow=full but feel to trust in
the Lord the god of Jacob I have learned in my tra=vels that man
is treche[r]ous and selfish but few excep=ted Brother ‹Sidney› is
a man whom I love but is not capa[b]le of that pure and stedfast
love for those who are his benefa=ctors as should ~~posess~~ p‹o›sess
the breast of ~~a man~~ ‹a ~~Pred~~› President of the Chu[r]ch of
Christ [p. 20] this with some other little things such as a selfish
and indipendance of mind which to often manifest distroys the
confidence of those who would lay down their lives for him but
notwithstanding these th=ings he is ‹a› very great and good man
a man of great power of words and can ‹gain› the friendsh=ip of
his hearrers very quick he is a man whom god will uphold if he
will continue faithful to his calling O God grant that he may for
the Lords sake Amen [p. 21] the man who willeth to do well we
should extoll his virtues and speak not of his faults behind his
back a man w=ho willfuly turneth away from his friend without a
cause is not ~~lightly to be forgiven~~ ‹easily forgiven› the kindness
of a man ‹should› ~~is~~ never ~~to~~ be forgotten that person who never
forsaketh his trus=t should ever have the hi=ghest place for
regard in our hearts and our love shou=ld never fail but incr=ease
more and more and this [is] my disposition and sentiment &c
Amen [p. 22] Brother Frederick ~~is a man who~~ ‹is one of those
men›in whom I place the greatest confidence and trust for I have
found him ever full of love and Brotherly kindness he is not a
man of many words but is ever wining because of his constant
mind he shall ever have place in my heart and is ever intitled to
my confiden‹ce›/ [33]He is perfectly honest and upright, and seeks
with all his heart to mag=nify his presidency in the church of
ch[r]ist, but fails in many in=stances, in consequence of a ~~lack~~

‹want› of confidence in him=self: God grant that he may [p. 23]
overcome all evil: Blessed be brother Frederick, for he shall never
want a friend; and his generation after him shall flourish. The Lord
hath ap=pointed him an inheritance upon the land of Zion. Yea,
and his head shall blossom ‹And he shall be› as an olive branch
that is bowed down with fruit: even so; Amen.

And again, blessed be brother Sidney, also not=withstanding he
shall be high and lifted up, yet he shall bow down under the yoke
like unto an ass that [p. 24] coucheth beneath his burthen; that
learneth his master's ‹will› by the stroke of the rod: thus saith the
Lord. Yet the Lord will have mercy on him, and he shall bring
forth much fruit; even as the ~~vun~~‹vine› of the choice grape when
her clusters are ‹is› ripe, before the time of the gleaning of the
vintage: and the Lord shall make his heart merry as with sweet
wine because of him who putteth forth his hand and lifteth him up
~~from~~ ‹out of›[a] deep mire, and pointeth him out the way, and
guideth his [p. 25] feet when he stumbles; and humbleth him in his
pride. Blessed are his generations. Nevertheless, one shall hunt
after them as a man hun=teth after an ass that hath strayed in the
wilderness, & straitway findeth him and bringeth him into the fold.
Thus shall the Lord watch over his generation that they may be
saved: even so; Amen.

/[34]on the 13th and 14th days of October [1833] I baptised the
following person[s][35] in in Mount Pleasant viz [p. 26]
    Moses Chapman Nickerson[36]
    Eleser [Eleazer] Freeman Nickerson
    Prechard Ramon Stowbridge
    Andrew Rose[37]
    Harvey John Cooper
    Samuel Mc Alester
    Eliza Nickerson[38]
    Mary Gates[39]
    Mary Birch[40]
    Lidia Baeley [Lydia Baily][41]
    Elisabeth Gibbs[42]

Phebe Cook[43]
Margrett Birch
Esther Birch

25th Nove[mber 1833] Brother Orson Hyde[44] & John Gould[45] [p. 27] returned from Zion and brough[t] the melen=cholly intelegen[ce] of the riot in Zion[46] with the inhabitants in pers[ec]uting the brethren.

---

the 4th Dec[ember 1833] commenc=ed distributing the type–and commen=ced setting on the 6 [December 1833] and being prepa=red to commence our Labours in the printing buisness I ask God in the [p. 28] name of Jesus to estab=lish it for ever and cause that his word may speedily go for[th to] the Nations of the earth to the accomplishing of his great work in bringing about the restoration of the house of Israel[47]

Nov[ember] 22d–1833 my brother Carlos Smith came to live with me and also learn the printing art[48] [p. 29] on the 9 of Dec[ember 1833] bro Phi[neas] Young[49] came to board with me to board rent & lodge at one dollar & twenty five cents p[er] week

Bro Wilbor Denton[50] came to board 11 Dec[ember 1833] at one Dollar and twenty five cents per week.

‹1833› Dec. 18 This day the Elders assembled togeth[er] in the printing office [p. 30] and then proceded to bow down before the Lord and dedicate the printing press and all that per=tains thereunto to God by mine own hand and confirmed by bro Sidney Rigdon and Hyrum Smith[51] and then proceded to take the first proof sheet of the star edited by Bro Oliv[er] Cowd[er]y blessed of the Lord is bro Oliver nevertheless there are [p. 31] are two evils in him that he must needs for=sake or he cannot altogeth[er] escape the buffitings of the adver[sar]y if he shall forsak[e] these evils he shall be forgiven and shall be made like unto the bow which the Lord hath set in the heavens he shall be a sign and an ensign unto the nations. behold he is blessed of the Lord for his constancy [p. 32] and steadfastness in the work of the Lord wherefore he shall be blessed in his generation and they shall never be cut off and he shall be helped out of many troubles and if he keep the command=ments and harken unto the ‹council of the› Lord ~~his and~~ [and] his rest shall be glorious and again blessed of the Lord is my father and also my mother and my brothers and my sisters for they shall [p. 33] yet find redemption in the house of the Lord and their ofsprings shall be a blessing a Joy and a comfort unto them blessed is my mother for her soul is ever fill[ed] with benevolence and phylanthropy and notwithstanding her age yet she shall receive strength and shall be comforted in the midst of her house and she shall have eternal life and blessed is my father for the hand of the Lord shall be [p. 34] over him for he shall see the affliction ‹of his children› pass away and when his head is fully ripe he shall behold himself as an olive tree whose bran=ches are bowed down with much fruit he shall also possess a mansion on high blessed of the Lord is my brother Hyrum for the integrity of his heart he shall be girt about with truth and faithful=ness shall be the strength of his loins [p. 35] from generation to generation he shall be a shaft in the hand of his God to exicute Judgment upon his enemies and he shall be hid by the hand of the Lord that none of his secret parts shall be discovered unto his hu[r]t his name shall be accounted a blessing among men and when he is in trouble and great tribulation hath come upon him [p. 36] he shall remember the God of Jacob and he will shield him from the power of satan and he shall receive ‹councel› ~~counel~~ in the house of the most high that he may be streng[t]hened in hope that the going ‹of his feet› may be established for eve[r] blessed of the Lord is bro Samuel[52] because the Lord shall say unto him Sam[ue]l, Sam[ue]l, therefore he shall be made a teache[r] in [p. 37] the house of the Lord and the Lord shall ma=ture his mind in Judgment and thereby he shall obtain the esteem and fellowship of his brethren and his soul shall be establis=hed and he shall ben=efit the house of the Lord because he shall obtain answ=er to prayer in his faithfulness—

Bro William[53] is as the fi[e]rce Lion [p. 38] who devideth not the spoil because of his strength and in the pride of his heart he will neglect the more weighty matters until his soul is bowed down in sorrow and then he shall re=turn and call on the name of his God and shall find forgiveness and shall wax valient therefor he shall be saved unto the ut=ter most and as the [p. 39] roaring Lion of the forest in the midst of his prey so shall the hand of his gen=eration be lifted up against those who are set on high that fight against the God of Israel fearless and unda[u]nted shall they be in battle in avenging the [w]rongs of the innocent and relieving the oppressed ther[e]for the blessings of the God of Jacob [p. 40] shall be in the midst of his house notwithstan=ding his rebelious heart and ‹now› O God let the residue of my fathers house ever come up in remembrance before thee that thou mayest save them from the hand of the oppressor and establish their feet upon the rock of ages that they may have place in thy house and be saved in thy Kingdom [p. 41] and let all these things be even as I have said for Christs sake Amen

Dec[ember] 19 [1833] This day Bro William Pratt[54] and David Pattin[55] took their Journey to the Land of Zion for the purpose of bearing dispatches to the Brethren in that place from Kirtland O may God grant it a blessing for Zion as a kind Angel from heaven Amen [p. 42]

January 16th 1834 this night at Brother Jinkins Salisbury[56] came from home Oh Lord keep us and my Family safe untill I can return to them again Oh my God have mer=cy on my Bretheren in Zion for Christ Sake Amen

---

/[57]January 11, 1834. This evening Joseph Smith Jr, Frederick G. Williams, Newel K. Whitney,[58] John Johnson,[59] Oliver Cowdery, and Orson Hyd[e] united in prayer and asked the Lord to grant the fol=lowing petition: [p. 43]
Firstly, That the Lord would grant that our lives might be precious in his sight, that he would watch over our per=sons and give his angels cha=rge concerning us and our families that no evil nor un=seen hand might be permitted to harm us.[60]

Secondly, That the Lord would also hold the lives of all the United Firm,[61] and not suffer that any of them shall be taken.

Thirdly, That the Lord would grant that our brother Jo=seph might prevail over [p. 44] his enemy, even Docter P. Hurl=but, who has threatened his life, whom brother Joseph has ‹caused to be› taken with a precept; that the Lord would fill the heart of the court with a spirit to do justice, and cause that the law of the land may be magnified in bringing him to justice.[62]

Fourthly, That the Lord would provide, in the order of his Providence, the bishop of this church with means sufficient to discharge every debt that the Firm owes, in due season, that [p. 45] the Church may not be braught into disrepute, and the saints be afflicted by the hands of their enemies.

Fifthly, That the Lord would protect our printing press from the hands of evil men, and give us means to send forth his word, even his gos=pel that the ~~ey~~ ears of all may hear it, and also that we may print his scrip=tures, and also that he would give those who were appointed to con=duct the press, wisdom sufficient that the cause [p. 46] may not be hindered, but that men's eyes may thereby be opened to see the truth.

Sixthly, That the Lord would deliver Zion, and gather in his scattered people, to possess it in peace; and also, while in their dispersion, that he would provide for them that they perish not with hunger nor ~~fam~~ cold. And finally, that God in the name of Jesus would gather his elect speedily, and unveil his face that his saints [p. 47] might behold his glory and dwell with him; Amen.

On the 13th of March A.D. 1833, Docter P. Hurlbut came to my house; I conversed with him consid=erably about the book of Mormon. He was ordained to the office of an elder in this Church under the hand of Sidney Rigdon on the **18th** [63] of March in the same year above written. According to my best recollection, I heard him say, in the [p. 48] course of conversing with him, that if he ever became con=vinced that the book of Mormon was false, he would be the cause of my destruction, &c.

He was tried before a counsel of high priests on the 21st day of June, 1833, and his license re=stored to him again, ~~it~~ ‹he›

previously having been ~~taken by the church at~~ ‹cut off from the›
Church by the bishop's court. He was finally cut off from the
church [p. 49] a few days after having his license restored, on the
21st of June./ [64]and then saught the dis=truction of the saints in
this place and more particularly myself and family and as the Lord
has in his mercy Delivered me out of his hand till the present and
also the church that he has not prevailed viz the 28 day of Jany
[p. 50] 1834 for which I off[er] the gratitud[e] of my heart to
Allmighty God for the same and on this night Bro Oliv[er] and bro
Frederick and my self bowed before the Lord being agred and united
in pray[er] that God would continue to deliver me and my brethren
from ‹him› that he may not prevail again[st] us in the law suit that
is pending [p. 51] and also that God would soften down the hearts
of E Smith J Jones Lowd & Lyman and also Bardsly[65] that they
might obey the gospel or if they would not repent that the Lord
would send faithful saints to purchase their farms that this stake
may be streng=thened and ‹its› ~~the~~ borders enlarged **O Lord grant
it for Christ Sake Amen [p. 52]**

/[66]31 Janu[ar]y 1834 it is my prayer to the Lord that three thousand
subscriber[s] may be added to the Star in the term of three yea[rs]

**Wensdy ‹Febuary› 26th [1834] started from home to obtain
volenteers for Zion**[67]

**Thursday 27th [February 1834] ~~star=ted Started~~ stayed at Br
Roundays**[68]

**28th [February 1834] stayed at a strangers who entertained us
very kindly ‹in› Westleville [Wesleyville, Erie County,
Pennsylvania]**

March 1th [1834] arived at Br Lewis[69] **and on the 2d [March
1834] the Sabath Brother Barly [Parley Pratt]**[70] **preached in this
place and I preached in the evening had a good [p. 53] meeting
there is a small church in this place tha[t] seem to be strong in
th[e] faith Oh may God keep them in the faith and save them and
lead them to Zion——————**

March 3d [1834] this morning intend[ed] to start on our Journy to <the> east <But did not start>[71] O may God bless us with the gift of utterance to ac=complish the Journy and the Errand on which we are sent and return soon to the land of Kirtland [p. 54] and <find> my Family all well O Lord bless my little chil=dren with health and long life to do good in th[is] generation for Christs sake Amen————————

/[72]Kirtland Geauger [Geauga County] Ohio
Thom[p]son [Geauga County]———— ————
Springfield Erie [County]   Pensy[l]
Elkcrick [Elk Creek, Erie County]   vania
Westfield [Chautauque, New York]————
Laona Chautauque N york
Silver Creek [Chautauque, New York]————
Perrysburgh Cateragus [Cattaraugus County, New York]
Collins Genesee [County, New York]
China [Genesee County, New York] [p. 55]
Warsaw [Genesee County, New York]————
Geneseeo
        Levingston [Geneseo, Livingston County, New York]
Sentervill [Centreville, Allegany County, New York]
Cattlin Alleghany
Spafford ~~Spafford~~
        Onondaga [County, New York]

John Gould payed me on papers–$1.50

/[73]Journal of P[arley Pratt] and J[oseph Smith]

March 4th [1834] took our Journy from Westfield [Chatauque County, New York] <accompanyed By Br gould> rode 33 miles arrived in **Vilanova** s<t>aid all night with a Brother Mc Bride,[74] next morning went 4 m;s to Br Nicisons [Nickerson's][75] found him and [p. 56] his house hold full of faith and of the holy spirit we cald the church together and Related unto them what had hapened to our

Brethren in Zion opened to them the prophesyes and revelations concerning the order of the gethering of Zion and the means of her Redemtion and Brother Joseph Prophesyed to them and the spirit of the Lord came mightily upon them and with all redyness the yo[u]ng and midle aged volenteered for Zion [p. 57] same evening held 2 meetin<gs> 3 or 4 miles Apart.

next day March 6th [1834] held another Mee=ting at Bro Nicisons the few un Believeers that atended were outragious and the meet=ing ended in compleet confusi<on>

March 7 [1834] started ~~toards~~ on our Journy accompany<ed> By Br Nicison Leaving Brs goold [John Gould] and Mathews[76] to Prepare <and gether up> the companys in the churches in that region and meet us in Ohio Reddy for Zion the first of May we arrived after dark to the [p. 58] county seat of Cataraugus cald Elicutville [Ellicottville] tryed every tavern in the place But Being Court time we found no room But were compeled to ride on in a ~~d~~ dark muddy rainy night we found shelter in rideing 1 mile Paid higher for our fare than tavern price

March 8th [1834] continued our journy came to Palmers=ville [Farmersville] to the house of Elder Mc gown[77] were Invited to go to Esq **walkers**—[78] to spend the evening [p. 59] we found them verry frien<dly> and somewhat Believeing tarryed allnight

sunday 9 [March 1834] held meeting in a school house had grea<t> attentian found a few desyples who were firm in faith and after meeting found many Believeing and could hardly get away from them we apointed A meeting in freedom [Cattaraugus County, New York] for Monday 10th [March 1834] and are now at Mr Cowderyes[79] in the full Enjoyment of <all> the Blessings Both temporal and spiritual [p. 60] of which we stand in need or are found worthy to receive held meting on Monday ~~moved~~ Preachd to crowd[ed] <congregat[ion]> at eve preacht again to a hous crowded full to overflo=wing after meting I proposed if any wished to obey if

they would make it manifest we would stay to administer at another
meeting a young man of the methodist order arose and testified his
faith in the ful=ness of ‹the› gospel and desired to Be Baptised we
Appointed another meting and the next [p. 61] day tuesday 11th
[March 1834] held meeting and Baptised Heman hide[80] after which
we rode 9 m;s Put up with . . . . ‹Stewards tavern› next
day rode 36 m;s to fauther Bosleys.[81]

13 [March 1834] thursday held meting I Prea‹chd›

friday 14th [March 1834] in F[ather] Beamans[82]

March 15th [1834] at Father Beamans and Brother Sidny and
Lyman[83] ari=ved at his house to ‹the› Joy of our Souls in Lyvona
[Livonia, Livingston County, New York]

Sunday 16th [March 1834] Brother Sidney preached to a very
large congregation ‹in Geneseo›

Monday 17 [March 1834] Brother B̶a̶ [p. 62] B̶r̶o̶ Parly preached
in the afternoon [84]

Tusd[a]y 18th [March 1834] Stayed at Father Boslys all day

Wensday 19th [March 1834] Started for home arrived at Brother
Whitheys[85] tarri=ed all night &c

Thursday 20th [March 1834] Started on ‹our› Journy at noon
took dinner at Brother Joseph Holbrooks,[86] and at night w̶e̶ tryed
three times to git keept in the name of Deciples, and could not be
keept, [p. 63] after night we found a man who would keep us for
mony thus we see that there ‹is› more p̶l̶ place for mony than for
Jesus ‹Deciples or› the Lamb of God, the name of the man is
W̶i̶l̶s̶o̶n̶ ̶R̶a̶u̶b̶e̶n̶ ̶W̶i̶l̶s̶o̶n̶ ——————————————Reuben Wilson[87] that
would not keep us without mony he ‹lived in China [Genesee
County, New York]›&c.—

March 21th [1834] came to a man by the name of Starks 6 th miles East of Springville [Erie County, New York][88] [p. 64]

22d [March 1834] came and tarri[e]d with vincen nights[89] in P̶ Perrysburg Co– of Cattaraugus——

23d [March 1834] came to Father Nickersons Perrysb=urg the same Co[unty] NY held a meeting &c.

24th [March 1834] this ⟨day⟩ am not able to start for h̶e̶ home but feel dete=rmined to go on the morrow morning——

25th [March 1834] came from Father Nickerson to Father Leweses [Job Lewis] in [p. 65] Westfield Father Nick=erson came with me

26th [March 1834] Came from Wes=tfield to Elk kreek [Erie County, Pennsylvania] stayed with Elder Hunt on free cost

27th [March 1834] came to spri=ngfield found Brother Sidney and came to within 16 miles from Painsville

28th [March 1834] Came home found my Family all well and the Lord be praised for this blessing

29th [March 1834] at home had much [p. 66] Joy with ⟨my⟩ Family

30th [March 1834] Sabb⟨a⟩th at home and went to hear Brother Sidney Preach the word of life &c.——

31th [March 1834] Monday this day came to Sharden [Chardon, Geauga County, Ohio] to tend the Court against Docter P Hurlbut[90] &c

3̶2̶d̶ Tusday [April 1, 1834] this day at Brother Riders[91] and the Court has not braught on our tryal yet we are ingaged in makeing out some supenies &c——for witnesses this is m̶ [p. 67]

~~this~~ Ap[r]el 1st [1834] Tusday my soul delighteth in the Law of the Lord for he forgiveth my sins and ‹will› confound mine Enimies the Lord shall destroy him who has lifted his heel against me even that wicked man Docter P. H[u]rlbut he ‹will› deliver him to the fow=ls of heaven and his bones shall be cast to the blast of the wind ‹for› he lifted his ‹arm› against the Almity therefore [p. 68] the Lord shall destroy him

---

/⁹²Wednesday [April 2, 1834] attended court at Chardon, Thursday [April 3, 1834] the same. Friday [April 4, 1834] morning returned home. Saturday [April 5, 1834] returned to Chardon ‹as witness for fath[er] Johnson› in the evening returned home.⁹³ Mr. Bussle ⁹⁴ the State's Att'y for Portage County called on me this eve=ning: He is a gentlemanly appearing man, and treat=ed me with respect.

/⁹⁵on the 7th day of April [1834] Bros Newel Oliver Frederick Heber⁹⁶ and myself meet [p. 69] in the counsel room and bowed down befor[e] the Lord and prayed that he would furnish the means to deliver the firm⁹⁷ from debt and ‹be› set at liberty and also that I may pre=vail against that wicked Hurlbut and that he be put to shame accordingly on the 9 [April 1834] after an im=partial trial the Court decided that the said Hurlbut was bound over under 200 dollars [p. 70] bond to keep the peace for six month[s] and pay the cost which amounted to near three hundred dollars⁹⁸ all of which was in answer to our prayer for which I thank my heavenly father

Remember to carry the bond between AS– Gilbert⁹⁹ & NK Whitney and have them exchang‹d› when I go to Zion¹⁰⁰

on ‹Thursday› the 10 [April 1834] had a co[u]ncel [p. 71] of the united firm at which it was agreed that the firm should be desolv[ed] and each one have their stewardship set off to them

Fryday 11 [April 1834] attended meeting and restored Father Tyler to the Church

Satterday 12 [April 1834] went to the lake [Erie] and spent the day in fishing and visiting the brethren in that place and took my horse from Father [John] Johnson and let brother Frederick have him to keep.

13 Sunday [April 1834] was sick and could not attend meeting [p. 72]

Monday 14 [April 1834] purch[as]ed some hay and oats and got them home

Tuesday 15 [April 1834] drawed a load of hay & ‹on Wensday 16 [April 1834]› plowed and sowed oats for Brother Frederick and on Thursday the 17 [April 1834] attended a meeting agreeable to appoint[ment] at which time the important subjects of the deliverence of Zion and the building of the Lords house in [p. 73] Kirtland by bro Sidney after which bro Joseph arose and requested the brethren and sisters to contr[i]bute all the money they could for the deliverence of Zion and received twenty nine dollars and sixty eight cts

---

/[101]April 18 [1834] left Kirtland in compa=ny with brothers Sidney Rigdon, Oliver Cowdery, ‹and› Zebedee Coltrin[102] for New Portage to attend a conference. Travelled to W.W. Williams'[103] in [p. 74] Newburgh [Cuyahoga County, Ohio] and took dinner, after which we travelled on, and after dark were hailed by a man who desired to ride. We were checked by the Spirit and refused: he professed to be sick; but in a few minutes was joined by two others who followed us hard, cursing and swearing, but we were successful in escaping their hands through the providence of the Lord, and stayed at a tavern where we were treat=ed with civility. Next morn=ing, 19 [April 1834] started, and arrived at brother Joseph Bozworth's ‹in› ~~Cop~~ [p. 75] Copley, Medina County, where we took dinner.[104] Bro. J. Bozworth was strong in the faith—he is a

good man and may, if faithful, do much good. After resting a
while, we left, and soon arrived at brother Johnathan Tayler's,[105] in
Norton, where we were received with kindness.

We soon retired to the wil=derness where we united in prayer and
suplication for the blessings of the Lord to be given unto his
church: We called upon the Father in the name of Jesus to go with
the breth[r]en who were [p. 76] going up to the land of Zion, to
give brother Joseph strength, and wisdom, and understand=ing
sufficient to lead the people of the Lord, and to gather back and
establish the saints upon the land of their inheritances, and
organize them according to the will of heaven, that they be no
more cast down for=ever. We then united and laid on hands:
Brothers Sidney, Oliver, and Zebedee laid hands upon bro. Joseph,
and confirmed upon him all the blessings necessary to qualify him
to ~~do~~ <stand> before the Lord in his high calling; and [p. 77] he
return again in peace and triumph, to enjoy the society of his
breth[r]en. Brothers Joseph, Sidney, and Zeb=edee then laid hands
upon bro. Oliver, and confirmed upon him the blessings of wisdom
and understanding sufficient for his station; that he be qualified to
as=sist brother Sidney in ar=ranging the church covenants[106] which
are to be soon pub=lished; and to have intelligence in all things to
do the work of printing. Brother[s] Joseph, Oliver, Zebedee then
laid [p. 78] hands upon bro. Sidney, and confirmed upon him the
bles=sings of wisdom and knowl=edge to preside over the Church
in the abscence of brother Joseph, and to have the spir=it to assist
bro. Oliver in conducting the Star, and to arrange the Church
cove=nants, and the blessing of old age and peace, till Zion is built
up & Kirtland established, till all his enemies are under his feet,
and of a crown of eternal life ~~at the~~ <in the> Kingdom of God with
us. [p. 79] We, Joseph, Sidney, and Oliver then laid hands up=on
bro. Zebedee, and con=firmed the blessing of wisdom to preach the
gospel, even till it spreads to the islands of the sea, and to be spared
to see three score years and ten, and see Zion built up and Kirtland
established forever, and even at last to receive a crown of life. Our
hearts rejoiced, and we were [p. 80] comforted with the Holy
Spirit, Amen.

~~18~~ 20th. [April 1834] Sunday, Brother Sidney Rigdon entertained a large con=gregation of saints, with an interesting discourse upon the "Dispensation of the ful=ness of times," &c.

21 [April 1834] Attended conference[107] and had a glorious time, some few vol=unteered to go to Zion, and others donated $66.37 for the bene=fit of the scattered breth[r]en in Zion.

Returned to Kirtland on the 22d [April 1834] and found all well. [p. 81]

23. [April 1834] Assembled in council[108] with breth[r]en Sidney, Frederick, Newel, John Johnson and Oliver and united in asking the Lord to give bro. Zebedee Coltrin in=fluence over our bro. Ja=cob Myre, [109] and obtain from him the money which he has gone to borrow for us, or cause him to come to this place & give it himself.

/[110]April 30th [1834] this day paid the ~~amount~~ <sum> of fifty dollars on the following mem=orandom to the [p. 82] following persons viz

Milton Holmes[111]	$15.00
Henry Herriman[112]	7.00
Sylvester Smith[113]	10.00
Wm Smith	5.00
Harvey Stanl[e]y[114]	5.00
William Smith	5.00
N K Whitn[e]y	3.00
	$50.00

Money received of the following brethren consecrated for the deliver[y] of Zion

By letter from East	$10.00	
Do [ditto] "	50.00	
Do "	100.00	[p. 83]
By Letter	$07 00	

Wm Smith	.5 00	
Wm Cahoon[115]	.5 00	
Harvey Stanley	.5 00	
Received of Martin Harris	47 00	
/[116]Rec[e]ived of Dexter Stillman[117]	10.	
Do of Lyman Johnson[118]	5.00	
Do of Sophia Howe	7.60	[p. 84]

/[119]August 21st 1834. This day brother
Freder=ick Williams returned from Cleveland and told us
con=cerning the plague,[120] and after much consultation we agreed
that bro. Fred=erick should go do Cleve=land and commence
admin=istering to the sick, for the purpose of obtaining ~~means~~
‹blessings for them, and› for the ~~work of~~ ‹glory of› the Lord:
Accordingly we, Joseph, Frederick, and Oliver united in prayer
before the Lord for this thing. [p. 85.]

Now, O Lord, grant unto us this blessing, in the name of Jesus
Christ, and thy name shall have the glory forever; Amen.

August 30, 1834. Received of the Church by the hand of Jared
Carter[121] from the east of consecrated money $3.00

Sept. 4, 1834. This day Edward [Edmund] Bosley said that if he
could obtain the management of his property in one year he would
put it in for the printing of the word of the Lord. [p. 86]

November 29. 1834. This evening Joseph and Oliver united in
prayer for the contin=uance of blessings, after giving thanks for the
relief which the Lord had lately sent us by opening the hearts of
certain brethren from the east to loan us $430.
After conversing and re=joicing before the Lord on this occasion
we agreed to enter into the fol=lowing covenant with the Lord,
viz:–
That if the Lord will [p. 87] prosper us in our busi=ness, and open
the way be=fore ‹us› that we may obtain means to pay our debts,
that we be not troubled nor brought into disre=pute before the

world nor his people, that after that of all that he shall give us we will give a tenth, to be bestowed upon the poor in his Church, or as he shall command, and that we will be faithful over that which he has entrus=ted to our care ~~and~~ that we [p. 88] may obtain much: and that our children after us shall remember to observe this sacred and holy cove=nant: ~~after us.~~ And that our children and our chil=dren's [children] may know of the same we here subscribe our names with our own hands before the Lord:

Joseph Smith Jr

/[122]Oliver Cowdery.

And now, O Father, as thou didst prosper our father Jacob, and bless [p. 89] him with protection and prosperity where ever he went from the time he made a like covenant before and with thee; and as thou didst, even the same night, open the heavens unto him and manifest great mercy and favor, and give him promises, so wilt thou do by us his sons; and as his blessings prevailed above the blessings of his Progenitors unto the utmost bounds of the [p. 90] everlasting hills, even so may our blessings prevail ~~above~~ <like> his; and may thy servants be preserved from the power and influence of wicked and unrighteous men; may every weapon formed against us fall upon the head of him who shall form it; may we be blessed with a name and a place among thy saints here, and thy sanc=tified when they shall rest. Amen. [p. 91]

Sabbath evening, No=vember 30, 1834. While reflecting upon the goodness and mercy of the Lord, this evening, a prophecy was put into our hearts, that in a short time the Lord would arrange his providen=ces in a merciful man=ner and send us assist=ance to deliver us from debt and bon=dage. [p. 92]

Friday Evening, December 5, 1834. According to the directions of the Holy Spirit breth[r]en Joseph Smith Jr. Sidney, Frederick G. Williams, and Oliver Cowdery, assembled to converse upon the welfare of the Church, when brother Oliver Cowdery was ordained an assistant President[123]of the High and Holy Priesthood un=der

the hands of brother Joseph Smith Jr. saying, "My brother, in the
name of Jesus Christ who ~~died~~ was crucified for the sins of the
world, I lay my hands upon thee, and ordain thee an assist=ant
President of the high and holy priest=hood in the Church of the
Latter Day Saints["] [p. 93][124]

/[125]Please to send the Paper that Has formerly Been sent to John
C[..]p[..]ton send it Now to Nathan Chase at West Lodi
Cataraugus County N.Y

Receive[d] of Elisha C Hubbard one Dollar for Papers
                    Perysburgh[126] [p. 103]

Hazard Andr[e]ws 1 paper Fairview Postoffi[ce] Cattaragus County

---

I have sent the money 25 cents by David Mo[....] as he was to send
the paper to Mis Taylor to Rushford but I wish to have it come in
my name as above

Direct Samuel Mcbride & James Mcbride[127] Papers to Nashville
Post office Shitauqua County

I wish you to send me one more Paper monthly and send one
Monthly Paper to Eleazer & Samuel & Richard Nickerson South
Dennis in the County of Barnsta[ble] Massachusetts[128]
                    J[ohn] Nickerson [p. 104]

/[129]The voice of the Spirit is, that brother Sidney speak to the
congregation this day, first, Brother Joseph next, bro. Oliver
[next?] and if time bro Zebedee [Coltrin][130]
                    Joseph Smith Jr
                    Oliver Cowdery [p. 105]

Diary, 1832-1834, p. 1. Handwriting of Joseph Smith. See text, pp.
15-16. (LDS Church Archives.)

Diary, 1832-1834, pp. 2-3. Handwriting of Joseph Smith. See text, pp. 16-17. (LDS Church Archives.)

Diary, 1832-1834, pp. 4-5. Handwriting of Joseph Smith. See text, p. 17. (LDS Church Archives.)

Diary, 1832-1834, pp. 6-7. Handwriting of Joseph Smith and Sidney Rigdon. See text, pp. 17-18. (LDS Church Archives.)

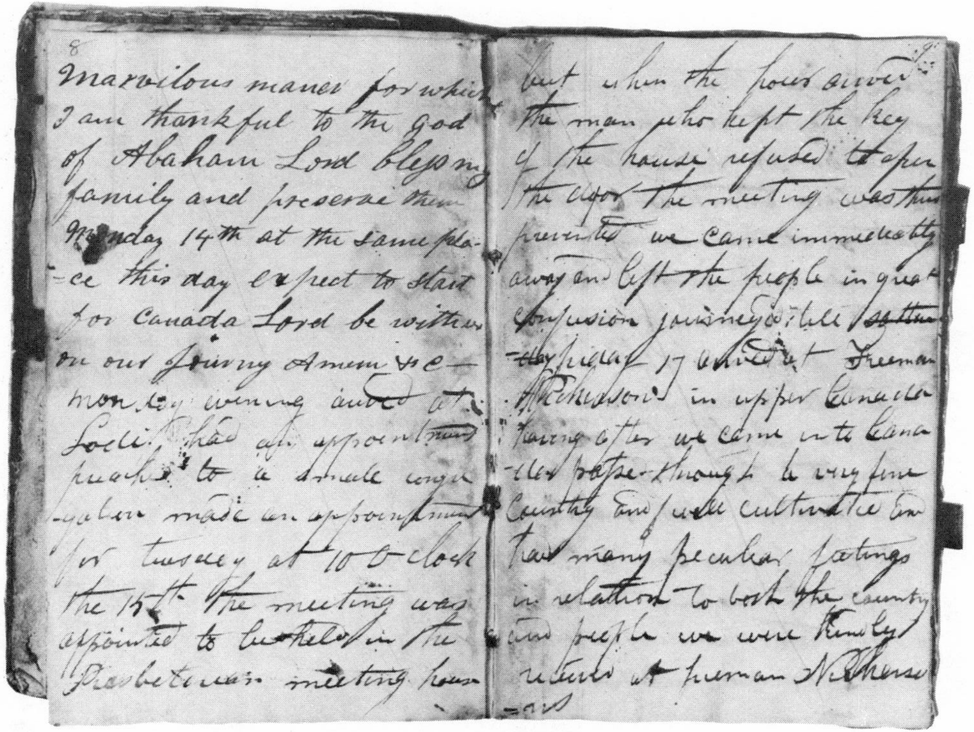

Diary, 1832-1834, pp. 10-11. Handwriting of Sidney Rigdon. See text, pp. 18-19. (LDS Church Archives.)

Diary, 1832-1834, pp. 14-15. Handwriting of Sidney Rigdon and Joseph Smith. See text, pp. 19-20. (LDS Church Archives.)

Diary, 1832-1834, pp. 16-17. Handwriting of Sidney Rigdon and Joseph Smith. See text, p. 20. (LDS Church Archives.)

Diary, 1832-1834, pp. 18-19. Handwriting of Oliver Cowdery and Joseph Smith. See text, pp. 20-21. (LDS Church Archives.)

November 19th 1833 the [fever] the
13th untill this date nothing
of note has transpired since
the great day on the [business] the
day night some what [strong] my
I will but feel to [strengthen]
the [trust] the god of Jacob
as I have [learned] no my tri-
-al that man is trickery
and selfish but few except
[tee] Brother Sidney
is a man whom
I love but is not equal of
that [firm] and [steadfast] love
to those who are his [friends]
[tors] as should [support]
[him] the [beauty] of
President of the Church

this with some other little
things such as a selfish and
indifference of mine which
to [often] manifest [during] the
confidence of those who would
lay down their lives for him
but notwithstanding these
things he is very [great] and good
man a man of great [power]
words and cast the [priesthood]
of his [harness] very [quick]
he is a man whom [you will]
uphold if he will continue
[faithful] to his calling O
[grant] that he may for
the Lords sake Amen

Diary, 1832-1834, pp. 20-21. Handwriting of Joseph Smith. See text, p. 21. (LDS Church Archives.)

Diary, 1832-1834, pp. 22-23. Handwriting of Joseph Smith and Oliver Cowdery. See text, pp. 21-22. (LDS Church Archives.)

Diary, 1832-1834, pp. 42-43. Handwriting of Frederick G. Williams, Joseph Smith, and Oliver Cowdery. See text, p. 25. (LDS Church Archives.)

Diary, 1832-1834, pp. 52-53. Handwriting of Frederick G. Williams and Joseph Smith. See text, p. 27. (LDS Church Archives.)

Diary, 1832-1834, pp. 54-55. Handwriting of Joseph Smith and an unidentified scribe. See text, pp. 27-28. (LDS Church Archives.)

Diary, 1832-1834, pp. 58-59. Handwriting of Parley P. Pratt; "walkers" inserted by Joseph Smith. See text, p. 29. (LDS Church Archives.)

62

day tuesday 11th held meeting and
Baptised 1 woman Miller after
which we rode 2 miss [...]
with [...] ... x next day rode
3 6 miss to Jonathan Burtsys [...]
13th thursday held meeting of [...]
[...] 14th [...] of [...]
March 15th at [...]
[...] and Brother
Sidney and Lyman [...]
[...] at his house [...]
of our souls [...]
Sunday 16th Brother
Sidney preached to a
very large congregation
Monday 19 Brother [...]

63

[...] preached
in the afternoon
Tuesday 18th stayed at
Father Bosleys all day
Wednesday 19 started
for [...] arrived at
Brother Whitneys horn
ed all night &c
Thursday 20th started
on my journey at noon
took dinner at Brother
Joseph Holbrookes and
at night stayed three
times to get height un th[e]
name of [...] and
could not [...]

Diary, 1832-1834, pp. 62-63. Handwriting of Parley P. Pratt and Joseph Smith. See text, p. 30. (LDS Church Archives.)

Diary, 1832-1834, pp. 64-65. Handwriting of Joseph Smith. See text, pp. 30-31. (LDS Church Archives.)

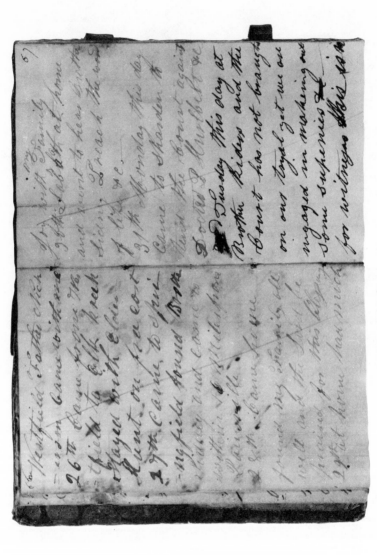

Diary, 1832-1834, pp. 66-67. Handwriting of Joseph Smith. See text, p. 31. (LDS Church Archives.)

Diary, 1832–1834, pp. 68–69. Handwriting of Joseph Smith, Oliver Cowdery, Frederick G. Williams. See text, p. 32. (LDS Church Archives.)

Diary, 1835-1836

/¹Sketch Book for the use of Joseph Smith, jr.

September 22, 1835. This day Joseph Smith, jr. labored with Oliver Cowdery, in obtaining and writing blessings. We were thronged a part of the time with company, so that our labor, in this thing, was hindered; but we obtained many precious things, and our souls were blessed. O Lord, may thy Holy Spirit be with thy servants forever. Amen.

September 23.th [1835] This day Joseph Smith, Jr. was at home writing blessings for my most beloved Brotheren ‹I› have been hindered by a multitude of visitors but the Lord has blessed our Souls this day. May Godd grant ‹to› con=tinue his mercies unto my house, this ‹night› day for Chr=ist sake. This day my Soul has desired the salvati=on of Brother Ezra, Thayr.² Also Brother Noah, Packard. Came to my house and let the Chap=pel Committee have one thousand dollers, by loan, for the building the house of the Lord; Oh may God bless him with an hundred fold! even of the ‹things of [the]› Earth, for this ritious act. My heart is full of desire to day, to ‹be› blessed of the God, of Abraham; with prosperity, untill I will be able to pay all my depts; for it is ‹the› delight of my soul to ‹be› honest. Oh Lord that thou knowes[t] right well! help me and I will give to the poor.³————————

September 23d 1835 This day Brothers William, ~~Tibbets~~ John, and Joseph Tibbits Started for Mosoura⁴ the place designated for Zion or the Saints gathering they Came to bid us farewell the Brotheren Came in to pray with them and Brother David Whitmer⁵ acted as spokesman he prayed in the spirit a glorious time suc=ceded his prayr Joy filled our hearts and we [p. 1] blessed them and bid them God speed ~~and~~ and promiced them a safe Journy and took them ‹by the hand› and bid them farewell for ‹a› season Oh! may God grant them long life and good days these blessings I ask ‹upon them› for Christ sake Amen

September 24th 1835 This day the high Cou=ncil met at my house to take into consid=[e]ration the redeemtion of Zion and it was the voice of the spirit of the Lord that we petition to the Governer that is those who have been driven out ‹should› ~~to~~ do so to be set back on their Lands next spring and we go next season to live or dy ~~to this end so the dy is east~~ in Jackson County we truly had a good time and Covena[n]ted to strugle for this thing u[n]till death shall desolve this union and if one falls that the rest be not ~~dis ha~~ discouraged but pe[r]sue this object untill it is acom=plished which may God grant u[n]to us in the name of Christ our Lord

September 24th 1835 This day drew up an Arti‹c›le of inrollment for the redemtion of Zion[6] that we may obtain volenteers to go ~~me~~ next spring ‹to Mo—› I ask God in the name of Jesus that we may obtain Eight hundred men ‹or one thousand› well armed and that they may acomplish this great work even so Amen————[p. 2]

/[7]Friday 25th September [1835]. This day I remained at home: nothing of note transpired. ~~The twelve all returned from the east to day.~~

26th [September 1835]. This evening, the twelve having returned from the east this morning,[8] we met them, and conversed upon some matters of difficulty which ware existing between some of them, and president Rigdon, and all things were settled satisfactorily.[9]

27th Sunday [September 1835]. Attended meeting: brethren, Thomas B. Marsh,[10] David W. Patten, Brigham Young[11] and Heber C. Kimball preached and broke bread. The Lord poured out his Spirit, and my soul was edified.

28th [September 1835]. High council met and tried brother Gladden Bish=op: he was reproved, repented, and was reordained.[12] The next was Lorenzo L. Lewis for fornication: he was cut off from the Church.

29th [September 1835] High Council met to-day and tried brother Allen Avery:[13] he was acquited from any charge. Also Brother Phineas H. Young[14] who was also acquited: also bro. Lorenzo Young,[15] who confessed his error and was forgiven. In all these I acted on the part of the defence for the accused to plead for mercy. The Lord blessed my soul, and the coun=cil was greatly blessed, also. Much good will no doubt, result from our labors during the two days in which we were occupied on the buisness of the CCh Church.

30th [September 1835]. Stayed at home and visited many who came to enquire after the work of the Lord.

October 1, 1835. This after noon labored on the Egyptian alphabet,[16] in company with brsr. O. Cowdery and W.W. Phelps:[17] The system of astronomy was unfolded.

2nd [October 1835]. To-day wrote a letter[18] to be published in the Messenger and Advocate. [p. 3]

/[19]Saturday 3d Oct [1835] held a high council on the case of Elder John Gould for giving credence to false and slanderous reports instigated to Injure bro Sidney Rigdon and also Dean Gould[20] for thretning bro Sidney Rigdon and others in authority of the Elders.[21] after due deliberation the[y] both confessed and wer[e] acquited. In the afternoon waited on the twelve most of them at my house and exhibited to them the ancient reccords in my possession and gave explanation of the same thus the day passed off with the blessings of the Lord

Sunday 4 [October 1835] started early in the mornin[g] with brother J. Carrell[22] to hold a meeting in Perry [Geauga County, Ohio] when about a mile from home we saw two Dears playing in the field which diverted our minds by giving an impatus to our thoughts upon the subject of the creation of God we conversed upon many topicks and the day passed off in a very agreeable manner and the Lord blessed our souls when we arived at Perry we were disappointed of a meeting through misaran=gements but conversed freely ~~upon~~ with Bro John Correls relatives which allayed much prejudice as we trust may the lord have mercy on their souls

Monday 5th [October 1835] returned home being much fatiegued riding in the rain spent the remainder of the day in reading and meditation &c and [p. 4] in the evening attend[ed] a high councel of the twelve apostles. had a glorious time and gave them many instruction[s] concerni=ng their duties for time to come. told them that it was the will of God they should take their families to Missouri next season, also attend this fall the solemn assembly[23] of the first Elders for the organization of the school of the prophets,[24] and attend to the ordinence of the washing of feet and to prepare the[i]r hearts in all humility for an endowment with power from on high to which they all agreed with one accord, and seamed to be greatly rejoiced may God spare the lives of the twelve with one accord to a good old age for christ the redeemers sake amen

Tuesday 6 [October 1835] At home ~~father or~~ Elder Stevens[25] came to my house and loaned F G Williams and Co six hundred Dollars which greatly releaved us out of our present difficulties may God bless and preserve his soul for ever —— Afternoon called to visit my father who was very sick with a fever some better towards evening spent the rest of the day in reading and meditation

Wednesday 7 [October 1835] went to visit my fathe[r] find him very low administered some mild herbs agreeable to the commandment may God grant to restore him immedi=ately to health for christ the redeemers sake Amen This day bro NK Whitney and Bro Hyrum Smith started for buffalo [New York] to purchase good[s] to replenish the committe store by land in the stage may God grant in the name of Jesus that their lives may [p. 5] be spared and they have a safe Journey and no accident or sickness of the least kind befall them that they may return in health and in safety to the bosom of their families

Blessed of the lord is bro [Newel] Whitney even the bishop of the church of the latter day saints, for the bishoprick shall never be taken away from him while he liveth and the time cometh that he shall overcome all the narrow mindedness of his heart and all his covetous desires that so easily besetteth him and ‹he› shall deal with a liberal hand to the poor and the needy the sick and the afflicted the widow and the fatherless and marviously and miraculously shall the Lord his God provid[e] for him, even that he shall be blessed with ‹all the ~~the~~ › a fullness of the good thing[s] of this earth and his seed after him from generation to generation and it shall come to pass that according to to the measure that he meeteth out with a liberal hand unto the poor so shall it be measured to him again by the hand of his God even an hundred fold Angels shall guard ‹his› house and shall guard the lives of his posterity, and they shall become very great and very numerous on the earth, whomsoever he blesseth they shall be blessed. whomsoever he curseth they shall be cursed. and when his enemies seek him unto his hurt and distruction let him rise up and curse and the hand of God shall be upon his enemies in Judgment [p. 6] they shall be utterly confounded and brought to dessolation, therefor he shall be preserved unto the utmost and his ‹life› ~~day~~ shall be precious in the sight of the Lord he shall rise up and shake him=self as a lion riseth out of his nest and roareth untill he shaketh the hills and as a lion goeth forth among the lesser beasts, so shall the goings forth of him ‹be› whom the Lord hath anointed to exalt the poor and to humble the rich, therefore his name shall be on high and his rest among the sanctified this afternoon recommenced translating the ancient reccords[26]

/[27]Thursday 8th [October 1835] at home nothing of note of note transpired ~~of~~ as we now recollect. I attended on my Father with feelings of great anxiety—

Friday 9th [October 1835] at home nothing worthy of note transpired on this day waited on ‹my Father›

Saturday 10th [October 1835] at home, visited the house of my Father found ‹him failing very fast›—

Sunday 11th [October 1835] visited my Father ‹again› who was verry sick ‹in secret prayer in the morning the Lord said my servant thy father shall live› I waited on him all this day with my heart raised to god in the name of Jesus Christ that he would restore him to health again, that I might be blessed with his company and advise esteeming it one of the greatest earthly blessings, to be blessed with the society of Parents, whose mature years and experience renders them capable of administering the most wholsom advice; at Evening Bro. David Whitmer came in we called on the Lord in mighty prayer in the name of Jesus Christ, and laid our hands on him, and rebuked the diseas[e] and God heard and answered our prayers to the great Joy and satisfaction of our souls, our aged Father arose and dressed himself shouted and praised the Lord called [p. 7] Br Wm Smith who had retired to rest that he might praise the Lord with us by joining in Songs of praise to the most High

Monday 12th [October 1835] rode to Willoughby in company with my wife to purchase some goods at W. Lyons Store on our return we found a Mr. Bradly lying across the road he had been thrown ~~from~~ from his waggon [and] was much injured by the fall

Tuesday 13th [October 1835] visited my Father who was verry much recovered from his sickness indeed, which caused us to marvel at the might power and condesension of our Heavenly Father in answering our prayers in his behalf

Wednesday 14th [October 1835] at home

Thursday 15th [October 1835] Laboured in Fathers orchard gathering apples

Friday 16th [October 1835] was called into the printing ‹office›
to settle some difficulties in that department, at evening on the
same day I baptised Ebenezer Robinson[28] the Lord poured out his
spirit on us and we had a good time

Saturday 17th [October 1835] called my family together and
aranged my domestick concerns and ~~domestic~~ dismissed my
boarders

Sunday 18th [October 1835] attended meeting in the chapel
con=firmed several who had been baptised[29] and blessed several
~~blessings~~ children with the blessings of the new and everlasting
covenant Elder Parley P. Pratt preach[e]d in the fore noon, and
Elder John F. Boynton in the after noon, we had an interesting
time[30]

Monday 19th [October 1835] at home, exibited the records of
of antiquity to a number who called to see them

Tuesday 20th [October 1835] at home preached at night in the
School-house–

Wednesday 21st [October 1835] at home nothing [p. 8] of note
transpired

Thursday 22d [October 1835] at home attending to my
domestick concerns–

Friday 23d at home ~~attended the prayer meeting~~ ‹see page 50›[31]

Saturday 24th Mr Goodrich and his lady ~~called~~ called to see the
antient Records also called at Doct. F G. Williams to see the
mummies, Brs. Hawks[32] & Carpen‹-ter› from Michigan visited us
& taried over Sunday and attended meeting—

Sunday 25th [October 1835] attended meeting President
Rigdon preached in the fore noon, Elder Lyman Johnson in the

afternoon, after which Elder S. Bronson joined Br. Wm Perry[33] &
Sister Eliza Brown in matrimony, and I blessed them with long life
and prosperity in the name of Jesus Christ, at evening I attended
prayer meeting opened it and exorted the brethren & Sister[s]
about one hour, the Lord pourd out his spirit and some glorious
things were spoken in the gift of toungs, and interp[r]eted
concer=ning the redemption of Zion

Monday 26th [October 1835] went to Chardon to attend the
county Court in company with Brs Hyrum Samuel & Carloss
Smith, Br. Samuel was called in question before this Court for not
doing military duty, and was fined because we had not our
conference minuets with us for testimony to prove that F G.
Williams was clerk of the conference–this testimony we should
have carried with us had it not been for the neglect of our Council,
or Lawyer, who did not put us in possession of this information this
we feel was a want of fidelity to his client, and we concider it a base
insult <practised> upon us on the account of our faith, that the
ungodly might have unlawful power over us and trample us under
their unhallowed feet; & in consequence of this neglect a fine was
imposed on Br Samuel [p. 9] of $20. including costs, for which
~~Lawsuit~~ he was obliged to sell his cow, to defray the expenses of the
same, and I say in the name of Jesus Christ that the money that
they have thus unjustly taken shall be a testimony against them and
canker & eat their flesh as fire

Tuesday 27th in the morning I was called to visit at Br Samuel
Smiths his wife was confined an[d] in a verry dangerous situation,[34]
Br. Carloss took one of my horses and went to Chardon after Doct.
Williams I went out into the field and bowed before the Lord and
called upon him in mighty prayer in her behalf the word of the
Lord came unto me saying my Servant Fredrick shall come and
shall have wisdom given him to deal prudently and my handmaden
shall be delivered of a living child & be spared, he come in a bout
one hour after that and in the course of about 2 hours she was
delivered and thus what God had manifested to me was fulfilled
every whit, on the night of the same day I preached in the School
house to a crowded congregation

Wednesday 28th at holm attending to my family concerns &c

Thursday 29th [October 1835] Br W. Parish[35] commenced
writing for me. Father & Mother Smith visit[ed] us and while we
set writing Bishop Partrige[36] passed our window just returned from
the East– Br Parish commenced writing for me at $15.00 pr month
I paid him $16.00 in advance out of the committee Store Br Parrish
agrees to board himself, for which I agree to <allow him> four
Dollars more pr. month making $19.00. I was then called to appear
before the high Council which was [p. 10] setting to give my
testimony in an action brought aga=inst Br. David Eliot for
whiping his Daughter unrea=sonably my testimony was in his
favour, returned to our writing room, went to Dr. Williams after
my large Journal,[37] made some observations to my Scribe
concerning the plan of the City which is to be built up hereafter on
this ground consecrated for a stake of Zion[38] while at the Doct[or's]
Bishop E Pa[r]trige came in, in compa=ny with President Phelps, I
was much rejoiced to see him, we examined the mumies, returned
home and my scribe commenced writing in <my> Journal a history
of my life, concluding President Cowdery['s] 2d letter to W. W.
Phelps, which president Williams had begun Bishop Whitney &
his wife with his Father & Mother[39] called to Visit us, his parents
having lately arived here from the East called to make enquiry
concerning the coming forth of the book of Mormon, Bishop
Partrige & some others came in I then set down and ~~taught~~ <related
to> them the history of the coming forth of the book the
administra=tion of the Angel to me the rudiments of the gospel of
Christ &c they appeared well satisfyed & I expect to baptise them
in a few days, or this is my feelings upon the subject altho they
have not made any request of this Kind at present, went to the
council,[40] the Presiden=cy arose and adjourned on my return Elder
Boynton[41] observed that long debates were bad. I replyed that it
was generally the case that to[o] much altercation was ~~generally~~
indulged in, on both sides and their debates protracted to an
unprofitable length; we were ~~seated~~ called to super, after being
seated around the table Bishop Whitney observed to Bishop

Partrige that ‹the› thought had just occured to his mind that perhaps in about one yea[r] from this time they might be seated together around a table ~~in~~ on the land of Zion [p. 11] ~~Sister Emma~~ ‹my wife› observed that she hoped it might be the case that not only they but the rest of the of the company present might be seated around her table in the land of promise; the same sentiment was reciprocated from the company round the table and my heart responded amen God grant it, I ask in the name of Jesus Christ, after super I went to the high council in company with my wife and some others that belong to my house hold I was solicited to take a seat with the presidency and preside in a case of Sister Eliots[42] I did so my Mother was called as testimony and began to relate circumstances that had been brought before the church and settled I objected against such testi=mony the complainant Br. William Smith arose and accused me of invalidating or doubting my mothers testimony which I had not done nor did I desire to do I told him he was out of place & asked him to set down he refused I repeated my request he become enraged I finally ordered him to set down he said he would not unless I knocked him down I was agitated in my feeling on the account of his stubournness and was about to ~~call~~ leave the house, but my Father requ[e]sted me not to ‹do so› I com=plyed the house was brought to order after much debate upon the subject and we proceded to buisness & br. Eliot & his wife were both cleared from the charges prefered against them

Friday 30th [October 1835] at home Mr. Fransis Porter[43] ~~called~~ from Jefferson Co. New York a member of the Methodist Church, called to make some inquiry about lands in this place whether there is any farmes for sale that are valuable and whether [p. 12] a member of our church could move into this vicinity and purchase lands and enjoy his own possessions & property without making it common Stock, he had been requested to do so by some breth=ren who live in the town of Leroy Jeff[erson] Co N.Y I replyed that I had a valuable farm joining the Temple Lot that I would sell & that there is other lands for sale in this place and that we have no common stock business among us, that every man enjoys his own property, or can if he is disposed, consecrate liberally or illiberally to the support of the poor & needy, or the building up of Zion, he also enquired how many members there are in this church I told him that there is about five or six hundred who commune at our chapel and perhaps a thousand in this vicinity; at evening I was presented with a letter from Br. Wm Smith the purport of which is that he is censured by the brethren on the account of what took place at the council last night and wishes to have the matter settled to the un=derstanding of all, that he may not be censur=ed unjustly, concidering that his cause was a just one, and that he had been materially injured; I replied that I thought we parted with the best of feelings, that I am not to blame on the account of the dissatisfaction of others. I invited him to call and talk with me, and that I would ~~give~~ ‹talk with› him in the spirit of meekness and give him all the satisfaction I could– this reply was by letter copy retained

Saturday 31st [October 1835] in the morning br. Hyram Smith came in and said he had been much troub=led all night and had not slept any [p. 13] that something was wrong while talking br. Wm Smith came in according to my requ[e]st last night br. Hyram observed that he must go to the Store I invited him to stay he said he wo=uld go and do his business & return he did so while he was gone br. William introduced the subject of our difficulty at the council, I told him I did not want to converse upon the subject untill Hyrum returned, he soon came in I then proposed to relate the occurrences of the council before named and wherein I had been out of the way I would confess it and ask his forgivness, and then he should relate his story and make confession wherein he had done wrong ~~he said he had not done wrong~~ and then leave it to br. Hyrum Smith & br. Parish to decide the matter between us and I would agree to the decission & be satisfyed there with; he observed that he had not done wrong, and that I was al=ways determined to carry my points whether right or wrong and there fore he would not stand an equ=al chance with me; this was an insult, but I did not reply to him in a harsh manner knowing his inflamatory disposition, but tryed to reason with him and show him the propriety of a complyance with my request, I finally succeeded with the assistance of br. Hyrum in obtaining his assent to the propo=sition that I had made. I then related my story and wherein I had been wrong I confessed it and asked his forgivness after I got through he made his statements jusifying himself throughout in transgressing the order of the council & treating the authority of the Presidency with contempt; after he had got through br. Hyrum began to make [p. 14] some remarks, in the spirit of meekness, he became enraged, I joined my brother in trying to calm his stormy feelings, but to no purpose he insisted that we intended to add abuse to injury, his passion increased, he arose abruptly and declared that he wanted no more to do with ~~them~~ us or the church and said we might take his licence for he would have nothing to do with us, he rushed out at the door we tryed to prevail on him to stop, but all to no purpose, he went away in a passion, and soon sent his licence to me, he went home and spread the levvin of iniquity among my brethren and especially prejudiced the mind of br. Samuel as I soon learned that he was in the street exclaiming against me, which no doubt our enemys rejoice at, and where the matter will end I know not, but I p[r]ay God to forgiv[e] him and th[e]m, and give them humility and repentance, the feelings of my heart I cannot express on this occasion. I can only pray my heav=enly Father to open their eyes that they may dis=cover where they stand, that they may extricate themselves from the snare they have fallen into—after dinner I rode out in company with my wife and children, br. carloss & some others, we went to visit br. Roundy & family who live near Willoughby, we had an interesting visit at br. Roundy['s] as soon as I returned I was called upon to baptise Samuel Whitney & his Wife and Daughter after baptism we returned to their house and offered our thanks, in prayer I obtained a testimony that Br. William would return ~~and~~ to the church and repair the wrong he had done [p. 15]

Sunday morning November 1st 1835 Verily thus Saith the Lord
unto me, his servant Joseph Smith jr min[e] anger is kindle[d]
against my servant Reynolds Cahoon because of his iniquities his
covetous and dishonest principles in himself and family and he
doth not pur=ge them away and set his house in order therefore if
he repent not chastisment awaiteth him even as it seemeth good in
my sight therefore go and declare unto him these words I went
imediately and del[i]vired this message accord=ing as the Lord
commanded me I called him in & read what the Lord had said
concerning him, he acknowledged that it was verily so & expressed
much humility—I then went to meeting Elder Carrill [John Corrill]
preached a fine discourse, in the afternoon President Phelps
continued the servises of the day by reading the 5th chapt. of
Mathew also the laws regulating the High Council and made some
remarks upon them after which sacrament was administered I then
confirmed a num=ber who had been baptised & blessed a number
of children in the name of Jesus Christ with the blessings of the
new and everlasting covenant, notice was then given that the
Elders School[44] wou[l]d commence on the on the morrow, I then
dismissed the meeting.

Monday morning 2d [November 1835] was engaged in
regu=lating the affairs of the School, I then had my team prepared
& Sidney Oliver Frederick ~~and~~ my scribe and a number of others
went to Willoughby to Hear Doct[or] Piexotto[45] deliver a lectu=re
on the ~~profession~~ theory & practice of Physic [medicine] [p. 16] we
called at Mr. Cushmans, had our horses put in the Stable took
dinner, attended the lecture was treated with great respect
throughout; returned home Lyman Wight came from Zion to
day;—George & Lyman Smith[46] also from the East the question
was agitated whether Frederick G. Willia=ms or Oliver Cowdery
Should go to New York to make arangements respecting a book
bindery they refered to me for a decision, and thus cam[e] the word
of the Lord unto me saying it is not my will that my servant
Frederi=ck should go to New York, but inasmuch as he wishes to go
and visit his relatives that he may warn them to flee the wrath to

come let him go and see them, for that purpose and let that be his only business, and behold in this thing he shall be blessed with power ~~while~~ to overcome their prejudices, Verily thus saith the Lord Amen.

~~Thus came~~ Tuesday 3d [November 1835] Thus came the word of the Lord unto me ~~saying~~ concerning the Twelve ‹saying› behold they are under condemnation, because they have not been sufficiently humble in my sight, and in consequence of their covetous desires, in that they have not dealt equally with each other in the division of the moneys which came into their hands, never‹the›less some of them dealt equally therefore they shall be rewarded, but verily I say unto you they must all humble themselves before me, before they will be accounted worthy to receive an endowment to go forth in my name unto all nations, as for my Servant William let the Eleven humble themselves in prayer and in faith [p. 17] and wait on me in patience and my servant William shall return, and I will yet make him a polished shaft in my quiver, in bringing down the wickedness and abominations of men and their shall be none mightier than he in his day and generation, neverthe=less if he repent not spedily he shall be brou=ght low and shall be chastened sorely for all his iniquities he has commited against me. nevertheless the sin which he hath sined against me is not even now more grevious than the sin with which my servant David W. Patten and my servant Orson Hyde and my serv=ant Wm E. McLellen have sinded against me, and the residue are not sufficiently humble before me, behold the parable which I spake concerning a man having twelve Sons, for what man amon[g] you having twelve Sons and is no respecter to them and they serve him obediantly and he saith unto the one be thou clothed in robes and sit thou here, and to the other be thou clothed in rages [rags] and sit thou there, and looketh upon his sons and saith I am just, ye will answer and say no man, and ye answer truly, therefore Verely thus saith the Lord your God I appointed these twelve that they should be equal in their ministry and in their porti=on and in their evangelical rights, wherefore they have sin[n]ed a verry grevious sin, in as=much as they have made themselves unequ=al and have not hearkned unto my voice therfor let them repent speedily and pre=pare their hearts for the solem[n] assembly [p. 18] and for the great day which is to come Verely thus saith the Lord Amen.

I then went to assist in organizing the Elders School called to order and I made some rem=arks upon the object of this School, and the great necessity there is of our rightly improving our time and reigning up our minds to ~~the~~ a sense of the great object that lies before us, viz, that glorious end=owment that God has in store for the faithful I then dedicated the School in the name of the Lord Jesus Christ. after the School was dismissed I attended a patriarchal meeting at Br Samuel Smiths, his wifeses parents were blessed also his child & named Susanah, at evening I preach[e]d at the School-house to a crowded congregation

Wednesday 4th [November 1835] in morning, at home attended school ~~all~~ during the school hours, made rapid progress in our studies, in the evening, lectured on grammar, at home on this day King Follet[47] arived at this place from Zion

Thursday 5th [November 1835] attended School ~~all day,~~ Isaac Morley[48] came in from the east this morning I was called to visit Thomas Burdick[49] who was sick, I took my scribe with me and we p[r]ayed for and laid our hands on him in the ‹name› of the Lord Jesus and rebuked his affliction—Wm E. McLellen & Orson Hyde came in and desired to hear the revelation concerning the Twelve,[50] my scribe read to ~~him~~ them they expressed some little dissatisfaction but after examining their own hearts, they acc=knowledged it to be the word of the Lord [p. 19] and said they were satisfied; after School Brigham Young came in and desired also to hear, it read ~~also~~ after hearing it he appeared perfectly satisfied; in the eveni=ng lectured on Grammar

Friday morning 6th [November 1835] at home. attended School during the school hours returned and spent the evening at home I was this morning introduced to a man from the east, after hearing my name he ~~replied~~ remarked that I was nothing but a man: indicating by this expression that he had sup=posed that a person, <to> whom the Lord should see fit to reveal his will, must be something more than a man, he seems to have forgotten the saying that fell from the lips of St. James, that Elias was a man of like passions like unto us, yet he had such power with God that He in answer to his prayer, shut the heavens that they gave no rain for the space of three years and six months, and again in answer to his prayer the heavens gave forth rain and the earth brought forth fruit;[51] and indeed such is the darkness & ignorance of this generation that they look upon it as incredible that a man should have any intercourse with his Maker.

Saturday 7th [November 1835] spent the day at home attending to my domestic concerns; The word <of the Lord> came to me saying, behold I am well pleased with my servant Isaac Morley and my servant Edward Partridge, because of the integrity of their harts in laboring in my vinyard for the salvation of the souls of men, Verely I say unto you their sins are [p. 20] forgiven them, therefore say unto them in my name that it is my will that they should tarry for a little season and attend the school, and also the solem assembly for a wise purpose in me, even so amen

Sunday 8th [November 1835] went to meeting in the morning at the us[u]al hour, Z. Snow[52] preached a verry interesting discourse, in the after noon J. Young[53] preached; after preaching Isaac Hill[54] came forward to make some remarks by way of confession, he had been previously excommunicated from the church for lying & for an attempt to seduce a female; his confiss=ion was not satisfactory to my mind <Uncle> John Smith[55] arose and made some remarks respecting the dealings of the high council on the case of the said Hill, that is that he sho=uld make a public confession of his crime and have it published in the messenger and Advocate, he proposed that Mr Hill should now make his confession before the congregatio<n> and then

immediately observed that he had forgiven Mr Hill, which was in
contradiction to the sentiment he first advanced, this I attr=ibuted
to an error in Judgment not in design President Rigdon then arose
and verry abrup=tly militated against ‹the sentiment of› Uncle
John, which had a direct tendency to destroy his influence and
bring him into disrepute in the eyes of the church, which was not
right, he also misrepresented Mr Hills case ~~wh~~ and spread darkness
rather than light upon the subject a vote ~~was then called~~ of the
church was then called on his case and he was restored without any
further confession; that he should [p. 21] be received into the
church by babtism which was administered acordingly. after I came
home I took up a labour with uncle John and convinced him that
he was wrong & he made his confession to my satisfaction; I then
went and laboured with President Rigdon and succeded in
convin=cing him also of his error which he confessed to my
satisfaction.

The word of the Lord cam[e] unto me saying that President
Phelps & President J[ohn] Whitmer are under condemnation
before the Lord, for their errors ‹for which they made satisfaction
the same day›;[56] I also took up a labour with J[ohn] Carrill for
~~leaving the meeting before~~ ‹not partaking of the› sacra=ment, he
made his confession; also my wife for ~~the same~~ leaving the meeting
before sacram=ent she made no reply, but manifested cont=rition
by weeping

Monday morning 9th [November 1835] after breckfast ~~Sister~~
‹Mary› Whitcher came in and wished to see me, ~~she~~ I granted her
request she gave a rela=tion of her griveances which were,
unfathomable at present, and if true sore indeed, and I pray my
heavenly Father to bring the truth of her case to light, that the
reward due to evil doers may be given them, and ‹that› the
afflicted & oppressed may be delivered;–while setting in my house
between the hours of ten & 11 this morning a man came in, and
introduced him=self to me, calling ‹himself› by the name of Joshua
the Jewish minister,[57] his appearance was some thing singular,
having a beard about 3 inches in length which is quite grey, also his

hair is long and considerably silvered with age [p. 22] I should
think he is about 50 or 55 years old, tall and strait slender built of
thin visage blue eyes, and fair com=plexion, he wears a sea green
frock coat, & pantaloons of the same, black fur hat with narrow
brim, and while speaking frequently shuts his eyes with a scowl on
his countinance: I made some enquiry after his name but received
no definite answer; we soon comm=enced talking upon the subject
of religion and af=ter I had made some remarks concerning the
bible I commenced giving him a relation of the circum=stances
connected with the coming forth of the book of Mormon, as
follows—being wrought up in my mind, respecting the subject of
religion and looking at the different systems taught the children of
men, I knew not who was right or who was wrong and I considered
it of the first importance that I should be right, in matters that
involve eternal consequ[e]nces; being thus perplexed in mind I
retired to the silent grove and bow[e]d down before the Lord, under
a realising sense that he had said (if the bible be true) ask and you
shall receive knock and it shall be opened seek and you shall find
and again, if any man lack wisdom let him ask of God who giveth
to all men libar=ally and upbradeth not; information was what I
most desired at this time, and with a fixed determination to obtain
it, I called upon the Lord for the first time, in the place above
stated or in other words I made a fruitless attempt to p[r]ay, my
toung seemed to be swolen in my mouth, so that I could not utter, I
heard a noise behind me like some person walking towards me, I
strove again to pray, but could not, the noise of walking seem=ed
to draw nearer, I sprung up on my feet, ~~and~~ [p. 23] and looked
around, but saw no person or thing that was calculated to produce
the noise of wal=king, I kneeled again my mouth was opened and
my toung liberated, and I called on the Lord in mighty prayer, a
pillar of fire appeared above my head, it presently rested down upon
me ~~head~~, and filled me with Joy unspeakable, a personage appeard
in the midst of this pillar of flame which was spread all around, and
yet nothing consumed, another personage soon appeard like unto
the first, he said unto me thy sins are forgiven thee, he testifyed
unto me that Jesus Christ is the Son of God; ‹and I saw many

angels in this vision> I was about 14 years old when I received this
first communication; When I was about 17 years old I saw another
vision of angels in the night season after I had retired to bed I had
not been a sleep, ~~when~~ but was me=ditating upon my past life and
experience, I was verry concious that I had not kept the
commandments, and I repented hartily for all my sins and
transgression, and humbled myself before Him <whose eyes are over
all things>, all at once the room was iluminated above the
brightness of the sun an angel appeared before me, his hands and
feet were naked pure and white, and he stood between the floors of
the room, clothed with ~~in~~ purity inexpressible, he said unto me I
am a messenger sent from God, be faithful and keep his
commandments in all things, he told me of a sacred record which
was written on plates of gold, I saw in the vision the place where
they were deposited, he said the Indians were the literal
descendants of Abraham he explained many ~~things~~ of the
prophesies to [p. 24] me, one I will mention which is ~~this~~ in
Malachi 4 chapt. behold the day of the Lord cometh &c. also that
the Urim and Thumim, was hid up with the record, and that God
would give me powre to translate it, with the assistance of this
instrument he then gradually vanished out of my sight, or the
vision closed, while meditating on what I had seen, the angel
appeard to me again and related the same things and much more,
also the third time bearing the same tidings, and dep=arted; during
the time I was in this vision I did not realize any thing ~~else~~ around
me except what was shown me in this communication: after the
vision had all passed, I found that it was nearly day-light, the
family soon arose, I got up also:—on that day while in the field at
work with my Father he asked me if I was sick I replyed, I had but
little strenght, he told me to go to the house, I started and went
part way and was finally deprived ~~deprived~~ of my stren=gth and fell,
but how long I remained I do not know; the Angel came to me
again and comm=anded me to go and tell my Father, what I had
seen and heard, I did so, he wept and told me that it was a vision
from God to attend to it I went and found the place, where the
plates were, according to the direction of the Angel, also saw

them, and the angel as before; the powers of darkness strove hard
against me. I called on God, the Angel told me that the reason
why I could not obtain the plates at this time was because I was
under transgression, but to come again in one year from that time,
I did so, but did not obtain them [p. 25] also the third and the
fourth year, at which time I obtained them, and translated them
into the english language, by the gift and power of God and have
been preaching it ever since.

   While I was relating this brief history of the establishment of
the Church of Christ in these last days, Joshua seemed to be highly
entertained after I had got through I observed that, the hour of
worship & time to dine had now arived and invited him to tarry,
which he concented to,

   After dinner the conversation was resumed and Joshua
proceded to make some remarks on the prophesies, as follows:

   He observed that he was aware that I could bear stronger meat
than m=any others, therefore he should open his mind the more
freely:– Daniel has told us that he is to stand in his proper lot, in
the latter days according to his vision he had a right to shut it up
and also to open it again after many days, or in the latter times;
Daniels Image whose head was gold, and body, armes, legs and feet
was composed of the different materials descr=ibed in his vision
represents different governm=ents, the golden head was ‹to
represent› Nebuchadnazer King of Babylon, the other parts other
kings & forms of gove=rnment, which I shall not now mention in
detail, but confine my remarks, more particularly to the feet of the
Image: The policy of the wicked spir=it, is to separate what God
has joined togather and unite what He has separated, which he has
succeded in doing to admiration, in the present state of society,
which is like unto Iron and clay, there is confusion in all things,
both [p. 26] both Political and religious, and notwithstanding all
the efforts that are made to bring about a un=ion, society remains
disunited, and all attempts to ‹unite her› are as fruitless, as to
attemp[t] to unite Iron & Clay.

   The feet of the Image, is the government of these united States,
other Nations & Kingdoms are looking up to her, for an example,

of union fredom and equal rights, and therefore worship her, like as Daniel saw in the vision, although they are begining to loose confidence in her, seeing the broils and discord that distract, her political & religious hor=izon; this Image is characteristic of all governmen=ts and institutions or most of them; as they begin with a head of gold and terminate in the contemp=[t]ible feet of Iron & clay: making a splendid app=earance at first, proposing to do much more than the[y] can perform, and finally end in degradation and sink, in infamy; we should not only start to com[e] out of Babylon but leav[e] it entirely lest we are overthrown in her ruins, we should keep improving and reforming;– twenty-four hours for improvement now, is worth as much as a year, a hundred years ago; the spirit of the Fathers that was cut down, or those that were under the altar, are now rising, this is the first resurection the Elder that falls first, will rise last; we should not form any opinion only for the present, and leave the result of futurity with God: I have ris=en up out of obscurity, but was looked up to when but a youth, in temporal things: It is not necess=ary that God should give us all things at first or in his first commission to us, but in his second. John saw the angel deliver the gospel in the last days, which would not be necessary if [p. 27] it was already, in the world, this expression would be inconsistent, the small lights that God has given, is sufficient to lead us out of babylon, when we get out we shall have the greater light. I told Jo[s]hua that I did not understand him concerning the resurection and wishd him to be more explanitory on the subject; he replied that he did not feel im=pressed by the spirit to unfold it further at present, but perhaps he might at some other time.

I then withdr[e]w to do some buisness with another gentleman that called to see me. He [Joshua] informed my Scribe that he was born in Washington County Town of Cambr=idge New York. he says that all the rail=roads canals and other improvements are performed by spirits of the resurection.

The silence spoken of by John the Revelator which is to be in heaven for the space of half an hour, is between 1830 & 1851, during which time the judgments of God will be poured out after that time there will be peace.

Curiosity to see a man that was reputed to be a Jew, caused many to call during the day and more particularly at evening Suspicions were entertained that said Joshua was the noted Mathias of New York, spoken so much of in the public prints on account of the trials he underwent in that place before a court of justice, for murder mansl=aughter comtempt of court whiping his Dau=ghter &c for the two last crimes he was imp=risoned, and came out about 4 months [p. 28] since, after some, equivocating he confessed that he was realy Mathias: after supper I proposed that he should deliver a lecture to us, he did so sitting in his chair; he commenced by say=ing God said let there be light and there was light, which he dwelt upon through his disco=urce, he made some verry exelent remarks but his mind was evidently filled with dar=kness, after he dismissed his meeting, and the congregation disperced, he conversed freely upon the circumstances that transpired in New York. His name is Robert Mathias, he say[s] that Joshua, is his priestly name.

During all this time I did not contradict his sentiments, wishing to draw out all that I could concerning his faith; the next morning

Tuesday 10th [November 1835] I resumed the conversation and desired him to enlighten my mind more on his views respecting the resurection, he says that he posses[ses] the spirit of his fathers, that he is a litteral decendant of Mathias the Apo=stle that was chosen in the place of Judas that fell and that his spirit is resurected in him, and that this is the way or schem[e] of eternal life, this transmigration of soul or spirit from Father to Son: I told him that his doctrine was of the Devil that he was in reality in possession of [a] wicked and depraved spirit, although he professed to be the spir=it of truth, itself, <& he said> also that he possesses the soul of Christ; he tarried until Wednesday 11th, after breckfast I told him, that my God told me that his God is the Devil, and I could not keep him any longer, and he must depart, and so I for once cast out the Devil in bodily shape, & I believe a murderer [p. 29] on monday th[e] 9th Mr. [Alvah] Beeman of N.Y came here to ask advice of me concerning purchasing lands, whether it is best for him to purchase in this vicinity and move into this church, or not,

he says that he cannot arrange his buisness so as to go to the
Missouri next spring; I advised him to come here, and settle untill
he could move to Zion

Wednesday morning 11th [November 1835] at home attended
School during school Hours, returned home and spent the evening,
around my fire-side, teaching my family the science of grammar; it
commensed snowing this after=no[o]n, the wind is verry heavy
indeed

Thursday 12th [November 1835] attended School again, during
school Hours, rain & snow is still falling, it is about one inch in
dept[h], the wind is verry heavy, and the weather extremly
unpleasant, the labour[er]s who commenced finis=hing the out side
of the ~~house~~ Chappel were oblieged to brake off from their buisness
at the commencement of this storm viz on the 11th they
commenced plasturing and finishing the outside on monday the 2.
Inst. this job is let to A. Millet[58] & L[orenzo] Young, ‹at $1,000›
they have progressed rapidly since they commenced.
   J. Bump[59] has the job of plastering the inside of the house
through out at $15.00, he commenced on Monday the 9th and is
continueing it notwithstanding the inclemency of the weather.
This evening viz the 12th at 6 oclock meet [met] with the council
of 12. by their request, 9 of them were present [p. 30] council
opened by singing & prayer, and I made some remarks as follows:–I
am happy in the enjoyment of this opportunity of meeting with this
council on this occasion, I am satisfyed that the spirit of the Lord is
here, and I am satisfied with all the breth[r]en present, and I need
not say that you have my utmost confidence, and that I intend to
uphold, you to the uttermost, for I am well aware that you ~~do and
delight in so do=ing~~ have to sustain my character ~~my character~~
against the vile calumnies and reproaches of this ungodly
generation and that you delight in so doing:–darkness prevails, at
this time as it was, at the time Jesus Christ was about to be
crucified, the powers of darkness strove to obscure the glorious sun
of righteousness that began to dawn upon the world, and was soon

to burst in great blessings upon the heads of the faithful, and let me
tell you brethren that great blessings awate us at this time and will
soon be poured out upon us if we are faithful in all things, for we
are even entitled to greater blessings than they were, because the[y]
had the person of Christ with them, to instruct them in the great
plan of salvation, his personal presence we have not, therefore we
need great faith on account of our peculiar circumstances and I am
determined to do all that I can to uphold you, although I may do
many things ‹invertarilly [inadvertently?]› that are not right in the
sight of God; you want to know many things that are before you,
that you may know how ~~how~~ to prepare your selves for the [p. 31]
great things that God is about to bring to pass; but there is on[e]
great deficiency or obstruction, in the way that deprives us of the
greater blessings, and in order to make the foundation of this
church complete and permanent, we must remove this
obstruct=ion, which is to attend to certain duties that we have not
as yet attended to; I supposed I had established this church on a
perma=nent foundation when I went to the Miss=ouri and indeed I
did so, for if I had been taken away it would have been eno=ugh,
but I yet live, and therefore God requires more at my hands:–The
item to which I wish the more particularly to call your attention to
night is the ord=inance of washing of feet, this we have not done as
yet but it is necessary now as much as it was in the days of the
Saviour, and we must have a place pre=pared, that we may attend to
this ordi=nance, aside from the world; we have not desired much
from the hand of the Lord, with that faith and obediance that we
ought, yet we have enjoyed great blessings, and we are not so
sensible of this as we should be: when or wher[e] has God suffered
one of the witnesses or first Elders of this church to fall? never nor
nowhere amidst all the calamities and judgments that have befallen
the inhabitants of the earth his almighty arm has sus=tained us,
men and Devils have raged and spent the[ir] malice in vain. [p. 32]
we must have all things prepared and call our solem assembly as the
Lord has commanded us, that we may be able to accomplish his
great work: and it mu[s]t be done in Gods own way, the house of
the Lord must be prepared, and the sol=em assembly called and

organized in it according to the order of the house of God and in it
we must attend to the ordinance of washing of feet; it was never
intended for any but official members, it is calcul=ated to unite our
hearts, that we may be one in feeling and sentiment and that our
faith may be strong, so that satan cannot over thro=w us, nor have
any power over us,—the endowment you are so anxious about you
cannot comprehend now, nor could Gab=riel explain it to the
understanding of yo=ur dark minds, but strive to be prepared in
your hearts, be faithful in all things that when we meet in the
solem assembly that is such as God shall name out of all the official
members, will meet, and we must be clean evry whit, let us be
faithful and silent brethren, ⟨and⟩ if God gives you a
m=anifestation, keep it to yourselves, be watchful and prayerful,
and you shall have a prelude of those joys that God will pour out on
that day, do not watch for iniquity in each other if you do you will
not get an endowment for God will not bestow it on such; but if we
are faithful and live by every word that procedes forth from the
mouth of God I will venture to prophesy that we shall get a [p. 33]
blessing that will be worth remembering if we should live as long as
John the Revelator, our blessings will be such as we have not
realized before, nor in this generation. The order of the house of
God has and ever will be the same, even after Christ comes, and
after the terminat=ion of the thousand years it will be the same,
and we shall finally roll into the celestial Kingdom of God and
enjoy it forever:—you need an endowment brethren in order that
you may be prepared and able to over come all things, and those
that reject your testimony will be damned the sick will be healed
the lame made to walk the deaf to hear and the blind to see
through your instrumentality; But let me tell you that you will not
have power after the endowment to heal those who have not faith,
nor to benifit them, for you might as well expect to benefit a devil
in hell as such an one, who is possessed of his spirit and are
will=ing to keep it for they are habitations for devils and only fit for
his society but when you are endowed and prepared to preach the
gospel to all nations kindred and toungs in there own languages you
must faithfully warn all and bind up the testimony and seal up the

law and the destroying angel will follow close at your heels and
execu=te his tremendeous mission upon the children of
disobediance, and destroy [p. 34] the workers of iniquity, while the
saints will be gathered out from among them and stand in holy
places ready to meet the bride groom when he comes.—
    I feel disposed to speak a few words more to you my brethren
concerning the endowm=ent, all who are prepared and are
suff=iciently pure to abide the presence of the Savi=our will see
him in the solem assembly.
    The brethren expressed their gratifycation for the instruction I
had given them, we then closed by prayer.—I then returned home
and retired to rest

    Friday 13th [November 1835] attended school during school
hours, returned home after School; Mr Messenger of Bainbridge
Chenango Co. N[ew] Y[ork] came in to make some enquiry about
H. Peck's[60] family he is a Universalian Minister we entered into
conversation upon religious subjects, we went to President Rigdon's
and spent the evening in convers=ation, we preachd the gospel to
him, and bore testimony to him of what we had seen and heard, he
attempted to raise some obje=ctions but the force of truth bore him
down, and he was silent, although un=believing; returned home
and retired to rest

    Saturday morning 14th [November 1835] Thus came the word
of the Lord unto me saying: verily thus saith the the Lord unto my
servant Joseph concerning my servant Warren [Parrish] behold
[p. 35] his sins are forgiven him because of his desires to do the
works of righteousness therefore in as much as he will continue to
hearken unto my voice he shall be blessed with wisdom and with a
sound mind even above his fellows, behold it shall come to pass in
his day that he shall <see> great things shew forth themselves unto
my people, he shall see much of my ancient records, and shall
know of hiden things, and shall be endowed with a knowledge of
hiden languages, and if he desires and shall seek it at my hand, he
shall be privileged with writing much of my word, as a scribe unto

me for the benefit of my people, therefore this shall be his calling
until I shall order it otherwise in my wisdom and it shall be said of
him in a time to come, behold Warren the Lords Scribe, for the
Lords Seer whom he hath appointed in Israel: Therefore ‹if he
will› keep my commandments he shall be lifted up at the last day,
even so Amen

A Gentleman called this after noon by the name of Erastus
Holmes of Newbury Clemon [Clermont] Co. Ohio, he called to
make enquiry about the establish=ment of the church of the
latter=day Saints and to be instructed more perfectly in our
doctrine &c I commenced and gave him a brief relation of my
experience while in my [p. 36] juvenile years, say from 6 years old
up to the time I received the first visitation of Angels which was
when I was about 14. years old and also the the visitations that I
received afterward, concerning the book of Mormon, and a short
account of the rise and progress of the church, up to this, date he
listened verry attentively and seemed highly gratified, and intends
to unite with the Church he is a verry candid man indeed and I am
much pleased with him.

On Sabath morning the 15th [November 1835] he went with
me to meeting, which was held in the Sch=ool-house on account
of the Chappel not being finished plastering. President Rigdon
prea=ched on the subject of men's being called to preach the gospel
and their qualifications &c we had a fine discourse it was verry
interesting indeed. Mr. Holmes was well satisfied, he came home
with me and dined.

Said Holmes has been a member of the Methodist Church, and
was excommunicated for receiving, the Elders of the church of the
latter-day Saints into his house

Went to meeting in the afterno[o]n, before part=aking of the
sacrament Isaac Hills case was agitated again, and settled after
much controversy, and he retained in the church by making an
humble acknowled[g]ement before the church, and concenting to
have his confession published in the Messenger and advocate, after
which the ordinance of the Lord['s] Supper was administered, and

the meeting closed, verry late,—returned home and spent the
evening.— [p. 37]

Monday the 16th [November 1835] at home, dictated a letter
for the Advocate, also one to Harvey Whitlock.[61] Father [Alvah]
Beeman called to council with me Elder Strong[62] and some others
/[63]Copy of the Letter from Harvey Whitloc[k]
Dear sir having a few leisure moment[s] I have at last concluded
to do what my own Judgment has long dictated would be right but
the allurements of many vices has long retarded the hand, that
would wield the pen to make intelligent the communication that I
wish to send to you: And even now that ambition which is a
prevaling and predoment principles among the great mass of
natural men even now forbids that plainness of sentiment with
which I wish to ~~unbosom my feelings~~ write. For know assuredly sir
to you I wish to unbosom my feelings, and unravil the secrets of my
heart: as before the omnicient Judge of all the earth.

Be not surprised when I declare unto you, as the spirit will bear
record that my faith is firm and unshaken in the things of the
everlasting gospel as it is proclaimed by the servants of the latter-
day saint[s].

Dear brother Joseph (If I may be allow=ed the expression)
when I considder the happy times and peaseful moments, and
pleasant seasons I have enjoyed with you, ~~and~~ and this people;
contrasted with my now degraded state; together with the high,
and important station I have held before [p. 38] God: and the abyss
into which I have fallen, is a subject that swells/[64] my heart to big
for utterance, and language is overwhelmed with feeling, and
looses its power of description. and as I desire to know the will of
God concerning me; Believing it is my duty to m=ake known unto
you my real situation.

I shall therefore, dispasionately procede to give a true and
untarnished relation; I need not tell you that in former times, I
have preached the word; and endeavored to be instant in season
[and] out of season, to reprove rebuke exhort and faithfully to
discharge that trust repo=sed in me. But oh! with what grief &

lame=ntable sorrow and anguish do I have to relate that I have
fallen, from that princely station where unto our God has called
me. Reasons why are unnecessary. May the fact suffice; and believe
me when I tell you, that I have sunk myself, (since my last
separation from this boddy) in crimes of the deepest dye, and that I
may the better enable you to understand what my real sins are, I
will mention (although pride forbids it) some that I am not guilty
of, my ‹hands› have not been stained with inocent blood; neither
have I lain couched around the cottages of my fellow men to seize
and car=ry off the booty; nor have I slandered my ne=ighbor, nor
bourn fals testimony, nor taken unlawful hire, nor oppressed the
widdow nor fatherless, neither have I persecuted the Saints. But
my hands are swift to do iniq= uity, and my feet are fast running in
the paths of vice and folly; and my heart [p. 39] quick to devise
wicked imaginations: nevertheless I am impressed with the sure
thought that I am fast hastning into a ~~whole~~ world of disembodied
beings, without God & with but one hope in the world; which is to
know that to er[r] is human, but to forgive is divine: much I might
say in relation to myself and the original difficulties with the
church, which I will forbear, and in asmuch as I have been charged
with things that I was not guilty of I am now more than doubly
guilty. and am now willing to forgive and forget only let me know
that I am within the reach of mercy; If I am not I have no
reflections to cast, but say that I have sealed my own doom and
pronounced my own sentence. If the day is passed by with me may I
here beg leave to entreat of those who are still toiling up the ruged
assent to make their way to the realms of end= less felicity, and
delight, to stop not for anchors here below, follow not my
exam=ple. but steer your course onward inspite of all the combined
powers of earth and hell, for know that one miss step here is only
retrievable by a thousand groans and tears before God. Dear
Brother Joseph, let me entreat you on the rec=eption of this letter,
as you regard the salvation of my soul, to enquire at the hand of the
Lord in my behalf; for I this day in the presence of God, do
cove=nant to abide the word that may be given, for I am willing to
receive any [p. 40] chastisement that the Lord sees I deserve.

Now hear my prayer and suffer me to br=eak forth in the agony
of my soul. O ye Angels! that surround the throne, ‹of God›
Princes of heaven, that excell in strength, ye who are clothed with
transcendant brightness, plead O plead for one of the most
wretched of the sons of men. O ye heavens! whose azure arches rise
immensely high and st=rech immeasurably wide, grand
ampith=eater of nature, throne of the eternal God bow to hear the
prayer of a poor wretched bewildered way wanderer to eternity. O
thou great Omnicient & omnipresent Jehovah, thou who siteth
upon the throne, before whom all things are present, thou maker
moulder & fashioner of all things visible and invisable breath o
breath into the ears of thy servant the Prophet, words su[i]tably
ad=apted, to my case, and situation, speak once more, make
known thy will conc=erning me, which favours I ask in the name
of the Son of God amen

N.B I hope you will not let any buis=iness prevent you from
answering this lett=er in hast
                    Yours Respectfully
                    Harvey Whitlock
to Joseph Smith [p. 41]

      Copy of a Letter sent Harvy Whitlock in answer to his

                                    Kirtland Nov. 16th 1835
Bro Harvey Whitlock
      I have received your letter of the 28th Sept. 1835, and I have
read it twice, and it gave me sensations that are better imagined
than discribed; let it suffice, that I say the verry flood-gates of my
heart were broken up: I could not refrain from weeping. I thank
God, that it has entered into your heart, to try to return to the
Lord, and to his people; if it so be, that he will have mercy upon
you.
      I have inquired of the Lord concerning your case, these words
came to me
      Verily thus saith the Lord unto you: let him who was my

servant Harvey, return unto me;–and unto the bosom of my
Church, and forsake all the sins wherewith he has offended against
me and persue from hence forth a virtuous and upright life, and
remain under the direction of those whom I have app=ointed to be
pillars, and heads of my church, and behold, saith the Lord, your
God; his sins shall be blotted out from under heaven, and shall be
forgotten from among men, and shall not come up in mine ears,
nor be recorded as ‹a› me=morial against him, but I will lift [p. 42]
him up as out of deep mire, and he shall be exalted upon the
high places, and shall be counted worthy to stand ammong
princ=es, and shall yet be made a polished shaft in my quiver, of
bringing down the strong holds of wickedness, among those who
set themselves up on high, that they may take council against me,
and against annoint=ed ones in the last days.

   Therefore let him prepare himself speed=ily and come unto
you; even to Kirtland and inasmuch as he shall harken unto all
your council from henceforth he shall be restored unto his former
state, and shall be saved unto the uttermost, even as the Lord your
God livith Amen.

   Thus you see my dear Brother the willing=ness of our heavenly
Father to forgive sins and restore to favour all those who are willing
to humble themselves before him, and confess their sins and
forsake them, and return to him with full purpose of heart (acting
no hypocrisy) to serve him to the end.

   Marvle not that the Lord has condescen=ded to speak from the
heavens and give you instructions whereby you may learn your
duty: he has heard your prayers, and witnessed your humility; and
holds forth the hand of paternal affection, for your return; the
angels rejoice over you, while the saints are willing to receive you
again into fellowship.

   I hope on the recept of this, you will ~~not~~ loose ~~any~~ no time in
coming to [p. 43] Kirtland: for if you get here in season, you will
have the privilege of attending the School of the prophets, which
has already commenced and, also receive instruction in doctrine,
and principle, from those whom God has appointed whereby you
may be qualified to go forth, and declare the true doctrines of the

Kingdom according to the ~~true doctr=ines of the~~ mind and, will of God. and when you come to Kirtland, it will be explained to you why God has condes=cended to give you a revelation according to your request.

Please give my respects to you[r] family, and bee assured I am yours in the bonds of the new and everlasting covenant

Joseph Smith Jun

on this evening, viz the 16th [November 1835] a council was called at my house to council with ~~Father~~ Alva Beeman on the subject of his moov=ing to the Missourie; I had previously told him that the Lord had said that he had better go to the Missourie, next Spring: however he wished a council, called, the cou=ncil met President D[avid] Whitmer arose and said the spirit manifested to him that it was his duty to go; also others bore the same testimony.

The same night ~~that~~ I received the word of the Lord on Mr. H[o]lmes case, he had desired that I would inquire at the hand of the Lord whether it was [p. 44] his duty to be baptised here, or wait until he returned home:–The word of the Lord ca=me unto me saying, that Mr. Holmes had better not be baptised here, and that he had better not return by water, also that there were three men that were seeking his destruction, to be ware of his ene[m]ys

Tuesday 17th [November 1835] exibited ‹the Alphabet› ~~some~~ of the ancient records to Mr. Holmes and some others, went with him to F G. Williams to see the Mumies, we then took the parting hand, and he started for home, being strong in the faith of the gospel of Christ and determined to obey the requiremen=ts of the same.

I returned home and spent the day dictating and comparing letters.

This has been a fine pleasant day altho=ugh cool, this Evening at early candlelight I pr[e]ached at the School house, returned home and retired to rest,

Wednesday 18th [November 1835] at home in the fore noon, untill about 11 oclock. I then went to Preserved Harris's,[65] to preach his fathers funeral Sermon, by the request of the family I preached on the subject of the resurection, the congregation were verry attentive My wife my mother and my scribe went with me to the funeral, we rode in a waggon, had a pleasant ride, the weather was pleasant, when we went, but cloudy and cool when we returned [p. 45] at evening Bishop Whitney his wife Father and Mother, and Sister in law, came in and invited me and my wife to go with them & visit Father Smith & family my wife was unwell and could not go; however I and my Scribe went, when we got there, we found that some of the young Elders, were about engaging in a debate, upon the subject of miracles, the q[u]estion was this; was or was it not the design of Christ to Est=ablish his gospel by miracles.

After an interesting debate of three hours or more, during which time much talent was displayed, it was desided by the presidents of the debate in the negative; which was a righteous descision I discovered in this debate, much warmth displayed, to much zeal for mastery, to much of that enthusiasm that chara=cterizes a lawyer at the bar, who is determined to defend his cause right or wrong. I therefore availed myself of this favorable opportunity, to drop a few words upon this subject by way of advise, that they might improve their minds and cultivate their powers of intellect in a proper manner, that they might not incur the displeasure of heaven, that they should handle sacred things verry sacredly, and with due deference to the opinions of others and with an eye single to the glory of God. [p. 46]

Thursday 19th went in company with Doct. Williams & my scribe to see how the work=men prospered in finishing the house; the masons on the inside had commenced puting on the finishing coat of plastureing. on my return I met L[l]oyd & Lorenzo Lewis[66] and conversed with them upon the subject of their being disaffected. I found that they were not so, as touching the faith of the chu=rch but with some of the members:

I returned home and spent the day in translating the Egyptian records: ~~on~~ this has been a warm & pleasant day——

Friday 20th [November 1835] in morning at home: the weather
is warm but rainy, we spent the day in translating, and made rapid
progress

At Evening, President Cowdery returned from New York,
bringing with him a qu=antity of Hebrew books for the benefit of
the school, he presented me with a Hebrew bible, lexicon &
grammar, also a Greek Lex=icon and Websters English Lexicon.

President Cowdery had a prosperous jo=urney, according to the
prayers of the saints in Kirtland

Saturday 21st [November 1835] at home, spent the day in
examining my books and study=ing ‹the› ~~my~~ hebrew alphabet, at
evening met with our hebrew class to make some arrangments
about a Teacher, it was decided by the voice of the School to send
[p. 47] to N. York for a Jew to teach us the language, if we could
get released from the engagement we had made with Doct.
Piexotto to teach the language, having asertained that he was not
qualified to give us the knowledge we wish to acqu=ire

Sunday 22d [November 1835] went to meeting at the us[u]al
hour. Simeon Ca[r]ter[67] preached from the 7th Chapt of Mathew;
President Rigdon's brother in Law & Some other relat=ives were at
meeting, in the after noon the meeting was held in the School-
house also in the evening had a meeting, and Elder [Andrew
Jackson] Squires who had withdrawn from the Church made
application, to return after giving him a severe chastisment, he was
recieved, and his licence restored to him; when the case of Elder
Squires was introduced, we organized into a regular council.
Sylvester Smith was chosen Clerk and after conciderable
altercation upon the subject & keen rebuke he was restored by the
voice of the council & church & the clerk ordered to give him his
licence as above stated.[68] On this night we had a snow storm

Monday 23d [November 1835] several brethren called to
converse with me, and see the records; rec'd a letter from Jared

Carter, spent the day in conversing, and in studying, the hebrew,
language

This has been a stormy day [p. 48]

Tuesday 24th [November 1835] at home, spent the fore noon
instructing those that called to inquire concerning the things of
God, in the last da=ys: in the after-noon, we translated some of the
Egyptian, records; I had an invitation to attend a wedding at Br.
Hiram Smith's in the evening also to solemnize the matrimonial
ceremony, <between Newell Knight[69] & Lydia Goldthwaite[70]> I
and my wife, went, when we arrived a conciderable company, had
collected, the bridegroom & bride came in, and took their seats,
which gave me to understand that they were ready. I requesteded
them to arise and join hands. I then remarked that marriage was an
institution of h[e]aven institu[te]de in the garden of Eden, that it
was necessary that it should be Solemnized by the authority of the
everlasting priesthood, before joining hands however, we attended
prayers. I then made the remarks above stated; The ceremony was
original <with me> it was in substance as follows. You covenant to
be each others companions through life, and discharge the duties of
husband & wife in every respect to which they assented. I then
p[r]onounced them husband & Wife in the name of God and also
~~pronounced~~ the blessings that the Lord confered upon adam & Eve
in the gar=den of Eden, that is to multiply and replen=ish the
earth, with the addition of long life and prosperity; dismissed them
and returned home.—The weather is freezing cold, some snow on
the ground [p. 49]

Wednesday 25th [November 1835] spent the day in
Translating.–To-day Harvey Redfield[71] & Jesse Hitchcock[72] arived
here from Missourie; the latter says that he has no doubt, but that a
dose of poison was administered to him in a boll of milk but God
deli-<vered him>

Thursday 26th [November 1835] at home, we spent the day in
transcribing Egyptian characters from the papyrus.–I am severely

afflicted with a cold.–to day Robert Rathbone[73] and George
Morey[74] arrived from Zion

Friday 27th [November 1835] much afflicted with my cold, yet
able to be about and I am determined to overcom in the name of
the Lord Jesus Christ,– spent the day in ~~stud~~ reading Hebrew at
home.
    The weather continues cold and unp=leasant.–Br. Parrish my
scribe being aff=licted with a cold, asked me to lay my hands on
him in the name of the Lord I did so, and in return I asked him to
lay his hands on me & we were both relieved.–

    ‹See page 9th› Copy of a prayer offered up on the 23d day of
Oct 1835, by the foll=owing individuals, at 4 oclock P.M. viz.
Joseph Smith Jn, Oliver Cowdery, David Whitmer, Hirum Smith
John Whitmer, Sidn[e]y Rigdon, Samuel H. Smith, Frede=rick G.
Williams, and Wm. W. Phelps, assem=bled and united in prayer,
with one voice before the Lord for the following blessings:
    That the Lord will give us means su=fficient to deliver us from
all our afflictions and difficulties, wherein we are placed by means
of our debts; that he will open the way and deliver Zion in the
app=[p. 50]ointed time and that without the shedd=ing of blood;
that he will hold our lives precious, and grant that we may live to
the common age of man, and never fall into the hands nor power of
the mob in Missourie nor in any other place; that he will also
preserve our posterity, that none of them fall even to the end of
time; that he will give us the blessings of the earth sufficient to
carry us to Zion, and that we may purchase inher=itances in that
land, even enough to carry on ‹and accomplish› the work unto
which he was appointed us; and also that he will assist all others
who desire, according to his commandme=nts, to go up and
purchase inheritances, and all this easily and without perplexity,
and trouble; and finally, that in the end he will save us in his
Celestial Kingdom. Amen.
                                        Oliver Cowdery Clerk

Saturday 28th [November 1835] at home, spent the morning in compareing our journal.–

~~This~~ Elder Josiah Clark called this mor=ning to see me, he lives in Cam[pb]el County K[entuck]y about three miles above Cincinate.

I am conciderably recovered from my cold, & I think I shall be able in a few days to translate again, with the blessing of God.–The weather is still cold and sto=rmy, the snow is falling, & winter seems to be closing in ~~verry fast~~, all nature shrinks before the chilling blasts of rigid winter.–

Elder Clark above mentioned, has been biten by a mad dog some three or four [p. 51] years since, has doctered much, and received some benefit by so doing, but is much afflicted notwithstanding, he came here that he might be benefited by the prayers of the church, acco=rdingly we prayed for and layed our hands on him, in the name of the Lord Jesus Christ and anointed him with oil, and rebuked his affliction, praying our heavenly Father to hear and answer our prayers according to our faith

Sunday morning 29th [November 1835] went to m=eeting at the us[u]al hour Elder Morley preachd and Bishop Partridge in the afternoon; their discourses were well adapted to the times in which we live, and the circumstances un=der which we are placed, their words were words of wisdom, like apples of gold in pictures of silver, spoken in the simple acc=ents of a child, yet sublime as the voice of an angels, the saints, appeared to be much pleased with the beautiful discourses of these two fathers in Israel; after these servises closed, three of the Zion brethren came forward and recieved their blessing

Solon Foster[75] was ordained to the office of an Elder; the Lord's supper was then administered, and the meeting closed. returned home and spent the evening. The storm continues, the weather is verry cold [p. 52]

Monday morning 30th [November 1835] yet the snow is falling and is sufficiently deep for ~~slay~~ sleighing, this is an uncommon

storm for this country, at this season of the year spent the day in
writing a letter for the Messenger & Advocate on the Subject of
the Gathering;[76]– this afternoon, Henry Capron[77] called to see me,
he is an old acquaintance of mine, from Manchester New York,
shewed him the Egyptian re=cords

Tuesday December 1st 1835, at home spent the day in writing,
for the M & Advoc=ate, the snow is falling and we have fine
sleighing.

Wednesday 2nd [December 1835] a fine morning I made
preparation, to ride to Painsvill[e], with my wife and ~~children,~~
family, also my Scr=ibe, we had our sleigh and horses prepared and
set out, when we ~~arived~~ were passing through Mentor Street, we
overtook a team with two men on the sleigh. I politely asked them
to let me pass, they granted my req=uest, and as we passed them,
they bawled out, do you get any revelation lately, with an adition
of blackguard that I did not understand, this is a fair sample of the
character of Mentor Street inhabitants, who are ready to abuse and
scandalize, men who never laid a straw in their way, and infact
those whos faces they never saw, and cannot bring an acusation,
against, either [p. 53] of a temporal or spir[i]tual nature; except our
firm belief in the fulness of the gospel and I was led to marvle ~~that~~
~~God~~ at the long suffering and condescention of our hea=venly
Father, in permitting, these ungodly wretches, to possess, this
goodly land, which is ~~the~~ indeed as beautifully situated and its soil
as fertile, as any in this region of country, and its inhabitance, ~~as~~
wealthy even blessed, above measure, in temporal things, and fain,
would God bless, them with, ~~with~~ spiritual blessings, even eter=nal
life, were it not for their evil he=arts of unbelief, and we are led to
~~cry in our hearts~~ mingle our prayers with those saints that have
suffered the like treatment before us, whose souls are under the
altar crying to the Lord for vengance upon those that dwell upon
the earth and we rejoice that the time is at hand when, the wicked
who will not repent will be swept ‹from the earth› with the besom
of destruction and the earth become an inheritance for the poor
and the meek.——

when we arived at Painsvill[e] we called at Sister Harriet
How[e']s,[78] and left my wife and family to visit her while we rode
into Town to do some business, ~~returned~~ called and visited H.
Kingsbury—[79] Returned and dined with Sister How[e], and
returned home, had a fine ride the sleighing is ~~fine~~ <good> and
weather pleasant——[p. 54]

Thursday the 3d [December 1835] at home, wrote a letter to
David Dort,[80] Rochester Michigan, another to Almyra Scoby[81]
Liberty Clay co., Mo. at home all day,–at evening, was invited
with my wife, to attend, at Thomas Caricoes,[82] to join W[arren]
Parrish & Martha H. Raymond in mattrimony, we found a verry
pleasant and respectable company waiting when, we arived, we
opened our interview with singing & prayer, after which, I
delivered an ad=dress, upon the subject of matrimony, I then
in=vited the <parties> ~~couple~~ to arise, who were to be joined in
wedlock, and, solemnized the institution in a brief manner, and
pronounced them husband and wife in the name of God according
to the articles, and covenants of the <Church of the> latter day
saints, closed by singing and prayer, took some refreshment, and
retired; having spent the evening, agreeab=ly

Friday 4th [December 1835] to day, in compa=ny with Vinson
Knights, we drew, three hundred and fifty Dollars, out of
Painsvill[e] Bank, on three months credit, for which we gave, the
names of F G. Williams & Co N.K. Whitney John Johnson, &
~~Newel~~ Vinson Knights, I also settled with Br. Hiram Smith, and
V. Knights, and paid said [K]nights ~~$2045~~ two hundred and forty
five dollars, I also paid, or have it in my power to pay, J. Lewis for
which, blessing, I feel hartily, to thank my heavenly Father, and
ask him, in the name of Jesus Christ, to enable us to extricate
[p. 55] ourselves, from all ~~the~~ embarasments whatever that we may
not be brought into disre=pute, in any respect, that our enemys
may not have any power over us;—spent the day at home, devoted
some time in studying <the> he=brew language.—this has been a
warm day with, some rain; our snow is melting verry fast,—This

evening, a Mr. John Holister of Portage County Ohio called to see me on the subject of religion, he is a member of the close communion ba=ptise Church, he said he had come to enquire concerning the faith of our church having heard many reports of the worst character about us, he seemed to be an honest enqui[r]er after truth. I spent the evening in talking with him, I found him to be an honest candid man, and no particular peculiarities about him, only his simplisity, he tarried over night with me, and acknowledged in the ‹morning› that although he had thought he knew something about religion he was now sensible that he knew but little, which was the greatest, trait of wisdom that I could discover in him

Saturday 5th [December 1835] the weather is cold and freezing, and the snow is falling moderately, and there is a pros=pect of sleighing again, spent the fore=noon in studying, hebrew with Doct. Williams & President Cowdery, I am labouring under some indisposition of health. laid down and slept a while, and [p. 56] and arose feeling tolerable well through the blessings of God.—I received a letter to day from Reuben McBride, Vilanova [Chautauque Co.] N. Y also another from Parley Pratts mother in law[83] from Herkimer Co. N. Y of no consequence as to what it contained, but cost me 25 cents for postage, I mention this as it is a common occurence, and I am subjected to a great deal of expence in this way,[84] by those who I know nothing about, only that they are destitute of good manners, for if people wish to be benefited with information from me, common respect and good breeding wou[l]d dictate, them to pay the postage on their letters.—

Sunday 6th [December] 1835, went to meet=ing at the us[u]al hour. G. Carter[85] preached a splendid discourse, in the after ‹noon› we had an exortation, and communion.–Br. Draper[86] insisted on leaving the meeting, some 2 or 3 we=eks since, before communion, and would not be prevailed upon to tarry a few moments although, we invited him to do so as we did not wish to have the house thrown into confusion, he observed that he would not if we excluded him from the chu=rch, to day, he attempted to make a confession, but it was not satisfactory to me, and I was constrained by the spirit to deliver him over to the bufetings of satan untill he should humble himself, and repent, of his sins, and make a satisfact=ory confession before the church—[p. 57]

Monday 7th [December 1835] received a letter from Milton Holmes, and was much rejoiced to hear from, him, and of his prosperity in proclaiming the gospel, wrote him a letter requesting, him to return to this place,
Spent the day in reading the hebrew. Mr. John Hollister[87] called and to take the parting hand with me, and remarked that he had been in darkness all his days, but had now found the light and intended to obey it. also a num=ber of brethren called this Evening to see the records. I exibited and explained them to their satisfaction. We have fine sleighing

Tuesday morning the 8th [December 1835] at holm spent the day in reading hebrew in company with, President Cowdery Doct. Williams Br. H. Smith & O. Pratt.
In the evening I preached, as us[u]al at the School House, had great liberty in speaking the congregation, were attentive, after the servises closed the brethren proposed to come and draw wood for me

Wednesday 9th [December 1835] at home, the wind is strong and chilly, from the south, and their is a prospect of a storm Elder [Noah] Packard came in this morning and made me a present, of 12 dollars which he held in a note against me, may God bless him for his liberality, also James Aldrich, sent me my note by the hand of Jesse Hitchcock, on which [p. 58] there was 12 dollars due, and may God bless him for his kindness to me
also the brethren whose names are written below opened the[ir] hearts in great liberality and payed me at the committee Store the sums set oposite their respective names

| John Corrill | $5.00 |
| Levi Jackman[88] | 3.25 |

John Corrill	$5.00
Levi Jackman[88]	3.25
Elijah Fordham[89]	5.25
James Emett[90]	5.00
Newel Knight	2.00
Truman Angell[91]	3.00
Wm Felshaw[92]	3.00
Emer Harris[93]	1.00
Truman Jackson[94]	1.00
Samuel Rolph[95]	1.25
Elias Higbee[96]	1.00
Albert Brown[97]	3.00
Wm F. Cahoon[98]	1.00
Harlow Crosier	.50
Salmon Gee[99]	.75
Harvey Stanley	1.00
Zemira Draper[100]	1.00
George Morey	1.00
John Rudd[101]	.50
Alexander Badlam[102]	1.00
	———
	40.50

with the adition of the 2 notes above   24.00

My heart swells with gratitude inex=pressible w‹h›en I realize the great condescen=tion of my heavenly Fathers, in opening the hearts of these, my beloved brethren [p. 59] to administer so liberally, to my wants and I ask God in the name of Jesus Christ, to multiply, blessings, without num=ber upon their heads, and bless me with much wisdom and understanding, and dis=pose of me, to the best advantage, for my brethren, and the advancement of thy cause and Kingdom, and whether my days are many or few whether in life or in death I say in my heart, O Lord let me enjoy the society of such brethren

To day Elder Tanner[103] brought me the half of a fat[e]ned hog
for the be[ne]=fit of my family.

And a few days since Elder S[hadrach] Roundy brought me a
quarter of beef and may all the blessings, that are named above, be
poured upon their heads, for their kindness toward me—

Thursday morning 10th [December 1835] a beautiful morning
indeed, and fine sleighing, this day my brethren meet according, to
previous arangement, to chop and haul wood for me, and they have
been verry industrious, and I think they have supplyed me with my
winters wood, for which I am sincerely grateful to each and every,
one of them, for this expression of their goodness towards me And
in the name of Jesus Christ I envoke the rich benediction of
heav[e]n to rest upon them ~~even all~~ and their families, and I ask my
heavenly Father [p. 60] to preserve their health's and those of their
wives and children, that they may have stren=gth of body to
perform, their labours, in their several ocupations in life, and the
use and activity of their limbs, also powers of intellect and
understanding hearts, that they may treasure up wisdom, ~~and~~
understanding, ~~until~~ and inteligence, above measure, and be
preserved from plagues pestilence, and famine, and from the power
of the adversary, and the hands of evil designing, men and have
power over all their enemys; and the way be prepared be=fore
them, that they may journey to the land of Zion and be
established, on their inherit=ances, to enjoy undisturbe[d] peace
and happi=ness for ever, and ultimately to be crowned with
everlasting life in the celestial Kingdom of God, which blessings I
ask in the name of Jesus of Nazareth. Amen

I would remember Elder Leonard Rich[104] who was the first one
that proposed to the brethren to assist me, in obtaining wood for
the use of my family, for which I pray my heavenly Father, to bless
<him> with all the blessings, named above, and I shall ever
remember him with much gratitude, for this testimony, of
benevolence and respect, and thank the great I am, for puting into
his heart to do me this kindness, and I say in my heart, I will trust
in thy goodness, and mercy, forever, for thy wisdom and

benevolence <O Lord> is unbounded and beyond the comprehension of men and all of thy ways cannot be found out [p. 61]

This afternoon, I was called in company with President David Whitmer, to visit Sister Angeline Works,[105] who lives at Elder Booths[106] we found her verry sick, and so much deranged, that She did not recognize her friends, and intimate acquaintences we prayed for and layed hands on her her in the name of Jesus Christ, and commanded her in his name to receive he[r] senses, which was immediately restored ~~to her~~ we also ~~asked a healing blessing~~ prayed that she might be restored to health, she said she was better.– On our return we found the brethren engaged, in putting out the board kiln which had taken fire, and after labour=ing for about one hour, against this dist=ructive, element they succeded in conquering it, and, probably will save about one fourth part of the lumber, that was in it, how much loss the committee have sustained by this fire I do not know but it is conciderable ~~as~~ there was much lumber in the kiln

There was about 200 brethren engaged on this occasion and displayed, much activity, and interest, for which they dese=rve much credit.

This evening I spent at hom[e], a nu=mber of brethren called to see the records which I exibited to them, and they were much pleased with their interview [p. 62]

~~Thursday~~ Friday morning the 11th [December 1835] a fire broke out in a shoe-makers shop owned by Orson Johnson,[107] but was soon, extinguished, by the active exertions of the brethren, but the family were much alarmed, the shop being connected with their dwelling house, they carryed their furniture into the street, but not much damage was sustained.– This is a pleasant morning, and their is a prospect of a thaw

Spent the day at home, in reading, and in=structing those who called for advise.– to day Elder Dayly & his wife left for home.

~~Friday~~ Saturday morning 12th [December 1835] at home, spent the fore noon in reading, at about 12 o clock a number of young

person[s] called to see the ~~records~~ Egyptian records I requested my
Scribe to exibit them, he did so, one of the young ladies, who had
been examining them, was asked if they had the appearance of
Antiquity, she observed with an air of contempt that they did not,
on hear=ing this I was surprised at the ignorance she displayed, and
I observed to her that she was an anomaly in creation for all the
wise and learned that had ever examined them, without hesitation
pronounced them antient, I further re=marked that, it was
downright wickedn=ess ignorance bigotry and superstition that
caused her to make the remark, and that I would put it on record,
and I have done so because it is a fair sam=ple of the prevailing
spirit of the times [p. 63] showing that the victims of priestcraft and
superstition, would not believe though one should rise from the
dead.

At evening attended a debate, at Br. Wm. Smiths, the
question proposed to debate upon was, as follows.– was it necessary
for God to reveal himself to man, in order for their happiness.– I
was on the affirmative and the last one to speak on that side of the
question,– but while listning, with interest to the, ingenuity
displayed, on both Sides of the qu[e]stion, I was called, away to
visit, Sister Angeline Work[s], who was suposed to be dan=gerously
sick, Elder Corrill & myself went and prayed for and layed hands
on her in the name of Jesus Christ, She appeard to be better,—
returned home

Sunday morning the 13th [December 1835] at the us[u]al hour
for meeting viz. at 10 ocl[oc]k attended meeting, at the School
house on the flats, Elder J. Hitchcock preachd a verry feeling
discourse indeed, in the after=noon Elder Peter Whitmer,[108] related
his exper=iance, after which President F G. Williams related his
also, they both spoke of many things connected with the rise and
progress of this church, which were interesting, and the Saints,
listened with much attention, after these serv[ic]es closed, the
sacrament of the Lords Supper was administered, under the
super=intendance of President D. Whitmer, who presided over the
meeting during the day. I then made som[e] remarks respecting

[p. 64] prayer meetings and our meeting was broug=ht to a close, by invoking the blessings of heaven.

We then returned home. I ordered my horse saddled and myself and Scribe, rode to Mr. E. Jennings,[109] where I joined Eb[e]nezer Robinson and Angeline Works, in matrimony, according to pre=vious arangements. Miss ‹Works› had so far recoverd from her illness, that she was able to sit in her easy chair while I pronounced the ma=riage ceremony.–

We then rode to Mr. [Isaac] McWithy's a distance of about 3 miles from Town, where I had been Solicited, to attend and solemnize, the matri=monial covenant betwen Mr. E. Webb & Miss E. A. McWithy, the parents and many of the conne=ctions of both parties were present, with a large and respectable company of friends, who were invited as guests; and after making the nec=essary arangements the company come to order, and the Groom & bride, with the attend=ants politely came forward, and took their seats, and having been requested, to make some preliminary remarks upon the sub=ject of matrimony, touching the design of the All Mighty in this institution, also the duties of husbands & wives towards eac[h] other, and after opening our interview with singing and prayer, I delivered a lecture of about 40 minuits in length, during this time all seem=ed to be interested, except one or two ind=ividuals, who manifested, a spirit of grovling contempt, which I was constrained to reprove and rebuke sharply, after I had ~~been~~ closed my remarks. I sealed the matrim= [p. 65]onial ceremony in the name of God, and pronounced the blessings of heaven upon the heads of the young married couple we then closed by returning thanks.

A sumptuous feast was then spread and the company were invited to seat them=selves, at the table by pairs, male & female commencing with the oldest, and I can only say that the interview was conducted with propriety and decorum, and our hearts were made to rejoice, while together, and ~~all~~ cheerfulness prevailed, and after spending the evening agreeably untill 9, oclock, we pronounc[e]d a blessing, upon the company and withdrew, and returned home

To day the board kiln, took fire again

Monday 14th [December 1835] this morning a number of brethren from New York call[ed] to visit me, and see the Egyptian records. Elder [Martin] Harris also returned this morning from Palmyra N. York. Br. Frazier Eaton, of the same place called and paid me a visit, a verry fine man also Sister Harriet How[e] called to pay us a visit

After dinner we went to attend the funeral of Sylvester Smiths youngest child.[110] in the evening meet according to notice previously given to make arangements to guard against fire, and organized a com=pany for this purpose, counciled also on other affairs of a temporal nature.

To day Samuel Branum came to my house, much afflicted with a swelling on his left arm, which was occasioned by a bruise [p. 66] on his elbow, we had been called to pray for him and anoint him with oil, but his faith was not sufficient to effect a cure, and my wife prepared a poultice of herbs and applyed to it and he tarryed with me over night

Spent the day at home reading hebrew, and visiting friends who called to see me.

~~To day I received a letter from Elder Orson Hyde from his own hand~~

Tuesday 15th [December 1835] spent the day at home, and as us[u]al was blessed with much company, some of which called to see the records Samuel Brannum, is verry sick in conseq=uence of his arm, it being much inflamed

This afterno[o]n Elder Orson Hyde, handed me a Letter, the purport of which is that he is dissatisfyed with the committee,[111] in their dealings, with him in temporal affairs, that is that they do not deal as liberally ~~in~~ <with> him as they do with Elder William Smith, also requested me to reconcile the revelation, given to the 12,[112] since their return from the East,

That unless these things and others named in the letter, could be reconciled to his mind his honour would not stand united with them.— this I believe is the amount of the contents of the letter although much was written, my feelings on this occasion, were much laserated, knowing that I had dealt in righteousness with him in all things and endeavoured to promote his happin=ess and well being, as much as lay in my power, and I feel that these reflections are [p. 67] ungrateful and founded in jealousy and that the adversary is striving with all his subtle devises and influence to destroy him by causing a division amon[g] the twelve that God has chosen to open the gospel Kingdom in all nations, but I pray my Heavenly Father in the name of Jesus of Nazareth that he may be delivered from the power of the destroyer, ~~and~~ that his faith fail not in this hour of temptation, and prepare him and all the Elders to receive an end=ument, in thy house, even according to thine own order from time to time as thou seeest them worthy to be called into thy Solemn Assembly [p. 68][113]

Wednesday morning the 16th [December 1835] the we=ather is extremely cold, this morning I went to the council room, to lay before the preside=ncy the letter that I received yesterday from Elder O. Hyde, but when I arived, I found that I had lost said letter, but I laid the substance of it as far as I could recollect before the council, but they had not time to attend to it on the account of other buisness, accordingly we adjourned untill Monday Evening the 20th Inst.

Returned home Elder McLellen Elder B. Young and Elder J[ared] Carter called and paid me a visit, with which I was much gra=tified. I exibited and explaind the Egy=ptian Records to them, and explained many things to them concerning the dealings of God with the ancients and the formation of the planetary System, they seemed much pleased with the interview.

This evening according to adjournment I went to Br. Wm. Smiths, to take part in the debate that was commenced on saturd=ay evening last.— after the debate was conc=luded, and a desision given in favour of the affirmative of the question, some altercati=on took place, upon the impropr[i]ety of continueing the school fearing that it would not result in good.

Br. Wm opposed these measures and insisted on having another question pro=posed, and at length become much enraged particularly at me and used [p. 69] violence upon my person, and also upo[n] Elder J. Carter and some others, for which I am grieved beyond expression, and can only pray God to forgive him inasmuch as he repents of his wickedness, and humbles himself before the Lord

Thursday morning 17th [December 1835] at home.– quite unwell.— This morning Elder Orson Hyde called to see me, and presented me with a copy of the letter that he hand=ed me on Tuesday last, which I had lost
The following is a copy

Dec. 15th 1835
President Smith
Sir you may esteem it a novel circumstance to receive a written commu=nication from me at this time.
My reasons for writing are the following. I have some things which I wish to communicate to you, and feeling a greater liberty to do it by writing alone by myself, I take this method; and it is generally the case that you are thronged with buisness and not convenient to spend m=uch time in conversing upon subjects of the following nature. Therefore let these excu=ses paliate the novelty of the circumstance and patiently hear my recital.
After the committee had received their stock of fall and winter goods, I went to Elder Cahoon[114] and told him that I was destitute of a cloak and wanted him to trust me until Spring for materials to make one. He told me that [p. 70] he would trust me until January, but m=ust then have his pay as the payments for the goods become due at that time. I told him that I know not from whence the money wou=ld come and I could not promise it so soon.
But in a few weeks after I unexpectedly obtained the money to buy a cloak and applyed imm=ediately to Elder C for one and told him that I had the cash to pay for it, but he said that the materials for cloaks were all sold and that he could not accommodate me, and I will here venture a guess that he has not realized the cash for one cloak pattern.

A few weeks after this I called on Elder Cahoon again and told him that I wan=ted cloth for some shirts to the amount of 4 or 5 Dollars I told him that I would pay him in the spring and sooner if I could.

He ~~told me~~ let me have it not long after, my school was established and some of the hands who laboured on the house attended and wished to pay me at the Committee Store for their tuition.– I called at the Store to see if any nego‹ti›ation could be made and they take me off where I owed them, but no such negotiation could be made. These with some other circumstances of like char=acter called forth the following reflections.

In the first place I gave the committee $275 in cash besides some more and during the last season have traveled thro the middle and Eastern states to suport and uphold the store and in so doing have reduced my=self to nothing in a pecuniary point. Under [p. 71] these circumstances this establishment refused to render me that accomodation which a world=lings establishment would have gladly done, and one too, which never ‹received› a donation from ~~my~~ me nor in whose favour I never raised my voice or exerted my influence.

But after all this, thought I, it may be right and I will be still—— Un[t]il not long since I asertained that Elder Wm Smith could go to the store and get whatever he pleased, and no one to say why do ye so, until his account has amounted to seven Hundred Dollars or there abouts and that he was a silent partner in the conce[r]n, yet not acknow=ledged ‹as› such fearing that his creditors would make a hawl upon the Store.

While we were abroad this last season we strain[e]d every nerve to obtain a little something for our familys and regularly divided the monies equally for ought that I know, not knowing that William had such a fountain at home from whence he drew his support. I then called to mind the revelation in which my=self, McLellen and Patten were chastened and also the quotation in that revelation of the parable of the twelve sons: as if the origi=nal meaning refer[e]d directly to the twelve apostles of the church of the Latter day Saints. I would now ask if each one of the twelve has not an equal right to the same accomodations from that Store provided they are alike faithful. If not, with such a combination [p. 72] mine honor be not thou united.

If each one has the same right, take the baskets off from our noses or put one to Will=iams nose or if this cannot be done, reconcile the parable of the twelve sons with the sup=erior priveleges that William has.

Pardon me if I speak in parables or parody.

A certain shepherd had twelve sons and he sent them out one day to go and gather his flock which were scattered upon the mountains and in the vallies afar off they were all obedient to their fathers mand=ate, and at Evening they returned with the flock, and one son received wool enough to make him warm and comfortable and also rec[eive]d of the flesh and milk of the flock, the other eleven received not so much as one kid to make merry with their friends

These facts with some others have dis=qualified my mind for studying the Hebr=ew Language at present, and believing, as I do, that I must sink or swim, or in other wor=ds take care of myself, I have thought that I should take the most efficient means in my power to get out of debt, and to this end I p[r]oposed taking the school, but if I am not thought competent to take the charge of it, or worthy to be placed in that station, I must devise some other means to help myself; altho having been ordained to that office under your own hand with a p[r]omise that it should not be taken from me.— [p. 73] Conclusion of the whole matter is sutch I am willing to continue and do all I can provided we can share equal benefits one with the other, and upon no other pr=inciple whatever. If one has his suport from the "publick crib" let them all have it. But if one is pinched I am willing to be, provided we are all alike.

If the principle of impartiality and equality can be observed by all I think that I will not peep again——

If I am damned it will be for doing what I think is right.– There have been two applications made to me to go into business since I

talked of taking the school, but it is in the world and I had rather
remain in Kirtland if I can consistently
All I ask is Right I Am Sir with Respect Your obt. servt.

Orson Hyde

To President J. Smith jn
Kirtland Geauga Co. Ohio [p. 74]

Elder O. Hyde called and read the foregoing letter himself and, I
explained upon the objec=tions, he had set forth in it, and
satisfyed his mind upon every point, perfectly and he observed after
I had got through, that he was more than satisfyed, and would
attend the hebrew school, and took the parting hand with me with
every expression of friendship that a gentleman, and a Christian
could ma=nifest, which I felt to reciprocate, with ~~the~~ cheerfulness
and entertain, the best of feeling for him, and most cheerfully
forgive him the ingratitude which was manifisted in his letter,
knowing that it was for want of corect information, that his mind
was disturbed as far as his reflections related to me.

But on the part of the committe, he was not treated, right in all
thing[s], however all things, are settled amicably, and no hard=ness
exists between us or them

My Father & Mother called this evening to see me upon the
subject of the difficulty, that transp=ired at their house on
wednesd[a]y evening between me and my Br. William, they were
sorely afflicted in mind on the account of that occurrence. I
conversed with them, and ~~showed~~ convinced them that I was not
to blame in taking the course I did, but had acted in righteousness,
in all thing[s] on that occasion

I invited them to come and live with me, they concented to do
so as soon as it is practicable [p. 75]

Friday morning 18th Inst. [December 1835] at home Br. Hyrum
Smith called to see me and read a letter ~~to me~~ that he received
from William, in which he asked, his [⸳⸳⸳⸳⸳] ~~for~~= forgivness

for the abuse he offered to him, at the debate, he tarried, most of
the fore noon, and conversed freely with me, upon the subject, of
the difficulty, existing betw=een me and Br. William, he said that
he was, perfectly satisfied, with the course I had taken, with him,
in rebuking, him in his wickedness,— but he is wounded to the
verry soul, with the conduct of William, and altho he feels the
tender feelings of a brother, toward him yet he can but look upon
his conduct as an abomination in the sight of God

And I could pray in my heart that all my brethren were like
unto my beloved brother Hyrum, who posseses the mildness of a
lamb, and the integrity of a Job and in short the meekness and
humility of Christ, and I love him with that love that is stronger
than death; for I never had occasion to rebuke him, ~~and~~ nor he me
which he declared when he left me to day [p. 76]

18th Inst. [December 1835]

Copy of a letter from Br. William Smith

Br. Joseph— Though I do not know but I have forfeited all
right and title to the word brother, in concequence of what I have
done, for I concider myself, that I am unw=orthy to be called one,
after coming to myself and concidering upon what I have done I
feel as though it was a duty, to make a humble confession to you for
what I have done or what took place the other evening— but leave
this part of the sub=ject at present.— I was called to an acco=unt by
the 12, yesterday for my conduct; or they desired to know my mind
or det=ermination and what I was going to do I told them that on
reflection upon the many difficulties that I had had with the church
and the much disgrace I had brought upon my=self in concequence
of these things and also that my health would not permit me to go
to school to <make> any preperations for the endument and that
my health was such that I was not able to travel, ~~I told them~~ that it
would be better for them to appoint one in the office that would be
better able to fill it, and by doing this they would throw me into the
hands of the church, and leave me where I was before I was
chosen—

Then I would not be in a situation [p. 77] to bring so much disgrace upon the cause, when I fell into temptation, and perhaps by this I might obtain Salvation you know my passions and the danger of falling from so high a station, and thus by withdraw=ing from the office of the apostleship while their is salvation for me, and remaining a member in the church; I feel a fraid if I do'nt do this it will be worse for me, some other day

And again my health is poor and I am not able to travel and it is ne=cessary that the office should not be idle— And again I say you know my passions and I am a fraid it will be worse for me, by and by

do so if the Lord will have mercy on me and let me remain as a member in the church, and then I can travel and preach, when I am able— do not think that I am your enemy for what I have done, perhaps you may say or ask why I have not remembered the good that you have done to me— When I reflect upon the ingury I have done you I must con=fess that I do not know what I have been ~~doing~~ about— I feel sorry for what I have done and humbly ask your forgiveness— I have not confid=ence as yet to come and see you for I feel ashamed of what I have done, and as I feel now I feel as thou=[p. 78]gh all the confessions that I could make verbally or by writing would not be suff=icient to atone for the transgression— be this as it may I am willing to make all the restitution you shall require. If I can stay in the church as a member— I will try to ma=ke all the satisfaction possible——

yours with respect
William Smith

Do not cast me off for what I have done but strive to save me in the church as a member I do repent of what I have done to you and ask your forgiveness— I concider the transgression the other evening of no small magnitude,— but it is done and I cannot help it now— I know brother Joseph you are always willing to forgive.

But I sometimes think when I ref=lect upon the many inguries I have done you I feel as though a confession was not hardly sufficient— but have mercy on me this once and I will try to do so no more—

The 12, called a council yesterday and sent over after me and I went over

This council rem[em]ber was called together by themselves and not by me

Wm S [p. 79]

Kirtland Friday Dec 18th 1835
Answer to the foregoing Letter from Br. William Smith a Copy

Br. William having received your letter I now procede to answer it, and shall first procede, to give a brief naration of my feel=ings and motives, since the night I first came to the knowledge, of your having a debating School, which was at the time I happened in with, Bishop Whitney his Father and Mother &c— which was the first that I knew any thing about it, and from that time I took an interest in them, and was delighted with it, and formed a determination, to attend the School for the purpose of obtain=ing information, and with the idea of imp=arting the same, through the assistance of the spirit of the Lord, if by any means I should have faith to do so; and with this intent, I went to the school on ‹last› Wednesday night, not with the idea of braking up the school, neither did it enter into my heart, that there was any wra=ngling or jealousy's in your heart, against me;

Notwithstanding previous to my leaving home there were feelings of solemnity, rolling across my breast, which were unaccountable to me, and also these feelings continued by spells to depress my ~~feelings~~ ‹spirit› and seemed to manifest that all was not right, even after the ~~debate~~ school commenced, and during the debate, yet I strove to believe that all would work together for good; I was pleased with the power of the arguments, that were aduced, and did [p. 80] not feel to cast any reflections, upon any one that had spoken; but I felt that it was ~~my~~ ‹the› duty of old men that set as presi=dents to be as grave, at least as young men, and that it was our duty to smile at solid arguments, and sound reasoning, and be im=presed with solemnity, which should be man=ifest in our countanance, when folly and that which militates against truth and righteousn=ess, rears its head

Therefore in the spirit of my calling and in view of the
authority of the priesthood that has been confered upon me, it
would be my du=ty to reprove whatever I esteemed to be wrong
fon=dly hoping in my heart that all parties, would concider it right,
and therefore humble themsel=ves, that satan might not take the
advantage of us, and hinder the progress of our School.

Now Br. William I want you should bear with me,
notwithstanding my plainness—

I would say to you that my feelings, were grieved at the
interuption you made upon Elder McLellen, I thought, you should
have concidered your relation, with him, in your apostle ship, and
not manifest any division of sentiment, between you, and him, for
a surrounding multitude to take the advan=tage of you:—
Therefore by way of entreaty, on the account of the anxiety I had
for your inf=luence and wellfare, I said, unto you, do not have any
feeling, or something to that amount, why I am thus particular, is
that if you, have misconstrued, my feelings, toward you, you may
be corrected.— [p. 81]

But to procede— after the school was closed Br. Hyrum,
requested the privilege, of speaking, you objected, however you
said if he would not abuse the school, he might speak, and that you
would not allow any man to abuse the school in your house.—

Now you had no reason to suspect that Hyrum, would abuse the
school, therefore my feelings were mortifyed, at those unnecessary
observations, I undertook to reason, with you but you manifested,
an inconciderate and stuborn spirit, I then dispared, of benefiting
you, on the account of the spirit you manif=ested, which drew from
me the expression that you was as ugly as the Devil.

Father then commanded silence and I formed a determination,
to obey his mandate, and was about to leave the house, with the
impr=ession, that you was under the influence of a wicked spirit,
you replyed that you, would say what you pleased in your own
house, Father replyed, say what you please, but let the rest hold
their toungs, then a reflection, rushed through my mind, of the,
anxiety, and care I ha[d] had for you and your family, in doing what
I did, in finishing your house and providin[g] flour for your family

&c and also father had possession in the house, as well, as your self;
and when at any time have I transgressed, the commandments of
my father? or sold my birthright, that I should not have the
privilege of spea=king in my fathers house, or in other words in my
fathers family, or in your house, [p. 82] (for so we will call it, and
so it shall be,) that I should not have the privilege of reproving a
younger brother, therefore I said I will speak, for I built the house,
and it is as much mine as yours, or something to that effect, (I
should have said that I helped finish the house,) I said it merely to
show that it could not be, the right spirit, that would rise up for
trifli=ng matters, and undertake to put me to sil=ence, I saw that
your indignation was kin=dled against me, and you made towards
me, I was not then to be moved, and I thought, to pull off my loose
coat, least it should tangle me, and you be left to hurt me, but not
with the intention, of hurt=ing You, but you was to soon for me,
and having once fallen into the hands of a mob, and ~~now~~ been
wounded in my side, and now into the hands of a brother, my side
gave way, after having been rescued, from your grasp, I left your
house, with feel=ings that were indiscriba[b]le, the scenery had
changed, and all those expectations, that I had cherished, when
going to your house, of brotherly kindness, charity forbearance and
natural affection, that in duty binds us not to make each others
offenders for a word.

But alass! abuse, anger, malice, hatred, and rage ‹with a lame
side› with marks, of violence ‹heaped› upon ~~my body~~ me by a
brother, were the reflec=tions of my disapointment, and with these
I returned home, not able to sit down, or rise up, without help, but
through the blessings of God I am now better.—— [p. 83] I have
received your letter and purused it with care. I have not
entertained a feeling of malice, against you, I am, older than you
and have endured, more suffering, have been mar[r]ed by mobs, the
labours of my calling, a series of persecution, and injuries,
continually heaped upon me, all serve to debilitate, my body, and
it may ‹be› that I cannot boast of being stronger, than you, if I
could, or could not, would this be an honor, or dishonor to me, if I
could boast like David of slaying a Goliath, who defied the armies

of the living God, or like Paul, of contending with Peter face to
face, with sound arguments, it might be an honor, But to mangle
the flesh or seek revenge upon one who never done you any wrong,
can not be a source of sweet reflection, to you, nor to me, neither
to an hon=orable father & mother, brothers, and sisters, and when
we reflect, with what care ~~our parents~~ and with what unremiting
diligence our parents, have strove to watch over us, and how many
hours, of sorrow, and anx=iety, they have spent over our cradles
and bedsides, in times of sickness, how careful we ought to be of
their feelings in their old age, it cannot be a source of swe[e]t
reflection to us to say or do any thing that will bring their grey hairs
down with sorrow to the grave.

In your letter you asked my forgivness, which I readily grant,
but it seems to me, that you still retain an idea, that I have given
you reasons to be angry or disaffected with me.

Grant me the privilege of saying then, [p. 84] that however
hasty, or harsh, I may have spoken, at any time to you, it has been
done for the express purpose of endeavouring, to warn exhort,
admonish, and rescue you, from falling into difficulties, and
sorrows which I foresaw you plunging into, by giving way to that
wicked spirit, which you call your passions, which you should curbe
and break down, and put under your feet, which if you do not you,
never can be saved, in my view, in the Kingdom of God.

God requires the will of his creatures, to be swallowed up in his
will.

You desire to remain in the church, but forsake your
apostleship, this is a stratigem of the evil one, when he has gained
one advantage, ~~your~~ he lays a plan for anoth=er but by maintaining
your apostleship in rising up, and making one tremendous effort,
you may overcome your passions, and please God and by forsaking
your apostleship, is not to be willing, to make that sacrafice that
God requires at your hands and is to incur his displeasure, and
without pleasing God do not think, that it will be any better for
you, when a man falls one step he must regain that step again, or
fall another, he has still more to gain, or eventually all is lost.

I desire brother William that you will humble yourself, I freely

forgive you and you know, my unshaken and ~~unshaken~~
unchangable disposition I ~~think~~ know in whom I trust, I stand
upon [p. 85] the rock, the floods cannot, no they shall not
overthrow me, you know the doctrine I teach is true, and you know
that God has blessed me, I brought salvation to my fathers house,
as an instrument in the hand of God, when they were in a
m=iserable situation, you know that it is my duty to admonish you
when you do wrong this liberty I shall always take, and you shall
have the same privilege, I take the privilege, to admonish you
because of my birthright, and I grant you the privilege because it is
my duty, to be humble and to receive rebuke, and instruction, from
a brother or a friend.

    As it regards, what course you shall persue hereafter, I do not
pretend to say, I leave you in the hands of God and his church.
Make your own desision, I will do you good altho you mar me, or
slay me, by so doing my garments, shall be clear of your sins, and if
at any time you should concider me to be an imposter, for heavens
sake leave me in the hands of God, and not think to take vengance
on me your self.

    Tyrany ursurpation, and to take mens rights ever has and ever
shall be banished from my heart.

    David sought not to kill Saul, although he was guilty of crimes
that never entered my heart.

    And now may God have mercy upon my fathers house, may
God take [p. 86] away enmity, from betwen me and thee, and may
all blessings be restored, and the past be forgotten forever, may
humble repentance bring us both to thee ‹O God› and to thy
power and protection, and a crown, to enjoy the society of father
mother Alvin Hyrum Sophron[i]a Samuel Catharine Car=loss Lucy
the Saints and all the sanctified in peace forever, is the prayer of
                                    ~~This from~~ Your brother
                                    Joseph Smith Jun

To William Smith——

    Saturday morning the 19th [December 1835] at home wrote the
‹above› letter to Br. Wm. Smith **I have had many ~~sollam~~**

<solemn> feelings this day Concerning my Brothe[r] William and
have prayed in my heart to fervently that the Lord will not ~~him~~
<cast him> off but he may return to the God of Jacob and magnify
his apostleship and calling may this be his happy lot for the Lord
of Glorys Sake Amen

Sunday the 20th [December 1835] At home all day and took
solled [solid] Comfort with my Family had many serious
reflections also Brothers Palmer and Tailor Came to see me I
showed them the sacred record to their Joy and sati[s]fac=tion O
may God have mercy upon these men and keep them in the way
of Everlas=ting life in the name of Jesus Amen [p. 87]

Monday morni[n]g 21st [December 1835] At home Spent this
[day] in indeavering to treasure up know[l]edge for the be[n]ifit of
my Calling the <day> pas[s]ed of[f] very pleasantly for which I
thank the Lord for his blessings to my soul his great mercy over
my Fam=ily in sparing our lives O Continue thy Care over me
and mine for Christ sake

Tusday 22d [December 1835] At home ~~this~~ Continued my
studys O may God give me learning even Language and indo[w]
me with qualifycations to magnify his name while I live I also
deliv[er]ed an ad=dress to the Church this Evening the Lord
blessed my Soul, my scribe also is un=well O my God heal him
and for his kindness to me O my soul be thou greatful to him and
bless him and he shall be blessed ~~of for ever~~ of God for=ever I
believe him to be a faithful friend to me therefore my soul
delighteth in him Amen

                                                    Joseph Smith Jr

/[115]Wednesday 23d [December 1835] In the forenoon at home
stud[y]ing the greek Language and also waited upon the brethren
who came in and exhibiting to them the papirus, in the afternoon
visited brother Leonard Rich with the relatives of bro Oliver
Cowdery had not a very agreeable visit for I found them [p. 88]

filled with prejudice against the work of the Lord and their minds
blinded with superstition & ignorence &c

Thirsday 24th [December 1835] At home in the forenoon in
the afternoon assisted in running <out> a road across my farm by
the commissionor[s] who were appoint[e]d by the court for the
same——

Fryday 25th [December 1835] At home all this day and enjoyed
myself with my family it being Chris<t>mas day the only time I
have had this privilege so satisfactorily for a long time

Saturday 26 [December 1835] commenced studeing the Hebrew
Language in company with bros Parrish & Williams in the mean
time bro Lyman Sher=man[116] came in and requested to have the
word of the lord through me for said he I have been wrought upon
to make known to you my feelings and desires and was promised to
~~have~~ that I should have a revelation ~~and~~ which should make
known my duty
    last evening a brother from the east called upon me for
instruction whose name is Jonathan Crosby
also in the course of the day two gentlemen called upon me while I
was cutting wood at the door and requested an interview with the
head of the church which I agreed to grant them on Sunday
morning the 27 Inst [p. 89] The following is a revelation given to
Lyman Sherman this day 26 Dec 1835[117]
    Verily thus saith the Lord unto you my servant Lyman your sins
are forgiven you because you have obeyed my voice in coming up
hither this morning to receive councel of him whom I have
appointed
    Therefore let your soul be at rest concerning your spiritual
standing, and resist no more my voice, and arise up and be more
careful henceforth in observing your vows which you have made
and do make, and you shall be blessed with exceding great
blessings. Wait patiently untill the time when the solemn assembly
shall be called of my servants then you shall be numbered with the

first of mine elders and receive right by ordination with the rest of mine elders whom I have chosen

Behold this is the promise of the father unto you if you continue faithful– and it shall be fulfilled upon you in that day that you shall have right to preach my gospel wheresoever I shall send you from henceforth from that time. Therefore strengthen your brethren in all your conversation in all your prayers, and in all your exhor=tations, and in all your doings, and behold and lo I am with you to bless you and deliver you forever Amen

/[118]Sunday morning 27th [December 1835] at the us[u]al hour, attended meeting at the School house, President Cowdery delivered a verry able and interesting discourse— in the after part of the day Br. [p. 90] Hyrum Smith & Bishop Partri[d]ge, delivered each a short and ‹interesting› lecture, after which the sacrament of the Lords supper ‹was administered› and dis=missed our meeting—

Those Gentlemen that proposed to have an interview with me on this morning, did not come, and I conclu=de they were trifling characters

Monday morning the 28th [December 1835] having prefered a charge against Elder Almon Babbit[119] for traducing my cha=racter, he was this morning called before the High Council, and I atten=ded, with my witnesses, and subst=antiated my charge against him and he in part acknowledged his fault but not satisfactory to the council, and after parleying with him a long time, and granting him every indulgence, that righ[t]eousness require the council adjourned without obta=ining a full confession from him—

On this day the council of the seven=ty meet to render an account of their travels and ministry, since they were ordained to that apostleship, the meeting was interesting indeed, and my heart was made glad while listning to the relations of those that had been la=bouring, in the vinyard of the Lord with such marvelous success, and I pray God to bless them with an increas[e] of faith, and power, and keep them [p. 91] all with the indurance of faith in the name of Jesus Christ, to ~~Amen~~ the end

Tuesday morning the 29th [December 1835] at home untill about 10. oclock I then went to attend a blessing meeting at Oliver Olneys,[120] in company with my wife, & father and mother who had come to live with me, also my scribe went with us a large company assembled and Father Smith arose and made some preliminary remarks, which were verry applicable, on occasions of this kind, after which ~~he opened the meeting by~~ a hymn was sung and he opened the meeting by prayer about 15 persons then received a patri=archal blessing under his hands[121]– the servises were then dismissed, as they commenced, viz. by singing and prayer.– a table was then spread and crowned with the bounties of nature, and after invoking the bene=diction of heaven upon the rich rep=ast, we fared sumptuously, and suf=fice it to say that we had a glorious meeting, through out and I was much pleased with the harmony and decorum that existed among the brethren and sisters, we returned home and ~~spent the evening~~—at early candlelight I went and pr[e]ach[e]d at the school house to a crowded congregation, who listened [p. 92] with attention, while I delivered a lecture of about 3, hours in length, I had liberty in speaking, some presbyterians were present, as I after learned, and I expect that some of my sayings set like a garment that was well fited, as I exposed their abominations in the language of the scriptures, and I pray God that it may be like a nail in a sure place, driven by the master of assemblies. Col. Chamberlains Son called to day

Wednesday 30 [December 1835] spent the day in reading hebrew at the council room, in company with my scribe which gave me much sattisfacti=on, on the account of his returning health, for I delight in his company
~~Friday morning Jany. 1st 1836~~

Thursday morning 31st [December 1835] at home, after attending to the duties of my family, retired to the council room, to persue my stud=ies, the council of the 12 convened in the ‹upper› room in the printing office directly over the room wher[e] we were convened, in our studies, they sent for me and the presidency, (or

part of them,) to receive council from us on the subject of the
council, which is to be held on Saturday next

In the after noon I attended at the Chapel to give directions,
concerning [p. 93] the upper rooms, and more espec=ially the west
room which I intend ocupying, for a translating room, which will
be prepared this week

Friday morning Jany. 1st 1836
this being the beginning of a new year, my heart is filled with
gratitude to God, that he has preserved my life and the lives of my
family wh=ile another year has rolled away, we have been,
sustained and upheld in the midst of a wicked and perverse
gener=ation, and exposed to all, the afflictions temptations and
misery that are inci=dent to human life, for which I feel to humble
myself in dust and ashes, as it were before the Lord— but
notwithst=anding, the gratitude that fills my heart on retrospecting
the past year, and the multiplyed blessings that have crowned our
heads, my heart is pained within me because of the difficulty that
exists in my father's family, the Devil has made a violent attack on
Br. Wm and Br Calvin [122] and the powers of darkness, seeme lower
over their minds and not only theirs but cast a gloomy shade over
the minds of my ~~my parents and some of my~~ brothers and sisters,
which prevents them from seeing things as they realy are, and the
powers of Earth & hell seem combined to overthrow us and the
church by [p. 94] causing a division in the family, and indeed the
adversary is bring[ing] into requis=ition all his subtlety to prevent
the Saints from being endowed, by causing division among the 12,
also among the 70, and bickerings and jealousies among the Elders
and offici=al members of the church, and so the leaven of iniquity
foments and spreads among the members of the church.

But I am determined that nothing on my part shall be lacking
to adjust and amicably dispose of and settle all family difficulties,
on this day, that the ensuing year, and years, be they many or few
may be spent in righteousness before God, and I know that the
cloud will burst and satans kingd=om be laid in ruins with all his
black designs, and the saints come forth like gold seven times tried

in the fire, being made perfect throug[h] sufferings, and
temptations, and the blessings of heaven and earth multiplyed
upon our heads which may God grant for Christ sake Amen——
     Br. William came to my house and Br. Hyrum, also, Uncle
John Smith, we went into a room in company with father, and
Elder Martin Harris, ~~and~~ father, Smith then opened our interview
by prayer after which, he expressed his feelings on the ocasion in a
verry feeling and pathetic manner even with all the sympathy of a
father whose feeling[s] were wounded deeply on the [p. 95] account
of the difficulty that was existing in the family, and while he
addressed us the spirit of God rested down upon us in mighty
power, and our hearts were melted Br. William made an humble
confession and asked ~~our~~ my forgiveness for the abuse he had
offered me and wherein I had been out of the way I asked his
forgivness, and the spirit of confession and forgiveness, was mutual
among us all, and we covenanted with each other in the sight of
God and the holy angels and the brethren, to strive from hence
forward to build each other up in righteousness, in all things and
not listen to evil reports concerning each other, but like brethren,
indeed go to each other, with our grievances in the spirit of
meekness, and be reconciled and thereby promote our own
happiness and the happiness of the family and in short the
happiness and well being of all.— my wife and mother, ~~Uncle John~~
& my scribe was then called in and we repeated the covenant to
them that we had entered into, and while gratitude swelled our
bosoms, tears flowed from our ey[e]s.– I was then requested to close
our interview which I did with prayer, and it was truly a jubilee and
time of rejoiceing [p. 96]

     Saturday morning 2nd [January 1836] acording to previous
arangement, I went to council at 9 oclock.– this council was
called, to set in judgment, on a complaint, prefered against Br.
William, by Elder Orson Johnson[123] the council organized and
opened by prayer and proceded to buisness, but before enter=ing on
the trial Br. William arose and humbly confessed the charges
prefered against him and asked the forgivness of the council and

the whole congregation a vote was then called to know whether his confession was satisfactory, and whether the brethren would extend the hand of fellowsh=ip to him again, with cheerfulness the whole congregation raised their hands to receive him

Elder Almon Babbit also confessed ~~his~~ the charges which I prefered against him in a previous council,[124] and was received into fellowship, and some other buisness was transacted, in union and fellowship and the best of feelings seemed to prevail among the brethren, and our hearts were made glad on the occasion, and there was joy in heaven, and my soul doth magnify the Lord for his goodness and mercy endureth forever— council adjo=urned with prayer as us[u]al——

Sunday morning 3d [January 1836] went to meeting at the us[u]al hour President Rigdon, delivered a fine lecture upon the subject of revelation, in the afternoon I confirmed about 10 or 12 persons who [p. 97] had been baptised, among whom was M C. Davis who was baptized at the intermission to day— Br William Smith made his confession to the church to their satisfaction, and was cordially received into fellowship again, the Lords supper was administered, and br. William gave out an appointment to preach in the evening, at early candlelight, and preach[e]d a fine discourse, and this day has been a day of rejoicing to me, the cloud that has been hanging over us has burst with blessings on our heads, and Satan has been foiled in his attempts to destroy me and the church, by causing jealousies to arise in the hearts of some of the brethren, and I thank my heavenly father for, the union and harmony which now prevails in the Church

Monday morning 4th [January 1836] meet and organized our hebrew School according to the arangements that were made on saturday last, we had engaged Doct[or] Piexotto to teach us in the hebrew language, when we had our room prepared. we informed him that we were ready and our room prepared and he agreed to wait on us on this day and deliver his introductory lecture yesterday he sent us word that he [p. 98] could not come untill wedensday next a vote was called to know whether we would, submit to such treatment or not and carried in the negative, and Elder Sylvester Smith appointed as clerk to write him on the subject and inform him that his servises, were not wanted, and Elders Wm E MC,Lellen & Orson ‹Hyde› J̶o̶h̶n̶s̶o̶n̶ despached to Hudson Semenary,[125] to hire a teacher, they were appointed by the voice of the School, to act f̶o̶r̶ in their beh=alf— however we concluded to go on with our school and do the best we can untill we can obtain a teacher, and by the voice of the school I concented, to ren=der them all the assistance I am able to, for the time being – we are ocupying the translating room for the use of the School untill another room can be prepared, this is the first day that we have ocupied ‹it› t̶h̶i̶s̶ r̶o̶o̶m̶ which is the west room in the upper part of the Chappel, which was concecrated this m=orning by prayer offered up by father Smith

This is a rainy time and the roads are extremely mudy meet this evening at the Chapel to make arangements for a Singing School after some altercation, a judicio=us arangement was made, a comittee of 6 was chosen, to take charge of the singing department, [p. 99]

Tuesday 5th [January 1836] attended the Hebrew School, divided them into classes, had some debate with Elder Orson Pratt, he manifested a stubourn spirit, which I was much grieved at

Wedenesday 6th [January 1836] attended School again, and spent most of the fore noon in setling, the unplesant feelings that existed in the breast of Elder O. Pratt and after much controversy, he confessed his fault and asked the forgivness of the whol[e] school and was cheerfully forgiven by all

Elder Mc.Lellen returned from Hudson, and reported to the school that he had hired a Teacher, to teach us the term of 7. weeks for $320. that is 40. Schollars for that amount, to commence in about 15. days hence.– he is highly celebr=ated as a hebrew schollar,[126] and proposes to give us sufficient knowledge in the above term of time to read and translate the language [p. 100]

Conference Minuits

at a conference held at the School house on Saturday the 2d Jan
1836 the following individuals were appointed by the voice of the
conference to be ordained to the office of Elders in the church of
the latter day saints under the hands of President Joseph Smith Jr
Sidney Rigdon Clerk——

    Vincent [Vinson] Knight
    Thomas Grover[127]
    Elisha [Elijah] Fordham   Eld[e]rs
    Hyram Dayton[128]
    Samuel James[129]
    John Herrott

Thursday 7th [January 1836] attended a sump=tuous feast at
Bishop N K. Whitneys this feast was after the order of the Son of
God the lame the halt and blind wer[e] invited accord=ing to the
in[s]truction of the Saviour

our meeting was opened by singing and prayer offered up by
father Smith, after which Bishop Whitneys father & mother were
bless[ed] and a number of others, with a patriarchal blessing, we
then received a bountiful refreshment, furnished by the liberality of
the Bishop the company was large, before we parted we had some
of the Songs of Zion sung, and our hearts were made glad while
partaking of an antipast of those [p. 101] Joys that will be poured
upon the head of the Saints w[h]en they are gath=ered together on
Mount Zion to enjoy each others society forever more even all the
blessings of heaven and earth and where there will be none to
molest nor make us afraid—
    returned home and spent the evening

Friday 8th [January 1836] Spent the day in the hebrew School,
and made rapid progress in our studies

Saturday 9th [January 1836] attended School in the fore noon
at about 11. oclock received the following note

Thus saith the voice of the spirit to me, if thy Brother Joseph Smith jn will attend the feast at thy house this day (at 12 ocl) the poor & lame will rejoice at his presence & also think themselves honored——

Yours in friendship & Love

9th Jany 1836   N[ewel] K. W[hitney]

I dismissed the School in order to attend to this polite invitation, with my wife father & mother

We attended the feast, a large congregation assembled a number was blessed under the hands of father Smith, and we had a good [p. 102] time, returned home and spent the evening

Sunday 10th [January 1836] went to the meeting at the us[u]al hour Elder Wilber Denton & Elder J[enkins] Salisbury, preached in the fore noon, in the after noon Br. Samuel & Br. Carloss Smith, they all did well concidering their youth, and bid fair to make useful men in the vinyard of the Lord, administered the sacrament and dismissed

at the intermission to day 3, were baptised by Elder Martin Harris——

returned home and spent the evening——

Monday morning 11th [January 1836] at home There being no school I spent the day at home, many brethren called to see me, among whom was Alva Beamon from New York Jenesee Co. he has come to attend the Solemn Assembly— I delight in the society of my friends & brethren, and pray that the blessings of heaven and earth may be multiplyed upon their heads

Tuesday morning 12th [January 1836] at home,– this day I called on the presidency of the church, and made arangements to meet tomorrow at 10, oclock A.M [p. 103] to take into concideration the subject of the Solemn Assembly— This after noon, a young man called to see the Egyptian manuscripts, and I exibited them to him, he expressed great satisfaction, and appeared verry anxious to obtain a know=ledge of the translation.— also a man was introduced to me by the name of Russel Wever[130] from Cambray Niagary Co. N. Y. this man is a preacher, in the church that is called Christian or Unitarian, ~~some~~ he remarked that he had but few minuits to spend with me, we entered into conver=sation, and had som[e] little controversy upon the subject of prejudice, but soon come to ~~the~~ an understanding, he spoke of the gospel and said he believed it, adding that it was good tidings of great joy— I replyed that it was one thing, to proclaim good tid=ings and another to tell what those tidings are, he waived the conversation and withdrew—— he was introduced by Joseph Rose——[131]

Wednesday morning 13th [January 1836] at 10, oclock A. M meet in council with all the presidency of Kirtland and Zion ~~that~~ together with ‹all› their councilors that could be found in this place[132] however some of the councellors were absent, both of Kirtland and Zion The presidency of the Seventy were also present, and many more [p. 104] of the Elders of the church of the latterday Saints—— come to order, sung Adam-ondi-ahman and opened by prayer offered up by Joseph Smith Sen——

I ~~President John Smith~~ presided on the occasion

After the council was organized and opened ~~President Joseph Smith jr~~ I made some ~~verry pertinent~~ remarks in my introductory lecture before the authority of the church, this morning, in general terms, laying before them, the buisness of the day which was to suply some deficiencies in the ~~council~~ Bishop['s] coun[c]il in this place ‹also in the high *council*› after some altercation upon the most proper manner of proc[e]ding Elder Vinson Knight was nominated by the Bishop and seconded by the presidency vote called of that body and caried vote was then called from the high council of Zion and carried vote was then called from the twelve and carried— vote then called from the council of the Seventy and carried vote then called from the Bishop and his council from Zion and carried— Elder Knight was received by the universal voice and concent of all the authority of the Church as a councilor in the Bishops coun=cil ‹in› this place, to fill the place of Elder Hyrum

Smith, who is ordained to the [p. 105] Presidency of the high
council of Kirtland

He was then ordained under the hands of Bishop N K. Whitney
to the office of a councillor also to that of high priest

Council adjourned for one hour by singing the song, come let
us rejoice in the day of Salvation

council assembled at one oclock P. M organized and proceded
to buisness The first buisness this afternoon was to supply some
deficiencies in the high council in Kirtland, the stake of Zion John
P. Greene[133] was nominated and seconded by the presidency vote
taken and carried in his favour by the una=nimous voice of the all
the authority of the church— he supplyes the place of President O.
Cowdery who is elected to the presidency of the high council in
this place

Elder Thomas Grover was nominated to supply the place of
Luke Johnson[134] who is chosen and ordained one of the twelve
Apostles— the nomination was seconded and vote carried in his
favour by all the authority present and he is received as a councilor
in the high council in Kirtland

Elder Noah Packard was next nominated and seconded to
supply the place of Sylvester Smith[135] who is ordained to the
presidency of the Seventy— vote called and carried [p. 106] in his
favour and Elder Packard was received by the unanimous vote of all
the authority present as a high councilor in Kirtland

Elder John Page[136] was nomin=ated, but was not present and his
name droped

Elder Joseph Kingsbury[137] was nominated and seconded, to fill
the place of Orson Hyde, who is chosen and ordained one of the
twelve, vote called and carried unanimously and Elder Kingsbury
was received as a hi[g]h councilor in Kirtland

Elder Samuel James, was nominated and seconded to fill the
place of Joseph Smith Sen– vote called and carried unanimously in
his favour and Elder James was received as a high councilor in
Kirtland

The new elected councilors were then called forward in order as
they were elected, and ordained under the hands of President's

Rigdon Joseph Smith Sen and Hyrum Smith to the office of High
Priests and council=ors in this place, viz. Kirtland the Stake of
Zion.– many great and glor=ious blessings were pronounced upon
the heads of thes[e] councilors by president S. Rigdon who was
spokesman on the occasion

Next proceded to supply the deficiencies in the Zion high
council [p. 107] which were two viz. Elder's John Murdock [138] and
Solomon Hancock[139] who were absent— Elder's Alva Bemon and
Isaac Mc Withy were nominated and seconded, to s[u]pp=ly their
place for the time being vote taken of the whole assembly and
carried in their favour, to serve as coun=cilors in the high council
of Zion, for the present

Elder Nathaniel Miliken and Thomas Carrico, were
nom=inated and seconded to officiate as doorkeepers in the house
of the Lord, vote called and carried, by the unanimous voice of the
assembly

President's Joseph Smith Jn S. Rigdon W. W. Phelps
D. Whitmer H. Smith, were nominated and seconded to draft rules
and regula=tion[s] to govern the house of the Lord vote called and
carried by the unanimous voice of the whole assembly

The question was agitate[d] whether whispering, should be
allowed in our councils and assemblys

A vote was called from the whole assembly and carried in the
negative, that no whisper=ing shall be allowed nor any one allowed
(except he is called upon or asks permission,) to speak
[p. 108] loud in our councils or assemblies, upon any concideration
whatever, and no man shall be interupted while speaking unless he
is speaking out of place, and every man, shall be allowed to speak
in his turn— Elder Miliken objected to of=ficiate in the house of
the Lord as door keeper on account of his health, and was released
by the voice of the assembly

The minuits of the council were then read, and council
adjourned untill Friday the 15th Inst. at 9. ocl A.M. at the ‹west›
school room in the up=per part of the Chapel

President S. Rigdon made a request to have some of the
pres=idency lay their hands upon him and rebuke a severe

affliction, in his face which troubles him most at night— Eld[e]r's
H. Smith and D. Whitmer by my request laid hands upon him and
pra=yed for him and rebuked his dis=ease in the name of the Lord
Jesus Christ,– the whole assembly ~~said~~ responded—Amen

Elder D[avid] W. Patten also made a request in behalf of his
wife for our prayers for her, that she might be healed.– I offered up
a pray[er] for her recovery, the assembly responded Amen [p. 109]

President Rigdon then arose and made some verry appropriate
remarks touching the enduement, and dismissed the assembly by
prayer—

W[arren] Parrish Scribe

This has been one of the best days that I ever spent, there has
been an entire unison of feeling expressed in all our p[r]oceedings
this day, and the Spirit of the God of Israel has rested upon us in
mighty power, and it has ‹been› good for us to be here, in this
heavenly place in Christ Jesus, and altho much fatiegued with the
labours of the day, yet my spiritual reward has been verry great
indeed

Returned home and spent the evening

Thursday morning the 14th [January 1836] at 9. oclock, meet
the hebrew class at the school room in the Chapel, and made some
arange=ments, about our anticipated Teacher Mr J. Sexias of
Hudson, Ohio—[140]

I then retired to the council room in the printing office, to
me[e]t, my colleagues who were appointed, with my self to draft
rules and regula=tions to be observed in the house of the Lord in
Kirtland built by the Church of the latter day saints, in the year of
our Lord 1834 which are as follows [p. 110]

1st— It is according to the rules and regula=tions of all regular and
legal organized bodies to have a president to keep order.–
2nd— The body thus organized are under obligation to be in
subjection to that auth=ority—
3d— When a congregation assembles in this house they shall

submit to the follow=ing rules, that due respect may be pa=yed to the order of worship—viz.

1st— no man shall be interupted who is appointed to speak by the presidency of the church, by any disorderly person or persons in the congregation, by whisper=ing by laughing by talking by men=acing Jestures by getting up and run=ning out in a disorderly manner or by offering indignity to the manner of worship or the religion or to any off=icer of said church while officiating in his office in any wise whatever by any display of ill manners or ill bree=ding from old or young rich or poor male or female bond or free black or white believer or unbeliever and if any of the above insults are offered such measures will be taken as are lawful to punish the aggressor or aggressors and eject them out of the house

2nd— An insult offered to the presid=ing Elder of said church, shall be considered an insult to the whole [p. 111] body, also an insult offered to any of the officers of said church while officiating shall be considered an insu=lt to the whole body—

3d— All persons are prohibited from going up the stairs in times of worship

4th— All persons are prohibited from exploring the house except waited upon by a person appointed for that purpose—

5th— All persons are prohibited from going into the several pulpits except the officers who are appointed to officiate in the same

6th— All persons are prohibited from cutting marking or maring the inside or outside of the house with a knife pencil or any other instrument whatever, under pain of such penalty as the law shall inflict—

7th— All children are prohibited from assembling in the house above or below or any part of it to play or for recreation at any time, and all parents guardians or masters shall be ameneable for all damage that shall accrue in consequence of their children—

8th— All persons whether believers or unbelievers shall be treated with due respect by the authorities of the Church—[p. 112]

9th— No imposition shall be practised upon any member of the church by depriving them of their ‹rights› in the house— council adjourned sini di [sine die]

returned home and spent the after no[o]n,– towards evening
President Cowdery returned from Columbus, the capital of this
State,[141] I could not spend much time with him being under
obligation to attend at Mrs. Wilcox[']s to join Mr. John Webb and
Mrs Catharine Wilcox in matrimony also Mr. Thos Carrier and
Miss Elizabeth Baker at the same place, I found a large company
assembled, the house was filled to overflo=wing, we opened our
interview by singing and prayer suited to the occasion after which I
made some remarks in relation to the duties that are incu=mbent
on husbands and wives, in par=ticular the great importance there is
in cultivating the pure principles of the in=stitution, in all its
bearings, and connexions with each other and Society in general

    I then invited them to arise and join hands, and pronounced
the ceremony according to the rules and regulations of the Church
of the latter day Saints

    ~~Closed~~ after which I pronounced such blessings upon their
heads as the Lord put into my heart ~~even~~ the blessings of Abraham
Isaac and Jacob, and dismissed by singing and prayer

    we then took some refreshment [p. 113] and our hearts were
made glad with the fruit of the vine, this is according to pattern,
set by our Saviour himself, and we feel disposed to patron=ize all
the institutions of heaven

    I took leave of the congregation and retired

    Friday the 15th [January 1836] at 9 oclock A.M meet in council
agreeably to the adjou=rnment, at the council room in the Chapel
organized the authorities of the church agreeably to their respective
offices in the same, I then made some observation respecting the
order of the day, and the great responsibility we are under to
trans=act all our buisness, in righteousness before God, inasmuch
as our desisions will have a bearing upon all mankind and upon all
generations to come

    Sung the song Adam-ondi-ahman and open[ed] by prayer—&
proceeded to buisness, by reading the rules and regula=tions to
govern the house of the Lord in Kirtland,– The vote of the
presidency was called upon these rules, and ~~carried~~ passed by the

unanimous voice of this presidency ‹viz.› of the high council, some object=ions were raised by president Cowdery, but waived, on an explination

The privilege of remarking upon the rules above named, was next granted [p. 114] to ‹the› high councillors of Kirtland, and after much altercation, their vote was called and unanimously passed, in favour of them

The investigation was then thrown bef=ore ~~the~~ the ‹high› council of Zion, some objections or inquiry, was made upon some particular items, which were soon settled, and their vote called ~~called~~ and passed unanim=ously in favour of them——

The twelve next investigated the subject of these rules, and their vote called and passed unanimously in favour of them—— Counsel adjourned for an hour— 1, oclock P.M in council, come to order, and proceded to buisness

The subject of the rules to govern the house of the Lord, come next in order before the counsel of the Seventy, their vote called and carried unanimously

The vote of the Bishop ‹of Zion› and his counsi=llors was then called, and after some debate was passed unanimously

The question was then thrown before the Bishop in Kirtland and his counsellors their vote called and carried in their favo=ur—— The above rules hav[e] now passed through the several quorums, in their order, and passed by the unanimous vote of the whole, and are therefore received and established as a law to govern the house of the Lord in this place,— In the investigati[o]n of this subject, I found that many who had deliberated upon this subject [p. 115] were darkened in their minds, which drew forth, some remarks from me, respect-ing the privileges of the authorities of the church, that they should, each speak in his turn, and in his place, and in his time and season, that their may be perfect order in all things, and that every man, before he, makes an objection to any, item, that is thrown before them for their concideration, should be sure that they can throw light upon the subject rather than spread darkness, and that his objections be founded in righteousness which may be done by applying ourselves closely to study the mind

and will of the Lord, whose Spirit always makes manifest, and
demonstrates to the underst=anding of all who are in possession, of
his Spirit—

Elder Carloss Smith was nomin=ated and seconded, to be
ordained to the high priesthood—also to officiate as president to
preside over that body in ~~this place~~ Kirtland— The vote was called
of the respective quorums in their order and passed through the
whole house by their unanimous voice—

Eld[e]r Alva Beemon, was nom=inated and seconded to
officiate as president of the Elders in Kirtland Elder Beemon arose
and asked permission to speak, and made the following remarks—
Brethren you [p. 116] know that I am young and I am old and
ignorant and kneed much instr=uctions, but I wish to do the will of
the Lord— The vote of the several authorities was then called and
carried unanimous=ly—

William Cowdery[142] was nominated and seconded to officiate as
president over the priests of the Aaronic priesthood in Kirtland,
the vote of the assembly was called, beginning at the Bishops
cou=ncil and passing through the several au=thorities untill it
come to the presidency of the high counsil in Kirtland and received
their sanction having ‹been› carried, unanim=ously in all the
departments, below

Oliver Olney was nominated and seconded to preside over the
teach=ers in Kirtland ~~and~~ The vote of the assembly was called and
passed unanimously

Ira Bond[143] was nominated and seconded to preside over the
deacons in Kirtland – vote called and passed unanimously

Eld[e]r Carloss Smith was called forward to the seat of the
presidency and ordained to the office's whereunto he was elected
and many blessings pronounced [p. 117] upon his head, by Joseph
Smith Jr. S. Rigdon and Hyrum Smith who were appointed to
ordain him

Also Eld[e]r Beemon received his ordination under the hands of
the same, to the office whereunto he had been elected, and many
blessings pronounced upon his head

Bishop Whitney ‹and his counselors› then proceded to ordain

Wm. Cowdery to the office whereunto he had been called, viz. to preside over the priests of the Aaronic priesthood in Kirtland, many blessings were sealed upon his head—

also Oliver Olney to preside over the teachers, in Kirtland with many blessings— also Ira Bond to preside over the deacons in Kirtland, with many blessings upon his head

next proceeded to nominated doorkeepers in the house of the Lord the officers of the several quorums were nominated seconded and carried that each should serve in their turn as doorkepers,– also that Nathaniel Miliken Thomas Carrico Samuel Rolph and Amos R. Orton[144] were elected to the office of doorkeepers [p. 118]

nominated and seconded that the presidency of the high counsel hold the keys of the outer and inner courts of the Lords house in Kirtland, except one of the vestries ‹keys› which is to be held by the Bishopric of the Aaronic Priesthood

the vote of the assembly called and carried unanimously

nominated and seconded that John Carrill [Corrill] be appointed to take charge of the house of the Lord in Kirtland immediately The vote of the assembly called and passed unanimously

President Rigdon then arose and delivered his charge to the assem=bly, his remarks were few and app=ropriate— adjourned by singing and prayer[145]

W. Parrish Scribe

Saturday morning the 16th [January 1836] by request I meet with the council of the 12 in company with my colleagues FG Williams and S. Rigdon

Council organized and opened by singing and prayer offered up by Thomas B. Marsh president of the 12

He arose and requested the privi=lege in behalf of his colleagues of sp=eaking, each in his turn without being interupted; which was granted them— Elder Marsh proceeded [p. 119] to unbosom his feelings touching the mission of the 12, and more par=ticularly respecting a certain letter which they received from the presidency of the high council in Kirtland, while attending a conference in the

~~East~~ State of Maine— also spoke of being plased in our council, on
·friday last below the council's of Kirtland and Zion having been
previously placed next [to] the presidency, in our assemblies— also
observed that they were hurt on account of some remarks made by
President H. Smith on the trial of Gladden Bishop[146] who had been
previously tried before the council of the 12, while on their mission
in the east,[147] who had by their request thrown his case before the
high council in Kirtland for investigation, and the 12 concidered
that their proceedings with him were in some degree,
discountenanced—

~~The remaining~~ Elder Marsh then gave way to his brethren and
they arose and spoke in turn untill they had all spoken acquiessing
in the observations of Elder Marsh and mad[e] some additions to his
remarks which are as follows— That the letter in question which
they received from the presidency, in which two of their numbers
were suspended, and the rest severely chastened, and that too upon
testimony which was unwarantable, and particular~~ly~~ stress was laid
upon a certain letter which the presidency had received from Dr.
[p. 120] W[arren] A. Cowdery of Freedom New York in which he
prefered charges against them which were false,[148] and upon which
~~they~~ ‹we› (the presiders) had acted in chastning them and
therefore, the 12, had concluded that the presidency had lost
confidence in them, and that whereas the church in this place, had
carressed them, at the time of their appointment, to the
appostleship they now treated them coolly and appear to have lost
confidence in them also —

They spoke of their having been in this work from the
beginning almost and had born[e] the burden in the heat of the day
and passed through many trials and that the presidency ought not
to ~~have~~ suspect their fidelity nor loose confid=ence in them,
neither have chastised them upon such testimony as was lying
~~before~~ before them— also urged the necessity of an explanation
upon the letter which they received from the presidency, and the
propriety of their having information as it respects their duties,
authority &c that they might come to ‹an› understanding in all
things, that they migh[t] act in perfect unison and harmony before

the Lord and be prepared for the endu=ment— also that they had prefered a charge against Dr Cowdery for his un=christian conduct which the presidency had disregarded— also that President O. Cowdery on a certain occasion had made use of language to one of the [p. 121] twelve that was unchristian and unbecom=ing any man, and that they would not submit to such treatment

The remarks of all the 12 were made in a verry forcible and explicit manner yet cool and deliberate,/ [149] I arose

I observed that we had heard them patiently and in turn should expect to be heard patiently also; and first I remarked that it was necessary that the 12 should state whether they were determined to persevere in the work of the Lord, whether the presidency are able to satisfy them or not; vote called and carried in the affirmative unani‹m›ously; I then said to them that I had not lost confidence in them, and that they had no reason to suspect my confidence, and that I would be willing to be weighed in the scale of truth today in this matter, and risk it in the day of judgment; and as it respects the chastning contained in the letter in question which I acknowledge might have been expressed in too harsh language; which was not intentional and I ask your forgiveness in as much as I have hurt your feelings; but nevertheless, the letter that that Elder Mclellen wrote back to Kirtland while the twelve were at the east was harsh also and I was willing to set the one against the other; I next proceeded to explain the subject of the duty of the twelve; and their authority which is next to the present presidency, and that the arangement of the assembly in this place on the 15 inst/ [150]in placing the high councils of Kirtland and next the presidency was because the buisness to be transacted was buisness that related to that body in particular which was to [p. 122] fill the several quorum's in Kirtland; not beca[u]se they were first in office, and that the arangement was most Judicious that could be made on the occassion also the 12, are not subject to any other than the first presidency; viz. myself S. Rigdon and F G. Williams— I also stated to the 12, that I do not continue countinanc[e] the harsh language of President Cowdery to them neither in myself nor any other man, although I have sometimes spoken to harsh from the impulse of the

moment and inasmuch as I have wounded your feelings brethren I
ask your forgivness, for I love you and will hold you up with all my
heart in all righteousness before the Lord, and before all men, for
be assured brethren I am willing to stem the torrent of all
opposition, in storms in tempests in thunders and lightning by sea
and by land in the wilderness or among fals[e] brethren or mobs or
wher=ever God in his providence may call us and I am determined
that neither hi=ghts nor depths principalities nor pow=ers things
present or to come nor any other creature shall separate me from
you; and I will now covenant with you before God that I will not
listen too nor credit, any derogatory report against any of you nor
condemn you upon any testimony beneath the heavens, short of
that testimony which is infalible, untill I can see you face to face
and know of a surity [p. 123] and I do place unlimited confidence in
your word for I believe you to be men of truth, and I ask the same
of you, when I tell you any thing that you place equal confidence in
my word for I will not tell you I know anything which I do not
know— but I have already consumed more time than I intended to
when I commenced and I will now give way to my colleagues

President Rigdon arose next and acquiessed in what I had said
and acknowledged to the 12, that he had not done as he ought, in
not citing Dr. Cowdery to trial on the charges that were put into
his hands by the 12, that he had neglected his duty in this thing,
for which he asked their forgiveness, and would now attend to it if
they desired him to do so, and ~~Elder~~ ‹Presdt› Rigdon also
obser=ved to the 12 ~~that~~ ‹if he› ~~he might~~ had spo=ken, or
reproved too harshly, at any time and had injured their feelings by
so doing he asked their forgivness.—

President Williams arose and acquiessed in the above
sentiments expressed by myself and President Rigdon, in full and
said many good things

The President of the 12, then called a vote of that body to
know whether they were perfectly satisfied with the [p. 124]
explenation which we had given them and whether they would
enter into the covenant we had proposed to them, which was most
readily manifested in the affirmative by raising their hands to

heaven, in testimony of their willingness and desire to enter into this covenant and their entire satisfaction with our explanation, upon all the difficulties that were on their minds, we then took each other by the hand in confirmation of our covenant and their was a perfect unison of feeling on this occasion, and our hearts over flowed with blessings, which were pronounced upon each others heads as the Spirit gave us utterance my scribe is included in this covenant ~~with~~ and blessings with us, for I love him, for the truth and integrity that dwelleth in him and may God enable us all, to perform our vows and covenants with each other in all fidelity and rightiousness before Him, that our influence may be felt among the nations of the earth in mig=hty power, even to rend the Kingdom of darkness in sunder, and triumph over priestcraft and spiritual wicked=ness in high places, and brake in pieces all ~~other~~ Kingdoms that are opposed to the Kingdom of Christ, and spread the light and truth of the everlasting gospel from the rivers to the ends of the earth

Elder Beemon call[ed] for council upon the subject of his returning home he wished to know whether it was best for him to return before the Solemn Assembly [p. 125] or not, after taking it into concider=ation the council advised him to tarry we dismissed by singing and prayer and retired

W. Parrish *Scribe*

Sunday morning the 17th [January 1836] /[151]Attended meeting at the schoolhouse at the usual hour a large congregation assembled; I proceeded to organ=ize the several quorums present; first, the presidency; then the twelve, and the seventy all who were present also the counsellors of Kirtland and Zion. President Rigdon then arose/ [152]and observed that instead of preaching the time would be occupied, by the presidency and twelve in speaking each in their turn untill they had all spoken, the Lord poured out his spirit upon us, and the brethren began to confess their faults one to the other and the congregation were soon overwhelmed in tears and some of our hearts were too big for utterance, the gift of toungs, come upon us also like the rushing of a m=ighty wind, and my soul was filled with the glory of God.

In the after noon I joined three couple in matrimony, in the
publick congregation, whose names are as follows— Wm F.
Cahoon[153] and Maranda Gibbs ~~Larona Cah~~ Harvy Stanly and
Larona Cahoon—[154] also Tunis Rapleye[155] and Louisa Cutler,[156]—
We then administered the Lord['s] supper and dismissed the
congregation; ‹which› was so dense that it was [p. 126] verry
unpleasant for all— we were then invited to Elder Cahoons to a
feast which was prepared on the occasion, and had a good time
while partaking of the rich repast that was spread before us, and I
verily realized that it was good for brethren to dwell togeth=er in
unity, ~~even~~ like the dew upon the m=ountains of Israel, where the
Lord commands blessings, even life for ever more,

Spent the evening at home

Monday the 18th [January 1836] attended the hebrew
school,— This day the Elders School was removed into the Chapel
in the room adjoining ours – nothing very special transpired

Copy of a Letter
Willoughby January 5th 1836

To Elder W. Parrish

Sir I have received an open note from Mr. Sylvester Smith
informing me that your School concidered itself dissolved from all
ingagements with me, for this I was not unprepared. But he adds
that I must excuse him for saying that I appear to be willing to trifle
with you in regard to appointments time, &c–

This insinuation is unworthy of me beneath my sence of
honour, and I [p. 127] could hope unwaranted by any mean
suspicion of your whole body— I wrote for books to New York by
Mr. Cowdery – not but ~~I could~~ I could not have taught the
rudiments without them – but because I wished to make my
instruction philosophically availing as well as mere elementary. In
this object I thought myself confirmed by *you*, my books have not
come as yet & are probably lost— of the pecuniary value I seek
not.— I borowed a book of Elder Boynton, & told him, believing
him to be responsible that Wednesday would be best for me to
deliver a publick lecture owing to my engagements here. I here was

deliver a publick lecture owing to my engagements here. I here was *officially* informed when the School was to be *opened* by me.—

The addition of insult to wrong may be gratifying to small minds— mine is above it, scorns and repud[i]ates it.—

I am verry respectfully Your verry ob. Servt.

Daniel L M. Piexotto

/[157]The Answer

Kirtland Jan 11th 1836

Dr. Piexotto,

Sir, I received yours of the 5th Inst in which you manifested much indignation and considered your hounour highly insulted by us as a body, if not by me as an indiv=idual, and deprecated our conduct because we informed you that you appear[e]d willing to trifle with us, as it [p. 128] respects our engagement with you to teach our Hebrew class I have acted in this matter as agent for the School; the time agreed upon for you to commence, was not to be protracted, at farthest later than Dec 15th and the class have ever till now, considered themselves bound by the engagement I made with you.– When Elder Cowdery and myself called, you set a time that you would come over to Kirtland and have our agreement committed to writing, but did not come, some were disp=leased, I excused you; some days passed without our hearing from you: at length Dr Williams called and you specified another time that you would come, (which is some 2 or 3 weeks since) the class were again disappointed, I again plead an excuse for you; on last saturday week, or in other words on the 2 Inst our class met and agreed to organize ~~the~~ on Monday morning the 4 Inst, at 9 oclock A.M. and by the voice of the school I was appointed to wait on you, and advertize your honour that we were ready, and should expect you to attend at that ~~hau~~ hour; presuming that you would be ready at this late period to fulfill your engagement if you ever intended to; and accordingly I called, and informed you of the arang<e>ments we had made, but on account of your arang<e>ments at the *Medical University*[158] I was willing to exceed my instructions, and let you name the hour that you would wait on us on that day, which was at 4 oclock P.M.

Sunday the 3 inst, I learned from Elder Boyanton [Boynton] that it would be most convenient for you to call on Wedensday, the school knew nothing of this as a body, on Monday morning we met, and I was called upon to report which I did; I also stated what I had [p. 129] heard from Elder Boyanton, the voice of the class was called to know, whether they considered themselves any longer under obligation to you, and whether they would wait any longer for you, and carried in the negative.

Now sir, what could I say in your behalf? I answer, nothing; I should have considered it an insult to have asked 40 men who had laid by every other consideration to attend this school, to lay upon their oars 3 days longer with the impression on their minds, (and justly too) that it would be altogether uncertain whether you would come then or not.

With these things lying before us, we are told by your *honour* that it may be gratifying to small minds to add *insult* to *wrong;* and you also informed me in your note, that you was not unprepared for the inteligence it contained, which is virtually saying that you intended the abuse you have heaped upon us.

I assure you sir that I have ever entertained the best of feelings towards you, and have recognized you as a friend in whom I could repose unlimited confid=ence and whith whom I have acted in good faith, and I am not a little surprized on this occasion, that you should treat us with such marked contem‹pt› and then upbraid us with adding insult to wrong; small as you may consider our minds, we have suffi=cient discernment to discover this insult, although offered by your *honour,* and sufficient good manners not to insult or wrong any man.

Respectfully your most obedient humble servant
                                    Warren Parrish

P.S. The note that we sent you, was well sealed when it was put into the hands of the messenger; which you infor=med me you recieved open, yours
                                    W.P. [p. 130]

/[159]Monday morning the 18th at 9 oclock, attended the hebrew school, nothing special transpir[e]d on this day— spent the evening at home with my family——[160]

Tuesday the 19th [January 1836] spent the day at school, the Lord blessed us in our stud=ies.– this day we commenced reading in our hebrew bibles with much success, it seems as if the Lord opens our minds, in a marvelous manner to understand his word in the origi=nal language, and my prayer is that God will speedily indu us with a knowledge of all languages and toungs, that his servants may go forth for the last time, to bind up the law and seal up the testimony

Form of Marriage Certificate ——
I hereby certify that agreeably to the rules and regulations of the Church of Christ of Latter-Day Saints, on matrimony, were joined in marriage Mr. William F. Cahoon and Miss Nancy M. Gibbs, both of this place, on Sabbath the 17th instant.
Joseph Smith Jun
Kirtland Ohio Jan. 18th 1836 Presiding Elder of said Church
[p. 131]

Wednesday morning 20th [January 1836] attended school at the us[u]al hour, and spent the day in reading and lecturing, and made some advancement in our studies,— At evening I attended at John Johnsons with my family, on a matrimonial occa=sion, having been invited to do so, ~~and~~ to join President John F. Boynton and Miss Susan Lowell in marriage, a large and respectable company assembled, and were seated by Eld[e]r's O. Hyde & W. Parrish in the following order— The presidency and their companions in the first seats the twelve apostles in the second the 70, in the third, and the remainder of the congre=gation seated with their companions
After the above arangments were made Eld[e]r Boynton & his Lady with their atte=ndants, came in and were seated in front of the presidency – a hymn was sung, after which I adressed a throne of grace,— I then arose and read aloud a licence granting any minister of the gospel the priviledge of solemnizing the rights of matrimony, and after calling for objection if any there were, against the anticipated alliance between Eld[e]r Boynton & Miss Lowell and waiting sufficient time, I observed that all forever after this must hold their peace—

I then envited them to join hands and I pronounced the
ceremony according to the rules and regulations of the church of
the Latter-day Saints, in the name of [p. 132] God, and in the
name of Jesus Christ I pronounced upon them the blessings of
Abraham Isaac and Jacob and such other blessings as the Lord put
into my heart, and being much under the in=fluence of a cold I
then gave way and President S. Rigdon arose and delivered a verry
forcible address, suited to the occ=asion, and closed the servises of
the evening by prayer.— Eld[e]r O. Hyde Eld[e]r L. Johnson &
Eld[e]r W. Parrish who served on the occasion, then presented the
pres=idency with three servers filled with glasses of wine, to bless,
and it fell to my lot to attend to this duty, which I cheerfully
di=scharged, it was then passed round in order, then the cake, in
the same order, and suffise it to say our hearts were made ~~cheerful
and~~ glad, while partaking of the bounty of the earth, which was
pres=ented, untill we had taken our fill, and Joy filled every bosom,
and the countena=nces of old, and young, alike, seemed to bloom
with the cheerfulness and smiles of youth and an entire unison of
feeling seemed to pervade the congregation, and indeed I doubt
whether the pages of history can boast of a more splendid and
inocent wedding and feast than this for it was conducted after the
order of heaven, who has a time for all thing[s] and this being a
time of rejoicing, we hartily embraced it, and conducted our=selves
accordingly— Took leave of the [p. 133] company and returned
home. ——

Thursday morning the 21st [January 1836] This morning a
minister from Conne[c]ticut by the name of John W. Olived called
at my house and enquired of my father if ~~Smith~~ the pro[p]het live's
here he replied that he did not understand him. Mr. Olived asked
the same question again and again and recieved the same answer.
he finally asked if Mr. Smith lives here, father replyed O yes Sir I
understand you now.— father then stept into my room, and
informed me that a gentleman had called to see me, I went into the
room where he was, and the first question he asked me, after
passing a compliment, was to know how many members we have in

our church, I replyed to him, that we hav[e] ~~about~~ between 15
hundred and 2,000 in this branch.— He then asked me wherein we
differ from other christian denomination[s] I replyed that we
believe the bible, and they do not.– however he affirmed that he
believed the bible, I told him then to be baptised,– he replied that
he did not realize it to be his duty— But when [I] laid ~~him~~ before
him the principles of the gospel, viz. faith and repentance and
baptism for the remission ‹of sins› and the laying on of hands for
the reseption of the Holy Ghost ‹he manifested much surprise›—I
then observed that the [p. 134] hour for school had arived, and I
must attend The man seemed astonished at our doctrine but by no
means hostile

At about 3. oclock P.M I dismissed the school and the
presidency, retired to the loft of the printing office, where we
attended to the ordinance of washing our bodies in pure water,[161]
we also perfumed our bodies and our heads, in the name of the Lord
at early candlelight, I meet with the presid=ency, at the west
school room in the Chapel to attend to the ordinance of
annointing our heads with holy oil— also the councils of ~~Zion~~
Kirtland and Zion, meet in the two ad=joining rooms, who waited
in prayer while we attended to the ordinance,– I took the oil in my
‹left› ~~right~~ hand, father Smith being seated before me and the rest
of the pre=sidency encircled him round about.— we then streched
our right hands to heaven and blessed the oil and concecrated it in
the name of Jesus Christ— we then laid our hands on our aged
fath[er] Smith, and invoked, the blessings of heaven,– I then
annointed his head with the concecrated oil, and sealed many
blessings upon him, ~~head,~~ the presidency then in turn, laid their
hands upon his head, beginning at the eldest, untill they had all
laid their hands on him, and pronounced such blessings, upon his
head as the Lord put into their hearts— all blessing him to be our
patraark [Patriarch], ~~and~~ ‹to› annoint our [p. 135] heads, and
attend to all duties that pertain to that office.— I then took the
seat, and father annoint[ed] my head, and sealed upon me the
blessings, of Moses, to lead Israel in the latter days, even as moses
led him in days of old,– also the blessings of Abraham Isaac and

Jacob.– all of the presidency laid their hands upon me and
pronounced upon my head many prophesies, and blessings, many
of which I shall not notice at this time, but as Paul said, so say I, let
us come to vissions and revelations,– The heavens were opened
upon us and I beheld the celestial Kingd=om of God, and the glory
thereof, whether in the body or out I cannot tell,– I saw the
transcendant beauty of the gate that enters, through which the
heirs of that King=dom will enter, which was like unto circling
flames of fire, also the blasing throne of God, whereon was seated
the Father and the Son,– I saw the beautiful streets of that
Kingdom, which had the appearance of being paved with gold— I
saw father Adam, and Abraham and Michael and my father and
mother, my brother Alvin[162] that has long since slept, and marvled
how it was that he had obtained this an inheritance ‹in› that
Kingdom, seeing that he had departed this life, before the Lord
‹had› set his hand to gather Israel the ‹second time› and had not
been baptised for the remission of sins— Thus said came the voice
‹of the Lord› unto me saying all who have [p. 136] died with[out] a
knowledge of this gospel, who would have received it, if they had
been permited to tarry, shall be heirs of the celestial Kingdom of
God— also all that shall die henseforth, with‹out› a knowledge of
it, who would have received it, with all their hearts, shall be heirs
of that Kingdom, for I the Lord ‹will› judge all men according to
their works according to the desires of their hearts— and again I
also beheld the Terrestial Kingdom I also beheld that all children
who die before they arive to the years of accountabil=ity, are saved
in the celestial Kingdom of heaven— I saw the 12, apostles of the
Lamb, who are now upon the earth who hold the keys of this last
ministry, in foreign lands, standing together in a circle much
fatiegued, with their clothes tattered and feet swolen, with their
eyes cast dow=nward, and Jesus ‹standing› in their midst, and they
did not behold him, the Saviour looked upon them and wept— I
also beheld Elder McLellen in the south, stand=ing upon a hill
surrounded with a vast multitude, preaching to them, and a lame
man standing before him, supp=orted by his crutches, he threw
them down at his word, and leaped as an heart [hart], by the
mighty power of God

Also Eld[er] Brigham Young standing in a strange land, in the
far south=west, in a desert place, upon a rock in the midst of about
a dozen men of colour, who, appeared hostile [p. 137] He was
preaching to them in their own tou=ng, and the angel of God
standing above his head with a drawn sword in his hand
protec[t]ing him, but he did not see it,— and I finally saw the 12 in
the celestial Kingdom of God,— I also beheld the redemption of
Zion, and many things which the toung of man, cannot discribe in
full.— Many of my brethren who received this ordinance with me,
saw glorious visions also,– angels ministered unto them, as well as
my self, and the power of the highest rested upon, us the house was
filled with the glory of God, and we shouted Hosanah to ~~the~~ God
and the Lamb

I am mistaken, concerning my rece=iving the holy anointing
first after father Smith, we received ‹it› in turn according to our
age, (that is the presidency,)

My Scribe also recieved his anointing ‹with us› and saw in a
vision the armies of heaven protecting the Saints in their return to
Zion— & many things that I saw

The Bishop of Kirtland with his counsellors and the Bishop of
Zion with his counsellors, were present with us, and received their,
annoint=ing under the hands of father Smith and confirmed by the
presidency and the glories of heaven was unfolded to them also—

We then invited the counsellors of Kirtland and Zion ~~and
Kirtland~~ into our room, and President Hyrum [p. 138] Smith
annointed the head of the presid=ent of the counsellors in Kirtland
and President D. Whitmer the head of the president, of the
counsellors of Zion—

The president of each quorum then annointed the heads of his
colleagues, each in his turn beginning, at the eldest

The vision of heaven was opened to these also, some of them
saw the face of the Saviour, and others were ministered unto by
holy angels, and the spirit of prop[h]esy and revelation was poured
out in mighty power, and loud hosanahs and glory to God in the
highest, saluted the heavens for we all communed with the
h[e]avenly host's,— and I saw in my vision all of the presidency in

the Celestial Kingdom of God, and, many others who were present[163]

Our meeting was opened by singing and prayer offered up by the head of each quorum, and closed by singing and invoking the benediction of heaven with uplifted hands, and retired between one and 2. oclock in the morning [p. 139]

Friday morning the 22nd [January 1836] attended at the school room at the us[u]al hour.– But insted of persuing our studies/ [164] we ~~commenced~~ spent the time in rehearsing to each other the glorious scenes that transpired on the preceding evening, while attending to the ordinance of holy anointing.— At evening we met at the same place, with the council of the 12 and the presidency of the 70 who were to receive this ordinance; the high councils of Kirtland and Zion were present also: we called to order and organized; the Presidency then proceeded to consecrate the oil; we then laid our hands upon Elder Thomas B. Marsh who is the president of the 12 and ordained him to the authority of anointing his brethren, I then poured the concecrated oil upon his head in the name of Jesus Christ and sealed such blessings upon him as the Lord put into my heart; the rest of the presidency then laid their hands upon him and blessed him each in their turn beginning at the eldest; he then anointed ‹and blessed› his brethren from the oldest to the youngest, I also laid my hands upon them and prounounced many great and glorious [blessings] upon their heads; the heavens were opened and angels ministered unto us.

The 12 then proceeded to anoint and bless the presidency of the 70 and seal upon their heads power and authority to anoint their brethren; the heavens were opened upon Elder Sylvester Smith and he leaping up exclaimed, The horsemen of Israel and the chariots thereof. ~~President Rigdon arose/~~ [165]Br. Carloss Smith was also, annointed and ~~ordained~~ blessed to preside over the high priesthood.— President Rigdon, arose to conclude the servises of the evening [p. 140] by invoking the benediction of heaven ~~of heaven~~ upon the Lords anointed ‹which he did› in an eloquent manner the congregation shouted a loud hosannah the gift of toungs, fell upon us in mighty pow[e]r, angels mingled ~~themselves~~ their voices with ours, while their presence was in our mid=st, and unseasing prases swelled our bosoms for the space of half an hour,— I then observed to the brethren that it was time to retire, we accordingly <closed> our interview and returned home at about 2. oclock in the morning/ [166]& the spirit & visions of God attended me through the night[167]

Saturday 23rd [January 1836] attended at the school room as usual & we came together filled with the spirit as on the past evening & did not fe[e]l like studying but commenced conversing upon heavenly things & the day was spent agreably & profitably– <Elder> ~~& other~~Alvah Beaman had been tempted to doubt the things which we recd. on saturday evening & he made an humble confession & asked forgiveness of the school whi[c]h was joyfully given – & the ~~old man~~ said he would try to resist Satan in future

Sunday Jany 24 [1836] Met the several quorems in the room under the printing office & after organizing & op[e]ning by prayer called upon the High council of Kirtland to proceede and confess their sins as th[e]y might be directed by the spirit– & they occupied the first part of the day and confessed & exhorted as the spirit led.– P.M. attended again & saw <the> Bread & wine administered to the quorems & brethren who were present—— In the evening met the Presidency in the room over the printing room & counseled on the subject of endowment & the preperation necessary for [p. 141] the solemn Assembly which is to be called when the House of the Lord is finished[168]

Jany. 25. Monday [1836]— Recd a line from my scribe informing me of his ill health as follows– Brother Joseph, My great desire to be in your com=pany & in the Assembly of the Saints where God opens the heavens & exhibits the treasures of eternity is the only thing that has stimulated me for a number of days past to leave my house; for be

assured, dear brother, my bod=ily affliction is severe; I have a
violent ‹cough› more especially nights, which deprives me of my
appetite, & my strength fails, & writing has a particular tendency
to injure my lungs while I am under the influence of such a cough I
therefore, with reluctance send your journal to you untill my health
improves

     Yours in heart [haste] Warren Par‹r›ish
P.S. Brother Joseph, pray for me, & ask the prayers of the class on
my account also.

 Appointed Elder Sylvester Smith acting Scribe for the time
being or till Eld[er] Parrish shall recover his health— spent the day
at home receiving visiters &c

 Tuesday 26 [January 1836] Mr. Seixas arived from Hudson to
teach the hebrew Langu[a]ge & I attended upon the organizing of
the class for the purpose of receiving his lectures in hebrew
grammar– his hours of instruction are from ten to eleven A.M. &
from two to three P.M. his intro=duction pleased me much. I think
he will be a help to the class in learning the hebrew

 Wednesday [27 January 1836] attended school as usual & other
matters which came before me to attend to [p. 142]

 Thursday ‹28› [January 1836] attended school at the usual
hours In the evening met the quorems of High Priests in the west
room of the upper loft of the Lord,s house & in company with my
council of the presidency – consecrated & anointed the
cou[n]sellors of the President of the High priesthood & having
instructed them & set the quorem in order I left them to perform
the holy anointing— & went to the quorem of Elders in the other
end of the room. I assisted in anointing the coun=sellors of the
President of the Elders & gave them the instruction necessary for
the occasion & left the President & his council to anoint the Elders
while I should go to the adjoining room & attend to organizing &
instructing of the quorem of the Seventy—

I found the Twelve Apostles assembled with this quorem & I proceeded with the quorem of the presedincy to instruct them & also the seven presidents of the seventy Elders to call upon God with uplifted hands to seal the blessings which had been promised to them by the holy anointing As I organized this quorem with the presedincy in this room, Pres. Sylvester Smith saw a piller of fire rest down & abide upon the heads of the quorem as we stood in the midst of the Twelve.

When the Twelve & the seven were through with their sealing prayers I called upon Pres. S. Rigdon to seal them with uplifted hands & when he he had done this & cried hossannah that all [the] congregation should join him & shout ho=sannah to God & the Lamb & glory to God in the highest— It was done so & Eld[er] Roger [p. 143] Orton saw a ~~flaming~~ ‹mighty› Angel riding upon a horse of fire with a flaming sword in his hand followed by five others – encircle the house & protect the saints even the Lords anointed from the power of Satan & a host of evil spirits which were striving to disturb the saints——

Pres. Wm Smith one of the Twelve saw the h[e]avens op[e]ned & the Lords host protecting the Lords anointed. Pres. Z[ebedee] Coltrin one of the seven saw the saviour extended before him as up=on the cross & [a] little after crowned with a glory upon his head above the brightness of the sun after these things were over & a glorious vision which I saw had passed I instructed the seven presidents to proceede & anoint the seventy & returned to the room of the High Priests & Elders & attended to the sealing of what they had done with uplifted hands, the Lord had assisted my bro. Carloss the Pres. of the High Priests to go forward with the anointing of the High priests so that he had performed it to the acceptance of the Lord, notwithstand=ing he was verry young & inexperienced in such duties & I f[e]lt to praise God with a loud hossannah for his goodness to me & my fathers family & to all the children of men – praise the Lord all ye his saints– praise his holy name after these quorems were dismissed I retired to my home filled with the spirit & my soul cried hossannah to God & the Lamb through ‹the› silent watches of the night & while my eyes were closed in sleep the visions of the Lord were sweet unto me & his glory was round about me praise the Lord. [p. 144]

Friday 29 [January 1836] – attended school & read hebrew—— recd the following line from the Presidency of the Elders–

                          Kirtland Jany. 29. AD. 1836
     To the Presidents of the Church of Latter day saints. Beloved Bret[hren] feeling ourselves amenable to you for our proceedings as the presidency of the first quorem of Elders in Kirtland, & believing that we are to be govorned by you; we desire to know if we are to receive all those who are recommended to us by Elders for ordaination, or shall we recei=ve none only those who have written recommendations from you. please answer our request
                                 Alvah Beman   Pres.
E.M. Green   Clk   Reuben Hadlock[169] Counsel
                             John Morton[170]

Answered the above verbally & attended to various duties. P.M. I called in all my Father,s family & made a feast– ‹& related my feeling towards them› My father pronounced the fol=lowing Patriarchial blessings

     Henry Garrett, born in Deerfield, Onieda Co. N.Y. Sept 5. AD. 1814— Bro. I bless thee by the authority of the Priesthood Lord had eye upon thee, Satan seek destruction relatives also I seal thee unto life. power to tread the adversa[r]y under thy feet & be useful reclaim friends. be a son of God, an heir jointly with Jesus Christ. stand on the earth if faithful till thou hast recd all the desires of thy heart which are in righteousness, the Lord shall bless thy chil[dren] after thee with the blessings of Abraham Isaac & Jacob, shall walk with companion to the [p. 145] House of God & see his glory fill the house & thou shalt receive all the blessings which thy heart can desire– I seal these blessings upon thee in the name of Jesus Amen—

Charles H. Smith born in Potsdam St. Lawrence Co Ny. April 16. 1817— Thou art in thy youth— satan will lay many snares for thee but I secure thee by the power of the holy priesthood from his grasp. thou hast no father— an orphan. The Lord shall watch over thee & keep thee & thou shalt receive the priesthood & be mighty in word, save fathers house receive all the blessings of the Earth even of A[braham] I[saac] & Jacob – stand on earth till Redeamer com[es] & do all that the power of the holy priesthood can qualify thee for. I seal these blessings upon thee in the name of Jesus Amen—

Marietta Carter born in Benson, Rutland Co. Vt. April 1. AD. 1818— Thou art an orphan & the Lord shall bless thee more than thy own father could do if he had not been taken from thee– thy name is written in the Book of life– become a companion & a mother– Lord bless thy children & some of them shall prophecy– thy father laid down his life for the redemption of Zion– his spirit watches over thee– thy heart shall be filled with light not sleep in the dust– see thy Redeamer come in the clouds of heaven. & be caught up to meet him & be ever with him– these blessings I seal upon thee in the name of Jesus Amen [p. 146]

Angeline Carter born in Benson Rutland Co. V.t. Aug[u]st 26 ‹1823› Thou art a child– thy heart is pure & Satan shall have no power over thee because of thy blessing God shall be thy father, an heir with Jesus– observe the words of thy friends who care for thee & seek to please them. The Lord will give thee children & wisdom to teach them righteousness, & they shall be blest of the Lord & call thee blessed, a daughter of Abraham live till satisfied with life. I seal the[e] up unto eternal life in the name of Jesus Amen—

Joanna Carter born in Putnam Ny— Nov. 26. AD. 1824— I seal the blessings of a father, thy father is no more. blessings of Abraham Isaac & Jacob. strength health healed of all infirmities. Satan have no power to afflict– Lord guard thee by his holy Angels – name written in heaven – eyes opened to see visions Angels minister unto thee– a companion– lead thee to the house of

God– see the glory of God fill the house– see the end of this
generation– have power to stand against all the power of satan &
overcome through the faith which is in Jesus. I seal thee up unto
eternal life in the name of the Lord Jesus Amen—

Nancy Carter born in Benson Rutland Co. V.t. Feby. 26 AD.
1827— Thou art a child– the Lord loves thee Satan shall seek in
vain to destroy thee– Lord raise friends for thee which shall guard
thee from the destroyer. thy name is written in heaven live to see
the winding up of this generation [p. 147] Angels shall watch over
thee in thy youth Eyes op[e]ned– see thy God– raise children in
right=eousness & they shall be blest & call thee blessed because of
thy diligence in teaching them the doctrine of the kingdom. I seal
all these blessings upon thee in the name of Jesus Amen[171]
          Written & recorded by Sylvester Smith scribe

This was a good time to me & all the family rejoiced together– we
continued the meeting till about eight oclock in the evening &
related the goodness of God to us in op[e]ning our eyes to see the
visions of heaven & in sending his holy Angels to minister unto us
the word of life– we sang the praise of God in anim=ated strains &
the power of love & union was felt & enjoyed—

Saturday 30 [January 1836] Attended school as usual, & waited
upon several visiters & showed them the record of Abraham– Mr
Seixas our hebrew teacher examined them with deep interest &
pronounced them to be original beyound all doubt, he is a man of
excellent understanding– & has a knowledge of many languages
which were spoken by the Anti[e]nts– he is an honorable man so
far as I can judge as yet— in the evening went to the upper rooms
of the Lord's house & set the different quorems in order–instructed
the Presidents of the seventy concerning the order of their
anointing & requested them to proceed & anoint the seventy
having set all the quorems in order I re=[p. 148]turned to my house
being weary with continual anxiety & labour in puting all the
Authorities in & in striving to purify them for the solemn
assem=bly according to the commandment of the Lord

Sunday 31. [January] 1836   Attended divine service in the schoolhouse organized the several quorems of the Authoraties of the church– appointed door keepers to keep order about the door because of the crowd & to prevent the house from being excess=ively crowded– The high council of Zion occupied the first part of the day in speaking as they were led & relating experi[e]nces trials &c.– P.M. house came to order as usual & Pres. Sidney Rigdon delivered a short discours[e] & we attended to the breaking of bread the season was as interesting as usual– In the evening my father attended to the blessing of three Brethren at Pres. O. Cowderies– spent the evening at home

Monday Febuary 1 [1836]. attended scholl as usual– & in company with the other committe organized another class of 30 to receive Mr Seixas Lectures on the hebrew– in the evening attended to the organizing of the quorems of High priests– Elders– Seventy & Bishops in the uper rooms of the house of the Lord & after blessing each quorem in the name of the Lord I left them & returned home
had an other interview with Mr. Seixas our hebrew teacher & related to him some of the dealings of God to me– & gave him some of the evidences of the work of the latter days— he listned candidly & did not appose [p. 149]

Tuesday Febuary 2. AD. 1836—Attended school as usual & various duties went to the schoolhouse in the evening & heard an animated discourse delivered by Pres. S. Rigdon he touched the outlines of our faith– showed the scat=tering & gathering of Israel from the scriptures & the stick of Joseph in the hands of Eaphraim & The law of Eaphraim aside from that of Moses It was an interesting meeting– the spirit bore record that the Lord was well pleased!——

Wednesday 3 [February 1836] attended our hebrew lecture P.M. & studied with O. Cowdery & Sylvester Smith P.M.—— received many visiters & showed the records of Abraham– my father blest three with a patri=archial blessing– Eld[er] A[lvah] Beman handed in the names of seventy of his quorem– designed for another seventy if God will—

Thursday 4 [February 1836] attended school & assisted in forming a class of 22 to read at 3.o clock P.m. the other 23 reads at 11 o.clock the first class recit[e]s at a quarter before 10 ‹AM› & the second at a quarter before 2– p.m. we have a great want of books but are determined to do the best we can– may the Lord help us to obtain this language that we may read the scrip=tures in the language in which they were given

Friday 5 [February 1836] Attended school & assisted the committe to make arangements for supplying the third & fourth classes with books– concluded to divide a bible into several parts for the benefit of said classes continued my studies in the hebrew– rec[eive]d several visiters & attended various duties— [p. 150]

Saturday 6 [February 1836] called the anointed together to receive the seal of all their blessings. The High Priests & Elders in the council room as usual– The Seventy with the Twelve in the second room & the Bishop in the 3– I laboured with each of these quorems for some time to bring [them] to the order which God had shown to me which is as follows– first part to be spent in solemn prayer before god without any talking or confusion & the conclusion with a sealing pray=er by Pres. Sidney Rigdon when all the quorems are to shout with one accord a solemn ho=sannah to God & the Lamb with an Amen— amen & amen– & then all take seats & lift up their hearts in silent prayer to God & if any obtain a prophecy or vision to rise & speak that all may be edified & rejoice together I had considerable trouble to get all the quorems united in this order– I went from room to room repeatedly & charged each separately– assuring them that it was according to the mind of God yet notwithstanding all my labour– while I was in the east room with the Bishops quorems I f[e]lt by the spirit that something was wrong in the quorem of Elders in the west room– & I immedi=ately requested Pres. O. Cowdery & H. Smith to go in & see what was the matter– The quorem of Elders had not observed the order which I had given them & were reminded of it by Pres. Carloss Smith & mildly requested to observe order & continue in prayer & requested – some of them replied that they had a teacher of their own & did not wish to be troubled by others this caused the spirit of the Lord to withdraw [p. 151] This interrupted the meeting & this quorem lost th[e]ir blessing in a great measure–[172] the other quorems were more careful & the quorem of the seventy enjoyed a great flow of the holy spirit many arose & spok testifying that they were filled with the holy spirit which was like fire in their bones so that they could not hold their peace but were constrained to cry hosan=nah to God & the Lamb & glory in the highest. Pres. Wm Smith one of the twelve saw a vision of the Twelve & seven in council together in old England & prophecied that a great work would be done by them in the old co[u]ntries & God was already beginning to work in the hearts of the p[e]ople– Pres. Z. Coltrin one of the seven saw a vision of the Lords Host– & others were filled with the spirit & spake in tongues & prophecied– This was a time of re=joicing long to be remembered! praise the Lord—

/[173]Sunday Feby 7. 1836 attended ~~the~~ meeting at the us[u]al hour the quorums, were seated according to their official standing in the church,– The Bishop of Zion and his counsellors ocupied the fore noon in confession and exortation– The Bishop of Kirtland and his counsellors, occu=pied, the stand in the after noon,– the discourses of these two quorums were verry interesting, a number of letters of commendation were presented and read, a vote called and all received into the church in Kirtland.– bread was broken and blessed, and while, it was passing President Rigdon, commenced speaking from Acts 2d [chapter] and continued about 15, minuits. his [p. 151][174] reasoning was cogent,– the wine was then blessed and passed after which meeting, dism=issed—— at evening meet with the presidency in the loft of the Printing-office, in company with the presidency of the 70, to chose other 70. also– Blessed one of the Zion brethren,– dismissed and retired—

Monday morning the 8th [February 1836] attended School at
the us[u]al hour.– nothing worthy of note transpired– in the
afternoon lectured in upper room of the printing office with some of
the brethren,– at evening ~~Mr~~ visited Mr Seixas, in company with
President's Rigdon & Cowdery, he converses freely, is an
interesting man— This day Elder Parrish my scribe, received my
journal again,[175] his health is so much improved that he thinks he
will be able, with the blessing of God to perform this duty

Tuesday the 9th [February 1836] spent the day in studying the
hebrew language,– we have pleasant weather and fine sleighing—
Spent the evening at home

Wednesday morning the 10th [February 1836] at home at 10.
oclock met at School room to read hebrew
   In the afternoon, read in the upper room of the printing-office –
at 4. oclock called at the School room in the chapel, to make some
arrangments, concerning the classes—on my return home I was
informed that Br. Hyrum Smith had cut himself [p. 152] I
immediately repaired to his house and found him badly wounded in
his ‹left› arm, he had fallen on his axe, which caused a wound
about 4 or 5 inches in length Dr. Williams was sent for
immediately ~~and~~ who when he came in sewed it up and dressed it,
and I feel to thank God that it is no worse, and I ask my heavenly
Father in the name of Jesus Christ to heal my brother hyrum ~~Smith~~
of his wound, and bless my fathers family one and all, with peace
and plenty, and ultimately eternal life——

/[176]Feb 8th 1836. Met in council, meeting opened with prayer
by President Hyrum Smith; Levi Jacks‹on›[177] supplied the place ~~of~~
of Joseph Coe.[178]
   Sister [*blank*] entered a complaint against Joseph Keeler, after
hearing the testimony the Councillors proceeded to give their
council after which Pres. Hyrum Smith arose and made some
remarks, the same was agreed to by President David Whitmer after
which the Presidency gave room for the parties to speak both of

which made a few remarks, the Pres[ident] then decided that
Joseph Keeler be acquited a vote of the council was called, the
council agreed to the decision of the Presidency
                                        Jesse Hitchcock Clerk.

/[179]Thursday mornin[g] 11th Feby 1836
at home– attended the School and read hebrew with the morning
Class– spent the afternoon in reading, and exibiting the
Egy=[p]tian records to those who called to see me and heavens
blessings have attended me.– [p. 153]

Friday 12th [February 1836] spent the day in reading hebrew,
and attending to the duties of my family, and the duties of the
church, nothing very special transpired meet this evening to make
arangements concerning ‹ordinations›[180]

Saturday 13th [February 1836] spent the fore noon in reading
Hebrew.— at noon I prepared a horse and sleigh, for Professer
Seixas, to go to Hudson to visit his family

Sunday 14th [February 1836] attended to the ordinance of
baptism, before meeting— at the us[u]al hour attended meeting,
the presi=dents of the 70, expressed their feelings, on the occasion,
and their faith in the book of Mor=mon, and the revelations,—
also their entire confidence in ‹all› the quorums that are organized
in the church of Latter day Saints— had a good time. the spirit of
God rested upon the congregation;— administered the Sacrament
and confirmed, a number who had been baptised, and dismissed

Kirtland Feb 12th 1836. I met in the School room in the chapel
in company with the several quorums to take into conciderations
the subject of ordinations, as mentioned at the top of this page
    opened by singing and prayer I then arose and made some
remarks upon the object of our meeting, which were as follows—
first that many are desir=ing to be ordained to the ministry, who
are [p. 154] not called and consequ[e]ntly the Lord is displeased—

Secondly, many already have been ordained who ought [not] to
hold official stations in the church because they dishonour
them=selves and the church and bring persecut=ion swiftly upon
us, in consequence of their zeal without k[n]owledge— I requested
the quor=um's to take some measures to regulate the same. I
proposed some resolutions and rem=arked to the brethren that the
subject was now before them and open for discussion
    The subject was taken up and discussed by President's S.
Rigdon O. Cowdery Eld[e]r M. Harris and some others, and
resolutions drafted, by my scribe who served as clerk on the
occasion— read and rejected— it was then proposed that I should
indite resolutions which I did as follows
1st— Resolved that no one be ordained to any office in the church
in this stake of Zion at Kirtland without the unanimous voice of
the several ~~quorums~~ bodies that constitute this quorum who are
appointed to do church buisness in the name of said church—viz
the presidency of the church & council [of] the 12. apostles of the
Lamb and 12 high counsellors of Kirtland the 12, high
counsellors of Zion, the Bishop of Kirtland & his counsellors the
Bishop of Zion and his counsellors—the 7 presidents of the
Seventies; untill otherwise ordered by the said quorums.— [p. 155]
2nd— And further resolved that no one be ordained in the
branches of said church abroad unless they are recomm=ended by
the ~~church~~ voice of the respective branches of the church to which
they belong to a general conference appointed by the heads of the
church, and from that conf=erence receive their ordination——[181]

    Monday the 15th [February 1836] attended the Hebrew School
at the usual hour,– spent the afternoon in reading hebrew, and
receiving and waiting upon visitors— on this day we commenced
translating the Hebrew language, under the instruction of professor
Seixas, and he acknowledg's that we are the most forward of any
class he ever taught, the same length of time[182]

    Tuesday the 16th [February 1836] atten[d]ed School at the
usual hour and resumed our translating and made rapid progress

many called to day to see the House of the Lord, and to visit me and see the Egy[p]tian manuscripts— we have [p. 156] extremely cold weather and fine sleighing

Wednesday the 17th [February 1836] attend[ed] the school and read and translated with my class as usual, and my soul delights in reading the word of the Lord in the original, and I am determined to persue the study of languages untill I shall become master of them, if I am permitted to live long enough, at any rate so long as I do live I am determined to make this my object, and with the blessing of God I shall succed to my sattisfaction,– this evening Elder Coe called to make some arangements about the Egyptian records and the mummies, he proposes to hire a room at J[ohn] Johnsons Inn and exibit them there from day to day at certain hours, that some benefit may be derived from them— I complied with his request, and only observed that they must be managed with prudence and care especially the manuscripts

Thursday the 18th [February 1836] spent the day as usual in attending to my fam=ily concerns, ~~and~~ receiving and waiting upon those who called for instruction and attending to my studies,

Friday the 19th [February 1836] attended with the morning class and translated– professor Seixas [p. 157] handed me the names of a few whom he had selected from the first class, and requ=ested us to meet together this afternoon and lecture, which we did in the upper room of the printing-office— The names are as follows President's S. Rigdon O. Cowdery W.W. Phelps– Bishop E. Partridge Eldr's E. McLellen O. Hyde O. Pratt Sylvester Smith myself and Scribe– these professor Seixas requested to meet one hour earlyer on the following morning— I conversed with Mr. Seixas upon the subject of religion, at my house this afternoon, he listened with attention and appe=ared interested with my remarks, and I believe the Lord is striving with him, by his holy spirit, and that he will eventually embrace the new and everlasting covenant, for he is a chosen vessel unto the Lord to do his people good,— but

I forbear lest I get to prophesying upon his head— this evening
President Rigdon and myself called at Mr. Seixas lodgings and
conversed with him upon the subject of the School, had a pleasant
interview[183]

Saturday morning the 20th [February 1836] at home attending
to my domestick con=cerns, at 9 oclock attended the school and
translated with the morning class— spent the after-noon with my
class in the printing-office—— spent the evening at home [p. 158]

Sunday the 21st Feb 1836 Spent the day at home, in reading
meditation and prayer— I reviewed my lessons in Hebrew— On
this day some 3 or 4 persons were baptised and the powers of
darkness seem to be giving way on all sides. many who have been
enemies to the work of the Lord are beginning to enquire in to the
faith of the Latter day Saints and are friendly

Monday the 22nd [February 1836] translated Hebrew with the
1st class in the morning— returned home and, made out my return
to the county clerk on 11. marriages which I have solemnized
within 3. months past 8, by license from the clerk of the court of
common pleas in Geauga county Ohio, and 3, by publishment,
sent them to chardon by Elijah Fuller—[184] I baptised John O.
Waterman.[185] I spent the afternoon translating ~~at~~ with my scribe
Eld[e]r W. Parrish at his house at 4. oclock. meet, Professor Seixas
and the school committee at [the] printing office to make some
arangements for the advancement of the several classes
      The lower room of the chapel is now prepared for painting—
      This afternoon the sisters met to make the veil of the Temple[186]
Father Smith presided over them and gave them much good
instruction, closed by singing & prayer [p. 159]

Tuesday the 23d [February 1836] read and trans=lated
Hebrew— This afternoon the sisters met again at the chapel[187] to
work on the ve[i]l toward the close of the day I met with the
presidency & many of the brethren in the house of the Lord— I

made some remarks from the pulpit upon the rise and progress of
the church of Christ of Latter day Saints and pron=ounced a
blessing upon the Sisters for the liberality in giving their servises so
cheerfully to make the veil for the Lord's house also upon the
congregation and dismissed

Wednesday the 24th attended to my studies as us‹u›al— at
evening met the quorums at the school-room in the chapel to take
into concideration the propriety or impropriety of ordaining a large
number of individuals who wish to be ordained to official stations
in the church– each individuals nam[e] was presented and the
voice of the ass=embly called and all of them except 7. were
rejected—[188] Their ordinations defered untill another time— O.
Hyde O. Cowdery and Sylvester Smith were nominated and
seconded to draft and ‹make› regulations concerning licenses—
vote of the assembly called and unanimously passed[189]

Thomas Burdick nominated and seconded to officiate as clerk
to record licenses, and receive pay for his sirvises accordingly
[p. 160] vote called and passed unanimously also nominated and
seconded that the 12, and presidents of the 70, be see that the calls
for preaching in the region round about Kirtland be attended to,
and filled by judicious Elders of this church—
adjourned, and closed by singing and prayer—

Thursday the 25th of Feb 1836 attended to my studies as usual,
and made some proficiency.– in the after=noon I was called upon
by President Rigdon to go and visit his wife who was verry sick,– I
did so in company with my scribe, we prayed for her and annointed
her in the name of the Lord and she began to recover from that
verry hour— Returned home and spent the evening

Friday the 26th [February 1836] attended and read hebrew with
the first class in the morning– spent the afternoon in the printing
office– settled som[e] misun=derstanding between Br. Wm Smith
and professor Seixas—

Saturday morning the 27th [February 1836] I prepared my horse
and sleigh for Mr Seixas to ride to Hudson to visit his family, he is
to return on monday next— attended with my class at the printing
office [p. 161] both in the fore and afternoon, and lectured on, and
translated Hebrew— we have cold weather and fine sleighing[190]

Sunday the 28th [February 1836] This morning two gentlemen
late from Scotland called to see me, to make inquiry about the
work of the Lord in these last days, they treated me with respect,
and the interview was pleasing to me, and I pres=ume interesting
to them, they attended our meeting, with me, and expressed a
satisfaction in what they heard
They spoke of Irvin[191] the oriental reformer and his
prop[h]esies— after meeting, I returned home and spent the after
part of the day and evening in read=ing and translating the Hebrew

Monday the 29th [February 1836] spent the day in studying as
usual.— A man called to see the house of the Lord in company
with another gentleman, on entering the door they were politely
invited by the gent[l]eman who has charge of the house to take of[f]
their hats one of them complyed with the request unhesitatingly
while the other observed that he would not take of[f] his hat nor
bow to Jo Smith but that he had made Jo bow to him at a certain
time—he was imm=ediately informed by Eld[e]r Morey the keeper
of the house that his first buis=ness was to leave it ~~the house~~ for
when [p. 162] a man imposed upon me he was imposed upon
himself, the man ma=nifested much anger, but left the house.—
for this independence and resolution of Eld[e]r Morey I respect him
and for the love he manifests toward me, and may Israels God bless
him and give him an ascendency over all his enemies—
This afternoon Professor Seixas returned from Hudson, and
brought a few more bibles and one grammar of his 2d edition.—
the weather is warm & our sleighing is failing fast

Tuesday March the 1st 1836 attended School, in the fore noon
in the afternoon at the printing office and read and translated with

my class untill 4. oclock— returned home and attended to my
domestic concerns

We have fine sleighing which is uncommon in this country at
this season of the Year

Wednesday the 2nd [March 1836] persued my studies as usual—
at 7 oclock in the evening, the first class met, agreeably to the
request of Mr. Seixas at Eld[e]r O. Hydes to spend one hour in
translating,— dismissed and returned home

Thursday the 3d [March 1836] attended to my studies in the
hebrew.— some misunderstanding, took place between [p. 163]
Professor Seixas and some of the schollars respecting the sale of
some Bibles,– his feelings were much hurt appearantly, he made
some remarks concerning it to each class at noon he called on the
School committee with his feelings much depressed— we gave him
all the satisfaction we could in righteousness, and his feelings were
measur[a]bly allayed

/[192]This evening the several quorums met agreeably to
adjou=r[n]ment and were organized according to their official
standing in the church.[193]

I then arose and made some remarks on the object of our
meeting which are as follows.
1st To receive or reject certain resolutions that were drafted by a
commitee chosen for that purpose at a preceeding meeting
respecting licenses for elders and other official members.
2nd To sanction by the united voice of the quorum[s] certain
resolutions respecting ordaining members; that had passed through
each quorum seperately for without any alteration or amendment
except‹ing› in the quorum of the twelve.

The council opened by singing and prayer. President O.
Cowdery then arose and read the resol=utions[194] respecting licenses
three times, the third time he read the article ‹resolutions› he gave
time and oppertunity after reading each article for objections to be
made if any there were; no objections were made— I then observed
that these resolutions must needs pass through each quorum

seperately begining at the presidency/ [195]and concequently it must
first be thrown into the hands of the president of the Deacon[s] &
his council as equal rights & privileges are my motto, and one
[p. 164] man is as good as another, if he behaves as well, and that
all men should be esteemed alike, without regard to distinction's of
an official nature,— the resolutions passed through the quorum of
the Deacons by their unanimous voice

It was then thrown before the president of the Teachers and his
council and passed unanimously—

Next into the hands of the President of the priests & his
council and passed unanimously

Then into the hands of the Bishop's council of Kirtland &
passed unanimously

from them to the Bishop of Zion & his council & passed
unanimously—

Next into the hands of the president of the ~~high priests & his~~
Elders & his council & passed unanimously

From them into the hands of the president of the High-Priests
& his council and passed unanimously

Next into the hands of the presidents of the 70. & passed
unanimously

from them to the high council of ‹Zion› ~~Kirtland~~ & passed
unanimously—

from them to the high council of Kirtland & passed
unanimously—

~~& Lastly in~~ and then into the hands of the 12, & passed
unanimously

& lastly into the hands of the presidency of the Church & all
the quorums and rec[eive]d their sanction.— having now passed
through all the quorums, the resolutions are received as a Law to
govern the Church [p. 165]

I was nominated & seconded for a standing chairman & F.G.
Williams for clerk to isue licenses to the official members of the
church S. Rigdon for chairman protem & O. Cowdery clerk – vote
called from the several quorums in their order & passed
unanimously

I then made some remarks on the am=endment of the 12. upon the resolutions recorded on pages 155 & 156. President T. B. Marsh made some observations after me, & then called a vote of his quorum, to asertain whether they would repeal their amendment or not 9. of the 12. vote[d] in the affirmative & 3. in the negative,[196] and the original bill was passed, which is recorded on the pages above named— dismissed by prayer & retired 1/2 past 9. oclock[197]

Friday the 4th ~~Feby~~ ‹March› 1836 attended school as usual— The sleighing is failing fast, the icy chains of winter seem to be giving way under the influence of the returning Sun, & spring will soon open to us with all his charms

Saturday the 5th[198] Attended School— in the afternoon the board kiln to[ok] fire & the lumber principally consumed– this is the 5 or 6 time it has burnt this winter if my memory serves me corectly—

Sunday the 6th [March 1836] Spent the day at home in the enjoy=ment ‹of the society› of my family, around the social fireside [p. 166][199]

~~March the 7th Monday~~
Monday March 7th 1836 Spent the day in attending to my studies
At Evening met with my class at Professor Seixas['s] Room, & translated the 17th chapter of Genesis,— after the class was dismissed I was requested to tarry with the rest of the School committee, to make some arange=ments about paying Mr. Seixas for his ~~tuition~~ instruction, & to engage him for another q[uarte]r we did not arive at any thing definite upon this point,– however ~~he~~ Mr Seixas has agreed to ~~stay~~ ‹teach us› 3, weeks longer, after having a vacation of 2, weeks at the expiration of this course, & perhaps a q[uarte]r

Tuesday the 8th [March 1836] Attended school & translated most of the 22. chapter of Gen. after my class were dismissed, retired to the printing office and translated 10. verses of Ex 3d [chapter] which with the 1st & 2nd Psalms are our next lesson

Wednesday the 9th [March 1836] Attended School as usual— ~~This day the snow is falling~~

Thursday 10th [March 1836] Attended School, in the morning, in the afternoon, read Hebrew in the office at evening went down to [the] Professor['s] room to be instructed by him, in the language on the account of the storm the class did not meet. [p. 167]

Friday the 11th [March 1836] meet with the morning class, at 9. oclock,– at 10. went into the office and made a divission of our class for private studies for our better accommodation, & advancement in the language we are persuing
    Presidents Rigdon Phelps & Cowdery and myself meet at the printing office Eld[e]r's O. Pratt Sylvester Smith & Bishop Partri[d]ge, at L[uke] Johnson's
    Eld[e]r's McLellen O. Hyde & W. Parrish on the flats—[200] this evening our class met at Mr Seixas['s] room & spent an hour in our studies,— class dismissed & retired except the school committee, who tarried and made some arangements with Mr Seixas about continuing longer with us & bringing his family to this place
    This has been a very stormy day and the snow is, still falling fast, & the prospect is fair for another run of sleighing which is uncommon for this country at this season of the Year

Saturday the 12th [March 1836] engaged a team to go to Hudson after Mr Seixas family <& goods> also a Horse and cutter for himself & wife,— we have cold weather & fine sleighing— I was informed to day that a man by the name of Clark froze to death last night near this place, who was under the influence of ardent spirits: O my God how long will this monster intemperance [p. 168] find it's victims on the earth, me thinks until the earth is swept with the wrath and indignation of God, and Christ's King=dom becomes universal. O come Lord Jesus and cut short thy work in rightieousness.

Eld[e]r Solomon Hancock received a letter to day, from Missouri bearing the painful inteligence, of the death of his wife.[201] May the Lord bless him and comfort him in this hour of affli=ction

Sunday the 13th of March 1836 met with the presidency & some of the 12, and counseled with them upon the subject of removing to Zion this spring, we conversed freely upon the importance of her redemption, and the necessity of the presidency removing to that place, that their influence, might be more effectually, used in in gathering the saints to that country, and we finally come to the resolution to emigrate on or before the 15th of May next, if kind providence smiles, upon us and openes the way before us

Monday the 14th [March 1836] Attended School as usual Professor Seixas returned from Hudson with his <family>

Tuesday the 15 [March 1836] At School in the fore=noon in the afternoon, met in the printing office, recd, and waited upon those who called to see me, and attended to my domestick concerns—at evening met in the printing office & recd a lecture, on grammar [p. 169]

Wednesday the 16th [March 1836] persued my studies in the Hebrew language,— at evening met the quorum of singers in the chapel, they per=formed admirably, concidering the advantages they have had

Thursday the 17th [March 1836] At school in the morning, in the afternoon in the office at evening, met with the quorums in the west school-room of the Lord's House to receive or reject certain individuals whose names were presented for ordination's a number were received, by the united voice of the assembly[202]

Friday the 18th [March 1836] attended School with the morning class.— at 10. oclock, went to the school house to attend the funeral of Susan Johnson, daughter of Esekiel Johnson,[203] she is a member of the church of Latter day Saints & remained strong in the faith, untill, her spirit, took it's exit from time to eternity

May God bless and comfort her aff=licted parents, family connexions, and friends— President Rigdon delivered a fine discourse on the occasion, and much solem=nity prevailed

Saturday the 19th [March 1836] Read Hebrew with the morning class.— Spent the day in attending [p. 170] to my domestick concerns, and the affairs of the church

Sunday the 20th March 1836 attended the house of worship, as usual the quorum of high priests, delivered short addresses to the congregation, in a very feeling, and impressive manner,— at the intermission at noon one individual was baptised—in the afternoon, administered the Lords Supper, as we are wont to do on every Sabbath, and the Lord blessed our souls with the out pouring of his spirit, and we were made to rejoice in his goodness,

Monday the 21st [March 1836] at school in the mo=rning– after school went to the printing office and prepared, a number of Elders licences, to send by Elder Palmer to the court [in] Medina County in order to obtain licenses to marry, as the court in this county will not grant us this privelege.— To day 10 persons were baptized, in this place

Tuesday the 22nd [March 1836] read Hebrew with the morning class,— to day 5, young men were received into the church by baptism, in this place— This is a stormy day, the snow is nearly a foot deep, an uncommon storm, for this season of the year [p. 171]

Wednesday the 23d ‹Mch› 1836 attended School— This is a pleasant day and fine sleighing— 2, more were received into the church by baptism

Thursday the 24th [March 1836] attended School as usual in the evening, met with my class at the printing office, and recd a lecture from Professor Seixas upon the Hebrew language

After we were dismissed, we called at the School-room to hear the ‹choir› ~~quire~~ of Singers perform, which they did admirably

On this day 5. more were recd into the Church by baptism——

Friday the 25th [March 1836] attend[ed] School with the morning class— also at 5 oclock P.M and recd a lecture upon the Hebrew Grammar— We have pleasant weather and good sleighing—

Saturday the 26th [March 1836] At home attending to my domestick concerns in the morning.— after brekfast met with the presidency to make arangements for the solemn assembly which occupied the remainder of the day[204]

Sunday morning the 27th [March 1836] The congregation began to assemble ‹at the chapel› at about 7 oclock one hour earlier than the doors were to be opened many brethren had come in from the region's [p. 172] round about to witness the dedication of the Lords House and share in his blessings and such was the anxiety on this occasion that some hundreds, (probably five or six,) assembled ~~collected~~ before the doors were opened——
The presidency entered with the door kepers and aranged them at the inner and outer doors also placed our stewards to receiv[e] donations from those who should feel disposed to contribute something to defray the expenses of building the House of the Lord— ‹we also dedicated the pulpits & consecrated them to the Lord› The doors were then opened President Rigdon President Cowdery and myself seated the congregation as they came in, ~~we received about~~ and according to the best calculation we could make we received between 9 ‹hundred› and 10,00 which is as many as can be comfortably situated we then informed the door keepers that we could rec[e]ive no more, and a multitude were depr=ived of the benefits of the meeting on acco=unt of the house not being

sufficiently capacious to receive them, and I felt to regret that any of my brethren and sisters should be deprived of the meeting, and I recommended them to repair to the School-house and hold a meeting which they did and filled that house ‹also› and yet many were left out—

The assembly were then organized in the following manner.— viz.[205] [p. 173]

West end of the house——

Presdt. F G. Williams Presdt. Joseph Smith, Sen and Presdt. WW. Phelps occupied the 1st pulpit for the Melchisedic priesthood— Presdt. S. Rigdon myself and Presdt Hyrum Smith in the 2nd— Presdt. D. Whitmer Presdt. O. Cowdery and Presdt. J. Whitmer in the 3d— The 4th was occupied by the president of the high-priests and his couns=ellors, and 2 choiresters— The 12. Apostles on the right in the 3 highest seats— The presdt of the Eldrs his clerk & counsellors in the seat immed=iatly below the 12— The high council of Kirtland consisting of 12, on the left in the 3, first seats— the 4th seat below them was occupied by the pres=idency's Eldr's W A. Cowdery & W. Parrish who served as scribes.— The pulpits in the east end of the house for the Aaronic priesthood were occupied as follows.— The Bishop of Kirtland and his counsellors in the 1st pulpit.— The Bishop of Zion and his counsellors in the 2nd— The presdt. of the priests and his counsellors in the 3d— The presdt. of the Teachers and his counsellors ‹& one choirister› in the 4th— The high council of Zion consisting of [p. 174] 12 counsellors on the right— The presdt of the Deacons and his counsillors in the seat below them— The 7 presdts of the Seventies on the left— The choir of singers were seated in the 4 corners of the room in seats prepared for that purpose— recd by contribution $960.00[206]

9 oclock A.M the servises of the day were opened by Presdt S. Rigdon by reading 1st the 96 Psalm secondly the 24th Psalm— the choir then sung hymn on the 29th page of Latter day Saints collection of hymn's— prayer by Presdt Rigdon choir then sung hymn on 14th page[207] Presdt Rigdon then ‹read› the 18, 19, & 20,

verses of the 8th Chapter of Mathew and preached more
particu=larly from the 20th verse.— his prayer and address were
very forcible and sublime, and well adapted to the occasion.— after
he closed his sermon, he called upon the several quorums
commenceing with the presidency, to manifest by rising up, their
willingness to acknowledge me as a prophet and seer and uphold
me as such by their p[r]ayers of faith, all the quorums in their turn,
cheerfully complyed with this request he then called upon all the
congregation of Saints, also to give their assent by rising on their
feet which they did unanimously

 After an intermission of 20, minutes the servises of the day
were resumed, by singing Adam ondi ahman.[208] / [209]I then made a
short address and called upon the several quorums, and all the
congregation of saints to acknowledge the Presidency as Prophets
and Seers, and uphold them by their prayers, they all covenanted
to do so by rising; I then called upon the quorums and congregation
of saints to acknowledge the 12 [p. 175] Apostles who were present
as Prophets and Seers and special witnesses to all the nations of the
earth, holding the keys of the kingdom, to unlock it or cause it to
be done among ~~all nations~~ them; and uphold them by their prayers,
which they assented to by rising, # I then called upon the quorums
and congregation of saints to acknowledge the high council of
Kirt=land in all the authorities of the Melchisedec prie=sthood and
uphold them by their prayers which they assented to by rising. I
then called upon the quoru‹ms› and congregation of saints to
acknowledge and upho‹ld› by their prayer's the Bishops of Kirtland
and Zion and their counsellors, ~~the Presidents of the Priests~~ in all
the authority of the Aaronic priesthood, which they did by rising. I
then called upon the quorums and congregation of saints to
acknowledge the high-council of Zion, and uphold them by their
prayers in all the authority of the high pries=thood which they did
by rising. I next called upon the quorums and congregation of
saints to acknowledge the Presidents of the seventys who act as
their represe=nt[at]ives as ‹Apostles and› special witnesses to the
nations to assist the 12 in opening the gospel kingdom, among all
people and to uphold them by their prayer's which they did by

rising— I then called upon the quorums and all the saints to
acknowledge [the] president of the Elders and his counsellors and
uphold them by their prayers which they did by rising— The
quor=ums and congregation of saints were then called upon to
acknowledge and uphold by their prayers the Presidents of the
Priests, Teachers, and Deacons and their counsellors, which they
did by rising.

\# N.B. The Presidents ~~were~~ of the seventy's were acknowledged
first after the 12 Apostles [p. 176]

The hymn on the hundred and 14 page was then sung,[210] after
which I offered to God the following dedication prayer.[211]

Prayer,

At the dedication of the Lord's House in Kirtland Ohio March 27,
1836.— by Joseph Smith, jr. President of the Church of the Latter
Day Saints.

Thanks be to thy name, O Lord God of Israel, who keepest
covenant and shewest mercy unto thy servants, who walk uprightly
before thee with all their hearts; thou who hast commanded thy
servants to build an house to thy name in this place. (Kirtland.)
And now thou beholdest, O Lord, that so thy servants have done,
according to thy commandment. And now we ask the[e], holy
Father, in the name of Jesus Christ, the Son of thy bosom, in in
whose name alone salvation can be administered to the children of
men: we ask the[e], O Lord, to accept of this house, the
workmanship of the hands of us, thy servants, which thou didst
command us to build; for thou know=est that we have done this
work through great trib=ulation: and out of our poverty we have
given of our substance to build a house to thy name, that the Son
of Man might have a place to manifest himself to his people.

And as thou hast said, in a revelation given unto us, calling us
thy friends, saying— "Call your solemn asse=mbly, as I have
commanded you; and as all have not faith, seek ye diligently and
teach one another words of wisdom; yea, seek ye out of the best
books words of wisdom: Seek learning; even by study, and also by
faith, Organize yourselves; prepare every ~~thing~~ needful thing, and

establish a house, even a house of prayer, a house [of] fasting, a house of faith, a house of learning [p. 177] a house of glory, a house of order, a house of God: that your incomings may be in the name of the Lord, that your outgoings may be in the name of the Lord: that all your salutations may be in the name of the Lord, with uplifted hands to the Most High."

And now, Holy Father, we ask thee to assist us, thy people with thy grace in calling our solemn assembly, that it may be done to thy honor, and to thy divine acceptance, and in a manner that we may be found worthy in thy sight, to secure a fulfilment of the promises which thou hast made unto us thy people, in the revelatio[n]s given unto us: that thy glory may rest down upon thy people, and upon this thy house, which we now dedicate to thee; that it may be sanctified and consecrated to be holy, and that thy holy presence may be continually in this house; and that all people who shall enter upon the threshold of the Lord's house may feel thy power and be constrained to acknowledge that thou hast sanctified it, and that it is thy house, a place of thy holiness.

And do thou grant, holy Father, that all those who shall worship in this house, may be taught words of wisdom out of the best books, and that they may seek learning, even by study, and also by faith, as thou hast said; and that they may grow up in thee and receive a fulness of the Holy Ghost, and be organized according to thy laws, and be prepared to obtain every needful thing and that this house may be a house of prayer, a house of fasting, a house of faith, a house of glory, and of God, even thy house: that all the incomings of thy people, into this house, may be in the name of the Lord; that all their outgoings, from this house, may be in the name of the Lord; that all their salutations may be in the name of [p. 178] [the] Lord, with holy hands uplifted to the Most High; and that no unclean thing shall be permitted to come into thy house to pollute it.

And when thy people transgress, any of them, they may speedily repent and return unto thee, and find favour in thy sight, and be restored to the blessings which thou hast ordained, to be poured out upon those who shall rever=ance thee in this thy house.

And we ask, holy Father, that thy servants may go forth from
this house, armed with thy power, and that thy name may be upon
them and thy glory be round about them, and thine angels have
charge over them, and from this place they may bear exceeding
great and glorious tidings, in truth, unto the ends of the earth, that
they may know that this is thy work, and that thou hast put forth
thy hand, to fulfil that which thou hast spoken by the mouths of
thy prophets conce=rning the last days.

We ask the[e], holy Father, to establish the people that shall
worship and honorably hold a name and stan=ding in this thy
house, to all generations, and for eterni‹ty› that no weapon formed
against them shall prosper; that he who diggeth a pit for them shall
fall into the same himself; that no combination of wickedness shall
have power to rise up and prevail over thy people, upon whom thy
name shall be put in this house: and if any people shall rise against
this people, that thine anger be kindled against them: and if they
shall smite this people, thou wilt smite them— thou wilt fight for
thy people as thou didst in the day of battle, that they may be
delivered from the hands of all their enemies.

We ask thee, holy Father, to confound, and astonish and bring
to shame, and confusion, all those who have [p. 178] spread lying
reports abroad over the world against thy servant or servants, if
they will not repent when the everlasting gospel shall be
procla=imed in their ears, and that all their works may be brought
to nought, and be swept away by the hail, and by the judgments,
which thou wilt send upon them in thine anger, that their may be
an end to lyings and slanders against thy people: for thou knowest,
O Lord, that thy servants have been innocent before thee in
bearing record of thy name for which they have suffered these
things, therefore we plead before thee for a full and com=plete
deliverence from under this yoke. Break it off O Lord: break it off
from the necks of thy servants, by thy power, that we may rise up in
the midst of this generation and do thy work!

O Jehovah, have mercy upon this people, and as all men sin,
forgive the transgressions of thy people, and let them be blotted out
forever. Let the anointing of thy ministers be sealed upon them

with power from on high: let it be fulfilled upon them as upon those on the day of Pentacost: let the gift of tongues be poured out upon thy people, even cloven tongues as of fire, and the interpretation thereof. And let thy house be filled, as with a rushing mighty wind, with thy glory.

Put upon thy servants the testimony of the covenant that where they go out and proclaim thy word, they may seal up the law, and prepare the hearts of thy saints for all those judg<e>ments thou art about to send, in thy wrath, upon the inhabitants of the earth because of their transgressions, that thy people may not faint in the day of trouble. [p. 179]

And whatever city thy servants shall enter, and the people of that city receive their testimony let thy peace and thy salvation be upon that city, that they may gather out from that city the righteous, that they may come forth to Zion, or to her stakes, the places of thine appoi=ntment, with songs of everlasting joy,– and until this be acomplished let not thy judgements fall upon that city.

And whatever city thy servants shall enter, and the people of that city receive not their testimony of thy servants, and thy servants warn them to save themselves from this untoward generation let it be upon that city according to that which thou hast spoken, by the mouths of thy prophets; but deliver thou, O Jehovah, we beseech thee, thy servants from their hands, and cleanse them from their blood. O Lord, we delight not in the destruct=ion of our fellow men: their souls are precious before thee; but thy word must be fulfilled:– help thy servants to say, with thy grace assisting them, thy will be done, O Lord, and not ours.

We know that thou hast spoken by the mouth of thy prophets, terrible things concerning the wicked in the last days, that thou wilt pour out thy judgements, without measure; therefore, O Lord, deliver thy people from the calamity of the wicked, enable thy servants to seal up the law and bind up the testimony, that they may be prepared against the day of burning.

We ask thee, holy Father, to remember those who have been driven by the inhabitants of Jackson county Missouri, from the lands of their inherit=ance, and break off, O Lord, this yoke of affliction [p. 180] that has been put upon them. Thou knowest, O Lord, that they have been greatly oppressed and afflicted, by wicked men, and our hearts flow out in sorrow because of their grevious burdens. O Lord, how long wilt thou suffer this people to bear this affliction, and the cries of the innocent ones to ascend up in thine ears, and their blood to come up in testimony before thee and not make a display of thy power in their behalf?

Have mercy, O Lord, upon that wicked mob, who have driven thy people, that they may cease to spoil, that they may repent of their sins, if repentance is to be found; but if they will not, make bare thine arm, O Lord, and redeem that which thou didst appoint a Zion unto thy people, And if it cannot be otherwise, that the cause of thy people may not fail before thee, may thine anger be kindled and thine indignation fall upon them that they may be wasted away, both root and branch from under heaven; but inasmuch as they will repent, thou art gracious and merciful, and will turn away thy wrath, when thou lookest upon the face of thine anointed.

Have mercy, O Lord, upon all the nations of the earth: have mercy upon the rulers of our land may those principles which were so honorably and nobly defended: viz, the constitution of our land, by our fathers, be established forever. Remember the kings, the princes, the nobles, and the great ones of the earth, and all people; and the churches: all the poor, the needy and the afflicted ones of the earth, that their hearts may be softened when thy servants shall go out from thy house, O [p. 181] Jehovah, to bear testimony of thy name, ‹that› their prejudices may give way before the truth, and thy people may obtain favour in the sight of all, that all the ends of the earth may know that we thy servants have heard thy voice, and that thou hast sent us, that from among all these thy servants, the sons of Jacob, may gather out the righteous to build a holy city to thy name, as thou hast commanded them.

We ask thee to appoint unto Zion other stakes besides this one, which thou hast appointed, that the gath=ering of thy people may roll on in great power and majesty, that thy work may be cut short in righteousness.

Now these words, O Lord, we have spoken before thee, concerning the revelations and commandments which thou hast given unto us, who are i[de]ntified with the Gentiles;– But thou knowest that we have a great love for the children of Jacob who have been scatt=ered upon the mountains; for a long time in a cloudy and dark day.

We therefore ask thee to have mercy upon the chil=dren of Jacob, that Jerusalem, from this hour, may begin to be redeemed; and the yoke of bondage may begin to be broken off from the house of David, and the children of Judah may begin to return to the lands which thou didst give to Abraham, their father, and cause that the remnants of Jacob, who have been cursed and smitten, because of their transgression, to be converted from their wild and savage condition, to the fulness of the everlasting gospel, that they may lay down their weapons of bloodshed and cease their rebellions. And may [p. 182] all the scattered remnants of Israel, who have been driven to the ends of the earth, come to a knowledge of the truth, believe in the Messiah, and be redeemed from oppression, and rejoice before thee.

O Lord, remember thy servant Joseph Smith jr. and all his afflictions and persecutions, how he has covenanted with Jehovah and vowed to thee O mighty God of Jacob, and the commandments which thou hast given unto him, and that he hath sincerely strove to do thy will.– Have mercy, O Lord, upon his wife and children, that they may be exalted in thy presence, and preserved by thy fostering hand.– Have mercy upon all their immediate connexions, that their preju=dices may be broken up, and swept away as with a flood, that they may be converted and redee=med with Israel and know that thou art God.

Remember, O Lord, the presidents, even all the presidents of thy church, that thy right hand may exalt them with all their families, and their immediate connexions, that their names may be perpetuated and had in everlasting remembrance from generation to generation.

Remember all thy church, O Lord, with all their families, and all their immediate connexions, with all their sick and afflicted ones, with all the poor and meek of the earth, that the kingdom which thou hast set up without hands, may become a great mountain and fill the whole earth, that thy church may come forth out of the wilderness of darkness, and shine forth fair as the moon, clear as the sun, and terrible as an army with banners, and be adorned as a bride for that day when [p. 183] thou shalt unveil the heavens, and cause the mountains to flow down at thy presence, and the valleys to be exalted, the rough places made smooth, that thy glory may fill the earth. That when the trump shall sound for the dead, we shall be caught up in the cloud to meet thee, that we may ever be with the Lord, that our garments may be pure, that we may be clothed upon with robes of righteousness, with palms in our hands, and crowns of glory upon our heads, and reap eternal joy for all our sufferings.

O Lord, God Almighty, hear us in these our petitions, and answer us from heaven, thy holy habitation, where thou sittest enthroned, with glory, honour, power majesty, might, dominion, truth, justice judgement, mercy and an infinity of fulness, from everlasting to everlasting.

O hear, O hear, O hear us, O Lord, and answer these petitions, and accept the dedication of this house, unto thee, the work of our hands, which we have built unto thy name; and also this church to put upon it thy name. And help us by the power of thy spirit, that we may mingle our voices with those bright shi=ning seruphs, around thy throne with accumu[la]tions of praise, singing hosanna to God and the Lamb: and let these thine anointed ones be clothed with salvation, and thy saints shout aloud for joy.
Amen and Amen.

/[212]Sung Hosanah to God and the Lamb[213] after which the Lords supper was administered

I then bore testimony of the administering of angels.— Presdt Williams also arose and testified that while Presdt Rigdon was making [p. 184] his first prayer an angel entered the window and <took his> seated ~~himself~~ between father Smith, and himself, and remained their during his prayer Presdt David Whitmer also saw angels in the house

We then sealed the proceedings of the day by a shouting hosanah to God and the Lamb 3 times sealing it each time with Amen, Amen, and Amen and after requesting all the official members to meet again in the evening we retired—[214] met in the evening and instructed the quorums respecting the ordinance of washing of feet which we were to attend to on wednesday following

Monday the 28, M[ar]ch 1836 Attended school—nothing worthy of note tra=nspired

Tuesday, the 29th Attended school, which was the last day of our course of lectures in Hebrew by Professor Seixas,— ~~After we dismissed made some arrangements for our meeting on the morrow; attended to my domestick concirns, nothing very special transpired~~
~~At evening I met with the presidency in the Temple of the Lord and the Lord commanded us to tarry and san[c]tify ourselves by washing our feet~~
At 11 oclock A.M. Presidents Joseph Smith Jun Frederick G. Williams, Sidney Rigdon, Hyrum Smith, and Oliver Cowdery met in the most holy place in the Lords house and sought for a revelation from Him to teach us concerning our going to Zion, and other im=[p. 185]portant matter[s] after uniting in prayer, the voice of the Spirit was that we should come into this place three times, and also call the other presidents, the two Bishops and their councils (each to stand in his place) and fast through the day and also the night and that during this, if we would humble ourselves, we should receive further communic=ation from Him.

After this word was received, we immediately sent for the other brethren who came. The presi=dency proceeded to ordain George Boosinger to the high priesthood and annoint him.

This was in consequence of his having adm=inistered unto us in temporal things in our distress. And also because he left the place just previous to the dedication of the Lords house to bring us the temporal means prev=iously named.

Soon after this, the word of the Lord came to us through Presdt J. Smith Jun that those who had entered the holy place must not leave the house untill morning but send for such things as were

necessary, and also, that during our stay we must cleans[e] our feet
and partake of the sacrament that we might be made holy before
Him, and thereby be qualified to officiate in our calling upon the
morrow in washing the feet of the Elders.

Accordingly we proceeded and cleansed our faces and our feet,
and then proceeded to wash each others feet.– president S. Rigdon
first washed presdt J. Smith jun and then in [p. 186] turn was
washed by him— after which president Rigdon washed presdt J.
Smith Sen. and Hyrum Smith ‹prsdt› J. Smith Jun washed presdt
F. G Williams, and then pres. Hyrum Smith washed president
David Whitmer's feet and president Oliver Cowdery's, then pres D.
Whitmer washed pres. W. W. Phelps feet and in turn pres Phelps
washed pres John Whitmers feet.

The Bishops and their councils were then washed: After which
we partook of the bread and wine. The Holy S[p]irit rested down
upon us and we continued in the Lords house all night prophesying
and giving glory to God

/²¹⁵Wednesday morning 8 o clock March 30th 1836 According
to appointment the presidency, the 12, the seventies, the high
co‹u›neils councils, the Bishops and their entire quorums, the
Elders, and all the official members in this stake of Zion amounting
to about 300 met in the temple of the Lord to attend to the
ordinance of washing of feet, I ascended the pulpit and remarked to
the congregation that we had passed through many trials and
afflictions since the organization of this church and that this is a
year of Jubilee to us and a time of rejoicing, and that it was
expedient for us to prepare bread and wine sufficient to make our
hearts glad, as we should not probably leave this house until
morning; to this end we should call on the brethren to make a
contribution, the stewards passed round and took up a liberal
contribution and messengers were dispatched for bread and wine,
tubs [of] water and towels were prepared and I called the house to
order, and the presidency proceeded to wash the feet of the 12
pronoun=cing many prophecy's and blessings upon them in the
name of the Lord Jesus, the brethren began to prophesy [p. 187]
upon each others heads, and cursings upon the enimies of Christ

who inhabit Jackson county Missouri continued prophesying and
blessing and sealing them with Hosanna and Amen until nearly 7
o clock P.M. the bread ‹& wine› was then brought in, and I
observed that we had fasted all the day, and lest we faint; as the
Saviour did so shall we do on this occasion, we shall bless the bread
and give it to the 12 and they to the multitude, after which we
shall bless the wine and do likewise; while waiting ~~for the wine~~ I
made the following remarks, that the time that we were requi=red
to tarry in Kirtland to be endued would be fulfilled in a few days,
and then the Elders would go forth and each must stand for
himself, that it was not necessary for them to be sent out two by
two as in former times; but to go in all meekness in sobriety and
preach Jesus Christ & him crucified not to contend with others on
the account of their faith or systems of religion but pursue a steady
course, this I delivered by way of commandment, and all that
observe them not will pull down persecution upon ~~your~~ ‹their›
heads, while those who do shall always be filled with the Holy
Ghost, this I pronounced as a prophesy sealed with a Hosanna &
amen. Also that the seventies are not called to serve tables or
preside over churches to settle difficulties, but to preach the gospel
and build them up, and set others who do not belong to these
quorums to preside over them who are high priests – the twelve also
are not to serve tables, but to bear the keys of the kingdom to all
nations, and unlock them and call upon the seventies to follow
after them and assist them. The 12 are at liberty to go wheresoever
they will [p. 188] and if one shall say, I wish to go to such a place
let all the rest say Amen.

The seventies are at liberty to go to Zion if they please or go
wheresoever they will and preach the gospel and let the redemtion
of Zion be our object, and strive to affect it by sending up all the
strength of the Lords house where=ever we find them, and I want
to enter into the following covenant, that if any more of our
brethren are slain or driven from their lands in Missouri by the mob
that we will give ourselves no rest until we are avenged of our
enimies to the uttermost, this covenant was sealed unanimou=sly
by a hosanna and Amen— I then observed to the quorums that I

had now completed the organization of the church and we had passed through all the necessary ceremonies, that I had given them all the instruction they needed and that they now were at liberty after obtaining their lisences to go forth and bui=ld up the kingdom of God, and that it was expedient for me and the presidency to retire, having spent the night previous in waiting upon the Lord in his temple, and having to attend another dedication on the morrow, or conclude the one commenced on the last sabbath for the benifit of those of my brethren and sisters who could not get into the house on the former occasion but that it was expedient for the brethren to tarry all night and worship before the Lord in his house I left the meeting in the charge of the 12 and retired at about 9 o clock in the evening; the brethren continued exhorting, prophesying and speak=ing in tongues until 5 o clock in the morning – the Saviour made his appearance to some, while angels minestered unto others, and it was a penticost and enduement indeed, long to be remembered for the sound shall go forth from this place into all the [p. 189] world, and the occurrences of this day shall be hande[d] down upon the pages of sacred history to all generations, as the day of Pentecost, so shall this day be numbered and celebrated as a year of Jubilee and time of rejoicing to the saints of the most high God.

Thursday morning 8 o clock March 31st [1836]   This day being set apart to perform again the cerem=onies of the dedication for the benifit of those who could not get into the house on the preceeding sabbath I repaired to the temple at 8 o clock A.M. in company with the presidency, and arranged our door-keepers and stewards as on the former occasion, we then opened the doors and a large congregation entered the house and were comfortably seated, the authorities of the church were seated, in their respective order and the services of the day were commenced prosecuted and term=inated in the same manner as at the former dedication and the spirit of God rested upon the congregation and great solemnity prevailed.

/²¹⁶Friday th[e] 1st day of April 1836 At home most of the day, many brethren called to see me, some on temporal & some on spiritual buisiness, among the number was Leeman Copley,²¹⁷ who testified against me in a suit I brought against Doctor P. Hulbut for threatning my life, he confessed that he bore a fals[e] testimony against me, in that suit but verily thought at the time that he was right but on calling to mind a̶l̶l̶ all the circumstances connected t̶h̶e̶ with the things that transpired at the time he was [p. 190] convinced that he was wrong, and humbly con=fessed it and asked my forgivness, which was readily granted, he also wished to be received into the chur=ch again by baptism, and was received according to his desire, he gave me his confession in writing

/²¹⁸Saturday April 2d [1836] Transacted business (although of a temporal nature), in compa=ny with S. Rigdon, O. Cowdery, J. Whitmer F. G. Williams, D. Whi[t]mer & W.W. Phelps, which was to have a bearing upon the redemption of Zion. The positive manner in which he [Joseph Smith] expressed himself on this, ‹his› favorite theme, was directly calculated to produce conviction in the minds of those who heard him, that his whole soul was engaged in it, notwith=standing on a superficial view of the same subject they might differ from him in judgement. It was determined in council, after mature deliberation, that he and O. Cowdery should act in concert in ra=ising funds for the accomplishment of the aforesaid object. As soon as the above plan was settled, he and O. Cowdery set out together, and their success was such in one half day, as to give them pleasing anticipations, a̶n̶d̶ assure them that they were doing the will of God and that his work prospered in their hands

Sabbath April 3d [1836] He attended meeting in the Lords House, assisted the other Presidents of the Church in seating the congregation and then became an attentive listener to the preaching from the Stand. T. B. Marsh & D. W. Patten spoke in the A.M. to an attentive audience of about 1000 persons. In the P.M. he assisted the other Presidents in distributing the elements

of the Lords Supper to the church, receiving them from the ~~Hands~~
"Twelve" whose privilige it was to officiate in the sacred desk this
day. After having performed this service to his brethren, he retired
to the pulpit, the vails being dropped, [p. 191] and bowed himself
with O. Cowdery, in solemn, but silent prayer to the Most High.
After rising from prayer the following vision was opened to both of
them.[219]

The vail was taken from their minds and the eyes of their
understandings were opened. They saw the Lord standing upon the
breast work of the pulpit before them, and under his feet was a
paved work of pure gold, in color like amber: his eyes were as a
flame of fire; the hair of his head was like the pure snow, his
countenance shone ab=ove the brightness of the sun, and his voice
was as the sound of the rushing of great waters, even the Voice of
Jehovah, saying, I am the first and the last, I am he who liveth, I
am he who was slain. I am your Advocate with the Father. Behold
your sins are forgiven you. You are clean before me, therefore, lift
up your heads and rejoice, let the hearts of your brethren rejoice
and let the hearts of all my ~~brethren~~ ⟨people⟩ rejoice, who have
with their might, built this house to my name. For behold I have
accepted this house and my name shall be here; and I will manifest
myself to my people, in mercy, in this House, yea I will appear unto
my servants and speak unto them with mine own voice, if my
people will keep my commandments and do not pollute this Holy
House. Yea the hearts of thousands and tens of thousands shall
greatly rejoice in consequence of the blessings which shall be
pour=ed out, and the endowment with which my servants have
already been endowed and shall hereafter be endowed in this
House. And the fame of this House shall spread to foreign lands,
and this is the beginning of the blessing, which shall [p. 192] be
poured out upon the heads of my people. even so Amen.
After this vision closed, the Heavens were again opened unto them
and Moses appeared before them and committed unto them the
keys of the gathering of Israel from the four parts of the Earth and
the lead=ing of the ten tribes from the Land of the North. After
this Elias appeared and committed the dispens=ation of the gospel

of Abraham, saying, that in them and their seed all generations after them should be blessed. After this vision had closed, another great and glorious vision burst upon them, for Elijah, the Prophet, who was taken to Heaven without tasting death, also stood before them, and said, behold the time has fully come which was spoken of by the Mouth of Malachi, testifying, that he should be sent before the great and dreadful day of the Lord come, to turn the hearts of the Fathers to the children, and the chil=dren to the fathers, lest the whole earth be smitten with a curse. Therefore, the keys of this dispensation are committed into your hands, and by this ye may know that the great and the dreadful day of the Lord is near, even at the doors [p. 193]

Kirtland Temple, Kirtland, Ohio, 1908. (George E. Anderson Collection, LDS Church Archives.)

Sketch Book for the use of
Joseph Smith, jr.

September 22, 1835. This day Joseph Smith, jr.
labored with Oliver Cowdery, in obtaining and
writing blessings. We were through a part of the
time with company, so that our labor in this thing
was hindered; but we obtained many precious things, and
our souls were blessed. O Lord, may thy Holy Spirit be with
thy servants forever. Amen.

September 23d. This day Joseph Smith, Jr. was at home
writing blessings for my most beloved Brethren, I have
been hindered by a multitude of visitors but the Lord
has blessed our souls this day. May God grant to continue his mercies unto my house, this night, for Christ Sake. This day my soul has desired the salvation of Brother Ezra Thayer. Also Brother Noah
Packard. Came to my house and let the Chappel Committee have one thousand dollars by loan,
for the building the house of the Lord; Oh may
God bless him with an hundred fold even of the
things of the Earth, for this righteous act. My heart is full of
desire to day, to be blessed of the God, of Abraham
with prosperity, until I will be able to pay all
my debts; for it is, the delight of my soul to be honest
Oh Lord that thou knowest right well help me
and I will give to the poor.

September 23d 1835. This day Brother William
Tibbets John, and Joseph Tibbets started for
Missouri the place designated for Zion or the
Saints gathering they came to bid us farewell
the Brethren came in to pray with them and
Brother David Whitmer acted as spokesman
he prayed in the Spirit a glorious time suc-
ceeded his prayer, joy filled our hearts and we

Diary, 1835-1836, p. 1. Handwriting of Oliver Cowdery and Joseph
Smith. See text, p. 58. (LDS Church Archives.)

blessed them and [...] them God [...] and and promised them a safe journey and took them by the h[and] [...] them farewell for season Oh! may God grant them long life and good days these blessings I ask [...] for Christ sake Amen

September 24th 1835

This day the high Council met at my house to take into consideration the redemption of Zion and it was the voice of the Spirit of the Lord that we petition to the Governer that is those who have been driven out [...] to do so to be set back on their Lands next Spring and we go next season to live or dy to this [...] [...] is cast in Jackson County we truly had a good time and Covenated to Strugle for this thing until death [...] dissolve this union and if one falls that the rest be not [...] discouraged but pesue this object untill it is accomplished which may God grant unto us in the name of Christ our Lord

September 24th 1835

This day drew up an Article of inrollment for the redemption of Zion that we may obtain volenteers to go next Spring to Missouri I ask God in the name of Jesus that we may obtain Eight hundred men or one thousand well armed and that they may acomplish this great work even so Amen

Diary, 1835–1836, p. 2. Handwriting of Joseph Smith. See text, pp. 58–59. (LDS Church Archives.)

and looked around, but saw no person or thing
that was calculated to produce the noise of walking; I kneeled again my mouth was opened and
my tongue liberated, and I called on the Lord in
mighty prayer, a pillar of fire appeared above
my head, it present ly rested down upon me,
and filled me with joy unspeakable, a
personage appeared in the midst of this pillar
of flame which was spread all around, and yet
nothing consumed, another personage soon appeared
like unto the first, he said unto me thy sins are
forgiven thee, he testified unto me that Jesus Christ
is the Son of God; I was about 14 years old
when I received this first communication: When
I was about 17 years old I saw another vision of
angels, in the night season after I had retired to
bed I had not been a sleep, but was meditating upon my past life and experience,
I was very conscious that I had not kept the
commandments, and I repented heartily for
all my sins and transgression, and humbled
myself before Him; all at once the room was
illuminated above the brightness of the sun
an angel appeared before me, his hands and
feet were naked pure and white, and he
stood between the floors of the room, clothed with
purity inexpressible, he said unto me I
am a messenger sent from God, be faithful
and keep his commandments in all things,
he told me of a sacred record which was
written on plates of gold, I saw in the vision
the place where they were deposited, he said the
Indians were the literal descendants of Abraham
he explained many things of the prophesies to

Diary, 1835-1836, p. 24. Handwriting of Warren Parrish. See text, pp. 75-76. (LDS Church Archives.)

away enmity from between me and thee
and may all blessings be restored, and the
past be forgotten forever, may humble
repentance bring us both to thee, o Lord
thy power and protection, and a crown to
enjoy the society of father mother alvin
Hyrum Sophrona Samuel Catharine Car
loss Lucy the Saints and all the sanctifyed
in peace forever is the prayer of

Your brother

Joseph Smith Jun

To William Smith

Saturday morning the 19th
at home wrote the letter to Br Wm Smith
I have had many solemn fulings this day concerning
my Brother William and have prayed in my heart to
fervently that the Lord will not cast him off but
he may return to the God of Jacob and magnify
his apostleship and calling may this be his
happy lot for the Lord of Glorys Sake Amen

Sunday the 20th
At home all day and took solled
comfort with my family had many
serious reflections also Brother Palmer
and Taylor came to see me I showed them
the sacred record to their joy and satifac
tion O may God have mercy upon these
men and keep them in the way of everlas
ting life in the name of Jesus Amen

Diary, 1835-1836, p. 87. Handwriting of Warren Parrish and Joseph Smith. See text, pp. 116-17. (LDS Church Archives.)

88

Monday Morning 21st
At home & Spent this in indeavering to
treasure up knowledge for the beifit of my
calling the day passed of very pleasantly for
which I thank the Lord for his blessings
to my Soul his great mercy over my Family in sparing our lives O continue thy
Care over me and mine for Christ sake

Tuesday 22d At home
Continued my Study O may God give
me learning even Language and indo-
me with qualifications to magnify his
name while I live I also delivered an address to the Church this Evening the Lord
blessed my Soul, my scribe also is unwell O my God heal him and for
his kindness to me O my Soul be thou
greatful to him and bless him and he
shall be blessed of God for ever of God for
ever I believe him to be a faithful
friend to me therefore my Soul
delighteth in him Amen
                              Joseph Smith Jr

Wednesday 23d
In the fore noon at home Studying
the greek Language and also waiting
upon the brethren who came in and
exhibiting to them the papyrus, in the
afternoon visited brother Leonard Rich with
the relatives of bro Oliver Cowdery had not
a very agreeable visit for I found them

Diary, 1835-1836, p. 88. Handwriting of Joseph Smith and Frederick G. Williams. See text, p. 117. (LDS Church Archives.)

Diary, 1835-1836, p. 150. Handwriting of Sylvester Smith. See text, pp. 155-56. (LDS Church Archives.)

177

The hymn on the hundred and 14 page
was then sung, after which I offered to God
the following dedication prayer.

Prayer.

At the dedication of the Lords House in Kirtland Ohio
March 27, 1836 — by Joseph Smith, jr.
President of the Church of the Latter Day Saints.

Thanks be to thy name, O Lord God of Israel, who
keepest covenant and shewest mercy unto thy servants,
who walk uprightly before thee with all their hearts;
thou who hast commanded thy servants to build an
house to thy name in this place. (Kirtland.) And now
thou beholdest, O Lord, that so thy servants have done
according to thy commandment. And now we ask thee, holy
Father, in the name of Jesus Christ, the Son of thy bosom, in
in whose name alone salvation can be administered to
the children of men: we ask thee, O Lord, to accept of this
house, the workmanship of the hands of us, thy servants,
which thou didst command us to build; for thou knew-
est that we have done this work through great tribulations; and out of our poverty we have given of our
substance to build a house to thy name, that the son
of Man might have a place to manifest himself to
his people.

And as thou hast said, in a revelation given unto us,
calling us thy friends, saying — "Call your solemn assembly as I have commanded you; and as all have not
faith, seek ye diligently and teach one another words
of wisdom; yea, seek ye out of the best books words of
wisdom; Seek learning, even by study, and also by faith.
"Organize yourselves; prepare every thing needful;
and establish a house, even a house of prayer,
a house fasting, a house of faith, a house of learning

Diary, 1835-1836, p. 177. Possibly the handwriting of Jesse Hitchcock.
See text, pp. 174-75. (LDS Church Archives.)

...convinced that he was wrong, and humbly confessed it and asked my forgiveness, which was readily
granted, he also wished to be received into the church again by baptism, and was received according to
his desire, he gave me his confession in writing—

                    Saturday April 2

Transacted business of a temporal nature in company with S. Rigdon, O. Cowdery, _____ & _____ , D. Whitmer,
& W. W. Phelps, which was to have a bearing upon the redemption
of Zion. The _____ was _____ with he expressed
himself on this, his favourite theme, was directly calculated
to produce conviction in the minds of those _____ , I saw
him that his whole soul was engaged in it, _____ the
standing on a superficial view of the same subject,
they might differ from him in judgement. It was
determined in council, after mature deliberation,
that he and O. Cowdery should act in concert in raising funds for the accomplishment of the aforesaid
object. As soon as the above plan was settled, he
and O. Cowdery set out together, and their _____ was
such in one half day as to give them pleasing
anticipations, and _____ them that they were doing the
will of God, and that his work prospered in their ha-

                    Sabbath April 3

He attended meeting in the Lords House, assisted the other
Presidents of the Church in seating the congregation and
then became an attentive listener to the preaching from the
stand, T. B. Marsh & D. W. Patten spoke in the A.M. to an
attentive audience of about 1000 persons. In the P.M.
he assisted the other Presidents in distributing the Elements
of the Lords Supper to the church, receiving them from the
_____ Twelve, whose privilege it was to officiate in the
sacred desk this day. After having performed this service
to his brethren, he retired to the pulpit, the veils being dropp-

Diary, 1835-1836, p. 191. Handwriting of Warren Parrish and Warren A. Cowdery. See text, pp. 185-86. (LDS Church Archives.)

History, 1838

The writing of Joseph Smith's *History of the Church* in its present form was begun on April 30, 1838, at Far West, Missouri. How much was completed before the Prophet left Missouri in the Spring of 1839 is not known; but by May 2 the writing had progressed to the eighth page of the manuscript, which contains the account of obtaining the Book of Mormon plates. Since work on the history is mentioned on only two additional days following May 2, probably not much more was written while Joseph was in Missouri.[1]

Less than three weeks after the Prophet arrived in Quincy, Illinois, in 1839, he moved his family to Commerce, sixty miles to the north, where he began to establish a new gathering place for the Saints. In the midst of this resettlement activity, he renewed work on his history. On June 11 James Mulholland[2] wrote that Joseph "commenced to dictate and I to write history."[3] Recognizing that succeeding portions of the *History* were also dictated, I have included only the beginning pages of this work here.

Owing to the many reports which have been put in circulation by evil disposed and designing persons in relation to the rise and progress of the Church of ⟨Jesus Christ of⟩Latter day Saints, all of which have been designed by the authors thereof to militate against its character as a church, and its progress in the world; I have been

induced to write this history so as to disabuse the publick mind,
and put all enquirers after truth into possession of the facts as they
have transpired in relation both to myself and the Church as far as I
have such facts in possession.

In this history I will present the various events in relation to
this Church in truth and righteousness as they have transpired, or
as they at present exist, being now the eighth year since the
organization of said Church. I was born in the year of our Lord One
thousand Eight hundred and five, on the twenty third day of
December, in the town of Sharon, Windsor County, State of
Vermont. ‹see page Note A 131›[4] My father Joseph Smith Senior
‹see Note E page 2. adenda.[5] My Father› left the State of Vermont
and moved to Palmyra, Ontario, (now Wayne) County, in the
State of New York when I was in my tenth year. or ‹thereabout.›[6]

In about four years after my father's arrival at Palmyra, he
moved with his fa=mily into Manchester in the same County of
Ontario. His family consisting of eleven souls, namely, My Father
Joseph Smith, My Mother Lucy Smith whose name previous to her
marriage was Mack, daughter of Solomon Mack, My brothers
Alvin (who ‹died Nov. 19th: 1823 in the 25 year of his age.›[7] is
now dead) Hyrum, Myself, Samuel-Harrison, William, Don
Carloss, and my Sisters Soph[r]onia, Cathrine and Lucy. Sometime
in the second year after our removal to Manchester, there was in
the place where we lived an unusual excitement on the subject of
religion. It commenced with the Methodists, but soon became
general among all the sects in that region of country, indeed the
whole district of Country seemed affected by it and great [p. 1]
multitudes united themselves to the different religious parties,
which created no small stir and division among the people, Some
crying, "Lo here" and some Lo there. Some were contending for
the Methodist faith, Some for the Presbyterian, and some for the
Baptist; for notwithstanding the great love which the converts to
these different faiths expressed at the time of their conversion, and
the great Zeal manifested by the respective Clergy who were active
in getting up and promoting this extraordinary scene of religious
feeling in order to have everybody converted as they were pleased

to call it, let them join what sect they please[d;] yet when the
Converts began to file off some to one party and some to another, it
was so that the seemingly good feelings of both the Priests and the
Converts were ~~mere pretence~~ more pretended than real, for a scene
of great confusion and bad feeling ensued; Priest contending
against priest, and convert against convert so that all their good
feelings one for another (if they ever had any) were entirely lost in
a strife of words and a contest about opinions.

I was at this time in my fifteenth year. My Fathers family
~~was~~<ere> proselyted to the Presbyterian faith and four of them
joined that Church, Namely, My Mother Lucy, My Brothers
Hyrum, Samuel Harrison, and my Sister Soph[r]onia.

During this time of great excitement my mind was called up to
serious reflection and great uneasiness, but though my feelings were
deep and often pungent, still I kept myself aloof from all these
parties though I attended their several meetings <as often> as
occasion would permit. But in process of time my mind became
somewhat partial to the Methodist sect, and I felt some desire to be
united with them, but so great was the confusion and strife amongst
the different denominations that it was impossible for a person
young as I was and so unacquainted with men and things to come
to any certain con=clusion who was right and who was wrong. My
mind at different times was greatly excited ~~for~~ the cry and tumult
were so great and incessant. The Presbyterians were most decided
against the Baptists and Methodists, and used all their powers of
either reason or sophistry to prove their errors, or at least to make
the people think they were in error. On the other hand the Baptists
and Methodists in their turn were equally Zealous in endeavoring
to establish their own tenets and disprove all others.

In the midst of this war of words, and tumult of opinions, I
often said to myself, what is to be done? Who of all these parties
are right? Or are they all wrong together? And if any one of them
be right which is it? And how shall I know it?

While I was laboring under the extreme difficulties caused by
the contests of these parties of religionists, I was one day reading
the Epistle of James, First Chapter and fifth verse which reads, "If

any of you lack wisdom, let him ask of God, that giveth to all men liberally and upbraideth not, and it shall be given him. Never did any passage of scripture come with more power to the heart of man that this did at this time to mine. It seemed to enter with great force into every feeling of my heart. I reflected on it again and again, knowing that if any person needed wisdom from God, I did, for how to act I did not know and unless I could get more wisdom than I then had would never know, for the teachers of religion of the different sects understood the same [p. 2] passage of scripture so differently as ‹to› destroy all confidence in settling the question by an appeal to the Bible. At length I came to the conclusion that I must either remain in darkness and confusion or else I must do as James directs, that is, Ask of God. I at last came to the determination to ask of God, concluding that if he gave wisdom to them that lacked wisdom, and would give liberally and not upbraid, I might venture. So, in accordance with this, my determination to ask of God, I retired to the woods to make the attempt. It was on the morning of a beautiful clear day early in the spring of Eighteen hundred and twenty. It was the first time in my life that I had ‹made› such an attempt, for amidst all ‹my› anxieties I had never as yet made the attempt to pray vocally.

After I had retired into the place where I had previously designed to go, having looked around me and finding myself alone, I kneeled down and began to offer up the desires of my heart to God, I had scarcely done so, when immediately I was ‹siezed› upon by some power which entirely overcame me and ‹had› such astonishing influence over me as to bind my tongue so that I could not speak. Thick darkness gathered around me and it seemed to me for a time as if I were doomed to sudden destruction. But exerting all my powers to call upon God to de=liver me out of the power of this enemy which had siezed upon me, and at the very moment when I was ready to sink into despair and abandon myself to destruction, not to an im=aginary ruin but to the power of some actual being from the unseen world who had such a marvelous power as I had never before felt in any being. Just at this moment of great alarm I saw a pillar ‹of› light exactly over my head above the

brightness of the sun, which descended ~~gracefully~~ gradually untill it
fell upon me. It no sooner appeared than I found myself delivered
from the enemy which held me bound. When the light rested upon
me I saw two personages (whose brightness and glory defy all
description) standing above me in the air. One of ‹them› spake
unto me calling me by name and said (pointing to the other) "This
is my beloved Son, Hear him." My object in going to enquire of the
Lord was to know which of all the sects was right, that I might
know which to join. No sooner therefore did I get possession of
myself so as to be able to speak, than I asked the personages who
stood above me in the light, which of all the sects was right, (for at
this time it had never entered into my heart that all were wrong)
and which I should join. I was answered that I must join none of
them, for they were all wrong, and the Personage who addressed
me said that all their Creeds were an abomination in his sight, that
those professors were all corrupt, that "they draw near to me with
their lips but their hearts are far from me, They teach for doctrines
the commandments of men, having a form of Godliness but they
deny the power thereof." He again forbade me to join with any of
them and many other things did he say unto me which I cannot
write at this time. When I came to myself again I found myself
lying on ‹my› back looking up into Heaven. ‹B See Note P 132›[8]
Some few days later after I had this vision I happened to be in
company with one of the Methodist Preachers who was very active
in the before mentioned religious excitement and conversing with
him on the subject of religion I took occasion to give him an
account of the vision which I had had. I was greatly surprised at his
behaviour, he treated my communication not only lightly but with
great contempt, saying it was all of the Devil, that there was no
such thing as visions or revelations in these days, that all such
things had ceased with the [p. 3] apostles and that there never
would be any more of them. I soon found however that my telling
the story had excited a great deal of prejudice against me among
professors of religion and was the cause of great persecution which
continued to increase and though I was an obscure boy only
between fourteen and fifteen years of age ‹or thereabouts,›[9] and my

circumstances in life such as to make a boy of no consequence in
the world, yet men of high standing would take notice sufficiently
to excite the public mind against me and create a hot per=secution,
and this was common ‹among› all the sects: all united to persecute
me. It has often caused me m serious reflection both then and
since, how very strange it was that an obscure boy of a little over
fourteen years of age and one too who was doomed to the necessity
of obtaining a scanty maintainance by his daily labor should be
thought a character of sufficient importance to attract the attention
of the great ones of the most popular sects of the day so as to create
in them a spirit of the bitterest persecution and reviling. But
strange or not, so it was, and was often cause of great sorrow to
myself. However it was nevertheless a fact, that I had had a vision.
I have thought since that I felt much like as Paul did when he made
his defence before King Aggrippa and related the account of the
vision he had when he saw a light and heard a voice, but still there
were but few who beleived him, some said he was dishonest, others
said he was mad, and he was ridiculed and reviled, But all this did
not destroy the reality of his vision. He had seen a vision he knew
he had, and ‹all› the persecution under Heaven could not make it
otherwise, and though they should persecute him unto death yet he
knew and would know to his latest breath that he had both seen a
light and heard a voice speaking unto him and all the world could
not make him think or believe otherwise. So it was with me, I had
actualy seen a light and in the midst of that light I saw two
personages, and they did in reality speak ‹un›to me, or one of
them did, And though I was hated and persecuted for saying that I
had seen a vision, yet it was true and while they were persecuting
me reviling me and speaking all manner of evil against me falsely
for so saying, I was led to say in my heart, why persecute ‹me› for
telling the truth? I have actually seen a vision, "and who am I that
I can withstand God" or why does the world think to make me
deny what I have actually seen, for I had seen a vision, I knew it,
and I knew that God knew it, and I could not deny it, neither dare
I do it, at least I knew that by so doing ‹I› would offend God and
come under condemnation. I had now got my mind satisfied so far

as the sectarian world was concerned, that it was not my duty to
join with any of them, but continue as I was untill further directed,
~~for~~ I had found the testimony of James to be true, that a man who
lacked wisdom might ask of God, and obtain and not be upbraided.
I continued to pursue my common avocations in life untill the
twenty first of September, One thousand Eight hundred and twenty
three, all the time suffering severe persecution at the hand of all
classes of men, both religious and irreligious because I con=tinued
to affirm that I ‹had› seen a vision. During the space of time which
intervened between the time I had the vision and the year
Eighteen hundred and twenty three, (having been forbidden to
join any of the religious sects of the day, and being of very tender
years and persecuted by those who ought to have been my friends,
and to have treated me kindly [p. 4] and if they supposed me to be
deluded to have endeavoured in a proper and affectionate manner
to have reclaimed me) I was left to ~~all kinds of~~ temptations, and
mingling ‹with› ~~all kinds of~~ society I frequently ‹fell› into many
foolish errors and displayed the weakness of youth and the
~~corruption~~ ‹foibles›[10] of human nature which I am sorry to say led
me into divers temptations ~~to the gratification of many appetites~~
offensive in the sight of God. ‹See Note C. p. 133›[11] In
consequence of these things I often felt condemned for my
weakness and imperfections; when on the evening of the above
mentioned twenty first of september, after I had retired to my bed
for the night I betook myself to prayer and supplication to
Almighty God for forgiveness of all my sins and follies, and also for
a manifestation to me that I might know of my state and standing
before him. For I had full confidence in obtaining a divine
manifestation as I had previously had one. While I was thus in the
act of calling upon God, I discovered a light appearing in the room
which continued to increase untill the room was lighter than at
noonday ~~and~~ ‹when› immediately a personage ‹appeared› at my
bedside standing in the air for his feet did not touch the floor. He
had on a loose robe of most exquisite whiteness. It was a whiteness
beyond any ‹thing› earthly I had ever seen, nor do I believe that
any earthly thing could be made to appear so exceedin[g]ly white

and brilliant, His hands were naked and his arms also a little above
the wrists. So also were his feet naked as were his legs a little above
the ankles. His head and neck were also bare. I could discover that
he had no other clothing on but this robe, as it was open so that I
could see into his bosom. Not only was his robe exceedingly white
but his whole person was glorious beyond description, and his
countenance truly like lightning. The room was exceedingly light,
but not so very bright as immediately around his person. When I
first looked upon him I was afraid, but the fear soon left me. He
called me by name and said unto me that he was a messenger sent
from the presence of God to me and that his name was Nephi
‹Moroni›.[12] That God had a work for me to do, and that my
‹name› should be had for good and evil among all nations kindreds
and tongues. or that it should be both good and evil spoken of
among all people. He said there was a book deposited written upon
gold plates, giving an account of the former inhabitants of this
continent and the source from whence they sprang. He also said
that the fullness of the everlasting Gospel was con=tained in it as
delivered by the Saviour to the ancient inhabitants. Also that
there were two stones in silver bows and these (put ‹stones
fastened›in to a breast plate) which constituted what is called the
Urim & Thummin deposited with the plates, and ‹the possession
and use of these stones› that was what constituted seers in ancient
or former times and that God ‹had› prepared them for the purpose
of translating the book. After telling me these things he
commenced quoting the prophecies of the old testa=ment, he first
quoted part of the third chapter of Malachi and he quoted also the
fourth or last chapter of the same prophecy though with a little
variation from the way it reads in our Bibles. Instead of quoting the
first verse as reads in our books he quoted it thus, "For behold the
day cometh that shall burn as an oven, and all the proud ‹yea› and
all that do wick=edly shall burn as stubble, for ‹they day› that
cometh shall burn them saith the Lord of hosts, that it shall leave
them neither root nor branch." And again he quoted the fifth verse
thus, "Behold I will reveal unto you the Priesthood by the hand of
Elijah the prophet before the coming of the great and dreadful day

of the Lord." He also quoted the next verse differently. [p. 5] "And
he shall plant in the hearts of the children the promises made to
the fathers, and the hearts of the children shall turn to their
fathers, if it were not so the whole earth would be utterly wasted at
his coming." In addition to these ~~quotations~~ he quoted the
Eleventh Chapter of Isaiah saying that it was about to be fulfilled.
He quoted also the third chapter of Acts, twenty second and
twenty third verses precisely as they stand in our new testament.
He said that that prophet was Christ, but the day had not yet come
when "they who would not hear his voice should be cut off from
among the people," but soon would come.

He also quoted the second chapter of Joel from the twenty
eighth to the last verse. He also said that this was not yet fulfilled
but was soon to be. And he further stated the fullness of the
gentiles was soon to come in. He quoted many other passages of
scripture and offered many explanations which cannot be
mentioned here. Again he told me that when I got those plates of
which he had spoken (for the time that they should be obtained
was not yet fulfilled) I should not show ‹them› to any person,
neither the breastplate with the Urim and Thummin only to those
to whom I should be commanded to show them. If I did I should be
destroyed. While he was conversing with me about the plates the
vision was opened to my mind that I could see the place where the
plates were deposited and that so clearly and distinctly that I knew
the place again when I visited it.

After this ~~conversation~~ communication I saw the light in the
room begin to gather imme=diately around the person of him who
had been speaking to me, and it continued to do so untill the room
was again left dark except just round him, when instantly I saw as it
were a conduit open right up into heaven, and he ascended up till
he entirely disappeared and the room was left as it had been before
this heavenly light had made its appearance.

I lay musing on the singularity of the scene and marvelling
greatly at what had been told me by this extraordinary messenger,
when in the midst of my meditation I suddenly discovered that my
room was again beginning to get lighted, and in an instant as it

were, the same heavenly messenger was again by my bedside. He commenced and again related the very same things which he had done at his first visit without the least variation which having done, he informed me of great judgements which were coming upon the earth, with great desolations by famine, sword, and pestilence, and that these grievous judgments would come on the earth in this generation: Having related these things he again ascended as he had done before.

By this time so deep were the impressions made on my mind that sleep had fled from my eyes and I lay overwhelmed in astonishment at what I had both seen and heard; But what was my surprise when again I beheld the same messenger at my bed side, and heard him rehearse or repeat over again to me the same things as before and added a caution to me, telling me that Satan would try to tempt me (in conse=quence of the indigent circumstances of my father's family) to get the plates for the purpose of getting rich, This he forbid me, saying that I must have mo no other object in view in getting the plates but to glorify God, and must not be influenced by any other motive but that of building his kingdom, otherwise I could not get them. After this third visit he again ascended up into heaven as before and I was again left to ponder on the [p. 6] strangeness of what I had just experienced, when almost immediately after the heavenly messenger had ascended from me the third time, the cock crew, and I found that day was approaching so that our interviews must have occupied the whole of that night. I shortly after arose from my bed, and as usual went to the necessary labors of the day, but in attempting to labor as at other times, I found my strength so exhausted as rendered me entirely unable. My father who was laboring along ‹with› me discovered something to be wrong with me and told me to go home. I started with the intention of going to the house, but in attempting to cross the fence out of the field where we were, my strength entirely failed me and I fell helpless on the ground and for a time was quite unconscious of any thing. The first thing that I can recollect was a voice speaking unto me calling me by name. I looked up and beheld the same messenger standing over my head

surrounded by light as before. He then again related unto me all
that he had related to me the previous night, and commanded me
to go to my father and tell him of the vision and commandments
which I had received.

I obeyed. I returned back to my father in the field and rehearsed
the whole matter to him. He replyed to me, that it was of God, and
to go and do as commanded by the messenger. I left the field and
went to the place where the messenger had told me the plates were
deposited, and owing to the distinctness of the vision which I had
had concerning it, I knew the place the instant that I arrived
there. *[13] Under a ~~stound~~ stone of considerable size, lay the plates
deposited in a stone box, This stone was thick and rounding in the
mid=dle on the upper side, and thinner towards the edges, so that
the middle part of it was visible above the ground, but the edge all
round was covered with earth. Having removed the earth ~~off the
edge of the stone,~~ and obtained a lever which I got fixed under the
edge of the stone, and with a little exertion raised it up, I looked in
and there indeed did I behold the plates, the Urim and Thummin
and the Breastplate as stated by the messenger The box in which
they lay was formed by laying stones together in some kind of
cement, in the bottom of the box were laid two stones crossways of
the box, and on these stones lay the plates and the other things
with them. I made an attempt to take them out but was forbidden
by the messenger and was again informed that the time ‹for›
bringing them forth had not yet arrived, neither would untill four
years from that time, but he told me that I should come to that
place precisely in one year from that time, and that he would there
meet with me, and that I should continue to do so untill the time
should come for obtaining the plates. Accordingly as I had been
commanded I went at the end of each year, and at each time I
found the same messenger there and received instruction and
intelligence from him at each of our interviews respecting what the
Lord was going to do, and how and in what manner his kingdom
was to be conducted in the last days. As my father's worldly
circum=stances were very, ‹limited› we were under the necessity of
laboring with our hands, hiring by days works and otherwise as we

could get opportunity, sometimes we were at home and some times abroad and by continued labor were enabled to get a comfortable maintenance.

In the year Eighteen hundred and twenty four my fathers family met with a great affliction by the death of my eldest brother Alvin.[14] In the month of October Eighteen hundred and twenty five I hired with an old Gentleman, by name of Josiah Stoal [p. 7] who lived in Chenango County, State of New York.[15] He had heard something of a silver mine having been opened by the Spaniards in Harmony, Susquahana County, State of Pensylvania, and had previous to my hiring with him been digging in order if possible to discover the mine. After I went to live with ‹him› he took me among the rest of his hands to dig for the silver mine, at which I continued to work for nearly a month without success in our undertaking, and finally I prevailed with the old gentleman to cease digging after it. Hence arose the very prevalent story of my having been a money digger.

During the time that I was thus employed I was put to board with a Mr Isaac Hale of that place, Twas there that I first saw my wife, (his daughter) Emma Hale. On the eighteenth of January Eighteen hundred and twenty seven we were married while yet I was employed in the service of Mr Stoal. Owing to my still continuing to assert that I had seen a vision, persecu=tion still followed me, ‹and my wife's father's family was very much› and so much was my wife's father excited, that he was greatly opp=osed to our being married, in so much that he would not suffer us to be married at his house, I was therefore under the necessity of taking her elsewhere, so we went and were married at Mr St the house of Mr Stoal. ‹Squire Tarbill in the South Bainbridge. Chenango County, New York.› Immediately after my marriage I left Mr Stoals, and went to my father's and farmed with him that season.

At length the time arrived for obtaining the plates, the Urim and Thummin and the breastplate. On the twenty second day of September, One thousand Eight hundred and twenty seven, having went as usual at the end of another year to the place where they were deposited, the same heavenly messenger delivered them up to me with this charge that I should be responsible for them. That if I should let them go carelessly or ‹through› any neglect of mine I should be cut off, but that if I would use all my endeavours to preserve them untill ‹he› (the messenger) ~~called~~ should call for them, they should be protected.

I soon found out the reason why I had received such strict charges to keep them safe and why it was that the messenger had said that when I had done what was required at my hand, he would call for them, for no sooner was it known that I had them than the most strenious exertions were used to get them from me. Every stratagem that could be ~~resorted~~ invented was resorted to for that purpose. The persecution became more bitter and severe than before, and multitudes were on the alert continualy to get them from me if possible but by the wisdom of God they remained safe in my hands untill I had accomplished by them what was required at my hand, when according to arrangement the messenger called for them, I delivered them up to him and he has them in his charge un=till this day, being the Second day of May, One thousand Eight hundred and thirty eight.

The excitement however still continued, and rumour with her thousand tongues was all the time employed in circulating tales about my father's family and about myself. If I were to relate a thousan‹d›th part of them it would fill up volumes. The persecution however became so intolerable that I was under the necessity of leaving Manchester and going with my wife ‹to› Susquahanah County in the State of Pensyllvania. While preparing to start (being very poor and the persecution so heavy upon us that there was no probability that we would ever be otherwise) in the midst of our afflictions we found a friend in a Gentleman by ‹the› name of Martin Harris, who came to us and gave me fifty dollars [p. 8] to assist us in our affliction, Mr Harris was a resident of Palmyra township Wayne County in the State of New York and a farmer of respectability. By this timely aid was I enabled to reach the place of my destination in Pensylvania, and immediately after my arrival there I commenced copying the characters of ~~all~~ the plates. I copyed a considerable number of them and by means of

the Urim and Thummin I translated some of them which I did
between the time I arrived at the house of my wife's father in the
month of December, and the February following. Sometime in this
month of February the aforementioned Mr Martin Harris came to
our place, got the characters which I had drawn off of the plates
and started with them to the City of New York. For what took
place relative to him and the characters I refer to his own account
of the circumstances as he related them to me after his return
which was as follows. "I went to the City of New York and
presented the Characters which had been translated, with the
translation thereof, to Professor <Charles> Anthony a gentleman
celebrated for his literary attainments. Professor Anthony stated
that the trans=lation was correct, more so than any he had before
seen translated from the Egyptian.

I then shewed him those which were not yet translated, and he
said that they were Egyptian, Chaldeak, Assyriac, and Arabac, and
he said that they were true charac=ters. He gave me a certificate
certifying to the people of Palmyra that they were true char=acters
and that the translation of such of them as had been translated was
also correct.

I took the Certificate and put it into my pocket, and was just
leaving the house, when Mr Anthony called me back and asked me
how the young man found out that there were gold plates in the
place where he found them. I answered that an Angel of God had
revealed it unto him. He then said to me, let me see that
certificate, I accordingly took it out of my pocket and gave it [to]
him when he took it and tore it to pieces, saying that there was no
such thing now as ministring of angels, and that if I would bring
the plates to him, he would translate them. * <I informed him that
part of the plates were sealed, and that I was forbidden to bring
them. he replied "I cannot read a sealed book."> I left him and
went to Dr Mitchel who sanction=ed what Professor Anthony had
said respecting both the Characters and the translation."[16]

Mr Harris having returned from this tour he left me and went
home to Palmyra, arranged his affairs, and returned again to my
house about the twelfth of April, Eighteen hundred and twenty

eight, and commenced writing for me while I translated from the plates, which we continued untill the fourteenth of June following, by which time he had written one hundred and sixteen ‹pages› of manuscript on foolscap paper. Some time after Mr Harris had began to write for me, he began to tease me to give him liberty to carry the writings home and shew them, and desired of me that I would enquire of the Lord through the Urim and Thummin if he might not do so. I did enquire, and the answer was that he must not. However he was not satisfied with this answer, and desired that I should enquire again. I did so, and the answer was as before. Still he could not be contented but insis=ted that I should enquire once more. ~~after~~ After much solicitation I again enquired of the Lord, and permission was granted him to have the writings on certain condit=ions, which were, that he shew them only to his brother. Preserved Harris, his own wife, his father, and his mother, and a Mrs Cobb a sister to his wife. In accordance with this last answer I required of him that he should bind himself in a covenant to me [p. 9] in the most solemn manner that he would not do otherwise than had been directed. He did so. He bound himself as I required of him, took the writings and went his way.

Notwithstanding however the great restrictions which he had been laid under, and the solemn=ity of the covenant which he had made with me, he did shew them to others and by strat=agem they got them away from him, and they never have been recovered nor obtained back again untill this day. In the mean time while Martin Harris was gone with the writings, I went to visit my father's family at Manchester. I continued there for a short season and then returned to my place in Pensylvania. Immediately after my return home I was walking out a little distance, when Behold the former heavenly messenger appeared and handed to me the Urim and Thummin again (for it had been taken from me in consequence of my having wearied the Lord in ask=ing for the privilege of letting Martin Harris take the writings which he lost by tran=sgression) . . . .

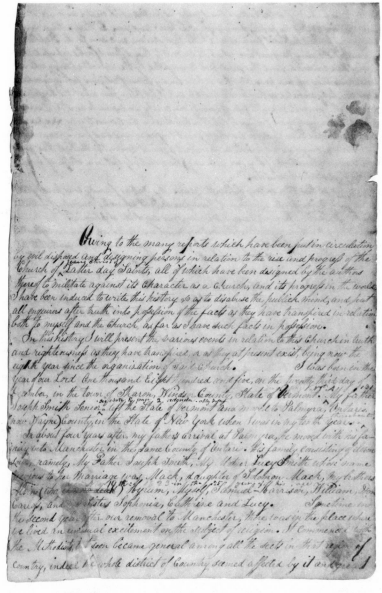

History, 1838, vol. A-1, p. 1. Handwriting of James Mulholland; insertions were written by Willard Richards. See text, pp. 196-97. (LDS Church Archives.)

Historical Sketch, March 1, 1842

John Wentworth, born in Sandwich, New Hampshire, in 1815, graduated from Dartmouth College in 1836 and then went to Michigan to find a job teaching school. Disappointed in his efforts, he went later that year to Chicago, Illinois, a village of twenty-five hundred, in search of other employment. Within a month, he became editor and, within three years, owner of the weekly *Chicago Democrat*, the town's first newspaper. Wentworth eventually became one of Illinois' foremost citizens, both in accomplishment and stature. At six foot six and three hundred pounds, "Long John" Wentworth was elected to the United States House of Representatives in 1843, and at twenty-eight years of age was the youngest member of that body. He subsequently served two more terms in the Congress and was elected mayor of Chicago in 1857. He was appointed to the Illinois state board of education, and at one time held title to more Cook County real estate than any other man in Chicago.[1]

In 1842, Wentworth, then the twenty-six-year-old Chicago editor, wrote to the Prophet Joseph Smith, requesting a "sketch of the rise, progress, persecution and faith of the Latter-day Saints" for a New Hampshire friend of his—George Barstow.[2] Joseph Smith's response is dated March 1, 1842.

I was born in the town of Sharon Windsor co., Vermont, on the 23d of December, A. D. 1805. When ten years old my parents removed to Palmyra New York, where we resided about four years, and from thence we removed to the town of Manchester.

My father was a farmer and taught me the art of husbandry. When about fourteen years of age I began to reflect upon the importance of being prepared for a future state, and upon enquiring the plan of salvation I found that there was a great clash in religious sentiment; if I went to one society they referred me to one plan, and another to another; each one pointing to his own particular creed as the summum bonum of perfection: considering that all could not be right, and that God could not be the author of so much confusion I determined to investigate the subject more fully, believing that if God had a church it would not be split up into factions, and that if he taught one society to worship one way, and administer in one set of ordinances, he would not teach another principles which were diametrically opposed. Believing the word of God I had confidence in the declaration of James; "If any man lack wisdom let him ask of God who giveth to all men liberally and upbraideth not and it shall be given him," I retired to a secret place in a grove and began to call upon the Lord, while fervently engaged in supplication my mind was taken away from the objects with which I was surrounded, and I was enwrapped in a [p. 706] heavenly vision and saw two glorious personages who exactly resembled each other in features, and likeness, surrounded with a brilliant light which eclipsed the sun at noon-day. They told me that all religious denominations were believing in incorrect doctrines, and that none of them was acknowledged of God as his church and kingdom. And I was expressly commanded to "go not after them," at the same time receiving a promise that the fulness of the gospel should at some future time be made known unto me.

On the evening of the 21st of September, A. D. 1823, while I was praying unto God, and endeavoring to exercise faith in the precious promises of scripture on a sudden a light like that of day, only of a far purer and more glorious appearance, and brightness burst into the room, indeed the first sight was as though the house was filled with consuming fire; the appearance produced a shock that affected the whole body; in a moment a personage stood before me surrounded with a glory yet greater than that with which I was already surrounded. This messenger proclaimed himself to be an angel of God sent to bring the joyful tidings, that the covenant which God made with ancient Israel was at hand to be fulfilled, that the preparatory work for the second coming of the Messiah was speedily to commence; that the time was at hand for the gospel, in all its fulness to be preached in power, unto all nations that a people might be prepared for the millennial reign.

I was informed that I was chosen to be an instrument in the hands of God to bring about some of his purposes in this glorious dispensation.

I was also informed concerning the aboriginal inhabitants of this country, and shown who they were, and from whence they came; a brief sketch of their origin, progress, civilization, laws, governments, of their righteousness and iniquity, and the blessings of God being finally withdrawn from them as a people was made known unto me: I was also told where there was deposited some plates on which were engraven an abridgement of the records of the ancient prophets that had existed on this continent. The angel appeared to me three times the same night and unfolded the same things. After having received many visits from the angels of God unfolding the majesty, and glory of the events that should transpire in the last days, on the morning of the 22d of September A. D. 1827, the angel of the Lord delivered the records into my hands.

These records were engraven on plates which had the appearance of gold, each plate was six inches wide and eight inches long and not quite so thick as common tin. They were filled with engravings, in Egyptian characters and bound together in a volume, as the leaves of a book with three rings running through the whole. The volume was something near six inches in thickness, a part of which was sealed. The characters on the unsealed part were small, and beautifully engraved. The whole book exhibited many marks of antiquity in its construction and much skill in the

art of engraving. With the records was found a curious instrument
which the ancients called "Urim and Thummim," which consisted
of two transparent stones set in the rim of a bow fastened to a
breastplate.

Through the medium of the Urim and Thummim I translated
the record by the gift, and power of God.

In this important and interesting book the history of ancient
America is unfolded, from its first settlement by a colony that came
from the tower of Babel, at the confusion of languages to the
beginning of the fifth century of the Christian era. We are
informed by these records that America in ancient times has been
inhabited by two distinct races of people. The first were called
Jaredites and came directly from the tower of Babel. The second
race came directly from the city of Jerusalem, about six hundred
years before Christ. They were principally Israelites, of the
descendants of Joseph. The Jaredites were destroyed about the time
that the Israelites came from Jerusalem, who succeeded them in the
inheritance of the country. The principal nation of the second race
fell in battle towards the close of the fourth century. The remnant
are the Indians that now inhabit this country. This book also tells
us that our Saviour made his appearance upon this continent after
his resurrection, that he planted the gospel here in all its fulness,
and richness, and power, and blessing; that they had apostles,
prophets, pastors, teachers and evangelists; the same order, the
same priesthood, the [p. 707] same ordinances, gifts, powers, and
blessing, as was enjoyed on the eastern continent, that the people
were cut off in consequence of their transgressions, that the last of
their prophets who existed among them was commanded to write
an abridgement of their prophesies, history &c., and to hide it up
in the earth, and that it should come forth and be united with the
bible for the accomplishment of the purposes of God in the last
days. For a more particular account I would refer to the Book of
Mormon, which can be purchased at Nauvoo, or from any of our
travelling elders.

As soon as the news of this discovery was made known, false
reports, misrepresentation and slander flew as on the wings of the

wind in every direction, the house was frequently beset by mobs, and evil designing persons, several times I was shot at, and very narrowly escaped, and every device was made use of to get the plates away from me, but the power and blessing of God attended me, and several began to believe my testimony.

On the 6th of April, 1830, the "Church of Jesus Christ of Latter-Day Saints," was first organized in the town of Manchester, Ontario co., state of New York. Some few were called and ordained by the spirit of revelation, and prophesy, and began to preach as the spirit gave them utterance, and though weak, yet were they strengthened by the power of God, and many were brought to repentance, were immersed in the water, and were filled with the Holy Ghost by the laying on of hands. They saw visions and prophesied, devils were cast out and the sick healed by the laying on of hands. From that time the work rolled forth with astonishing rapidity, and churches were soon formed in the states of New York, Pennsylvania, Ohio, Indiana, Illinois and Missouri; in the last named state a considerable settlement was formed in Jackson co.; numbers joined the church and we were increasing rapidly; we made large purchases of land, our farms teemed with plenty, and peace and happiness was enjoyed in our domestic circle and throughout our neighborhood; but as we could not associate with our neighbors who were many of them of the basest of men and had fled from the face of civilized society, to the frontier country to escape the hand of justice, in their midnight revels, their sabbath breaking, horseracing, and gambling, they commenced at first ridicule, then to persecute, and finally an organized mob assembled and burned our houses, tarred, and feathered, and whipped many of our brethren and finally drove them from their habitations; who houseless, and homeless, contrary to law, justice and humanity, had to wander on the bleak prairies till the children left the tracks of their blood on the prairie, this took place in the month of November, and they had no other covering but the canopy of heaven, in this inclement season of the year; this proceeding was winked at by the government and although we had warrantee deeds for our land, and had violated no law we could obtain no redress.

There were many sick, who were thus inhumanly driven from
their houses, and had to endure all this abuse and to seek homes
where they could be found. The result was, that a great many of
them being deprived of the comforts of life, and the necessary
attendances, died; many children were left orphans; wives, widows;
and husbands widowers.—Our farms were taken possession of by
the mob, many thousands of cattle, sheep, horses, and hogs, were
taken and our household goods, store goods, and printing press,
and type were broken, taken, or otherwise destroyed.

Many of our brethren removed to Clay where they continued
until 1836, three years; there was no violence offered but there
were threatnings of violence. But in the summer of 1836, these
threatnings began to assume a more serious form; from threats,
public meetings were called, resolutions were passed, vengeance
and destruction were threatened, and affairs again assumed a fearful
attitude, Jackson county was a sufficient precedent, and as the
authorities in that county did not interfere, they boasted that they
would not in this, which on application to the authorities we found
to be too true, and after much violence, privation and loss of
property we were again driven from our homes.

We next settled in Caldwell, and Davies counties, where we
made large and extensive settlements, thinking to free ourselves
from the power of oppression, by settling in new counties, with
very few inhabitants in them; but here we were not allowed to live
in peace, but in 1838 we were again attacked by mobs [p. 708] an
exterminating order was issued by Gov. Boggs, and under the
sanction of law an organized banditti ranged through the country,
robbed us of our cattle, sheep, horses, hogs &c., many of our
people were murdered in cold blood, the chastity of our women was
violated, and we were forced to sign away our property at the point
of the sword, and after enduring every indignity that could be
heaped upon us by an inhuman, ungodly band of maurauders, from
twelve to fifteen thousand souls men, women, and children were
driven from their own fire sides, and from lands that they had
warrantee deeds of, houseless, friendless, and homeless (in the
depth of winter,) to wander as exiles on the earth or to seek an

asylum in a more genial clime, and among a less barbarous people.

Many sickened and died, in consequence of the cold, and hardships they had to endure; many wives were left widows, and children orphans, and destitute. It would take more time than is allotted me here to describe the injustice, the wrongs, the murders, the bloodshed, the theft, misery and woe that has been caused by the barbarous, inhuman, and lawless, proceedings of the state of Missouri.

In the situation before alluded to we arrived in the state of Illinois in 1839, where we found a hospitable people and a friendly home; a people who were willing to be governed by the principles of law and humanity. We have commenced to build a city called "Nauvoo" in Hancock co., we number from six to eight thousand here besides vast numbers in the county around and in almost every county of the state. We have a city charter granted us and a charter for a legion the troops of which now number 1500. We have also a charter for a university, for an agricultural and manufacturing society, have our own laws and administrators, and possess all the privileges that other free and enlightened citizens enjoy.

Persecution has not stopped the progress of truth, but has only added fuel to the flame, it has spread with increasing rapidity, proud of the cause which they have espoused and conscious of their innocence and of the truth of their system amidst calumny and reproach have the elders of this church gone forth, and planted the gospel in almost every state in the Union; it has penetrated our cities, it has spread over our villages, and has caused thousands of our intelligent, noble, and patriotic citizens to obey its divine mandates, and be governed by its sacred truths. It has also spread into England, Ireland, Scotland and Wales: in the year of 1839 where a few of our missionaries were sent over five thousand joined the standard of truth, there are numbers now joining in every land.

Our missionaries are going forth to different nations, and in Germany, Palestine, New Holland, the East Indies, and other places, the standard of truth has been erected: no unhallowed hand can stop the work from progressing, persecutions may rage, mobs may combine, armies may assemble, calumny may defame, but the truth of God will go forth boldly, nobly, and independent till it has penetrated every continent, visited every clime, swept every country, and sounded in every ear, till the purposes of God shall be accomplished and the great Jehovah shall say the work is done.

We believe in God the Eternal Father, and in his son Jesus Christ, and in the Holy Ghost.

We believe that men will be punished for their own sins and not for Adam's transgression.

We believe that through the atonement of Christ all mankind may be saved by obedience to the laws and ordinances of the Gospel.

We believe that these ordinances are 1st, Faith in the Lord Jesus Christ; 2d, Repentance; 3d, Baptism by immersion for the remission of sins; 4th, Laying on of hands for the gift of the Holy Ghost.

We believe that a man must be called of God by "prophesy, and by laying on of hands" by those who are in authority to preach the gospel and administer in the ordinances thereof.

We believe in the same organization that existed in the primitive church, viz: apostles, prophets, pastors, teachers, evangelists &c.

We believe in the gift of tongues, prophesy, revelation, visions, healing, interpretation of tongues &c.

We believe the bible to be the word of God as far as it is translated correctly; we also believe the Book of Mormon to be the word of God.

We believe all that God has revealed, all that he does now reveal, and we be= [p. 709]lieve that he will yet reveal many great and important things pertaining to the kingdom of God.

We believe in the literal gathering of Israel and in the restoration of the Ten Tribes. That Zion will be built upon this continent. That Christ will reign personally upon the earth, and that the earth will be renewed and receive its paradasaic glory.

We claim the privilege of worshipping Almighty God according to the dictates of our conscience, and allow all men the same privilege let them worship how, where, or what they may.

We believe in being subject to kings, presidents, rulers, and magistrates, in obeying, honoring and sustaining the law.

We believe in being honest, true, chaste, benevolent, virtuous, and in doing good to *all men;* indeed we may say that we follow the admonition of Paul "we believe all things we hope all things," we have endured many things and hope to be able to endure all things. If there is any thing virtuous, lovely, or of good report or praise worthy we seek after these things.[3] Respectfully &c.,
                                    JOSEPH SMITH.

Part 2
Letters
and
Documents

—A Mark Hofmann forgery —

Note on Anthon Transcript, February 1828

In recording the circumstances of the coming forth of the Book of Mormon, Joseph Smith wrote that on September 21, 1823, a heavenly messenger revealed to him the existence of an ancient record written upon gold plates containing an account of former inhabitants of the American continent, and that buried with the plates in a hill not far from his home in Palmyra, New York, were the means for their translation. Four years later Joseph received custody of the record and "translators." As news of his acquisitions spread, "strenuous exertions" were made to get them from him. "Every stratagem that could be invented was resorted to for that purpose," finally forcing him to leave his home and move to his wife's parents' place in Harmony, Pennsylvania. He arrived there in December 1827 with timely assistance from Martin Harris, a well-to-do Palmyra farmer.

Harris played a key role in furnishing monetary and clerical assistance for the translation and publication of the Book of Mormon. In February 1828, before Joseph commenced work on the record, Harris was sent to language authorities in the East with a copy of characters from the plates for their perusal. Among those he visited was Professor Charles Anthon of Columbia College in New York City, who later described his encounter with the "plain-looking countryman." Anthon recalled his meeting Harris with disdain and described the transcript as a hoax: "The characters were arranged in columns, like the Chinese mode of writing, and presented the most singular medley that I ever beheld. Greek, Hebrew and all sorts of letters, more or less distorted, either through unskilfulness or from actual design, were intermingled with sundry delineations of half moons, stars, and other natural objects, and the whole ended in a rude representation of the Mexican zodiac."[1]

Joseph's summary of the incident appears in the following note he jotted on the back of the transcript. Although undated, it was probably written shortly after Harris returned from New York City.

[Harmony, Pennsylvania February 1828?]

These C‹h›aractors were dilligently coppied by my own han=d from the plates of gold and given to Martin Harris ‹who took them› to new york Citty but the learned could not tra=nslate it because the Lord would not open it up to them in fulfilment of the prop‹h›icy of Isa‹i›h written in the 29th Chapter and 11 verse

Joseph Smith Jr.

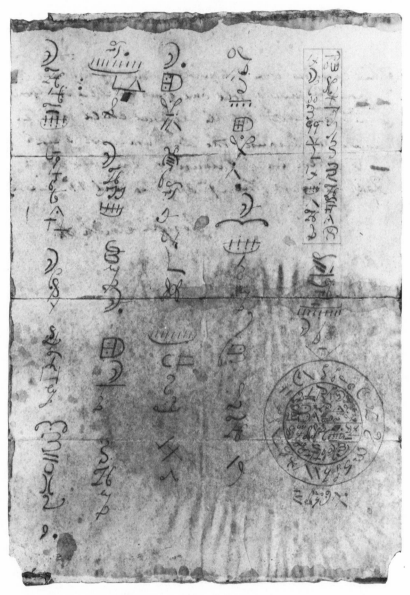

Anthon Transcript, 1828, p. 1. (LDS Church Archives.)

Note on Anthon Transcript, February 1828, p. 2. Handwriting of Joseph Smith. See text, p. 224. (LDS Church Archives.)

To Oliver Cowdery,
October 22, 1829

To finish the translation of the Book of Mormon in the face of growing opposition against him in Pennsylvania, Joseph Smith left Harmony in June 1829 and moved to the Peter Whitmer home in Fayette, New York. Upon completing the translation, Joseph negotiated with the Palmyra publisher, Egbert B. Grandin, to print 5,000 copies of the book for $3,000, ordered a complete copy of the manuscript made as insurance against loss of the original, and then, leaving Oliver Cowdery to supervise the publication, with strict instructions for protecting the manuscript, returned to his home in Pennsylvania. On October 22, less than three weeks after arriving there, Joseph wrote the following letter to Oliver Cowdery.[1]

Harmony—Oct. 22d 1829

Respected Sir I would in form you that I arrived at home on sunday morning the 4th after having a prosperous Journey, and found all well the people are all friendly to ‹us› except a few who are in opposition to evry thing unless it is some thing that is exactly like themselves and two of our most formadable persacutors are now under censure and are cited to a tryal in the church for crimes which if true are worse than all the Gold Book business. we do not rejoice in the affliction of our enimies but we shall be glad to have truth prevail there begins to be a great call for our books in this country the minds of the people are very much excited when they find that there is a copy right obtained[2] and that there is really [a] book, about to be printed I have bought a horse of Mr. Stowell and want some one to come after it as soon as convenient Mr. Stowell has a prospect of getting five or six hundred dol=lars he does not know certain that he can get it but he is a going to try and if he can get the money he wants to pay it in immediately for books we want to hear from you and know how you prosper in the good work, give our best respects to Father & Mother and all our brothers and Sisters, to Mr. Harris and all the company concerned tell them that our prayers are put up daily for them that they may be prospered in evry, good word and work and that they may be preserved from sin here and and from the consequence of sin hereafter and now dear brother be faithful in the discharge of evry duty looking for the reward of the righteous and now may God of his infinite mercy keep and pre=serve us spotless untill his coming and receive us all to rest with him in eternal repose through the attonement of Christ our Lord Amen

Joseph Smith Jr

Oliver H. Cowdery

To Hyrum Smith,
March 3, 1831

In the fall of 1830, four missionaries (Oliver Cowdery, Peter Whitmer, Jr., Parley P. Pratt, and Ziba Peterson) were called to preach the restored gospel "in the wilderness among the Lamanites," as the Indians were known to believers in the Book of Mormon.[1] Traveling through the area of Parley Pratt's former residence in Ohio's Western Reserve, the missionaries added some three hundred converts to the new faith, including an influential Campbellite minister, Sidney Rigdon.

After requesting that an overseer be sent from New York to care for the young flock in Ohio, the missionaries, accompanied by one of their converts, Frederick G. Williams, continued their journey west. Traveling in a season remembered as "the winter of the deep snow," they reached their destination at Independence, Missouri, near the Indian lands of the frontier, in December.[2]

To sustain the group, Whitmer and Peterson found employment in a tailor shop while the others crossed the Kansas River, eager to present their message to the Delaware and Shawnee Indians. But as word of their activity spread, opposition from sectarian missionaries and Indian agents forced them to leave the Indian lands. Consequently, they turned their attention to the white population of Jackson County.[3]

Back in New York, Joseph Smith had no sooner sent John Whitmer to preside over the new converts in Ohio than he received a revelation that directed all of the Saints in New York to gather there. The Prophet arrived in Kirtland on February 1, 1831, and a month later wrote this letter to his brother Hyrum who was presiding over the Saints at Colesville, New York.[4]

Kirtland Geauga County Ohio
March 3th 1831

  Brother Hyram
we arived here safe and are all well I hav[e] been engageed in regulating the Churches here as the deciples are numerous and the devil has made many att‹e›mpts to over throw them[5] it has been a serious Job but the Lord is with us and we have overcome and have all things regular the work is brakeing forth on the ‹right› hand and on the left and there is a great Call for Elders in this place we hav[e] recieved a leter from Olover [Oliver Cowdery] dated independence Jackson County Missouri Janua=ry the 29th 1831 these are the words which he has written saying– My ~~dealy~~ dearly beloved bretheren after a considerable lengthy journy I ~~arived~~ avail myself of the first opertunity of communicating to you a knowledge of our situation that you may be priviledged of writing to us for we have not heard any thing from you since we left you last fall we arived ~~here~~ at this place a few days since which is about 25 miles from the Shawney indians on the south side of the Kan=sas River at its mouth & delewares on the north I have had two intervi‹e›ws with the Chief of ~~[-] that~~ the delewares who is ‹a› very old & venerable looking man[6] after ~~haveing~~ laying before him & eighteen or twenty of the Council of that nation the truth he said that ‹he› ~~hand they~~ he and they were very glad for what I their Brother had told them and they had recived it in their hearts &c– But how the matter will go with this tribe to me is uncirtain nether Can I at presen‹t› Conclude mutch about it the wether is ~~mutch~~ is quite severe and the snow is Considerable deep which

makes it at present quite dific=cult traveling about I have but a
short time to write to you my bloved Bretheren as the mail leves
thi[s] place in ~~morni~~ the morning [p. 1] but I wish some of you to
write ‹to› me immediate=ly a full letter of all your affairs and
then I will write to you the situation of all the western tribes &c
thus reads most of the letter Saying to us the god of my father
Jacob be with you all amen I remain in Christ your Brother
forever

Oliver

My Dearly Beloved Brother Hyrum
    I ‹have› had much Concirn about you but I always remember
you in ~~your~~ ‹my› prayers Calling upon god to keep ‹you› Safe in
spite ‹of› men or devils I think ‹you› had better Come into this
Country immediately for the Lord has Comm=anded us that we
should Call the Elders of this Chursh to gether unto this plase as
soon as possable
    March forth this morning after being Colled out of my bed in
the night to go a small distance I went and had ~~and~~ an awful
strugle with satan ‹but› being armed with the power of god he
was cast out and the woman is Clothed in hir right mind the Lord
worketh wonders in this land
    I want to see you all may the grace of God be and abide with
you all even so Amen

your Brother forever
Joseph Smith Jr

    PS if you want to ~~to~~ write to Oliver direct your letter ~~direct
your~~ to independence Jackson County misouri [p. 2]

    Harrison and O[r]son prat[7] arrived here on Feb 27th they left
our folks well David Jackways[8] has threatened to take father with
a sup=reme writ in the spring you had ‹beter› Come to fayette
and take father along with you Come in a one horse wagon ~~if~~ if

you Can do not Come threw Bufalo for th[e]y will lie in wait for
you God protect you I am Joseph [p. 3]

Mr. Hyram Smith
Harpers Vill B‹r›oom Co.
N. Y.

Kirtland Mills. O
3 March   25

Kirtland, Geauga County Ohio

Brother Hyrum   March 3, 1831

we arived here safe and are all well I have
been engaged in regulating the Churches here
as the deciples are numerous and the devil has
made many attempts to over throw them it has
been a serious Job but the Lord is with us and
we have overcome and have all things regular
the work is breaking forth on the right hand and on the
left and there is a great Call for Elders in this
place we too recieved a liter from Oliver dated
Independence Jackson County Missouri Janu-
ry the 29th 1831 then are the words which he has
written saying My dearly beloved bretheren
after a considerable lengthy journy I avail oavil
myself of the first oppertunity of communicating to
you a knowledge of our situation that you may
be priviledged of writing to us for we have not
heard any thing from you since we left you
last fall we arived here at this place a few
days since which is about 25 miles from the
Shawney indians on the south side of the Kansas River at its mouth & deleware on the north
I have had two interviews with the Chief of the
the deleware who is a very odd & venerable
looking man after having laying before him
& eighteen or twenty of the Council of that nation
the truth he said that they he and they
were very glad for what I their Brother had
told them and they had recieved it in their
hearts &c But how the matter will go with the
tribe to me is uncirtain nether Can I at present
conclude mutch about it the wether is
is quite severe and the snow is considerably
deep which makes it at present quite dific-
ult traveling about I have but a short time
to write to you my beloved Brethren as the
mail leves this place in the morning

To Hyrum Smith, March 3, 1831, p. 1. Handwriting of Joseph Smith.
See text, pp. 230-31. (LDS Church Archives.)

but I wish some of you to write to me immediately a full letter of all your affairs, and then I will write to you the situation of all the western tribes &c. Then reads most of the letter. Saying to us the god of my father Jacob be with you all amen I remain in Christ your Brother forever Oliver

My Dearly Beloved Brother Hyrum I had much concern about you but I always remember you in my prayers calling upon god to keep you safe in spite of men or devils I think you had better come into this Country immediately for the Lord has commanded us that we should call the Elders of this Church together unto this place as soon as possible

March forth this morning after being Called out of my bed in the night to go a small distance I went and had an awful struggle with satan but being armed with the power of god he was cast out and the woman is clothed in her right mind the Lord worketh wonders in this land

I want to see you all may the grace of god be and abide with you all even so Amen

yours Brother forever

Joseph Smith Jr

P.S if you want to write Oliver direct your letter to independence Jackson County missouri

To Hyrum Smith, March 3, 1831, p. 2. Handwriting of Joseph Smith.
See text, p. 231. (LDS Church Archives.)

To Hyrum Smith, March 3, 1831, p. 3. Handwriting of Joseph Smith.
See text, pp. 231-32. (LDS Church Archives.)

To Hyrum Smith, March 3, 1831, p. 4. Handwriting of Joseph Smith. See text, p. 232. (LDS Church Archives.)

To Emma Smith,
June 6, 1832

With the designation of Kirtland, Ohio, as one gathering place and Jackson County, Missouri, as another, there developed two centers of Mormon activity beginning in 1831.[1] The foundation of the Church membership in Missouri consisted mainly of the early converts from the Fayette-Colesville area of New York, while the Ohio membership was made up largely of Sidney Rigdon's followers in the area of Kirtland. In consequence of this dual concentration, a certain spirit of jealousy arose between the members in the two places. This derived from the fact that the Prophet resided in Ohio, that most of those in high Church positions came from there, and that the Missouri Saints had not participated in rapid developments in Church organization. To allay these feelings Joseph Smith and other Church leaders were directed by revelation to "sit in council" with the Saints in Missouri, "otherwise Satan seeketh to turn away their hearts." Hence, the Prophet, Newel K. Whitney, Sidney Rigdon, and Jesse Gause traveled to Missouri in April 1832. On April 26, meetings commenced at Independence in which personal grievances were settled and important Church business transacted.[2]

Ten days later Joseph, Newel, and Sidney left Independence to return to Ohio by stagecoach. Between Vincennes and New Albany, Indiana, a runaway occurred in which Newel's leg was badly broken, preventing further travel.[3] Con-

sequently, Rigdon proceeded on to Kirtland and Joseph remained with his disabled companion at the Porter tavern in
Greenville, Indiana,[4] until the leg was healed sufficiently to
continue the journey. While detained at Greenville in the
month of June, the Prophet wrote this letter to his wife Emma.

June 6th Greenville Floid Co[5] ~~1823~~
                            1832
Dear Wife
    I would inform you that Brother Martin has arrived here and
braught the pleasing news that our Familys were well when he
left there which Greately Cheared our hearts and revived our
Spirits we thank our hevenly Father for his Goodness ~~uto~~ unto us
and ⟨all of you⟩ ~~you~~ Martin arrived on Satterday the Same week
he left Chagrin[6] haveing a prosperous time we are all in good
health Brother Whitneys leg is gaining and he thin⟨ks⟩ he Shall
be able to to perform his Journy so as to get home ⟨about⟩ ~~as
Soon as~~ the 20th my Situation is a very unpleasent one[7] although
I will endeaver to be Contented the Lord asisting me I have
visited a grove which is Just back of the town almost every day
where I can be Secluded from the eyes of any mortal and there
give vent to all the feelings of my heart in meaditation and prayr I
have Called to mind all the past moments of my life and am left to
morn ~~w~~ ⟨and⟩ Shed tears of sorrow for my folly in Sufering the
adversary of my Soul to have so much power over me as he has
⟨had in times past⟩ but God is mercif⟨ul⟩ [p. 1] and has
fo[r]given my Sins and I r[e]joice that he Sendeth forth the
Comferter unto as many as believe and humbleeth themselves
before him I was grieved to hear that Hiram had ⟨lost⟩ his little
Child[8] I think we Can in Some degree Simpathise with him but
we all must be reconciled to our lots and say the will ⟨of the
Lord⟩ be done [-] Sister Whitney[9] wrote a letter to ~~h[--]~~ ⟨her
husband⟩ which ~~which~~ was very chearing ~~but~~ and being unwell at
that time and filled with much anxiety it would have been very

Cons‹o›ling to me to have received a few lines from you but as
you did not take the trouble I will try to be conte=nted with my
lot knowing that God is my friend in him I shall find comfort I
have given myf life into his hands I am prepared to go at his Call I
desire to be with Christ I Count not my life dear to me only to do
his will I am not pleased to hear that William Mclelin has come
back and disobayed the voice of him who is altogether Lovely for
a woman I am astonished at Sister Emaline yet I cannot belive she
is not a worthy sister[10] I hope She he will ‹find› him true and
kind to her but have no reason to [~] expect it his Conduct merits
the disapprobation of every true follower of Christ [p. 2] but this
is a painful subject I hope you will excuse my warmth of feeling
in mentioning this sub subject and also my inability in convaying
my' ideas in writing I am happy to find that you are still in the
faith of Christ and at Father Smiths I hope you will Comfort
Father and Mother in their trials and Hiram and Jerutia Jerusha
and the rest of the Family tell Sophronia I remember her and
Kalvin in my prayrs my respects to the rest I Should Like [to] See
little Julia and once more take her on my knee and converse with
you on the all the subjects whi=ch concerns us things I cannot is
not prud=ent for me to write I omit all the important things
which could I See you I could make you acquainted with tell
Brother Williams that I and Brother Whitney will arrange the
business of that farm when we Come give my respects to all the
Brotheren Br– Whitney['s] Family tell them he is Chearfull and
patient and a true Brother to me I subscr=ibe myself your
Husband the Lord bless you peace be with [you] so Farewell
untill I return

Joseph Smith Jr— [p. 3]
(martin will come with us)
Greenville Ind
June 7th 18 3/4

Mrs Emma Smith
Kirtland Geauga Co
Ohio

June 6th Greenville Floyd Co [Indiana] 1832

Dear Wife

I would inform you that Brother Martin has arrived here and braught the pleasing news that our Familys wear well when he left there which Greatly Cheared our hearts and revived our Spirits we thank our heavenly Father for his Goodness unto us and all of you, Martin arrived on Satterday the Same week he left Chagrin haveing a prosperous time we are all in good health Brother Whitneys leg is gaining and he thinks he shall be able to perform his Journy so as to get home about the 20th my Situation is a very unpleasent one although I will endeavor to be contented the Lord asisting me I have visited a grove which is just back of the town almost every day where I can be Secluded from the eyes of any mortal and there give vent to all the feelings of my heart in meaditation and prayr I have Called to mind all the past moments of my life and am left to mourn and Shed tears of sorrow for my folly in Sufering the adversary of my Soul to have so much power over me as he has had in times past but God is mercifull

To Emma Smith, June 6, 1832, p. 1. Handwriting of Joseph Smith. See text, p. 238. (Chicago Historical Society.)

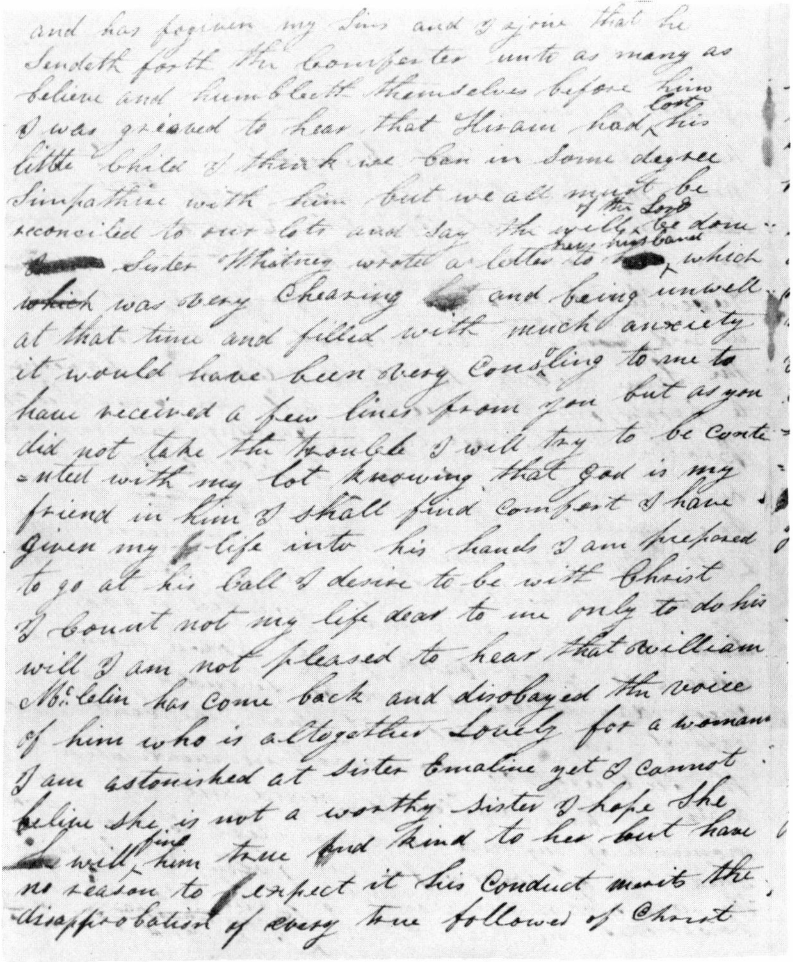
and has forgiven my sins and I rejoice that he
Sendeth forth the Comforter unto as many as
believe and humbleeth themselves before him
I was grieved to hear that Hiram had lost his
little child I think we can in some degree
Simpathise with him but we all must be
reconciled to our lots and say the will of the Lord be done
Sister Whitney wrote a letter to her husband which
~~which~~ was very chearing and being unwell
at that time and filled with much anxiety
it would have been very consoling to me to
have received a few lines from you but as you
did not take the trouble I will try to be conte-
-nted with my lot knowing that God is my
friend in him I shall find comfort I have
given my life into his hands I am prepared
to go at his Call I desire to be with Christ
I count not my life dear to me only to do his
will I am not pleased to hear that William
McLelin has come back and disobayed the voice
of him who is altogether Lovely for a woman
I am astonished at Sister Emaline yet I cannot
believe she is not a worthy sister I hope She
will find him true and kind to her but have
no reason to expect it his Conduct merits the
disapprobation of every true follower of Christ

To Emma Smith, June 6, 1832, p. 2. Handwriting of Joseph Smith. See text, p. 238-39. (Chicago Historical Society.)

but this is a painful subject I hope you will
excuse my warmth of feeling in mentioning this
Subject and also my inability in conveying my ideas
in writing I am happy to find that you are still
in the faith of Christ and at Father Smith I
hope you will comfort Father and Mother in
their trials and Hiram and _____ Jerusha
and the rest of the Family tell Sophronia I
remember her and Kalvin in my prayrs my
respects to the rest I Should Like See little
Julia and once more take her on my knee and
converse with you on the all the Subjects whi—
—ch Concerns us things I Cannot is not prud—
ent for me to write I omit all the important
things which could I see you I could make
you acquainted with tell Brother Willi_____ that
I and Brother Whitney will arrange the
business of that farm when we come give
my respects to all the Brothern Br Whitney
Family I tell them he is Chearfull and
patient and a true Brother to me I Subscr—
—ibe myself your Husband the Lord bless
you peace be with So Farewell untill I return

Joseph Smith Jr

To Emma Smith, June 6, 1832, p. 3. Handwriting of Joseph Smith. See
text, p. 239. (Chicago Historical Society.)

To William W. Phelps,
July 31, 1832

Upon his arrival in Kirtland after the delay at Greenville, Indiana, Joseph Smith learned that all was not well with the Saints he had left in Missouri. In the first place, the spirit of discord that had seemed to dissolve amid expressions of fellowship when he was there had again manifested itself. Furthermore, the settlement of the Saints in Missouri was not proceeding in accordance with the rules set forth for those desirous of migrating to Zion.[1] On July 31 Joseph defined the situation in this letter to William W. Phelps.

Hyram[2] July 31– 1832

Broth[er] William I have received your letter dated 30th June and procede this morning to answer it. I sit down to dictate for Broth[er] Frederick[3] to write but cannot write my feelings, neither can toungue, or language paint them to you. I only can observe that I could wish, that my heart, & feelings thereof might for once be laid upon before [you], as plain as your own nat=ural face is to you by looking in a mirror; verily I say ~~unto you~~ my only hope and confidence is in that God who gave me being in whom there is all power who now is present before me & my heart is naked before his eyes continually he is my comfe[r]ter & he forsaketh me not in the seventh trouble and in the mean time I have learned by sad exper‹i›ance there is no confidence to be placed in in man that the

spirit of man is as cold as the northern blast and had I not
considered the great care and multitude of busi=ness which is
crowding upon your mind I could not have excused the cold and
indifferent manner in which your letter is writen, true you have
expressed fellowship, but the spirit which I ~~possess~~ enjoy, the
feeling of my soul enquires does this letter give me the important
information which I stood in need of at the present critical moment
from your hand concerning yourself your family & business & the
faith & fellowship & prosperity of the breth=ren in Zion &c let
your own heart and the integrity of your own soul answer this
question & excuse the warmth of feeling of your unworthy yet
affectionate brother in the Lord travling through affliction and
great tribulation, you informed me that you wrote a few lines to
bear up our strength in the glorious labour wherewith our saviour
hath been pleased to call us, I rejoice exceedingly for the little
strength & information God has been plesed to give me through
your letter— viz—to hear that our brethren from this place &
Nelson have arived safe in Zion⁴ and as I trust without accident this
is the mercy of our God, but in the disch=arge ‹of my Duty,› must
inform you that they left here under this dis=pleasure of heaven for
several reasons now what I write I write without sparing any (or the
feeling of any) knowing that God will bear me up in what I write, I
will give you some of the rea=sons, firstly making a mock of the
profession of faith in the commandments by proceding contrary
thereto in not complying [p. 1] with the requirements of them in
not obtaining reccommends &c⁵ seccondly, that the church should
procede to receive Wm McLelin into there fellowship &
communion on any other conditions, then the filling [of] his
mission to the South countries according to the commandment of
Jesus Christ,⁶ I cite your minds to this saying he that loveth Father
or Mother wife & children more than me is not worthy of me thus
saith the Lord Thirdly the unorganized & confused state in leaving
here, and the evil surmisings which were among them & neglect of
duty &c more then this I do not wish to mention, now therefore
the buffitings of the advesary be upon all those ‹among you› who
are eniquitous persons and rebelious, I would inform them they do

not have my right hand of fellowship, but I will leave this subject
for will not my God and your God do right, I return to your let=ter
you informed me slightly that you heard of the accident to broth[er]
Whitney at Greenvill Id [Indiana] A question how did you hear,
did any of you receive letters writen by any of us informing you of
the crit=ical situation we were placed in, if so how did you treat
them if not so have you writen to us to give us that information
which would be calculated to releave the mind of its painful
anxciety concerning you, whether that fellowship and brotherly
love con=tinued among you towards us which you professed when
we left you, it is true we received a letter from brother John Carl
[Corrill] by the hand of Broth[er] [Sidney] Gilbert after we arived
home from Indiana who had arived here before us, but what did it
contain, it gave us this inteligence, that the Devel had been to
work with all his inventive immagination to reward us for our toils
in travling from this country to Zion amidst a crooked & perverse
generation leaving our familys in affliction amidst of death upon
the mercy of mobs[7] & of brethren who you know sometimes are
found to be u[n]stable unbeleiving, unmerciful & unkind, and in
this trying situation to keep in the commandment of God we took
our lives in our hands and traveled through evry combination of
wickedness to your country for your salvation & for our travail &
our toils, suffering & privations as I said before [p. 2] we learned by
Broth[er] Johns letter that the devel had set to work to reward us by
stirring up your hearts (I mean those who were engaged in this
wickedness) by raking up evry fault, which those eyes that are filled
with beams could see in looking for motes in the eyes of those who
are laboring with tender and <prayerful> hearts continually for
there salvation, and not being content with bringing up those
things which had been settled & forgiven & which they dare not
bring to our faces but many with which we were charged with were
absolutely false & could not come from any other sours [source]
than the father of all lies & this is the thanks & the reward the
ad=visary saught to reward us by the instrumentality of those who
should have been our staff & after our detention on the road I often
times wandered alone in the lonely places seeking consolation of

him who is ‹alone› able to console me, while my my beloved
Brother Whitney (who is without gile) poured out his soul with
much weeping upon his pillow for you or for Zion while I in ‹the›
lonely places communed with him who is altogether lovely
witnessed your case & viewed the conspiricy with much grief and
learned the displeasure of heaven and veewed the frowns of the
heavenly hosts upon Zion & upon all the earth, and my Brethren I
would inform you that I do not fellowship the letter which was
writen to me by Bro John & neither the spirit thereof, I do not
plead guilty of the charges made against me in that letter. I have
not given occasion of offence to the brethren or sisters in Zion,
neither of Jealous=y, or evel surmisings. I have ever been filled
with the greatest anxiety for them, & have taken the greatest
intrest for there welfare. I am a lover of the cause of Christ and of
virtue chastity and an upright steady course of conduct & a holy
walk, I dispise a hypocrite or a covenant breaker, I judge them not,
God shall Judge them according to there works, I am a lover even
of mine enimies for an enimy seeketh to destroy openly, I can pray
for those who dispitefully use and persicute me, but for all I can not
hope, and now I conjure ~~you~~ and exhort mine accusers and the
hypocrite in Zion in the love of Christ [p. 3] yea in the name of
Jesus of Nazreth to remember the covenant which they have made
with God, and to me & repent of their iniquities and give
satisfaction to the in=nocent whom they have injured I appeal to
your conciences, and if appealing to your conciences, by all the ties
which bind man to man which are st[r]onger than death will not
open your eyes & let you see the state & standing which you are in
and bring you to repentance I then appeal to a higher court even
the court of heaven the tribunal of the great God & there I & my
Brethren (I mean Broth[ers] Sidney & Newel) will meet ~~them~~ you
to be weighed in the ballance and there the innocent shall not
suffer and the guilty go unpunished for the Lord God Almighty will
do right I bear you record that my self Bro Sidney & Newel as far as
any thing that I know have ever maintained the purest desires for
your welfare and do still our object in going to Zion was altogether
to keep the com=mandment of ~~God~~ the most high, when Bro

Sidney learned the feelings of the Brethren in whom he had placed
so much confidence for whom he had endured so much fateague &
suffering & whom he loved with so much love his heart was grieved
his spirits failed & for a moment he became frantick & the advisary
taking the advantage, he spake unadvisedly with his lips after
receiving a severe chastisement resigned his commision and
became a private member in the church, but has since repented
like Peter of old and after a little suffering by the buffiting of ~~the~~
Satan has been restored to his high standing in the church of God,
now this is a warning to all to whom this knowledge may come,
and he that thinks he stands, let him take heed least he fall, tell
Bro Edward [Partridge] it is very dangerous for men who have
received the light he has received to be a seek=ing a ‹after› sign,
for there shall no sign be given for a sign except as it was in the
days of Lot. God sent angels to gather him & his family out of
Sodom while the wicked were distroyed by a devou=ring fire behold
this is an exsample; but I must return to your letter again you
complain that there have already [p. 4] to[o] many deciples arived
there for the means, tell brother Edward to remember Ananias &
Sophria, remember also that your own wick=edness hedge up your
own ways, you suffer your children; your ignorant & unstable
Sisters & weak members who are acquainted with your evil hearts
of unbelief to write wicked and discouraging letters to there
reletives who have a zeal but ‹not› according to knowledge and
prophecy falsly which excites many to believe that you are put=ting
up the Indians to slay the Gentiles which exposes the lives of the
Saints evry where you observe that God has been merciful, very
true then never forget to revere his holy name for ever, that
circum=stances are as well with you as they are, you requested me
to pre=serve all the origeonal copies of the commandments, my
reasons for not sending the remainder, & also the Vision[8] I think
will give you satisfaction towards me I have much care and
tribulation calculated to weigh down and distroy the mind and in
times past they have been snatched from under my hand as soon as
given I will send them to you as soon as possable, but I will exhort
you to be careful not to alter the sense of any of them for he that

adds or diminishes to the prop[h]ecies must come under the condemnation writen therein, you mention concerning the translation[9] I would inform you that they will not go from under my hand during my natural life for correction, revisal or printing and the will of [the] Lord be done therefore you need not expect them this fall, Brother Frederick is employed to be a scribe for me of the Lord—we have finished the translation of the New testament great and ~~marvilous~~ glorious things are revealed, we are making rapid strides in the old book and in the strength of God we can do all things according to his will the rage of the enemy is abating in this regeon of the country and while God is rem[em]bering mercy unto us and making us mighty to the pulling down the strong hold of Satan, having sent down the Angel of God to trouble the waters that a few more sick folk may be healed he is streaching forth his hand in awful [p. 5] Judgment upon all the face of the earth, we have infor=mation which may be relyed upon that the cholera[10] is cutting down its hundreds in the city of New York p[e]r day also is raging in Boston Charleston Rochiste[r] Albany & Buffalo and in all the large citys in the eastern country, we have Just received a letter from sister Elmira Scoba[11] who is now at Detroit to visit her friends she states that the cholera is raging in that city to an alarming degree,[12] hundreds of families are a fleeing to the country and the country people have be=come alarmed and torn up the bridges and stopped all communication and even shot peoples horses down under them who attempt to cross the river or any express two steam boats loaded with troops for the Indian expedition while going up [the] Detroit river the cholera made its attact upon the soldiers about fifty died the rest disbanded (about six hundred in number) and the last account we have of them they could find no quarters among the inhabitants and were a dying in the sheds and fields and nobody to bury them while between us and you the Indians are a spreading death and devestation wherever they go[13] no force has as yet been brought sufficient to stand before them frequent cases of the cholera occures on steem boats and ⟨other⟩ water crafts on the Lakes the dysentary and the Cholera Morbus are the prevailing deseases as far as our infor=mation

extends and is so malignant that it baffles the skill of the most
eminent Phisicians we have news from our brethren who have gone
to the east God is with them pul=ling down the strong holds of
Satan two brethren are here from ~~the east~~ Newhampshire & one
from Vermont who are Elders and worthy young men who were
brought in by the hands of Bros. Lyman Johnson & Orison Pratt
who are like Peter & John building up the cause of God wherever
they go and healing the sick they have baptized better then sixty
since they left here[14] we also here from many others whose good
success in gaining converts to the redeemers [p. 6] cause is a proof
of there faithfulness in the high calling I would exhort Bros Oliver
& John to be ware of seducing spirits and stand firm in the liberty
wherein they have been set free and never be weary in well doing
which is also my exhortation to all those in Zion that love the
appear=ing of our Lord and saviour Jesus Christ. I went to Kirtland
last week and held a meeting on the Lord[s] day and found the
brethren strong in the faith and enjoying the sweet influence of the
holy spirit cheering there hearts and enlarging there understandings
and binding there souls to gethe[r] that nothing but death can
break asunder we found the brethren in the injoyment of tolerable
health except Sister Elliott whom the Doctors ‹(two of them)› had
given over & Bro Sidney[s] seccond daughte[r] but were restored ~~to
health~~ by the prayer of faith, Father Johnsons family & mine are
enjoying tolerable health inso much we cannot com=plain. Sister
Sarah Jackson came to live with us yesterday you have the prayers
of us all daily and I think I can say almost hourly and in this day of
calamity the saints & sinner[s] hearts are almost failing them for
fear and are crying to whom shall we go or whethe[r] shall we flee O
my God spare Zion that it may be a place of Reffuge and of safety. I
have a partickular request to make of Bro John Whitmer that is as
soon as you receive this letter for him to assertain the exact
num=ber of Deciples that have arived in Zion & how many have
received there inheritence and the stat[e] and standing of each
branch o[f] the church and of this inteligence communicate to us as
soon as it can be done by letter such as is not wisdom to publish in
the paper, I exhort Bro John also to remember the commandment

to him to keep a history of the church & the gathering and be sure to shew him self approoved whereunto he hath been called

This is a copy of a letter writen to Broth[er] Wm Phelps, July 31—1832 from Hyram except a few words on the wrappe[r] by way of exhortation complementary &c

Joseph Smith Jr.

Copy of a letter writen to Broth[er]
William Phelps Zion
Editor of the Evening & Morning Star

To Emma Smith,
October 13, 1832

As partners in a prosperous Kirtland, Ohio, mercantile firm, Newel K. Whitney and Sidney Gilbert played a key role in the economic development of Mormon communities in Ohio and Missouri. After their baptism in the fall of 1830, these men gave nearly all their time and means to the cause of the Church.

Traveling to Independence, Missouri, with Joseph Smith in 1831, Gilbert heard the revelation designating Jackson County as the place for the city of Zion and calling him to remain there and establish a store, profits from which would be used to assist those migrating there.[1]

In March 1832 a business partnership known as the United Order, or United Firm, was established by revelation in Kirtland, Ohio. The purpose of the organization was to consolidate business activity for the benefit of the Church.[2] When Joseph Smith, Newel Whitney, Jesse Gause, and Sidney Rigdon, members of the Firm, traveled to Missouri in April 1832, one item of business transacted was to consolidate the mercantile activities of the Church in Missouri and Ohio under the United Firm. The Missouri branch was to be called Gilbert, Whitney and Company. The Ohio branch was to be called Newel K. Whitney and Company. Gilbert and Whitney were to be agents of the Firm. During the meetings held by the Prophet in Missouri, Whitney was directed to negotiate a $15,000 loan to assure the stability of the Firm. He was also called by revelation to travel among the branches of the Church to solicit funds for the poor and to warn the people in certain eastern cities of the desolation that would come upon those who rejected the gospel.

To fill these assignments, Whitney headed east in the fall of 1832 accompanied by Joseph Smith.[3] Summarizing his travels, he later wrote: "My leg was not perfectly well, but I proceeded with Joseph . . . to New York, Providence and Boston, and through New England. We visited Bishop [Benjamin T.] Onderdonk of the Episcopal Church of the United States while at N. York,[4] and returned back to Kirtland. This journey was taken to fulfill the revelation."[5]

While Whitney was engaged in New York City purchasing goods for the mercantile business, the two men lodged at the Pearl Street House on Manhattan Island.[6] From his room there on October 13, Joseph wrote the following letter to Emma.

Oct 13 1832
P Pearl Street House N Y

My Dear Wife
   This day I have been walking through the most splended part of the City of n New Y–[7] the buildings are truly great and wonderful to the astonishing ‹of› to eve[r]y beholder and the lan=guage of my heart is like this can the gre=at God of all the Earth maker of all thing[s] magnificent and splendid be displeased with man for all these great inventions saught out by them my answer is no it can not be seeing these works are are calculated to mak[e] men comfortable wise and happy therefore not for the works can the Lord be displeased only aganst man is the anger of the Lord Kindled because they Give him not the Glory therefore their iniquities shall ‹be› visited upon their heads and their works shall

be burned up with unquenchable fire the inequity of the people is
pri=nted in every countinance and nothing but the dress of the
people makes them look fair and butiful all is deformity their is
something in every countinance that is disagreable with few
exceptions Oh how long Oh Lord Shall this order of things exist
and darkness cover the Earth and gross darkness cover the people
after beholding all that I had any desire to behold I returned to
my room to meditate and calm my mind and behold the thaughts
of home of Emma and Julia[8] rushes upon my mind like a flood and
I could wish for [p. 1] [a] moment to be with them my breast is
filld with all the feelings and tenderness of a parent and a
Husband and could I be with you I would tell you many things
yet when I ref=lect upon this great city like Ninevah not
desearning their right hand from their left yea more then two
hundred <thousand> souls my bow=els is filled with compasion
towards them and I am determined to lift up my voice in this City
and leave the Event with God who holdeth all things in his hands
and will not suffer an hair of our heads unnoticed to fall to the
ground there is but few Cases of the cholra in this City[9] now and
if you should see the people you would not ~~that~~ know that they
~~people~~ had ever heard of the <cholra> I hope you will excuse me
for writting this letter so soon after w[r]iting for I feel as if I
wanted to <~~say~~> ~~you~~ say something to you to com=fort you in
your beculier triel and presant affliction[10] I hope God will give
you strength that you may not faint I pray God to soften the
hearts of those arou[n]d you to be kind to you and take <the>
burdon of[f] your shoulders as much as posable and not afflict you
I feel for you for I know you[r] state and that others do not but
you must cumfort yourself knowing that God is your friend in
heaven and that you hav[e] one true and living friend on Earth
your Husband

Joseph Smith Jr [p. 2]

PS while Brother Whitney [is] Selecting goods I have
nothing to [do] but to sit in my room and pray for him that he

may have strength to indure his labours for truly it is [a] tedious
Job to stand on the feet all day to select goods its wants good
Judgement and a long acquantence with goods to git good ones
and a man must be his own Judge for no one will Judge for him
and it is much pepleccity [perplexity] of mind I prefer reading and
praying and holding comuneion with the holy spirit and writing to
‹you› then walking the streets and beholding the distraction of
man I have ‹had› some conversation with few which gave
satisfaction and one very butiful young gentleman from Jersy
whose countinance was very sollam he came and set by my side
and began to converce with me about the Cholra and I learned he
had been seased with it and came very near die[i]ng with it he said
the Lord had spared him for some wise pu[r]pose I took advantage
of this and opened a long discours with him he received my
teaching ~~with~~ appearan[t]ly with much pleasure and becam[e]
very strongly attacth to me we talkd till late at nig=ht and
concluded to omit ‹conversation› till the next day but having
some business to do he was detai=ned untill the boat was ready to
go out and must leave he came to me and bid me Farewell ‹and we
parted› with much reluctance Brother Whitney is received with
great kindness by all his old acquaintance[s] he is faithful in prayr
and fervant in spirit and ~~he~~ we take great comfort together there
is about one hundred boarders and sometimes more in this house
every ‹day› from one to two from all parts of the world I think
you would hav[e] laughed right harty if you could [have] been
whe[r]=e you could see the waiters to day noon [as they] waited
on the table both Black and white and molato runing bowing and
maneuvering but I must conclude I remain your affectionate
Husband until Death

Joseph Smith Junior [p. 3]

Emma Smith
Kirtland Geauga Co
Ohio

To Emma Smith, October 13, 1832, p. 1. Handwriting of Joseph Smith. See text, pp. 252-53. (RLDS Church Archives.)

moment to be with them my breast is filled
with all the feelings and tenderness of a parent
and a Husband and could I be with you I
would tell you many things yet when I reflect
upon this great City like Ninevah not
descerning their right hand from their left
yea more then two hundred thousand souls my bowels is filled with compasion towards them
and I am determined to lift up my voice
in this City and leave the event with God
who holdeth all things in his hands and will
not suffer an hair of our heads unnoticed
to fall to the ground there is but few Cases
of the Cholra in this City now and if you
should see the people you would not know that
know that they had ever heard of the cholra
I hope you will excuse me for writing
this letter so soon after writing for I feel
as if I wanted to say something to you to comfort you in your peculier trial and present
affliction I hope God will give you strength
that you may not faint I pray God to soften
the hearts of those around you to be kind
to you and take the burden of your shoulders
as much as posable and not afflict you
I feel for you for I know your state and
that others do not but you must comfort
yourself knowing that God is your friend
in heaven and that you have one true and
living friend on Earth your Husband
                                    Joseph Smith Jr

To Emma Smith, October 13, 1832, p. 2. Handwriting of Joseph Smith.
See text, p. 253. (RLDS Church Archives.)

P. S. while Brother Whitney is selecting goods I have
nothing to do but to set in my room and pray for him that
he may have strength to endure his labours for truly
it is tedious job to stand on the feet all day to select
goods its wants good judgment and a long acquaintance
with goods to get good ones and a great variety also
his own judge for no my will judge for him and
it is much perplexity of mind I prefer reading and
praying and holding communion with the holy Spirit
and writing to you than walking the streets and beholding
the distraction of man I have seen some conversation with
few which gave me satisfaction and one very butiful
young gentleman from Jersey whose countinance was
very sollam he came and set by my side and began to
converse with me about the cholera and I learned he
had been seased with it and came very near dying
with it he said the Lord had spared him for some
wise purpose I took advantage of this and opened a
long discours with him he received my teaching
liberally with much pleasure and became very
strongly attached to me we talked till late at nig[ht]
and I concluded to invite till the next day
but having some business to go out and meet
and untill the boat was ready to go and we part[ed]
he came to me and bid me farewell with
much reluctance Brother Whitney by all his acquaintance he
is faithful in prayer and pursant in spirit
and so we take great comfort together there
is about one hundred boarders and sometimes more
in this house every day from one to two from
all parts of the world I think you would have
laughed right harty if you could have [been present]
if you could see the waiters to day noon wai[ting]
on the table both Black and white and mulato
runing boring and maneuvering but I must
conclude I remain Yours affectionate Husband
untill Death Joseph Smith Junior

To Emma Smith, October 13, 1832, p. 3. Handwriting of Joseph Smith.
See text, pp. 253-54. (RLDS Church Archives.)

To William W. Phelps,
November 27, 1832,
January 11, 1833

The 1831 revelations that designated Jackson County, Missouri, as a gathering place of the Saints and location for the city of Zion also directed Edward Partridge, the recently appointed bishop, to administer the law of consecration and oversee the settlement of the Saints in that land. They also gave specific instructions for those who planned to go there. The Saints were advised to avoid disorder and haste in migrating, to purchase the land they settled on so that outsiders "may not be stirred up unto anger,"[1] to bring a certificate of recommendation from their former presiding Church officer, and to consecrate their property for the assistance of the poor.[2] The Church newspaper in Missouri admonished prospective inhabitants of Zion to "prepare temporally and spiritually . . . settle all . . . concerns with the world, and owe no man," to "overcome the world" and be ready, when they arrived at the place of gathering, "to consecrate all to the Lord," otherwise they could not hold communion with their brethren nor "expect an inheritance according to the regulations and order of the church."[3]

As the influx of Mormons to Jackson County increased, the rules governing the migration were often ignored. One witness noted that the gathering fostered an irrational enthusiasm: "The church got crazy to go up to Zion. . . . The rich were afraid to send up their money to purchase lands, and the poor crowded up in numbers, without having any places provided, contrary to the advice of the bishop and others, until the old citizens began to be highly displeased."[4] At one point, a conference of high priests lamented, "We feel more like weeping over Zion than we do like rejoicing over her."[5]

In the midst of these developments, Joseph Smith wrote to William W. Phelps, the Church newspaper editor in Jackson County on November 27, 1832, and again on January 11, 1833.

Kirtland Nov 27th 1832

Brother Wm Phelps I say brother because I feel so from the heart and altho it is not long since I wrote a letter unto you yet I feel as tho you would excuse me for writing this as I have many things which I wish to communicate some things which I will mention in this letter which are laying ‹great› with weight upon my mind I inform you I am well and family God grant that you may enjoy the same and yours and all the brethren and sisters who remember to enquire afte[r] the commandments of the Lord and the welfare of Zion and such a being as me and while I dictate this letter I fancy to myself that you are saying or thinking something simmiler to these words my God great and mighty art thou therefore shew unto thy servant what shall becom[e] of all these who are assaying to come up unto Zion in order to keep the commandments of God and yet rec[e]ive not there inher[i]tance by consecration by order or deed from the bishop the man that God has appointed in a legal way agreeable to the law given to organize and regulate the church and all the affairs of the same; Bro Wm in the love of God having the most implicit confidence in you as a man of God having obtained this confidence by a vision of heaven therefore I will procede to unfold to you some of the feelings of my heart and procede to answer the questions firstly, it is the duty of the lord[s] clerk whom he has appointed to keep a hystory and a general church receord of all things that transpire in Zion and of all

those who consecrate properties and receive inhertances legally
from the bishop and also there manner of life and the faith and
works and also of all the apostates who apostatize after receiving
ther inher[i]tances ~~in that day shall not find an inheritance among
the saints of the~~ [p. 1a] ~~most high therefore it shall be done unto
them as unto the Children of the priest as you will find recorded in
the second chapter and sixty first and second verses of Ezra now
Brother william if what I have said is true how careful then had
men aught to be what they do in the last days lest they think they
stand should fall because they keep not the ‹Lo[r]d[s]›
commandments whilest you who obey who do the will of the lord
and keep his commandments have need to rejoice with unspeakabl
Joy for such shall be exalted very high and shall be lifted up in
triumph above all the kingdoms of the world but I must drop this
subject at the begining, O Lord when will the time come when Bro
Wm thy servant and myself behold the day that we may stand
together and gaze upon eternal wisdom engraven upon the heavens
while the magesty of our God holdeth up the dark curtain until we
may read the record of eternity to the fulness of our immortal souls,
O Lord God deliver us in thy due time from the little narrow prison
almost as it were total darkness of paper pen and Ink and a crooked
broken scattered and imperfect Language, I would inform~~ seccondly
it is conterary to the will and commandment of God that those
who receive not their inheritance by consecration agreeable to his
law which he has given that he may tithe his people to prepare
them against the day of vengence and burning should have there
names enrolled with the people of God, neithe[r] is the[ir]
geneology to be kept or to be had where it may be found on any of
the reccords or hystory of the church there names shall not be
found neithe[r] the names of their fathers or the names of the[ir]
chil=dren writen in the book of the Law of God saith [p. 2] the
**Lord of hosts yea thus saith the still small voice which whispereth
through and pierceth all things and often times it maketh my
bones to quake while it maketh manifest saying and it shall come
to pass that I the Lord God will send one mighty and strong
holding the scepter of power in his hand clothed with light for a**

covering whose mouth shall ~~utt~~ utter words Eternal words while
his bowels shall be a fou=ntain of truth to set in order the house
of God and to ar=ange by lot the inheritance of the saints whose
names are found and the names of their fathers and of their
chi=ldren enroled in the Book of the Law of God while tha=t man
who was called of God and appointed that puteth forth his hand
to steady the ark of God shall fall by the shaft of death like as a
tree that is smitten by the vivid shaft of lightning and all they who
are not found writen in the book of remmemberance shall find
none inheritence in that day but they shall be cut assunder and
their por=tion shall be appointed them among unbelievers where
is wailing and gnashing of teeth these things I say not of myself
therefore as the Lord speaketh he will also fu=lfill and they who
are of the high Priesthood whose names are not found writen in
the book of the Law or that are found to have appostitised or to
have been cut off out of the church as well as the lesser
Priesthood or the mem=bers in that day shall not find an
inheritence among the saints of the most high therefore it shall be
done unto them as unto the children of the Priest as you will find
recorded in the second chapter and sixty first and second verses of
Ezra now Broth– William if what I ~~say~~ have said is true how
careful then had men aught to be what they do in the last days lest
they are cut ~~as=sunder~~ short of their expectations and they that
think [they] stand should fall because they keep not the Lords
commandments whilst you who do the will of the Lord and keep
his comman=dments have need to rejoice with unspeakable Joy
for such shall be exalted very high and shall be lifted up in ~~triu~~ [p.
3] triumph above all the kingdoms of this world but I must drop
this subject at the begining Oh Lord when will the time come
when Brothe[r] William thy Servent and myself ~~sha~~ behold the
day that we may stand together and gase upon Eternal wisdom
engraven upon the hevens while the mages=ty of our God holdeth
up the dark curtain <until> we may read the round of Eternity to
the fullness and satisfaction of our immortal souls Oh Lord God
deliver us in thy due time from the little narrow prison almost as

it were totel darkness of paper pen and ink and a crooked
bro=ken scattered and imperfect language I would inform you
that I have obtained ten subscribers for the Star and received pay
their names and place of residence [are] as follows, John
McMahhan, James McMahhan, James White, William Brown,
Henry Kingery, Micayer Dillions, Abraham Kingery, John A
Fisher, David Houghs, Thomas Singers, the papers and and all to
be sent to Guyndotte ~~the paper are all to be sent to~~ Post office
Verginea except David Houghs his is to be sent to Wayne
‹County› ~~Township~~ Worster ~~County~~ ‹Township› Ohio,[6]
Vienna Jaqis[7] has not r[e]ceived her Papers pleas inform her
Sister ‹Hariet› that Shee is well and give my respects to her tell
her that Mrs Angels Brother came after her and the child soon
after she went from here all he wanted ~~wanted~~ was the child No
more ‹my› love for all the Brotheren yours in bonds Amen

                          Joseph Smith Jr–

     William W Phelps

     PS send the evening and morning star to Brothe[r] Joseph
Wakefield Watertown Jeffers[on] County New York all to be from
first No.

                          Joseph [p. 4]

Kirtland January 11– 1833

~~Bro~~ Brother William
     I Send you the Olieve leaf[1] which we have plucked from the tree
of Paradise, the Lords message of peace to us, for though our Brethren
in Zion, indulge in feelings towards us, which are not according to
the requirements of the new covenant yet we have the satisfaction
of knowing that the Lord approves of us & has accepted us, &
established his name in kirtland [p. 18] for the salvation of the
nations, for the Lord will have a place from whence his word will

go forth in these last days in purity, for if Zion, will not purify
herself so as to be approved of in all things in his sight he will seek
another people for his work will go on untill Isreal is gathered
& they who will not hear his voice must expect to feel his wrath,
Let me say unto you, seek to purefy yourselves, & also all the
inhabitants of Zion lest the Lords anger be kindled to fierceness,
repent, repent, is the voice of God, to Zion, & yet strange as it may
appear, yet it is true mankind will presist in self Justification until
all their eniquity is exposed & their character past being redeemed,
& that which is treasured up in their hearts be exposed to the gaze
of mankind, I say to you—(& what I say to you, I say to all) hear
the ‹warning› voice of God lest Zion fall, & the Lord swear in his
wrath the inhabitants of Zion shall not enter into my rest, The
Brethren in Kirtland pray for you unceasingly, for know=ing the
terrors of the Lord, they greatly fear for you; you will see that the
Lord commanded us in Kirtland to build an house of God, &
establish a school for the Prophets, this is the word of the Lord to
us, & we must—yea the Lord helping us we will obey, as on
conditions of our obedience, he has promised ‹us› great things, yea
‹even› a visit from the heavens to honor us with his own presence,
we greatly fear before the Lord lest we should fail of this great
honor which our master proposes to confer on us, we are seeking
for humility & great faith lest we be ashamed in his presence, our
hearts are greatly greaved at the spirit which is breathed both in
your letter & that of Bro G——s the very spirit which is wasting
the strength of Zion like a pestalence, and if it is not detected &
driven from you it will ripen Zion for the threatened Judgments of
God, remember God sees the secret springs of human action, &
knows the hearts of all living, Br suffer us to speak plainly for God
has respect to the feelings of his saints & he will not let them be
tantalized with impunity. tell Br G–t that low insinuations God
hates, but he rejoices in an honest heart and knows better who is
guilty than he does, we send him this worning voice & let him fear
greatly for himself lest a worse thing overtake him, all we can say
by way of conclusion is, if the fountain of our tears are not dried up

we will ‹still› weep for Zion, this from your brother who trembles
greatly for Zion,–and for the wrath of heaven which awaits her if
she repent not,— P.S. I am not in the habit of crying peace, when
there is no peace, and knowing the th[r]eatened Judgments of God.
I say Wo, unto them who are at ease [p. 19] in zion fearfulness will
speedily lay hold of the hypocrite, I did not expect that you had
lost commandments, but thought from your letters you had
neglected to read them, otherwise you would not have writen as
you did, it is in vain to try to hide a bad spirit from the eyes of them
who are spiritual for it will shewe itself in speaking & in writing as
well as all our other conduct, it is also useless to mak[e] great
pretentions when the heart is not right before God, for God looks
at the heart, and where the heart is not right the Lord will expose it
to the view of his faithful saints, we wish you to render the Star as
interesting as possable by setting forth the rise progress and faith of
the church, as well as the doctrine for if you donnot render it more
interesting than at present it will fall, and the church suffer a great
Loss thereby — — — —

Joseph Smith Jr

To William W. Phelps, November 27, 1832, Joseph Smith Letterbook 1, p. 1a. Handwriting of Frederick G. Williams. See text, pp. 259-60. (LDS Church Archives.)

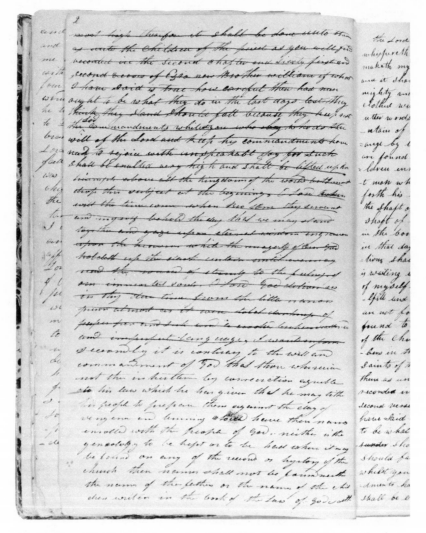

To William W. Phelps, November 27, 1832, Joseph Smith Letterbook 1, p. 2. Handwriting of Frederick G. Williams. See text, p. 260. (LDS Church Archives.)

the Lord of host yea thus saith the still small voice which
whispereth through and pierceth all things and often times it
maketh my bones to quake while it maketh manifest saying
and it shall come to pass that I the Lord God will send one
mighty and strong holding the scepter of power in his hand
clothed with light for a covering whose mouth shall
utter words Eternal words while his bowels shall be a foun
tain of truth to set in order the house of God and to ar
range by lot the inheritance of the Saints whose names
are found and the names of their fathers and of their chil
dren enroled in the Book of the Law of God while tha
t man who was called of God and appointed that putteth
forth his hand to steady the ark of God shall fall by
the shaft of death like as a tree that is smitten by the vivid
shaft of lightning and all they who are not found writ[ten]
in the book of remembrance shall find none inheritance
in that day but they shall be cut assunder and their por
tions shall be appointed them among unbelievers where
is wailing and gnashing of teeth these things I say not
of myself therefore as the Lord speaketh he will also fu
lfill and they who are of the high Priesthood whose names
are not found written in the book of the Law or that are
found to have apostatized or to have been cut off out
of the Chhrch as well as the lesser Priesthood or the mem
bers in that day shall not find an inheritance among the
Saints of the most high therefore it shall be done unto
them as unto the children of the Priest as you will find
recorded in the Second Chapter and sixty first and
second verses of Ezra now Broth William if what I say
have said is true how careful then had men aught
to be what they do in the last days lest they are cut as
sunder short of their expectations and they that think they stand
should fall because they keep not the Lords commandments
whilst you who do the will of the Lord and keep his comman
dments have need to rejoice with unspeakable joy for such
shall be exalted very high and shall be lifted up in tri

To William W. Phelps, November 27, 1832, Joseph Smith Letterbook 1, p. 4. Handwriting of Joseph Smith and Frederick G. Williams. See text, pp. 261-62. (LDS Church Archives.)

To Mr. Editor, January 4, 1833

As the year 1833 dawned, conditions in the world seemed ominous to the Saints: "Appearances of troubles among the nations became more visible this season than they had previously been since the Church began her journey out of the wilderness. The ravages of the cholera were frightful in almost all the large cities on the globe. The plague broke out in India, while the United States, amid all her pomp and greatness, was threatened with immediate dissolution. The people of South Carolina, in convention assembled (in November), passed ordinances, declaring their state a free and independent nation; and appointed Thursday, the 31st day of January, 1833, as a day of humiliation and prayer, to implore Almighty God to vouchsafe His blessings, and restore liberty and happiness within their borders. President Jackson issued his proclamation against this rebellion, called out a force sufficient to quell it, and implored the blessings of God to assist the nation to extricate itself from the horrors of the approaching and solemn crisis."[1]

On Christmas Day 1832, Joseph Smith had conveyed a revelation and prophecy to the Church "concerning wars that will shortly come to pass, beginning at the rebellion of South Carolina which will eventually terminate in the death and misery of many souls."[2] Less than two weeks later, he sent the following letter to N. C. Saxton, the editor of a Rochester,

New York, newspaper, written, as he subsequently indicated,
"by the commandment of God."

Kirtland 4th Jany. 1833–

Mr. Editor Sir,
    Considering the Liberal prisciples upon which your interesting
and valuable paper is published and myself being a subscriber and
feeling a deep intrist in the cause of Zion and in the happiness of
my brethren of mankind I cheerfully take up my pen to contribute
my mite at this every [very] interesting and important period
    For some length of time I have been carfully viewing the state
of things as now appear throug[h]out our christian Land and have
looked at it with feelings of the most painful anxiety while upon
the one hand beholding the manifeste withdrawal of Gods holy
Spirit and the vail of stupidity which seems to be drawn over the
hearts of the people and upon the other hand beholding the
Judgments of God that have swept and are still sweeping hundreds
and thousands of our race (and I fear unprepared) down to the
shades of death with this solemn and alarming fact before me I am
led to exclaim ["]O that my head were waters and mine ey[e]s a
fountain of tears that I might weep day and night &c." I think that
it is high time for a christian world to awake out of sleep and cry
mightely to that God day and night whose anger we have Justly
incured. Are not these things a sufficient stimulant to arouse the
faculties and call forth the energies of evry man woman and child
that poseses feeling of sympathy for his fellow[s] or that is in any
degree endeared to the buding cause of our glorious Lord; I leave an
inteligent community to answer this important question with a
confession that this is what has caused me to overlook my own
inability and expose my weakness to a learned world but trusting in
that God who has said these things are hid from the wise and
prudent and reve[a]led unto babes I step forth into the field to tell
you what the Lord is doing and what you must do to enjoy the

smiles of your saviour in these last day[s]—The time has at last
~~come~~ arived when the God of Abraham of Isaac and of Jacob has
set his hand again the seccond time to recover the remnants of his
people which have [p. 14] been left from Assyria, and from Egypt
and from Pathros &.c. and from the Islands of the sea and with
them to bring in the fulness of the Gentiles and establish that
covenant with them which was promised when their sins should be
taken away. See Romans 11. 25, 26, & 27 and also Jeremiah 31.
31, 32, & 33, This covenant has never been established with the
house of Isreal nor with the house of Judah for it requires two
parties to make a covenant and those two parties must be agreed or
no covenant can be made. Christ in the days of his flesh proposed
to make a covenant with them but they rejected him and his
proposals and in consequence thereof they were broken off and no
covenant was made with them at that time but their unbelief has
not rendered the promise of God of none effect; no, for there was
another day limited in David which was the day of his power and
then his people *Isreal,* should be a willing people and he would
write his laws in their hearts and print them in their thoughts their
sins and their eniquities he would remember no more, Thus after
this chosen family had rejected Christ and his proposals the heralds
of salvation said to them "lo we turn ‹un›to the gentiles," and the
gentiles received the covenant and were grafted in from whence
the chosen family were broken off but the Gentiles have not
continued in the goodness of God but have departed from the faith
that was once delivered to the saints and have broken the
~~everlasting~~ covenant in which their fathers were established see
Isaiah 24th 5th and have become high minded and have not feared
therefore but few of them will be gathered with the *chosen family*
Has not the pride highmindedness and unbelief of the Gentiles
provoked the holy one of Israel to withdraw his holy spirit from
them and send forth his Judgments to scourge them for their
wick=edness; this is certianly the case, Christ said to his deciples
Mark 16, 17 & 18 that these signs should follow them that believe;
In my name shall they cast out Devils they shall speak with new

tongues they shall take up serpants and if they drink any deadly
thing it shall not hurt them they shall lay hands on the sick
and they shall recover, and also in connection with this read
1 Corinthians 12 Chapt, By the foregoing testamonies or through
the glass of the foregoing testamonies we may look at the Christian
world and see the apostacy there has been from [p. 15] the
Apostolic platform, and who can look at this, ~~and~~ and not exclaim
in the language of I<s>aiah, ["]the earth is defiled under the
inhabitants thereof because they have transgressed the Laws,
changed the ordinances and broken the everlasting covenant"
    The plain fact is this, the power of God begins to fall upon the
Nations, and the light of the latter day glory begins to break forth
through the dark atmosphere of sectarian wickedness and their
iniquity rools [rolls] up into view and the Nations of the Gentiles
are like the waves of the sea casting up mire and dirt or all in
commotion and they hastily are preparing to act the part allotted
them when the Lord rebukes the nations, when he shall rule them
with a rod of iron & break them in peaces like a potters vessel, The
Lord has declared to his servants some Eighteen months since that
he was then withdrawing his spirit from the earth, and we can see
that such is the fact for not only the churches are dwindling away,
but there are no conversions, or but very few, and this is not all,
the governments of the earth are thrown into confusion &
division, and distruction to the eye of the spiritual beholder seemes
to be writen by the finger of an invisable hand in Large capitals
upon almost evry thing we behold — — — — — — — — — — — — — — — —
    And now what remains to be done under circumstances like
these, I will proced to tell you what the Lord requires of all people
high and low, rich and poor, male and female, ministers & people
professors of religion, and nonproffessors in order that they may
enjoy the holy spirit of God to a fulness, and escape the
Judg=ments of God, which are almost ready to burst upon the
nations of the earth — Repent of all your sins and be baptized in water
for the remission of them, in the name of the father, and of the
son, and of the Holy Ghost, and receive the ordinance of the
laying on of the hands of him who is ordained and sealed unto this

power, that ye may receive the holy spirit of God, and this
according to the holy scriptures, and of the Book of Mormon; and
[p. 16] the only way that man can enter into the Celestial
kingdom. These are the requesitions of the new Covenant or first
principles of of the Gospel of Christ; then add to you[r] faith virtue
and to virtue knowledge and to knowledge temperance, and to
temperance patience, and to patience, brotherly kindness and to
brotherly kindness charity (or Love) and if these things be in you
and abound, they make you to be neither baran nor unfruitful in
the knowledge of our Lord Jesus Christ — — — — — —

The Book of Mormon is a record of the forefathers of our
western Tribes of Indians, having been found through the
ministration of an holy Angel translated into our own Language by
the gift and power of God, after having been hid up in the earth for
the last fourteen hundred years containing the word of God, which
was delivered unto them, By it we learn that our western tribes of
Indians are desendants from that Joseph that was sold into Egypt,
and that the land of America is a promised land unto them, and
unto it all the tribes of Israel will come. with as many of the
gentiles as shall comply with the requesitions of the new
co[v]en=ant. But the tribe of Judah will return to old Jerusalem.
The City, of Zion, spoken of by David in the 102 Psalm will be
built upon the Land of America and the ransomed of the Lord shall
return and come to it with songs and ever=lasting joy upon their
heads, and then they will be delivered from the overflowing scourge
that shall pass through the Land But Judah shall obtain deliverence
at Jerusalem see Joel 2. 32. Isaiah 26, 20 & 21, Jer. 31, 12, Psalm
50. 5, Ezekiel 34, 11. 12 & 13, These are testamonies that the
good Shepherd will put forth his own sheep and Lead them out
from all nations where they have been scattered in a cloudy and
dark day, to Zion and to Jerusalem beside many more testamonies
which might be brought— And now I am prepared to say by the
authority of Jesus Christ, that not many years shall pass away before
the United States shall present such [p. 17] a scene of *bloodshed* as
has not a parallel in the hystory of our nation pestalence hail
famine and earthquake will sweep the wicked off this generation

from off the face of this Land to open and prepare the way for the
return of the lost tribes of Israel from the north country—The
people of the Lord, those who have complied with the requisitions
of the new covenant have already commenced gathering togethe[r]
to Zion which is in the State of Missouri. Therefore I decl=are unto
you the warning which the Lord has commanded me to declare
unto this generation, rem[em]bering that the eyes of my maker are
upon me and that to him I am accountable for evry word I say
wishing nothing worse to my fellow men then their eternal
salvation therefore fear God, and give glory to him for the hour of
his Judgment is come. Repent ye Repent, ye and imbrace the
everlasting Covenant and flee to Zion before the over=flowing
scourge overtake you, For there are those now living upon the earth
whose eyes shall not be closed in death until they see all these
things which I have spoken fulfilled Rem[em]ber these things, call
upon the Lord while he is near and seek him while he may be found
is the exhortation of your unworthy servant

Joseph Smith Jr

To N. E. Sexton Rochester N Y.

To N. C. Saxton,
February 12, 1833

Noting that the letter he had sent on January 4 to the Rochester newspaper editor had appeared in abbreviated form, Joseph again addressed Mr. Saxton on February 12 urging the importance of publishing the document in its entirety.[1]

To N C Sexton [Saxton] Rochester

Dear sir

I was somewhat disappointed on receiv=ing my paper with only a part of my letter inserted in it. The letter which I wrote you for publication I wrote by the [p. 27] commandment of God, and I am quite anxious to have it all laid before the public for it is of *importance* to them, But I have no clame upon you, neither do I wish to urge you beyond that which is reasonable to do it. I have only to appeal to your extended generosity to all religious societies that claim that Christ has come in the flesh and also tell you what will be the consequence of a neglect to publish it– some parts of the letter were very severe upon the wickedness of sectarianism – I acknowledge and the truth, remember is hard and severe against all iniq=uity and wickedness, but this is no reason why it should not be published but the very reason why it should, It lays the axe at the root of the tree and I long to see many of the sturdy oaks which I have long cumbred the ground fall prostrate. I now say unto you that if you wish to clear your garments from the blood of your readers I exhort you to publish that letter *entire* but if not the sin be upon your head—

Accept sir the good wishes and tender regard of your unworthy servant—

Joseph Smith Jr

Kirtland 12th Feby. 1833

—A Mark Hofmann forgery—

To Emma Smith,
March 6, 1833

According to the law upon which Zion was to be built in Jackson County, Missouri, an inheritance in that land depended upon the consecration of property and means for the benefit of the poor. The assistance of the poor was an important function of the law of consecration, administered by Bishop Edward Partridge, which was to govern those who migrated to Zion, and of the United Order or Firm, established to correlate Church business functions in Ohio and Missouri.[1] Both Isaac Morley, counselor to Edward Partridge, and Frederick G. Williams, an 1833 member of the United Firm, played key roles in this organization. It was probably in this context that the March 1833 request was made upon Joseph Smith's plow, as indicated in the following letter to his wife.

March 6th 1833

Dear Wife
 Brother Williams has this day ‹received› word from Brother Morely that we should commit the cross plow unto the hands of the poor you will therefor please to trust it to Brother Williams by ‹his› hand I send this I subs‹c›ribe myself your Hus=band

    Joseph Smith Jr

Emma Smith

March 6th 1833

Dear Wife

(Brother Williams has this day received
from Brother Morly that we should commit
the cows now in the hands of the poor gone
will therefor please to trust it to Brother Williams
by hand & And this I subscribe myself your Hus
=band

Emma Smith

Joseph Smith jr

To Emma Smith, March 6, 1833. Handwriting of Joseph Smith. See text, p. 277. (Brent F. Ashworth.)

To Newel K. Whitney
[1833-1834]

Doctor Philastus Hurlbut, born February 3, 1809, in Chittendon County, Vermont, was given the name Doctor because of the superstition that a seventh son would possess supernatural qualities of medical skill. He met Joseph Smith in March 1833 in Kirtland, Ohio, where the two men "conversed considerably about the Book of Mormon." But soon after Hurlbut was baptized and ordained an elder, he was excommunicated for immoral conduct. Whereupon he joined with anti-Mormons in Kirtland in vigorous opposition to Joseph Smith.

After threatening the Prophet's life, which netted him a $200 court fine and a restraining order to keep the peace, Hurlbut was hired by a local committee "to obtain affidavits showing the bad character of the Mormon Smith Family," and to "completely divest Joseph Smith of all claims to the character of an honest man, and place him at an immeasurable distance from the high station he pretends to occupy."[1] Hurlbut traveled in Ohio, New York, and Pennsylvania collecting statements that were eventually published in Eber D. Howe's seminal anti-Mormon book *Mormonism Unvailed*, in 1834.[2]

Although undated, the following note from Joseph Smith to Newel K. Whitney, a fellow officer of the United Firm, was written sometime between June 23, 1833, and April 10, 1834.[3]

279

[Kirtland, Ohio]

    Brother Whitney I write this because I forgot to tell you of some things that you ⟨ought to⟩ know ~~wer~~ Docter P. Hurlbut is commenceing an un=just suit against Brother Hyram to git the prope[r]ty of this farm⁴ which belongs to the firm Brother Hyram ⟨or⟩ ~~mot~~ father has ⟨not got⟩ any property here but one cow ~~a peace~~ each I have a ⟨bill⟩ for all the rest made over to me more than one year ago for Books and what they owed me and it will involve me ~~in~~ or the firm if we let them take this property which you ⟨may⟩ rest asured belongs to us a word to the wise is sufficie⟨nt⟩

                        Joseph Smith Jr

Brother Whitney I write this because I forgot
to tell you of some things that you[?] know
Docter P. Hurlbut is commencing an un-
-just suit against brother Hyram to git
the property of this farm which belongs
to the firm brother Hyram nor father
had any property here but one cow &
each I have a bill for all the rest made
over to me more than one year ago for
Books and what they owed me and it will
involve me in or the firm if we let them
take this property which you really[?] und-
belong to us a word to the wise is sufficient

Joseph Smith Jr

To Newel K. Whitney [1833-1834]. Handwriting of Joseph Smith. See
text, p. 280. (University of Utah Library.)

To William Phelps, John Whitmer, Edward Partridge, Isaac Morley, John Corrill, and Sidney Gilbert, August 10, 18, 1833

Within two years of the 1831 announcement that Jackson County, Missouri, would be the site for their city of Zion, approximately one thousand Latter-day Saints (comprising about one-third of the total population of the county) had settled in that area. But the sudden influx of a large body of northerners in a predominantly Southern state created a situation that was to prove disastrous for the newcomers. Specific charges made against the Mormons by the old settlers, based upon the cultural differences of the two peoples, became the focal point of action to drive the Saints from the county. On July 20, 1833, a mob gathered at Independence and destroyed the Church printing shop and the storehouse and goods of the Gilbert and Whitney store, tarred and feathered Bishop Edward Partridge, and forced the signing of an agreement stipulating that the Mormons leave the county before the coming year.[1]

Immediately after this disaster, Oliver Cowdery was sent to Ohio to confer with Joseph Smith. Cowdery arrived in Kirtland on August 9 and the next day wrote a letter back to Missouri in which he gave what he termed reliable advice: "It is wisdom that you look out another place to locate on. Be wise in your selection and commence in the best situation you can find. . . . Another place of beginning will be no injury to Zion in the end. . . . Do not remove any faster to your new home than you bound yourselves to. . . . There was no other way to save the lives of all the church in Zion, or the most; and any who are dissatisfied with that move are not right. . . . This great tribulation would not have come upon Zion had it not been for rebellion. . . . It was necessary that these things should come upon us; not only justice demands it, but there was no other way to cleanse the Church."

Appended to the Cowdery letter were a few lines by Joseph Smith. This postscript and a lengthy epistle dated August 18 contain Joseph Smith's initial reaction to news of the Missouri violence.

Kirtland Mills Ohio
Aug 10th 1833.

Dear Brethren, W, J, E, I, J, and S, and all others who are willing to lay down their lives for the cause of our Lord Jesus Christ:
. . . .
P.S. Brethren if I were with you I should take an active part in your sufferings, and although nature shrinks, yet my spirit would not let me forsake you unto death, God helping me. Oh be of good cheer, for our redemption draweth near. Oh, God save my brethren in Zion. Oh brethren give up all to God, forsake all for Christ's sake

J[oseph] S[mith]

Kirtland, August 18, 1833.

Brother William, John, Edward, Isaac, John and Sidney.
   O thou disposer of all Events, thou dispencer of all good! in the name of Jesus Christ I ask thee to inspire my heart indiht my thaughts guide my peen to note some kind word to these my Brotheren in Zion that like the rays of the sun upon the Earth wormeth the face thereof so let this word I write worm the hearts of my Brotheren or as the gentle rain decen[d]eth upon the earth or the dews upon the mountains refresheth the face of nature and Causeth her to smile so give unto thy servent Joseph have a word

that shall refresh the hearts and revi[v]e the spir[i]ts yea souls of
those afflicted ones who have been called to leave their homes and
go to a strange land not knowing what should befall them behold
this is like Abraham a strikeing ‹evidence› of their acceptance
before the ‹Lord› in this thing but this is not all ‹they are› ~~but~~
called to contend with the beast of the wilderness for a long time
whos[e] Jaws ‹are› ~~were~~ open to devour them thus did Abraham
and also Paul at Ephesus bhold thou art like ~~him~~ ‹them› and
again the affliction of my Brotheren reminds me of Abraham
offering up Isaac his only son but my Brothren have been called
to give up even more than this their wives and their children yea
and their own life also O Lord what more dost thou require at
their hands before thou wilt come and save them may I not say
thou wilt yea I will ‹say› Lord thou wilt save them out of the
hands of their enemies thou hast tried them in the fu[r]nace of
affliction a furnace of thine own choseing and couldst thou have
tried them more then thou hast O Lord then let this suffice and
from henceforth ‹let› this ‹be› reco[r]ded ‹~~be~~› in heaven for
thine angels to look upon and for a testimony against all those
ungodly men who have commited those ungodly deeds [forever
and] ever and ‹yea›~~let~~ thine anger ‹is› ~~be~~ enki=ndled against
them ~~and~~ ‹let › ~~them~~ ‹and they shall› be consumed before thy
face and be far removed from Zion O ‹they will go› ~~let them~~ go
down to ‹the› pit and give pl[a]ce for thy saints for thy spirit will
not always strive with man therefore I fear for all these things yet
O Lord glorify thyself thy will be done and not mine but I must
conclude my pray[er] my heart being full of real desire for all
such are not [so] reprobate that they cannot be saved————————

    Dear Brotheren in fellowship and ‹love› towards you and
with a broken heart and a contrite spirit I take the pen to address
you but I know not what to say to you and the thaught ‹that› this
‹~~of~~› letter will be so long coming to you my heart faints within
me I feel to exclaim O Lord let the desire of my heart be felt and
realized this moment ‹upon your hearts› and teach you all things
thy servent would communicate to ~~would~~ you my Brotheren
since the intel=igence of the Calamity of Zion has reached the

ears of the wicked there is no saifty for us here but evevery man has to wach their houses every night to keep off the mobers[1] satan has Come down in great wrath upon all the Chirch of God and th[ere] is no saifty only in the a[r]m of Jehovah none else can deliver and he will not deliver unless we do prove ourselves faithful to him in the severeest trouble for he that will have his robes washed in the blood of the Lamb must come up throught great tribulation even the greatest of all affliction but know this when men thus deal with you and speak all maner of evil of you falsly for the sake of Christ that he is your friend and I verily know that he will spedily deliver Zion for I have his immutible covenant that this shall be the case but god is pleased to keep it hid from mine eyes the means how exactly the thing will be done the chirch in Kirtland concluded with one accord to die with you or redeem you and never at any time have I felt as I now feel that pure love and for you my Brotheren the wormth and Zeal for you[r] safty that we can scarcely hold our spirits but wisdom I trust will keep us from madness and desperation and the power of the Go[s]pel will enable us to stand and [p. 1] and bear with patience the great affliction that is falling upon us on all sides for we ‹are› no safer here in Kirtland then you are in Zion the cloud is gethering around us with great fury and all pharohs host or in other words all hell and the comb[ined] powrs of Earth are Marsheling their forces to overthrow us and we like the chilldre=n of Is‹s›arel with the red Sea before us them and the Egyptions ready to fall upon them to distroy them and no arm could diliver but the arm of God and this is the case with us we must wait on God to be gratious and call on him with out ceaseing to make bare his arm for our defence for naught but the arm of the almighty can save us we are all well here as can be expe=cted yea altogether so with the exception of some little ailments feavers &c.——

Brother Oliver is now Sitting before me and is faithful and true and his heart bleeds as it were for Zion yea never did the hart pant for the cooling streem as doth the heart of thy Brothe[r] Oliver for thy salvation yea and I may say this is the Case with

the whole Chirch and all the faithful Oliver will or aught rather
to stay with me or in this land ~~unti~~ until I am permitted to Come
with him for I know that if God shall spare my life that he will
permit me to settle on an inhe[r]i=tance on the land of Zion ‹in
due time› but when I do not know but this I do know that I have
been keept from going ‹up› as yet for your sakes and the day will
come that Zion will be keept for our sakes therefore be of good
cheer and the cloud shall pass over and the sun shall shine as
clear and as fair as heaven itself and the Event shall be glorious
Oliver can stay here to good advantage and have his wife come to
him and he can be instrumental of doing great good in this place
and god will ‹give› Brother william more help and grace to stand
as an ensign to the people for it must be lifted up [–] and cursed
sha[ll] every man be that lifts his arm to ‹hinder› this great work
and god is my witness of this truth it shall be done and let all the
saints say amen————————

Dear Brotheren we must wait patiently until the Lord come[s]
and resto[res] unto us all things and build the waist places again
for he will do it in his time and now what shall I say to cumfort
your hearts well I will tell you that you have my whole
confidence yea there is not one doubt in ‹my heart› not one place
in me but what is filld with perfect confidince and love for you
and this affliction is sent upon us not for your sins but for the sins
of the chirch and that all the ends of the Earth may know that
you are not speculiting with them for Lucre but you are willing to
die for the cause you have espoused you know that the chirch
have treted lightly the com=mandments of the Lord and for this
cause they are not worthy to receive them yet god has suffered it
not for your sins but that he might ‹pre›prare you for a grateer
work that you might be prepared for the endowment from on high
we cast no reflections upon you we are of one heart and one mind
on this subject which I speak in the name of the chirch all seem to
wax strong as th[e]y see the day ‹of› tribulation approcing and if
our kingdom were of this world then we would fight but our
weapons are not carnal yet mighty and ‹will› bind satan ere long
under our feet we shall get a press immediately in this place and

print the Star until you can obtain deliverence and git up again[2] if
god permit and we believe he will we think it would be wise in
you to try to git influence by offering to print a paper in favor of
the goverment as you know we are all friends to the Constitution
yea true friends to that Country ~~we hav~~ for which our fathers
bled in the mean time god will send Embasadors to the authorities
of the government and sue for protection and redress that they
may be left with out excuse that a ritious Judgement might be
upon them [p. 2] and thus the testimony of the Kingdom must go
unto all and there are many ways that God disigns to bring about
his ritious purposes and in the day of Judgement he disigns to
make us the Judges of the ~~whole world~~ generation in which we
live O how unsearchable are the depths of his mysteries and his
ways past finding out Brotheren the testamony which you have
given of your honesty and the truth of this work will be felt
Ete[r]naly by this generation for it will be proclaimed to [the]
ends of the Earth that there are men now liveing who have
offered up their lives ~~for this~~ as a testimony of their religion our
Brotheren in the East will handle this testimony to good
advantage it seems to inspire every heart to a lively sence of
faith and to arm them ‹with› double fortitude and power and the
harder the persicution the greater the gifts of God upon his chirch
yea all things shall work together for good to them who are
willing to lay down their lives for Christ sake we are suffering
great persicution on account of one man by the name of Docter
Hurlburt who has been expeled from the chirch for lude and
adulterous conduct and to spite us he is lieing in a wonderful
manner and the peopl are running after him and giveing him
mony to brake down mormanism which much endangers ‹our
lives› at pre=asnt but god will put a stop to his carear soon and all
will be well my heart this moment ‹is made› glad for Zion we
have Just received you[r] letter containing the bond with which
our enemies bound themselves to distroy Zion and also the
blessing ‹of› god in poreing out ~~upon~~ his spirit upon you and we
have had the word of the Lord that you shall [be] deliverd from
you[r] dainger and ‹shall› again flurish in spite of hell [this] god

has communicated to me by the gift of the holy ghost that this
should be ‹the case› after much p[rayer] and suplication and also
that an other printing office must be built the Lord knows how
and also it is the will of the Lord that the Store shou[ld] be kept
and that ‹not› one foot of ‹land› ~~the~~ perchased should ‹be› given
to the enimies of god or sold to them but if any is sold let it be sold
to the chirch we cannot git the consent of the Lord that we shall
give the ground to the enemies yet let those who are bound to
leave the land ~~to~~ make a show as if to do [it] untill the Lord
delivr[s] a word to the wise is sufficien‹t› therefore Jud[g]e what
I say for know assuredly that every foot of ground that falls into
the hands of the enimies with consent is not easy to be obtained g
again O be wise and not let the knowledge I give unto ‹you› be
known abroad for your saks hold fast that which you have
received trust in god considder Elijah when he prayed for rain go
often to your holy plases and ‹look› for a cloud of light to apper
to your help O God I ask thee in the name of Jesus of nazereth to
save all things concerning Zion and build up her wai[s]=t places
and restore all things O god send forth Judge=ment unto victory
O come down and cause the mou[n]=tans to flow down at thy
presance and now I conclude by telling you that we wait the
Comand of God to do whatever he plese and if ‹he› shall say go
up to Zion and defend thy Brotheren by ‹the sword› we fly and
we count not ~~dear~~ our live[s] dear to us I am your Brother in
Christ

Joseph Smith Jr [p. 3]

/³Edward Pa‹r›trige
Independence
Jackson County
Missouri [p. 4]

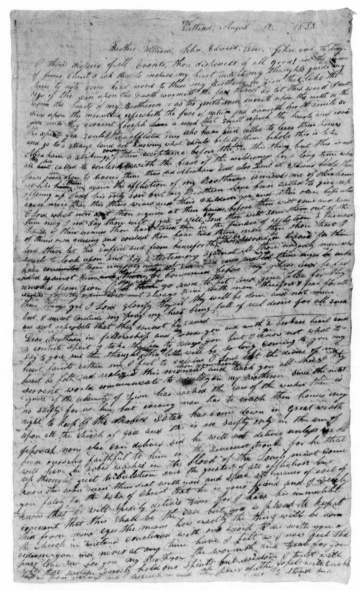

To William Phelps and Others, August 18, 1833, p. 1. Handwriting of
Joseph Smith. See text, pp. 283-85. (LDS Church Archives.)

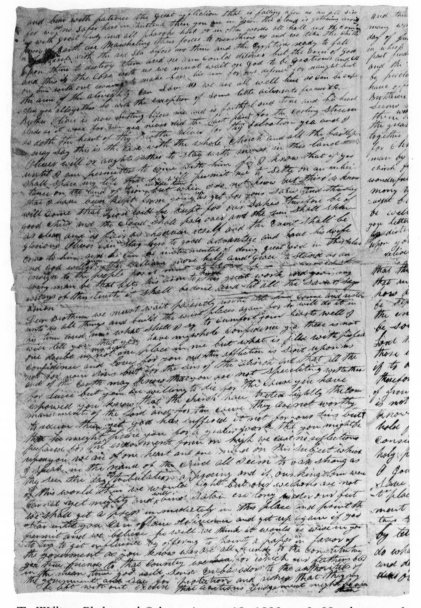

To William Phelps and Others, August 18, 1833, p. 2. Handwriting of Joseph Smith. See text, pp. 285-87. (LDS Church Archives.)

To William Phelps and Others, August 18, 1833, p. 3. Handwriting of Joseph Smith. See text, pp. 287-88. (LDS Church Archives.)

To William Phelps and Others, August 18, 1833, p. 4. Handwriting of Frederick G. Williams. See text, p. 288. (LDS Church Archives.)

To Vienna Jacques,
September 4, 1833

Vienna Jacques, born at New Rowley, Massachusetts, in 1787, at an early age moved to Boston, where, "in her self-reliant way, by patient toil and strict economy," she accumulated considerable wealth. After joining the Methodist Church, but still feeling dissatisfied in her spiritual aspirations, she continued seeking. In 1831 she heard that a prophet had risen up in the west and published a sacred record containing the fulness of the gospel. Procuring the book but failing to comprehend its message, she set it aside; then one evening as she pondered a theme for her daily meditation, a vision of the Book of Mormon was presented to her mind, and she prayed for an impression of its truth. The resulting manifestation motivated her to travel to Kirtland, Ohio, where she was baptized. Such were her impressions of Mormonism that she donated all of her wealth to the Church. Her contribution came at a particularly needful time and was an important factor in the purchase of Missouri land for the settlement of the Saints. When the time came for her own removal to Missouri, she was promised an inheritance by revelation: "And again, verily I say unto you, it is my will that my handmaid Vienna Jacques should receive money to bear her expenses, and go up unto the land of Zion . . . and receive an inheritance from the hand of the bishop."[1]

Vienna arrived in Jackson County in time to witness the

violence that erupted there in July 1833. A short time later she received the following letter from Joseph Smith.

Kirtland Sept 4th 1833——

Dear Siste[r]

——Having a few Leisur moments I sit down to communicate to you a few wordes which I know I am under obligation to improve for your satisfaction if it should be a satisfaction for you to receive a few words from your unworthy brother in Christ, I received your Letter some time since containing a history of your Journey and your safe arival for which I bless the Lord I have often felt a whispering since I received your letter like this Joseph thou art indebted to thy God for the offering of thy Sister Viana which proved a savior of life as pertaining to thy pecunary concern therefor she should not be forgotten of thee for the Lord hath done this and thou shouldst remember her in all thy prayers and also by letter for she oftentimes calleth on the Lord saying O Lord inspire thy servant Joseph to communicate by letter some word to thine unworthy handmaid canst thou not speak peaceably unto thine handmaid and say all my sins are forgiven and art thou not content with the chastisement wherewith thou hast chastised thy handmaid yea sister this seams to be the whisperings of a spirit and Judge ye what spirit it is I was sensable, when you left Kirtland that the Lord would chasten you but I pray‹ed› fervently in the name of Jesus that you might live to receive your inheritance agreeable to the commandment which was given concerning you I am not at all astonished at what has happened to you neither to what has happened to Zion and I could tell all the whys & wherefores of all there calamities but alas it is in vain to warn and give precepts for all men are naturally disposed to walk in their own paths as they are pointed out by their own fingers and are not willing to considder and walk in the path which is pointed out by another saying this is the way walk ye in it altho he should be an unering director and the Lord his God sent him neverthe=less I do not feel disposed to

cast any reflections but I feel to cry mightily unto the Lord that all
things might work together for good which has happened yea I feel
to say O Lord let Zion be comforted let her waste places be built up
and established an hundred fold [p. 1] let thy saints come unto Zion
out of every nation let hir be exalted to the third heaven and let
thy Judgments be sent forth unto victory and after this great
tribulation let thy blessings fall upon thy people and let thy
handmaid live till her soul shall be sat=isfied in beholding the glory
of Zion notwithstanding her present affliction she shall yet arise
and put on her beautiful garments and be the Joy and ~~praise~~ ‹glory›
of the whole earth therefore let your heart be comferted live in
strict obedience to the commandments of God and walk humble
before him and he will exalt thee in his own due time the brethren
in this place are gaining ground in spiritual things and are trying to
overcome all things that is not well pleasing to their heavenly
father ~~we have common~~ there has many brethren mooved to this
place from different parts of the country so much so that one house
is not sufficient to contain them for public worship and we have
divided and hold meetings in two sepperate places namely at the
school house on the flats and Uncle John Smiths who lives on
brother Coes place we have commenced building the house of the
Lord in this place and are making great progress in it so much so
that I feel great hopes that by spring it will be finished so that we
can have a place to worship where we shall not be molested a few
days since Brother Ball and Sister Elizabeth Chan arived here from
boston broth[er] ball has gone about three miles from this place to
work at his trade and Sister Elizab=eth lives with me at present
Agnes & Mary[2] Lives with father Smith————————————
I will assure you that the Lord has respect unto the offering you
made he is a God that changes not and and his word cannot fail
remember what he has said in the book of mormon respecting those
who should assist in bringing this work forth we frequently have
intelligence from our elder[s] abroad that are proclaming the word
that God is working with them for they have attained to great faith
insomuch that signs do follow them that believe [p. 2] Brother
David Pattin[3] has Just returned from his tour ~~from~~ ‹to› the east and

gives us great satisfaction as to his ministry he has raised up a
church of about Eighty three members in that part of the country
where his friends live in the state of New York many were healed
through his instrumantality several criples were restored as many as
twelve that were afflicted came at a time from a distan[ce] to be
healed he ‹and others› administered in the name of Jesus and they
were made whole thus you see that the Laborers in the Lords
vineyard are Labouring with their mights while the day lasts
knowing the night soon cometh wherein no man can work I wish
you to say to brother Partridge that we received his letter of the 13
August directed to Bro Frederick requesting an explination on the
Plan of the house which is to be built in Zion and also of the City
Platt that ‹the› broth[ren] whom we have recently sent to Zion
will giv[e] them all the information they need about it[4] I have but
little time to write at present for I am Labouring on the house of
the Lord with my own hands therefor I must bid you farewell and
subscribe myself your unworthy brother in Christ amen

[Joseph Smith Jr.]
Viana Jaquish [Vienna Jacques] [p. 3]

Kirtland Mills 0
Sept 11

Viana Jacquish
Independence Jackson [County]
Missouri

To Silas Smith,
September 26, 1833

Among the most devoted supporters of Joseph Smith's religious claims were members of his own family. Although a universalist who did not affiliate with any of the religious institutions of his day, the Prophet's father, Joseph, Sr., was a devout student of the Bible and believed in his son's divine calling. At an early date he testified that God had called his son "by name out of the heavens,"[1] and was the first to accept his boy's testimony of the appearance, in September 1823, of the heavenly messenger Moroni.

In the fall of 1828 the elder Joseph wrote to his father's family in Stockholm, New York, that his son had had "several remarkable visions,"[2] and shortly after the Book of Mormon was published he traveled to Stockholm to show the book to his family. With one exception, all of Joseph Smith, Sr.'s, living brothers accepted the message of the Restoration. John was baptized in 1832, and Asael and Silas in 1835. About two years before he was baptized, Silas (1779-1839), a veteran of the War of 1812, received this letter from his nephew, Joseph Smith, Jr.

Kirtland Mills Ohio sept 26 [1833]

Respected Uncle Silas

It is with feelings of deep interest for the well=fare of mankind which fills my mind on the reflection that all were formed by the

297

hand of him who will call the same to give an impartial account of
all their works on that great day to which you and myself in
common with them are bound, that I take up my pen and seat
myself in an attitude to address a few though imperfect lines to you
for your perusal.

I have no doubt but that you will agree with me that men will
be held accountable for the things which they have and not for the
things they have not or that all the light and intell=igence
communicated to them from their benifficen[t] creator wh=ether it
is much or little by the same they in justice will be judged, and that
they are required to yield obedience and improve upon that and
that only which is given for man is not to live by bread alone but by
every word that proceeds [p. 228] out of the mouth of God

Seeing that the Lord has never given the world to unders=tand
by anything heretofore revealed that he had ceased forever to speak
to his creatures when saught unto in a proper manner why should it
be thought a thing incredible that he should be pleased to speak
again in these last days for their salvation Perhaps you may be
surprized at this assertion that I should say for the salvation of his
creatures in these last days since we have already in our possesion a
vast volume of his word which he has previously given—But you will
admit that the word spoken to Noah was not suff=icent for
Abraham or it was not required of Abraham to leave the land of his
nativity and seek an Inheritance in a strange ~~land~~ Country upon
the word spoken to Noah but for himself he obtain=ed promises at
the hand of the Lord and walked in that perf=ection that he was
called the friend of God Isaac the promi=sed seed was not required
to rest his hope upon the promises made to his father Abraham but
was priviledged with the assu=rance of his approbation in the sight
of Heaven by the direct voice of the Lord to him If one man can
live upon the revelat=ions given to another might not I with
propriety ask why the n=ecessity then of the Lord speaking to Isaac
as he did as is record=ed in the 26 chapter of Genesis for the Lord
there repeats or rath=er promises again to perform the oath which
he had previously sworn unto Abraham and why this repet[it]ion to
Isaac Why was not the first promise as sure for Isaac as it was for

Abraham. Was not Isaac Abraham's son And could he not place implicit confidence in the word of his father as being a man of God.

Perhaps you may say that he was a very peculiar man and different from men in these last days consequently the Lord favored him with blessings peculiar and different as he was different from men in this age I admit that he was a peculiar man and was not only peculiarly blessed but greatly bless=ed. But all the peculiarity that I can discover in the [p. 229] man or all the difference between him and men in this age is that he was more holy and more perfect before God and came to him with a purer heart and more faith than men in this day.

The same might be said on the subject of Jacobs history Why was it that the Lord spake to him concerning the same prom=ise after he had made it once to Abraham and renewed it to Isaac why could not Jacob rest contented upon the word spoken to his fathers When the time of the promise drew nigh for the deliverance of the children of Israel from the land of Egypt why was it necessary that the Lord should begin to speak to them The promise or word to Abraham was that his seed should serve in bondage and be afflicted four hun=dred years and after that they should come out with great substance Why did they not rely upon this promise and when they had remained in Egypt in bondage four hundred [years] come out without waiting for further revelation but act entirely upon the promise given to Abraham that they should come out.

Paul said to his Hebrew brethren that God b[e]ing more abu=ndantly willing to show unto the heirs of his promises the immu=tability of his council ["]confirmed it by an oath." He also exhorts them who throug[h] faith and patience inherit the pro=mises.

["]Notwithstanding we (said Paul) have fled for refuge to lay hold of the hope set before us which hope we have as an an=chor of the soul both sure and steadfast and which entereth into that within the vail." Yet he was careful to press upon them the necessity of continuing on untill they as well as those who inherited the promises might have the assurance of their salvat=ion confirmed to them by an oath from the mouth of him who ~~cannot~~

could not lie for that seemed to be the example an=ciently and
Paul holds it'out to his brethren as an object atta=inable in his day
and why not I admit that by reading [p. 230] the scriptures of truth
saints in the days of Paul could learn beyon‹d› the power of
contradiction that Abraham Isaac and Jacob had the promise of
eternal life confirmed to them by an oath of the Lord but that
promise or oath was no assurance to them of their salvation but
they could by walking in the footsteps ‹and› continuing in the
faith of their fathers obtain for themselves an oath for confirmation
that they were meet to be partake[r]s of the inheri=tance with the
saints in light.

   If the saints in the days of the Apostles were priviledged to take
the saints for example and lay hold of the same promises and attain
to the same exhalted priviledges of knowing that their names were
writen in the Lambs book of life and that they were sealed there as
a perpetual memorial before the face of the most high will not the
same faithfulness the same pur=ity of heart and the same faith bring
the same assurance of eternal life and that in the same manner to
the children of men now in this age of the world

   I have no doubt but that the holy prophets and apostles and
saints in ancient days were saved in the Kingdom of God. Neither
do I doubt but that they held converse and com=munion with
them while in the flesh as Paul said to the cori=nthian brethren
that the Lord Jesus showed himself to above 500 saints at one time
after his resure[c]tion. Job said that he knew that his Redeemer
lived and that he should see him in the flesh in the latter days. I
may believe that Enoch wa=lked with God³ I may believe that
Abraham communed with God and conversed with angels. I may
believe that Isaac obtained a renewal of the covenant made to
Abraham by the direct voice of the Lord. I may believe that Jacob
conversed with holy angels and heard the word of his Maker. that
he wrestled with the angel until he prevailed and obtained a
blessing I may believe that Elijah was taken to Heaven in a chariot
of fire with fiery horses I may believe that the [p. 231] saints saw the
Lord and conversed with him face to face aft=er his resurection I
may believe that the Hebrew Church came to Mount Zion and

unto the city of the living God the *Heave[n]=ly* Jerusalem and to an inumerable company of angels. I may believe that they looked into Eternity and saw the Judge of all, and Jesus the Mediator of the new covenant; but will all this purchase an assurance for me, or waft me to the regions of Eternal day with my garments spotless, pure, and white? Or, must I not rather obtain for myself, by my own faith and dilligence, in keeping the commandments of the Lord, an assurance of salvation for myself And have I not an equal priviledge with the ancient saints? and will not the Lord hear my prayers, and listen to my cries, as soon [as] he ever did to their's if I come to him in the manner they did or is he a respecter of persons?

I must now close this subject for the want of time; and I may say with propriety at the begining; we would be pleased to see you in Kirtland and more pleased to have you embrace the New Covenant. I remain.

Yours affectionately
Josep[h] Smith Jr

To Moses Nickerson,
November 19, 1833

Amidst his anxiety over the trials of the Church in Missouri, Joseph Smith left Kirtland on October 5, 1833, in company with his counselor Sidney Rigdon and a recent convert, Freeman Nickerson, on a proselyting mission among Nickerson's relatives and friends in Canada. The three men arrived on October 18 at Mt. Pleasant, Upper Canada, where they spent eleven days meeting and teaching the people.[1] Before departing on October 29, Joseph baptized fourteen people and organized a branch of the Church, with members of the Nickerson family as a nucleus. One of these was Freeman's son, Moses Nickerson, the recipient of a letter sent by the Prophet on November 19 after his arrival back in Kirtland, Ohio.

Kirtland Mills, Geauga County, Ohio, Nov. 19, 1833

Brother Moses, We arrived at this place on the 4th ult. [ultimo] after a fateagueing journey, during which time we [p. 62] were blessed with health as usual. We parted with father and mother Nickerson at Buffalo. They were both in good health, and expressed a degree of satisfaction for the prosperity and bles=sings of their journey. Since our arrival here, bro. Sidney has been afflicted with sore eyes, which is probably the reason why you have not previously heard from us, as he was calcu=lating to write you immediately. But, though I expect that he will undoubtedly write you soon, as his eyes are considerably better, yet lest you should be impatient to learn something concerning us, I have thought that perhaps a few lines from me, though there may be a lack of fluency in address according to the *literate* of the age, may be received with a degree of satisfac=tion on your part, at least, when you call to mind the near relation with which we are united by the everlasting ties of the gospel of our Lord Jesus Christ.

We found our families, and the church in this place well, generally: nothing of consequence transpired while we were abscent, except the death of one of our brethren, a young man of great worth as a private citizen among us, the loss of whom we justly mourn. We are favored with frequent intelligence from different sections of our country respecting the progress of the gospel; and our prayers are daily to our Father, that it may pre greatly ~~prevail~~ ‹spread,› even till all nations shall hear the glorious news and come to a[c]knowledge of the truth.

We have received letters from our breth[r]en in Mis=souri of late, but we cannot tell from their contents the probable extent that those persons who are desirous to expel them from that country, will carry their unlawful and unright=eous purposes. Our brethren have applied to the Executive of that State, who has promised them all the assistance that the civil law can give; and in all probability with us, a suit has been com=menced ere this.

We are informed, however, that those persons are very violent, and th[r]eaten immediate excision upon all those who profess this ~~faith~~ doctrine. How far they will [p. 63] be suffered to execute their th[r]eats we know not, but we trust in the Lord, and leave the event with him to govern in his own wise providence.

I shall expect a communication from you on the reception of this, and hope you will give me in=formation concerning the brethren, their health, faith, &c. Also inform me concerning our friends with whom we formed acquaintance.

You are aware, no doubt, dear brother, that anxieties in=expresible crowd themselves continually upon my mind for the saints, when I consider the many temptations with which we are subject from the cunning and flattery of the great adversary of our souls. And I can truely say, that with much fervency I have called upon the Lord in behalf of our b[r]ethren in Canada. And when I call to mind with what rediness they received the word of truth by the ministry of bro. Sidney and myself, I am truely under great obligation to humble myself in thankfulness before him.

When I contemplate the rapidity with which the great and glorious day of the coming of the Son of Man advances, when he shall come to receive his saints unto himself where they shall dwell in his presence and be crowned with glory & immortality; when I consider that soon the heavens are to be shaken, and the earth tremble and reel to and fro; and that the heavens are to be unfolded as a scroll when it is fol=ded ‹rolled› up, that every mountain and island are to flee away ‹away–› I cry out in my heart, What manner of person ought I to be in all holy conversasion and godliness!

You remember the testimony which I bore in the name of the Lord Jesus, concerning the great work which he has brought forth in the last days. You know my manner of commu=nication, how that in weakness and simpleness I de=clared to you what the Lord had brought forth by the min=istering of his holy angels to me, for this generation. I pray that the Lord may enable you to treasure these things up in your mind, for I know that his Spirit will bear testimony to all who seek diligently after knowledge [p. 64] from him. I hope you will search the scriptures, to see wheth=er these things are not also consistant with those things that the ancient prophets and apostles have written.

I remember brother Freeman and Wife, Ranson also, and sister Lydia, and little Charles, with all the brethren and sisters. I intreat for an interest in all your prayers before the throne of mercy in the name of Jesus. I hope that the Lord will grant that I may see you all again, and above all that we may overcome and set down together in the Kingdom of our Father.

We contemplate with much pleasure a visit from you next spring, ‹and before if consistant with your business,› and hope we shall not be disappointed. So I close, by subscribing myself your brother in the bonds of the gospel,

Joseph Smith Jr.

PS. I said that father and mother Nickerson were well when we parted with them at Buffalo, but you will recollect that father's eyes ‹were› very sore while at your place: when we left him they were not well but considerably improved.

J.

To Moses Nickerson, November 19, 1833, Joseph Smith Letterbook 1, p. 63. Handwriting of Oliver Cowdery. See text, pp. 302-3. (LDS Church Archives.)

To Edward Partridge, William W. Phelps, John Whitmer, Algernon Sidney Gilbert, John Corrill, Isaac Morley and All the Saints Whom It May Concern, December 10, 1833

On July 23, 1833, three days after mob violence had destroyed the Mormon press and other property in Independence, Missouri, Church leaders there were forced to sign an agreement that they would leave Jackson County by the end of the year and that the remainder of their people would be out by the following April. When Oliver Cowdery arrived with this news in Kirtland, Joseph Smith sent Orson Hyde and John Gould to Missouri to advise the Saints in their situation. On September 28, Hyde and W. W. Phelps outlined Mormon grievances in a petition to Missouri Governor Daniel Dunklin. The governor responded that the laws of the land were sufficient for any redress, whereupon the Mormon leaders initiated procedures to bring the matter before the courts. As news of this development spread, the anti-Mormon reaction in Jackson County was predictable. By November 7 the entire Mormon population had been driven from the county.

Although conflicting reports had reached Joseph Smith a few days earlier, on November 25 the Prophet received "the melancholy intelligence" that the Missouri Saints had been driven from the "land of their inheritance."[1] That same day he responded in a letter to the Church in Missouri.

Kirtland Mills Ohio December 10th, 1833

Beloved brethren; E. Partridge, W.W. Phelps J Whitmer A S
Gilbert J Carrel I Morley, and all the saints whom it may concern.

This morning the mail brought bros. Partridge & Carrels letters
& also bro Williams, all mailed at Liberty Nov. 19th which gave us
the melancholy inteligence of your flight from the land of your
inheritance having been dri=ven before the face of your enemies in
that place

From previous letters we had learned that a number of our
brethren have been slain, but we could not learn from those refered
to above as there had been but one, that was bro Barber and bro
Dibble wounded in the bowels,[2] we were thankful to learn that no
more were slain, and our daily prayers are, that the Lord will not
suf=fer his saints who have gone up to his land to keep his
commandments, to stain his holy mountain [p. 70] with their
blood. I cannot learn from any com=munication by the spirit to me
that Zion has forfeited her claim to a celestial crown
not=withstanding the Lord has caused her to be thus afflicted;
except it may ~~it may~~ be some individuals who have walked in
disobedience and forsaken the new covenants; all such will be
made manifest by their works in due time. I have always expected
that Zion would suffer sore affliction from what I could learn from
the com=mandments which have been given.[3] but I would remind
you of a certain clause in one which says that after *much* tribulation
cometh the *blessing.*[4] by this and also others, and also one received
of late,[5] I know that Zion, in the own due time of the Lord will be
redeemed, but how many will be the days of her purification,
tribulation and affliction, the Lord has kept hid from my eyes; and
when I enquire concerning this subject the voice of the Lord is, Be
still, and know that I am God! all those who suffer for my name
shall reign with me, and he that layeth down his life for my sake
shall find it again. Now there are two things of which I am ignorant
and the Lord will not show me—perhaps for a wise purpose in
himself. I mean in some respects, and they are these, Why God
hath suffered so great calamity to come upon Zion; or what the
great moving cause of this great affliction is. ~~These two things~~ and

again by what means he will return her back to her inheritance
with songs of everlasting Joy upon her head. These two things
brethren, are in part kept back that they are not plainly ‹shewn
unto me, but there are some things that are plainly› manifest, that
has incured ‹th[e]› displeasure of ~~displeasure~~ the Almighty. when I
contemplate upon all things that have been [p. 71] manifested, I
am sensable that I aught not to murmer and do not murmer only in
this, that those who are innocent are compelled to suffer for the
iniquities of the guilty; and I cannot account for this, only on this
wise, that the saying of the savior has not been strictly observed: If
thy right eye offend thee pluck it out. and cast it from thee ‹or if
thy right arm offend thee pluck it of[f] and cast it from thee›. Now
the fact is, if any of the members of our body are disordered, the
rest of our body will be effected with them and then all is brought
into bondage together. And yet notwithstanding all this, it is with
difficulty that I can restrain my feelings; when I know that you my
brethren with whom I have had so many happy hours, sitting as it
were in heavenly places in Christ Jesus, and also have=ing the
witness which I feel, and even have felt, of the purity of your
motives—are cast out, and are as strangers and pilgrims on the
earth, exposed to hunger, cold, nakedness peril, sword &c I say
when I contemplate this, it is with difficulty that I can keep from
complaining and murmering against this dispensation; but I am
sensible that this is not right and may God grant that
notwithstanding your great afflictions and sufferings there may not
any thing sepperate us from the Love of Christ. Brethren, when we
learn your sufferings it awakens evry sympathy of our hearts; it
weighs ~~us~~ us down; we cannot refrain from tears yet we are not able
to realize only in part your sufferings. And I often hear the brethren
saying they wish they were with you that they might bear̶ a part of
your sufferings; and I myself should have been with you had not
God prevented it in the order of his providence, that the yoke of
affliction might be less grievous upon you; God having forewarned
me concerning these things for your sakes; and also bro Oliver,
could not lighten your afflictions by tarrying longer with you, for
his presence would have so much the more enraged your enemies;

therefore, God hath dealt mercifully with us. O brethren, let us be thankful [p. 72] that it is as well with us as it is, and we are yet alive that peradventure, God hath Laid up in store great good for us in this generation, and grant that we may yet glorify his name, I feel thankful that there have no more denied the faith; I pray God, in the name of Jesus that you all may be kept in the faith, unto the end, let your suffering, be what they may, it is better that you should die in the ey[e]s of God, then that you should give up the Land of Zion, the ~~inhabitant~~ inher=itances which you have purchased with your monies; for evry man that giveth not up his inheritances, though he should die yet when the Lord shall come, he shall stand upon it, and with Job in his flesh he shall see God. Therefore this is my council that you retain your lands even unto the uttermost, and seeking ⟨evry⟩ lawful means to obtain redress of your enemies &c &c and pray to God day and night to return you in peace and in safety to the Lands of your in=heritance and, when the Judge fails you, appeal unto the Executive, and when the Exe=cutive fails you, appeal unto the President, and when the President fails you, and all laws fail you and the humanity of the people fails you, and all things else fails you but God alone, and you continue to weary him with your importunings, as the poor woman the unjust Judge, he will not fail to exicute Judgment upon your enemies and to ave=nge his own elect that cry unto him day and night— Behold he will not fail you he will come with ten thousands of his saints and all his advisaries shall be distroyed by the breath of his lips! all those that keep their inheritances not=withstanding they should be pealed and driven [p. 73] shall be likened unto the wise virgins who took oil in their lamps, But all those who are unbelieving and fearful, will be likened unto the foolish virgins, who took no oil in their lamps; and when they shall return, and say unto the saints, give us of your lands, behold there will be no room found for them. As respects giving *deeds* I would advise to give deeds as far as the brethren have legal and Just claims for them and then let evry man answer to God for the disposal of them. I would suggest some Ideas to bro William P. not knowing as they will be of any real benefit, but suggest them for consideration I would be glad that he were here, but dare not advise, were it possable for him to come, not kno=wing what shall befall us, as we are under very heavy and serious threatening from a great many people in this place. But purhaps, the people in Liberty may feel willing, God having power to soften the hearts of all men, to have a press established there; and if not, in some other place; any place where it can be the most convenient and it is possable to get to it: God will be willing to have it in any place where it can be practiculer [practicable?] and safe. we must be *wise* as serpe‹n›ts and harmless as doves. Again I desire that bro William would collect all the information, and give us a true history of the begining and rise of Zion, and her calamities &c Now hear the prayer of your unworthy Brothe[r] in the bonds of the new and everlasting covenant: O my God! thou who hast called and chosen a few through thy weak instrument by commandment and sent them to Missouri a place which thou didst call *Zion* and commanded thy servants to consecrate unto thyself for a place of a refuge, and of safety for the gathering of thy saints, to be built up a holy city unto thyself and as thou hast said that none [p. 74] other place should be appointed like unto this therefore I ask thee in the name of Jesus Christ, to return thy people unto their homes, & there inher=itances, to enjoy the fruit of their Labors; that all the waste places may be built up; that all the enemies of thy people, who will not ~~return~~ repent and re turn unto thee be distroyed from off the face of that Land; and let an house be built and established unto thy name, and let all the losses that thy people have sustained be rewarded unto them, even more than four fold; that the bor=ders of Zion be enlarged forever, and let her be established no more to be thrown down; and let all thy saints when they are scattered as sheep, and are persecuted, ~~and~~ flee unto Zion, and be established in the midst of her, and let her be organized according to thy law and let this prayer even ~~before~~ be recorded before thy face; give thy holy spirit unto my brethren: unto whom I write: send thy angels to guard them and to deliver them from all evil; and when they turn there faces towards Zion and bow down before thee and pray may their sins never com up before thy face neithe[r] have place in the book of thy remem=brance and may they depart from all their eniquities, provide ~~bread~~ ‹food› for them as thou doest for the ravens, provide clothing to cover there nakedness, and ‹houses that they may› ~~cause that they~~ dwell therein give unto them friends in abundance, and let their names be recorded in the Lambs book of life eternally before thy face Amen finely, brethren, the grace of our Lord Jesus Christ be with you all unto his coming and Kingdom, Amen

Joseph Smith J[r]

To Edward Partridge,
William W. Phelps, and
Others of the Firm,
March 30, 1834

Following the expulsion of the Latter-day Saints from
Jackson County in November 1833, the immediate question
facing the exiles was how to regain their lost land and possessions. At first, the answer seemed clear when Missouri Attorney General Robert Wells told Mormon representatives that
upon application, "an adequate force" would be sent to restore
them to their lands.[1] But after formally petitioning Daniel
Dunklin, the state's chief executive, William W. Phelps reported that the governor was willing, "but as the constitution
gives him no power to guard us when back, we are not willing to
go."[2] And John Corrill elaborated that for the Saints to return
to their lands would be futile unless the governor would "leave a
force there to help protect; for the mob say that three months
shall not pass before they will drive us again."[3]

In February 1834, Church leaders met in Kirtland to consider "when, how and by what means Zion was to be redeemed
from her enemies." At this meeting provisions were made for
the creation of an armed force that could protect the Saints
once they were returned to their lands. Immediately, four pair
of elders (including Joseph Smith and Parley P. Pratt) were sent
to eastern branches of the Church to solicit funds and volunteers.[4]

Two days after Joseph's return to Kirtland, after an absence

of about a month, he wrote the following letter to the Church
in Missouri.

To Edward, Williams, and others of the firm.
Kirtland, March 30, 1834.

Dear Brethren:

We have received several communications from you of late; but
the most of us being absent, brother Oliver laid them over till
council could be had; and I now seat myself to dictate to answer
them all in one.

Since brothers, Parley & Lyman, arrived⁵ I have written a few
lines with my own hand in letters which have already gone: one
from this place, and one from Freedom N.Y. but was not able to
write the more weighty matters, and did not think to say anything
more than to comfort your hearts if possible, and keep you from
fainting, while God, in his wisdom, and in the order of his
providence, is preparing all things before his face for the
redemption of Zion. We r‹e›joice greatly on learning that you and
the brethren, so many of them, are yet spared in the midst of those
who wear the form of human beings, but are less merciful than the
prowling beast of the wilderness. We would inform you that with
very few exceptions the Church in this place are all well; and every
man, woman & child, that belongs to the Church, as far as I have
any knowledge of the matter, are crying day & night to God for the
deliverance and prosperity of Zion; and many are preparing with all
zeal to do all that lies in their power to accomplish the great work,
and it will be seen in due time, that the saints in this region are not
slack towards you considering their circumstances, & their great
poverty, & afflictions & persecutions with which they are called to
suffer in this part as well as you in that region; for the more we
[p. 30] try to live Godly in Christ Jesus, the more we are made to
feel the weight of persecution, inflicted by those who are under
the inf=luence of the enemy of the souls of men. But let this
suf=fice: I shall proceed first to answer some of the most important
items contained in your last communications, the more part which

gave us much satisfaction. We admire the confi=dence & love which our brethren have manifested in them, in giving us *sharp, piercing, & cutting* reproofs, which are calculated to wake us up & make us search about ourse=lves, & put a double watch over ourselves in all things that we do. And we acknowledge that it is our duty to receive all reproofs & chastisements given of the spi=rit of the most Holy One. And if being chastised and reproved of what we are guilty, seems not to be joyous for the present but grievous, O, how wounding, & how poignant must it be to receive chastisements & reproofs, for things that we are not guilty of from a source we least expect them, arising from a distrus=tful, a fearful, & jealous spirit. However, we feel to make all allowances, & reflect seariously & consider upon all sides before we make an effort to throw off the yoke, lest we should be found in anywise blamable before God. There are some items contained in bro. William's letters by the way of reproof, that we feel to give, we think some reasonable excuses, that you may ‹know› how far you have reason to give reproof, that you may not have wrong feelings concerning those to whom you are espoused in Christ Jesus who always will be found *true* to all con=fidence that shall be imposed in them.

Firstly, you have given us to understand that there are glaring errors in the Revelation, or rather, have shown us the most glaring ones, which are not calculated to suit the refinement of the age in which we live, of the great men, &c. We would say, by way of excuse, that we did not think so much of the orthography, or the manner, as [p. 31] as we did of the subject matter; as the word of God means what it says; & it is the word of God, as much as Christ was God, although *he* was born in a stable, & was rejected by the manner of his birth, notwithstanding he was God. *What a mistake!* the manner of his birth, & the source from which he sprang caused him to be rejected & cast out, & to be taken & put to death. Whereas ‹had› he pleased the great men, the high priests, the lawyers, & the learned, he might have escaped. But supposing we should happen to make as great a mistake as the Lord did, & come under the censure of big men & fall in the same way, what would be the cons=equence? The fact was, there was no room in the *Inn;*

& when man cannot do as they would, they must do as they can; for God set the example before them.

For there was no room in the Inn! but there was room found in the *stable*; & here was utterly a fault in the eyes of the ["]laughing philosophers;" but it is not given to us to understand that he altered his cou‹r›se to please any man. And who was it that triumphed? was it the "laughing philosophers," or *him* who never deviated from the will of him who sent him? Now the fact is, if we have made any mistakes in punctuation, or spelling, it has been done in consequence of brother Oliver, having come from Zion in great afflictions, through much fatigue and anxiety, and being sent contrary to his expectations to New York, and obtai[ni]ng press and Types, and *hauling* them up in the midst of *mobs*, when he and I, and all the church in Kirtland had to lie every night for a long time upon our arms to keep off *mobs*, of forties, of eighties, & of hundreds to save our lives and the press, and that we might not be scattered & driven to the four winds!⁶ And all this in the midst of every kind of confu=sion & calamity, & in the sorrowful tale of Zion, for the sake of Zion, that the word of God might be printed & sent forth by confidential brethren to the different churches; for the churches are just like you—they will not receive anything but by [p. 32] revelation! for when you *hint* they will ask a question, and if by any means in the heat of zeal you would hit them a *kick* it never fails to turn over the *dish*. Therefore, when we give them a hint, and they ask a question, we sometimes answer them plainly; but all this is a wonder and a mystery; but it wont do to *kick*, therefore to unfold the mystery we must of necessity send out the word of ~~the mystery we must of~~ God unto the different churches, or they could not be made to understand, that they, with their moneys, and their young men & their middle aged, must, in order to do the will of God, redeem the land which had been purchased, & the children of Zion—and if by chance in doing all this ‹we› should have to suffer peril by false brethren. For men are as liable in this generation to turn aside from the holy commandments, as were the children of Israel when Aaron bought the golden calf at the expense of all the jewelry, & riches of the children of Israel, while

Moses tarried yet forty days in the mount, that he might receive the law of the everlasting gospel upon tables of stone, written by the finger of of God, while they, the children of Israel, were delivered over, & bowed down and worshiped the dumb idol, and said, These be our Gods that brought us up out of the land of Egypt. And Moses being angry destroyed the tables of stone, and the golden calf and made the children of Israel drink the substance of their God, which they said brought them up out of the land of Egypt. Therefore, I say, if we should suffer peril among false brethren, should it be accounted a strange thing? But here comes up another question, a great mystery! How did the revelation come to be garbled by the printers of the day, published and sent to Jackson Co. and elsewhere? But if all these things, upon a little reflection had been rightly considered and understood, there would have been no mystery, nor any question asked. Not a sigh—not a lingering thought—not a grief, or a single reflection cast upon the innocent, a virgin, *the spouse of Zion!* Suffice it to say, that the revelation went into the hands of the world by stealth, through the means of *false* brethren, and lest it should reach the ears of the President and Governor, with a false coloring, being misrepresented, [p. 33] wisdom dictated that we should send it in its own proper light. And if truth, and the word of God will not bear off the Palms and bring us the victory, shall we, who profess to be men of God conde=scend to folly? Shall we turn aside from the word of God and seek to save our lives, and that we may please men? If men will seek occasion against the truth, will they not seek occasion even if we should shun the truth? The fact is, beloved brethren, we seek not gold or silver or this world's goods, nor honors nor the applause of men; but we seek to please him, and to do the will of him who hath power not only to destroy the body; but to cast the soul into hell! Ah! men should not attempt to steady the ark of God! But enough on this subject.

Now concerning employing Mr. Wells of Jefferson C'ty. as counsellor &c. We think it would be advisable. You may consider that you have our consent: We speak to wise men! Judge ye what we say! Employ, then, Mr. Wells, and although we have neither gold nor silver, we have run into debt for the press, and also to obtain money to pay the New York debt for Zion, and have received but a very few dollars for the Star and printing as yet, no means of speculation to gain or make money, yet we think that the money can be had, and that there will be no difficulty on this subject: and this, while you are writing to us to reprove us, and telling us, that your dependence for money is on your eastern brethren, and at the same time saying *"Dont buy your gold too dear!"* this is the way that we buy our gold! Now, brethren, let me tell you, that it is my dispos=ition to give and *forgive,* and to bear & to *forbear,* with all long suffering and patience, with the foibles, follies, weaknesses, & wickedness of my brethren and all the world of mankind; and my confidence and love toward you is not slackened, nor weakened. And now, if you should be called upon to bear with us a little in any of our weaknesses and follies, and should, with us, receive a rebuke to *yourselves,* dont be offended, dont in anywise let it *hit* you, so as to turn over the dish! And when you & I meet face to face, I [p. 34] anticipate, without the least doubt, that all matters between us will be fairly understood, and perfect love prevail; and [the] sacred covenant by which we are bound together, have the uppermost seat in our hearts.

We expect that a number of our able brethren will come on soon and go to Zion; and should you have no other way of obtaining moneys, you can sell them your lands, let them go on to them, protect them on the same, till your suits are determined, and then, (if you succeed) you will have means to purchase more, and if not they will receive you into their bosoms. We see no other way now; but the Lord may open other ways in time. Brs. Parley and Lyman are both in the east; but we expect they will leave here for the west by the first of may, and go as soon as they can, so should you be organized by the time they arrive, perhaps it would be well. You must act wisdom for yourselves in many things, as you are better prepared to judge in many things than we are. Many things are familiar with some of us, which we *cannot* com=municate by letter; but will be brought about in their times. You ought to be prepared to go back at a moment's warning, and we are inclined to think that it was a wise step in employing the Att'y Gen. for he will investigate and learn the truth, and then [the] Governor will investigate also.

Once more I design coming unto [you]; but when, it has not been revealed: whether it will be with Parley & Lyman I cannot now say; but *once more* I design to come *mob* or no *mob, enemy* or no *enemy!* There needs be no difficulty in relation to the revelations; for they show plainly from the face of them, that no blood is to be shed except in self-defense; and that the law of God as well as man gives us a privilege. If you make yourselves acquainted with the revelations, you will see that this is the case, though we should not publish any more than we are obliged to of necessity for the Church's sake. We have nothing to fear if we are faithful: God will strike through kings in the day of his wrath but what he will deliver his people; and what do you suppose he could do with a few *mobbers* [p. 35] in Jackson County, where, ere long, he will set his feet, when earth & heaven shall tremble!

Be united, brethren, in all your moves, and stand by each other even unto death that you may prevail.

I remain your brother in the new covenant.

Joseph Smith, Jun.

P.S. To bro. William——You say "my press, my types, &c." Where, our brethren ask, did you get them, & how came they to be *"yours?"* No hardness, but a caution, for you know, that it is, *We,* not *I,* and all things are the Lord's, and he opened the hearts of his Church to furnish these things, or *we* should not have been privi=leged with using them.

To Edward, Williams, and others of the firm.

Kirtland, March 30, 1834.

Dear Brethren:

We have received several communications from you of late, but the most of us being absent, brother Vinson have them over till council could be had, and we now seat myself to dictate to, answer them all in one.

Since brothers, Parley & Lyman, arrived I have written a few lines with my own hand in letters which I have already, gone; one from this place, and one from Freedom N.Y. but was not able to write the more weighty, matters, and did not think to say any thing more than to comfort your hearts if possible, and keep you from fainting, while God in his wisdom, and in the order of his providence, is preparing all things before us to bring for the redemption of Zion. We feel greatly on learning that you and the brethren so many of them, are yet spared in the midst of those who wear the form of human beings, but are less merciful than the prowling beast of the wilderness. We would inform you that with very few exceptions the Church in this place are all well; and every man, woman, & child, that belong to the Church, as for as I have any knowledge of the matter, are crying day & night to God for the deliverance and prosperity of Zion; and many are preparing with all zeal to do all that lies in their power to accomplish the great work, and it will be seen in due time, that the saints in this region are not slack towards you considering their circumstances, & their great poverty, & afflictions & persecutions with which they are called to suffer in this part as well as you in that region; for the more we

To Edward Partridge and Others, March 30, 1834, Oliver Cowdery Letterbook, p. 30. Handwriting of Thomas Burdick. See text, p. 314. (Huntington Library.)

To Emma Smith,
May 18, June 4, 1834

In a letter dated February 4, 1834, Governor Dunklin wrote Mormon leaders in Missouri, "I am very sensible indeed of the injuries your people complain of, and should consider myself very remiss in the discharge of my duties were I not to do everything in my power consistent with the legal exercise of them, to afford your society the redress to which they seem entitled. One of your requests needs no evidence to support the right to have it granted; it is that your people be put in possession of their homes, from which they have been expelled. But what may be the duty of the Executive after that, will depend upon contingencies." The Governor informed his correspondents that a military guard would protect the witnesses and officials of the impending court of inquiry to be held in Jackson County to investigate the Mormon expulsion. He added, "Under the protection of this guard, your people can, if they think proper, return to their homes in Jackson County, and be protected in them during the progress of the trial in question."[1] But nothing was said about protection for the Saints after the trial was over. To provide this protection, Joseph Smith organized Zion's Camp. Originally intended to consist of five hundred men, only 130 with twenty baggage wagons left Kirtland for Missouri in the first week of May 1834.

Two letters written by Joseph Smith to Emma survive his march to Missouri. The first, dated May 18, is postmarked from

Richmond, Indiana, just after the Camp crossed the Ohio bor-
der; the other was written June 4 as they arrived at the Mississippi River.

18th May Camp of Israel in Indiana State ‹town of Richmond›

My Dear Wife
    meeting being over I sit down in my tent to write a few lines to
you to let you know that you are on my mind and that I am
sensible of the dutes of a Husband and Father and that I am well
and I pray God to let his blessings ~~to~~ rest upon you and the
children and all that are a round you untill I return to your
society the few lines you ~~roa~~ wrote and sent by the ha[n]d of
Brother Lyman gave me satisfaction and comf=ort and I hope you
will continue to communica=te to me by your own hand for this
is a consola=tion to me ~~that~~ to convirse ‹with› you in this way in
my lonely moments which is not easily discribed I will indeavour
to write every Su[n]day if I can and let you know how I am ‹and›
Brother Fredri=ck² will write to Oliver³ and give him the names
of the places we pass through and a history of our jou[rn]ey from
time to time so that it ‹will› not be nessary for me to endevou[r]
to write it but feel a satisfaction to write a few lines with my own
hand in this way I can have the privelege to communicate some of
my feelings that I should not dare to reveal as you know that
‹my› situation is a very critacal one Brother Jinkins and William
Jese and Jeorge are all well⁴ and are humble are detirmined to be
faithful and finally all the Kirtland Broth[r]en are well and cannot
fail I must close for I cannot write on my knees sitting on the
ground to edifica=tion O may the blessings of God rest upon you
is the prayre of your Husband until death

                        [Joseph Smith, Jr.]

Emma Smith [p. 1]

/⁵Mrs. Emma Smith
Kirtland Mills Geauga County Ohio [p. 2]

On the banks of the Mississippi,
June 4th 1834

My Dear Companion, I now embrace a few moments to dictate a few words that you may know how it is with us up to this date.

We arrived this morning on the banks of the Mississippi, and were detained from crossing the river, as there was no boat that we could cross in, but expect a new one to be put into the river this evening, so that we are in hopes, to be able to cross to morrow, and proceed on our journey.[1] A tolerable degree of union has prevailed among the brethren or camp up to the present moment, and we are all in better circumstances of health apparently than when we started from Kirtland with the exception of Alden Childs[2] who is sick with the Mumps attended with [p. 56] considerable fever in consequence of taking cold—and bro Foster[3] who came from Genseeo who was taken last evening with the Typhus Fever, but are both better to day, and we are in hopes will be able to proceed on their journey to morrow, I have been able to endur[e] the fatigue of the journey far beyond my most sanguine expectations, except have been troubled some with lameness, have had my feet blistered, but are now well, and have also had a little touch of my side complaint, Bro Harper Riggs[4] is now able to travel all day & his health is improving very fast, as is the case with all the weakly ones, Addison Wren[5] has been an exceeding good boy and has been very obedient to me in all things, as much so as tho I was his own father, and is healthy and able to travel all day. William has been some unwell, but is now enjoying good health George has been afflicted with his eyes, but they are getting better, and in fine, all the Camp is in as good a situation as could be expected; but our numbers and means are altogether too small for the accomplishment of such a great enterprise, but they are falling daily and our only hope is that whilst we deter the enemy, and terrify them for a little season (for we learn by the means of some spies we send out for that pur=pose that they are greatly terrified) notwithstanding they are endeavoring to make a formidable stand,

and their numbers amount to several hundred, and the Lord shows us to good advantage in the eyes of their spies, for in counting us the[y] make of our 170 men from five to seven hundred and the reports of the people are not a little calculated [to] frighten and strike terror through their ranks for the general report is that four or five hundred Mormons are traveling through the country well armed, and disciplined; and that five hundred more has gone a south west [course] and expect to meet us, and also another company are on a rout North of us, all these things serve to help us, and we believe the hand of the Lord is in it, Now is the time for the Church abroad to come to Zion. It is our prayer day and night that God will open the heart of the Churches to pour in men and means to assist us, for the redemption of Zion and upbuilding of Zion. We want the Elders in Kirtland to use every exertion to influence the Church to come speedily to our relief. Let them come pitching their tents by the way, remembering to keep the sabbath day according to the articles and covenants the same as at home, buying flour and cooking their own provision which they can do, with little trouble, and the expence will be trifling. We have our company divided into messes of 12 or 13—each having a cook and cooking utensils, all that is necessary; so that we are not obliged to trouble any mans house, and we buy necessaries such as butter, sugar and honey, so that we live as well as heart can wish. After we left the eastern part of the State of Ohio we could get provision on an average as follows; flour by the hundred $1.50, bacon from 4 1/2 to 6 dollar[s] per Hundred butter from 6 to 8 cents pr pound, honey from 3 to 4 shilling the gallon, new milk from 4 to 6 ct pr gallon. The whole of our journey, in the midst of so large a company of social honest and sincere men, wandering over the plains of the Nephites, recounting [p. 57] occasionaly the history of the Book of Mormon, roving over the mounds of that once beloved people of the Lord, picking up their skulls & their bones, as a proof of its divine authenticity, and gazing upon a country the fertility, the splendour and the goodness so indescribable, all serves to pass away time unnoticed, and in short were it not at every now and then our thoughts linger with inexpressible anxiety for our wives and our children our kindred according to the flesh who are entwined around our hearts; and also our brethren and friends; our whole journey would be as a dream, and this would be the happiest period of all our lives. We learn this journey how to travel, and we look with pleasing anticip=ation for the time to come, when we shall retrace our steps, and take this journey again in the enjoyment and embrace of that society we so much love, which society can only cause us to have any desire or lingering thoughts of that which is below. We have not as yet heard any thing from Lyman and Hyrum[6] and do not expect to till we get to salt river Church, which is only fifty miles from this place. Tell Father Smith and all the family, and brother Oliver to be comforted and look forward to the day when the trials and tribulations of this life will be at an end, and we all enjoy the fruits of our labour if we hold out faithful to the end which I pray may be the happy lot of us all.

From your's in the bonds of affliction.

Joseph Smith Jr

N.B. The enclosed bill we could not get changed and is of no use to us now, and we send [it] to you & sister Williams[7] to be divided between you, that you may be able to procure such necessaries as you need &c.

town of Richmond

18th May Camp of Israel in Indiana State
My Dear Wife

meeting being over I sit down in my tent to write
a few lines to you to let you know that you are
on my mind and that I am sensible of the duties
of a Husband and Father and that I am well
and I pray God to let his blessings to rest
upon you and the Children and all that are
a round you untill I return to your society
the few lines you wrote and sent by the hand
of Brother Lyman gave me satisfaction and comf
ort and I hope you will continue to communica
te to me by your own hand for this is a consola
tion to me to converse with you in this way in
my lonely moments which is not easily discribed
I will indeavour to write every Sunday if I can
and let you know how I am and Brother Fredrick
ck will write to Oliver and give him the names of
the places we pass through and a history of our journey
from time to time so that it will not be necesary for me
to endevour to write it but feel a satisfaction to
write a few lines with my own hand in this way
I can have the privelege to communicate some of
my feelings that I should not dare to reveal
as you know that my Situation is a very critical
one Brother Jinkins and William Fisk and George are
all well and are humble are determined to be
faithful and finally all the Kirtland Brothen are
well ma cannot quit I must close for I cannot
write on my knees sitting on the ground to edifica
tion O may the blessings of God rest upon you
is the prayre of your Husband until death

Emma Smith

To Emma Smith, May 18, 1834, p. 1. Handwriting of Joseph Smith. See
text, p. 322. (RLDS Church Archives.)

To Emma Smith, May 18, 1834, p. 2. Handwriting of Frederick G. Williams. See text, p. 322. (RLDS Church Archives.)

To Lyman Wight,
Edward Partridge, John Corrill,
Isaac Morley, and Others of the
High Council, August 16, 1834

When news reached Jackson County that a Mormon army was being organized to help reinstate their exiled brethren to their lands in Missouri, local reaction was immediate. Zion's Camp had not left Kirtland before some 170 Mormon buildings still standing in Jackson County were burned.[1] As the Camp neared Clay County, Missouri, threats of violence and opposition intensified. In this setting, Mormon representatives informed Governor Dunklin that they were ready to avail themselves of the promised military guard to reinstate them upon their lost lands.[2] According to Parley P. Pratt, the governor acknowledged the justice of the demand "but frankly told us he dare not attempt the execution of the laws in that respect, for fear of deluging the whole country in civil war and bloodshed."[3]

Without the promised support and faced with the futility of trying to protect the entire Mormon population with such a small force, Joseph Smith terminated the mission of Zion's Camp.[4]

After organizing a high council and regulating local Church affairs in Clay County, the Prophet returned to Kirtland, arriving about August 1 "after a tedious journey from the midst of enemies, mobs, cholera, and excessively hot weather."[5] On the sixteenth he dictated the following letter to Church leaders in Missouri.

Kirtland August 16th 1834

Dear Brethren Lyman Wight Edward Partrige John Carrill Isaac
Morley and others the high council of the Church of the Latter
Day Saints—
    Afte[r] so long a time I dictate a few lines to you to let you
know that I am in Kirtland and that I found all well on my arival,
as pertaining to health &c but ~~found~~ our common advisary had
taken the advantage of our brothe[r] Sylvest[er] Smith and others
who gave a false colloring to allmost every transaction from the
time that we left Kirtland untill we returned, and thereby stirred up
a great difficulty in the Church against me⁶ accor=dingly I was met
in the face and eyes as soon as I had got home with a catalogue that
was as black as the author himself and the cry was Tyrant,! Pope!!
King!!! Usurper!!!! Abuser of men!!!!! Ange[l]!!!!!! False
prophet!!!!! Prophecying Lies in the name of the Lord and taking
consecrated monies!!!!!!! and every other lie to fill up and
complete the cattelogue that was necissary to perfect the Church to
be meet for the devourer the shaft of the ~~devouring~~ ‹distroying›
Angel! and in consequence of having to combat all these I have
not been [p. 84] able to regulate my mind so as to write to give you
counsel and the information that you needed, but that God who
rules on high and thunder[s] Judgments upon Israel when they
transgress has given me power from the time that I was born (into
this kingdom) to stand and I have succeeded in putting all
gainsayers and enemies to flight unto the present time and not
withstanding the advisary laid a plan which was more subtle than
all others, I now swim in good *clean* ~~pure~~ water with my *head* out! as
you will see by the next star⁷
    I shall now procede to give you such council as the spirit of the
Lord may dictate you will reccollect that your business must be
done by your high council:⁸ you will rec=collect that the first elders
are to receive their endowment in Kirtland before the redemption
of Zion you will reccollect that your high council will have power
to say who of the first Elders among the Children of Zion are
accounted worthy; and you will also reccollect that you have my

testamony in behalf of certain ones previously to my departure you
will reccollect that the sooner that these ambassadors of the most
high are dispatched to bear testamony to lift up a warning voice
and to proclaim the everlasting gospel and to use every convincing
proof, and facculty with this generation while on their Journey . . .
‹to Kirtland›[9] They should awaken ‹the› sympathy of the people I
would reccommend to brother Phelps (If he is yet there) to write a
petition such as will be approved of by the high council and let
there be every signer obtained that can be in the State of Missouri
and while they are on their Journey to this country that
peradventure we may learn [p. 85] whethe[r] we have friends or not
in these United States,

This petition to be sent to the Govonor of Missouri to solicit
him to call on the President of the United States for a guard to
protect our brethren in Jackson County upon their own Lands from
the insults and abuses of the MOB

And I would reccomend to brother Wight to enter complaint to
the Govonor as often as he receves any insults or injury, and in
case that they pro=cede to endeavor to take life or tear down
homes, and if the citizens of Clay co, do not befriend us to gather
up the little army and be set over Immediately into Jackson County
and trust in God and do the ~~worst~~ ‹best› he can in ~~defending~~
maintaining the ground, but in case the excitement continues to be
allayed and peace prevails use every effort to prevail on the
churches to gather to those regions and situate themselves to be in
readiness to move into Jackson Co. in two years from the Eleventh
of September next which is the appointed time for the redemption
of Zion, *If* Verely ~~If~~ I say unto you *If* the Church with one united
effort performs their duties If they do this the work shall be
complete If they do not this in all humility making prep=eration
from this time forth like Joseph in Egypt laying up store against the
time of famine every man having his tent, his horses, his charrots
his armory his cattle his family and his whole substance in readiness
against the time ‹when› it shall be said *To your tents O Isral!!* and
let not this be noised abroad let every heart beat in silence and
every mouth be shut.

Now my beloved brethren you will learn by this we have a great work to do, and but little time to do it in and if we dont exert ourselves to the utmost in gathering up the strength of the Lords house that this thing may be accomplished behold their remaineth a scorge[10] [p. 86] also, Therefore be wise this once O ye children of Zion! and give heed to my councel saith the Lord!

I would inform bro Edward that the bill I recieved of him was good and when I can get ‹our› ~~other~~ money changed for another I will mail it to him the brethren as yet have generally ~~been~~ arived from Clay Co. in health notwithstanding the warm season. I would also in=form bro Edward that I am not satisfied with bro Hulett conserning the colt and so long as unrig=hteousness acts are suffered in the church it can=not [be] sanctified neither Zion be redeemed.

And also, that I was obliged to leave the consecrated horn in Illinois also bro William E McLelin who was sick we expect when he recovers that he will come to Kirtland—he was humble, and I entertain no doubt as to his standing while he continues so we have a desire to Learn conserning the Cholera and whether sister Bunnel is yet alive; as well as all deaths, the names and standing of those who are called away &c. The Cholera is raging in Detroit Cleaveland Fairport Buffalow and other places, we found it in Chariton as we came through and almost every other place,[11] it ‹is› an awful and solomn day, but this is only the forebodings of what is to come, The church seems to be in a languid cold disconsolate state, and as the revolution of the earth is once in 24 hours so we may look for revolutions among this wicked and perverse generation and also in the Church of Christ! When the head is sick the whole body is faint, for when the church lifts up the head the Angel will bring us good tidings even so Amen

Joseph Smith Jr

To Oliver Cowdery, September 24, 1834

Alexander Campbell was born in 1788 at Shaw's Castle, County Antrim, Ireland. Trained for the ministry by his father, a Presbyterian minister, and further educated at the University of Glasgow, Campbell emigrated to America in 1809, joining his father who had preceded him to Pennsylvania. Disturbed by the "rule of faith" of the Presbyterian creed, the Campbells in 1810 formed an independent society at Brush Run, Pennsylvania, based upon Baptist views and usages. But believing baptism necessary for the remission of sins, contrary to the Baptist avowal that the new life was complete before baptism, the Campbells were expelled from the Baptist communion in 1827. Objecting to any human creed, and regarding the Bible as a sufficient rule of faith, they formed the Disciples of Christ, commonly known as Campbellites or Disciples. In 1823 Campbell began publishing the *Christian Baptist,* changed in 1829 to *Millennial Harbinger,* the official publication of his denomination.[1]

Followers of Campbell under the leadership of Sidney Rigdon provided the initial converts to Mormonism in Kirtland, Ohio, in the fall of 1830.[2] Having been the focus of attention by Campbell in the pages of the *Millennial Harbinger* in 1834, Joseph Smith responded in *The Evening and the Morning Star.*

Kirtland, Ohio, September 24, 1834.

DEAR BROTHER,——

    I have, of late, been perusing Mr. A. Campbell's "Millennial Harbinger." I never have rejoiced to see men of corrupt hearts step forward and assume the authority and pretend to teach the ways of God—this is, and always has been a matter of grief; therefore I cannot but be thankful, that I have been instrumental in the providence of our heavenly Father in drawing forth, before the eyes of the world, the *spirits* by which certain ones, who profess to be "Reformers, and Restorers of ancient principles," are actuated! I have always had the satisfaction of seeing the truth triumph over error, and darkness give way before light, when such men were *provoked* to expose the corruption of their own hearts, by crying delusion, deception, and false prophets, accusing the innocent, and condemning the guiltless, and exalting themselves to the stations of gods, to lead blind-fold, men to perdition!

    I have never been blessed, (if it may be called such,) with a personal acquaintance with Mr. Campbell, neither a personal interview, but the GREAT MAN, not unfrequently *condescends* to notice an individual of as obscure birth as myself, if I am at liberty to interpret the language of *his* "Harbinger," where he says, "*Joe* Smith! *Joe* Smith! imposture! imposture!" I have noticed a strange thing! I will inform you of my meaning, though I presume you have seen the same ere this. Mr. Campbell was very lavish of his expositions of the falsity and incorrectness of the book of Mormon, some time since, but of late, since the publication of the Evening and the Morning Star, has said little or nothing, except some of his back-handed *cants*. He did, to be sure, about the time the church of Christ was established in Ohio, come out with a lengthy article, in which he undertook to prove that it was incorrect and contrary to the former revelations of the Lord. Perhaps, he is of opinion that he so completely overthrew the foundation on which it was based, that all that is now wanting to effect an utter downfall of those who have embraced its principles is, to continue to *bark* and *howl,* and cry, *Joe* Smith! false prophet! and ridicule every man who may be disposed to examine the evidences which God has given to the world of its truth!

I have never written Mr. Campbell, nor received a communication from him but a public notice in his paper:—If you will give this short note a place in the Star you will do me a kindness, as I take this course to inform the gentleman, that while he is breathing out scurrility he is effectually showing the honest, the motives and principles by which he is governed, and often causes men to investigate and embrace the book of Mormon, who might otherwise never have perused it. I am satisfied, therefore he should continue his scurrility; indeed, I am more than gratified, because his cry of *Joe* Smith! *Joe* Smith! *false* prophet! *false* prophet! must manifest to *all* men the spirit he is of, and serves to open the eyes of the people.

I wish to inform him further, that as he has, for a length of time, smitten me upon one cheek, and I have offered no resistance, I have turned the other also, to obey the commandment of our Savior; and am content to sit awhile longer in silence and see the great work of God roll on, amid the opposition of this world in the face of every scandal and falsehood which may be invented and put in circulation.

I am your brother in the testamony of the book of Mormon, and shall ever remain.

JOSEPH SMITH jr.

TO OLIVER COWDERY.

To Oliver Cowdery,
December 1834

Philastus Hurlbut, upon returning to Ohio from his New York and Pennsylvania trip to find materials that would discredit Joseph Smith, began lecturing on the origin of Mormonism. In his efforts to blacken the Smith name, Hurlbut had gathered signatures to a number of affidavits from people who claimed acquaintance with the Smith family in New York and Pennsylvania. Strangely repetitious in phraseology and generalities, the affidavits portrayed the Smiths as indolent deceivers, "entirely destitute of moral character and addicted to vicious habits."[1]

In the spring of 1834 Hurlbut sold his material to Eber D. Howe, the editor of the *Painesville* (Ohio) *Telegraph*, who published it in his *Mormonism Unvailed* in November of that year. Concurrent with the appearance of the Howe book, the *Messenger and Advocate* began publication of what was intended to be "a full history of the rise of the church" to counteract distorted reports that had circulated. Oliver Cowdery, editor of the paper, in his introduction, wrote that "no sooner had the messengers of the fulness of the gospel, began to proclaim its heavenly precepts, and call upon men to embrace the same, than they were vilified and slandered by thousands who never saw their faces, and much less knew aught derogatory of their characters, moral or religious—Upon this unfair and unsaint like manner of procedure they have been giving in large *sheets* their own opinions of the incorrectness of our system, and *attested* volumes of our lives and characters."[2]

Having learned of the prospective history, Joseph Smith sent Oliver Cowdery the following letter which appeared in the December issue of the paper.

[December 1834]

Brother O. Cowdery:

Having learned from the first No. of the Messenger and Advocate, that you were, not only about to "give a history of the rise and progress of the church of the Latter Day Saints;" but, that said "history would necessarily embrace my life and character," I have been induced to give you the time and place of my birth; as I have learned that many of the opposers of those principles which I have held forth to the world, profess a personal acquaintance with me, though when in my presence, represent me to be another person in age, education, and stature, from what I am.

I was born, (according to the record of the same, kept by my parents,) in the town of Sharon, Windsor Co. Vt. on the 23rd of December, 1805.

At the age of ten my father's family removed to Palmyra, N.Y. where, and in the vicinity of which, I lived, or, made it my place of residence, until I was twenty one—the latter part, in the town of Manchester.

During this time, as is common to most, or all youths, I fell into many vices and follies; but as my accusers are, and have been forward to accuse me of being guilty of gross and outragious violations of the peace and good order of the community, I take the occasion to remark, that, though, as I have said above, "as is common to most, or all youths, I fell into many vices and follies," I have not, neither can it be sustained, in truth, been guilty of wronging or injuring any man or society of men; and those imperfections to which I alude, and for which I have often had occasion to lament, were a light, and too often, vain mind, exhibiting a foolish and trifling conversation.

This being all, and the worst, that my accusers can substantiate against my moral character, I wish to add, that it is not without a deep feeling of regret that I am thus called upon in answer to my own conscience, to fulfill a duty I owe to myself, as well as to the cause of truth, in making this public confession of my former uncircumspect walk, and unchaste conversation: and more particularly, as I often acted in violation of those holy precepts which I knew came from God. But as the "Articles and Covenants" of this church are plain upon this particular point, I do not deem it important to proceed further. I only add, that I do not, nor never have, pretended to be any other than a man "subject to passion," and liable, without the assisting grace of the Savior, to deviate from that perfect path in which all men are commanded to walk!

By giving the above a place in your valuable paper, you will confer a lasting favor upon myself, as an individual, and, as I humbly hope, subserve the cause of righteousness.

I am, with feelings of esteem, your fellow laborer in the gospel of our Lord.

JOSEPH SMITH Jr.

To Almira Scobey, June 2, 1835
To Sally Phelps, July 20, 1835

Zion's Camp disbanded near Fishing River in Clay County, Missouri, on June 22, 1834, when, in the face of renewed violence, Joseph Smith read a revelation stating that "the redemption of Zion" was being postponed "for a little season" and that it was not necessary for the Camp "to fight the battles of Zion." For those who had participated in the march to Missouri, the revelation promised a special "blessing and endowment" in the temple then being built at Kirtland.[1]

Among fifteen men subsequently named to receive this honor was the Church printer, William W. Phelps. Although newly appointed to the Missouri high council, Phelps was instructed to leave his family and plan to remain in Kirtland for a time to assist with Church printing. Leaving his wife and six of his seven children, Phelps started for Ohio with his eldest son (twelve-year-old William Waterman) and John Whitmer on April 25, 1835. He arrived in Kirtland three weeks later.[2]

During the next eleven months, while living in the home of the Prophet in Kirtland, Phelps's only contact with his family was through the letters he wrote. On two occasions Joseph availed himself of the opportunity to fill unused space in a Phelps letter with a message of his own. One letter, written by William to his wife Sally on June 2, 1835, contains a few lines of Joseph to his cousin Almira Scobey, who, along with Sally

338

Phelps, was living in Liberty, Missouri, at the time.[3] Another, dated July 20, was directed by Joseph to Sally Phelps.

[Kirtland, Ohio, June 2, 1835]

Cousin Almyra, Scoby
    Brother W W phelps has left a little space for me to occupy and I gladly improve it, I would be glad to see the Children of Zion and del[i]ver the ‹word› of Eternal life to them from my own mauth but cannot this year nevertheless the day will come that I shall injoy this priviluge I trust. and we all shall receive an inheritance in the land of refuge which is so much to be desired seeing it is under the direction of the Allmighty therefore let us live faithful before the Lord and it shall be well with us I feel for all the Chilldren of Zion and pray for them in all my prayrs peace be multiplyed unto their redeemtion and favor from God Amen

Joseph Smith Jr

[Kirtland, Ohio, July 20, 1835]

    D Sister phelps as Brother phelps has given me an oportu=nity in his ~~paper~~ letter, I gladly improve it, how far it may be to your edifycation I know not, but trust you will receive it in a maner that shall answer my intention in so doing—for my intention is to give you a word of consolation to streng[th]=en you in the absence of your most worthy Companion, and husband whose Merits and exper‹i›ance and acquirements, but few can compete with in this generation and fewer I fear will ever appretiate the worth of such men; men upon whom God in his wi[s]dom hath bestowed gifts, that duly q‹u›alify them to lead men in the way of life and salvation. I consid=er in some degree how great a trial you muste have in this sepira=tion, but I think I may safely say, that you may rest with a firm reliance that God will so order it

that you may not be seperated only but for a short season, and
then ‹your Joy will be full› and if faithful ‹he will› return and
teach you things that have been hid from the wise and prudent,
hiden things of old times as Moses said in Deut. 33d ‹chap› 19th
verse for they shall suck of the abundance of t[he] [se]as and of
the tre[as]ures hid in the sand. Some of these things have begun
[to] come forth therefore Lift up your heart and be glad; be
comforted be faithful: pray in faith; and in fine say to all the
saints in Zion as the Lord God livith the [re]demtion of Zion is
nigh at hand, and we shall live to see it

J. Smith Jr.

To Almira Scobey, June 2, 1835. Handwriting of Joseph Smith. See text, p. 339. (LDS Church Archives.)

To Sally Phelps, July 20, 1835. Handwriting of Joseph Smith. See text, pp. 339-40. (Reproduction from Improvement Era 45 [August 1942]: 529.)

To Brethren,
June 15, 1835

Shortly after the organization of the Church in 1830, Joseph Smith commenced what he called a "new translation" of the Bible. By 1833, the work had progressed to the point that extracts were printed in *The Evening and the Morning Star* in Missouri and plans were announced to publish the completed translation simultaneously at Independence, Missouri, and Kirtland, Ohio. However, the expulsion of the Saints from Jackson County interrupted this. An April 1834 revelation urged that Martin Harris contribute money for the printing of the scriptures and that a copyright be secured for the publication.[1]

It is not clear what Harris's circumstances were, but this letter of the Prophet to brethren of the Church on June 15, 1835, indicates that other sources of funding for the publication were necessary.

Kirtland June 15, 1835

Dear brethren in the Lord,

I send you my love and warmest wishes for your prosperity in the great cause of our Redeemer.

We are now commencing to prepare and print the New Translation, together with all the revelations which God has been pleased to give us in these last days, and as we are in want of funds to go on with so great and glorious a work, brethren ‹we› want you should donate and loan us all the means or money you can that we may be enable[d] to accomplish the work as a great means towards the salvation of men.

My love to my relatives &c
                    your brother in the bonds of the New Covenant

Joseph Smith Jr

To Hezekiah Peck,
August 31, 1835

In March 1831, at the age of twenty-nine, the Book of Mormon witness John Whitmer was called by revelation as Church historian and began writing the history he designated "The Book of John Whitmer." Later that year he was sent to Jackson County, Missouri, with Oliver Cowdery to carry Church revelations for publication. Early in 1835, having in the meantime been appointed an assistant president of the Church in Missouri, Whitmer returned to Kirtland, Ohio, where he worked on the temple, participated in its dedication, and edited the *Messenger and Advocate*. While in Kirtland, continuing to add to his history, he wrote that letters were received by the presidency concerning difficulties among officers of the Church in Zion. When Joseph Smith responded to the situation on August 31, 1835, Whitmer copied the letter in his history.[1] As noted therein, Joseph had dictated the original and addressed it to Hezekiah Peck,[2] one of the Church leaders in Missouri.

Kirtland Aug. 31, 1835.

The Presiding of Kirtland and Zion say that the Lord has manifested by revelation of his spirit: that the high priest[s], Teachers, Priests and deacons, or in other words all the officers in the land of Clay Co. Mo. belonging to the church are more or less in transgre=sion, because they have not enjoyed the spirit of God

345

sufficiently to be able to comprehend their duties respecting them=selves, and the welfare of Zion. Thereby having been left to act, in a manner that is detrimental to the interest, and also a hindrance, to the redemption of Zion.

Now if they will be wise, they will humble themselves in a peculiar manner that God may open the eyes of their under=standing, It will be clearly manifest that the design and purposes of the Almighty; are with regard to them and the children of Zion; that they should let the high counsel which is appointed of God, and ordained for that purpose, ‹make and› regulate all the affairs of Zion: and that it is the will of God, that her chil=dren should stand still, and see the salvation of her redemption; and the officers of the church should go forth, inasmuch as they can have their families in comfortable circumstances; and gather up the saints, even the strength of the Lords house. And those who cannot go forth consis[t]=ently with the will of God their circumstan=ces preventing them; remain in deep humility: and in as much, they do any thing [p. 77] confine themselves to teaching the first principles of the Gospel: not endeavoring to institute regulations or laws for Zion, without having been appointed of God.

Now we say there is no need of ordaining in Zion, or appointing any more officers: but let all those that are ordained magnify themselves before the Lord; by going into the vineyard and cleansing their garments from the blood of this generation. It is one thing to be ordained to preach the gospel, and to push the people together to Zion, and it is another thing to be annointed to lay the foundation and build up the City of Zion, and execute her laws. There=fore it is certain that many of the Elders have come under great condemnation, in endeavoring to steady the ark of God, in a place where they have not been sent.

The high counsel and bishops court have been established to do the business of Zion, and her children are not bound, to accknowledge any of those who feel dis=posed to run to Zion and set themselves to be their rulers. Let not her children be duped in this way, but let them prove those who say they are apostles, and

are not. The Elders have no right to regulate Zion, but they have a
right to preach the gos=pel. They will all do well to repent and
humble themselves, and all the church, and also we, ourselves
receive the admonition and do now endeavor and pray to this end
[p. 78] When the children of Zion are stranger[s] in a strange land
their harps must be hung upon the willows: and they cannot sing
the songs of Zion: but should mourn and not dance. Therefore
brethren, it remains for all such to be exercised with prayer, and
contin=ual suplication, until Zion is redeemed. We realize the
situation that all the brethren and sisters must be in, being
deprived of their spir=itual privileges, which are enjoyed by those
who set in heavenly places in Christ Jesus; where there are no mobs
to rise up and bind their consciences. Nevertheless, it is wisdom
that the church should make but little or no stir in that region, and
cause as little excitement as posible and endure their affli=ctions
patiently until the time appointed—and the Governor of Mo.
fulfils his promise in setting the church over upon their own lands.
We would suggest an idea that it would be wisdom for all the
mem=bers of the church on the return of the Bish=op, to make
known to him their names places of residince &c. that it may be
known where they all are when the Governor shall give directions
for you to be set over on your lands

Again it is the will of the Lord, that the church should attend
to their com=munion on the sabbath day, and let them remember
the commandment which says "talk not of Judgment" we are
com=manded not to give the childrens bread unto the dogs; neither
cast our pearl before [p. 79] swine, least they trample them under
their feet, and turn again and rend you. There=fore–let us be wise
in all things, and keep all the commandments of God, that our
salvation may be sure; having our armour ready and prepared
against the time ap=pointed; and having on the whole armour of
righteousness, we may be able to stand in that trying day. We say
also that if there are any doors open for the Elders to preach the
first principles of the gospel: let them not keep silence: rail not
against the sects, neither talk against their tenets. But preach
Christ and him crucified, love to God, and love to man, observing

always to make mention of our republic=an principles, thereby if posible, we may allay the prejudice of the people, be meek and lowly of heart, and the Lord God of our fathers shall be with you for evermore Amen. Sanctioned and signed by the Presidents

> Joseph Smith Jr.
> Oliver Cowdery
> Sidney Rigdon
> F. G. Williams
> W. W. Phelps
> John Whitmer

P.S. Br Hesakiah Peck

We remember your family, with all the fi[r]st families of the church, who first embraced the truth, we remember your losses and sorrows our first ties are not broken, we [p. 80] participate with you in the evil as well as the good, in the sorrows as well as the joys, our union we trust is stronger than death, and shall never be severed. Remember us unto all who believe in the fulness of the gospel of our Lord and Saviour Jesus Christ. We hereby authorize you Hezekiah Peck, our beloved brother to read this epistle and communicate it unto all the brotherhood in all that region of Country. Dictated by me your unworthy brother, and fellow laborer in the testimony of the book of Mormon. Signed by my own hand in the token of the everlasting covenant.

> Joseph Smith Jr.

To Emma Smith,
August 19, 1836

In July 1836, faced with heavy financial obligations, Joseph Smith, Sidney Rigdon, Oliver Cowdery, and Hyrum Smith traveled to Salem, Massachusetts. According to Ebenezer Robinson, the trip to Salem was motivated, at least in part, by the claim of a Church member named William Burgess "that a large amount of money had been secreted in the cellar of a certain house in Salem, Massachusetts, which had belonged to a widow, and he thought he was the only person now living who had knowledge of it, or to the location of the house." Convinced of the veracity of the claim, Burgess took steps "to try and secure the treasure."

The Prophet and his associates left Kirtland on July 25. But upon arriving in Salem, Mr. Burgess was unable to identify the particular house because "time had wrought such a change" to the area since he was last there. Although Joseph Smith and his friends found a house "they felt was the right one" and rented it, they failed to locate the treasure, and returned to Kirtland in September after a revelation had directed their attention to the human "treasure" in the city.[1]

The following letter of Joseph to his wife, Emma, was written from Salem on August 19.

Salem, Mass., August 19th, 1836.

My beloved Wife:—Bro. Hyrum is about to start for home
before the rest of us, which seems wisdom in God, as our business
here can not be determined as soon as we could wish to have it. I
thought a line from me by him would be acceptable to you, even if
it did not contain but little, that you may know that you and the
children are much on my mind. With regard to the great object of
our mission, you will be anxious to know. We have found the
house since Bro. Burgess left us, very luckily and providentially, as
we had one spell been most discouraged. The house is occupied,
and it will require much care and patience to rent or buy it. We
think we shall be able to effect it; if not now within the course of a
few months. We think we shall be at home about the middle of
September. I can think of many things concerning our business,
but can only pray that you may have wisdom to manage the
concerns that involve on you, and want you should believe me that
I am your sincere friend and husband. In haste. Yours &c.,

                            Joseph Smith, Jr.
        Emma Smith

To John Corrill and the Church in Zion, September 4, 1837

One of the darkest hours of Joseph Smith's life occurred at Kirtland, Ohio, in 1837. With economic conditions as the focal point following the collapse of the Kirtland bank, a spirit of discord threatened dissolution of the Church. According to Brigham Young, "Disaffection and apostacy . . . prevailed so extensively that it was difficult for any to see clearly the path to pursue. . . . The knees of many of the strongest men in the church faltered." George A. Smith wrote that "the hearts of many of the strong trembled, and a severe attempt" was made to overthrow Joseph Smith and replace him as Prophet. During this time, dissenters were "very violent in their opposition" to Joseph Smith and all who supported him.[1]

While Joseph was absent on Church business in Canada during the summer, dissenters led by Warren Parrish interrupted a meeting presided over by Joseph Smith, Sr., and tried to seize control of the temple. Only alert action by police prevented bloodshed. Upon the Prophet's return, a conference was convened to deal with matters and restore stability. During the conference, three members of the Quorum of Twelve and four members of the Kirtland High Council were rejected.

The day after the conference, on September 4, 1837, Joseph appended a copy of the conference minutes with this letter to John Corrill and the Saints in Missouri.

Sept 4th A.D. 1837
Kirtland Geauga Co. Ohio

Joseph Smith Jr Prest of the Church ‹of Christ› of Latter Day
Saints in all the world To John Corroll & the whole Church in
Zion [p. 18] Sendeth greeting,
    Blessed be the God of and father of our Lord Jesus Christ Who
has blessed you with many blessings in Christ. And who has
delivered you many times from the hands of your Enimies And
planted you many times in an heavenly or holy place, My res=pects
& love to you all, and my bless=ings upon all the faithfull & true
harted in the new & everlasting covenant & for as=much as I have
desired for a long time to see your faces, & converse with you &
instruct you in those things which have been revealed to me
portaining to the Kingdom of God in the last days, I now write
unto you offering an appolegy, My being bound with bonds of
affliction by the workers of ini=quity and by the labours of the
Ch=urch endeaveroung in all things to do the will of God, for the
Salvation of the Church both in temporal as well as spiritual
things. Bretheren we have wai=ded through a Scene of affliction
and sor=row thus far for the will of God, that lan=guage is
inadequate to describe pray ye therefore with more earnestness for
our redemption. You hav[e] und[o]=ubtedly been informed by letter
& otherwise of our difficulties in Kirtla=nd which are now about
being Settled and that you may have a knowledge of the same I
subscribe to you the following minutes of the comittee of the whole
Church of Kirtland the authorities &c. refering you to my brother
Hyrum & br. T.B. Marsh for further particulars also that you [p.
19] may know how to proceed to set in order & regulate the affairs
of the Church in Zion whenever they become disorganized

[Minutes for September 3, 1837, follow.]

Joseph Smith Jr.

Diary Entry, March 13, 1838

To the Presidency of the Church in Kirtland, March 29, 1838

Feelings against Joseph Smith in Kirtland, Ohio, reached such proportions by January 1838 that Joseph was forced to leave the town to save his life. According to his history, "A new year dawned upon the Church in Kirtland in all the bitterness of the spirit of apostate mobocracy; which continued to rage and grow hotter and hotter, until Elder Rigdon and myself were obliged to flee from its deadly influence. . . . On the evening of the 12th of January, about ten o'clock, we left Kirtland, on horseback, to escape mob violence, which was about to burst upon us under the color of legal process to cover the hellish designs of our enemies, and to save themselves from the just judgment of the law."[1]

Destitute and traveling in extremely inclement weather, Joseph and his family arrived in Far West, Missouri, on March 13. A month later he began dictating a record of his experience, beginning with his arrival in Missouri, to his clerk George W. Robinson who wrote it down in a volume he titled "The Scriptory Book of Joseph Smith Jr., President of the Church of Jesus Christ, of Latterday Saints in all the World." Robinson had been appointed general church recorder at a conference in Kirtland the previous September. On April 6, 1838, his appointment was reaffirmed by the vote of the Church in Far West, and in addition he was named "scribe for the first presidency."[2] Six days later Robinson began writing at

Joseph Smith's dictation the volume that has become an important documentary source for events involving Joseph Smith
and the Church in Missouri between March 13 and September
10, 1838.

The Scriptory Book consists of journal entries describing
the Prophet's activities, interspersed with copies of revelations,
letters, and other documents of historical value. With the exception of the first two pages, the journal portion of the record
was written by Robinson as he observed Joseph's comings and
goings. The beginning entry, dictated by Joseph Smith, is presented here with a letter recorded in the same volume dated
March 29 to Church leaders still in Kirtland, the original of
which may also have been a dictation, or a holograph.

On the 13th day of March I with my family and some others
arrived within 8 milds of Far West and put up at brother Barnerds
to tarry for the night. Here we ware meet by an escort of
brether=en from the town who came to make us welcome to their
little Zion. On the next day as we ware about entering the town
Many of the brether=en came out to meet us who also withe open
armes welcomed us to their boosoms. We were immediately
received under the hospitable roof of George W. Harris[3] who
treated us with all kindness possible. here we refreshed ourselves
withe much sattisfaction after our long and tedious Journey and the
bretheren braught in such necessaries as we stood in need of for our
presant comfort and necessities.

After being here two or three days my Brother Samuel arrived
with his family an[d] shortly after his arrival while walking with
him & cirtain other bretheren the following sentiments occured to
my mind.

Motto of the Church of Christ of Latterday Saints

The Constitution of our country formed by the Fathers of
Liberty.

Peace and good order in society Love to God and good will to
man.

All good and wholesome Laws; And virtue and truth above all things

And Aristarchy live forever!!!

But Wo, to tyrants, Mobs, Aristocracy, Anarchy and Toryism: And all those who invent or seek out unrighteous and vexatious lawsuits under the pretext or color of law or office, either religious or political.

Exalt the standard of Democracy! Down [p. 16] with that of Priestcraft, and let all the people say Amen! that the blood of our Fathers may not cry from the ground against us.

Sacred is the Memory of that Blood which baught for us our liberty.

	Signed	Joseph Smith Jr
		Thomas B. Marsh
		D. W. Patten
		Brigham Youngs
		Samuel H. Smith
Geo. W. Robinson		George M. Hinkle
		John Corrill

Far West March 29th A.D. 1838

To the ~~first~~ Presidency of the Church of Jesus Christ of Latter Day Saints in Kirtland

Dear & well beloved brotheren. Through the grace & mercy of our God, after a long & tedious Journey of two months & one day, I and my family arrived in the City of Far West Having been met at Huntsville 120 Miles from this by broth=eren with teams & money to forward us on our Journey When within eight miles of the City of Far West We were met by an [p. 23] escort of bretheren from the City Who were T. B. Marsh John Corril Elias Higby & Severel others of the faithfull of the West Who received us with open armes and warm hearts and welcomed us to the bosom of their Sosciety On our arrival in the City we were greeted on Every hand by the Saints who bid us welcom[e]; Welcome; to the land of their inheritance. Dear bretheren you may be assured that so friendly a

meeting & reception paid us will for our long seven years of
Servictude persecution & affliction in the mi=dst of our enimies in
the land Kirtland yea verily our hearts were full and we feel
greatfull to Almighty God for his kindness unto us. The particulars
of our journey brotheren cannot well be writen but we trust that
the same God w‹h›o has prot=ected us will protect you also, and
will sooner or later grant us the privilege of seeing each other face
‹to› face & of rehersing all our sufferings We have herd of the
destruction of the printing office¹ which we presume to believe
must have been occasioned by the Parrishites² or more properly the
Aristocrats or Anarchys as we believe, The Saints here have
provided a room for us and daily necessary's which is brought in
from all parts of the Co. to make us comf=ortable, so that I have
nothing to do but to attend to my spiritual concerns or the spiritual
affairs of the Church The difficulties of the Church had been
Ajusted before [my] arrival here by a Judicious High Council With
T. B. Marsh & D W Patten who acted as Pres. Pro. Tem. of the
Church of Zion being appointed by the voice of the Council &
Church Wm. W. Phelps & John Whitmer having been cut off from
the Church,³ D Whitmer remains as yet. The saints at this time are
in union & peace & love prevails throughout, in a word Hea=ven
smiles upon the saints in Caldwell. Various & many have been the
falshoods writen from thence [p. 24] to this place, but have
prevailed nothing, we have no uneasiness about the power of our
enimies in this place to do us harm Br Samuel H Smith & family
arrived here soon after we did in go[o]d health, Br B Young Br D.
S. Miles⁴ & Br L. Richards⁵ arrivd here when we did. They were
with us on the last of our journey which aded much to our
sattisfaction. They also are well They have provided places for their
families & are now about to break the ground for seed. Being under
the hand of wicked vex‹at›ious Lawsuits for seven years past my
buisness was so dangerous that I was not able to leave it, in as good
a situation as I had antisipated, but if there are any wrongs, They
shall all be noticed so far as the Lord gives me ability & power to do
so, Say to all the brotheren that I have not forgotten them, but
remember them in my pr=ayers, Say to Mother Beamon that I
remember her, Also Br Daniel Carter⁶ Br St[r]ong & family Br

Granger & family, Finally I cannot innum=erate them all for the
want of room I will just name Br Knights the Bishop &c.. My best
respects to them all ~~for the want of room~~ & I commend them and
the Church of God in Kirtland to our Heavenly Father & the word
of his grace, which is able to make you wise unto Salvation I would
just say to Br. Marks, that I saw in a vision while on the road that
whereas he was closely persued by an innumerable concource of
enimies and as they pressed upon him hard as if they were about to
devour him, It had seemingly attained some degre of advantage
over him But about this time a chariot of fire came and near the
place and the Angel of the Lord put forth his hand unto Br. Marks
& said [p. 25] unto him thou art my son come *here*. And
immedia=tely he was caught up in the Chariot and rode away
triumphantly out of their midst and again the Lord said I will raise
th[ee] up for a blessing unto many people Now the particulars of
this whole matter cannot be writen at this time but the vision was
evidently given to me that I might know that the hand of the Lord
would be on his behalf

J Smith Jr

I transmit to you the folowing motto of the Church of Jesus
Christ of Latter day Saints Recorded on Pages 16 & 17 of J Smith
Jr Scriptory Record Book A:

We left Pres. Rigdon 30 miles this side of Parris Illinois in
consequence of the sickness of Br. G. W. Robinsons wife, on
yesterday br Robinson arrived here who informed us that his
fatherin Law (S. Rigdon) was at Huntsville detained there on
account of the ill health of his wife, They will proba[b]ly be here
soon, Choice seeds of all kinds of fruit also Choice breed of Cattle
would be in much demand also best blood of horses garden seeds of
every description also hay seed of all sorts, all of these are much
needed in this place

Verry respe[c]tfully I subscribe myself your Servent in Christ our
Lord & Savior

Joseph Smith Jr
Prest of the Church of
Jesus Christ of
Latterday Saints

— A Mark Hofmann forgery —

To Hyrum Smith,
May 25, 1838

On May 18, 1838, Joseph Smith and Sidney Rigdon left Far West, Caldwell County, Missouri, at the head of an expedition northward into Daviess County for the purpose of locating land and making claims to further facilitate the settlement of the Latter-day Saints in that part of Missouri. While there, they selected the site for a city to be named Adam-ondi-Ahman. On May 24, the Prophet, whose wife was imminently expecting the birth of a child, returned to Far West, and the next day he addressed the following note to his brother Hyrum at "Plattis-grove."[1] The document is the only known Joseph Smith holograph written at Far West, Missouri.

[Far West, Missouri, May 25, 1838]

Verily thus Saith the Lord unto Hyram Smith if he will come strateaway to Far West and in=quire of his brother it shall be shown him how that he may be freed from de[b]t and ob=tain a grate treasure in the earth even so Amen [p. 1]

Mr Hyram Smith
Plattisgrove[2] [p. 2]

358

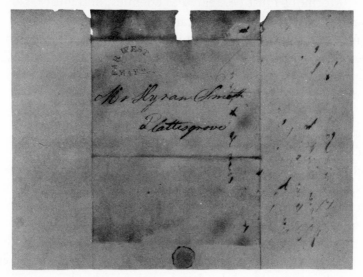

To Hyrum Smith, May 25, 1838. Handwriting of Joseph Smith. See text, p. 358. (LDS Church Archives.)

To Emma Smith,
November 4, 1838

The conflict between Mormon and non-Mormon that pre-
cipitated the expulsion of the Saints from Jackson County in
1833 flared again in northern Missouri in 1838. Beginning with
an election day confrontation at Gallatin, Daviess County, on
August 6, acts of violence, fed by bigotry and misunderstanding, proceeded in somber succession, culminating on October
27 with Governor Lilburn Boggs's order to militia units that
"the Mormons must be treated as enemies, and must be exterminated or driven from the State." Three days later an army of
some twenty-five hundred state militia, led by General Samuel
D. Lucas, approached the Mormon community of Far West
with its five hundred defenders for what appeared to be a final
showdown.[1]

On October 31, in an effort to defuse the tense situation,
Joseph Smith, Sidney Rigdon, Parley P. Pratt, Lyman Wight,
and George W. Robinson approached the camp of General
Lucas[2] under a flag of truce only to be seized and held as prisoners. Parley P. Pratt recalled: "We were marched into camp surrounded by thousands of savage looking beings, many of whom
were dressed and painted like Indian warriors. These all set up a
constant yell, like so many bloodhounds let loose upon their
prey, as if they had achieved one of the most miraculous vic-
tories that ever graced the annals of the world."[3]

The next day, after Hyrum Smith and Amasa Lyman were

also confined and an order to execute the prisoners was refused by General Alexander Doniphan, General Lucas ordered the Mormons taken to his fourth division militia headquarters in Independence, where they arrived on November 4 in the midst of a driving rain. Parley Pratt described the situation: "We were provided with a comfortable house, and a noble fire, as the storm was very severe. There we spent the time in conversation with the throngs who flocked to see us until supper, when we were guarded to a hotel and a splendid supper was set before us. After refreshing ourselves we were guarded back to our house and provided with papers and writing materials and candles and Br. Smith, Br. Robinson and myself now sit at the same stand scribbling each to our respective families while Brs. Wight, Rigdon, Hiram Smith, and Br. Lyman are in conversation with the visitors and guards. . . . Indeed were it not for the absence of our families we should almost forget that we are prisoners. We believe that this journey saved our lives from the hands of furious men and will result in good."[4]

The letter written by Joseph Smith to his wife on this occasion follows.

November 4th 1838
Indipenda[n]ce Jackson Co— Mo—

My dear and beloved companion, of my bosam, in tribulation, and affliction, I woud inform you that I am well, and ~~I am~~ that we are all of us in good spirits as regards our own fate, we have been protected by the Jackson County boys, in the most genteel manner, and arrived here in ‹the› midst of a splended perade, ~~this~~ a little after noon, instead ‹of› going to ~~J~~ goal [jail] we have a good house provided for us and the kindst treatment, I have great anxiety about you, and my lovely childre=n, my heart morns ‹and› bleeds for the broth=eren, and sisters, and for the slain ‹of

the⟩ peop=le of God, I Colonal Hinkle,[5] proved to be a trator, to
the Church, he is worse than a hull[6] who betraid the army at
detroit, he decoyed ⟨us⟩ unawares God rewa=rd him, I Jhon Carl[7]
~~told~~ ⟨general Wilson⟩ ~~was a going~~ told general, wilson,[8] that he
was a going to leave the Church, general Willson says he thinks
much less of him now then before, why I mention this is to have
you careful not to trust them, if we are permited to ~~be~~ stay any
time here, we ⟨have⟩ obtained a promice that ~~they~~ we may have
our families brought to us, what God may ~~do~~ do for us I do not
~~kow~~ know but I hope for the best always in all ~~s~~ circumstances
although I go unto death, I will trust in God, what outrages may
be committed by the mob I know not, but expect there will be but
little ⟨or⟩ no restr=aint Oh may God have mercy on us, [p. 1]
when we arrived at the river last night an express came to gene[r]al
Willson from geneal Clark of Howard County[9] claiming the right
of command ordering us back where ⟨or what place⟩ God only
knows, and there is some feelings betwen the offercers,[10] I do not
know where it will end, it ⟨is⟩ said by some that general Clark, is
determi=ned to exterminate~~ng~~ God has spare=d some of us thus
far perhaps he will extend mercy in some degree toward us ⟨yet⟩
some of the people of this place have told me that some of the
mormans may settle in this county as others ⟨men⟩ do ~~the peg~~ I
have some hopes that some thing may turn out for good to the
afflicted saints, I want you to stay where you are untill you here
from me again, I may send for you to ~~bl~~ bring you to me, I cannot
learn much for certainty in the situation that I am in, and can
only pray for deliverance, untill it is meeted out, and take every
thing as it comes, with patience and fortitude, I hope you will be
faithful and true to every trust, I cant write much in my
situa[t]=ion, conduct all matters as your circum=stances and
necesities require, may God give you wisdom and prudance and
sobriety which ⟨I⟩ have every reason to believe you will, those
little ⟨childrens⟩ are subjects of my medita=tion continually, tell
them that Father is yet alive, God grant that he may see them
again Oh Emma for God sake [p. 2] do not forsake me nor the
truth but remember me, if I do ⟨not⟩ meet you again in this life

may God grant that we may ‹may we› meet in heaven, I cannot express my feelings, my heart is full, Farewell Oh my kind and affectionate Emma I am yours forever your Hu[s]band and true friend

[Joseph Smith, Jr.]

To Mrs—
Emma Smith
Far West Mo
Coldwell Co. Mo– [p. 3]

November 4th 1838

Indipendace Jackson Co. Mo

My dear and beloved companion, of my
bosam, in tribulation, and affliction, I would
inform you that I am well, and that
that we are all of us in good spirits as
regards our own fate, we have been
protected by the Jackson County boys,
in the most genteel manner, and arived
here in the midst of a splended perade, this
a little after noon, instead of going to goal
we have a good house provided for us
and the kindest treatment, I have great
anxiety about you, and my lovely children
= n, my heart morns and bleeds for the breth
= ren, and Sisters, and for the Slain of the peop
= le of God, Colonal, Hinkle, proved to
be a traitor, to the Church, he is worse
than a hull who betraid the army at
detroit, he decoyed us unawares god reward
= rd him, John Carl, was going
told general, wilson, that he was a
going to leave the Church, general Willson
says he thinks much less of him now
then before, why I mention this is to
have you careful not to trust them
if we are permited to stay any
time here, we have obtained a promise that they
be may have our families brought to us
what God may do for us I do not know
know but I hope for the best, always in
all circumstances although I go unto
death, I will trust in God, what outrages
may be committed by the mob I know not
but expect there will be but little or no resto
= aint Oh may god have mercy on us,

To Emma Smith, November 4, 1838, p. 1. Handwriting of Joseph Smith.
See text, pp. 361-62. (RLDS Church Archives.)

when we arrived at the river last night
an express came to geneal Willson from
geneal Clark of Howard County, claiming
the right of command ordering us back
where or what place God only knows, and there is some
feelings between the officers I do not
know where it will end, it is said by
some that general Clark, is determi
ned to extermination God, has spared
some of us thus far perhaps he will
extend mercy in some degree toward
us yet Some of the people of this place have
told me that Some of the mormans
may settle in this County as others men to
them peg I have some hopes that Some
thing may turn out for good to the
afflicted Saint, I want you to Stay
where you are untill you here from
me again, I may send for you to
bring you to me, I cannot learn
much for certainty in the situation
that I am in, and can only pray for
deliverance, untill it is meeted out,
and take every thing as it comes,
with Patience and fortitude, I hope
you will be faithful and true to every
trust, I cant write much in my situa
tion, conduct all matters as your circum
stances and necessities require, may God
give you wisdom and prudance and sobriety
which I have every reason to beleave you
will, those little childrens are Subjects of my medita
tion continually, tell them that Father
is yet alive, god grant that he may see
them again Oh Emma for God Sake

To Emma Smith, November 4, 1838, p. 2. See text, p. 362. (RLDS Church Archives.)

do not forsake me nor the Truth but remember me, if I do not meet you again in this life may God grant that we may meet in heaven, I cannot express my feelings, my heart is full, Farewell Oh my kind and affectionate Emma I am yours forever your Husband and true friend

To Emma Smith, November 4, 1838, p. 3. See text, pp. 362-63. (RLDS Church Archives.)

To Emma Smith,
November 12, 1838

Four days after Joseph Smith and his associates were brought to Independence, an order came from General John B. Clark to move them to Richmond in Ray County. In the absence of a sufficiently large jail there, the men were thrust into an old log house, chained together, and placed under heavy guard.[1] On November 12 a court of inquiry, presided over by Judge Austin A. King of the Missouri fifth judicial circuit,[2] convened in the Richmond courthouse to consider charges of "treason, murder, arson, burglary, larceny, and stealing" against the Mormon prisoners. Anticipating a just and speedy hearing, Joseph wrote this letter to his wife on the day the court opened.

November 12th, 1838, Richmond

My Dear Emma,

we are ~~pr~~ prisoners in chains, and under strong guards, for Christ sake and for no other cause, although there has been things that were unbeknown to us, and altogether beyond our controal, that might seem, to the mob to be a pretext, for them to persacute us, but on examination, I think that the authorities, will discover our inocence, and set us free, but if this blessing cannot be ~~done~~ obtained, I have this consolation that I am an innocent man, let what will befall me, I recieved your letter which I read over and over again, it was a sweet morsal to me. Oh God grant that I may have the privaliege of seeing once more my

367

lovely Family, in the injoyment, of the sweets of liberty, and
sotia͞ial life, to press them to my bosam and kissng their lovely
cheeks would fill my heart with unspeakable ~~great~~ grattitude, tell
the chilldren that I am alive and trust I shall come and see them
before long, comfort their hearts all you can, and try to be
comforted yourself, all you can, the[re] is no possible dainger but
what we shall be set at Liberty if Justice can be done ⟨~~and~~ and⟩
that you know as well as myself, the tryal will begin to day for
some of us, Lawyer Rice[3] and we expect Doniphan,[4] will plead
our cause, we could ⟨git⟩ no others in time for the tryal, they are
able men and ⟨will⟩ do well no doubt, Brother Robison[5] is
chained next to me he ~~he~~ has a true heart and a firm mind,
Brother Whight,[6] is next, Br. Rigdon, next, Hyram, next, Parely,
next Amasa, next, and thus we are bound together in chains as
well as the cords of everlasting love, we are in good spirits and
rejoice that we are counted worthy to be per=secuted for christ
sake, tell little Joseph, he must be a good boy, Father loves him
⟨with⟩ a per=fect ~~H~~love, he is the Eldest must not hurt those that
⟨are⟩ smaller then him, but cumfor⟨t⟩ them tell little Frederick,
Father, loves him, with all his heart, he is a lovely boy. [p. 1] Julia
is a lovely little girl, I love hir also She is a promising child, tell
her Father wants her to remember him and be a good girl, tell all
the rest that I think of them and pray for them all, Br Babbit[7] is
waitting to carry our letters for us ~~the~~ colonal ⟨price⟩[8] is ~~wa~~
inspecting them therefore my time is short ⟨the⟩ little ~~baby~~
Elexander is on my mind continuly Oh my affectionate Emma, I
want you to remember that I am ⟨a⟩ true and faithful friend, to
you and the chilldren, forever, my heart is intwined around
you[r]s forever and ever, oh may God bless you all amen ~~you~~ I am
your husband and am in bands and tribulation &c—

                    Joseph Smith Jr

        to Emma Smith

        P S write as often as you can, and if possible come and see me,
and bring the chilldren if possible, act according to your own

feelings, ⟨and⟩ best Judgement, and indeavour to be comforted, if possible, and I trust that all will turn out for the best. J yours,

J. S. [p. 2]

Mrs Emma Smith
Far West

Dear
Affectionate
Affectation [p. 3]

November 12th 1838 Richmond

My Dear Emma, we are prisoners in chains, and under strong guards, for Christ sake and for no other cause, although there has been things that were unbeknown to us, and altogether beyond our controal, that might seem to be a pretext for them to persecute us, but on examination I think that the authorities, will discover our inocency and set us free, but if this blessing cannot be obtained, I have this consolation that I am an innocent man, let what will befall me, I received your letter which I read over and over again, it was a sweet morsal to me, Oh God grant that I may have the privaliege of seeing once more my lovely Family, in the injoyment, of the sweets of liberty, and sotial life, to press them to my bosom and kiss their lovely cheeks would fill my heart with unspeakable gratitude, tell the children that I am alive, and trust I shall come and see them before long, comfort their hearts all you can, and try to comfort yourself, all you can, there is no possible danger but what we shall be set at liberty if justice can be done, and that you know as well as myself, the trial will begin to-day for some of us, Lawyer Rice, and we espect Donithan, will plead our cause, we could git no others in time for the trial, they are able men and as well no doubt, Brother Robison is chained next to me, he has a true heart and a firm mind, Brother Whight is next to Bro. Rigdon, next, Hyram, next, Parly next, Amasa, next, and thus we are bound together in chains as well as the cords of everlasting love, we are in good spirits and rejoice that we are counted worthy to be persicuted for christ sake, tell little Joseph, he must be a good boy, Father loves him with a perfect love, he is the Eldest must not hurt those that are smaller them him, but care for them, tell little Frederick, Father, loves him, with all his heart; he is a lovely boy.

To Emma Smith, November 12, 1838, p. 1. See text, pp. 367-68.
(RLDS Church Archives.)

Julia is a lovely little girl; I love her also,
she is a promising child; tell her, Father
wants her to remember him and be a
good girl; tell all the rest that I think
of them and pray for them all. Br
Babbitt is waiting to carry our letters;
for us. the colonal price is inspecting them;
therefore my time is short. little baby
Elexander is on my mind continuelly;
Oh my affectionate Emma, I want you
to remember that I am true and faithful
friend, to you; and the children, forever;
my heart is entwined around yours forever
and ever; Oh, may God bless you all,
amen. you I am your husband and
am in bands and tribulation &c
to Emma Smith &c   Joseph Smith Jr

P.S. I write as often as you can, and
if possible come and see me; and bring
the children if possible, act according
to your own feelings and best judgement,
and indeavour to be comforted, if possible,
and I trust that all will turn out
for the best. / yours, J. S.

To Emma Smith, November 12, 1838, p. 2. Handwriting of Joseph
Smith. See text, pp. 368-69. (RLDS Church Archives.)

To Emma Smith, November 12, 1838, p. 3. Handwriting of Joseph Smith. See text, p. 369. (RLDS Church Archives.)

To Emma Smith, December 1, 1838

To the Church in Caldwell County, December 16, 1838

For Joseph Smith, his associates, and some fifty other Mormons confined in Richmond during the November 1838 court of inquiry, the experience was anything but pleasant. Parley P. Pratt wrote that "it was a very severe spell of snow and winter weather, and we suffered much. During this time Elder Rigdon was taken sick from hardship and exposure, and finally lost his reason; but still he was kept in our miserable, noisy, and cold room, and compelled to sleep on the floor with a chain and padlock round his ankle, and fastened to six others; and here he endured the constant noise and confusion of an unruly guard . . . frequently composed of the most noisy, foul-mouthed, vulgar, disgraceful, indecent rabble, that ever defiled the earth." Beside this suffering and privation, the proceedings of the court, which lasted from November 12 to November 28, brought little hope. According to Parley Pratt, "The judge could not be prevailed on to examine the conduct of the murderers, robbers, and plunderers, who had desolated our Society. Nor would he receive testimony except against us. And by the deserters and apostates who wished to save their own lives and property at the expense of others; and by those who had murdered and plundered us from time to time, he obtained abundance of testimony, much of which was entirely false."[1]

Finally, the court found "probable cause" to charge Joseph Smith, Lyman Wight, Hyrum Smith, Alexander McRae, Caleb Baldwin, and Sidney Rigdon with "overt acts of treason" in Daviess and Caldwell Counties,[2] and to charge Parley P. Pratt and four others with murder in Ray County.[3] In the absence of adequate jail facilities in the counties where the alleged crimes took place, those charged with treason were consigned to the jail at Liberty in Clay County; the others were to remain at Richmond. All were to await trial the following year.

The prisoners sent to Liberty Jail were taken there on December 1 in a heavy wagon under armed guard. Upon his arrival, Joseph Smith wrote a brief letter to his wife. Two weeks later he wrote to the scattered and destitute Church members in Caldwell County. Both letters follow. The first is a holograph; the second was written for Joseph by an unknown person at the jail.

December 1st, 1838

My Dear companion I take this oppertunity to inform you that I we arrived in Liberty and [were] commited to Jaol this Evening but we are all in good spirits Captain bogard[4] will hand you this line my respects to all remain where you are at preasant J yours &c ———

Joseph Smith Jr [p. 1]

To Emma Smith
Far West [p. 2]

Liberty Jail Missouri. Dec 16th 1838

To the chur<c>h of latter day saints in Caldwell county and the saints scattered abroad and are persecuted and made desolate and are afflicted in divers manners for christ's sake and the gospel's, and whose perils are greatly augmented by the wickedness and corruption of false brethren. May grace, mercy, and peace, be and

abide with you and notwithstanding all your sufferings we assure
you that you have our prayers and fervent desires for your welfare
both day and night. We believe that that God who sees us in this
solitary place will hear our prayers & reward you openly. Know
assuredly dear brethren that it is for the testim=ony of Jesus that we
are in bonds and in prison. But we say unto you that we consider
our condition better, (notwithstanding our suffering) than those
who have persecuted us and smitten us and ⟨borne⟩ ~~bear~~ false
witness against us, and we most assuredly believe that those who
bear false witness against us ⟨do⟩ seem to have a great triumph over
us for the present. But we want you to remember Haman and
Mordecai[1] you know that Haman could not be satisfied so long as
he saw Mordecai at the king's gate, and he sought the life of
Mordecai and the peop=le of the jews. But the Lord so ordered that
Haman was hanged upon his own gallows. So shall it come to pass
with poor Haman in the last days. Those who have sought by their
unbelief and wickedness and by the principle of mobocracy to
destroy us and the people of God by killing and scattering them
abroad and wilfully and maliciously delivering us into the hands of
mur=derers desiring us to be put to death thereby having us dragged
about in chains and cast into prison, and for what cause: it is
because we were honest men and were determined to defend the
lives of the saints at the expense of our own. I say unto you that
those who have thus vilely treated us like Haman shall be hanged
upon their own gallows, or in other words shall fall into their own
gin and trap and ditch which they have prepared for us and shall go
backward and stumble and fall, and their names shall be blotted
out, and God shall reward them according to all their
abominations. Dear brethren do not think that our hearts faint as
though some strange thing had happened unto us for we have seen .
and been assured of all these things beforehand, and have an
assurance of a better hope than that of our persecutors. Therefore
God has made our shoulders broad that we can bear it. We glory in
our tribulation because we know that God is with us, that he is our
friend and that he will save our souls. We do not care for those that
kill the body they cannot harm our souls; we ask no favors at the

hands of mobs nor of the world, nor of the devil nor of his
emissaries the dissenters.[2] We have never dissembled nor will we
for the sake of our lives. Forasmuch then as we know that we have
been endeavoring with all our mights, minds, and strength [p. 1] to
do the will of God and all things whatsoever he has commanded us.
And as to our light speeches from time to time they have nothing
to do with the fixed principle of our hearts. Therefore it sufficeth us
to say that our souls were vexed from day to day. We refer you to
Is‹a›iah who considers those who make a man an offender for a
word and lay a snare for them that reproveth in the gate.[3] We
believe the old prophet verily told the truth. We have no
retraction to make, we have reproved in the gate and men have
laid snares for us we have spoken words and men have made us
offenders, and notwithstanding all this our minds are not darkened
but feel strong in the Lord. But behold the words of the savior, if
the light which is in you beco=me darkness behold how great is
that darkness. Look at the dissenters. And again if you were of the
world the world would love its own Look at Mr Hinkle. A wolf in
sheep's clothing. Look at his brother John Corrill Look at the
beloved brother Reed Peck who aided him in leading us, as the
savior was led, into the camp as a lamb prepared for the slaug=hter
and a sheep dumb before his shearer so we opened not our mouths
But these men like Balaam being greedy for a reward sold us into
the hands of those who loved them, for the world loves his own. I
would remember W. W. Phelps who comes up before us as one of
Job's com=forters. God suffered such kind of beings to afflict Job,
but it never entered into their hearts that Job would get out of it
all. This poor man who professes to be much of a prophet has no
other dumb ass to ride but David Whitmer to forbid his madness
when he goes up to curse Israel, and this ass not being of the same
kind of Balaams therefore the angel notwithstanding appeared unto
him yet he could not penetrate his understanding sufficiently so but
what he brays out cursings instead of blessings. Poor ass whoever
lives to see it will see him and his rider perish like those who
perished in the gain=saying of Core,[4] or after the same
condemnation. Now as for these and the rest of their company we

will not presume to say that the world loves them but we presume
to say that they love the world and we classify them in the error [of]
Balaam[5] and in the gainsaying of Core and with the company of
Cora and Dathan and Abiram.[6] Perhaps our brethren may say
because we thus write that we are offended at those characters, if
we are, it is not for a word neither because they reproved in the
gate. But because they have been the means of shedding innocent
blood. Are they not murderers then at heart? Are not their
consciences seared as with a hot iron? We confess that we are
offended [p. 2] but the saviour said that offences must come but
woe unto them by whom they come, and again blessed are ye when
all men shall revile you and speak all manner of evil against you
falsely for my sake, rejoice and be exceeding glad for great is your
reward in heaven for so persecuted they the prophets which were
before you. Now dear brethren if any men ever had reason to claim
this promise we are the men, for we know that the world not only
hates us but ~~but~~ speak all manner of evil of us falsely for no other
reason than because we have been endeavoring to teach the fulness
of the gospel of Jesus Christ after we were bartered away by Hinkle
and were taken into the militia camp we had all the evidence we
could have wished for that the world hated us and that most
cordially too. If there were priests of all the different sects they
hated us, if there were Generals they hated us, if there were
Colonels they hated us, and the soldiers and officers of every kind
hated us, and the most profane blasphemers and drunkards &
whoremongers hated us, they all hated us most cordia=lly. And
now what did they hate us for, purely because of the testimony of
Jesus Christ. Was it because we were liars? We know that it has
been reported by some but it has been reported falsely. Was it
because we have committed treason against the government in
Daviess County or of burglary, or of larceny or arson, or any other
unlawful act in Daviess county. We know that certain priests and
certain lawyers and certain judges who are the instigators aiders and
abettors of a certain gang of murderers and robbers who have been
carrying on a scheme of mobocracy to uphold their priestcraft
against the saints of the last days for a number of years and have

tried by a well contemplated and premeditated scheme to put down by physical power a system of religon that all the world by all their mutual attainments and by any fair means whatever were not able to resist. Hence, mobbers were encouraged by priests and Levites, by the Pharisees, Sadducees, and Essenees, and the Herodians, and the most ruthless, abandoned, and debauched, lawless inhuman and the most beastly set of men that the earth can boast of; and indeed a parallel cann‹o›t be found any where else; to gather together to steal to plunder to starve and to exterminate and burn the houses of the Mormons these are the characters that by their treason=able and avert acts have desolated and laid waste Daviess County these are the characters that would fain make all the world believe that we are guilty of the above named acts. But they represent us [p. 3] falsely; we say unto you that we have not committed treason, nor any other unlawful act in Daviess County was it for murder in Ray county against mob-militia who was a wolf in the first instance hide and Hair, teeth, and legs, and tail, who afterwards put on a militia sheepskin with the wool on, who can sally forth in the day time into the flock and snarl & show his teeth, and scatter and devour the flock and satiate himself upon his prey, and then sneak back into the brambles in ord=er that he might conceal himself in his well tried skin with the wool on. We are well aware that there is a certain set of priests & satellites and mobbers that would fain make all the world believe that we are the dogs that barked at this howling wolf that made such havoc among the sheep who when he retreated howled and bleated at such a desperate rate that if one could have been there he would have thought that all the wolves whether wrapped up in sheep skins or goat skins or any other skins and in fine all the beast[s] of the forest were awful=ly alarmed and cat‹c›hing the scent of innocent blood they sallied forth with a tremend‹u›ous howl and crying of all sorts and such a howling and such a tremenduous havoc never was known such a piece of inhumanity and relentless cruelty and barbarity cannot be found in all the annals of history. These are the characters that would make the world believe that we had committed murder by making an attack upon this howling wolf

while we were at home and in our beds and asleep and knew
nothing of that transaction any more than we know what is going
on in China while we are within these walls. Therefore we say
again unto you we are innocent of these things they have
represented us falsely Was it for committing adultery, we are aware
that false slander has gone abroad for it has been reiterated in our
ears. These are falsehoods also. Renegadoes, mormon dissenters are
running through the world and spreading various foul and libelous
reports against us thinking thereby to gain the friendship of the
world because they knew that we are not of the world and that the
world hates us; therefore they make a tool of these fellows by them
they do all the injury they can and after that they hate them worse
than they do us because they find them to be base traitors and
sycophants. Such characters God hates we cannot love them the
world hates them and we sometimes think the devil ought to be
ashamed of them. We have heard that it has been reported by some
that some of us should have said that we not only dedicated our
prop=erty but our families also to the Lord, and satan taking
advantage of this has transfigured it into lasciviousness such as a
community of wives [p. 4] which is an abomination in the sight of
God. When we consecrate our pro=perty to the Lord it is to
administer to the wants of the poor and nee=dy for this is the law of
God it is not for the purpose of the rich those who have no need
and when a man consecrates or dedicates his wife and children he
does not give them to his brother or to his neighbor for there is no
such law for the law of God is thou shalt not commit adultery thou
shalt not covet thy neighbor's wife. He that looketh upon a woman
to lust after her has committed adultery already in his heart. Now
for a man to consecrate his property and his wife & children to the
Lord, is nothing more nor less than to feed the hungry, clothe the
naked, visit the widow and the fatherless, the sick, and the
afflicted, and do all he can to administer to their relief in their
afflictions, and for him and his house to serve the Lord. In order to
do this he and all his house must be virtuous and shun every
appearance of evil. Now if any person has represented any thing
other wise than what we now write he or she is a liar and have

represented us falsely. And this is another manner ~~of~~ of of evil which
is spoken against us falsely. We have learned also since we have
been in prison that many false and pernicious things which were
calculated to lead the saints far astray and to do great injury ‹have
been taught by Dr. Avard[7]› as coming from the Presidency ~~taught
by Dr Avard~~ and we have reason to fear ‹that› many ‹other
~~things~~› designing and corrupt characters like unto him=self ‹have
been teaching many things› which the presidency never knew of
being taught in the church by any body untill after they were made
prisoners, which if they had known of, they would have spurned
them and their authors from them as they would the gates of hell.
Thus we find that there has been frauds and secret abominations
and evil works of darkness going on leading the minds of the weak
and unwary i‹n›to confusion and distraction, and palming it all the
time upon the presidency while meantime the presidency were
ignorant as well as innocent of these things, which were practicing
in the church in their name and were attending to their own family
concerns, weighed down with sorrow, in debt, in poverty, in
hunger assaying to be fed yet finding themselves receiving deeds of
charity but inadequate to their subsistence, and because they
received those deeds they were envied and hated by those who
professed to be their friends But notwithstanding we thus speak we
honor the church when we speak of the church, as a church, for
their liberality, kindness, patience, and long suffering, and their
continued kindness towards us. And now breth=ren we say unto
you, what can we enumerate more; is not all manner of evil of
every description spoken against us falsely, yea, we say unto [p. 5]
unto you falsely; we have been misrepresented and misunderstood
and belied and the purity of our hearts have not been known. And
it is through ignorance, yea, the very depth of ignorance is the
cause of it, and not only ignorance but gross wickedness on the part
of some and hypocrisy also who by a long face and sanctified prayers
and very pious sermons had power to lead the minds of the ignorant
and unwary and thereby obtain such influence that when we
approached their iniquities the devil gained great advantage &
would bring great sorrow upon our heads and in fine we have waded

through an ocean of tribulation, and mean abuse practiced upon us
by the ill bred and ignorant such as Hinkle, Corrill, and Phelps,
Avard, Reed Peck, Cleminson, and various others who are so very
ignorant that they cannot appear respectable in any decent and
civilized society, and whose eyes are full of adultery and cannot
cease from sin. Such characters as McLellin, John Whitmer, D.
Whitmer, O. Cowdery, Martin Harris, who are too mean to
mention and we had liked to have forgotten them. Marsh & Hyde
whose hearts are full of corruption, whose cloak of hypocrisy was
not sufficient to shield them or to hold them up in the hour of
trouble, who after having escaped the pollutions of the world
through the knowledge of God and become again entangled and
overcome the latter end is worse than the first. But it has happened
unto them according to the words of the savior, the dog has
returned to his vomit, and the sow that was washed to her
wallowing in the mire. Again if we sin wilfully after we have
received the knowledge of the truth, there remaineth no more
sacrifice for sin, but a certain fearful looking <for> of judgement
and fiery indignation to come which shall devour these adversaries.
For he who despiseth Moses' law died without mercy under two or
three witnesses of how much more severe punishment suppose ye
shall he be thought worthy who hath sold his brother and denied
the new and everlasting covenant by which he was sanctified
calling it an unholy thing and doing despite to the spirit of grace.
And again we say unto you that inasmuch as there be virtue in us
and the holy priesthood hath been conferred upon us, and the keys
of the kingdom hath not been taken from us, for verily thus saith
the Lord be of good cheer for the keys that I gave unto <you> are
yet with you Therefore we say unto you dear brethren in the name
of the Lord Jesus Christ we deliver these characters unto the
buffetings of satan untill the day of redemption that they may be
dealt with according to their works [p. 6] and from henceforth their
works shall be made manifest. And now dear and well beloved
brethren and when we say brethren we mean those who have
continued faithful in christ men, women, and children, we feel to
exhort you in the name of the Lord Jesus, to be strong in the faith

of the new and everlasting covenant, and nothing frightened at
your enemies. For what has happened unto us is an evident token
to them of damnation but unto us of salvation and that of God.
Therefore hold on even unto death, for he that seeks to save his life
shall ~~loose~~ lose it but he that los‹e›th his life for my sake and the
gospels shall find it sayeth Jesus Christ. Brethren from henceforth
let truth and righteousness prevail and abound in you and in all
things be temperate, abstain from every appearance of evil,
drunkenness, and profane language, and from every thing which is
unrighteous or unholy; also from enmity, and hatred, and
covetousness and from every unholy desires. Be honest one with
another, for it seemeth that some have come short of these things,
and some have been unch=aritable & have manifested greediness
because of their debts towards those who have been persecuted &
dragged about with chains without cause and imprisoned. Such
persons God hates and they shall have their turn of sorrow in the
rolling of the great wheel for it rol=leth and none can hinder. Zion
shall yet live though she seemeth to be dead. Remember that
whatsoever measure you meet out to others it shall be measured to
you again. We say unto you brethren be not afraid of your
adversaries contend earnestly against mobs, and the unlawful works
of dissenters and of darkness. And the very God of peace shall be
with you and make a way for your escape from the adver=sary of
your souls we commend you to God and the word of his grace
which is able to make us wise unto salvation. Amen.

Joseph Smith Jun.

To Emma Smith, December 1, 1838, p. 1. Handwriting of Joseph Smith. See text, p. 374. (LDS Church Archives.)

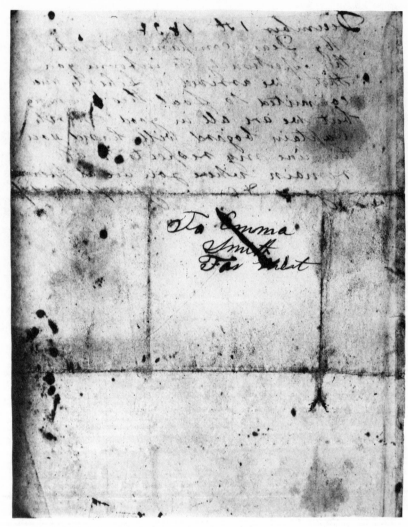

To Emma Smith, December 1, 1838, p. 2. Handwriting of Joseph Smith. See text, p. 374. (LDS Church Archives.)

To Presendia Huntington Buell,
March 15, 1839

Built in 1833 at a cost of $600, the jail at Liberty, Missouri, was a two-story structure approximately twenty-two feet square built of rough-hewn limestone. Inside the outer wall was another wall of oak logs. The two walls were separated by a twelve-inch space filled with loose rock, the whole presenting a formidable barrier four feet thick. The interior of the jail was divided into upper and lower rooms, the lower, or dungeon, lighted by two small windows grated with heavy iron bars. It was here on December 1, 1838, that Joseph Smith began four months and five days of confinement.[1]

In January 1839, after petitioning to have their case heard on a plea of habeas corpus, the prisoners were brought before Judge Joel Turnham of Clay County. This hearing gave Sidney Rigdon his freedom, but the rest of the prisoners were returned to the jail. Convinced that justice could not be obtained for them in that part of the state, the prisoners decided to try other means to gain their freedom. The result was two abortive jail-break attempts, one on February 6 and the other on March 4.

To discourage further thoughts of unauthorized departure, security at the jail was tightened. Visitors were watched closely and in some instances denied entrance altogether. One who came to the jail about this time was Presendia Huntington Buell,[2] whose brother William had been among the Mormon prisoners at Richmond. Presendia visited the jail twice, once in company with her father and once with Frederick G. Williams. The second time she was refused entrance. Knowledge of this prompted the following letter from Joseph Smith.

Liberty Jail March 15th 1839

Dear Sister

My heart rejoiced at the friendship you manifested in requesting to have conversation with us but the Jailer is a very Jealous man for fear some one will leave tools for us to get out with he is under the eye of the mob continually and his life is at Stake if he grants us any privileges he will not let us converse with any one alone Oh what joy it would be to us to see our friends it would have gladdened my heart to have the privilege of conversing with you but the hand of tyrany is upon us but thanks be to God it cannot last always and he that sitteth in the heavens will laugh at their calamity and mock when their fear cometh We feel Dear Sister that our bondage is not of long duration I trust that I shall have the chance to give such instructions as are communicated to us before long I suppose you wanted some instruction for yourself and also give us some information and administer consolation to us and to find out what is best for you to do I think that many of the brethren if they will be pretty still can stay in this country until the indignation is over and past but I think it would be better for brother Buel to leave and go with the rest of the Brethren if he keep the faith and at any rate for thus speaketh the Spirit concerning him I want him and you to know that I am your true friend I was glad to see you no tongue can tell what inexpressible Joy it gives a man to see the face of one who has been a friend after having been inclosed in the walls of a prison for five months it seems to me that my heart will always be more tender after this than ever it was before my heart bleeds continually when I contemplate the distress of the Church[3] Oh that I could be with them I would not shrink at toil and hardship to render them comfort and consolation I want the blessing once more to lift my voice in the midst of the Saints I would pour out my soul to God for their instruction it has been the plan of the Devil to hamper me and distress me from the beginning to keep me from explaining myself to them and I never have had opportunity to give them the plan that God has revealed to me for many have run without being sent crying tidings my Lord and have done much injury to the Church giving the Devil more power over those that walk by sight and not by faith [But trials]⁴ will only give us that knowledge to understand the minds of the Ancients for my part I think I never could have felt as I now do if I had not suffered the wrongs that I have suffered all things shall work together for good to them that love God Beloved Sister we see that perilous times have truly come and the things which we have so long expected have at last began to usher in but when you see the fig tree begin to put forth its leaves you may know that the Summer is nigh at hand there will be a short work on the Earth it has now commenced I suppose there will soon be perplexity all over the Earth do not let our hearts faint when these things come upon us for they must come or the word cannot be fulfilled I know that something will soon take place to stir up this generation to see what they have been doing and that their fathers have inherited lies and they have been led captive by the Devil to no profit but they know not what they do do not have any feelings of enmity towards any Son or Daughter of Adam I believe I shall be let out of their hands some way or another and shall see good days we can not do any thing only stand still and see the Salvation of God he must do his own work or it must fall to the ground we must not take it in our hands to avenge our wrongs Vengeance is mine saith the Lord and I will repay I have no fears I shall stand unto death God being my helper I wanted to communicate something and I wrote this &c Write to us if you can

J. Smith Jr.

To Mrs. Norman Buel
Clay Co. Mo.

To the Church of Latterday Saints at Quincy, Illinois, and Scattered Abroad, and to Bishop Partridge in Particular, March 20, 1839

To Emma Smith, March 21, 1839

With her husband imprisoned in Liberty Jail, Emma Smith and her children were among the Latter-day Saints who made their way across northern Missouri to Quincy, Illinois, in the winter of 1839. This experience was vivid in her mind when she wrote to Joseph on March 7: "I shall not attempt to write my feelings altogether, for the situation in which you are, the walls, bars, and bolts, rolling rivers, running streams, rising hills, sinking vallies and spreading prairies that separate us, and the cruel injustice that first cast you into prison and still holds you there, with many other considerations, places my feelings far beyond description. Was it not for conscious innocence, and the direct interposition of divine mercy, I am very sure I never should have been able to have endured the scenes of suffering that I have passed through, since what is called the Militia, came into Far West, under the ever to be remembered Governor's notable order. . . . We are all well at present, except Frederick, who is quite sick. Little Alexander who is now in my arms is one of the finest little fellows, you ever saw in your life, he is so strong that with the assistance of a chair he will run all round the room. . . . No one but God, knows the reflections of my mind and the feelings of my heart when I left our house and home, and allmost all of every thing that we possessed excepting our little children, and took my journey out of the State of Missouri, leaving you shut up in that lonesome prison. But the recollection is more than human nature ought to bear. . . . The daily sufferings of our brethren in travelling and camping out nights, and those on the other side of the river would beggar the most lively description. The people in this state are very kind indeed, they are doing much more than we ever anticipated they would; I have many more things I could like to write but have not time and you may be astonished at my bad writing and incoherent manner, but you will pardon all when you reflect how hard it would be for you to write, when your hands were stiffened with hard work, and your heart convulsed with intense anxiety. But I hope there is better days to come to us yet."[1]

On March 19, less than two weeks after the failure of the second jailbreak attempt, Joseph Smith received his wife's letter, along with letters from his brothers Don Carlos and William, and from Bishop Edward Partridge.[2] This correspondence called forth an immediate response. The following day Lyman Wight noted that the Prophet was "writing an epistle to the church,"[3] and on March 21 Joseph wrote to Emma. The lengthy letter produced on March 20 was signed by all the prisoners in the Liberty Jail and contained sentiments that were later published as sections 121-123 of the Doctrine and Covenants.[4] Although this epistle was addressed to the "church . . . scattered abroad and to Bishop Partridge in particular," Joseph sent it to his wife with instructions for his family to have the first reading and then convey it to the Church. The two documents, dated March 20 and 21, follow.

Liberty Jail Clay County Mo
March 20th 1839.

   To the church of Latterday saints at Quincy Illinois and scattered abroad and to Bishop Partridge in particular. your humble

servant Joseph Smith Jr prisoner for the Lord Jesus Christ's sake and
for the saints taken and held by the pow=er of mobocracy under the
exterminating reign of his excel=ancy the Governer Lilburn W.
Boggs in company with his fellow prisoners and beloved Brethren
Caleb Baldwin Lymon Wight Hyram Smith and Alexander McRae
send unto you all greeting. May the grace of God the father and of
our Lord and savior Jesus Christ rest upon you all and abide with
you for ever. May knoledge be multiplied unto you by the meorcy
of God. And may faith and virtue and knoledge and temperance
and pationce and Godliness and Brotherly kindness and charity be
in you and abo=und that you may not be baron in anything nor
unfrutefull. Forasmuch as we know that the most of you are well
acquainted with the rongs and the high toned injustice and cruelty
that is practiced upon us whereas we have been taken prisoners
charged falsly with evry kind of evil and thrown into prison
inclo=sed with strong walls surrounded with a strong guard who
continually watch day and knight as indefatigable as the devil is in
tempting and laying snayers for the people of God. Therefore
dearly and beloved Brethr=en we are the more ready and willing to
lay ~~elam~~ claim to your fellowship and love. For our curc=[p. 1]
umstances are calculated to awaken our spirits to a sacred
rememberance of evry thing and we think that yours are also and
that nothing therefore can seperate us from the love of God. and
fellowship one with another and that evry species of wickedness
and cruelty practised upon us will only tend to bind our harts
together and seal them together in love we have no need to say to
you that we are held in bonds without cause neither is it needfull
that you say unto us we are driven from our homes and smitten
without cause we mutually understand that if the inhabitance of
the state of Missouri had let the saints alone and had been as
desirable of peace as they ware there would have been nothing but
peace and quiatude in this <state> unto this day we should not have
been in this hell surrounded with demonds if not those who are
damned, they are those who shall be damned and where we are
compeled to hear nothing but blasphemos oaths and witness a scen
of blasphemy and drunkeness and hypocracy and debaucheries of

evry description. And again the cries of orphans and widdows
would ‹ not › have assended up to God. the blood of inocent women
and children yea and of men also would not have cried to God
against them ‹**it**› would ‹**not**› have stained the soyl of Missouri.
but oh! the unrelenting hand the inhumanity and murderous
disposition of this people it shocks all nature it beggers and defies
all discription. it is a tail of [p. 2] wo a lamentable tail yea a sorrifull
tail too much to tell too much for contemplation too much to
think of for a moment to much for human beings it cannot be
found among the hethans it cannot be found am=ong the nations
where Kings and tyrants are inth=roned it cannot be found among
the savages of the wilderness yea and I think it cannot be found
amo=ng the wild and ferocious beasts of the forist that a man
should be mangled for sport women be ~~violated~~ ‹robed› of all that
they have their last morsel for subsistan=ce and then be violated to
gratify the hell[i]sh desires of the mob and finally left to perish with
their helpless ofspring clinging around their necks but this is not all
after a man is dead he must be dug up from his grave and mangled
to peaces for no other purpose than to gratify their splean against
the religeon of god. They practise ‹these› things upon the saints
who have done them no rong who are inocent and virtuous who
loved the Lord their god and were willing to forsaik all things for
~~his~~ ‹Christ› sake these things are awfull to relait but they are verily
true it must needs bee that offences come, but WO! to them by
whom they come.[5] O God where art thou and where is the pavilion
that covereth thy hiding place how long shall thy hand be stayed
and thine eye yea thy pure eye behold from ~~from~~ the etearn=al
heavens the rongs of thy people and of thy servants [p. 3] and thine
ear be penetrated with their c[r]yes yea o Lord how long shall they
suffer these rongs and unlawfull oppressions before thine hart shall
be softened towards them and thy bowels be moved with
compassion to-words them. O Lord God almity maker of heaven
earth and seas and of all things that in them is and who controleth
and subjecteth the devil and the dark and benig[h]=ted dominion
of shayole. Streach forth thy hand let thine eye pierce let thy
pavilion be taken up let thy hiding place no longer be covered let

thine ear be inclined let thine hart be softened and thy bowels
moved with compassion toward us let thine anger be kindle[d]
against our enemis and in the fury of thine hart with thy sword
avenge us of our rongs remember thy suffering saint[s] oh our God
and thy servants will rejoyce in thy name for ever. Dearly and
beloved Brethr[en] we see that peralas times have come as was
testified of we may look then with most purfect asshurance for the
roling in of all those things that have been written and with more
confidence than ever before lift up our eyes to the luminary of day
and say in our harts soon thou wilt vail thy blushing face he that
said let there be light, and there was light hath spoken this word,
and again thou moon thou dimmer light thou luminary of night
shall ~~truru~~ ‹turn› to blood we see that evry thing is fulfilling and
the time shall soon come when the son of man shall [p. 4] desend
in the clouds of ‹heaven.› our harts do not shrink neither are our
spirits altogether broken at the grie=vious yoak which is put upon
us. We know that God will have our oppressors in derision that he
~~laf~~ ‹will laugh› at their calamity and mock when their fear comith
oh that we could be with you Brethren and unbosome our feeling to
you we would tell [you] that we should have been at ‹liberated› the
time Elder Rigdon was on the writ of habeas corp=us had not our
own lawyers interpreted the law contra=ry to what it reads against
‹us› which prevented us from introducing our evidence before the
mock court,[6] they have done us much harm ‹from› the begining
they have of late acknoledged that the law was misconstrewed and
tantalised our feelings with it and have intirally forsaken us and
have forfeited their oaths and their bonds and we have a come back
on them for they are co-workers with the mob. As nigh as we can
learn the publick mind has been for a long time turning in our favor
and the majority is now friendly and the lawyers can no longer
browbeat us by saying that this or that is a matter of publick
oppinion for publick oppinion is not willing to brook it for it is
begining to look with feelings of indigna=tion against our oppresors
and to say that the morm=ons were not in the fault in the least we
think that truth honor and virtue and inocence will eventu=ally
come out tryumphant we should have taken a habeas corpus before

the high Judge and escaped [p. 5] the mob in a summary way but unfortunatly for us the timber of the wall being verry hard our auger handles gave out and hindered us longer than we expected we applied to a friend and a verry slight un=cautious act gave rise to some suspition and before we could fully succeed our plan was discovered we had evry thing in readiness but the last stone and we could have made our escape in one minute and should have succeeded admirably had it not been for a little imprudance or over anxiety on the part of our fri=end. The sheriff and jailor did not blame us for our attempt it was a fine breach and cost the county a round sum[7] but publick oppinion says that we ought to have been permitted to have made our escape that then the disgrace would have been on us but now it must come on the state. that there cannot be any charge sustained against us and that the con=duct of the mob, the murders committed at hawns mill,[8] and the exterminating order of the Governer, and the one sided rascally proceedings of the Legislature has damned the state of Missouri to all eternity I would just name also that Genl Atchison[9] has proved himself to be as contemtible as any of them we have tryed for a long time to get our lawyers to draw us some petitions to the supream Judges of this state. but they uterly refused we have examined the law and drawn the petitions ourselvs and have obtained abundance of proof to counter act all the testimony [p. 6] that was against us, so that if the supream Judge dose ‹not grant› us our liberty he has got to act without cause contrary to honor evidence law or justice shearly to please the devil but we hope better things and tru=st that before many days God will so order our case that we shall be set at liberty and take up our habita=tion with the saints we received some letters last eve=ning one from Emma one from Don C. Smith and one from Bishop Partridge all breathing a kind and consoling spirit we were much gratified with there contence we had been a long time withou‹t› information and when we read those letters they were to our ‹souls› ~~soles~~ as the gentle air, ‹is› refreshing but our joy was mingled with greaf because of the suffering of the poor and much injured saints and we need not say to you that the flood gates of our harts were hoisted and our eyes were a fountain of tears

but those who have not been inclosed in the walls of a prison
without cause or provication can have but a little ideah how sweat
[sweet] the voice of a friend is one token of friendship from any
sorce whatever a wakens and calles into action evry simpathetick
feeling it brings up in an instant evry thing that is pased it sesses
[siezes] the presant with a vivasity of lightning it grasps after the
future with the fea‹r› sn=ess of a tiger it rhetrogrades from one
thing to an other untill finally all enmity malice and hatred and
past diferances misunderstandings and mis [p. 7] managements be
slain victoms at the feet of hope and when the hart is sufficiently
contrite ~~and~~ ‹then› the voice of inspiration steals along and
whispers[10] my son peace be unto thy soal thine advirsity and thy
afflictions shall be but a small moment and then if thou indure it
well God shall exalt the[e] on high thou shalt tryumph over all thy
foes thy friends do stand by the[e] and they shall hail the[e] agai‹n›
with warm harts and friendly hands thou art not yet as Job thy
friends do not contend again[st] the[e] neither charge the[e] with
transgretion as they did Job and they ‹who› do ~~the w~~ charge the[e]
with transgretion there hope shall be blasted and there prospects
shall melt away as the hory frost melteth before the burning rays of
the rising sun and also that God hath set to his hand and seal to
change the times and season‹s› and to blind their minds that they
may not understand his marvilos workings that he may prove them
also and take them in there own craftiness also because their harts
are corrupt and the thing which they are willing to bring upon
others and love to have others suffer may come upon them ‹selvs›
to the verry utmost that they may be disappointed also and their
hopes may be cut off and not many years hence that they and their
pasterity shall be swept from under heaven saith God that not one
of them [p. 8] is left to stand by the wall cursed are all those that
shall lift up the heal against mine anointed saith the Lord and cry
they have sined when they have not sined before me saith the Lord
but have done that which was meat in min‹e› eyes and which I
commanded them but those who cry transgresion do it becaus they
are the servants of sin and are the children of disobedi=ance
themselvs and those who swear false against my servants that they

might bring them unto bondage and death. Wo unto them because
they have offended my little ones they shall be severed from the
ordinances of mine house their basket shall not be full their houses
and their barnes shall famish and they themselvs shall be dispised
by those that flattered them they shall not have right to the
priesthood nor their posterity after them from generation to
generation it had been better for them that a millstone had been
hanged about their necks and they drownd in the depth of the see
wo unto all those that discomfort my people and drive and mur=der
and testify against them saith the Lord of host[s] a generation of
viper[s] shall not escape the damnation of hell behold mine eye
seeth and knoweth all their works and I have in reserve a swift
judgement in the season thereoff for them all for there is a time
appointed ~~for~~ ⟨to⟩ evry man [p. 9] according ~~their~~ ⟨as his⟩ work
shall be and now beloved Brethren we say unto [you] that in
asmuch as ~~good~~ ⟨God⟩ hath said that he would have a tried people
that he would purge them as gold now we think that this time he
has cho=sen his own crusible wherein we have been tryed and we
think if we get through with any degree of safty and shall have
keept the faith that it will be a sign to this generation alltogether
sufficient to leave them without excuse and we think also that it
will be a tryal of our faith equal to that of Abraham and that the
ansionts [ancients] will not have were off [whereof] to bost over us
in the day of judgment as being called to pass through heavier
afflictions that we may hold an even waight in the balances with
them but now after having suffered so grate a sacrifis and having
pased through so grate a seane of sorrow we trust that a Ram may be
caught in the thicket speedily to releave the sons and daughters of
Abr=aham from their ~~grate~~ ⟨**great**⟩ anxiety and to light up the
lamp of salvation upon their countinances that they may hold ~~up~~
⟨on⟩ now after having gone so far unto ever=lasting life. Now
brethren conserning the places for the location of the saints we
cannot counsyl you as we could if we were presant with you and
⟨as⟩ to the ~~thi~~ things that ware writen heartofore we did not
concider them any thing verry binding therfore we now say once
for all that we think it most proper that the general affairs of the

church which are nessisary [p. 10] to be concidered while your
humble servant remains in bondage s[h]ould be transacted by a
general conferance of the most faithfull and the most respectible of
the authorities of the church and a minute of those transactions
may be kept and fo[r]warded from time to time to your humble
servant and if there should be any corrections by the word ~~of the
word of~~ the Lord they shall be f[r]eely transmit=ted and your
humble servant will approve all ~~tha~~ things what soever is
acceptable unto God if any thing should have been sejusted
[suggested] by us or any names me=ntioned expt by commandment
or thus saith the Lord we do not concider it binding. therefore our
harts shall not be greaved if diferant arraingments should be
entered into nevertheless we would sejest the propriety of being
awar of an aspiring spirit which spirit has oftentim‹es› urged men
fo[r]wards to make foul speaches and influa=ance the church ~~and~~ to
reject milder councils and has eventually ‹been› ~~by~~ the means of
bringing much death and sorrow upon the church we would say be
awar of pride also for well and truly hath the wise man s[a]id that
pride goeth before distruction and a haughty spirit before a fall /[11]
and Again outward appearance is not always a Crite=rean for us to
Judge our fellow man but the lips betray the haughty and over
bari=ng imm[a]ginations of the heart, by his words ~~by~~ ‹and› his
deeds let him be scan‹e›d [p. 11] flaterly [flattery] also is a deadly
poison a frank an[d] open Rebuke provoketh a good man to
Emulation and in the hour of trouble he will be your best friend,
but on the other hand it will draw out all the corruption of a
corrupt heart And lying and the poison of asps shall be under their
tongues and they do cause the pure in heart to be cast in to prison
because they want them out of thare way, A fanciful and flowely
[flowery] and heated immagination be aware of be cause the things
of God Are of deep import and time and expear=iance and carful
and pondurous and solom though[ts] can only find them out. thy
mind O Man, if thou wilt lead a soul unto sal=vation must streach
as high as the utmost Heavens, and sear[c]h in to and contemplate
the ~~loest~~ ‹lowest› conside[r]ations of the darkest abyss, and
Expand upon the broad considerations of Eternal Expance, he must

commune with God. how much more dignifide and noble are the thoughts of God, than the vain immaginations of the human heart, none but fools, will triful, with the souls of men, how vane and trifling, have ben our spirits, our Conferencs our Coun[c]ils our ~~private~~ Meetings our pri[v]ate as well as public Conversations to low to mean to vulgar [p. 12] to condecending, for the dignifide Characters of the Cald and Chosen of God, according to the purposes of his ~~word~~ will from befo[re] the foundation of the world. to hold the keys of the mistres [mysteries] of those things that have ben kept hid from the foundation untill now, ~~for~~ <of> which som have tasted a little and which many of them are to be pored down from heaven upon the heads of babes, yea the weak obscure and dispizable ones of this earth. therefore We beseath of you bretheren that <you **bear**> ~~bare~~ with those [w]ho do not feel themselves more worth=ey than yourselves, while we Exort one another, to a reffermation, with one an[d] all. both old and young. teachers and taugh[t] both high and low rich and poor bond and free Male and female. let honesty and sobriety, and cander and solemnity, and virtue, and pureness, and meekness, and simplisity, Crown our heads in every place, and in fine becum as little Children without mallice guile or ~~high pockrichy~~ Hypokrisy: and now Bretheren after your tribulations if you do these things, and exercise fervent prayer, and faith in the sight of God Always he shall give unto you knowledge [p. 13] by his holy spirit yea by the unspeakable gift of the holy-Ghost that has not been revealed since the world was untill now which our fathers have wated with anxious expectation to be revealed in the last times which their minds were pointed to by the Angels as held in rese=rve for the fullness of their glory a time to come in the which nothing shall be with held whither there be one god or many gods they shall be manifest all thrones and dominions principalities and pow=ers shall be revealed and set forth upon all who have indured valiently for the gospel of Jesus Christ and also if there be bounds set to the heavens or to the seas or to the dry land or to the sun moon or starrs all the times of their revolutions all their appointed days month[s] and years and all the Days of their days, months and years, and all their glories laws and

set times shall be reveald in the days of the dispensation of the
fullness of times according to that which was ordained in the midst
of the councyl of the eternal God of all other Gods before this
world was that should be reserved unto the finishing and the end
thereoff ~~when~~ <when> evry man shall enter into his eternal
presants and into his imortal rest but I beg leave to say unto you
Brethren that ignorance supe[r]stition and bigotry placing itself
where it ought not is often times in the way of the prosperity of this
church/[p. 14] like the torant of rain from the mountains that
floods the most pure and christle stream with mire and dirt and
filthyness and obscures evry thing that was clear before and all hurls
along in one general deluge but time tethers <wethers> tide and
notwithstanding we are roled in for the time being by the mire of
the flood the next surge perad=venture as time roles on may bring
us to the fou=ntain as clear as cristal and as pure as snow while all
the filthiness flood wood and rubbish is left is left and purged out by
the way.[12] How long can rowling watters remain impure what
power shall stay the heavens as well might man streach forth his
puny arm to stop the Missouri River in its dicread cours or to turne
it up stream as to hinder the Almighty from pooring down knoledge
from <heaven> upon the heads of the Latter day saints what is
Boggs or his murderous party but wimbling willows upon the shore
to catch the flood wood as well might we argue that watter is not
watter because the the mountain torants send down mire and riles
the cristle stream altho afterwords ren<d>ers it more pure than
before or that fire is not fire because it is of a quenchable nature by
pooring on the flood, as to say that our cause is down because
runegadoes lyers preasts theavs and murderers who are all ali=ke
tenatious of their crafts and creeds have poord [p. 15] down from
their spiritual wickednes in high places and from their strong holds
of the divi[ne] a flud of dirt and mire and filthiness and vomit upon
our heads no God forbid hell may poor forth its rage like the
burning lavy of mount vesuvias or of Etna or of the most terible of
the burning mountains and yet shall mormonism stand. watter,
fire, truth, and god are all the same truth is [as] mormonism God is
the author of it he is our shield it is by him we received our birth, it

was by his voice that we were called to a dispensation of his gospel in the begining of the fullness of times it was by him we received the book of mormon and it was by him that we remain unto this day and by him we shall remain if it shall be for our glory and in his almighty name we are determined to indure tribulation as good soldiers unto the end but brethren we shall continue to offer further reflections in our next epistle you will learn by the time you have read this and if you do not learn it you may learn it that walls and ‹iron› doors ‹and screaking hinges› ~~is only calcu~~ and half scard to death Guards and jailors grining like some damn=ed spirit lest an inocent man should make his esc=ape to bring to light the damnible deeds of a murderous mob is cal[c]ulated in its verry nature to make the sole of an honest man feel stronger than the powers of hell. But we must bring our epistle to a close [p. 16].

we send our respects to Fathers, Mothers, wives, and children, Brothers, and Sisters. we hold them in the most sacred rememberance ~~I send this epistle to Emma that she may have the first perusal of it~~ we feel to inquire after Elder Rigdon if he has not forgotten us it has not been signified to us by his ~~pen~~ scrawl. Brother George W Robinson also and Elder Cahoon we remember him but would like to jog his memory a little on the fable of the [bear] and the two friends who mutually agreed to stand by each other and prehaps it would not be amis to mention Unkle John[13] and various others, a word of consolation and a blessing would not come amiss from any body while we are being so closly whispered by the Bair but we feel to excuse evry body and evry thing. Yea the more readily when we contemplate that we are in the hands of a wors[e] than a Bair for the Bair would not pray upon a dead carcus. Our respects and love and fellowship to all the virtious saints we are your Brethren and fellow sufferers and prisoners of Jesus Christ for the gospels sake and for the hope of glory which is in us. Amen.

Joseph Smith Jr
Hyrum Smith
Lyman Wight
Caleb Baldwin
Alexander McRae. [p. 17]

Continued to the church of Latter-day-saints.

We continue to offer further reflections to Bishop Partridge and to the church of Jesus Christ of Latter-day-saints whom we love with ferveant love and do allways bear them in mind in all our prayers to the throne of God. It still seams to bear heavily in our minds that the church would do well to secure to themslves the contract of the Land which is proposed to them by Mr Isaac Galland.[14] and ‹to› cultivate the friendly feelings of that gentleman in as much as ‹he› he shall proo=ve himself to be a man of honor and a friend to humanity. We really think that his letter breaths that kind of spirit if we can judge correctly. and Isaac Van Allen Esqr. the attorney General of Iowa Territory that peradventure such men may be wraught upon by the providence of God to do good unto his people. Governer Lucas[15] also. We sejust [suggest] the ideah of praying fervently for all men who manifest any degree of sympothy for the suffering children of God. we We think that peradventure the United States survayer ‹of the Iowa Territory› may be of grate benefeit to the church if it be the will of God ‹to this end› if ritious=ness should be manifested as the girdle of our loin‹s› It seems to be deeply impresed upon our minds that the saints ought to lay hold of evry door that shall seem to be opened for the saints ‹ unto them› to obtain foot hol hold on the Earth and be a making all the pre=perations that is within the power of posibles for the terible storms that are now gethering in the heavens with darkness and gloominess and thick darkness as spoken of by the prophets who [p. 1] cannot be now of a long time lingering. For there seems to be a whispering that the angels ‹of he‹a›ven› who have been intrusted with the council of these matters for the last days have taken council together and among the rest of the general affairs that have to be trasnsacted in there hono[r]=able council ‹they› have taken cognisance of the testi=mony of those who were murdered at Hawns mills and also those who were martered wi with D. W. Patten. and ‹else where and› have pased some desis=ions peradventure in favor of ‹the saints and›those who were called to suffer without cause. These

desisions will be made known in there time and ‹they will› s̶h̶a̶l̶l̶
take into concideration all those things that offend. We have a
fervant desire that in your general conferances that evry thing
should be discused with a grate deal of care and propriety lest you
grieve the holy spirit which shall be poured out at all times upon
your heads when you are exercised with those principals of
ritious=ness that are agreeable to the mind of God. and are
properly affected one toward another and are carefull by all means
to remember those who are in bondage and in heaviness and in
deep aflection for your sakes and if there are any among you who
aspire after their own aggrandisement and seek their own
oppulance while their brethren are groning in poverty and are
under sore trials and temptations they cannot be benefeited by the
interses=ions of the holy spirit which maketh inter=sesion for us
day and knight ‹with gronings that cannot be uttered›. We ought
at all times to be verry carefull that such highmindedness never
have place in our harts but condesend to men of low estate [p. 2]
and with all long suffering bare the infermities of the weak.[16]
Behold there are many called but few are chosen. And why are
they not chosen? Because their hearts are set so much upon the
things of this world and aspire to the honors of men that they do
not learn this one lesson. that the rights of priesthood are
inseperably connected with the powers of heaven and that the
powers of heaven cannot be controled nor handled only upon the
principals of rightiousness that they may be confered upon us it is
tru[e] but when we undertake to cover our sins t̶o̶ or to gratify our
pride or vaine ambition or to exercise controle or dominion or
comp=ulsion upon the souls of the children of men in any degree of
unritiousness behold the heavens with draw themselves the spirit of
the Lord is grieved and when it has with=drawn amen to the
priesthood or the au=thority of that man behold ‹ere› he is aware
h̶e̶ ̶i̶s̶ ̶a̶w̶a̶r̶e̶ he is left unto himself to kick aga=inst the pricks to
persecute the saints and to fight against God. We have learned by
sad experiance that it is the nature and disposition of almos‹t› all
men as soon as they get a little au=thority as they suppose they will
im=ediatly begin to exercise unritious do=minion hence many are

called, but few are chosen. No power or influance can or ought to
be maintained by virtue of the priesthood, only by persuasion by
long suffering, by gentleness and meakness and by love unfaigned,
by kindness [p. 3] by pure kno‹w›ledge which shall g‹e›ratly
enlarge the soul without highpocracy and with=out guile reproving
~~by~~ betimes with ~~shar~~ sharpness when moved upon by the holy ghost
and then sho‹w›ing forth afterwords an increas of love to ward him
whom thou hast reproved lest he esteem the[e] to be his enemy that
he may know that thy faithful=ness is stronger than the cords of
death thy bowells also being full of charity to ward all men and to
the household of faith and virtue garnish thy thoughts unseasingly
then shall thy confidence wax strong in the presants of God and
the doctrines of the priesthood destell upon thy soul as the dews
from heaven the Holy Ghost shall be thy constan‹t› companion
and thy septer an unchanging septer of ritiousness and truth and
thy dominion shall be an everlasting ‹dominion› and without
compulsory means it shall flow unto thee for eve[r] and ever[17] the
ends of the Earth shall inquire after thy name and fools shall have
thee in derision and hell shall rage against thee while the pure in
heart and the wise and the noble and the virtuous shall seak
counc=il and authority and blesings constantly from under thy
hand and thy people shall never be turned against ‹thee› by the
testimony of traters and altho‹**ugh**› their influance shall cast the[e]
into trouble and into barrs and walls thou shalt be had in honor
and but for a small moment and thy voice shall be more terible in
the midst of thine enemies than the **fierce**[18] Lion because of thy
ritious=ness and thy God shall stand by the[e] for ever [p. 4] and
ever. If thou art called to pass through tribulation if thou art in
perel among false brethren if thou art in perel amongst robbers if
thou art in peral by land or by sea if thou art accused with all maner
of false accusations if thine enemies fall upon the[e] if they tear
the[e] from the society of thy father and mother and brethren and
sisters and if with a dra=wn sword thine enemies tear the[e] from
the bosom of thy wife and of thine off springs and thine elder
~~one~~‹**son**› altho‹**ugh**› but six years of age shall cling to thy
gar=mont and shall say my father O[19] my father why cant you stay

with us o my father what are the men agoing to do with you and if
then he shall be thrust from the[e] by the sword and thou be draged
to prison and thine enemies prowl around the[e] like wolves for
blood of the Lamb and if thou should=est be cast into the pit and or
into the hand of murdere[r]s and the sentance of death pased upon
‹thee› if thou be cast into the deep if the bilowing surge conspire
against thee if the fearse wind become thine enemy if the heavens
gether bla=ckness and all the elements combine to hedge up thy
way and above all if the verry jaws of hell shall gap open her mouth
wide after thee know thou my son that all these things shall give
thee experiance ‹and shall be for thy good› The son of man hath
desended below them all art thou gr‹e›ater than he ‹therefore›
hold on thy way and the priesthood shall remain with thee ‹for›
their boun=ds are set they cannot pass thy days [p. 5] are known and
thy years shall not be numbered less therefore fear not what man
can do for God shall be with you for ever and ever ‹now
Brotheren› I would sejest for the concideration of the
co‹n›ferance of its being carefully and wisely understood by the
council or conference that our brethren scattered abroad that
‹who› understand the spirit of the gethering that they fall into the
places of refuge and safty that God shall open unto them betwean
Kirtland and Far West Those from the East and from the West and
from far countries let them fall in some where betwean those ‹two›
bound=eries in the most safe and quiet places they can find and let
this be the presant understanding unt=ill God shall open a more
effectual door for us for further conciderations. And again we
‹further› sejest for the concideration of the council that there be
no organizations of large bodies upon common sto stock princepals
‹in property› or of large companies of firms firm untill the Lord
shall signify it in a proper maner as it opens such a dredfull field for
the avericious and the indolent and corrupt hearted to pray upon
the inocent ‹and virtious and honest› we have reason to believe
that many things were intro=duced among the saints before God
had signi=fied the times and not withstanding the princi=ples and
plans may have been good ‹innocent and virtitous› yet aspi=ring
men or in other words men who had not the substance of Godliness

about them perhaps under=took to handle edge tools children you
know are fond of tools while they are not yet able to use them.
Time and experiance however is the only safe remidy against such
~~people~~ evils there are many teachers but perhaps not many fathers
there are times coming when God will signify many things which
are expedeant [p. 6] for the well being of the saints but the times
have not yet come but will come as fast as there can be found place
and reception for them[20] And again we would ~~sejest~~‹sugjest› for
your concideration the propriety of all the saints gether=ing up a
knoledge of all the facts and sufferings and abuses put upon them by
the people of this state and also of all the property and amount of
damages which they have sus=tained both of character ‹&›
personal injuries as well as real property and also the names of all
persons that have had a hand in their oppressions as far as they can
get hold of them and find them out. And perhaps a committe can
be appointed to find out these things and to take statements and
affidafe=its and also to gether up the libilous publications that are a
float and all that are in the maga=zines and in the Insiclopedias and
all the libillious histories that are published and that are writing
and by whom and pre=sent the whole concatination of
diabolic=alil~~y~~ rascality and nefarious and mur=derous impositions
that have been practised upon this people that we may not only
publish to all the world but present them to the heads of the
govern=ment in all there dark ‹and hellish› hugh as the last effort
which is injoined on us by our heavenly father before we can fully
and completely claim that promise which ~~sha~~ shall call him forth
from his hiding place and also that the whole nation may be left
without excuse before he can ~~let fall that which the~~ send forth the
power of his mig=hty arme it is an imperios duty that [p. 7] we owe
to God to angels with whom we shall be braught to stand and also
to our=selves to our wives and our children who have been made to
bow down with greaf sorrow and care under the most damning
hand of murder tyronny and appression sup=ported and urged on
and upheld by the influan=ce of that spirit which hath so strongly
rivited the creeds of the fathers who have inhereted lies upon
~~their~~‹the harts of the› children and filled the world with confusion

and has been growing stronger and stronger and is now the verry
main spring of all corruption ⟨the corruption in ⟨the⟩ world.⟩ and
the whole Earth grones under the wait of its iniquity. It is an iron
yok it is a strong band they are the verry hand cufs and chains and
shackles and ⟨fetters⟩ of hell therefore it is an imperious duty that
we owe not only to our own wives and children but to the widdow
and fatherless whose hu=sbands and fathers have been murdered
under its iron hand which dark and blackning deeds are enough to
make hell itse⟨l⟩f shudder and to stand aghas[t] and pail and the
hands of the verry devile ~~palsy~~ ⟨tremble⟩ and palsy and also it is an
imperi=ous duty that we owe to all the rising generation and to all
the pure in heart which there are many yet on the Earth among all
sects parties and denom=inations who are blinded by the suttle
craftiness of men where by they ly in wait to decieve and only kept
from the truth because they know not where to find it therefore
that we should waist and ware out our lives in bringing to light all
the hidden things of dar=kness where in we kno⟨w⟩ them and they
are truly manifest from heaven. These should then be [p. 8]
attended to with greate earnestness Let no man count them as
small things for there is much which lieth in futurity petaining to
the saints which depends upon these things you know brethren that
a verry large ship is benefeited verry much by a verry small helm in
the time of a storme by being kept work ways with the wind and the
waves therefore dearly beloved brethren let us chearfully do all
things that layeth in our power and then may we stand still with
the utmost asur=ance to see the salvation of God and for his arm to
be revealed. And again I would fur=ther sejest the impropriety of
the organization of bands or companies by covenant or oaths by
penal=ties or secrecies but let the time past of our experia=nce and
suferings by the wickedness of Doctor Avard suffise and let our
covenant be that of the everlasting covenant as is contained in the
Holy writ. and the things that God hath revealed unto us. Pure
friendship always becomes weakened the verry moment you
undertake to make it stronger by penal oaths and secrecy. Your
humble servant or servants intend from hence forth to
disa=p⟨p⟩robate ev⟨e⟩ry thing that is not in accordance with the

fullness of the gospel of Jesus Christ and is not of a bold and frank
and an upright nature they will not hold their peace as in times past
when they see iniquity begining to rear its head for fear of traitors
or the concequinces that shall flow by reproving those who creap in
unawairs that they may get something to destroy the flock we
believe that the experience of the saints in times past has been
sufficient that they will from henceforth be always ready to obey
the truth without having mens persons in admi[p. 9]=ration
because of advantage it is expediant that we should be awair of such
things. and we ought always to be awair of those prejudices which
sometimes so strongly presented themselves and are so congen=ial
to human nature against our neighbors friends and bretheren of the
world who choose to differ with us in opinion and in matters of
faith. Our religeon is betwean us and our God their religeon is
betwean them and their God there is a tie ~~which belongs~~ from God
that should be exercised to wards those of our faith who walk
uprightly which is peculiar to itself but it is without prejudice but
gives scope to the mind which inables us to conduct ourselves with
grater liberality to word all others ‹**that are not of our faith**› than
what they exercise to wards one an=other these principal[s]
approximate nearer to the mind of God because it is like God or
God like There is a principal also which we are bound to be
exercised with that is in common with all men such as governments
and laws and regulations in the civil conserns of life this principal
garen=tees to all parties sects and demominations and clases of
religeon equal ~~and [·]~~ coherent [and] indefeasible rights they are
things that pertain to this life therefore all are alike interested they
make our responcibilities ‹~~things~~› one toward another in matters of
corruptable ‹things› while the former principals do not distroy the
latter but bind us stronger and make our responcibili=ties not only
one to another but unto God also hence we say that the
constitution of the Unit[ed] States is a glorious standard it is
founded [in] the wisdom of God it is a heavenly banner it is to all
those who are privilaged with the sweats of its liberty like the
cooling shades and refresh[p. 10]=ing watters of a greate rock in a
thirsty and a weary land it is like a gr‹e›ate tree under whose

branches men from evry clime can be shielded from the burning raies of an inclemant sun. We bretheren are dep=rived of the protection of this glorious prin=cipal by the cruelty of the cruele by those who only look for the time being for pas=terage like the beasts ‹**of the field** only to fill them‹selves›› and forget that the mormons as well as the pr[e]sbitareans and those of evry other class and discription have equal rights to ~~pluck~~ ‹partake of› the fruit of the great tree of our national liberty but notwithstanding we see what we see and we feel what [we] feel and know what we know yet that fruit is no les presious and delisious to our taist we cannot be weaned from the milk nether can we be drawn from the breast neither will we deny our rele=geon because of the hand of oppresion but we will hold on untill death we say that God is true that the constitution of the united States is [true][21] that the Bible is true that the book of [mor]m[on] is true that the book of covenants [is] tru[e] that Christ is true that the ministering [angels sen]t forth from God are true and [that we know] that we have an house not made [with hands] eternal in the heavens, whose [builder and m]aker is God a consolation [which our opp]resers cannot feel when for[tune, or fate, sh]all lay its iron hand on them [as it has on us] now we ask what is man [remember breth]ren that time and chance hape[neth to all men] we shall continue our reflect=[ions in our nex]t We subscribe ourselves your sin=[cere friends and] bretherin in the bonds of the ever[p. 11]=lasting gospel prisoners of Jesus Christ for the sake of the gospel and the saints. we pronounce the blesing of heaven upon the heads of the ~~[¬]~~ the saints who seek to serve God with an un=devid[ed] heart ‹in the name of Jesus Christ› Amen.

> **Joseph Smith Jr,**
> Hyrum Smith
> Lyman Wight
> Caleb Baldwin
> Alexander McRae.

Mrs Emma Smith
Quincy Ill

Liberty Jail Clay Co Mo 1839 March 21st

Affectionate Wife

I have sent an Epistle to the church directed to you because I wanted you to have the first reading of it and then I want Father and Mother to have a coppy of it keep the original yourself as I dictated the matter myself and shall send an other as soon as posible I want to be with you very much but the powers of mobocra[c]y is to many for me at preasant I would ask if Judge Cleaveland[1] will be kind enough to let you and the children tarry there untill [I] can learn someth[i]ng fu[r]ther concerning my ~~lot~~ fate I will reward him well if he will and see that you do not ~~s~~suffer for any thing I shall have a little mony left when I come my Dear Emma I very well know your toils and simpathise with you if God will spare my life once more to have the privelege of takeing care of you I will ease your care and indeavour to cumfort your heart [p. 1] I wa[n]t ~~the~~ you to take the best care of the family you can which I believe you will do all you can I was sorry to learn that Frederick was sick but I trust he is well again and that you are all well I want you to try to gain time and write to me a long letter and tell me all you can and even if old major[2] is alive yet and what those little pratlers say that cling around you[r] neck do you tell them I am in prison ~~that~~ that their lives might be saved I want all the church to make out a bill of damages and apply to the uni=ted states court as soon as possible how‹ev›eve[r] they will find out what can be done themselves you expressed my feelings concerning the order and I blieve that there is a way to git redress for suck [such] things but God ruleth all things after the council of his own will my trust is in him the salvation of my soul is of the most importants to me for as much as I know for a certainty of Eternal things if the heveans linger it is nothing to ‹me› I must stear my bark safe which I intend to do I want you to do the same yours forever

Joseph Smith Jr.

Emma Smith [p. 2]

I want you <to> have the Epistole coppy-ed immedeately and let it go to the Bretheren firs[t] into the hands of Father for I want the production for my record if you lack for mony or for bread do let me know it as soon as possible my nerve trembles from long confinement but if you feel as I do you dont care for the imperfections of my writings for my part a word of consolation from any sourse is cordially recieved by us me I feel like Joseph in Egyept doth my friends yet live if they live do they remem=ber me have they regard for me if so let me know it in time of trouble my Dear Emma do you think that my being cast into prison by the mob of renders me less worthy of your friends=ship no I do not think so but when I was in prisen and ye viseted me inasmuch as you have don it to the least <of> these you have don[e] it to me these shall enter into life Eternal but no more your Husband

J Smith Jr [p. 3]

Mrs Emma Smith
Quincy Ilinoi [p. 4]

Liberty Jail, Liberty, Missouri, 1878. Joseph Smith and other Latter-day Saints were imprisoned here from December 1, 1838 to April 6, 1839. This photograph was given to Joseph F. Smith by Josie Schweich, a grand-daughter of David Whitmer. (LDS Church Archives.)

To the Church at Quincy, March 20, 1839, p. 1. Handwriting of Alexander McRae. See text, pp. 389-90. (LDS Church Archives.)

To Emma Smith, March 21, 1839, p. 1. Handwriting of Joseph Smith. See text, p. 408. (LDS Church Archives.)

I want that you to take the best care
of the family you can which I believe
you will do all you can I was sorry to learn
that Frederick was sick but I trust he is
well again and that you are all well I
want you to try to gain time and write to
me a long letter and tell me all you can
and even if old major is alive yet and what
those little prattlers say that cling around
you neck do you tell them I am in prison
that their lives might be saved
I want all the church to make out
a bill of damages and apply to the uni-
-ted States Court as soon as possible
however they will find out what can
be done themselves you express my
feelings concerning the order and I believe
that there is a way to get redress for
such things but God ruleth all things
after the council of his own will my
trust is in him the salvation of my
soul is of the most importance
to me for as much as I know
for a certainty of Eternal things
if the heavens linger it is nothing
to me I must steer my bark safe
which I intend to do I want you
to do the same yours forever Joseph Smith
Emma Smith

I want you to have the epistle copyed immediately and let it go to the
Brethren first into the hand[s] of Father
for I want the production for my
record if you lack [for] money or for
bread &c let me know it as soon as
possible my nerve trembl[e] from long
confinement but if you feel [as] I do
you dont care for the imperfections
of my writing for my part a word of
consolation from any source is
cordially received by me as I feel like
Joseph in Egypt doth my friends
yet remember [me] they [live] do they remember
[me?] ask them [if they have] regard for me if so
let me know it in time of trouble
my Dear Emma do you think that my
being cast into prison by the mob
renders me less worthy of your friendship no I do not think so but
when I was in prison and ye visited
me inasmuch as you have don it to
the least of these you have don it to
me these shall enter into life
eternal but no more
your husband J Smith jr

To Emma Smith, March 21, 1839, p. 3. Handwriting of Joseph Smith.
See text, p. 409. (LDS Church Archives.)

To Emma Smith, March 21, 1839, p. 4. Handwriting of Joseph Smith. See text, p. 409. (LDS Church Archives.)

To Isaac Galland,
March 22, 1839

In the fall of 1838, a group of Mormons who had lost their way while fleeing from Missouri toward Quincy, Illinois, and ended up on the Des Moines River in southeastern Iowa were the first Latter-day Saints to meet Isaac Galland.[1] A land broker with extensive holdings in the area, Galland offered to sell the destitute Saints twenty thousand acres at two dollars an acre with no interest and payable in twenty annual installments.

On February 26, 1839, Galland wrote David W. Rogers, one of the committee investigating a possible location for the Saints, that he had received assurances of goodwill for the Mormon people from the Governor of Iowa, and he expressed an interest in the plight of the Mormons still in Missouri, including Joseph Smith: "I wish to serve your cause in any matter which Providence may afford me the opportunity of doing, and I therefore request that you feel no hesitancy or reluctance in communicating to me your wishes, at all times and on any subject. The little knowledge which I have as yet of the doctrine, order or practice of the Church, leaves me under the necessity of acting in all this matter as a stranger, though, as I sincerely hope, as a friend, for such, I assure you I feel myself to be, both towards you collectively, as a people, and individually as sufferers. Accept, dear sir, for yourself and in behalf of the Church and people, assurance of my sincere sympathy in your sufferings and wrongs, and deep solicitude for your immediate relief from present distress."[2]

A short time later, David Rogers delivered the Galland letter to Joseph Smith at the Liberty Jail, and on March 22 the Prophet dictated this answer.

Liberty Jail, Clay co. Mo. March 22nd, 1839.

MR. ISAAC GALLAND; Dear Sir:

I have just been privileged with a perusal of a letter, put into my hands by Mr. D. W. Rogers, which letter was directed to him, dated February 26th, 1839. and signed, Isaac Galland. The contents of said letter expresses a sympathy and a good feeling towards the people and church of the Latter Day Saints, which I have the high honor, of being their religious leader; I say high honor, more especially, because I know them to be an honorable, a virtuous, and an upright people And that honor, vir[p. 51]tue, and righteousness is their only aim and object in this life. They are sir, a much injured, and abused people; and are greatly belied as to their true character. They have been fallen upon by a gang of ruffians and murderers, three times, in the state of Missouri; and entirely broken up, without having committed the first offence: or without there being the least shadow in the very slightest degree of evidence, that they have done ought of any thing derogatory to the laws, or character, of the state of Missouri. And this last time of their being broken up; it is either my misfortune, or good fortune, (for I rather count it good fortune to suffer affliction with the people of God,) in connection with others of my brethren, to be made a severe sufferer, by the hands of the above mentioned *rascals:* they are supported by some portions of the authorities of the State, either in consequence of prejudices, excited by foul calumnies, or else they themselves, are the fathers and instigators, of the whole diabolical and murderous proceeding.

I am bold to say sir, that a more nefarious transaction never has existed, since the days of Yore; than that which has been practiced

upon us.—Myself and those who are in prison with me, were torn
from our houses, with our wives and children clinging to our
garments, under the awful expectation of being exterminated. At
our first examination, the mob found one or two persons, of low
and worthless character, whom they compelled, at the peril of their
lives, to swear some things against us: which things, if they had
been even true, were nothing at all, and could not have so much as
disgraced any man under heaven. Nevertheless, we could have
proved, by more than five hundred witnesses, that the things were
false. But the Judge employed an armed force, and compelled us to
abandon the idea of introducing witnesses, upon the peril of the
lives of the witnesses. Under such circumstances, sir, we were
committed to this jail, on a pretended charge of treason, against
the State of Missouri, without the slightest evidence to that effect.
We collected our witnesses the second time, and petitioned a
habeas corpus: but were thrust back again into prison, by the rage
of the mob; and our families robbed, and plundered: and families,
and witnesses, thrust from their homes, and hunted out of the
State, and dare not return for their lives. And under this order of
things, we, held in confinement, for a pretended trial: whereas we
are to be tried by those very characters who have practiced those
things, yea the very characters who have murdered some hundred
men, women, and children,[3] and have sworn to have our lives also;
and have made public proclamation that these men must and
should be hung, whether they were innocent, or guilty. Such men
too, sir, have made this proclamation, as general Atchison, who is
considered one of the most prominent men in the State. This is
according to the information I have received, which I suppose to be
true. Their plea sir, is that the State will be ruined, if the Mormon
leaders are liberated, so that they can publish the real facts, of what
has been practised upon them.

We are kept under a strong guard, night and day, in a prison of
double walls and doors, proscribed in our liberty of conscience, our
food is scant, uniform, and coarse; we have not the privilege of
cooking for ourselves, we have been compelled to sleep on the floor
with straw, and not blankets sufficient to keep us warm; and when

we have a fire, we are obliged to have almost a constant smoke.
The Judges have gravely told us from time to time that they knew
we were innocent, and ought to be liberated, but they dare not
administer the law unto us, for fear of the mob. But if we will deny
our religion, we can be liberated. Our lawyers have gravely told us,
that we are only held now by the influence of long faced Baptists;
how far this is true, we are not able to say: but we are certain that
our most vehement accusers, are the highest toned professors of
religion. On being interogated what these men have done? their
uniform answer is, we do not know, but they are false teachers, and
ought to die. And of late boldly and frankly acknowledge, that the
religion of these men, is all that they have against them. Now sir,
the only difference between their [p. 52] religion, and mine, is,
that I firmly believe in the prophets and apostles, Jesus Christ,
being the chief corner stone. And speak as one having authority
among them, and not as the scribes, and am liberal in my
sentiments towards all men, in matters of opinion, and rights of
conscience, whereas they are not. But enough of this. I feel highly
gratified to learn of a man who had sympathy, and feelings of
friendship towards a suffering, and an injured, and an innocent
people: if you can do them any good, render them any assistance,
or protection, in the name of suffering humanity, we beseach you,
for God's sake, and humanity's sake, that you will do it. If you
should see Gov. Lucas, I wish you would have the kindness to state
to him, the contents of this letter; as we know him from
information to be a man of character and a gentleman. I would be
glad, therefore, if it were possible that he, and not only him, but
every other patriotic, and humane man, should know the real facts
of our sufferings: and of the unjust and cruel hand that is upon us. I
have been in this State one year, the 12th, day of this month; I
have never borne arms at any time. I have never held any office,
civil or military in this State. I have only officiated as a religious
teacher, in religious matters, and not in temporal matters. The
only occasion I have given, was to defend my own family, in my
own door yard, against the invasions of a lawless mob: and that I
did not at the expense of any man's life: but risked my own in

defence of an innocent family, consisting of a wife, five children, hired servants &c. My residence was in Far West. I was surrounded with a noble, generous, and enterprising society, who were friendly to the laws, and constitution of our country: they were broken up without cause, and my family now as I suppose, if living, are in Quincy, Illinois.

We are informed that the prisoners in Richmond jail, Ray county, are much more inhumanly treated than we are;[4] if this is the case, we will assure you, that their constitutions cannot last long, for we find ours wearing away very fast: and if we knew of any source whereby aid and assistance could be rendered unto us, we should most cordially petition for it: but where is liberty? Where is humanity? Where is patriotism? Where has the genius of the pedistal of the laws and constitution of our boasted country fled? Are they not slain victims at the feet of prejudice, to gratify the malice of a certain class of men, who have learned that their craft and creed cannot stand against the light of truth, when it comes to be investigated?—hence they resort to the vilest of the vile means, and to foul calumnies, and to physical force to do what? To deprive some fifty thousand, of the right of citizenship, and for what? because they are blasphemers? no: For this is contrary to their practice, as well as faith. Was it because they were tavern haunters, and drunkards? no. This charge cannot be substantiated against them as a people; it was contrary to their faith. And finally was it for any thing? no sir, not for any thing, only, that Mormonism is truth; and every man who embraced it felt himself at liberty to embrace every truth: consequently the shackles of superstition, bigotry, ignorance, and priestcraft, falls at once from his neck; and his eyes are opened to see the truth, and truth greatly prevails over priestcraft; hence the priests are alarmed, and they raise a hu-in-cry, down with these men! heresy! heresy! fanaticism! false prophet! false teachers! away with these men! crucify them! crucify them! And now sir, this is the sole cause of the persecution against the Mormon people, and now if they had been Mahomedans, Hottentots, or Pagans; or in fine sir, if their religion was as false as hell, what right would men have to drive them from their homes, and their country, or to exterminate them, so long as their religion did not interfere with the civil rights of men, according to the laws of our country? None at all. But the mind naturally being curious wants to know what those sentiments are, that are so at varience with the priests of the age, and I trust you will bear with me, while I offer to you a few of my reflections on this subject, and if they should not meet your mind, it may open a door for an exchange of ideas, and in the exercise of a proper liberality of spirit, it may not be unprofitable.

In the first place, I have stated above [p. 53] that Mormonism is truth, in other words the doctrine of the Latter Day Saints, is truth; for the name Mormon, and Mormonism, was given to us by our enemies, but Latter Day Saints was the real name by which the church was organized. Now, sir, you may think that it is a broad assertion that it is truth; but sir, the first and fundamental principle of our holy religion is, that we believe that we have a right to embrace all, and every item of truth, without limitation or without being circumscribed or prohibited by the creeds or superstitious notions of men, or by the dominations of one another, when that truth is clearly demonstrated to our minds, and we have the highest degree of evidence of the same; we feel ourselves bound by the laws of God, to observe and do strictly, with all our hearts, all things whatsoever is manifest unto us by the highest degree of testimony that God has committed us, as written in the old and new Testament, or any where else, by any manifestation, whereof we know that it has come from God: and has application to us, being adapted to our situation and circumstances; age, and generation of life; and that we have a perfect, and indefeasible right, to embrace all such commandments, and do them; knowing, that God will not command any thing, but what is peculiarly adapted in itself, to ameliorate the condition of every man under whatever circumstances it may find him, it matters not what kingdom or country he may be in. And again, we believe that it is our privilege to reject all things, whatsoever is clearly manifested to us that they do not have a bearing upon us. Such as, for instance, it is not binding on us to build an Ark, because God commanded Noah to build one.—It would not be applicable to our case; we are not looking for a flood. It is not binding on us to lead the children of Israel out of the land of Egypt, because God commanded Moses. The children of Israel are not in bondage to the Egyptians, as they were then; our circumstances are very different. I have introduced these for examples: and on the other hand, "Thou shalt not kill. Thou shalt not steal. Thou shalt not commit adultery. Thou shalt not bare false witness against thy neighbor. Thou shalt not covet thy neighbor's wife, nor his ox, nor his ass, nor his man servant, nor his maid servant, nor any thing that is thy neighbors."

These sentiments we most cordially embrace, and consider them binding on us because they are adapted to our circumstances. We believe that we have a right to revelations, visions, and dreams from God, our heavenly Father; and light and intelligence, through the gift of the Holy Ghost, in the name of Jesus Christ, on all subjects pertaining to our spiritual welfare; if it so be that we keep his commandments, so as to render ourselves worthy in his sight. We believe that no man can administer salvation through the gospel, to the souls of men, in the name of Jesus Christ, except he is authorized from God, by revelation, or by being ordained by some one whom God hath sent by revelation, as it is written by Paul, Romans 10: 14, "and how shall they believe in him, of whom, they have not heard? and how shall they hear without a preacher? and how shall they preach, except they be sent?" and I will ask, how can they be sent without a revelation, or some other visible display of the manifestation of God. And again, Hebrews, 5:4, "And no man taketh this honor unto himself, but he that is called of God, as was Aaron."—And I would ask, how was Aaron called, but by revelation?

And again we believe in the doctrine of faith, and of repentance. and of baptism for the remission of sins, and the gift of the Holy Ghost, by the laying on of hands, and of resurrection of the dead, and of eternal judgment. We believe in the doctrine of repentance, as well as of faith; and in the doctrine of baptism for the remission of sins as well as in the doctrine of repentance; and in the doctrine of the gift of the Holy Ghost by the laying on of hands, as well as baptism for the remission of sins; and also, in like manner, of the resurrection of the dead, and of eternal judgment. Now all these are the doctrines set forth by the appostles, and if we have any thing to do with one of them, they are all alike precious, and binding on us. And as proof, mark the following quotations. Mark 16 chap., 15-16 verses, "and he said [p. 54] unto them go ye into all the world and preach the gospel to every creature, and he that believeth and is baptized shall be saved, but he that believeth not shall be damned." Hear you will see the doctrine of faith: and again, Acts 2nd chap. 28 verse, "Then Peter said unto them repent and be baptized every one of you in the name of Jesus Christ for the remission of sins, and ye shall receive the gift of the Holy Ghost." Hear you see the doctrine of repentance and baptism for the remission of sins, and the gift of the Holy Ghost, connected by the promise inseperably. Now I want you to consider the high standing of Peter; he was now being endowed with power from on high and held the keys of the kingdom of heaven. Mathew 16th chap. 19th verse, and I will give unto you the keys of the kingdom of heaven, and whatsoever thou shalt bind on earth shall be bound in heaven, and whatsoever thou shalt loose on earth shall be loosed in heaven." This was the character, Sir, that made the glorious promise of the gift of the Holy Ghost, predicated upon the baptism for the remission of sins: and he did not say that it was confined to that generation, but see further: Act 2nd chap. 39th verse. "for the promise is unto you, and your children, and to all who are afar off, even as many as the Lord our God shall call." Then, Sir, if the callings of God extend unto us, we come within the perview of Peter's promise. Now where is the man who is authorized to put his finger on the spot and say, thus far shalt thou go and no farther: there is no man. Therefore let us receive the whole, or none. And again, concerning the doctrine of the laying on of hands. Act 8th chap. 14th to 17th verse. Now when the apostles, which were at Jerusalem, heard that Samaria had received the word of God, they sent unto them Peter and John; who, when they were come down, prayed for them, that they might receive the Holy Ghost; for as yet he was fallen upon none of them, only they were baptized in the name of the Lord Jesus.—Then laid they their hands upon them, and they received the Holy Ghost.—Acts 19th chap. 5th–6th verses.—When they heard this, they were baptized in the name of the Lord Jesus.—And when Paul had laid his hands upon them, the Holy Ghost came on them; and they spake with tongues and prophesied. We discover by these, the doctrine of the laying on of the hands.—And for the doctrine of the resurrection of the dead and of eternal judgment: Hebrews 6th chap. 2nd verse, of the doctrine of baptism, and of laying on of the hands, and of reserrection of the dead, and of eternal judgment. I consider these to be some of the leading items of the gospel, as taught by Christ and his apostles, and as received by those whom they taught. I wish you would look at these, carefully and closely, and you will readily perceive that the difference between me and other religious teachers, is in the bible; and the bible and them for it: and as far as they teach the gospel of Jesus Christ, as it is verily written, and are inspired, and called as was Aaron, I feel myself bound to bow with all defference to their mandates and teachings; but see Gallations, 1st chap. 6th to 10th verse. I marvel that you are so soon removed from him that called you into the grace of Christ, unto another Gospel; but there be some that trouble you, and would pervert the gospel of Christ. But though we, or an angel from heaven, preach any other gospel unto you than that which we have preached unto you, let him be accursed. As we said before, so say I now again, if any man preach any other gospel unto you than that ye have received, let him be accursed. For do I now persuade men or God? or do I seek to please men? for if I yet pleased men, I should not be the servant of Christ. Further, the 11-12 verses. But, I certify you, brethren, that the gospel which was preached of me is not after man; for I neither received it of man, neither was I taught it, but by the revelation of Jesus Christ.

Please sir, to pardon me for having obtruded thus lengthy upon your feelings, as you are a stranger to me; and I know nothing of you, only what I have read in your letter, and from that I have taken the liberty which I have. Be assured Sir, that I have the most liberal sentiments, and feelings of charity towards all sects, parties, and denominations; and the rights and liberties of concience, I hold most sa[p. 55]cred and dear, and dispise no man for differing with me in matters of opinion.

Accept Dear Sir, my best wishes for your welfare, and desire for further acquaintance, I close my letter, by giving you some quotations which you will have the goodness to read.

The second epistle of Paul to Timothy, 1: 5-7. 2: 10-14. 4: 2-7. Ephesians 4: 10-18. 1st Corinthians 12: 1-31. 8:3-6. Ephesians 4: 1-8. The 1st Epistle of John 1: Mathew, 3: 13-17. St. John 3: 1 16. 10: 1-50. 28: 18-20. St. Luke 24: 45-53. If you wish another address on this subject, you have only to let me know, and it shall be attended to.

Yours truly,
JOSEPH SMITH, Jr.

N. B. If Bishop Partridge, or if the church have not made a purchase of your land, and if there is not any one who feels a particular interest in making the purchase, you will hold it in reserve for us; we will purchase it of you at the proposals that you made to Mr. Barlow.[5] We think the church would be wise in making the contract. therefore, if it is not made before we are liberated, we will make it.

Yours &c.
JOSEPH SMITH, Jr.

To Emma Smith,
April 4, 1839

The court of inquiry that committed Joseph Smith and his associates to the Liberty Jail in November 1838 designated "the first thursday after the fourth monday in March next"[1] and the Daviess County court as the time and place for their trial. For the prisoners, the day of removal came none too soon, but it was more than a week after the designated day before they were taken from the jail. On the eve of their departure, Joseph wrote this final letter to Emma from Liberty.

Liberty, Jail, Clay Co. Mo,
Aprel, 4th 1839.

Dear— and affectionate— wife.

Thursday night I set down just as the sun is going down, as we peak throw the greats of this lonesome prision, to write to you, that I may make known to you my situation. It is I believe ⟨it is⟩ now about five months and six days since I have been under the *grimace,* of a guard night and day, and within the walls grates and screeking of iron dors, of a lonesome dark durty prison. With immotions known only to God, do I write this letter, the contemplations, of the mind under these circumstances, defies the pen, or tounge, or Angels, to discribe, or paint, to the human mid mind being, who never experiance[d] what I we experience. This night we expect; is the last night we shall try our weary Joints and bones on our dirty straw couches in these walls, let our

case hereafter be as it may, as we expect to start to mor=row, for
Davis Co, for our trial. We shall have a change of Venue to some
of the lower counties, for the final *trial,* as our *Lawyers* generaly
say, if law can be adheared to in Davis, as it grants us the
privaliege. But you are awere ~~of~~ what we may expect, of beings
that ‹have› conducted [themselves] as they have We lean on the
arm of Jehovah, and none else, for our deliverance, and if he dont
do it, it will not be done, you may be assured, for there is great
thirsting for our blood, in this state; not beca=use we are guilty of
any thing: but because they say these men ‹will› give an account
of what has been done to them; the wrongs they have
su=stain[ed] if it is known, it ‹will› ruin the State. So the mob
party have sworn, to have our lives, at all hasards, but God will
disapp=oint them we trust. We shall be moved from this [place] at
any rate and we are glad of it let what will become of ‹us› we
cannot ‹get› into a worse hole [p. 1] then this is, we shall not stay
here but one night besid=es this ‹if that ~~if that~~› thank God, we
shall never cast a lingering wish after liberty in clay county ~~no~~
Mo. we have enough of it to last forever, may God reward fals
swearers according to their works, is all I can wis=h them. My
Dear Emma I think of you and the children continualy, if I could
tell you my tale, I think you would say it was altoge=ther enough
for once, to grattify the malice of hell that I have suffered. I want
‹to› see little Frederick, Joseph, Julia, and Alexander, Joana,[2] and
old major. And as to yourself if you want to know how much I
want to see you, examine your feelings, how m=uch you want to
see me, and Judge for ‹you[r]self›, I would gladly ~~go~~ ‹walk› from
here to you barefoot, and bareheaded, and half naked, to see you
and think it great pleasure, and never count it toil, but do not
think I am babyish, for I do not feel so, I bare with fortitude all
my oppression, so do those that are with me, not one of us have
flinched yet, I want you ‹should› not let those little fellows,
forgit me, tell them Father loves them with a perfect love, and he
is doing all he can to git away from the mob to come to them, do
teach them all you can, that they may have good minds, be tender
and kind to them, dont be fractious to them, but listen to their
wants, tell them Father says they must be good children ‹and›

mind their mother, My Dear Emma there is great respo[n]sibility resting upon you, in preserveing yourself in honor, and sobr=iety, before them, and teaching them right things, to form their young and tender min=ds, that they begin in right paths, and not git contaminated when young, by seeing ungodly examples, I soppose you see [p. 2] the need of my council, and help, but ‹a› ~~as~~ combin=nation ‹of› things have conspired to place me where I am, and I know it ‹is› not my fault, and further if my voice and *council,* had been heeded I shou=ld not have been here, but I find no fault with you, attall I know nothing but what you have done the best you could, if there is any thing it is known to yourself, you must be your own Judge, on that subject: and if ether of ~~done~~ us have done wrong it is wise in us to repent of it, and for God sake, do not be so foolish as to y‹i›eld to the flattery of the Devel, faslshoods, and vainty, in this hour of trouble, that our affections be drawn, away from the right objects, those preasious things, God has given us will rise up in Judgement against us ~~in the day of judgement against us~~ if we do not mark well our steps, and ways. My heart has often been exceding sorrow=ful when I have thaught of these thing[s] for many considerations, one thing let [me adm]=onished you by way of my duty, do not [be] self willed, neither harber a spirit of re=vevenge: and again remember that he who is my enemys, is yours also, and nev=er give up an old tried friend, who has waded through all manner of toil, for your sake, and throw him away becau[se] fools may tell ‹you› he ‹has› some *faults;* these thing[s] have accured to ‹me› [as] I have been writing, I do[n't] speak of ‹them› because you do not know them, but because I want to stir up your pure mind by way of *rememberance:* all feelings of diss[at]=isfaction is far from my heart, I wish to act upon that principle of *generosity,* that will acqu‹it› myself in the preasance of [--] through the mercy of God You [*page cut away*]

[Joseph Smith Jr.] [p. 3]

Mrs ⁃ Emma Smith
Quincy Illinois

Liberty, Jail, Clay-County, April 4th 1839.

Dear and affectionate—Wife.

Thursday night I sit down just as the sun is going down, as we peak throw the grates of this lonesome prison, to write to you, that I may make known to you my situation. It is I believe now about five months and six days since I have been under the grimace of a guard night and day, and within the walls grates and screeking of iron dors, of a lonesome dark dusty prison. With immotions known only to God, do I write this letter, the contemplations, of the mind under these circumstances, defies the pen, or tounge, or angels, to discribe, or paint, to the human being, who never experiance what we experience. This night we expect; is the last night we shall try our weary joints and bones on our dirty straw couches in these walls, let our case hereafter be as it may, as we expect to start to morrow, for Davis Co, for our trial. We shall have a change of Venue to some of the lower counties, for the final trial, as our Lawyers generally say, if law can be adheared to in Davis, as it grants us the priviling. But you are aware of what we may expect, of beings that have conducted as they have We lean on the arm of Jehovah, and none else, for our deliverance, and if he dont do it, it will not be done, you may be assured, for there is great thirsting for our blood, in this State, not becaus we are guilty of any thing; but because they say these men will, give an account of what has been done to them, the wrongs they have sustain if it is known, it will, ruin the State. So the mob party have sworn, to have our lives, at all hasards, but God will disappoint them we trust, We shall be moved from this at ony rate and we are glad of it let what will become of us we cannot git into worse hole

then this is, we shall not stay here but one night beca
= se this, & thank God, we shall never cast a lingering
wish after liberty in clay county — Mo. we have
enough of it to last forever, may God reward false
swearers according to their works, is all I can wis
= h them. My Dear Emma I think of you and the
children continualy, if I could tell you my
tale, I think you would say it was altoge
them enough for once, to gratify the malice of
hell that I have suffered. I want to see little
Frederick, Joseph, Julia, and Alexander,
Joana, and old major, and as to yourself,
if you want to know how much I want
to see you, examine your feelings, how m
= uch you want to see me, and judge for yourself
I would gladly walk from here to you barefoot,
and bareheaded, and half naked, to see you and
think it great pleasure, and never count it
toil, but do not think I am babyish, for
I do not feel so, I bare with fortitude all
my oppressions, so do them that are with me
not one of us have flinched yet, I want
you should not let those little fellows, forgit me,
tell them Father loves them with a perfect
love, and he is doing all he can to git away
from the mob to come to them, do teach
them all you can, that they may have good
minds, be tender and kind to them, dont
be fractious to them, but listen to their wants
tell them Father says they must be good
children, and mind their mother, My Dear Emma
there is great responsibility resting upon you,
in preserving yourself in honor, and sobr
= iety, before them, and teaching them right
things, to form their young and tender min
= ds, that they begin in right paths, and not
git contaminated when young, by seeing
ungodly examples, I suppose you see

To Emma Smith, April 4, 1839, p. 2. Handwriting of Joseph Smith. See text, pp. 426-27. (Yale University Library.)

the need of my council, and help, but in combin
=nation things have conspired to place me where
I am, and I know it is not my fault, and further
if my voice and council, had been heeded I shou
=ld not have been here, but I find no fault
with you, attall I know nothing but what
you have done the best you could, if there is
any thing it is known to yourself, you must
be your own jadge, on that subject: and
if either of above us have done wrong it is
wise in us to repent of it, and for God
sake, do not be so foolish as to yield to
the flattery of the Devil, falshoods, and
vanity, in this hour of trouble, that our
affections be drawn away from the right
object, those precasious things, God has given
us will rise up in judgement against us
in the day of judgement against us if we
do not mark well our steps, and ways
My heart has often been exceeding sorrow
=ful when I have thought of these thing
for many considerations, one thing let
onisted you by way of my duty, do not
self willed, neither harber a spirit of re
= revenge: and again remember that he
who is my enimy, is yours also, and nev
= er give up an old tried friend, who has
waded through all manner of toil, for
your sake, and throw him away becaus
fools may tell you he, some faults, these thing
have accured to me I have been writing, I do
speak of them, because you do not know them, but
because I want to stir up your pure mind
by way of rememberance: all feelings of diso
= isfaction is far from my heart, I wish to ac
upon that principle of generosity, that will acqu
myself in the preasance of
through the mercy of God You

Journal Extract,
November 1839

On April 6, 1839, Joseph Smith and his fellow prisoners were taken from the Liberty Jail and hurried off to Daviess County. Two days later, a grand jury was convened at the house of Elisha B. Creekmore, near Gallatin, and was presided over by Thomas C. Burch, judge of Missouri's Eleventh Judicial Circuit. Indictments of riot, arson, burglary, treason, and receiving stolen goods were brought against the five Mormon prisoners.

Objecting to a trial in Daviess County on grounds that prejudice was extreme in that part of the State and that the judge had been counsel in the case, the prisoners were granted a change of venue to Boone County. A short time later, while traveling near Yellow Creek in Chariton County en route to Columbia, the Mormon prisoners were allowed to escape. After pursuing his course night and day, avoiding main roads, Joseph joined his family in Quincy, Illinois, on April 22, 1839.[1]

Following their expulsion from Missouri, the Latter-day Saints began to establish themselves in their new gathering place at Nauvoo, sixty miles north of Quincy. One of their first undertakings was the publication of a monthly paper, the *Times and Seasons*. Edited by Ebenezer Robinson and Don Carlos Smith, the first issue appeared in November 1839 with the promise, "We shall . . . endeavor to give a detailed history of the persecution and suffering, which the members of the church of Jesus Christ of Latter Day Saints, has had to endure in Missouri, and elsewhere, for their religion."[2] The first item published in the paper after the editor's prospectus was an "Extract, From the Private Journal of Joseph Smith Jr.," which contained his account of his Missouri experience.

On the fourteenth day of March, in the year of our Lord one thousand eight hundred and thirty eight, I with my family, arrived in Far West, Caldwell county Missouri, after a journey of more than one thousand miles, in the winter season, and being about eight weeks on our Journey; during which we suffered great affliction, and met with considerable persecution on the road.[3] However, the prospect of meeting my friends in the west, and anticipating the pleasure of dwelling in peace, and enjoying the blessings thereof, buoyed me up under the difficulties and trials which I had then to endure. However, I had not been there long before I was given to understand that plots were laid, by wicked and designing men for my destruction, who sought every opportunity to take my life; and that a company on the Grindstone forks of Grand river, in the county of Daviess, had offered the sum of one thousand dollars for my scalp: persons of whom I had no knowledge whatever, and who, I suppose, were entire strangers to me; and in order to accomplish their wicked design, I was frequently waylaid &c.; consequently, my life was continually in jeopardy.

I could hardly have given credit to such statements, had they not been corroborated by testimony, the most strong and convincing; as shortly after my arrival at Far West, while watering my horse in Shoal Creek, I distinctly heard three or four guns snap, which were undoubtedly intended for my destruction; however, I was mercifully preserved from those who sought to destroy me, by their lurking in the woods and hiding places, for this purpose.

My enemies were not confined alone, to the ignorant and obscure, but men in office, and holding situations under the

Governor of the State, proclaimed themselves my enemies, and
gave encouragement to others to destroy me; amongst whom, was
Judge King, of the fifth Judicial circuit, who has frequently been
heard to say that I ought to be beheaded on account of my religion.
Expressions such as these, from individuals holding such important
offices as Judge King's, could not fail to produce, and encourage
persecution against me, and the people with whom I was
connected. And in consequence of the prejudice which existed in
the mind of this Judge, which he did not endeavor to keep secret,
but made it as public as he could, the people took every advantage
they possibly could, in abusing me, and threatening my life;
regardless of the laws, which [p. 2] promise protection to every
religious society, without distinction.

During this state of things I do not recollect that either myself,
or the people with whom I was associated, had done any thing to
deserve such treatment, but felt a desire to live at peace, and on
friendly terms, with the citizens of that, and the adjoining
counties, as well as with all men; and I can truly say, "for my love
they were my enemies," and "sought to slay me without any cause,"
or the least shadow of a pretext.

My family was kept in a continual state of alarm, not knowing,
when I went from home, that I should ever return again; or what
would befall me from day to day. But notwithstanding these
manifestations of enmity, I hoped that the citizens would
eventually cease from their abusive and murderous purposes, and
would reflect with sorrow upon their conduct in endeavoring to
destroy me, whose only crime was in worshipping the God of
heaven, and keeping his commandments; and that they would soon
desist from harrassing a people who were as good citizens as the
majority of this vast republic—who labored almost night and day,
to cultivate the ground; and whose industry, during the time they
were in that neighborhood, was proverbial.

In the latter part of September, A.D. 1838, I took a journey, in
company with some others, to the lower part of the county of
Caldwell, for the purpose of selecting a location for a Town. While
on my journey, I was met by one of our brethren from Dewitt, in

Carroll county, who stated that our people, who had settled in that place, were, and had been for some time, surrounded by a mob, who had threatened their lives, and had shot at them several times; and that he was on his way to Far West, to inform the brethren there, of the facts. I was surprised on receiving this intelligence, although there had, previous to this time, been some manifestations of mobs, but I had hoped that the good sense of the majority of the people, and their respect for the constitution, would have put down any spirit of persecution, which might have been manifested in that neighborhood.

Immediately on receiving this intelligence, I made preparations to go to that place, and endeavor if possible, to allay the feelings of the citizens, and save the lives of my brethren who were thus exposed to their wrath. I arrived at Dewitt, about the first of October, and found that the accounts of the situation of that place were correct, for it was with much difficulty, and by travelling unfrequented roads, that I was able to get there; all the principal roads being strongly guarded by the mob, who refused all ingress as well as egress. I found my brethren, (who were only a handfull, in comparison to the mob, by which they were surrounded,) in this situation, and their provisions nearly exhausted, and no prospect of obtaining any more.

We thought it necessary to send immediately to the Governor, to inform him of the circumstances; hoping, from the Executive, to receive the protection which we needed, and which was guaranteed to us, in common with other citizens. Several Gentlemen of standing and respectability, who lived in the immediate vicinity, (who were not in any wise connected with the church of Latter Day Saints,) who had witnessed the proceedings of our enemies; came forward and made affidavits to the treatment we had received, and concerning our perilous situation; and offered their services to go and present the case to the Governor themselves. A messenger was accordingly despatched to his Excellency, who made known to him our situation. But instead of receiving any aid whatever, or even sympathy from his Excellency, we were told that "the quarrel was between the Mormons and the mob," and that "we might fight it out." In the mean time, we had petitioned the Judges to protect us. They sent out about one hundred of the militia, under the command of Brigadier General Parks;[4] but almost immediately on their arrival, General Parks informed us that the greater part of his men under Capt. Bogart had mutinied, and that he should be obliged to draw them off from the place, for fear they would join the mob; consequently he could afford us no assistance. [p. 3]

We had now, no hopes whatever, of successfully resisting the mob, who kept constantly increasing: our provisions were entirely exhausted and we being wearied out, by continually standing on guard, and watching the movements of our enemies; who, during the time I was there, fired at us a great many times. Some of the brethren died, for want of the common necessaries of life, and perished from starvation; and for once in my life, I had the pain of beholding some of my fellow creatures fall victims to the spirit of persecution, which did then, and has since prevailed to such an extent in Upper Missouri—men too, who were virtuous, and against whom, no legal process could for one moment, be sustained; but who, in consequence of their love to God— attachment to his cause—and their determination to keep the *faith*, were thus brought to an untimely grave.

Many houses belonging to my brethren, were burned; their cattle driven away, and a great quantity of their property destroyed by the mob. Seeing no prospect of relief, the Governor having turned a deaf ear to our entreaties, the militia having mutinied, and the greater part of them ready to join the mob; the brethren came to the conclusion to leave that place, and seek a shelter elsewhere; they consequently took their departure, with about seventy waggons, with the remnant of the property they had been able to save from their matchless foes, and proceeded to Caldwell. During our journey, we were continually harrassed and threatened by the mob, who shot at us several times; whilst several of our brethren died from the fatigue and privations which they had to endure, and we had to inter them by the wayside, without a coffin, and under circumstances the most distressing.

On my arrival in Caldwell I was informed by General Doniphan of Clay county, that a company of mobbers eight hundred strong, were marching towards a settlement of our people's in Daviess county. He ordered out one of the officers to raise a force and march immediately to what he called Wight's town and defend our people from the attacks of the mob, until he should raise the militia in his, and the adjoining counties to put them down. A small company of militia who were on their route to Daviess county, and who had passed through Far West, he ordered back again, stating that they were not to be depended upon, as many of them were disposed to join the mob; and to use his own expression, were "damned rotten hearted." According to orders Lieut. Colonel Hinkle marched with a number of our people to Daviess county to afford what assistance they could to their brethren. Having some property in that county and having a house building there, I went up at the same time. While I was there a number of houses belonging to our people were burned by the mob, who committed many other depredations, such as driving off horses, sheep, cattle hogs &c. A number, whose houses were burned down as well as those who lived in scattered and lonely situations, fled into the town for safety, and for shelter from the inclemency of the weather, as a considerable snow storm had taken place just about that time; women and children, some in the most delicate situations, were thus obliged to leave their homes, and travel several miles in order to effect their escape. My feelings were such as I cannot describe when I saw them flock into the village, almost entirely destitute of clothes, and only escaping with their lives. During this state of affairs General Parks arrived at Daviess county, and was at the house of Colonel Lyman Wight, when the intelligence was brought, that the mob were burning houses; and also when women and children were fleeing for safety. Colonel Wight who held a commission in the 59th regiment under his (General Parks) command, asked what was to be done. He told him that he must immediately, call out his men and go and put them down. Accordingly, a force was immediately raised for the purpose of quelling the mob, and in a short time were on their march with a determination to drive the mob, or die in the attempt; as they could bear such treatment no longer. The mob having learned the orders of General Parks, and likewise being aware of the determination of the oppressed, they broke up their encampments and fled. The mob seeing that they could not succeed by force, now [p. 4] resorted to stratagem; and after removing their property out of their houses, which were nothing but log cabins, they actually set fire to their own houses, and then reported to the authorities of the state that the Mormons were burning and destroying all before them.

On the retreat of the mob from Daviess, I returned to Caldwell, hoping to have some respite from our enemies, at least for a short time; but upon my arrival there, I was informed that a mob had commenced hostilities on the borders of that county, adjoining to Ray co. and that they had taken some of our brethren prisoners, burned some houses and had committed depredations on the peaceable inhabitants. A company under the command of Capt. Patten, was ordered out by Lieutenant Col. Hinckle to go against them, and stop their depredations, and drive them out of the county. Upon the approach of our people, the mob fired upon them, and after discharging their pieces, fled with great precipitation, with the loss of one killed and several wounded. In the engagement Capt Patten, (a man beloved by all who had the pleasure of his acquaintance,) was wounded and died shortly after. Two others were likewise killed and several wounded. Great excitement now prevailed, and mobs were heard of in every direction who seemed determined on our destruction. They burned the houses in the country and took off all the cattle they could find. They destroyed cornfields, took many prisoners, and threatened death to all the Mormons. On the 28 of Oct. a large company of armed soldiery were seen aproaching Far West. They came up near to the town and then drew back about a mile and encamped for the night. We were informed that they were Militia, ordered out by the Governor for the purpose of stopping our proceedings; it having been represented to his excellency, by wicked and designing men from Daviess, that we were the aggressors, and had committed

outrages in Daviess &c They had not yet got the Governors orders
of *extermination,* which I believe did not arrive until the next day.
On the following morning, a flag was sent, which was met by
several of our people, and it was hoped that matters would be
satisfactorily arranged after the officers had heard a true statement
of all the circumstances. Towards evening, I was waited upon by
Colonel Hinckle who stated that the officers of the Militia desired
to have an interview with me, and some others, hoping that the
difficulties might be settled without having occasion to carry into
effect the exterminating orders, which they had received from the
Governor. I immediately complied with the request, and in
company with Elders Rigdon and Pratt, Colonel Wight, and Geo.
W. Robinson, went into the camp of the militia. But judge of my
surprise, when instead of being treated with that respect which is
due from one citizen to another, we were taken as prisoners of war,
and were treated with the utmost contempt. The officers would not
converse with us, and the soldiers, almost to a man, insulted us as
much as they felt disposed, breathing out threats against me and my
companions. I cannot begin to tell the scene which I there
witnessed. The loud cries and yells of more than one thousand
voices, which rent the air and could be heard for miles; and the
horrid and blasphemous threats and curses which were poured upon
us in torrents, were enough to appal the stoutest heart. in the
evening we had to lie down on the cold ground surrounded by a
strong guard, who were only kept back by the power of God from
depriving us of life. We petitioned the officers to know why we
were thus treated, but they utterly refused to give us any answer, or
to converse with us. The next day they held a court martial, and
sentenced us to be shot, on Friday morning, on the public square,
as an ensample to the Mormons. However notwithstanding their
sentence, and determination, they were not permitted to carry
their murderous sentence into execution.

Having an opportunity of speaking to General Wilson,[5] I
inquired of him the cause why I was thus treated, I told him I was
not sensible of having done any thing worthy of such treatment;
that I had always been a supporter of the constitution and of

Democracy. His answer was "I know it, and that is the reason why I want to kill you or have you killed." The militia then went into the town and without any restraint whatever, plundered the [p. 5] houses, and abused the innocent and unoffending inhabitants. They went to my house and drove my family out of doors. They carried away most of my property and left many destitute.—We were taken to the town, into the public square; and before our departure from Far West, we, after much entreaties, were suffered to see our families, being attended all the while with a strong guard; I found my wife and children in tears, who expected we were shot by those who had sworn to take our lives, and that they should see me no more. When I entered my house, they clung to my garments, their eyes streaming with tears, while mingled emotions of joy and sorrow were manifest in their countenances. I requested to have a private interview with them a few minutes, but this privilege was denied me. I was then obliged to take my departure, but who can realize my feelings which I experienced at that time; to be torn from my companion, and leaving her surrounded with monsters in the shape of men, and my children too, not knowing how their wants would be supplied; to be taken far from them in order that my enemies might destroy me when they thought proper to do so. My partner wept, my children clung to me and were only thrust from me by the swords of the guard who guarded me. I felt overwhelmed while I witnessed the scene, and could only recommend them to the care of that God, whose kindness had followed me to the present time; and who alone could protect them and deliver me from the hands of my enemies and restore me to my family.

I was then taken back to the camp and then I with the rest of my brethren, viz: Sidney Rigdon, Hyram Smith, Parley P. Pratt, Lyman Wight, Amasa Lyman, and George W. Robinson, were removed to Independence, Jackson county. They did not make known what their intention or designs were in taking us there; but knowing that some of our most bitter enemies resided in that county, we came to the conclusion that their design was to shoot us, which from the testimony of others, I do think was a correct conclusion. While there, we were under the care of Generals Lucas and Wilson, we had to find our own board, and had to sleep on the floor with nothing but a mantle for our covering, and a stick of wood for our pillow. After remaining there a few days we were ordered by General Clark to return; we were accordingly taken back as far as Richmond, and there we were thrust into prison and our feet bound with fetters. While in Richmond, we were under the charge of Colonel Price from Chariton county, who suffered all manner of abuse to be heaped upon us. During this time my afflictions were great, and our situation was truly painful. After remaining there a few days we were taken before the court of inquiry, but were not prepared with witnesses, in consequence of the cruelty of the mob, who threatened destruction to all who had any thing to say in our favor: but notwithstanding their threats there were a few who did not think their lives dear so that they might testify to the truth, and in our behalf, knowing we were unlawfully confined; but the court who was predjudiced against us, would not suffer them to be examined according to law, but suffered the State's Attorney to abuse them as he thought proper. We were then removed to Liberty jail in Clay county, and there kept in close confinement in that place for more than four months. While there, we petitioned Judge Turnham[6] for a writ of habeas corpus, but on account of the predjudice of the jailor all communication was cut off; at length however, we succeeded in getting a petition conveyed to him, but for fourteen days we received no answer. We likewise petitioned the other Judges but with no success. After the expiration of fourteen days Judge Turnham ordered us to appear before him, we went and took a number of witnesses, which caused us considerable expense and trouble; but he altogether refused to hear any of our witnesses. The lawyers which we had employed refused to act; being afraid of the people. This being the case, we of course could not succeed, and were consequently remanded back to our prison house.—We were sometimes visited by our friends whose kindness and attention, I shall ever remember with feelings of lively gratitude, but frequently we were not suffered to have that privilege. Our victuals were of the coarsest [p. 6] kind, and served up in a manner which was disgusting. We continued in this situation, bearing up under the injuries and cruelties we suffered as well as we could, until we were removed to Daviess county, where we were taken in order to be tried for the crimes with which we had been charged. The grand jury (who were mostly intoxicated,) indicted us for treason, &c. &c.

While there, we got a change of venue to Boon county, and were conducted on our way to that place by a strong guard. The second evening after our departure the guard got intoxicated, we thought it a favorable opportunity to make our escape; knowing that the only object of our enemies was our destruction; and likewise knowing that a number of our brethren had been massacred by them on Shoal creek, amongst whom were two children; and that they sought every opportunity to abuse others who were left in that state; and that they were never brought to an account for their barbarous proceedings, but were winked at, and encouraged, by those in authority. We thought that it was necessary for us, inasmuch as we loved our lives, and did not wish to die by the hand of murderers and assasins; and inasmuch, as we loved our families and friends, to deliver ourselves from our enemies, and from that land of tyrany and oppression, and again take our stand among a people in whose bosoms dwell those feelings of republicanism and liberty which gave rise to our nation:—Feelings which the inhabitants of the state of Missouri were strangers to.—Accordingly we took the advantage of the situation of our guard and took our departure, and that night we travled a considerable distance. We continued on our journey both by night and by day, and after suffering much fatigue and hunger, I arrived in Quincy Illinois, amidst the congratulations of my friends and the embraces of my family.

I have now resided in this neighborhood for several weeks as it is known to thousands of citizens of Illinois, as well as of the State of Missouri, but the authorities of Mo., knowing that they had no justice in their crusade against me, and the people with whom I was associated, have not yet to my knowledge, taken the first step towards having me arrested.

Amongst those who have been the chief instruments, and

leading characters, in the unparallelled persecutions against the church of Latter Day Saints; the following stand conspicuous, viz: Generals Clark, Wilson, and Lucas, Colonel Price, and Cornelius Guilliam.[7] Captain Bogart also, whose zeal in the cause of oppression and injustice, was unequalled, and whose delight has been to rob, murder, and spread devastation amongst the Saints. He stole a valuable horse, saddle and bridle from me; which cost two hundred dollars, and then sold the same to General Wilson. On understanding this I applied to General Wilson for the horse, who assured me, upon the honor of a gentleman, and an officer, that I should have the horse returned to me; but this promise has not been fulfilled.

All the threats, murders, and robberies which these, officers have been guilty of, are entirely looked over by the Executive of the state; who, to hide his own iniquity, must of course shield and protect those whom he employed, to cary into effect his murderous purposes.

I was in their hands as a prisoner about six months, but notwithstanding their determination to destroy me, with the rest of my brethren who were with me; and although at three different times (as I was informed) we were sentenced to be shot, without the least shadow of law, (as we were not military men,) and had the time, and place appointed for that purpose; yet, through the mercy of God, in answer to the prayers of the saints, I have been preserved, and delivered out of their hands, and can again enjoy the society of my friends and brethren, whom I love: and to whom I feel united in bonds that are stronger than death: and in a state where I believe the laws are respected, and whose citizens, are humane and charitable.

During the time I was in the hands of my enemies; I must say, that although I felt great anxiety, respecting my family and friends; who were so inhumanly treated and abused; and who had to mourn the loss of the husbands and children, who had been slain; and after having been robbed of [p. 7] nearly all that they possessed be driven from their homes, and forced to wander as strangers in a strange country, in order, that they might save themselves and their little ones, from the destructions they were threatened with in Missouri; yet, as far as I was concerned, I felt perfectly calm, and resigned to the will of my heavenly Father. I knew my innocency, as well as that of the saints; and that we had done nothing to deserve such treatment from the hands of our oppressors: consequently, I could look to that God, who has the hearts of all men in his hands, and who had saved me frequently from the gates of death for deliverance: and notwithstanding that every avenue of escape seemed to be entirely closed, and death stared me in the face, and that my destruction was determined upon, as far as man was concerned; yet, from my first entrance into the camp, I felt an assurance, that I with my brethren and our families should be delivered. Yes, that still small voice, which has so often whispered consolation to my soul, in the debth of sorrow and distress, bade me be of good cheer, and promised deliverance, which gave me great comfort: and although the heathen raged, and the people imagined vain things, yet the Lord of hosts, the God of Jacob, was my refuge; and when I cried unto him in the day of trouble, he delivered me; for which I call upon my soul, and all that is within me, to bless and praise his holy name: For although I was "troubled on every side, yet not distressed; perplexed, but not in dispair; persecuted, but not forsaken; cast down, but not destroyed."

The conduct of the saints under their accumulated wrongs and sufferings, has been praise-worthy; their courage, in defending their brethren from the ravages of mobs; their attachment to the cause of truth, under circumstances the most trying and distressing, which humanity can possibly endure; their love to each other; their readiness to afford assistance to me, and my brethren who were confined in a dungeon; their sacrifices in leaving the state of Missouri, and assisting the poor widows and orphans, and securing them houses in a more hospitable land; all conspire to raise them in the estimation of all good and virtuous men; and has secured them the favor and approbation of Jehovah; and a name, as imperishable as eternity. And their virtuous deeds, and heroic actions, while in defence of truth and their brethren: will be fresh and blooming; when the names of their oppressors shall either be entirely forgotten, or only remembered, for their barbarity and cruelty. Their attention and affection to me, while in prison, will ever be remembered by me; and when I have seen them thrust away, and abused by the jailor and guard, when they came to do any kind offices, and to cheer our minds while we were in the gloomy prison house, gave me feelings, which I cannot describe, while those who wished to insult and abuse us, by their threats and blasphemous language, were applauded and had every encouragement given them.

However, thank God, we have been delivered; and although, some of our beloved brethren, have had to seal their testimony with their blood; and have died martyrs to the cause of truth; yet,

> Short, though bitter was their pain,
> Everlasting is their joy.

Let us not sorrow as "those without hope," the time is fast approaching, when we shall see them again, and rejoice together, without being affraid of wicked men: Yes, those who have slept in Christ, shall he bring with him, when he shall come to be glorified in his saints, and admired by all those who believe: but to take vengeance upon his enemies, and all those who obey not the gospel. At that time, the hearts of the widow and fatherless shall be comforted, and every tear shall be wiped from of their faces.

The trials they have had to pass through, shall work together for their good, and prepare them for the society of those, who have come up out of great tribulation; and have washed their robes, and made them white in the blood of the Lamb. Marvel not then, if you are persecuted, but remember the words of the Savior, "The servant is not above his Lord, if they have persecuted, me, they will persecute you also;" and that all the afflictions through which the saints have to pass, are in fulfillment of the words of [p. 8] the prophets, which have spoken since the world began. We shall therfore do well to discern the signs of the times, as we pass along, that the day of the Lord may not "overtake us as a thief in the night." Afflictions, persecutions, imprisonments and deaths, we must expect according to the scriptures, which tell us, that the blood of those whose souls were under the alter, could not be avenged on them that dwell on the earth, untill their brethren should be slain, as they were.

If these transactions had taken place among barbarrians, under the authority of a despot; or in a nation, where a certain religion is established according to law, and all others proscribed; then there might have been some shadow of defence offered. But can we realize that in a land which is the cradle of Liberty and equal rights and where the voice of the conquerors, who had vanquished our foes, had scarcely died away upon our ears, where we frequently mingled with those who had stood amidst the "battle and the breeze," and whose arms have been nerved in the defence of their country and liberty: whose institutions are the theme of philosophers and poets, and held up to the admiration of the whole civilized world. In the midst of all these scenes, with which we were surrounded, a persecution, the most unwarrantable, was commenced; and a tragedy, the most dreadful, was enacted, by a large portion of the inhabitants, of one of those free and independent States, which comprise this vast republic; and a deadly blow was struck at the institutions, for which our Fathers had fought many a hard battle, and for which, many a Patriot had shed his blood; and suddenly, was heard, amidst the voice of joy and gratitude for our national liberty, the voice of mourning, lamentation and woe. Yes, in this land, a mob, regardless of those laws, for which so much blood had been spilled, dead to every feeling of virtue and patriotism, which animated the bosom of freemen; fell upon a people whose religious faith was different from their own; and not only destroyed their homes, drove them away, and carried off their property, but murderd many a free born son of America. A tragedy, which has no parrallel in modern, and hardly in ancient times; even the face of the Red man would be ready to turn pale at the recital of it.

It would have been some consolation, if the authorities of the State had been innocent in this affair, but they are involved in the guilt thereof; and the blood of innocence, even of *children*, cry for vengeance upon them. I ask the citizens of this vast republic, whether such a state of things is to be suffered to pass unnoticed, and the hearts of widows, orphans and patriots, to be broken, and their wrongs left without redress? No! I invoke the genius of our constitution, I appeal to the patriotism of Americans, to stop this unlawful and unholy procedure; and pray that God may defend this nation from the dreadful effects of such outrages. Is there not virtue in the body politic? Will not the people rise up in their majesty, and with that promptitude and zeal, which is so characterestic of them, discountenance such proceedings, by bringing the offenders to that punishment which they so richly deserve; and save the nation from that disgrace and ultimate ruin, which otherwise must inevitably fall upon it?

JOSEPH SMITH JR.

To Henry G. Sherwood,
November 7, 1839

To Emma Smith,
November 9, 1839

After repeated efforts to obtain redress for their lost lands and property in Missouri had failed on the local and state level, the Latter-day Saints decided to approach the nation's highest authority. At a conference of the Church held in Nauvoo on October 7-8, 1839, Joseph Smith, Sidney Rigdon, and Elias Higbee were selected as a committee to lay the Mormon cause before the federal government.[1]

The committee left Nauvoo on October 29 in a two-horse carriage, accompanied by Orrin Porter Rockwell, but were forced to stop at Springfield when sudden illness prevented Sidney Rigdon from continuing the trip. While there, the Prophet wrote two letters, one, dated November 7, to the Nauvoo land agent, Henry Sherwood,[2] and the second, two days later, to his wife:

Springfield November 7th 1839

Mr. Henry. G. Sherwood
     you will please to pay John. A. Hicks[3] fifty Dollars and charge the same to me yours &c

Joseph Smith Jr

The Above order is for mony to bear our expences on the
road he will take a lot or land if you have any to please him if not
you can sell the lot that Br— Jonathan Hampton[4] was to have I
have seen him hes paid me the damage &c &c

Joseph Smith Jr

Springfild Ill
November 9th 1839

My Dear Wife
    perhaps you may thing strange That we are not fu‹r›ther on
our Jou[r]ny at this date but I will say that we have done all that
we could for the safty of Elder Rigdon on account of his week
state of hea[l]th and this morning we are under the ~~neces~~ nesesity
of leaveing him at Brother Snyders[1] and pesueing our Journy
without him we think he will soon recover his health as he is not
dangerously sick we regret that he cannot go on with us very ~~mut~~
much but cannot help ourselves but must comm=it him into the
hands of God and ~~pe~~ go on being fild with constant anxiety for
our Families and friends behind I shall be filled ‹with› constant
anxiety about you and the children until I hear from you and in a
perticular maner litle Frecerick it was so painful to leave him sick
I hope you will wa[t]ch over those tender ofsprings in a maner
that ‹is› bec‹~~is~~›=oming a mother and ‹a› saint and try to
cu[l]tiva=te their minds and learn ‹them› to read and be sober do
not let ‹them› be exposed to the wether to take cold and try to git
all the rest you can it will be a long and lonesome time ~~and~~
dureing my absence from you and nothing but a sense of
humanity could have urged me on to ~~a~~ so great a sacrafice but
shall I see so many perish and ‹not› seek redress no I will try this
once in the ‹name› of the Lord therefore be patient u‹n›till I
come and do the best you can I cannot write what I want but

believe me ‹my›feelings are of the best kind towards you all my hand cramps so I must close I am [*page cut away*]

[Joseph Smith Jr.]

To Emma Smith [p. 1]

Mrs Emma Smith
Commerce Hancock Co Ill— [p. 2]

Springfield November 7th 1839

Mr. Henry G. Sherwood

You will please to pay John A. Hicks fifty Dollars and change the same to me if Comes &c

Joseph Smith Jr

The above order is for money to bear our expences on the road he will take as lot or land if you have any to spare him if not your own sell the lot that Bro Jonathan Hampton was to have if I have seen him its paid me the damage &c &c

Joseph Smith

To Henry G. Sherwood, November 7, 1839. Handwriting of Elias Higbee and Joseph Smith. See text, pp. 447-48. (Illinois State Historical Library.)

Springfield S November 9th 1839

My Dear Wife

perhaps you may think it strange
That we are not further on our journy at this
date but I will say that we have done all
that we could for the safty of Elder Rigdon
on account of his week state of heath and
this morning we are under the necessity
of leaveing him at Brother Snyders and persuing
our journy without him we think he will soon
recover his heath as he is not dangerously sick
we regret that he cannot go on with us very
much but cannot help aurselves but must comm
it him into the hands of God and so go on
being fild with constant roraciety for our
Families and friends behind I shall be filled with
constant anxeity about you and the children
until I hear from you and in a perticular
maner little Fredrick it was so painful to
leave him sick I hope you will wach over
those tender offsprings in a maner that becom
ouring a mother affectionat and try to cultiva
te their minds and learn them to read and be sober
do not let them be esposed to the wether to take
cold and try to git all the rest you can
it will be a long and lonesom time
dureing my absence from you and nothing
but a sense of humanity could have
urged me on to so great a sacrafice
but shall I see so many perish and seek not
redress no I will try this once in the name of the
Lord therefore be patient utill I come and
do the best you can I cannot write what I
want but believe me my feelings are of the best
kind towards you all my hand cramps so I
must close I am

To Emma Smith

To Emma Smith, November 9, 1839, p. 1. Handwriting of Joseph Smith.
See text, pp. 448-49. (RLDS Church Archives.)

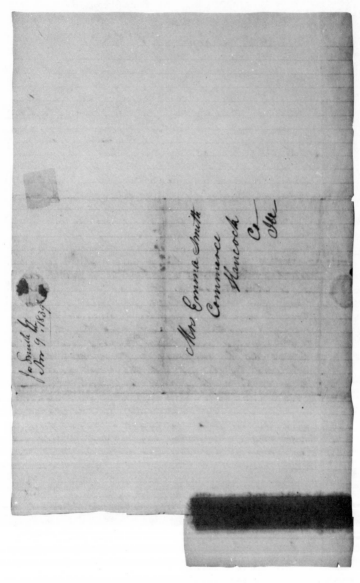

Mrs Emma Smith
Commerce
Hancock
Co—
Illi—

Jo Smith Jr
Nov 9, 1839

To Emma Smith, November 9, 1839, p. 2. Handwriting of Joseph Smith. Handwriting of Joseph Smith. See text, p. 449. (RLDS Church Archives.)

To Emma Smith,
January 20, 1840

To Mr. Editor, Sir,
January 22, 1840

Continuing their journey toward Washington, D.C., the Mormon committee on redress arrived in Columbus, Ohio, on November 18, 1839. There, due to poor traveling conditions, Sidney Rigdon's continued ill health, and the need for haste in reaching Washington, Joseph Smith and Elias Higbee proceeded on their way, leaving Porter Rockwell, Rigdon, and Robert Foster (Rigdon's doctor, who joined the company at Springfield, Illinois) to come as the sick man's health would permit.

The Prophet and Elias Higbee arrived in Washington, D.C., on November 28, found lodging at the corner of Missouri and Third Street, and the next day were received at the White House by President Martin Van Buren. The meeting with the President and ensuing contacts with other government officials were less than satisfactory to Joseph Smith. Prejudice against the Mormon people, strong state rights sentiment, and political aspiration seemed to militate against any hope for redress. Finally, convinced that nothing would come from prolonging his stay in Washington, Joseph started for home.[1]

Prior to his departure, while awaiting developments at Washington, the Prophet spent several weeks visiting the Saints in Pennsylvania and New Jersey. Two letters written from Chester County, Pennsylvania, reflect this phase of his eastern experience, one dated January 20, 1840, to Emma, and another from Brandywine on January 22 to the editor of the *Chester County Register and Examiner.*

~~Pheadelpha~~ ‹Chester Co Pa› 20th 1840

My Dear and beloved Wife

I recieved a letter from Hyram which cheared my heart to learn that my Family was all alive yet my heart mourns for those who have been taken from us[2] but not without hope for I shall see them again and be with them therefore we can be more reconciled to the dealings of God I am now makeing all hast[e] to arange my business to start for home I feel very ancious to see you all once more in this wor=ld the time seems long that I am deprived of your sosiety but the ‹lord› being my helper I will not be ~~mue~~ much longer I am determined to st[art] for home in a few days our bus=iness I expect is before the house of Congress now ‹and› I shall ~~shall~~ start for Washington in a few day[s] and from there home as soon as posible I am filled with consta=nt anxiety and shall be until I git home I pray God to spare you all untill I git home my dear Emma my heart is intwined arr=ound you and those little ones I want ‹you› to remember me tell all the chi[l]dren ~~ha~~ that I love them and will come home as soon as I can yours in the bonds of love your Husband u[n]till Death &c

Joseph Smith Jr

Emma Smith [p. 1]

Emma Smith
Commerce
Hancock ~~Co~~ County Ill. [p. 2]

Brandywine Chester Co Pa
Jan. 22d 1840
~~Faith of~~ the Latter Day Saints ~~in goverments and Laws in general~~

Mr. Editor Sir

For as much as many false rumers are a broad in the world
concerning my self and the fa=ith which I profess and that my
belief with regard to Earthly goverments and laws in gen=eral may
not be miss interpreted nor miss=understood I have thought proper
to present for your consideration and for the consideration of the
public (if you will do me the favour) through your valuable and
interesting paper my opinions concerning the same[1]

First I believe that goverments were instituted of God for the
benefit of man and that he holds men accountable for ~~their~~ their
acts in relation to them Either in making laws or administering
them for the good and safty of Society

Secondly I believe that no goverment can exist in peace except
such laws are framed and held inviolate as will secure to each
individual the free exercise of concience the right and controll of
property and the protection of life

Third I ~~We~~ believe that all gover‹n›ments necessarily re=quire
civel officers and magistrates to inforce the Laws of the Same and
that such as will administer the Laws ‹~~of the same~~› in equity and
justice should be sou=ght for and upheld by the voise of the people
(if a republic~~k~~) or the will of the Sovreign

Fourth I believe that ~~a~~ religion is ~~instuted~~ instituted of God and
that men are ameniable to him ‹and to him ~~onley~~› onley for the
exersise of it unless their religious opinion prompts them to infringe
upon the righ=ts and ‹liberty ~~privaleges~~› ~~privalegs~~ of others But I
do~~o~~ not be=lieve that human Law has a right to inter=fear in
prescribing rules of worship to bind the conciences of men nor ~~do~~
dictate forms for public or private devotion That the civel
magistrate shou=ld restrane crime but never controll concience
should punish guilt but never supress the freedom of the ‹soul›
[p. 1]

5 I believe that all men are bound to sustane and uphold the

respective governments in which they reside while protected in
their inherent and in alienable rights by the Laws of such
Govern=ments and that sedition and rebellion are un=becoming
every Citizen thus prote[c]ted and should be punished accordingly
and that all Governme=nts have a right to enact such laws as in
their own judgements are best calculated to secure the public
interest at the same time ‹however› holding sacred the freedom of
concience

6 I believe that every man should be honoured in his station
Rulers and magistrates as such be=ing plalaced [placed] for the
protection of the inocent and the punishment of the guilty and that
to the Law all men owe respect and deference as with out them
peace and harmony would be supplanted by anar=chy and
~~confusion~~ terror human Laws being in=stituted for the express
purposs of regulating our interests as individuals and Nations
between man and man and divine laws given of heav=en
prescribing rules on spiritual conserns for faith and worship both to
be answered by man to his maker

7 I believe that rulers states and ~~and~~ govern=ments have a
right and are bound to enact Laws for the protection of all
Citizen[s] in the free exercise of their religious belief. But I do not
be=lieve that they have a right in justice to deprive Citizens of this
privalege or proscribe them in their opinions so long as a regard and
reverence ~~are~~ is shown to the Laws and such religious opinions do
not Justify sedition nor conspiracy

8 I ~~do not~~ believe that the commission of crime should be
punished according to the nature of the offence that murder
treason Robbery theft and the breach of the general peace in all
rispects should be punished according to their criminalty and their
tendancy to evil among men by the Laws of that gov=ernment in
which the offence is committed and for the public peace and
tranquility all men should step forward and use their ability in
bringing ~~the~~ offenders aggainst good laws to ~~justice~~ punishment

9 I do not believe it just to mingle religious in=fluence with
civel government whereby one reli[p. 2]=gious Society is fostered

and another proscribed in its spiritual privaleges and the individual rights of its members as citizens denied

10 I believe that all religious Societies have a right to deal with its ‹their› members for disorderly conduct according to the rules and regulations of such so=cieties provieded that such dealing be for fellow=ship and good Standing but I doo not be=lieve that any religious Society has authority to try men for ‹on› the right of property or life to take away ‹from them› this worlds goods or put them in Je‹o›par=dy either life or limb neither to inflict any fisical punishment upon them they can onley excommunicate them from their society and with their with draw their ‹from their› fellowship

11 I believe that men should appeal to the Civel law for redress of all wrongs and grieve=ences where personal abuse is inflicted or the right of propperty or character infringed where such laws exist as will protect the Same but we ‹I› believe that all men are Justified in defending themsSelves their friends and prop=erty and the government from ‹the› unlawful assau=lts and encroachments of all persons in times of ex=ingencies where immediate appeal cannot be made to the Laws and relief afforded

12 I believe it just to preach the Gospel to the Nations of the Earth and warn the Righteous to Save themselves from the corruptions of the world But I do not believe it right to interfear with bond Servants neither preach the gospel to nor baptise them contrary to the will and wish of their masters nor to meddle with th or influence them in the least contrary to the wish to cause them to be dissatisfied with their sittuations in this life theirby jeopardiseing the lives of men Such interfearence we I believe to be unlawful and unjust and dangerous to the peace of every government allowing human beings to be held in servitude

13 It has been reported by some vicious or de[s]igning characters that the church of Latter Day Saints believe in having their pro[p]erty in common and also the leaders of sade church controlls saide propperty This is a base fabrication without the least the least shadow or collering [coloring] of any thi=ing to make it out of but on the contrary no persons feelings can be more

repugnant to such [p. 3] a principle than mine every person in this Church has a right to controll his own proppe[r]=ty and is not required to do any thing except by his own free voluntary act that he may impart to the poor according to the requirement of the gospel "Give to him that asketh thee and from him that would borrow of thee turn <not> thou ~~not~~ away" I Math 5 chap 42 v.

I believe in liveing a virtuous upright and holy life before God and feel it my duty to perswaid all men in my power to do the same. That they may cease to do evil and learn to do well and brake off ~~from~~ their Sins by Rigteousness I close this by subscribing my self your mo[st] obedient Servent

Joseph Smith Jr

To Emma Smith, January 20, 1840, p. 1. Handwriting of Joseph Smith.
See text, p. 454. (Chicago Historical Society.)

To Emma Smith, January 20, 1840, p. 2. Handwriting of Joseph Smith. See text, p. 454. (Chicago Historical Society.)

To Robert D. Foster,
March 11, 1840

When Sidney Rigdon became ill at the outset of the 1839 trip to Washington, D.C., he was cared for by Robert D. Foster, a physician the party had met when they arrived at Springfield, Illinois, on November 4. An Englishman by birth and a convert to the Church, Dr. Foster attended Rigdon until January 27, 1840, when Rigdon was left to recuperate at Philadelphia. During the remainder of the eastern trip, Dr. Foster was with Joseph Smith as he concluded his business in the nation's capitol and then returned to Illinois. After leaving Elias Higbee in Washington and Orrin Porter Rockwell in Dayton, Ohio, the two men continued the last leg of the "wearisome" journey alone, arriving home in the first week of March.[1] On March 11 Joseph wrote to Dr. Foster at Beverly, Adams County, Illinois.

Nauvoo March 11, 1840.

Sir,

After I left you, I came to my bro's house in Plymouth the same day; and there I learned that my father was sick, and that he was not expected to live—had called his children together &c. My Bro. William had left home for this place the day before I arrived there. But when I arrived here I found him a little better, but was quite low yet. Since that time, he has been much afflicted with the ague, but is now recov=ering. With that exception we are all well at pres=ent; and it is a general time of health here now.

I have delivered two discourses in this place since my return— giveing a brief history of our journey the reception we met with by the president &c. and the general feeling towards us in Washington and other places. The effect has been to turn the entire mass of the people, even to an individual, so far as I have learned on the other side of the great political question

I find that we have lost nothing by our change; but have gained friends and influence. The fact is, we were compelled to change in consequence of seeing a disposition manifest to turn a deaf ear to the cries of suffering innocence. When we can see a disposition in our chief magistrate to sacrifice the rights of the poor at the shrine of popularity, it is high time to cast off such an individual.

After haveing formed an acquaintance with you, and a very intimate one too, for the last 4 months, and I need not say an agreeable one ~~too~~, I feel quite anxious to see you after a short separation, I hope you can make it convenient to come up and see us soon. I want to get hold of your journal very much.

Our Church here is prospering, and many are comeing into it. Our Town is improveing very fast. It is almost incredible to see what amt. of labor has been performed here during the winter [p. 1] past. There is now every prospect of our haveing a good society, a peaceable habitation and a desirable residence here.

May the Lord prosper our righteous cause, and save us in the day of his comeing! As ever, I am your friend and Brother in the New and everlasting cov't.

Joseph Smith Jun.

Robt. D Foster M.D.
Beverley Adams Co
Illinois

P.S. Our Business in Washington has gone before ⟨a⟩ ~~the~~
committee on ⟨the⟩ judiciary without a dissenting voice. We have
recently received two letters from Judge Higbee to this effect.[2] He is
well, But pres't. Rigdon yet has the chills and fever.

Our best respects to Bro. Wilbur & family; and to all other
friends in that section

As before
J.S. Jun. [p. 2]

Sir,   Nauvoo, March 11, 1840.

After I left you, I came to my bro house in Plymouth the same day, and there I learned that my father was sick, and that he was not expected to live—had called his children together &c. My bro. William had left home for this place the day before I arrived there. But when I arrived here I found him a little better, but was quite low yet. Since that time, he has been much afflicted with the ague, but is now recovering. With that exception we are all well at present, and it is a general time of health here now.

I have delivered two discourses in this place since my return—giving a brief history of our journey the reception we met with by the president &c. and the general feeling towards us in Washington and other places. The effect has been to turn the entire mass of the people, even to an individual, so far as I have learned on the other side of the great political question.

I since that we have lost nothing by our change; but have gained friends and influence. The fact is, we are compelled to change in consequence of seeing a disposition manifest to turn a deaf ear to the cries of suffering innocence. When we can see a disposition in our chief magistrate to sacrifice the rights of the poor at the shrine of popularity, it is high time to cast off such an individual.

After having formed an acquaintance with you, and a very intimate one too, for the last 11 months, and I need not say an agreeable one too, I feel quite anxious to see you after a short separation. I hope you can make it convenient to come up and see us soon. I want to get hold of your journal very much.

Our Church here is prospering, and many are coming into it. Our Town is improving very fast. It is almost incredible to see what amount of labor has been performed here during the winter

To Robert D. Foster, March 11, 1840, p. 1. Handwriting of Orson Hyde. See text, pp. 461-62. (LDS Church Archives.)

To The High Council, June 18, 1840

To Newel K. Whitney, December 12, 1840

Agreement, May 14, 1841

At the October 20, 1839, meeting of the Nauvoo high council, Joseph Smith was named Church treasurer with power to oversee the pricing and sale of land in Nauvoo.[1] Subsequently, much of his time was involved in this work. On June 18, 1840, the Prophet petitioned the council for relief from the "anxiety and trouble necessarily attendant on business transactions" so that he might devote his time more effectively to spiritual concerns. The council responded by urging Joseph to continue as treasurer, since they knew of "no way to relieve him" from the responsibility of liquidating the debt on the city plot. They did, however, appoint Henry G. Sherwood to assist Joseph as clerk, and Alanson Ripley,[2] recently appointed bishop of Iowa, to "provide for the wants of the Presidency."[3]

The June 18 petition is presented here along with two holograph documents: the first, dated December 12, 1840, to Newel K. Whitney, bishop of Nauvoo's Middle Ward; and the second, dated May 14, 1841, specifying a land transaction with Ebenezer and Elender Wiggins. The holographs indicate that temporal matters continued to concern Joseph after the action of the high council.

To the Honorable the High Council of the Church of Jesus Christ of Latter Day Saints

The memorial of Joseph Smith Jr respec[t]=fully represents.

That after the Church of Jesus Christ had been inhumanly as well as unconstitutionally expelled from their homes which they had secured to themselves in the State of Missouri, ~~and having~~ ⟨they⟩ found a resting place in the State of Illinois altho very much scattered and at considerable distances from each other.

That after the escape of your memorial=ist [Joseph Smith] from his enemies, he, (under the direction of the authorities of the Church) took such steps as has secured to the Church the present Locations viz the Town plat of Nauvoo and lands in the Iowa Territory

That in order to secure said locations your memorialist had to become responsible for the payment of the same and had to use considerable exertion in order to commence a settlement and a place of gathering for the Saints, but knowing that from the genius of the constitution of the Church and for the well being of the saints that it was necessary so that the constituted Authorities of the Church might assemble together to act or to legislate for the good of the whole society and that the saints might enjoy those priviledges which they could not by being scattered so wide apart, induced your memorialist, to exert himself to the utmost, in order to bring about an object so necessary and so desireable to the saints at large

That under the then existing circum=stances your memorialist had necessarily to engage in the temporalities of the Church [p. 1] which he has had to attend to the present time which has greatly engaged his mind and taken up much of his time.

That your memorialist feels it a duty which he owes to God as well as to the Church to give his attention more particularly to those things connec=ted with the spiritual welfare of the saints (which have now become a great people) so that they may be built up in their most holy faith and be enabled to go on to perfection—

That the Church having erected an office where he can attend to the affairs of the Church without distraction, he thinks and verily believes that the time has now come when he should devote himself exclusively to those things which relate to spiritualities of the Church and commence the work of translating the Ejyptian

Records— the Bible —and wait upon the Lord for such revelations as may be suited to the condi=tion and circumstances of the church and in order to attend to those things, prays that your honorable body will relieve him from the anxi=ety and trouble necessarily attendant on business transactions by appointing some one ~~of the Bishops~~ to take charge of the City Plot and attend to the business transactions which have heretofore rested upon your Memorialist.

That should your Honors deem it propper to do so, your memorialist would respectfully suggest, that he would have no means of support whatever and therefore would request that some one might be appointed to see that all his necessary wants be provided for as well as sufficient means or appropriations for a Clerk or Clerks which he may require to aid him in his important work [p.2]

Your memorialist would further represent that as Elder H.G. Sherwood is conversant with the affairs of the City plot, he thinks that he would be a suitable person to act as Clerk in that business and attend to the disposing of the remaining lots &c &c

Your Memorialist would take this opportunity of congratulating your Honorable body on the peace and Harmony which exists in the Church and for the good feelings which seem to be manifest by all the saints – and hopes that inasmuch as every one devotes themselves for the good of the Church and the spread of the Kingdom that the Choisest blessings of Heaven will be poured upon us and that the Glory of the Lord will overshadow the inheritances of the Saints

Joseph Smith Jr

Nauvoo June 18th 1840 [p. 3]

To the Hon
The High Council of the
Church of Jesus Christ
of Latter Day Saints [p. 4]

Nauvoo Dec 12th 1840

Brother Whitney
Dear Sir
    I am at work in my office am under the ne=cesity to have
some help from time to time to help me along in my calling I
therefore desire you to let the bearer of this hav[e] some of that
dry wood to burn in the stove of my office and obliege your
humble servent

                              Joseph Smith

Nauvoo ‹May› 14th 1841

    Ebenezer F Wiggins and Ela‹en›der Wiggins¹ agrees to sell to
Joseph Smith h their farm containing two hundred and thirty two
acres of land on the following condi=tions the ‹they are› to have
a deed for one of the best ‹city› lots in Nauvoo ‹at 1000 dollars›
and one hundred dollers in goods in hand and the remainder to be
in mony to be paid in three yearly payme=nts with interest from
this date said Smith is to have the p=ossession of the primices
‹immedeately› with all the spring work and the crops now on the
same with the excepttion of the house ‹which they live in› which
they are to have a rea=sonable time to obtain one some where els
they are not to be distressed on account of the house the rents of
those who have rented any portion ‹of said farm› is to come to
said smith

                         Ebenezer. F. Wiggins
                         Elender – Wiggins—

Nauvoo Dec. 12th 1840

Brother Whitney

Dear Sir

I am at work in my office and under the ne-cessity to have some help from time to time to help me along in my calling I therefore desire you to let the bearer of this have some of that dry wood to burn in the Stove of my office and Oblige Your humble Servant

Joseph Smith

To Newel K. Whitney, December 12, 1840. Handwriting of Joseph Smith. See text, p. 468. (LDS Church Archives.)

Nauvoo May 14th 1841

Ebenezer F. Wiggins and Elder Wiggins agrees to sell to Joseph Smith their farm containing two hundred and thirty two acres of land on the following conditions they are to have a deed for one of the best lots in Nauvoo at 1000 dollars and one hundred dollars in goods in hand and the remainder to be in money to be paid in three yearly payments with interest from this date Said Smith is to have the immediate possession of the primises with all the spring work and the crops now on the same with the exception of the house which they are to have a reasonable time to obtain one elce where els they are not to be distressed on account of the house the rents of those who have rented any portion of said farm is to come to said Smith

Ebenezer F. Wiggins
Elender Wiggins —

100
1000
·100

2700
·100

3/1600

533-33

Agreement, May 14, 1841. Handwriting of Joseph Smith. See text, p. 468. (LDS Church Archives.)

To William W. Phelps,
July 22, 1840

Among the spiritual casualties during the trying times of
1838 in Missouri was William W. Phelps, one of the presidents
of the Church in Zion. Accused of selling his land in Jackson
County, contrary to counsel, and of using Church money for
his own purposes, he was excommunicated in March 1838.
Later that year, in the hearing before Judge Austin A. King at
Richmond, he testified, among other things, that Joseph Smith
had advocated resistance to all law and had engineered the
burning and plundering of Gallatin and Millport.[1] His testimony for the state, along with other dissenters, helped establish the case that committed the Mormon leaders to prison.

Following his excommunication, William W. Phelps
moved to Dayton, Ohio, where he was living when Orson
Hyde and John E. Page, en route to Europe, found him penitent and poverty stricken. Encouraged by his visitors, William
wrote to Joseph Smith on June 29, 1840, seeking to regain the
fellowship of his former associates: "I am alive, and with the
help of God I mean to live still. I am as the prodigal son, though
I never doubt or disbelieve the fulness of the Gospel. . . . I
have seen the folly of my way, and I tremble at the gulf I have
passed. So it is, and why I know not. I prayed and God answered, but what could I do? Says I, 'I will repent and live, and
ask my old brethren to forgive me, and though they chasten me
to death, yet I will die with them, for their God is my God. The

471

least place with them is enough for me, yea, it is bigger and better than all Babylon.' . . . I know my situation, you know it,
and God knows it, and I want to be saved if my friends will help
me. . . . I have done wrong and I am sorry. The beam is in my
own eye. I have not walked along with my friends according to
my holy anointing. I ask forgiveness in the name of Jesus Christ
of all the Saints, for I will do right, God helping me."[2]

Joseph Smith responded to these solicitations on July 22.

Nauvoo Hancock Co Ill.
July 22nd 1840

Dear Brother Phelps

I must say that it is with no ordinary feelings I endeavour to
write a few lines to you in answer to yours of the 29th Ultimo, at
the same time I am rejoiced at the priveledge granted me. You may
in some measure realise what my feelings, as well as Elder Rigdon's
& Bro Hyrum's were when we read your letter, truly our hearts
were melted into tenderness and compassion when we assertained
your resolves &c

I can assure you I feel a disposition to act on your case in a
manner that will meet the approbation of Jehovah (whose servant I
am) and agreeably to the principles of truth and righteousness
which have been revealed and inasmuch as long-suffering patience
and mercy have ever characterized the dealings of our heavenly
Father towards the humble and penitent, I feel disposed to copy the
example and cherish the same principles, by so doing be a Savior of
my fellow men

It is true, that we have suffered much in consequence of your
behavior—*the cup of gall already full enough* for mortals to drink, was
indeed *filled* to *overflowing* when you turned against us: One with
whom we had oft taken sweet council together, and enjoyed many
refreshing seasons from the Lord "Had it been an enemy we could
have borne it" In the day that thou stoodest on the other side, in

the day when Strangers carried away captive his forces, and
foreigners entered into his gates and cast lots upon Far West even
thou wast as one of them. But thou shouldst not have ["]looked on
[p. 157] the day of thy brother, in the day that he became a
stranger neither shouldst thou have spoken proudly in the day of
distress" However the Cup has been drunk, the will of our heavenly
Father has been done, and we are yet alive for which we thank the
Lord. And having been delivered from the hands of wicked men by
the mercy of our God, we say it is your privilidge to be delivered
from the power of the Adversary—be brought into the liberty of
God's dear children, and again take your stand among the Saints of
the Most High, and by diligence humility and love unfeigned,
commend yourself to our God and your God and to the church of
Jesus Christ

Believing your confession to be real and your repentance
genuine, I shall be happy once again to give you the right hand of
fellowship, and rejoice over the returning prodigal.

Your letter was read to the Saints last Sunday and an expression
of their feeling was taken, when it was unanimously resolved that
W.W. Phelps should be received into fellowship.

"Come on dear Brother since the war is past,
For friends at first are friends again at last."

Yours as Ever
Joseph Smith Jr

To Oliver Granger, July 1840

As the process of buying land and establishing the Saints in a new settlement got underway following the disaster in Missouri, one of the major problems confronting Joseph Smith was a lack of money. Besides the immediate expense of resettlement, debts incurred in Ohio prior to 1838 remained unpaid, and Church property in Kirtland, including the temple, had become encumbered with legal entanglements.[1] Having been suddenly forced to leave Ohio amidst threats of mob violence in January 1838, Joseph Smith had been unable to resolve business obligations contracted there. Later that year he had sent Oliver Granger,[2] an ex-sheriff and militia officer, a man of integrity and ability, back to Kirtland as a Church agent to settle unpaid debts. Although Granger remained in Ohio but a short time in 1838, his handling of affairs was effective. Consequently, when conditions permitted in 1840, he was again sent to Kirtland as agent. Shortly after Oliver's arrival, he received this letter from Joseph Smith.

[July 1840]

Brother Granger
Dr Sir

It was with great pleasure I received your's and Bro Richards'[3] Letter dated New York June 23rd 1840 and was very happy to be informed of your safe arrival in that place and your probability of

474

success and I do hope that your anticipa=tions will be realized and that you will be able to free the Lords House from all incumbrances, and be prospered in all your undertakings for the benefit of the Church, and pray that while you are exerting your influence to bring about an object so desireable, that the choicest blessings of heaven may rest down upon you. While you are endeavoring to do so and attending to the duties laid upon you by the authorities of the Church in this place, I am sorry to be informed not only in your letter but from other respectable sources of the strange conduct pursued in Kirtland by Elder Alman Babbit;[4] I am indeed surprised that a man having the experience which Bro Babbit has had should take any steps whatever calculated to destroy the con=fidence of the brethren in the presidency or any of the authorities of the church. In order to conduct the affairs of the kingdom in righteousness it is all important, that the most perfect harmony kind feeling, good understanding and confidence should exist in the hearts of all the brethren and that true charity – love one towards another, should characterize all their proceedings. If there are any uncharitable feelings, any lack of confidence, then pride and arrogancy and envy will soon be manifested and con=fusion must inevitably prevail and the authorities of the church set at nought; and under such circumstances Kirtland cannot rise and free herself from <the> captivity in which she is held and become a place of safety for the saints nor can the blessings of Jehovah rest upon her. If the saints in Kirtland deem me unworthy of their prayers when they assemble together, and neglect to bear me up at a throne of heavenly grace, it is a strong and convincing proof to me that they have not the spirit of God.

If the revelations we have received are true, who is to lead the people? If the keys of the kingdom have been committed to my hands, who shall open out the mysteries thereof. As long as my brethren stand by me and encourage me I can combat the predjudices of the world and can bear the contumely and abuse of the world with joy [p. 159] but when my brethren stand aloof– when they begin to faint and endeavour to retard my progress and enterprise then I feel to mourn but am no less determined to prosecute my task, being confident that altho my earthly friends may fail and even turn against me, yet my heavenly father will bear me off triumphant. However I hope that even in Kirtland, their are some who do not make a man an "offender for a word," but are disposed to stand forth in defence of righteousness and truth and attend to every duty enjoined upon them and who will have wisdom to direct them against any movement or influence calculated to bring confusion and disorder into the camp of Israel, and to discern between the spirit of truth and the spirit of error.

It would be gratifying to my mind to see the saints in Kirtland flourish, but think the time has not yet come and I assure you it never will until a different order of things be established and a different spirit be manifested. When confidence is restored, when pride shall fall and every aspiring mind be clothed with humility as with a garment and selfishness give place to benevolence and charity, and a united determination to live by every word which proceedeth out of the mouth of the Lord is observable, then and not till then can peace and order, and love prevail

It is in consequence of aspiring men that Kirtland has been forsa=ken. How frequently has your humble servant been envied in his office by such characters who endeavoured to raise themselves to power at my expense, and seeing it impossible to do so, resorted to foul slander and abuse and other means to effect my overthrow; such characters have ever been the first to cry out against the presidency, and publish their faults and foibles to [the] four winds of heaven.

I cannot forget the treatment I received in the house of my friends, these things continually roll across my mind and cause me much sorrow of heart, and when I think that others who have lately come into the church should be led to Kirtland instead of to this place by Elder Babbit, and having their confidence in the authorities lessened by such observations as he (Elder Babbit) has thought propper to make, as well as hearing all the false reports and exaggerated accounts of our enemies, I must say that I feel grieved in spirit, and cannot tolerate such proceedings neither will I, but will endeavour to dis abuse the minds of the saints and break down all such unhallowed proceedings. [p. 160]

It was something new to me when I heard there had been secret meetings held in the Lords house, and that some of my friends – faithful brethren, men enjoying the confidence of the church should be locked out. Such like proceedings are not calculated to promote union or peace but to engender strife and will be a curse instead of a blessing. To those who are young in the work I know they are calculated to and must be injurious to them. Those who have had experience and who should know better, than to reflect on their brethren, there is no excuse for them. If Bro Babbit and the other brethren wish to reform the Church and come out and make a stand against sin & speculation &c &c, they must use other weapons than lies, or their object can never be effected, and their labors will be given to the house of the stranger rather than to the house of the Lord

The proceedings of Bro Babbit were taken into consideration at a meeting of the Church at this place when it was unan=imously resolved that fellowship should be withdrawn from him until he make satisfaction for the conduct he has pursued of which circumstance I wish you to apprize him of without delay and demand his license

Dr Sir I wish you to stand in your lot and keep the station which was given you by revelation and the authorities of the Church; attend to the affairs of the Church with diligence and then rest assured on the blessings of heaven: It is binding on you to act as president of the Church in Kirtland until you are removed by the same authority which put you in, and I do hope, their will be no cause for opposition but that good feeling will be manifested in [the] future by all the brethren.

Bro Burdicks letter to Bro Hyrum was duly received for which he has our best thanks. It was indeed an admirable letter and worthy of its author the sentiments express'd were in accordance with the spirit of the gospel and the principles correct. I am glad that Bro Richards has continued with you and hope he has been of some service to you – give my love to him Our prospects in this place continue good. considerable numbers have come in this spring. There were some bickerings respecting your conduct soon after your departure but they have all blown over, and I hope there will never be any occasion for any more, but that you will commend yourself to God and to the saints by a virtuous walk and holy conversation

I had a letter from W.W. Phelps a few days ago informing me of his desire to come back to the Church if we would accept of him, he appears very humble and is willing to make every satisfaction that saints or God may require.

We expect to have an edition of the book of Mormon printed by the first of September it is now being sterotyped in Cincinnatti.

I rem[ain] &c &c

Joseph Smith Jr.

To the Twelve,
December 15, 1840

Although LDS missionary work in England began in 1837 through the efforts of Heber C. Kimball and Orson Hyde, two members of the Quorum of the Twelve, an 1838 revelation directed the entire quorum to "go over the great waters" to promulgate the gospel the following year.[1] The 1840-41 mission of the Twelve to England proved to be an important training ground for them, and it brought new life to the Church because of the immigration of English converts. The Twelve found England a field ripe for the harvest. By the time they returned to Nauvoo in 1841, approximately eight thousand people had been baptized, an extensive publication program had been launched, and a shipping agency had been established that had already sent one thousand converts to America.[2]

Their distance from Nauvoo and the slow means of communication forced the Twelve in England to make administrative decisions that had been previously reserved to the First Presidency. On September 5, 1840, Brigham Young and Willard Richards wrote the First Presidency that they had made use of their "own credit" to assist the poor to emigrate: "Brethren, our hearts are pained with the poverty & misery of this people, & we have done all we could to help as many off as possible to a land where they may get a morsel of bread, & serve God according to his appointment; & we have done it cheerfully as unto the Lord, & we desire to ask you have we done right?" Other

questions followed: "Shall we send all we can to America &
stay here ourselves?" "Have we done right in printing a hymn
book?" "Are we doing right in Printing the book of Mormon?"
"Are we doing right in staying here & leaving our families to be
a burden to the Church?" "We have heard . . . that Brothers
Joseph & Hyrum are coming to England next season. Is this
good news true?"[3]

On December 15, Joseph Smith responded to these and
other questions.

Nauvoo Hancock Co, Ills. Decr. 15. 1840

Beloved Brethren.

May Grace, Mercy, and Peace rest upon you, from God the
Father and the Lord Jesus Christ.

Having several communications laying before me, from my
Brethren the "Twelve" some of which have ere this merited a reply,
but ‹from› the multiplicity of business which necessarily engages
my attention I have delayed communicating to them, to the
present time. Be assured my beloved brethren, that I am no
disinterested observer of the things which are transpiring on the
face of the whole earth and amidst the general movements which
are in progress, none is of more importance, than the glorious work
in which you are now engaged, and consequently, I feel some
anxiety on your account, that you may, by your virtue, faith,
diligence, and charity, commend yourselves to one another, ‹to
the Church of Christ› and ‹to› your Father which is in heaven, by
whose grace you have been called to so holy a calling, and be
enabled to perform the great and responsible duties which rest upon
you. And I can assure you, that from the information I have
received; I feel satisfied, that you have not been remiss ‹in your
duty› but that your diligence and faithfulness have been such as
must secure you the smiles of that God, whose servants you are,
and the good will of the saints throughout the world.

The spread of truth throughout England is certainly pleasing; the contemplation of which, cannot but afford feelings of no ordinary kind in the bosoms of those who have had to bear the heat and burthen of the day, and who were its firm supporters, and strenuous advocates in infancy, while surrounded with circumstan=ces the most unpropitious, and its destruction threatened on all hands. But like the gallant Bark, that has braved the storm unhurt, spreads her canvass to the breese, and nobly cuts her way through the yielding wave, more conscious than ever of the strength of her timbers and the experience and ca=pabilities of her Captain, Pilate and crew.

It is likewise very satisfactory to ‹my› mind, that there has been such a good understanding existing between you, and that the saints have ‹so› cheerfully, hearkened to council and vied with each other in their labors of love; and in the promotion of truth and righteousness; this is as it should be in the Church of Jesus Christ. Unity is strength. "How pleasant [p. 1] it is for brethren to dwell together in Unity &c" Let the saints of the most high, ever cultivate this principle, and the most glorious blessings must result, not only to them individually but to the whole church—The order of the kingdom will be maintained—Its officers respected, and its requirements readily and cheer=fully obeyed. Love is one of the leading characteristics of Deity, and ou[gh]t to be manifested by those who aspire to be the sons of God. A man filled with the love of God, is not content with blessing his family alone but ranges through the world, anxious to bless the whole of the human family. This has been your feelings and caused you to forego the pleasures of home, that you might be a blessing to others, who are candidates for immortal=ity but who were strangers to the principals of truth and for so doing I pray that Heavens' choicest blessings may rest upon you.

Being requested to give my advice respecting the propriety of your returning in the spring, I will do so willingly. I have reflected on the subject some time and am of the opin=ion that it would be wisdom in you to make preparations to leave the scene of your labors in the spring. Having carried the testimony to that land, and

numbers having received it, consequently the leaven can now
spread, without your being obliged to stay. Another thing, there
has been some whisperings of the spirit; that there will be some
agitation, some excite=ment, and some trouble in the land in
which you are now laboring. I would therefore say in the mean
time be diligent, organize the churches and let every one stand in
his proper place, so that those who cannot come with you in the
spring may not be left as sheep without shepherds.

I would likewise observe that inasmuch as this place has been
appointed for the gathering of the saints, it is necessary that it
should be attended to, in the order which the Lord intends it
should; to this end I would say that as there are great numbers of
the saints in England, who are extreemly poor and not accustomed
to the farming business, who must have certain prepara=tions made
for them before they can support themselves in this country,
therefore to prevent confusion and disappointment when they
arrive here, let those men who are accustomed to making
machinery and those [p. 2] who can command a capital even if it
be but small, come here as soon as convenient and put up
machinery and make such other preparations as may be necessary,
so that when the poor come on they may have employment to
come to. This place has advantages for manufacturing and
commercial purposes which but very few can boast of; and by
establishing Cotton Factories, Founderies, Potteries &c &c would
be the means of bringing in wealth and raising it to a very
important elevation. I need not occupy more space on this subject
as its reasonableness must be obvious to every mind. In my former
epistle I told you my mind respec=ting the printing of the Book of
Mormon. Hymn Book &c &c– I have been favored by receiving a
Hymn Book from you and as far as I have examined it I highly
approve of it and think it to be a very valuable collection. I am
informed that the Book of Mormon is likewise printed, which I am
glad to hear, and should be pleased to hear that it was printed in all
the different languages of the earth. You can use your own pleasure
respecting printing the Book of Doctrine & Covenants, if there is a
great demand for them, I have not any objections, but would rather
encourage it.

I am happy to say, that as far as I have been made aquainted
with your movements, I have been per=fectly satisfied that they
have been in wisdom, and I have no doubt but the spirit of
the Lord has directed you and this proves to my mind that you have
been humble, and your desires have been for the salvation of your
fellow man, and not your own agrandizement and selfish interest.
As long as the saints manifest such a disposition their council will
be approved of, and their exertions crowned with suc=cess. There
are many things of minor importance, on which you ask council,
but which I think you will be perfectly able to decide upon as I you
are more conversant with the peculiar circumstances than I am,
and I feel great confidence in your united wisdom, therefore you
will excuse me for not entering into detail. If I should see any thing
that was wrong I should take the priviledge of making known my
mind to you and pointing out the evil. [p. 3]

If Elder Parley Pratt should wish to remain in England for some
time longer than the rest of the Twelve, he will feel himself at
liberty to do so; as he his family are with him consequently his
circumstances are somewhat different to the rest, and likewise it is
necessary that some one should remain who is conversant with the
rules, regulations &c & of the church and continue the paper
which is published; consequently taking all these things into
consideration I would not press upon Brother Pratt to return in the
spring.

I am happy to inform you that we are prospering in this place,
and that the saints are more healthy than formerly, and from the
decrease of sickness this season, when compared with the last, I am
led to the conclusion that this must eventually become a healthy
place.

There are at present about 3000 inhabitants in Nauvoo, and
numbers are flocking in daily; severeal stakes have been set off in
different parts of the country, which are in prospering
circumstances. Provisions are much lower than when you left.
Flour is worth about four dollars per barrel, corn 25 cents per
bushel: pottatoes about 20 cents and other things in abou[t] the
same proportion. There has been a very plentiful harvest indeed,
throughout the Union.

You will observe by the "Times & Season" that we are about building a Temple for the worship of our God in this place: preparations are now making, every tenth day is devoted by the brethren here for quarrying rock &c & we have secured one of the most lovely sites for it that there is in this region of country. It is expected to be considerably larger and on <a> more magnificent scale than the one in Kirtland and which will undoubtedly attract the attention of the great men of the <earth> We have a bill before the Legislature for the incorporation of the City of Nauvoo for the establishment of a Seminary and other purposes, which I expect will pass in a short time.

You will also have received intelligence of the death of my Father,[4] which event altho painful to the family and to the church generally, yet the sealing testimony of the truth of the work of the Lord was indeed satisfactory; the particulars of his death &c you will find in the Sep. number of the "Times and Seasons" Brother Hyrum succeeds him as patriarch of the Church, according to his last directions and benedictions.

Several persons of emmine[n]ce and distinction in society, have joined the Church, and [p. 3a][5] become obedient to the faith, and I am happy to inform you that the work is spreading very fast on this continent, Some of the Brethren are now in New Orleans, and we expect to have a gathering from the South.

I have had the pleasure of welcoming about one hundred of the Brethren from England who came with Elder Turley,[6] the remainder I am informed stoped in Kirtland, not having means to get any further. I think those that came here did not take the best possible rout or the least expensive. Most of the brethren have obtained employment of one kind or another and appear tolerably well contented and seem disposed to hearken to council. Brothers Robinson & Smith lately had a letter from Elders Kimball, Smith & Woodruff[7] in London which gave us information of the commencement of the work of the Lord in that City, which I was glad to hear. I am likewise informed that Elders have gone to Austrailia & to the East Indies I feel desireous that every providential opening of that kind should be filled, and that you

should, prior to your leaving England, send the gospel into as many
parts as you possibly can.

Beloved brethren, you must be aware in some measure of my
feelings when I contem=plate the great work which is now rolling
on, and the relationship which I sustain to it; while it is extending
to distant lands, and islands, and thousands are embracing it, I
realize in some measure my responsibility and the need I have of
support from above, and wisdom from on high; that I may be able
to teach this people, which have now become a great people, the
principles of righteousness, and lead them agreeably to the will of
heaven so that they may be perfected and prepared to meet the
Lord Jesus Christ, when he shall appear in great glory. Can I rely
on your prayers to your heavenly Father in my behalf? and on the
prayers of all my brethren & sisters in England? (whom having not
seen yet I love) that I may be enabled to escape every stra[ta]gem of
satan, surmount every difficulty, and bring this people, to the
enjoyment of those blessings, which are reserved for the righteous.
I ask this at your and their hands in the name of Jesus Christ.
[p. 2a]

Let the saints remember that great things depend on their
individual exertion, and that they are called to be co-workers with
us and with the holy spirit in accomplishing the great works of the
last days, and in consideration of the extent, the blessings, and the
glories of the same let every selfish feeling be not only buried, but
anihalated, and let love to God and man, predominate and reign
triumphant in every mind, that their hearts may become like unto
Enoch's of old so that they may comprehend all things, present,
past, and future, and "come behind in no gift waiting for the
coming of the Lord Jesus Christ". The work in which we are
unitedly engaged in, is one of no ordinary kind, the enemies we
have to contend against are subtle and well skilled in manuvering,
it behoves us then to be on the alert, to concentrate our energies,
and that the best feelings should exist in our midst, and then by the
help of the Almighty we shall go on from victory to victory and
from conquest unto conquest, our evil passions will be subdued, our
predjudices depart, we shall find no room in our bosoms for hatred,

vice will hide its deformed head, and we shall stand approved in the sight of heaven and be acknowledged "the sons of God" Let us realize that we are not to live to ourselves but to God by so doing the greatest blessings will rest upon us both in time and in Eternity.

I presume the doctrine of "Baptism for the dead" has ere this reached your ears, and may have raised some inquiries in your mind respecting the same. I cannot in this letter give you all the information you may desire on the subject, but aside from my knowledge independant of the Bible, I would say, that this was certainly practised by the antient Churches and St Paul endeavours to prove the doctrine of the ressurrection from the same, and says "else what shall they do who are baptised for the dead["] &c &c. I first mentioned the doctrine in public while preaching the funeral sermon of Bro Brunson,[8] and have since then given general instruc=tions to the Church on the subject. The saints have the priviledge of being baptised for those of their relatives who are dead, who they feel to believe would have embraced the gospel if they had been priviledged with hearing it, and who have received the gospel in the spirit through the instrumentality of those who may have been commissioned to preach to them while in prison. Without enlarging on the subject you will undoubtedly see its consistancy, and reasonableness, and [it] presents the the gospel of Christ in probably a more enlarged scale than some have viewed it. But as the performance of this right is more particularly confined to this place it will not be necessary to enter into particulars, at the same time I allways feel glad to give all the information in my power, but my space will not allow me to do it. [p. 1a]

We had a letter from Elder Hyde a few days ago, who is in New Jersey, and·is expecting to leave for England as soon as Elder Page reaches him.[9] He requested to know in his letter if converted Jews are to go to Jerusalem or to come to Zion. I therefore wish you to inform him that converted Jews must come here. If Elder Hydes & Pages testimony to the Jews at Jerusalem should be received then they may know "that the set time hath come": I will write more particular instructions to them afterwards. ~~your~~

Your families are well and generally in good spirits, and bear their privations with christian fortitude and patience.

Brother Richards' question respecting coming in the spring is answered. I shall be very happy to see him & his family & likewise Brother Fielding. Tell him that Bro Thompson is making preparations for his coming.

With respect to the rout best to be taken I think you will be better able to ⟨give⟩ advise than myself. But I would not advise coming round by the lakes. And it would not be prudent to come via New Orleans in the sickly season but in the spring or fall or winter it might do. Give my kind love to all the brethren, and sisters, and tell them I should have been pleased to have come over to England to see them, but am afraid that I shall be under the necessity of remaining here for some time, therefore I give them a pressing invitation to come and see me. I am Dr Brethren yours, affectionately

Joseph Smith [p. 4]

To the Travelling High Council and Elders of the Church of Jesus Christ of LDS in Great Britain

Do not understand me to say that all the Elders are to come with you, as it will be necessary for some to stay. [p. 4a]

J.

To the "Twelve" [p. 4]

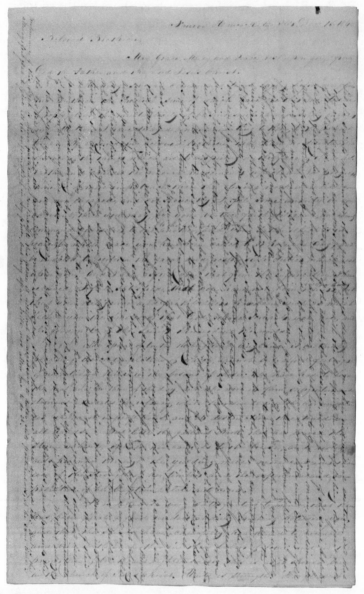

To the Twelve, December 15, 1840, pp. 1, 1a. Handwriting of Robert B. Thompson. Cross-written to save postage. See text, pp. 480-81, 485-86. (LDS Church Archives.)

To Oliver Granger,
January 26, 1841

Under the impression that Oliver Granger, the agent sent to settle Church debts in Kirtland, was planning to return to Nauvoo in the fall of 1840, Joseph Smith learned belatedly that Granger had no such intentions. In the meantime, a Church conference had convened in Nauvoo on October 3, 1840, at which Almon Babbitt had been appointed to preside over the stake at Kirtland, an appointment that would probably have fallen to Granger had his correspondence to the Prophet arrived before the conference.[1] Upon receiving the delayed correspondence, Joseph wrote to Oliver Granger on January 26.

City of Nauvoo Jany 26. 1841

Dear Brother Granger.

I wrote you a few days ago in answer to a letter recently received from you, expressing my surprise that I had not re=ceived the letters you mentioned; Since that time, I have to inform you that I have received two letters giving me an account of the proceeding of the Church in Kirtland and some of your business transactions. I am extreemly sorry that the person by whom you sent those letters did not hand them over to me sooner, however, I assure you, I was glad to ~~peruse~~ ‹read› them and felt very much satisfied with the perusal. I was likewise very much pleased with the spirit which was manifest by the saints in Kirtland and for their desire to promote the interests of the Kingdom.

If those letters had been received in their propper time, we probably might have acted differently at the last conference, but not having the information we desired, we acted to the best of our understanding, which I hope will prove advantageous to all parties. I hope you will not let any of the proceedings of last conference disturb your mind, for we understood you were intending to come here last fall, and consequently thought it ad=visable to appoint some one to preside in Kirtland. I should be glad if you would co-opperate with Elder Babbit and both lay your shoulders to the work, and if you do so I think you will be a blessing to the Church, and pros=perity will smile upon you.

I should be much pleased [p. 1] to receive a letter from you as oft as you can make it convenient and give me all the intelligence in your power. I am yet in the dark respecting the New York debts I should be much pleased to hear that they were settled.

Since writing the above I received yours of the 9th inst, and I assure you I was very much gratified to hear of your success in redeeming the "Lords House" &c I hope Dear Brother that success will attend all your efforts for the prosperity of the cause, so dear to the saints and that you will be abundantly rewarded by that God whose has called us to be co-workers with him and his holy spirit in these last days.

Be assured of my continued regard for your welfare and for the prosperity of the Saints in Kirtland, and I pray that they may prosper in every good word and work and after the afflictions and tribulations of mortality be crowned with everlasting joy in the celestial Kingdom of our God.

We continue to prosper in this place and expect to have a large encrease of inhabitants the next season. We are making preperation for some large and extensive buildings which we intend to erect soon.

With sentiments of respect, I am very respectfully yours, Affectionately

Joseph Smith [p. 2]

P.S. With respect to giving advise to the saints moving to Kirtland I would say, that I feel desireous that the Eastern brethren should come to this place but at the same time, those who had rather move to Kirtland than to this place are at liberty to do so.

I am pleased you have secured the keys of the Lords House, and should advise you and you are hereby requested to hold them until [I] come. ~~wh~~ I can=not say when I shall pay you a visit but I think not before the New York debts be settled, so if you are desireous to see me, you will have to exert yourselves to get the debts settled.

Please to write me all the par=ticulars of your transactions and let me know when we shall have the pleasure of seeing you here

J.S.

Dr Galland accompanied by some one of the brethren (perhaps Hyrum) intend to leave this place in a few days for the east, on business for the church, they will call at Kirtland and will be glad to see you as you may possibly give them such information as will be necessary for them in their business transactions.

J.S

To Amos Keeler,
March 16, 1841

Among the unpaid Kirtland debts that confronted Joseph Smith when he was able once again to turn his attention to the matter after his Missouri imprisonment was one involving the dry goods firm of Amos Keeler in New York City.[1] Early in March 1841, Mr. Keeler wrote Joseph on the subject and on the sixteenth received the following reply.

City of Nauvoo March 16, 1841

Sir, Yours of the 2nd Ul[t]imo was duly received but having been mislaid I have not been able to answer it until the present. It would have afforded me much pleasure could I have assisted you in your present circumstances, but having no means excepting those which I put into the hands of Mr Oliver Granger of Kirtland to apply on what debts were owing in New York &c I am not able [to] promise you any assistance.

From a communication I lately received from Mr Granger I was informed that he had effected a settlement with the merchants in New York, and I hoped that your firm was one of the number.

I suppose you are aware of the great loss of property I sustained while in Missouri, and my imprisonment &c for which I have not received any remuneration, and in consequence I was reduced to poverty & from which I have not been able to extricate myself—
I am very respectfully Yours &c

Joseph Smith

Amos Keeler Esqr

492

To Oliver Granger,
May 4, 1841

By 1841, Oliver Granger's understanding of the temporal affairs of the Church in Kirtland was such as to be almost indispensable to their satisfactory regulation and settlement. Having heard that the Church agent had been very ill, Joseph Smith wrote to him on May 4 urging that affairs be "straitened up" as soon as possible to avoid complications that would develop should Granger suddenly pass away. The concern proved to be well conceived, as Oliver died at the age of forty-nine,[1] less than four months after receiving this letter.

City of Nauvoo May 4, 1841

Dear Bro. Granger

Bro Hyrum having returned and given me a statement of his jour=ney and proceedings in the East, which have been very pleasing and satisfac=tory. I was sorry to hear that you had been so sick, and not able to attend to business as much [as] could be desired.

I have since heard that you have had a relapse, and that you were very sick again, this I was sorry to hear– However I hope you will yet recover and that we shall see you at this place before long.

I am very anxious indeed to have the matters which concern the First Presidency settled as soon as possible, for until they are I have to labor under a load that is intolerable to bear, I therefore respectfully reccommend to you to give a ~~whole~~ statement of the whole affairs to Dr Galland who is yet in the East,[2] and will be in

Kirtland soon, and get him to take the matter into his hands and get the business straitened up. This I must beg leave to urge upon you to do, for delays are dangerous, your health is precarious and if any thing should occur– [p. 1] so that you were to bid adieu to mortal=ity it would be impossible for me ever to get the run of the business and I should be again involved in difficulties from which it would be impossible for me to extricate myself. Now dear Brother I do hope you will see the reasonableness of this my request and assist Dr Galland in the affair.

I do not make these observations because I have lost confidence in you far from it, but I feel impressed to write what I have done from a sence of duty which I owe to the Church of Christ, to you and to myself.

I wish you to see that the judgment obtained on the mortgage on the house of the Lord, in the circuit court, be entered satisfied, and I will settle with you ‹the same› as if you held it yourself– Bro Carlos' House & Lot I want deeding to Mrs Agnas Smith and her heirs.[3]

I am happy to inform you, that things are going on well in this place, we have been greatly prospered, and many are flocking in from Europe & about 300 have arrived in less than a week, more are on the way. [p. 2]

I shall be anxous to hear from you, as soon as possible, relative to these matters &c

I am with great respect very respectfully

Joseph Smith

Mr Oliver Granger

The house and store encumbered by the debts for the "Plates" are now at liberty, ~~Bro Babbit~~ ‹that debt› having ‹been› settled ~~that debt~~ You can therefore let Bro. Babbit [have] control over them untill I settle with him. You will also keep possession of the

Keys of the House of the Lord until you receive further instructions from me.

Joseph Smith

Bro Hyrum sends his respects to you and family. [p. 3]

Mr. Oliver Granger
Kirtland Lake Co
Ohio [p. 4]

To Smith Tuttle,
October 9, 1841

The largest acquisition of land upon which Nauvoo was to be built occurred in August 1839 when approximately five hundred acres were obtained from Connecticut land speculators Horace R. Hotchkiss, John Gillett, and Smith Tuttle. Under the terms of agreement, the Latter-day Saints were to have immediate use of the land, but no deeds were to be issued until the debt was paid. The total amount of the purchase was $114,500, to be paid in twenty years. This figure included $3,000 annual interest payments which, along with other monetary demands, created a heavy financial burden upon the Saints. Difficulty in meeting the interest payments was immediate. At first, the method of making the payments on the Nauvoo land was by soliciting contributions from Church members and the selling of town lots. Another means of liquidating the obligation was to encourage Church members in the East to obtain Nauvoo land in exchange for their eastern property, which would then be used as payment to the Hotchkiss, Gillett, and Tuttle syndicate.

In the spring of 1841 Hyrum Smith and Isaac Galland were sent east with means to pay notes that were due and to regulate the eastern land exchange. However, illness almost immediately forced Hyrum to return to Nauvoo, and sometime later in the summer the Prophet learned that Galland had not completed the errand to Hotchkiss. The correspondence between Joseph Smith and members of the Connecticut land syndicate outline the difficult financial problems that faced the Prophet at Nauvoo and his tortured efforts to resolve them. On October 9, 1841, in response to a conciliatory letter by Smith Tuttle when a misunderstanding arose over the first interest payment, Joseph sent the following letter.[1]

Nauvoo, Ill. October 9th 1841

Smith Tuttle Esqr.
    Dear Sir, Your kind letter of Sept. last was rec'd. during our Conference which is just over, containing a full & particular explanation of every thing which gave rise to some feelings of disappoint=ment in relation to our business transactions; and I will assure you, it has allayed, on our part, every prejudise. It breaths the spirit of kindness & truth. I will assure you that we exceedingly regret that there have been any grounds for hardness and disappointment. But so far as I am concerned, I must plead innocence; and you will consider me so, when you come to know all the facts– I have done all that I could on my part. I will still do all that I can. I will not leave one stone unturned.— Now the facts are these. I sent my Brother Hyrum Smith & Dr. Galland with means in their hands.– say, not money, but with power to obtain every property or money which was necessary to enable them to fulfil the contract I made with Mr. Hotchkiss. My brother was under the necessity of returning, in consequence of ill health, to this place, leav=ing the business in the hands of Dr. Galland, with the fullest expectation that he would make over the property or money to Mr. Hotchkiss, and make every thing square, so far as the interest is concerned, if not the principal. He was instructed to pay

the interest that had accrued & would accrue up to the fall of 1842,
so as to be in ad=vance of our indebtedness. I had also made
arrangements with the eastern Churches, & had it in my power to
fork over land for the whole debt; & had expected that an
arrangement of that kind would have been entered into. I am well
assured that Dr. Galland did not lack ‹any› means whatever, to
pay the interest, at any rate, if not the principal; & why he has not
done according to my instruc=tions, God only knows.[2] I do not feel
to charge him with having done wrong, until I can investigate the
matter, and ascertain for a certainty where the fault lies. It [p. 1]
may be, that through sickness or disaster, this strange neglect has
happened. I would to God the thing had not happened. When I
read Mr. Hotchkiss' letter, I learned that he was dissatisfied. I
thought he meant to oppress me, & felt exceedingly mortified &
sorrowful in the midst of affliction, to think that he should distrust
me for a moment, that I would not do all that was within my
power. But upon hearing an explanation of the whole matter, my
feelings are changed; and I think you all have had cause for
complaining; but you will in the magnanimity of y[ou]r good
feelings, certainly not blame me when you find I have discharged
an honorable duty on my part. I regret exceedingly that I did not
know some months since, what I now know, so that I could have
made another exertion before it got so late. Cold weather is now
rolling in upon us. I have been confined here this season by
sickness & various other things that were beyond my control; such
as having been demanded by the Governor of Mo. of the Governor
of this State, & he not having moral courage enough to resist the
demand, although it was founded in injustice & cruelty. I
accordingly was taken pris=oner, & they put me to some ten or
eleven hundred dollars expense & trouble before I could be
redeemed from under the difficulty; lawyer's fees, witnesses– &c.
&c.– But I am now clear from them once more, & now in
contemplating the face of the whole subject, I find that I am under
the necessity of asking a little further indulgence, ‹say› until next
spring, so that I may be enabled to recover myself; and then if God
spares my life, & gives me power to do so, I will come in person to

y[ou]r country, & will never cease my labors until the whole matter
is completely adjusted to the fullest satisfac=tion of all of you. The
subject of your debt was presented fairly before our general
Conference, on the first of the month, of some ten thousand people
for their decission for the wisest & best course, in relation to
meeting your demands. The Twelve, as they are denominated in
the [p. 2] "Times & Seasons," were ordered by the Conference to
make arrangements in the eastern branches of the Church,
ordering them to go to you & turn over their property as you &
they could agree, & take up our obligations & bring them here, &
receive property here for them. & I have been ordered by the Genl.
Conference to write this letter to you, informing you of the
measures which are about be=ing taken to make all things right. I
would inform you that Dr. Galland has not returned to the western
Country as yet. He has a considerable amt. of our money in his
hands, which was to have been paid to you as we intended. He is
on his way for ought we know, & is retarded in his journey by some
misfortune or other. He may return, however, as yet, & give a just
and honorable account of himself. We hope this may be the case. I
am sorrowful on account of y[ou]r disap=pointments. It is a great
disappointment to me as well as to yourselves. As to the growth of
our place, it is very rapid; & it would be more so, were it not for
sickness & death. There have been many deaths which leaves a
melancholly reflection, but we cannot help it. When God speaks
from the heavens to call us hence, we must submit to his
mandate.– And for ~~yr.~~ your sincerity & friendship, gentlemen, we
have not the most distant doubt. We will not harbour any. We
know it is for your interest to do us good, & for our happiness &
welfare, to be punctual in the fulfilment of all our vows. And we
think for the future you will have no cause of complaint. We
intend to struggle with all the misfortunes of life, & shoulder them
all up handsomely & honorably, even like men. We ask nothing,
therefore, but what ought to be ‹required› ~~granted~~ between man &
man, & by those principles which bind man to man by kindred
blood, in bearing our own part in everything which duty calls us to
do as not in=ferior to any of the human race, & will be treated as

such, although differing with some in matters of opinion in things,
(viz:– religious matters,) for which we only feel ourselves amenable
to the Eternal God. And may God forbid that pride, ambition, a
want of humanity [p. 3] or any degree of importance, unjustly
should have any dominion in our bosoms. We are the sons of
Adam. We are the *free born sons of America,* and as having been
trampled upon, & our constitutional rights taken from us, by a
great many who boast themselves of being valient in freedom's
cause, which their hearts possess not a spark of its benign &
enlivening influence. This will afford a sufficient excuse, we hope,
for any harsh remarks that may have been dropped by us, when we
thought there was an assumption of supe=riority designed to gall
our feelings. We are very sensitive as a people; we confess it, but we
want to be pardoned for our sins, if any we have committed.

  With regard to the time when the first payment of interest
should be made, it appears we did not understand each other, but it
is a matter, which I hope we can amicably adjust when we see each
other. I do not intend that it shall prevent our making an
arrangement concerning the *whole matter,* for unless we can
accomplish this, it will be useless for us to think of proffiting by the
purchase. With sentiments of respect, I remain as ever yours &c.–

                    Joseph Smith

Smith Tuttle Esqr
New Haven,
Ct. [p. 4]

To John M. Bernhisel,
November 16, 1841

John M. Bernhisel, born at Loysville, Cumberland County, Pennsylvania, on June 23, 1799, launched a successful medical career after graduating from the University of Pennsylvania in 1827. He practiced medicine in Philadelphia before moving to New York City in 1832. Five years later, he joined the Latter-day Saints and at a conference on April 15, 1841, was appointed bishop over the Church in New York City. A cordial friendship developed between him and Joseph Smith.[1]

On September 8, 1841, Bishop Bernhisel wrote the Prophet that he was sending "a copy of Stephen's Incidents of Travel in Central America, Chiapas, and Yucatan,[2] which I hope you will do me the favor to accept . . . as a token of my regard for you as a Prophet of the Lord."[3] The next day, the letter, with Stevens's two-volume work, was given to Wilford Woodruff, who was passing through New York City on the final leg of a missionary journey to Europe, to be delivered at Nauvoo.

On November 16, Joseph acknowledged the gift.

Nauvoo November 16, 1841

Dear Sir
I received your kind present by the hand of Er Woodruff & feel myself under many obligations for this mark of your esteem &

friendship which to me is the more interesting as it unfolds &
developes many things that are of great importance to this
gen=eration & corresponds with & supports the testimony of the
Book of Mormon; I have read the volumes with the greatest
interest & pleasure & must say that of all histories that have been
written pertaining to the antiquities of this country it is the most
correct luminous & comprihensive.—

In regard to the land referred to by you I would simply state that
I have lands both in and out of the City some of which I hold deeds
for and others bonds for deeds when you come which I hope will be
as soon as convenient you can make such a selection from among
those as shall best meet with your needs & feelings. In gratefull
re=membrance of your kindness I remain your affec=tionate
Brother in the bonds of the
Everlasting Covenant

Joseph Smith

To Dr Bernhisel [p. 1]

Dr Bernhisel care of
Lucian R. Foster
No 13 Oliver St
New York [p. 2]

To Esquires Browning and Bushnell,
December 7, 1841

Among the unpaid debts of the Kirtland era were two notes
with the New York City mercantile firm of Halsted, Haines,
and Company totaling $4,719.23, containing thirty-two co-
signers, including Joseph Smith.[1] In the fall of 1841, Halsted
and Haines gave the bill to Quincy, Illinois, law partners
Nehemiah Bushnell and Orville H. Browning for collection.
Joseph responded to their solicitation on December 7, 1841.

Decr. 7th 1841

Esqrs. Browning & Bushnell,
Gentlemen,
     Your letter of [the] 23rd Ultimo, concerning two notes placed
in your hands by Messrs. Halsted Haines & Co against myself and
thirty one others for collection, was duly received.
     In reply I must inform you, that I am not in the possession of
means, belonging to me individually to liquidate those notes at
present. The reason is apparent to every one: I need not relate to
you the persecution I have suffered and the loss & confiscation of
all my effects at various times, as a reason of my inability; you know
it all, and so do the gentlemen whose notes you hold for collection.
But I wish you to say to them, that if they will give me my time,
(and no more than I must necessarily have,) they shall have their
pay in some way or other; that I have the means at command in the
east, which, with a sufficient indulgence, will enable me to pay

503

them every whit, but un=less this is granted me it will be impossible for me to do so. All I ask of those gentle=men and of this generation is, that they should not tie up my hands, nor thwart me in my opperations; if this is granted me, I pledge my word, yea my sacred honor that all that can in fairness be demanded at my hands, either now or at any time, shall ul=timately be adjusted to the satisfaction of all concerned. This is all that I can say at this time, or do, hoping that you will communicate to Mers. Halsted Haines & Co the contents or at all events the purport of this letter, together with my sincere regard for their welfare, and as re=gards you, Gentlemen, I remain

Very Respectfully yr. Obt. servt,

Joseph Smith

To Esquires Browning and Bushnell, December 7, 1841, Joseph Smith
Letterbook 2, p. 217. Handwriting of John S. Fullmer. See text, pp. 503-
4. (LDS Church Archives.)

To Nancy Rigdon,
1842

John C. Bennett, doctor, educator, military man, and writer, was born in Fairhaven, Massachusetts, in 1804. He received his schooling in Ohio and subsequently practiced medicine there and in Virginia. He participated in the founding of the college at New Albany, Indiana, and the medical college at Willoughby, Ohio, where he became Professor of Midwifery, Diseases of Women, and Children, and Medical Jurisprudence. After moving to Illinois in 1838, he practiced medicine, helped found the Illinois State Medical Society, was appointed brigadier general in the Illinois militia and, later, quartermaster general of the state. In 1840, he joined the Latter-day Saints and became closely associated with Joseph Smith, receiving prominent positions of trust in the Mormon community. His influence was instrumental in securing passage of the Nauvoo city charter by the Illinois legislature, and he became Nauvoo's first mayor, a major general in the Nauvoo Legion, and chancellor of the Nauvoo university.[1]

Within two years of his meteoric rise to prominence among the Latter-day Saints, Bennett's world collapsed when it was discovered that he had used his influence in the community and his knowledge of the practice of plural marriage in the Church as a guise for immoral purposes. Although the doctrine of plural marriage had been revealed to Joseph Smith as early as 1831, its practice was not introduced until some time later. By

July 12, 1843, when the revelation that authorized and defined the principle was put into writing (Doctrine and Covenants 132), the practice had already commenced on a limited basis but had not been publicized. When Bennett's licentious conduct was discovered he was cut off from the Church.

To vent his wrath following his excommunication, Bennett published a slanderous exposé and lectured widely against the Church, focusing particularly upon the practice of plural marriage at Nauvoo. Having been closely associated with prominent men of the community, he had knowledge of Church teachings and practices but portrayed them in a foul light. Among the writings published by Bennett during this time, however, was an authentic statement by Joseph Smith that exists in no other known source. The August 19, 1842, issue of the *Sangamo Journal* presented its readers with the following article, which Bennett claimed had been written as a letter by Joseph Smith to Nancy Rigdon after she had refused a proposal of plural marriage to him. John Rigdon, Nancy's brother, later confirmed that such a proposal had taken place, but he made no mention of the letter.[2] When the statement was reproduced in volume 5 of Joseph Smith's *History of the Church*, B. H. Roberts noted that although the occasion for the writing of the letter seemed clouded, it nevertheless was produced at the time the new law of marriage was being introduced by the Prophet and that it was "very likely" that the letter was written with a view of applying its contents "to the conditions created by introducing said marriage system."[3]

[1842]

[to Nancy Rigdon?]

Happiness is the object and design of our existence, and will be the end thereof if we pursue the path that leads to it; and this path

is virtue, uprightness, faithfulness, holiness, and keeping all the
commandments of God. But we cannot keep all the
commandments without first knowing them, and we cannot expect
to know all, or more than we now know, unless we comply with or
keep those we have already received. That which is wrong under
one circumstance, may be and often is, right under another. God
said thou shalt not kill,—at another time he said thou shalt utterly
destroy. This is the principle on which the government of heaven
is conducted—by revelation adapted to the circumstances in which
the children of the kingdom are placed. Whatever God requires is
right, no matter what it is, although we may not see the reason
thereof till long after the events transpire. If we seek first the
kingdom of God, all good things will be added. So with Solomon—
first he asked wisdom, and God gave it him, and with it every
desire of his heart, even things which may be considered
abominable to all who do not understand the order of heaven only
in part, but which, in reality, were right, because God gave and
sanctioned by special revelation. A parent may whip a child, and
justly too, because he stole an apple; whereas, if the child had
asked for the apple, and the parent had given it, the child would
have eaten it with a better appetite, there would have been no
stripes—all the pleasures of the apple would have been received,[4]
all the misery of stealing lost. This principle will justly apply to all
of God's dealings with his children. Every thing that God gives us
is lawful and right, and 'tis[5] proper that we should enjoy his gifts
and blessings whenever and wherever he is disposed to bestow; but
if we should seize upon these same blessings and enjoyments
without law, without revelation, without commandment, those
blessings and enjoyments would prove cursings and vexations in
the end, and we should have to go[6] down in sorrow and wailings of
everlasting regret. But in obedience there is joy and peace
unspotted, unalloyed, and as God has designed our happiness, the
happiness of all his creatures, he never has, he never will institute
an ordinance, or give a commandment to his people that is not
calculated in its nature to promote that happiness which he has
designed, and which will not end in the greatest amount of good

and glory to those who become the recipients of his laws and ordinances. Blessings offered, but rejected are no longer blessings, but become like the talent hid in the earth by the wicked and slothful servant—the proffered good returns of the giver, the blessing is bestowed on those who will receive, and occupy; for unto him that hath shall be given, and he shall have abundantly; but unto him that hath not, or will not receive, shall be taken away that which he hath, or might have had.

"Be wise to-day, 'tis madness to defer.

Next day the fatal precedent may plead;

Thus on till wisdom is pushed out of time," Into eternity. Our heavenly father is more liberal in his views, and boundless in his mercies and blessings, than we are ready to believe or receive, and at the same time is as[7] terrible to the workers of iniquity, more awful in the executions of his punishments, and more ready to detect every false way than we are apt to suppose him to be. He will be enquired of by his children—he says ask and ye shall receive, seek and ye shall find; but if ye will take that which is not your own, or which I have not given you, you shall be rewarded according to your deeds, but no good thing will I withhold from them who walk uprightly before me, and do my will in all things, who will listen to my voice, and to the voice of my servant whom I have sent, for I delight in those who seek diligently to know my precepts, and abide by the laws of my kingdom, for all things shall be made known unto them in mine own due time, and in the end they shall have joy.

To Edward Hunter,
January 5, 1842

During the winter of 1839-40 while in the East awaiting developments in his appeal to the federal government in the matter of the Mormon expulsion from Missouri, Joseph Smith visited the Edward Hunter family in West Nantmeal, Chester County, Pennsylvania. Although not a member of the Church at the time of the Prophet's visit, Edward Hunter was seriously impressed with the message of the Restoration, which he had first heard from a Mormon elder a short time previous to Joseph's visit.

Born in Newton, Delaware County, Pennsylvania, on June 22, 1793, Edward had engaged in agricultural pursuits during his early years. He also learned the trades of tanner, currier, and surveyor, and had experience as a merchant. He served three years as county commissioner before moving to Chester County at the age of forty. There he purchased a five-hundred-acre farm and married Ann Standly. A seeker after the true form of worship, with a vigorous sense of justice and fair play, Edward Hunter contributed land for and helped build the West Nantmeal Seminary, a community hall erected for educational and religious purposes, with the stipulation that persons of all persuasions be allowed to speak there. Upon hearing a Mormon missionary earlier in 1839 and receiving a spiritual manifestation of the truth of what he said, he subsequently opened his home to any Church representative who came his way. In October 1840, a few months after Joseph Smith visited the Hunters and preached in the Seminary, Edward was baptized. The following year he traveled to Nauvoo, where he purchased a farm and several town lots in preparation to move there. Returning to Pennsylvania, he disposed of much of his property and invested a considerable sum in merchandise for Joseph Smith's Nauvoo store. In June 1842, he joined the Saints in Illinois.[1] Five months before he left Chester County, Edward received this letter from the Prophet.

Nauvoo January 5" 1842

Mr Edward Hunter.
Beloved Brother,
　　I wrote you on the 21 ultimo, in reply to yours of the 27" of october, but lest by any means the letter should fail to reach you I will recapitulate very briefly some important itims therein contained.
　　The power of Attorney was duly executed by Mrs Smith & forwareded to the clerks office for seal of state, to be sent, from thence direct to you.
　　The goods are accepted and ‹will be› applied according to your request.
　　I have purchased 90 acres of woodland, a little up the River; have made proposals to Mr Foll. but am yet waiting his answer, from his eastern correspondent.
　　Steam Engines & mills of any description will do well here, the more of such things you can bring, the better.— for particulars on the foregoing I would refer you to my letter of the 21 ult which I hope you have received ere this.—
　　~~The~~
　　I am happy that it is my privilige to say to you that the large New Building which I had commenced when you were here, is now completed, and the doors are opened this day for the sale of goods

for the first time. The foundations of the building is somewhat
spacios, (as you will doubtless recollect.) for a country store, The
principal part of [p. 1] the building below, which is nearly 10 feet
high is devoted ~~to~~ exclusively to Shelves ‹&› drawers Except 1
door opening back into the space, on the left of which are the
cellar & chamber stairs & on the Right the counting Room; from
the space at the top of the chamber stairs, opens a door into the
Large front room, of the same size with the one below.—the walls
lined with counters, covered with reserve goods.— in f[r]ont of the
stairs opens the door to my private office, or where I keep the
sacred writings. with a window to the south, overlooking the River
below & the opposite shore for a great distance, ‹which› together
with the passage of boats in the season thereof, constitutes a
peculiarly interesting situation, in prospect & no less interesting
from its retirement from the bustle & confusion of the
neighborhood & city, and altogether is a place the Lord is pleased
to bless.—[2]

The painting of the store has been excuted by some of our
English brethren.—[3]& the counters, drawers– & pillars present a
very respectable representation of oak, mahogony & marble—for a
back woods establishment.–

The Lord has blessed our exertions in a wonderful manner. and
although some individuals have suceeded in detai[ni]ng goods to a
considerable amount for the time being, yet we have been enabled
to s[e]cure goods in the building Sufficient to fill all the shelves ‹&
soon as they were completed› & have some in reserve, both in loft
& cellar. Our assortment is tolerably good—very good considering
the different purchases made by differe[n]t individuals, at different
times, and under circumstances which controuled their choice to
some extent, but, I rejoice [p. 2] that we have been enabled to do
as well as we have, for the hearts of many of the poor brethren &
sisters will be made glad, with those comforts which are now within
their reach. The store has been filled to overflowing all day, & I
have stood behind the counter ‹all day myself› dealing out goods as
steady as any clerk you ever saw to oblige those who were
compelled to go without their ‹usual› Christmas & New years

dinners for the want of a little sugar, molasses, Raisons &c. &c.—
& to please myself also for I love to wait upon the Saints, and be a
servant to all hoping that I may be exalted in the due time of the
Lord.

It is highly necessary that the store be well supplied with
merchandise from this time forward, both for the interest of the
church generally & the comfort of the brethren individually and as
expences have been incurred already to a great amount in building
the store, Temple, "Nauvoo house" &c &c—a great many of the
goods on hand will have to pass away on orders previous contracts,
&c. & we shall be obliged to lean upon other resources ‹to a great
extent› rather than the profits of goods, this winter, to supply a
new stock in the spring, & for this reason as well as those before
stated, & also, for your gratification in learning of our prosperity, I
write you this early to disire you to have the money you are to get
on the power of Attorney, of Mrs Smith ready for disposal in
Philadelphia as soon as the rivers shall open, & I sincerely hope &
trust that nothing will prevent your getting the money as you
expect, so that it may be ready in deposit at Philadephia, or ~~or~~ so
that you can meet Mr Whitney ‹at Phila.› or someone who may go
for the goods at a time which may be appointed hereafter. So that
we may have an [p. 3] early supply, of a spring selection. as you are
aware that the first opening of a new assortment would be much to
the advantage of the establishment, and I wish you to give me the
earliest information possible, of any thing new, in relation to this,
matter. With Sentiments of high consideration I remain your
Brother in Christ,

Joseph Smith
pr. W. Richards, Scribe

Edward Hunter Esqr
West. Nantmeal
Chester County
Pensylvania [p. 4]

Note of Authorization,
February 24, 1842

Having learned the printing trade as a youth in New York, nineteen-year-old Ebenezer Robinson was employed in the Kirtland, Ohio, Mormon printing firm of F. G. Williams & Co. in 1835 when he was converted. In the ensuing years, Robinson's name was associated with Church printing in Ohio, Missouri, and Illinois. He wrote that following the expulsion of the Latter-day Saints from Missouri "an increased interest was manifest in the work, and calls were made for the Book of Mormon, but there were none on hand to supply the demand." He subsequently played an important role in the publication of the third (1840) American edition of the book.

In June 1839, he and Don Carlos Smith had been given the Church press, salvaged from the Missouri mobbings, with authorization to publish a paper—the *Times and Seasons*—at their own expense and to use the profits therefrom to support their families. As co-editor and proprietor of the Nauvoo printing establishment, Ebenezer Robinson traveled in 1840 to Cincinnati, Ohio, where he negotiated with the firm Shepard and Stearns to have stereotype plates made, from which was published the 1840 edition of the Book of Mormon.

As they prospered, Smith and Robinson agreed in December 1840 to divide their business. Don Carlos was to take the *Times and Seasons* and handbill printing, and Ebenezer was to take the book and fancy job printing, the stereotype foundry, and the book bindery. When Don Carlos Smith died in August 1841, Ebenezer became sole proprietor of the establishment until he sold it to the Church in February 1842. On February 24, about three weeks after ownership of the printing office passed out of Robinson's hands, Joseph Smith authorized him to use the stereotype plates to make another impression of the Book of Mormon.[1]

Nauvoo City Feb. 24th 1842

Ebenezer Robinson is intitled to the use of the sterotipe plates and coppy right for the print[in]g [of] fifteen Hundred Books of Morman

Joseph Smith

Witness N K Whitney

Note of Authorization, February 24, 1842. Handwriting of Joseph Smith.
See text, p. 515. (Illinois State Historical Library.)

To Edward Hunter,
March 9, 11, 1842

On February 10, Edward Hunter responded to Joseph Smith's January letter, informing the Prophet that he would be coming to Nauvoo in the spring. He wrote, "I have sold one of my Farms & the other I do not know whether I can sell it, the money matters is in a dreadfull situation Banks are breaking continually. I intend sending out 400. Dollars for the erection of the Temple, & Four hundred Dollars for Stock in Nauvoo House. I would like to send drafts on the State Bank of Illinois or St. Louis if you think it the most proper way of conveyance of funds, on this subject I wish to hear from you. I shall receive part of the sale of my property First of Aprile next at that time I would wish to send the Eight hundred Dollars I before mentioned & I wish to hear how the State Bank of Illinois stands & the Banks of St Louis those banks will be a very important subject to the brethren that are going out this spring – Myself and family purpose starting out to Nauvoo begining of May, the greater part of this branch are geting ready to go out this summer."[1]

Joseph answered Edward Hunter's letter on March 9.

Nauvoo City March 9th 1842,

Bro. Edward Hunter
Dear Sir
    I yesterday had the pleasure of Receiving your Letter of Feb.

10– am much pleased that you have effected a sale, and are so soon to be with us &c.——

I have purchased the lands you desired, and will use my influence to have the improvements made which you wish. Bro. Weiler² rec'd your Letter and says he will do what he can to have all done.

The Power of Attorney I will forward to you with all its due forms

The eight hun-dred dollars for the Temple & Nauvoo House I wish you to bring in goods, which I will give you stock & credit for, as soon as Received.

I wish you to invest as much money as you possibly can in goods, to bring here, and I will purchase them of you, when you come, if we can agree on terms, or you can have my new brick store to rent. I wish the business kept up by some one, in the building as it is a very fine house, and cost me [p. 1] a handsome amount to build it.– Some eight or ten thousand dollars worth of goods would be of great advantage to this place, therefore if you or some of the Brethren would bring them on, I have no doubt but that I can arrange for them in some way to your (or their) advantage.

As to money matters here, the State Bank is down, and we cannot tell you what Bank would be safe a month hence, I would say that Gold and Silver is the only safe money a man can keep these times, you can sell specie [coin] here for more premiums [bank notes] than you have to give, therefore there would be no loss, and it would be safe. The Bank you deposite in might fail before you had time to draw out again——

I am now very busily engaged in Translating, and therefore cannot give as much time to Public matters as I could wish, but will nevertheless do what I can to forward your affairs

I will send you a memorandum of such goods as will suit this market, yours affectionately

Joseph Smith [p. 2]

March 11. After diligent enquiry I have learned that the presiding Judge of this circuit is a great distance from this, & it will **not be possible** according to present appearances, to get an accknowled[g]ment of the Letter of Attorney until the former part of May. If you Sir & the parties concerned will proceed with the business Just as though you had the Letter, for the purpose of expediting the business, I pledge my honor that a duly authenticated letter of Attorney shall be forth coming at the earliest date possible.– & by so doing you will confer a favor on your friend, &c.

Joseph Smith
W. Richards. Scribe[3] [p. 3]

Mr. Edwd Hunter
West Nantmeal
Chester Co
Pennsylvania [p. 4]

To Jennetta Richards,
June 23, 1842

Perhaps Willard Richards's major contribution to the Church was the clerical assistance he gave Joseph Smith in keeping the Prophet's diary during the last two years of his life and the role he played in the compilation of the Prophet's history. Born in 1804 in Massachusetts, Willard Richards was baptized on the last day of 1836 by Brigham Young in Kirtland, Ohio. Six months later, he left with members of the Twelve on a proselyting mission to England. During the next four years, he labored as a missionary, published the *Latter-day Saints' Millennial Star*, was ordained an apostle, and met and married Jennetta Richards. While in England, Jennetta bore two sons, one of whom died there.

Returning to America in the summer of 1841, Willard left his family with relatives in Richmond, Massachusetts, and continued alone to Nauvoo, expecting to return for them after he was settled; but heavy ecclesiastical, civic and clerical responsibilities delayed his return to get his family for nearly a year. His departure on July 1, 1842, was probably motivated by a letter from Jennetta to Joseph Smith.[1] The Prophet's response to that letter was written on June 23, 1842.

Nauvoo June 23rd 1842

Sister Jennetta Richards;

    Agreabley to your request, in the midst of all the bustle, and
buisness of the day, and the care of all the Churches boath at home
and abroad, I now imbrace a moment to adress a few words to you
thinking peradventure it may be a consolation to you to know that
you too are remembered by me as well as all the saints. my hearts
desire and prayr to God is all the day long for all the saints and in
an especial and poticular manner for those whom he hath chosen
and anointed to bear the heaviest burthens in the heat of the day
among which number is your husband received a man in whom I
have the most implicit confidence and trust you say I have got him
so I have in the which I rejoice, for he has done me great good and
taken a great burden off my shoulders since his arrival in Nauvoo
never did I have greater intimacy with any man than with him may
the bless=ings of Elijah crown his head forever and ever. we are
about to send him in a few days after his dear familyy he shall have
our pray'rs fervently for his safe arrival to their imbraces and may
God speed his Journey and return him quickly to our society, and I
want you beloved Sister, to be a Genral in this matter, in helping
him along, which I know you will he will be able to teach you
many things which you never have heard you may have implicit
confidence in the same. I have heard much about you by the twelve
and in consequence of the great friendship that exists between your
husband and me and the information they all have given me of
your virtue and strong attachment to the truth of the work of God
in the Last Days I have formed a very strong Brotherly friendship
and attachment for you in the bonds of the Gosple, Although I
never saw you I shall be exceedingly glad to see you face to face and
be able to administer in the name of the Lord some of the words of
Life to your consolation and I hope that you may be kept steadfast
in the faith even unto the end, I want you should give my love and
tender reguard to Br Richards familey and those who are friendly
enough to me to enquire after me in that region of Country, not

having but little time to apportion to anyone & having stolen this oppertunity I therefore subscribe myself in haste your most obedient Brother in the fulness of the Gosple

Joseph Smith

P.S. Bro Richards having been with me for [p. 1] a long time can give you any information which you need and will tell you all about me. I shall be very anxious for his return he is a grate prop to me in my Labours.

Mrs. Jennetta Richards
Richmond
Massachusetts

Nauvoo June 23rd 1842

Sister Jennetta Richards:

Agreeable to your request in the midst of all the bustle, and business of the day and the care of all the churches both at home and abroad I now embrace a moment to address a few words to you thinking peradventure it may be a consolation to you to know that you too are remembered by me as well as all the saints. my hearts desire and prayer to God is all the day long for all the saints and in in especial and particular manner for those whom he hath chosen and anointed to bear the heaviest burthens in the heat of the day among which number is your husband, received a man in whom I have the most implicit confidence and trust you say I have got him so I have in those which I rejoice for he has done me great good and taken a great burden off my shoulders since his arrival in Nauvoo neither did I have greater intimacy with any man than with him may the blessings of Elijah crown his head forever and ever as are about to send him in a few days after his dear family he shall have our prayers fervently for his safe arrival to their embraces and may God speed his journey and return him quickly to our society and I want you beloved sister, to be a general in this matter, in helping him along. which I know you will be well be able to teach you many things which you never have heard you may have implicit confidence in the same. I have heard much about you by the twelve and in consequence of the great friendship that exists between your husband and me and the information they all have given me of your virtue and strong attachment to the truth of the work of God in the last days I have formed a very strong brotherly friendship and attachment for you in the bonds of the Gospel, although I never saw you I shall be exceedingly glad to see you face to face and be able to administer in the name of the Lord some of the words of life to your consolation and I hope that you may be kept stedfast in the faith even unto the end. I want you should give my love and tender regard to Mr Richards family and those who are friendly enough to me to enquire after me in that region of country, not having but little time to apportion to any one & having stolen this opportunity I therefore subscribe myself in haste your most obedient Brother in the fulness of the Gospel Joseph Smith

P.S. Mr Richards having been with me for

To Jennetta Richards, June 23, 1842, p. 1. Handwriting of William Clayton. See text, pp. 521-22. (LDS Church Archives.)

To Emma Smith,
August 16, 1842

To Wilson Law,
August 16, 1842

When an unknown assailant shot Lilburn W. Boggs at his Independence, Missouri, home on May 6, 1842, seriously wounding the Missouri exgovernor, the Mormons became prime suspects in consequence of Boggs's role in driving the Saints from Missouri four years earlier. Upon recovering sufficiently, Boggs accused Joseph Smith and Orrin Porter Rockwell of the crime and urged Missouri authorities to extradite them to Missouri for trial. His request fell upon receptive ears, and on August 8 Joseph Smith and Porter Rockwell were taken into custody in Nauvoo by an Adams County deputy sheriff sent by Illinois Governor Thomas Carlin. Sensing the danger of his situation, Joseph immediately appealed to the Nauvoo municipal court on a writ of habeas corpus. In the face of this complication, the sheriff departed for Quincy to determine the legality of the Nauvoo court to act in the case. Upon his departure, the sheriff left the arrested men in the custody of the Nauvoo city marshal but failed to leave the original writ of arrest, the only legal means of detaining the prisoners. Consequently, when he returned, his prisoners were gone. To Joseph Smith the arrest attempt was a case of harassment with no legal basis and justified his remaining out of sight until the matter could be resolved by an impartial court.

On August 11, while in hiding at his Uncle John Smith's across the Mississippi River in Zarahemla, Joseph sent word for trusted friends to meet him on the island in the river that night. At this meeting, it was decided that the Prophet should be taken to Edward Sagers's place via the river and Wiggins's farm on the northeast outskirts of Nauvoo. While there on the sixteenth, word came of the sheriff's renewed determination to serve his warrant, even if he had to "search every house in the city" to do it.[1] In the face of increased danger, plans were made for Joseph to leave on a moment's notice for the Wisconsin pine country.[2] In this setting, Joseph wrote on August 16 to Emma and to Wilson Law, recently appointed major general of the Nauvoo Legion's first cohort.

Nauvoo, August 16, 1842.

My Dear Emma:—I embrace this opportunity to express to you some of my feelings this morning. First of all, I take the liberty to tender you my sincere thanks for the two interesting and consoling visits that you have made me during my almost exiled situation. Tongue cannot express the gratitude of my heart, for the warm and true-hearted friendship you have manifested in these things toward me. The time has passed away since you left me, very agreeably; thus far, my mind being perfectly reconciled to my fate, let it be what it may. I have been kept from melancholy and dumps, by the kind-heartedness of brother Derby,[3] and his interesting chit-chat from time to time, which has called my mind from the more strong contemplations of things, and subjects that would have preyed more earnestly upon my feelings. Last night—in the night— brother Hyrum, Miller,[4] Law,[5] & others came to see us. They seemed much agitated, and expressed some fears in consequence of some manouverings and some flying reports which they had heard in relation to our safety; but after relating what it was, I was able to comprehend the whole matter to my entire satisfaction, and did not feel at all alarmed or uneasy. They think, however, that the Militia will be called out to search the city, and if this should be the case I would be much safer for the time being at a little distance off, until Governor Carlin could get weary and be made ashamed of his corrupt and unhallowed proceedings. I had supposed, however, that if there were any serious operations taking by the governor; that Judge Ralston[6] or Brother Hollister would have notified us; and cannot believe that any thing very serious is to be apprehended, untill we obtain information from a source that can be relied on. I have consulted wether it is best for you to go to Quincy, and see the Governor; but on the whole, he is a fool; and the impressions that are suggested to my mind, are, that it will be of no use; and the more we notice him, and flatter him, the more eager he will be for our destruction. You may write to him, whatever you see proper, but to go and see him, I do not give my consent at present. Brother Miller again suggested to me the propriety of my accompanying him to the Pine woods, and then he return, and bring you [p. 173] and the children. My mind will eternally revolt at every suggestion of that kind. More especially since the dream and vision that was manifested to me on the last night. My safety is with you, if you want to have it so. Any thing more or less than this cometh of evil. My feelings and council I think ought to be abided. If I go to the Pine country, you shall go along with me, and the children; and if you and the children go not with me, I don't go. I do not wish to exile myself for the sake of my own life, I would rather fight it out. It is for your sakes, therefore, that I would do such a thing. I will go with you then, in the same carriage and on Horse back, from time to time, as occasion may require; for I am not willing to trust you, in the hands of those who cannot feel the same interest for you, that I feel; to be subject to the caprice, temptations, or notions of anybody whatever. And I must say that I am pre-possessed somewhat, with the notion of going to the Pine country any how; for I am tired of the mean, low, and unhallowed vulgarity, of some portions of the society in which we live; and I think if I could have a respite of about six months with my family, it would be a savor of life unto life, with my house. Nevertheless if it were possible I would like to live here in peace and wind up my business; but if it should be ascertained to a dead certainty that there is no other remedy, then we will round up our shoulders and cheerfully endure it; and this will be the plan. Let my horse, saddle, saddle-bags, and valice to put some shirts and clothing in, be sent to me. Let brother Derby and Miller take a horse and put it into my Buggy with a trunk containing my heavier clothes, shoes and boots, &c. and let brother Taylor accompany us to his fathers, and there we will tarry, taking every precaution to keep out of the hands of the enemy, untill you can arrive with the children. Let brother Hyrum bring you. Let Lorain[7] and brother Clayton[8] come along and bring all the writings and papers, books and histories, for we shall want a scribe in order that we may pour upon the world the truth like the Lava from Mount Vesuvius. Then, let all the goods, household furniture, clothes and Store Goods that can be procured be put on the Boat, and let 20 or 30 of the best men that we can find be put on board to man it; and let them meet us at Prairie Du Chien; and from thence, we will wend our way like larks up the Mississippi untill the touring mountains and rocks, shall remind us of the places of our nativity, and shall look like safety and home; and then we will bid defiance to the world, to Carlin, Boggs, Bennett, and all their whorish whores, and motly clan, that [p. 174] follow in their wake, Missouri not excepted; and until the damnation of hell rolls upon them, by the voice, and dread thunders, and trump of the eternal God; then, in that day will we not shout in the victory and be crowned with eternal joys, for the battles we have fought, having kept the faith and overcome the world. Tell the children that it is well with their father, as yet; and that he remains in fervent prayer to Almighty God for the safety of himself, and for you, and for them. Tell Mother Smith that it shall be well with her son, whether in life or in death; for thus saith the Lord God. Tell her that I remember her all the while, as well as Lucy and all the rest; they all must be of good cheer. Tell Hyrum to be sure and not fail to carry out my instructions, but at the same time if the Militia does not come, and we should get any favorable information, all may be well yet. Yours in haste, your affectionate husband until death, through all eternity for evermore,

Joseph Smith

P.S.—I want you to write to Lorenzo Wasson,[9] and get him to make affidavit to all he knows about Bennett and forward it. I also want you to ascertain from Hyrum wether he will conform to what I have requested. And you must write me an answer per bearer, giving me all the news you have, and what is the appearance of things this morning.

J.S.

Head Quarters of Nauvoo Legion
August 16 1842

Major Gen. Law,[1]
Beloved brother and friend
    Those few lines which I received from you written on the 15th was to me like apples of Gold in pictures of silver.[2] I rejoice with exceeding great joy to be associated in the high and responsible stations which we hold, [with one] whose mind and feelings and heart is so congenial with my own. I love that soul that is so nobly entabernacled in that clay of yours. may God Almighty grant, that it may be satiated with seeing a fulfilment of every virtuous ~~desire~~ and manly desire that you possess. May we be able to triumph gloriously over those who seek our destruc=tion and overthrow, which I believe we shall. The news you wrote me was more favorable than that which was communicated by the brethren. They seemed a little agitated for my safety and advise me for the Pine Woods. But I succeeded admirably in calming all their fears. But nevertheless as I said in my former letter, I was willing to exile myself for months and years, if it would be for the safety and welfare of the people; and I do not know but it would be as well for me to take a trip to the Pine countries and remain untill arrangements can be made for my most perfect safety when I return. These are therefore to confer with you on this subject, as I want to have a concert of action in every thing that I do. If I [k]new that they would oppress me alone, and let the rest of you

dwell peaceably and quietly, I think It would be the wisest plan to absent myself for a little season if by that means we can prevent the profusion of blood. Please write and give me your mind on that subject and all other information that has come to hand today and what are the signs of the times. [p. 1] I have no news for I am where I cannot get much all is quiet and peaceable around. I therefore wait with earnest expectation for your advices. I am anxious to know your opinions on any course that I may see proper to take, for in the multitude of council there is safety.

I add no more, but subscribe myself your faithful and most obedient servant, friend and brother

> Joseph Smith
> Lieut Gen. of Nauvoo Legion of
> Illinois Millitia

Maj Gen Law

Reflections,
August 16, 23, 1842

On August 16, the same day Joseph Smith wrote to Emma from his place of seclusion at Sagers's north of Nauvoo, he also began dictating a lengthy expression of his feelings to his clerk William Clayton as he reflected upon the loyalty of trusted friends who had rallied to his support in times of crisis. Then, suddenly forced to leave amid rumors that his hiding place had been discovered, Joseph eventually returned to his home and secreted himself in his office where, on August 23 he continued dictating the sentiments he had begun on the sixteenth. Although William Clayton concluded his writing on the twenty-third with the notation that Joseph would "continue the subject again," nothing more was ever added.

August 16, 1842.

Brother Erastus H. Derby is one among the number of the faithful souls, who have taken as yet the greatest interest that possibly could have been imagined for the welfare of President Joseph. I therefore record the following blessing from the mouth of the President himself.

Blessed is Brother Erastus H. Derby, and he shall be blessed of the Lord; he possesses a sober mind, and a faithful heart; the snares therefore that are subsequent to befall other men, who are treacherous and rotten-hearted, shall not come nigh unto his doors, but shall be far from the path of his feet. He loveth wisdom, and shall be found possessed of her. Let there be a crown of glory, and a diadem upon his head. Let the light of eternal Truth shine forth upon his understanding; let his name be had in everlasting remembrance; let the blessings of Jehovah be crowned upon his posterity after him, for he rendered me consolation, in the lonely places of my retreat: How good and glorious, it has seemed unto me, to find pure and holy friends, who are faithful, just and true, and whose hearts fail not; and whose knees are confirmed and do not faulter; while they wait upon the Lord, in administering to my necessities; [p. 135] in the day when the wrath of mine enemies was poured out upon me. In the name of the Lord, I feel in my heart to bless them, and to say in the name of Jesus Christ of Nazareth that these are the ones that shall inherit eternal life. I say it by virtue of the Holy Priesthood, and by the ministering of Holy Angels, and by the gift and power of the Holy Ghost. How glorious were my feelings when I met that faithful and friendly band, on the night of the eleventh on thursday, on the Island, at the mouth of the slough, between Zarahemla and Nauvoo. With what unspeakable delight, and what transports of joy swelled my bosom, when I took by the hand on that night, my beloved Emma, she that was my wife, even the wife of my youth; and the choice of my heart. Many were the reviberations of my mind when I contemplated for a moment the many ~~passt~~ scenes we had been called to pass through. The fatigues, and the toils, the sorrows, and sufferings, and the joys and consolations from time to time [which] had strewed our paths and crowned our board. Oh! what a comingling of thought filled my mind for the moment, again she is here, even in the seventh trouble, undaunted, firm and unwavering, unchangeable, affectionate Emma. There was Brother Hyrum who next took me by the hand, a natural brother; thought I to myself, brother Hyrum, what a faithful heart you have got. Oh, may the eternal Jehovah crown eternal blessings upon your head, as a reward for the care you have had for my soul. O how many are the sorrows have we shared together, and again we find ourselves shackled with the unrelenting hand of oppression. Hyrum, thy name shall be written

in the Book of the Law of the Lord,[1] for those who come after thee
to look upon, that they may pattern after thy works. Said I to
myself here is brother Newel K. Whitney also, how many scenes of
sorrow, have strewed our paths together; and yet we meet once
more to share again. Thou art a faithful friend in whom the
afflicted sons of men can confide, with the most perfect safety. Let
the blessings of the eternal be crowned also upon his head; how
warm that heart! how anxious that soul! for the welfare of one who
has been cast out, and hated of almost all men. Brother Whitney,
thou knowest not how strong those ties are, that bind my soul and
heart to thee. My heart was overjoyed, as I took the faithful band
by hand, that stood upon the shore one by one. Wm. Law, Wm.
Clayton, Dimick B. Huntington,[2] George Miller, were there. The
above names constituted the little group. I do not think to mention
the particulars of the history of that sacred night, which shall
forever be remembered by me. But the names of the faithful are
what I wish to record in this place. These I have met in prosperity
and they were my friends, I now meet them in adversity, and they
are still my warmer friends. These love the God that I serve; they
love the truths that I promulge; they love those virtuous, and those
holy doctrines that I cherish in my bosom with the warmest feelings
of my heart; and with that zeal which cannot be denied. I love
friendship and truth; I love virtue [p. 164] and Law; I love the God
of Abraham and of Isaac and of Jacob, and they are my brethren,
and I shall live; and because I live, they shall live also. These are
not the only ones, who have administered to my necessity; whom
the Lord will bless. There is Brother John D. Parker,[3] and Brother
Amasa Lyman,[4] and Brother Wilson Law, and Brother Henry G.
Sherwood, my heart feels to reciprocate the unweried kindnesses
that have been bestowed upon me by these men. They are men of
noble stature, of noble hands, and of noble deeds; possessing noble
and daring, and giant hearts and souls. There is Brother Joseph B.
Nobles[5] also, I would call up in remembrance before the Lord.
There is brother Samuel Smith, a natural brother; he is, even as
Hyrum. There is Brother Arthur Millikin[6] also, who married my
youngest sister, Lucy. He is a faithful, an honest, and an upright

man. While I call up in remembrance before the Lord these men, I would be doing injustice to those who rowed me in the skiff up the river that night, after I parted with the lovely group; who brought me to this my safe and lonely and private retreat; brother Jonathan Dunham[7] and the other whose name I do not know. Many were the thoughts that swelled my aching heart, while they were toiling faithfully with their oars. They complained not of hardship and fatigue to secure my safety. My heart would have been harder than an adamantine stone, if I had not have prayed for them with anxious and fervent desire. I did so, and the still small voice whispered to my soul, these that share your toils with such faithful hearts, shall reign with you in the kingdom of their God; but I parted with them in silence and came to my retreat. I hope I shall see them again that I may toil for them and administer to their comfort also. They shall not want a friend while I live. My heart shall love those; and my hands shall toil for those, who love and toil for me, and shall ever be found faithful to my friends. Shall I be ungrateful? verily no! God forbid!

The above are the words, and sentiments, that escaped the lips of President Joseph Smith on the 16th day of August A D 1842, in relation to his friends: and has now quit speaking for the moment, but will continue the subject again.

Wm. Clayton, Clerk [p. 165]

August 23, 1842.

This day President Joseph has renewed the subject of conversation, in relation to his faithful brethren, and friends in his own words; which I now proceed to record as follows;

While I contemplate the virtues and the good qualifications and characteristics of the faithful few, which I am now recording in the Book of the Law of the Lord, of such as have stood by me in every hour of peril, for these fifteen long years past; say, for instance; my aged and beloved brother Joseph Knight, Senr.,[8] who was among the number of the first to administer to my necessities, while I was laboring, in the commencement of the bringing forth of the work of the Lord, and of laying the foundation of the Church of Jesus Christ of Latter Day Saints: for fifteen years has he been faithful and true, and even handed, and exemplary and virtuous, and kind; never deviating to the right hand or to the left. Behold he is a righteous man. May God Almighty lengthen out the old man's days; and may his trembling, tortured and broken body be renewed, and in the vigor of health turn upon him; if it can be thy will, consistently, O God; and it shall be said of him, by the sons of Zion, while there is one of them re-maining; that this man, was a faithful man in Israel; therefore his name shall never be forgotten. There are his son[s] Newel Knight and Joseph Knight[9] whose names I record in the Book of the Law of the Lord, with unspeakable delight, for they are my friends. There is a numerous host of faithful souls, whose names I could wish to record in the Book of the Law of the Lord; but time and chance would fail. I will mention therefore only a few of them as emblematical of those who are to[o] numerous to be written. But there is one man I would mention namely Porter Rockwell,[10] who is now a fellow-wanderer with myself, an exile from his home because of the murderous deeds and infernal fiendish disposition of the indefatigable and unrelenting hand of the Missourians. He is an innocent and a noble boy; may God Almighty deliver him from the hands of his pursuers. He was an innocent and a noble child, and my soul loves him. Let this be recorded for ever and ever. Let the blessings of salvation and honor be his portion. But as I said before, so say I again while I remember the faithful few who are now living, I would remember also the faithful of my friends who are dead, for they are many; and many are the acts of kindness, and paternal and brotherly kindnesses which they have bestowed upon me. And since I have been hunted by the Missourians many are the scenes which have been called to my mind. Many thoughts have rolled through my head, and across my breast. I have remembered the scenes of my childhood. I have thought of my father who is dead, who died by disease which was brought upon him through suffering

by the hands of ruthless mobs. He was a great and a good man. The
envy of knaves and fools was heaped upon him, and this was his lot
and portion all the days of his life. He was of noble stature, and
possessed a high, and holy, and exalted, and a virtuous mind. His
soul soared above all those mean [p. 179] and groveling principles
that are so subsequent to the human heart. I now say, that he never
did a mean act that might be said was ungenerous, in his life, to my
knowledge. I loved my father and his memory; and the memory of
his noble deeds, rest with ponderous weight upon my mind; and
many of his kind and parental words to me, are written on the
tablet of my heart. Sacred to me, are the thoughts which I cherish
of the history of his life, that have rolled through my mind and
have been implanted there, by my own observation since I was
born. Sacred to me is his dust, and the spot where he is laid. Sacred
to me is the tomb I have made to encircle o'er his head. Let the
memory of my father eternally live. ~~Let the faults and the follies~~
Let his soul, or the spirit my follies forgive. With him may I reign
one day, in the mansions above; and tune up the Lyre of anthems,
of the eternal Jove. May the God that I love look down from
above, and save me from my enemies here, and take me by the
hand; that on Mount Zion I may stand and with my father crown
me eternally there. Words and language, is inadequate to express
the gratitude that I owe to God for having given me so honorable a
parentage. My mother also is one of the noblest, and the best of all
women. May God grant to prolong her days, and mine; that we
may live to enjoy each other's society long yet in the enjoyment of
liberty, and to breathe the free air. Alvin my oldest brother, I
remember well the pangs of sorrow that swelled my youthful bosom
and almost burst my tender heart, when he died. He was the
oldest, and the noblest of my father's family. He was one of the
noblest of the sons of men: Shall his name not be recorded in this
book? Yes, Alvin; let it be had here, and be handed down upon
these sacred pages, forever and ever. In him there was no guile. He
lived without spot from the time he was a child. From the time of
his birth, he never knew mirth. He was candid and sober and never
would play; and minded his father, and mother, in toiling all day.

He was one of the soberest of men and when he died the angel of
the Lord visited him in his last moments. These childish lines I
record in remembrance of my childhood scenes. My Brother Don
Carlos Smith, whose name I desire to record also, was a noble boy.
I never knew any fault in him. I never saw the first immoral act; or
the first irreligious, or ignoble disposition in the child. From the
time that he was born, till the time of his death; he was a lovely, a
goodnatured, and a kind-hearted, and a virtuous and a faithful
upright child. And where his soul goes let mine go also. He lays by
the side of my father. Let my father, Don Carlos, and Alvin, and
children that I have buried be brought and laid in the tomb I have
built. Let my mother, and my brethren, and my sisters be laid there
also; and let it be called the Tomb of Joseph, a descendant of Jacob;
and when I die, let me be gathered to the tomb of my father. There
are many souls, whom I have loved stronger than death; to them I
have proved faithful; to them I [p. 181] am determined to prove
faithful, untill God calls me to resign up my breath. O, thou who
seeeth, and knoweth the hearts of all men; thou eternal,
omnipotent, omnicient, and omnipresent Jehovah, God; thou
Eloheem, that sitteth, as saith the psalmist; enthroned in heaven;
look down upon thy servant Joseph, at this time; and let faith on
the name of thy Son Jesus Christ, to a greater degree than thy
servant ever yet has enjoyed, be conferred upon him; even the faith
of Elijah; and let the Lamp of eternal life, be lit up in his heart,
never to be taken away; and let the words of eternal life, be poured
upon the soul of thy servant; that he may know thy will, thy
statutes, and thy commandments, and thy judgments to do them.
As the dews upon Mount Hermon, may the distillations of thy
divine grace, glory and honor in the plenitude of thy mercy, and
power and goodness be poured down upon the head of thy servant.
O Lord God, my heavenly Father, shall it be in vain, that thy
servant must needs be exiled from the midst of his friends; or be
dragged from their bosoms, to clank in cold and iron chains; to be
thrust within the dreary prison walls; to spend days of sorrow, and
of grief and misery there, by the hand of an infuriated, insensed and
infatuated foe; to glut their infernal and insatiable desire upon

innocent blood; and for no other cause on the part of thy servant, than for the defence of innocence, and thou a just God will not hear his cry? Oh, no, thou wilt hear me; a child of woe, pertaining to this mortal life; because of sufferings here, but not for condemnation that shall come upon him in eternity; for thou knowest O God, the integrity of his heart. Thou hearest me, and I knew that thou wouldst hear me, and mine enemies shall not prevail; they all shall melt like wax before thy face; and as the mighty floods, and waters roar; or as the billowing earth-quake's, devouring gulf; or rolling thunder's loudest peal; or vivid, forked lightnings flash; or sound of the Arch-Angels trump; or voice of the Eternal God, shall the souls of my enemies be made to feel in an instant, suddenly, and shall be taken, and ensnared; and fall back-wards, and stumble in the ditch they have dug for my feet, and the feet of my friends; and perish in their own infamy and shame, be thrust down to an eternal hell, for their murderous and hellish deeds.

After writing so much President Joseph left off speaking for the present but will continue the subject again. . . .

Wm Clayton, Clerk. [p. 181]

To the Whitneys, August 18, 1842

Newel K. Whitney had been a close friend to Joseph Smith ever since the Prophet arrived at Kirtland in February 1831. In addition to the community needs provided by the Whitney mercantile firm, Newel had given untiring service as bishop of the Church in Ohio. He had left strife-torn Kirtland with his family to join the Saints in western Missouri in the fall of 1838; but at St. Louis, after hearing reports of violence against the Church in western Missouri, he did not proceed further. Turning northward, he settled temporarily at Carrolton, Greene County, Illinois, and then at Quincy, in Adams County. In the spring of 1840 the Whitneys joined the exiled Saints at Commerce (Nauvoo), and later that year Newel was appointed bishop of one of the town's three wards.[1]

When the practice of plural marriage was introduced at Nauvoo in the early 1840s, the Whitney family were among those involved. Seventeen-year-old Sarah Ann Whitney was sealed[2] to Joseph Smith on July 27, 1842, her father performing the ceremony. Three weeks later Joseph wrote the following letter to Newel, Elizabeth Ann, and Sarah Ann. At the time, he was in seclusion at Carlos Granger's on the outskirts of Nauvoo. The letter reflects the crisis atmosphere that had forced him into hiding following the Boggs assassination attempt and the strain of conditions upon his family.

538

Nauvoo August 18th 1842

Dear, and Beloved, Brother and Sister, Whitney, and &c.—
    I take this oppertunity to communi[c]ate, some of my feelings,
privetely at this time, which I want you three Eternaly to keep in
your own bosams; for my feelings are so strong for you since
what has pased lately between us, that the time of my abscence
from you seems so long, and dreary, that it seems, as if I could not
live long in this way: and ‹if you› three would come and see me
in this my lonely retreat, it would afford me great relief, of mind,
if those with whom I am alied, do love me, now is the time to
afford me succour, in the days of exile, for you know I foretold
you of these things. I am now at Carlos Graingers, Just back of
Brother Hyrams farm, it is only one mile from town, the nights
are very pleasant indeed, all three of y̶ you c̶o̶m̶e̶ ‹can› come and
See me in the fore part of the night, let Brother Whitney come a
little a head, and nock at the south East corner of the house at
‹the› window; it is next to the cornfield, I have a room inti=rely
by myself, the whole matter can be attended to with most perfect
safty, I ‹know› it is the will of God that you should comfort
‹me› now in this time of affliction, or not at[ta]l now is the [p. 1]
time or never, but I hav[e] no kneed of saying any such thing, to
you, for I know the goodness of your hearts, and that you will do
the will of the Lord, when it is made known to you; the only
thing to be careful of; is to find out when Emma comes then you
cannot be safe, but when she is not here, there is the most perfect
safty: only be careful to escape observation, as much as possible, I
know it is a heroick undertakeing; but so much the greater
frendship, and the more Joy, when I see you I ‹will› tell you all
my plans, I cannot write them on paper, burn this letter as soon
as you read it; keep all locked up in your breasts, my life depends
up=on it. one thing I want to see you for is ‹to› git the fulness of
my blessings sealed upon our heads, &c. you w̶i̶ will pardon me
for my earnest=ness on ‹this subject› when you consider how
lonesome I must be, your good feelings know how to ‹make›

every allow=ance for me, I close my letter, I think Emma wont come tonight if she dont dont fail to come to night. I subscribe myself your most obedient, <and> affectionate, companion, and friend.

Joseph Smith

Nauvoo Augus 18th 1842

Dear, and Beloved, Brother and
Sister, Whitney, and &c.—
I take this opportunity to communicate
some of my feelings, privetely at
this time, which I want you three
Eternaly to keep in your own
bosams; for my feelings are so
strong for you since what has
passed lately between us, that the
time of my absence from you
seems so long, and dreary, that
it seems, as if I could not live
long in this way: and if you three would
come and see me in this my lonely
retreat, it would afford me great
relief, of mind, if those with whom
I am alied, do love me, now is the
time to afford me succour, in the
days of my exile, for you know I
foretold you of these things. I am
now at Carlos Graingers, Just back
of Brother Hyrams farm, it is only one
mile from town, the nights are
very pleasant, indeed, all three of
you can come and see me in the
fore part of the night, let Brother
Whitney come a little a head, and
nock at the south East corner of
the house at the window; it is next to
the cornfield; I have a room intirely by myself, the whole matter
can be attended to with most perfect
safty, I know it is the will of God that you
should comfort me now in this time
of affliction, or not at all now is the

time or never, but I have no need of saying
any such thing, to you, for I know the
goodness of your hearts, and that you
will do the will of the Lord, when it is
made known to you; the only thing
to be careful of, is to find out when
Emma comes then you cannot be
safe, but when she is not here, there
is the most perfect safty; only be
careful to escape observation, as
much as possible, I know it is a
heroick undertaking; but so much
the greater friendship, and the more
joy, when I see you I will tell you all
my plans, I cannot write them on
paper, burn this letter as soon as you
read it; keep all locked up in
your breasts, my life depends upon it; one thing I want to see you
for is to git the fulness of my blessing
sealed upon our heads, &c. you
will pardon me for my earnest-
ness on this subject when you consider how
lonesome I must be; your good
feelings know how to make every allow-
ance for me, I close my letter
I think Emma wont come tonight
if she dont dont fail to come tonight, I subscribe myself your
most obedient, and affectionate,
Companion, and friend

Joseph Smith

To the Whitneys, August 18, 1842, p. 2. Handwriting of Joseph Smith.
See text, pp. 539-40. (LDS Church Archives.)

To All the Saints,
September 1, 1842

Three weeks after Joseph Smith had gone into hiding following the attempted arrest in the Boggs affair, the Nauvoo Saints were pleased by his unexpected appearance at two public meetings, the first a special conference on August 29 at which volunteers were called to travel through the country to allay the false information promulgated by John C. Bennett, and the second, a gathering of the Female Relief Society on August 31. Joseph informed the sisters in the latter meeting that "important things" had been manifested to him during his absence respecting the doctrine of baptism for the dead "which I shall communicate to the Saints next Sabbath, if nothing should occur to prevent me." But before he could fulfill his promise, he was again forced into seclusion. On September 1 and again on September 6, Joseph wrote two letters to the Nauvoo Saints in which he dwelt at length on the subject of baptism for the dead.[1] Both were later canonized as sections 127 and 128 of the Doctrine and Covenants. The first of these is presented here.

September 1st 1842

To all the saints in Nauvoo

Forasmuch as the Lord has revealed unto me that my enemies both of Mo & this State were again on the pursuit of me, and inasmuch as they pursue me without cause and have not the least shadow or coloring of justice or right on their side in the getting up

543

of their prosecutions against me; and inasmuch as their pretensions are all founded in falsehood of the blackest die, I have thought it expedient and wisdom in me to leave the place for a short season for my own safety and the safety of this people. I would say to all those with whom I have business that I have left my affairs with agents and clerks who will transact all business in a prompt and proper manner and will see that all my debts are cancelled in due time, by turning out property or otherwise as the case may require, or as the circumstances may admit of. When I learn that the storm is fully blown over then I will return to you again. And as for the perils which I am called to pass through they seem but a small thing to me, as the envy and wrath of man has been my common lot all the days of my life and for what cause it seems mysterious, unless I was ordained from before the foundation of the world for some good end, or bad as you may choose to call it. Judge ye for yourselves, God knoweth all these things wether it be good or bad, but nevertheless deep water is what I am wont to swim in, it all has become a second nature to me and I feel like Paul to glory in tribulation for unto this day has the God of my Fathers [p. 1] delivered me out of them all and will deliver me from henceforth for behold and lo I shall triumph over all my enemies for the Lord God hath spoken it.

Let all the saints rejoice therefore and be exceeding glad for Israels God is their God and he will meet out a just recompense of reward upon the heads of all your oppressors. And again verily thus saith the Lord let the work of my Temple and all the works which I have appointed unto you be continued on and not cease; and let your diligence and your perseverance and patience and your works be redoubled, and you shall in no wise loose your reward saith the Lord of Hosts. And if they persecute you so persecuted they the prophets and righteous men that were before you; for all this there is a reward in heaven.

And again I give unto you a word in relation to the Baptism for your dead. Verily thus saith the Lord unto you concerning your dead when any of you are baptised for your dead let there be a recorder, and let him be eye=witness of your baptisms; let him hear with his ears that he may testify of a truth, saith the Lord; that in all your recordings it may be recorded in Heaven, that whatsoever you bind on earth may be bound in heaven; whatsoever you loose on earth may be loosed in heaven; for I am about to restore many things to the Earth, pertaining to the Priesthood saith the Lord of Hosts. And again let all the Records be had in order, that they may be put in the archives of my Holy Temple to be held in remembrance from generation to generation saith the Lord of Hosts.

I will say to all the saints that I desired with exceeding great desire to have addressed them from the stand on the subject of Baptism for the dead on the following sabbath but inasmuch as it is out of my power to do so I will write the word of the Lord from time to time on that subject and send it [to] you by mail as well as many other things. –

I now close my letter for the present for the want of more time, for the enemy is on the alert and as the saviour said the prince of this world cometh but he hath nothing in me. Behold my prayer to God is that you all may be saved and I subscribe myself your servant in the Lord, prophet and Seer of the Church of Jesus Christ of Latter day Saints

Joseph Smith

Mr W. Clayton
Nauvoo Hancock Co
Ill

To James Arlington Bennet, September 8, 1842

In April 1842, James Arlington Bennet, proprietor of a Long Island, New York, educational institution that bore his name, was appointed inspector-general of the Nauvoo Legion. A non-Mormon, Bennet's friendship was welcomed as a potential influence in the East to counter anti-Mormon sentiment then spreading in the wake of John C. Bennett's activities.[1]

When Willard Richards, Joseph Smith's secretary, traveled to Massachusetts to get his family in the summer of 1842, he stopped at the Arlington House on Long Island. He wrote of his experience, "We were most cordially welcomed by Gen. Bennett, Lady; and family consisting of one son and one daughter. His mansion is of the first order, surpassed by none in N[ew] York and few in England. . . . He is a gentleman and stands at the head of the elite of New York. He is a schollar and believing that every man should be the creator of himself, or the originator of his own resources, has applied himself with unremitting diligence to all the arts and sciences and subjects within his reach, and those not a few. His mind is of the highest order and stoops not to notice those little broils which distract the human family."

Willard Richards reported that Bennet regarded Joseph Smith "as great a prophet as Moses and a better man. But he does not believe in special revelation in any period of time. He belongs to no sect or party, and were he to join any, would as

546

soon join the Mormons as any other but does not conceive it would make him a better man to join any. If he joins any party with his present views, it would be to do them good, to defend the oppressed, for he hates persecution with a perfect hatred. One of the fundamental principles of his religion is that men should never take the life of an animal to gratify his appetite, but live on vegetables, and would Joseph make this a starting point in his creed he would join his church."

With respect to the Mormons and his Nauvoo Legion appointment, James Bennet believed "the Mormon Empire to be not of the west alone, but eventually to overrun the world. And although it is no honor to a man now to be a Mormon General . . . yet he accepts the appointment with the same good feelings it was intended by the Legion and is ready to repair to superintend the creation of fortifications &c. and suggests the appointment of George Clinton Beekman (grandson of Governor Geo. Clinton, Vice President of the United States) as his aid-de-camp, with the title of Col., if it meet the approbation of the Legion." Finally, he "wished to be remembered to the Prophet Joseph, [and] would be happy to receive a letter of his own dictation, signed by his own hand."[2]

Upon receiving Willard Richards's letter, Joseph granted Bennet's wish by dictating a letter to William Clayton and personally affixing his signature.

Nauvoo Sepr 8th 1842

Dear Sir—

I have just received your very consoling letter dated August 16th 1842; which I think, is the first letter you ever addressed to me, In which you speak of the arrival of Dr. W Richards, and of his person, very respectfully. In this, I rejoice, for I am as warm a friend to Dr Richards, as he possibly can be to me. And in relation to his almost making a Mormon of yourself, it puts me in mind of the saying of Paul in his reply to Agrippa Acts chapter 26 verse 29 "I would to God that not only thou, but also all that hear me this day, were both almost, and altogether such as I am, except these bonds." And I will here remark, my Dear sir; that Mormonism, is the pure doctrine of Jesus Christ; of which I myself am not ashamed. You speak also, of Elder Foster, president of the Church in New York, in high terms; and of Dr. Bernhisel of New York.[3] These men I am acquainted, with, by information, and it warms my heart to know that you speak well of them; and as you say could be willing to associate with them forever, if you never joined their church, or acknowledged their faith. This, is a good principle for when we see virtuous qualities in men, we should always acknowledge them, let their understanding be what it may, in relation to creeds and doctrine; for all men are, or ought to be, free; possessing inalienable rights, and the high and noble qualifications of the laws [p. 1] of nature, and of self preservation; to think, and act, and say as they please while they maintain a due respect, to the rights, and privileges of all other creatures; infringing upon none. This doctrine, I do most heartily subscribe to, and practise; the testimony of mean men, to the contrary, notwithstanding. But Sir, I will assure you, that my soul, soars far above all the mean, and grovelling dispositions of men, that are disposed to abuse me and my character; I therefore shall not dwell upon that subject. In relation to those men you speak of, referred to above; I will only say, that there are thousands of such men in this church; who, to be ⟨if a man is⟩ found worthy to associate with, will call down the envy of a mean world, because of their high and noble demeanor; and it is with unspeakable delight, that I contemplate them as my friends and brethren. I love them with a perfect love; and I hope they love me, and have no reason to doubt but they do.

The next in consideration, is John C. Bennett. I was, his friend; I am yet, his friend; as I feel myself bound to be a friend to all the sons of Adam, wether they are just or unjust; they have a degree of my compassion & sympathy. If he is my enemy, it is his own fault; and the responsibility rests upon his own head, and instead of [a]raigning his character before you; suffice it to say, that his own conduct wherever he goes, will be sufficient to recommend him to an enlightened public, wether for a bad man, or a good one. Therefore, whos[o]ever will associate themselves [p. 2] with him may be assured that I will not persecute them; but I do not wish their association; and what I have said may suffice on that subject, so far as his character is concerned. Now in relation to his book, that he may write, I will venture a prophecy, that whoever has any hand in the matter, will find themselves in a poor fix, in relation to the money matters. And as to my having any fears of the influence that he may have against me, or any other man, or set of men may have is the most foreign from my heart; for I never knew what it was, as yet, to fear the face of clay, or the influence of man. My fear, sir, is before God. I fear to offend him, and strive to keep his commandments. I am realy glad that you did not join John C. in relation to his book; from the assurances which I have, that it will prove a curse to all those who touch it. In relation to the honors that you speak of, both for yourself, and for Mr J. G. Bennett of the Herald,[4] you are ‹both› strangers to me; and as John C. Bennett kept all, his letters which he received from you, entirely to himself; and there was no correspon[den]ce between you and me that I knew of, I had no opportunity to share very largely, in the getting up of any of those matters. I could not, as I had not sufficient knowledge to enable me to do so. The whole therefore, was at the instigation of John C. Bennett, and a quiet submission on the part of the rest, out of the best of feelings. But as for myself, it was all done at a time when I was overwhelmed with a great many business cares, as well as the care of [p. 3] all the churches. I must be excused therefore for any wrongs that may have taken place, in relation to this matter. And so far as I obtain a knowledge of that which is right, shall meet with my hearty approval. I feel to tender you my most hearty & sincere thanks for every expression of kindness you have tendered toward me or my brethren, and would beg the privilege of obtruding myself a little while upon your patience in offering a short relation of my circumstances. I am at this time persecuted the worst of any man on the earth; as well as this people, here in this place; and all our sacred rights, are

trampled under the feet of the mob. I am now hunted as an hart by
the mob, under the pretense, or shadow of law, to cover their
abominable deeds. An unhallowed demand has been made from
the Governor of Missouri on oath of Governor Boggs, that I made
an attempt to assassinate him, on the night of the sixth of May,
when on that day ‹and on the seventh› it is well known ‹~~that~~ I
was attending the officers drill and answered to my name when the
role was caled› by the thousands that assembled here in Nauvoo,
that I was at my post in reviewing the Nauvoo Legion in the
presence of twelve thousand people; and the Gov. of the State of
Illinois ‹notwithstanding his being› knowing to all these facts,
‹yet he› immediately granted a writ, and by an unhallowed
usurpation, has taken away our chartered rights, and denied the
right of Habeus Corpus; and has now about thirty of the most
blood-thirsty kind of men ‹~~from Missouri~~› in this place in search
for me, threatening death, and destruction, and extermination
upon all the Mormons; and searching my house almost continually
from day to day, menacing, and threatening, [p. 4] and
intimidating an innocent wife and children; and insulting them in
a most diabolical manner, threatening their lives &c, If I am not to
be found; with a gang of Missourians with them, saying, they will
have me dead or alive, and if alive, they will carry me to Missouri
in chains; and when there, they will kill me at all hazards. And all
this is backt up, and urged on, by the Gov. of this State, with all
the rage of a demon, putting at defiance the constitution of this
State—our chartered rights, and the constitution of the United
States; for not as yet, have they done one thing that was in
accordance to them; while all the citizens of this city, *en masse*,
have petitioned the Governor with remonstrances, and overtures,
that would have melted the heart of an adamantine, to no effect.
And at the same time, if any of us open our mouths, to plead our
own cause, in the defence of law and justice, we~~th~~ are instantly
threatened with Militia & extermination Great God! When shall
the oppressor cease to prey and glut itself upon innocent blood.
Where is patriotism? Where is liberty? Where is the boast of this
proud, and haughty nation? O humanity! where has thou fled? hast

thou fled ‹forever.› I now appeal to you, sir, inasmuch as you have
subscribed yourself our friend; will you lift your voice, and your
arm, with indignation, against such unhallowed oppression? I must
say sir, that my bosom swells, with unutterable anguish, when I
contemplate the scenes of horror [p. 5] that we have pass'd through
in the State of Missouri and then look, and behold, and see the
storm, and cloud, gathering ten times blacker— ready to burst
upon the heads of this innocent people. Would to God that I were
able to throw off the yoke. Shall we bow down and be slaves? Is
there no friends of humanity, in a nation that boasts itself so much?
Will not the Nation rise up and defend us? If they will not defend
us, will they not grant, to lend a voice of indignation, against such
unhallowed oppression? Must the tens of thousands bow down to
slavery and degradation? Let the pride of the nation arise, and
wrench these shackles from the feet of their fellow citizens; and
their quiet, and peaceable, and innocent and loyal subjects. But I
must forbear, for I cannot express my feelings. The Legion, would
all willingly die in the defence of their rights; but what would this
accomplish? I have kept down their indignation, and kept a quiet
submission on all hands, and am determined to do so, at all
hazards. Our enemies shall not have it to say, that we rebel against
government, or commit treason; however much they may lift their
hands in oppression, and tyranny, when it comes in the form of
Government. We tamely submit, although it lead us to the
slaughter, and to beggary; but our blood be upon their garments,
and those who look tamely on, and boast of patriot=ism shall not
be without their condemnation. [p. 6] And if men are such fools, as
to let once, the precedent be established, and through their
prejudices, give assent, to such abomination, then let the
oppressors hand lay heavily throughout the world, untill all flesh
shall feel it together; and untill they may know, that the Almighty
takes cognizance of such things; and then shall church rise up
against church; and party against party; mob against mob; oppressor
against oppressor; army against army; and kingdom against
kingdom; and people against people; and kindred against kindred.
And where, sir, will be your safety, or the safety of your children. If

my children can be led to the slaughter with impunity, by the
hands of murderous rebels; will they not lead yours to slaughter,
with the same impunity? Ought not then, this oppression sir, to be
checked in the bud, and to be look'd down, with just indignation,
by an enlightened world; before the flame become
unexting=uishable, and, the fire devour the stubble. But, again I
say, I must forbear; and leave this painful subject. I wish you would
write to me in answer to this and let me know your views. On my
part, I am ready to be offered up a sacrifice, in that way that can
bring to pass, the greatest benifit, and good, to those who must
necessarily be interested, in this important matter. (I have dictated
this letter, while my clerk is writing for me; and) I would to God
that you could know all my feelings on this subject [p. 7] and the
real facts in relation to this people, and their unrelenting
persecution. And if any man, feels an interest in the welfare of
their fellow-beings, and would think of saying or doing any thing in
this matter, I would suggest the propriety of a committee of wise
men being sent, to ascertain the justice or injustice of our cause to
get in possession of all the facts; and then make report to an
enlightened world, wether we individually, or collectively, are
deserving such high-handed treatment.

In relation to the books that you sent here, John C. Bennett
put them into my store, to be sold on commission saying, that
when I were able, the money must be remitted to yourself. Nothing
was said about any conse=cration of the Temple.

Another calamity has befallen us; our Post Office in this place is
exceedingly corrupt. It is with great difficulty that we can get our
letters to and from our friends. Our letters are broken open and
robbed of their contents–our papers that we send to our
subscribers, are embezzled, and burned or wasted. We get no
money from our subscribers, and very little information from
abroad; and what little we do get, we get by private means, in
consequence of these things. And I am sorry to say, that this
robbing of the Post Office– of money, was carried on by John C.
Bennett, and since he left here, it is carried on by the means of his

confederat[es] I now subs-cribe myself your friend, and a patriot and lover of my country, pleading at their feet for protection, and deliverance by the justice of their constitu=tion. I add no more. Your most obedient servant

Joseph Smith.

P.S. I have dictated this letter while my clerk is writing for me

Nauvoo, Illinois, 1846. Unidentified daguerrotype. (Charles W. Carter Collection, LDS Church Archives.)

To Sidney Rigdon,
March 27, 1843

Among the early converts to Mormonism, Sidney Rigdon played a prominent role in Church government during the decade of the 1830s as a counselor to Joseph Smith. But by 1843 his influence had diminished, due partly to Rigdon's ill health and partly to a strained relationship that developed between him and the Prophet. Joseph was convinced that Rigdon was practicing "deception and wickedness" against him and the Church stemming from Rigdon's position as Nauvoo postmaster. For some time Joseph had regarded the office as "exceedingly corrupt," charging that the mail was being opened and destroyed and money stolen. To a correspondent in November 1842, he wrote, "Few if any letters for me can get through the post office in this place and more particularly letters containing money, and matters of much importance. I am satisfied that Sidney Rigdon and others connected with him have been the means of doing incalculable injury, not only to myself, but to the citizens in general; and . . . under such a state of things, you will have some idea of the difficulties I have to encounter, and the censure I have to bear through the unjust conduct of that man and others, whom he permits to interfere with the post office business."[1] In February 1843, Joseph appealed to Illinois Senator Richard M. Young, urging that an application for a change in the Nauvoo postmaster be expedited, "as the citizens generally are suffering severely from the impositions and dishonest conduct of the postmaster and those connected with the postoffice in this city."[2] Then, on March 27, the Prophet confronted Rigdon directly in this letter.

Nauvoo March 27, 1843

Sidney Rigdon Esqr.
Dear Sir,
    It is with sensations of deep regret and poignant grief that I sit down to dictate a few lines to you, this morning, to let you know what my feelings are in relation to your-self, as it is again[s]t my principles to act the part of a hypocrite, or to dissemble in any wise whatever, with any man. I have tried for a long time to smother my feelings, and not let you know, that I thought, that you were secretly and underhandedly, doing all you could, to take the advantage and injure me: but, whether my feelings are right or wrong, remains for Eternity to reveal. I cannot any longer forbear throwing of[f] the mask, and let you know of the secret wranglings of my heart; that you may not be deceived, in relation to them, and ‹that you may› be prepared, Sir, to take whatever cou[r]se you see proper in the premises. I am, Sir, honest, when I say that I believe, & am laboring under the fullest conviction that you are actually practising deception and wickedness against me and the church of Jesus Christ of Latter Day Saints. and that [p. 1] you are in connection with John C. Bennett, & Geo W. Robinson in the whole of their abomin[a]ble practices in seeking to destroy me and this people and that Jared Carter, is as deep S̶i̶r̶ in the mire, as you ‹, Sir,› are in the mire, in your conspiracies and that you are in the exercise of a trait[o]rous spirit against our lives and interest by combining with our Enemies and the murderous Missourians. My feelings, Sir, have been wrought upon to a very great extent, in relation to yourself, ever since soon after the first appearance of John C. Bennet in this place. there has been something dark & my[s]terious hovering over our business concerns that are not only palpa=b̶l̶e but altogether unaccountable in relation to the Post

office, and Sir from the very first of the pretentions of John C
Bennet, to secure to me the Post office, (which, by the by I have
‹never› desired, if I could have justice done me in that
department,) ‹without my occupancy› I have known, Sir, that it
was a fraud practiced upon me, and of the secret plottings &
conniving between, him & yourself in relation to the matter the
whole time, as well as many other things which I have kept locked
up in my own bosom but I am constrained at this time, to make
[p. 2] known my feelings to you. I do not write this with the
intention of insulting you or of bearing down upon you or with a
desire to take any advantage of you or with the inten=tion of ever
laying one straw in your way, detrimental to your character or
influence, or to suffer any thing whatever that has taken place,
which is within my observation, or that ‹has› come to my
knowledge to go abroad, betraying any confidence that has ever
been placed in me but I do assure you most sincerly that what I
have said I verily believe & this is the reason why I have said it,
that you may know the real convictions of my heart, not because I
have any malice or hatred, neither would I injure one hair of your
head, and I will assure you that these convictions are attended with
the deepest sorrow & remorse. I wish to God it were not so, & that
I could get rid of the ackings of my heart on that subject and I now
notify you. that unless something should take place to restore my
mind to its former confidence in you, by some acknowledg=ments
on your part or some explanations, that shall do away my
Jealousies, I must as a conscientious man, publish my withdrawal of
my fellowship from you, to the Church, through the medium of the
times & Seasons, and demand of the conference a hearing
concerning your case; that if on conviction of justifiable grounds,
they will [p. 2] demand your license. I could say much more but let
the above suffice for the present, yours in haste,[3]

Joseph Smith

Sidney Rigdon Esqr.
Post Office
Nauvoo [p. 3]

To Lucien Adams,
October 2, 1843

In October 1842, the *Maid of Iowa*, a small stern-wheeler steamboat, made its appearance on the Mississippi River. Built by Levi Moffit, an Augusta, Illinois, businessman, and by Dan Jones, an experienced riverboat captain, the boat was purchased by Joseph Smith and James Adams[1] the following year and began plying the rivers of the Mississippi Valley as a Mormon-owned freight-passenger-ferry-excursion boat.[2] When James Adams suddenly died of cholera in August 1843, his affairs, at least so far as the boat was concerned, were handled by his son Lucien,[3] who was the recipient of this Joseph Smith holograph note dated October 2, 1843. The bearer of the note, to whom Lucien was to pay the seventy-five dollars, was one George Stuart.

Nauvoo City Oct– 2d 1843

Mr. Lucian Adams
    Dear Sir   I have furnished the Steam boat the one hundred dollers you agreed to Send me as well as in every thing else and Set her a runing and She is like to do well She is now at St. Louis I am owing the bearer of this line Seventy five dollers in cash which I want you to pay him for me and I will apply it on you[r] Share of the boat I am most respect[f]uly you[r] Obedient Servent

Joseph Smith

557

Nauvoo City Oct 2ᵈ 1843
Mr Lucien Adams Dear
Sir I have furnished the
Steam boat the one hundred
dollers you agreed to Send me
as well as in every thing
else and Set her a running
and She is like to do well
She is now at St Louis
I am owing the bearer of this
line Seventy five dollers
in cash which I want
you to pay him for me
and I will apply it on
you Share of the boat
I am most respecfuly
you Obedient Servent
Joseph Smith

To Lucien Adams, October 2, 1843. Handwriting of Joseph Smith. See text, p. 557. (LDS Church Archives.)

To William Clayton
December 9, 1843

Having been freed early in 1843 from a harassing legal encounter with Missouri authorities, Joseph Smith was faced with another threat from that quarter following the unexpected triumph of the Democratic ticket in the Hancock County election that year. Violence was threatened on August 2 when newly elected Mormon officials arrived in Carthage to take their oath of office. Twice within a month, irate citizens met and drafted a lengthy anti-Mormon statement, one resolution of which urged the Missouri governor "to make another demand" upon Illinois "for the body of Joseph Smith" and committed themselves to serve as a posse if their services should be needed.[1]

In November and early December 1843, two Mormons living near Warsaw, Illinois, Daniel and Philander Avery, were kidnapped from Illinois and imprisoned in Missouri. Rumors circulated that others would be taken and that a legal process was being initiated against Joseph Smith. After deliberating upon the situation with the Nauvoo City Council on December 8, Joseph Smith as mayor ordered Nauvoo Legion commander Wilson Law to hold some of his men in readiness for any emergency. The next day Law wrote to Joseph Smith that to carry out his order it would be necessary to supply the men with "munitions of war" at the expense of the city, concluding, "You will therefore please to give orders to the commandants of co-

horts on their application to you on the city treasury for whatever amount you may think proper on the present occasion."²
On December 9, Joseph wrote this note to city treasurer William Clayton.

Nauvoo City Dec 9th 1843

Mr. Clayton Treasury for the City of Nauvoo
   you will Please pay out of the City funds in your hands Sixty
dollers to be paid to the commandants of Cohorts to be used in
case of defence
                              Joseph Smith
                              Mayor of said City

To William Clayton, December 9, 1843. Handwriting of Joseph Smith.
See text, p. 560. (LDS Church Archives.)

To Thomas Ford, January 1, 1844

When Daniel and Philander Avery were kidnapped and imprisoned in Missouri, Joseph Smith sent an affidavit by Delmore Chapman on December 6 outlining the situation and asked Governor Thomas Ford what should be done, noting that as mayor he would act according to his best judgment constitutionally "till I receive your instructions." He also asked if any portion of the Nauvoo Legion should be called out.[1]

On December 12, Governor Ford wrote that the militia could be mustered only to repel invasion, suppress insurrection, or meet some other emergency, but "not to suppress, prevent, or punish individual crimes." He added that kidnapping a citizen from Illinois to Missouri was indictable, but that "the Constitution and laws have provided no means whereby either the person or property taken away can be returned except by an appeal to the laws of Missouri. The Governor has no legal right to demand the return of either. . . . In every Country individuals are liable to be visited with wrong which the law is slow to redress and some of which are never redressed in this world." As to Joseph's request for relief from threats of extradition and harrassment by Missouri authorities, he replied that in August he had received many affidavits and evidence on the subject from Joseph and others. He wrote, "I have not read them and probably never will, unless a new demand should be made in which case they will receive a careful perusal and you may rest

assured, that no Steps will be taken by me but such as the Constitution and laws may require."[2]

On January 1, 1844, Joseph answered in this letter.

Nauvoo Jan'y 1 1844

Gov. Thomas Ford

Your Letter of the 12th Dec last is before me, and lest a wrong
im=pression may be imbibed, or may have been cherished by your
excellency or his friends relative to the late distur=bances of the mob
in this section as well as the outrageous act of kidnapping two citizens
of Illinois and my question whether I should call out any portion of the
Legion &c, let me say that there must have been a mis conception of
my idea as expressed in the letter, ‹and› as backed up by the affidavit
of Mr Chapman. We have never talked of sending men to Missouri ‹to
fight.› No you can not even compel a witness to go there much less an
armed force, but as Col. Levi Williams[3] (sworn to support the
constitution) had there, and still has, (if I am correctly informed
and the numerous affidavits are true) from one to three hun=dred
men well armed with rifles, pistols bowie [knives] &c to guard
himself from being taken by a warrant, now in the hands of some
constable; and as was affirmed, to kidnap a Mr Turner [p. 1] of this
city and others as reported, in addition to the two Averys already
there groaning in the prisons of Missouri I thought it advisable to
have a portion of the Legion ready to resist a mob. A burnt child
dreads the fire, and when my old friends, men women and children
look to me in the hour of danger for protection, and the wives and
children of kidnaped men beg with tears for Justice and protection I
am bound by my o[a]th of office and by all laws human and divine
to grant it. I have always said I should act constitutionally. I know I
have no power to call out men to go to Missouri, or to take Col
Williams. the constable can take such a posse as he pleases, or the
sheriff may, if necessary to affect the ends of Justice, call out the
power of the county, and I as Mayor of the city of Nauvoo, have

power when an armed mob has been organized for weeks, and carried off to another state innocent citizens, and flung them into prisons, and threaten to take more and if resisted, say they will slaughter the inhabitants of the city, and swear [p. 2] "if the Governor opens his mouth, they will punch a hole in him." I say I have power to call upon any portion of the Legion to resist them and keep the peace of the city, and from the good opinion I have of your excellency and the favorable reports from others of your excellencys honorable intentions for all laudable citizens, and a high minded spirit to magnify the Law and make it efficent. I know I shall merit your sanction for honest endeav[o]r to keep the peace, and shall be boul=stered up by the Governors cordial co=operation in every move that is virtuous, patriotic, and wise.

I would say Orin P. Rockwell has just returned from about ‹nine› months prison service in Missouri,[4] and tha‹t› he has had to walk upon the burning ploughshare, with bare feet. they are unblistered. and his garments are unscorched. he has suffered innocently. who will not see the injustice of Missouri? Mr Rockwell rec[eiv]ed an honorable acquittal from a Jury in the very hot bed of mobbery and Boggs violence. Mr Daniel [p. 2] Avery too, as per affidavit is fairly discharged. And what will your excel=lency direct as to the three Missourians named in Mr Averys affidavit who kidnaped him from Illinois?

Your Excellencys opinion that the Nauvoo Legion are ‹part of the› Militia of the State of Illinois, seems so consistent with the spirit and genius of the charter and the common law of the land, as well as the intention of our consti=tutions, that the Attorneys Generals opinions, to the contrary notwithstanding, are some what like an eclipse on the opposite side of the earth, *"to us in visible!"*

With a devout calculation to magnify the law and safely confide in it, and the integrity of its executors, I, as well as the Latter day Saints generally, will be sure that the Missourians, and disaffected Illinoisans, are law breakers, aggressors and made themselves guilty before we move with‹out› counsel, and not then but for self defence. We [always] let our enemies violate law. With highest consideration &c.

Joseph Smith

A Mark Hofmann forgery

Joseph Smith III Blessing, January 17, 1844

In March 1844, in anticipation of a time that others would be required to carry on the work he had begun, Joseph Smith conferred upon the Council of the Twelve "keys of authority" and the responsibility "of bearing off the kingdom." According to Orson Hyde, the Twelve received this commission on March 23, 1844, during a meeting of the Council of Fifty at Nauvoo. However, two months earlier, the Prophet had blessed his eleven-year-old son, Joseph Smith III, expressing a hope that he too would someday play a major role in the leadership of the Church. The blessing was given on January 17, 1844, at Nauvoo in a private council meeting attended by about two dozen people at Joseph Smith's red brick store, and it suggests that at that time the Prophet anticipated a place for his own posterity in the future leadership of the kingdom and that his hopes for them were not incompatible with the apostolic possession of the keys of authority.[1]

A blessing, given to Joseph Smith, 3rd, by his father, Joseph Smith, Jun., on Jany 17. 1844.

Blessed of the Lord is my son Joseph, who is called the third,— for the Lord knows the integrity of his heart, and loves him, because of his faith, and righteous desires. And, for this cause, has the Lord raised him up;—that the promises made to the fathers might be fulfilled, even that the anointing of the progenitor shall be upon the head of my son, and his seed after him, from generation to generation. For, he shall be my successor to the Presidency of the High Priesthood: a Seer, and a Revelator, and a Prophet, unto the Church; which appointment belongeth to him by blessing, and also by right.

Verily, thus saith the Lord: if he abides in me, his days shall be lengthened upon the earth, but, if he abides not in me, I, the Lord, will receive him, in an instant, unto myself.

When he is grown, he shall be a strength to his brethren, and a comfort to his mother. Angels will minister unto him, and he will be wafted as on eagle's wings, and be as wise as serpents, even a multiplicity of blessings shall be his. Amen.

Jany 17. 1844.
Joseph Smith 3
blessing

To Reuben McBride,
January 18, 1844

To Joseph Coe,
January 18, 1844

Following the untimely death of Oliver Granger in 1841, Reuben McBride[1] was appointed in his place as agent to regulate business affairs of the Church in Kirtland, Ohio. McBride's grasp of the local situation proved invaluable when a claim was made against Joseph Smith's Kirtland farm by Joseph Coe who was renting the place in January 1844. Coe, a charter member of the Kirtland high council in 1834 had helped purchase the Egyptian mummies in 1835. Two years later he allied himself with dissenters and left the Church. In a January 1844 letter to Joseph Smith, he claimed that his part in the purchase of the mummies had never been repaid and that an agreement to do so with Joseph's father through a gift of land had been ignored. "Cannot you make arangements with your brother William for his house and lot, or with Hyram for his, or let me have the use of this farm over which you are sole trustee in trust," he queried. He added that he would be glad to occupy the Prophet's Kirtland farm "for several years to come" provided he could "dictate the policy in relation to its management."[2]

Having learned that Coe had written to Joseph Smith, Reuben McBride notified the Prophet of the situation respecting him. Reuben stated that he had allowed Joseph Coe to rent the Prophet's farm at a reasonable fee of ninety dollars per year plus taxes, but that Coe had failed to pay the tax and half the rent in 1842, and although promising to settle the account, had paid nothing in 1843. Reuben added that the property tax was now due and that it would be difficult to raise enough money to keep the farm from being sold. He further noted that Joseph Coe did not intend to pay the rent or the tax because of his claims against the Church. "I give it as my belief that if he had the place and no one [were] here to see to it he would let it be sold for tax and bid it off himself and get a sheriff's deed of it, for he certainly would [have] let it be sold this year if I were not here," he concluded.[3]

On January 18 Joseph responded to both men, first to Reuben McBride and then to Joseph Coe.

Nauvoo January 18. 1844

Dear Brother

Your letter of the 1st instant was received last evening, its contents have been duly considered and I now proceed to reply.

I have also received a letter from Joseph Coe requesting me to let him have the place &c I shall answer his letter this morning. At the same time I want you to take measures to remove him from the farm forthwith, for I am tired of hearing the report of its liability to be sold for taxes &c I consider that he has treated me mean, and I am under no obligations to let him have the place on any terms, and do not intend he shall have it. I also want you to use all necessary means to collect that portion of the rent which is due from him, although I have little hopes of your being able to do much with him, but collect it if you can.

You had better rent the place to some responsible person who will give sufficient securities for the rent, at the same time binding them to keep all the Taxes regularly paid, and also to keep the place in sufficient repair. For if you do not put the person under sufficient bonds who rents the place, to pay the Taxes regularly you will be for ever harassed with arrearages and the land will be sold and consequently adding cost to cost until it use up the principal.

There is a straight way to do all things and it is invariably the safest and the best, and when good security is given, for a sufficient amount, there is no further trouble, or anxiety about the danger of losing either rent, or having it sold for Taxes.

As to the idea of suffering a part of it to be sold for Taxes, it is very far from meeting with my approbation. I do not want it to be sold on any pretext whatever, and lest there is a possibility that some part of it may have already been sold I wish you to make every necessary enquiry and see that it is all right and safe.

As to the choice of a person for a tenant I leave that to your own judgment, only be careful to have writings sufficiently strong to keep the premises safe and free from further trouble if possible. It matters little to me who occupies the premises so that the property is not wasted or destroyed, and the rent is duly paid.

We are doing well in Nauvoo, the city is in a flourishing condition, and it is a time of general good health, with some few exceptions.

Our enemies occasionally boil over, and vent their foam and rage; but it all blows over easy and we are now enjoying a pleasant calm.

The work prospers as ever, and the kindness of the God whom we serve, in preserving us and blessing us with good things causes our hearts to rejoice from day to day.

Praying that God may bless you and give you wisdom to do all things for the best I close for the present, in the mean time I remain as ever your undeviating friend and brother in the new and Everlasting Covenant.

Joseph Smith

Mr. R. McBride

Nauvoo Jany 18. 1844

Dr. Sir

I have received a letter from you dated the 1st inst., concerning some pretended claim you seem to think you have on the Mummies, and also requesting me to let you have the use of my farm for a longer Season &c, as a recompense for your interest in the Mummies.

I have received information from an authentic source, that Brother McBride has not been able to realize much rent from you for the place and also that you have neglected to pay ~~your~~ ⟨the⟩ taxes. Now I am satisfied that you know you wrong me when you thus expose my property for sale for the Taxes, and at the same time are reaping the fruits of it. I must confess that I feel very much dissatisfied with the course you are pursuing in relation to the matter. Brother McBride is my authorized Agent to attend to matters and affairs in Kirtland. I shall give him such instructions as I deem expedient about the matter.

The idea of your claiming an Interest in the Mummies astonishes me. You must either be under the influence of very corrupt feelings, or be very forgetful of your business transactions. However it may be that you have forgot some things, and I will therefore inform you by way of putting you in remembrance that I have got your Deed, executed by your own hand, in due form, for all the interest you ever held in the Mummies, and consequently dont feel under the necessity of listening to such unjust claims, nor taking any notice of them, only as above stated.

It is astonishing that any man can be so wicked and corrupt as to suffer the property of his benefactor and best friend to be sold in order to defraud him out of it by getting a Sheriffs Deed, surely the shades of darkness prevail over such a man; his heart must be hard as the nether-mill-stone, and virtue have no place in him. The tenor of your letter and other information I have received tells a black story of the situation of the Apostates in Kirtland.

On the place where Godliness and uprightness once dwelt, now dwells dishonesty, fraud, envy, lying, oppression and every evil work.

But enough on this subject, I must conclude and turn my attention to a more pleasing and profitable subject

Yours &c
Joseph Smith

Mr. Joseph Coe.

2

To Reuben McBride, January 18, 1844. Handwriting of Thomas Bullock. See text, pp. 568-69. (LDS Church Archives.)

To Joseph L. Heywood, February 13, 1844

Joseph L. Heywood was born in Grafton, Worcester County, Massachusetts, on August 1, 1815. He spent his early years on his father's farm. As a young man of twenty-two, he moved to Illinois, where, in the fall of 1839, he established a mercantile business in Quincy with his brother-in-law, Oliver Kimball. Three years later, he visited Joseph Smith and was converted to the Church. When the Latter-day Saints commenced their exodus from Nauvoo in 1846, Heywood, along with Almon Babbitt and John S. Fullmer, was chosen as one of the trustees to supervise the disposal of Church property. After arriving in the Salt Lake Valley in 1848, he was named postmaster of Salt Lake City and bishop of the Seventeenth Ward. He helped John M. Bernhisel at the nation's capitol obtain a territorial government for Utah and was appointed U.S. marshal for the newly created Utah Territory. As a colonizer, Heywood supervised the settling of Salt Creek, later Nephi, in Juab County, Utah, in 1851, and in the spring of 1855 accompanied Orson Hyde in the founding of the Mormon settlement at Carson Valley. In 1861 he moved to southern Utah, where he spent the remainder of his life and for many years was a Church patriarch. He died in Panguitch on October 16, 1910.[1]

Early in 1844, while still living in Quincy, Illinois, the young merchant invited Joseph Smith to visit him and the Saints in Quincy. The Prophet responded on February 13.

Nauvoo Feby 13th 1844

Dear Brother Heywood

I sit down at this time to acknowledge the receipt of, and reciprocate the friendly feelings manifest in, yours of the 7th inst, and although surrounded by a press of business shall take pleasure in spending a few moments to reply.

I would take the greatest pleasure imaginable in coming down to Quincy on a visit to see you and all my friends in your City would business & circumstance permit, but it would be a matter of impossibility almost for me [to] leave home at the present time in conse=quence of a multitude of business which I have daily to attend to; Moreover wisdom and prudence seem to forbid my coming on account of the bitter feeling which manifests itself in various places between this ~~place~~ and Quincy not that I have any apprehen=sions for my personal safety, for the same kind hand which hath hitherto been my shield and support would save me from the power of my wicked persecutors but ~~you know~~ something might grow out of it which would prompt my adversaries to get out another illegal writ and would eventually probably cost me ⟨some⟩ three or four thousand dollars as in other cases and under which I have still to labor to disadvantage. Under these considerations therefore, I am compelled to decline paying you a visit for the present, at the same [p. 1] time in connexion with Mrs Smith I tender my warmest acknowledgements for the invitation.

I am pleased to hear of the prosperity of your branch and hope it will continue, for although I never feel to force my doctrines ~~(or rather the doctrines revealed to me of God)~~ upon any person I rejoice to see prejudice give way to truth, and the traditions of men dispersed by the pure principles of the Gospel of Jesus Christ.

I should be pleased to have the privilege of forming an acquaintance with your partner Mr Kimball and his lady, and should they ever come up this way I hope they will call and see me.

As respects things in Nauvoo I have nothing to say but good. Although the mobocrats of this county breath out their shame with a continual foam and threaten extermination &c the citizens of Nauvoo are at peace, they fear no danger for the ~~sound~~ ‹report› of mobs have become so common, that the Mormons pay no attention to it whatever. Each man minds his own business and all are making improvements as fast as they can. In fact things in general seem prosperous and pleasing and I never saw a better feeling amongst the saints than at the present time.

My family have been some sick of late ~~but are now improving in health and are out of danger~~ ‹and continue so, especially my youngest boy›

Accept dear sir the warmest respects of myself and Mrs Smith & please present the same to your lady in the mean time I remain your friend and brother

Joseph Smith

To Barbara Matilda Neff, May 1844

John Neff, born in 1794 in Strasburg, Lancaster County, Pennsylvania, was a man of wealth and influence with extensive land, livestock, and other business holdings. In 1821 he married Mary Barr, also of Lancaster County, and the couple subsequently raised a family of ten children. In 1842 the Neffs joined the Church, and two years later they traveled to Nauvoo to meet the Prophet Joseph Smith.[1] During this visit, while staying in the Mansion House between May 8 and 13, 1844, twenty-two-year-old Barbara Matilda, the Neff's eldest daughter, collected autographs from prominent Nauvoo citizens. Among those who wrote in her book were William W. Phelps and Joseph Smith.[2] William W. Phelps wrote

> To Miss B[arbara] M[atilda] Neff
> Two things will beautify a youth
> That is: Let *virtue* decorate the *truth*
> and so you know; every little helps
> yours— W.W. Phelps

Continuing his clerk's train of thought, Joseph Smith added these lines.

The truth and virtue both are good
When rightly understood
But Charity is better Miss
That takes us home to bliss
and so forthwith
remember Joseph Smith

To Barbara Matilda Neff, May 1844. Handwriting of Joseph Smith. See text, p. 576. (LDS Church Archives.)

To Joel Hamilton Walker,
June 1, 1844

Having learned, probably from the newspapers, that Joseph Smith had petitioned the United States Congress for authority to raise a force of 100,000 volunteers to protect and defend the southern and western borders of the United States, including those Americans who had migrated into Texas and Oregon, Joel Hamilton Walker of Boston, Massachusetts, wrote to the Prophet on May 9, 1844, expressing an interest in the undertaking and offering his services. Walker, besides having "devoted much attention" to military study and having "an ardent love for the art," also claimed an academic and mercantile education and inquired if there were anything in Nauvoo "which would be for our mutual advantage."[1]

Joseph Smith's reply follows.

Nauvoo, Ill. June 1, 1844.

Sir:– Yours of May 9 is before ‹me› and according to my custom, I answer off hand. I have not yet ascertained whether Congress will, by special act, authorize me to protect our beloved country: if it should I have not a doubt but your services could be agreeably used.

As to what you could do in Nauvoo, I am unable to say. Gentlemen with a small capital, or a large one, can easily employ it to good advantage, our City is so rapidly improving.

578

Truth, virtue and honor combined with energy and industry, pave the way to exaltation, glory and bliss. Respectfully
I have the honor to be your Ob Sert

Joseph Smith

Joel Hamilton Walker
Boston Mass

To Mr. Tewksbury,
June 4, 1844

In April 1842, Freeman Nickerson, presiding elder of the Church in Boston, Massachusetts, reviewed the progress of the Church since his arrival there in May 1841. He wrote that after participating several months in the free discussions of religion at Winchester Hall, "one of the number which was called infidels," Abijah Tewksbury, was the first to be baptized. Tewksbury had opened his shipping office to preaching, and in September 1842 he represented the Boston Branch, consisting of seventy-seven members, at a conference held in Salem, Massachusetts. Church annals contain no further references to Tewksbury, but it is evident that he later left the Church.[1] Recording Joseph Smith's activities for the afternoon of June 4, 1844, in the Prophet's diary, Willard Richards noted, among other things, that Joseph "wrote Mr Tewksbury, Boston."

Nauvoo Ill. June 4, 1844.

Sir: We understand that you have been cut off from the church of Jesus Christ of Latter Day Saints, and feeling an ardent desire for the salvation of the souls of men, we take pleasure in feeling after you: and therefore would in the sincerity of men of God advise you to be rebaptised by Elder Nickerson ‹one of the servants of God› that you may again receive the sweet influences of

580

the holy Ghost, and enjoy the fellowship of the Saints ‹the law of God requires it and you cannot be too good› Patience is heavenly; obedience is noble: forgivness is merciful; and exaltation is Godly: and he that holds out faithful to the end shall in no wise lose his reward. A good man will endure all things to honor Christ, and dispose of the whole world and all in it to save his soul grace for grace is a heavenly decree, and union is power where wisdom guides

> Respectfully even
> Joseph Smith
> Hyrum Smith

To Washington Tucker, June 12, 1844

In the midst of the furor brought on by the *Expositor* affair,[1] Joseph Smith paused briefly on June 12 to answer a letter from an inquirer in Eldorado, Union County, Arkansas. On May 4, Washington Tucker had written of his interest in the Church after talking with a missionary and reading some Church litera- ture. Mr. Tucker reported that "hundreds who never before heard of the new revelation are opening their eyes and staring and gaping to know more about it" and that it was the general wish of a great many in Union County to have a minister sent who could instruct them more fully.[2] Joseph Smith responded in this letter.

Nauvoo Ill. June 12, 1844.

Sir:— Your letter dated May 4, has reached me, and its contents duly considered. A multiplicity of business keeps me from writing as freely to correspondents as I could wish, still my heart is large enough for all men and my sensibilities keen enough to have compassion for every case when justice mercy virtue, or humanity requires it, be pleased to accept my thanks for your very kind letter; study the bible; as many of our books as you can get; pray to the Father in the name of Jesus Christ, have faith on the promises made to the fathers, and your mind will be guided to the *truth*, An

582

Elder shall be sent as soon as the "Twelve" can make the necessary arrangements. In the gospel of our Lord Jesus Christ
I am your obdt Sevt

Joseph Smith

Washington Tucker
Edward
Ark

The building on the right is possibly the original Nauvoo Expositor building, Nauvoo, Illinois. The photograph was taken by B. H. Roberts in 1886. (LDS Church Archives.)

To Washington Tucker, June 12, 1844. Handwriting of John McEwan. See text, pp. 582-83. (LDS Church Archives.)

To Thomas Ford,
June 14, 1844

When Mormon dissenters (some of whom had been prominent in Church and civic affairs in Nauvoo) published a slanderous newspaper, the Nauvoo Expositor, on June 7, 1844, a situation developed that culminated in the death of Joseph and Hyrum Smith less than a month later. Perceiving the Expositor as a threat to the peace of the community, the Nauvoo City Council, after lengthy deliberations on June 8 and 10, declared the paper a public nuisance and instructed the mayor to remove the establishment and its contents "without delay, in such a manner as he shall direct." Whereupon Joseph Smith ordered the marshal to destroy the press, scatter the type, and burn all the copies of the paper, which order was executed about 8 P.M. on June 10. No sooner was this done than the proprietors of the Expositor brought legal action against Joseph Smith and other members of the Nauvoo City Council on a charge of riot. On June 12 Joseph was arrested by Constable David Bettisworth on a writ that ordered him to be brought before the Hancock County justice of the peace, Thomas Morrison, at Carthage, "or some other justice of the peace." Later that day, the Prophet was released on a petition of habeas corpus before the Nauvoo Municipal Court, and the other members of the city council were freed the next day.[1]

As news spread of the destruction of the Expositor and the seemingly flagrant ease with which Joseph Smith and the members of the city council avoided legal consequences, indignant county residents held meetings and adopted resolutions, and the Hancock County countryside took on the appearance of an armed camp as determined men prepared to take the law into their own hands. On June 14, amidst threats of open violence, Joseph summarized for Governor Ford the decision to destroy the *Expositor*.

Nauvoo June 14, 1844.

His Excellency Thomas Ford.

Sir— I write you this morning, briefly to inform you of the facts relative to the removal of the Press and fixtures of the "Nauvoo Expositor["] as a nuisance.

The 8th and 10th instant were spent by the city council of Nauvoo, in receiving testimony concerning the character of the Expositor, and the character and designs of the proprietors.

In the investigation it appeared evident to the council that the proprietors were a set of unprincipled men, lawless, debouchees, counterfeiters, Bogus Makers, gamblers, peace disturbers, and that the grand object of said proprietors was to destroy our constitutional rights and chartered pri=vileges; to overthrow all good and wholesome regulations in society; to strengthen themselves against the municipality; to fortify themselves against against the church of which I am a member, and destroy all our religious rights and privileges, by libels, slanders, falsehoods, perjury & stick=ing at no corruption to accomplish their hellish purposes. and that said paper of itself was libelous of the deepest dye, and very injurious as a vehicle of defamation,– tending to corrupt the morals, and disturb the peace, tranquillity and happiness of the whole community, and especially that of Nauvoo.

After a long and patient investigation of the character of the Expositor, and the characters and designs of its proprietors thereof – the constitution, the charter, [p. 1] (see adenda, to Nauvoo charter from the springfield charter, Sec 7) and all the best

authorities on the subject. (See Blackstone III, 5. and n. &c &c);
The city council decided that it was necessary for the "peace,
benefit, good order, and regulations" of said city. "and for the
protection of property" and for "the happiness and prosperity of the
citizens of Nauvoo" that said Expositor should be removed; and,
declaring said Expositor a nuisance, ordered the Mayor– to cause
them to be removed without delay, which order was committed to
the Marshall, by due process, and by him executed the same day.
by remov=ing the paper, press, and fixtures into the street, and
burning the same, all which was done without riot, noise, tumult,
or confusion, as has already be[en] proved before the municipality
of the city, and the particulars of the whole transactions may be
expec=ted in our next "Nauvoo Neighbor".

 I send you this hasty sketch that your Excellency may be aware
of the lying reports that are now being circulated by our enemies,—
that there has been a *"mob at Nauvoo"*, *"and blood and thunder"* and
"swearing that two men were killed" &c &c as we hear from abroad,–
are false,– false as Satan himself could invent, and that nothing has
been transacted here but what has been in perfect accordance with
the strictest principles of law and good [p. 2] order, on the part of
the authorities of this city,– and if your Excellency is not satisfied,
and shall not be satisfied, after reading the whole proceedings
which will be forth coming soon, and shall demand an
investigation of our municipality before Judge Pope or any legal
tribunal at the Capital, you have only to write your wishes – and
we will be forth coming: we will not trouble you to fill a writ or
send an officer for us.

 I remain as ever a friend to truth, good order and your Ex's.
humble Sert.

Joseph Smith

His Ex. Thomas Ford [p. 3]

His Excellency
Thomas Ford – Govr.
Springfield Illinois

Politeness of Mr S. James Special Messenger [p. 4]

To Thomas Ford, June 16, 1844

To Isaac Morley, June 16, 1844

To John Smith, June 17, 1844

In the face of public clamor against Joseph Smith and the Nauvoo City Council over the destruction of the *Expositor*, Judge Jesse B. Thomas, Justice of the Illinois Supreme Court and circuit judge of Adams and Hancock Counties, came to Nauvoo on June 16. He advised Joseph Smith that although he had been freed by action of the Nauvoo municipal court, he should go before another magistrate, not of the Mormon faith. This action, it was felt, would "allay all excitement, answer the law, and cut off all legal pretext for a mob." Hence, the following day, Joseph Smith and the others indicted with him appeared before Hancock County justice Daniel Wells, where, after "a long and close examination," they were again discharged.[1]

In the meantime, word came to Nauvoo that fifteen hundred Missourians were about to cross into Illinois, where they would join forces with others to harass the Saints in outlying areas and then proceed to the city and demand Joseph and Hyrum Smith. Joseph also received a letter from Isaac Morley, living at the Morley settlement, and one from his uncle, John Smith, at Macedonia, informing him of impending mob action. Isaac Morley, a colonel in the Nauvoo Legion, stated that he had been approached by a local committee and told that Joseph Smith and seventeen others had broken the law and that the Saints at Morley settlement had three alternatives:

take up arms and proceed with the outsiders to arrest Joseph Smith, take necessary effects and flee to Nauvoo, or give up their arms and remain quiet "until the fuss is over."[2] Joseph's response to the situation is found in his letters of June 16 to Governor Ford and Isaac Morley and June 17 to John Smith.

Nauvoo Ill: June 16. 1844

His Excellency
Thomas Ford

Sir I am informed from credible sources as well as from the proceedings of a public meeting at Carthage &c as published in the "Warsaw Signal" extra, that an energetic attempt is being made by some of the citizens of this and the surrounding counties to drive and exterminate "the Saints" by force of arms. And I send this information to your Excellency by a Special Messenger Hugh McFall – Adjutant ‹General – Nauvoo Legion –› who will give all particulars, and I ask at your hands, immediate council and protection.

Judge Thomas has been here and given his advice in the Case which I shall strictly follow until I hear from your Excellency – and in all cases shall adhere to the Constitution and Laws.

The Nauvoo Legion is at your service to quell all insurrections and support the dignity of the common weal.

I wish, urgently wish your Excellency to come down in person with your Staff, and investigate the whole matter, without delay and cause peace to be restored to the Country – and I know not but this will be the only means of stopping an effusion of blood

The information referred to above is before me, by affidavit

I remain Sir the friend of peace, and your Excellency's humble servant

Joseph Smith

His Excellency
Thomas Ford [p. 1]

His Excellency
Thomas Ford
Governor of Illinois
Springfield

per Gen: McFall [p. 2]

Head Quarters, Nauvoo
Legion, Lieut Gens office
Nauvoo June 16, 1844.

Col Isaac Morley

Sir In reply to yours of this date, you will take special notice
~~you will take special notice~~ of the movements of the mob party,
that is stirring up strife and endeavoring to excite rebellion to the
government, and destroy the saints, and cause all the troops of said
Legion in your vicinity to be in readiness to act at a moments
warning. And if the mob shall fall upon the saints by force of arms
defend them at every hazard, unless prudence dictates the retreat of
the troops to Nauvoo, in which case the mob will not disturb your
women and children. And if the mob move towards Nauvoo,
either come before them or on their rear, and be ready to cooperate
with the main body of the Legion– Instruct the companies to keep
cool, and let all things be done decently and in order. Give
information by affidavit before a magistrate, & special messengers
to the Governor of what has occurred, and every illegal
proceedings that shall be had on the subject without delay. Also
notify me of the same, and demand instruction and protection from
the governor.

> Joseph Smith,
> Lieut Gen Nauvoo Legion

Col Isaac Morley

Nauvoo June 17th 1844

Uncle John:—

Dear Sir:— The brethren from Ramus arrived here this morning, We were glad to see them and to hear that you were all alive in the midst of the ragings of an infatuated and blood thirsty mob. I write these few lines to inform you that we feel determined in this place not to be dismayed if hell boils over all at once. We feel to hope for the best, and determined to prepare for the worst. And we want this to be your motto in common with us, "that we will never ground our arms untill we give them up by death—" "*Free trade and sailors rights, protection of persons and property, wives and families*". If a mob annoy you, defend yourselves to the very last, and if they fall upon you with a superior force, and if you think you are not able to compete with them, retreat to Nauvoo. But we hope for better things, but remember if your enemies do fall upon you be sure and take the best and most efficient measures the emergency of the case may require. Remember the front and the rear of your enemies, because if they should come to Nauvoo to attack Nauvoo unlawfully, and by mob force, a little annoyance upon the rear with some bold fellows would be a very good thing to weaken the ranks of an enemy It is impossible to give you correct information what to do beforehand, but act according to the emmergency of the case [p. 1] but never give up your arms, but die first. The brethren will give you information of the conversation between us. We have sent to the Governor and are about to send again and we want you to send affidavits and demand the attention of the Governor, and request protection at his hand in common with the rest of us, that by our continual wearing we may get him to come in and investigate the whole matter.

I now conclude with my best wishes and must refer you to the brethren for further information.

Joseph Smith
Mayor of the City of Nauvoo
and Leutenant Gen of Nauvoo Ledgion

To Thomas Ford,
June 22, 1844

Anticipating an attack upon Nauvoo, Joseph Smith placed the city under martial law on June 18, ordering the police and Nauvoo Legion to see that no persons or property be allowed to pass in or out of the city without permission. Three days later, on June 21, alarmed by the excitement in Hancock County, Governor Ford arrived at Carthage to investigate the matter, "preserve the peace and enforce the laws." To better understand the situation, he immediately requested of Joseph Smith, the Nauvoo mayor, that one or more well-informed persons be sent to give him the Mormon side of the difficulties.[1] Immediately, John Bernhisel and John Taylor were dispatched to Carthage with information. The next morning the Prophet sent Lucien Woodworth with additional details and the following letter to Governor Ford.

Nauvoo Saturday Morning
June 22nd 1844

To His Excellency
Thomas Ford Governor
Dear Sir:— I this morning forward you the remainder of the affidavits which are ready to present to you ‹by the hands of a gentleman who is fully competent to give you›[2] information on the whole subject which have been the cause of the origin of our

592

present difficulties. I would respectfully recommend the bearers Col Woodworth as one of my aids & men [3] whose testimonies can be relied upon.

I presume you are already convinced that it would be altogether unsafe for me or any of the city council to come to Carthage on account of the vast excitement which has been got up by false report and libellous publications. Nothing would afford me a greater pleasure than a privilege of investigating the whole subject before your Excellency in person, for I have ever held my=self in readiness to comply with your orders and answer for my proceedings before any legal tribunal in the state.

I would hereby respectfully pray your Excellency to come to Nauvoo, if congenial with your feelings and give us a privilege of laying the whole matter before you in its true colors, and where abundance of testimony can be forthcoming to prove every point by disinterested persons; ‹men of character and of worth and notoriety› strangers, who were here all the time, but I am satisfied your Excellency does not wish men to expose the lives of the citizens of this place by requiring them to put themselves into the power of an infuriated, blood thirsty mob, a part of whom have already several times fired upon our people without the least shadow of cause or provocation. [p. 1]

I am informed this morning that some gentleman has made affidavit that he had a private conversation with me in which I stated that I had secret correspondence with you &c. If any person has been wicked enough to do this he is a perjured villian, for in the first place I do not suffer myself to hold private conversation with any stranger, and in the second place I have never even intimated any thing of the kind as having secret correspondence with your Excellency.

Our troubles are invariably brought upon us by falsehood & misrepresentations by designing men, we have ever held our=selves amenable to the law, and for myself Sir, I am ever ready to conform to and support the laws and constitution even at the expense of my life, I have never in the least offered any resistance to law, or lawful

process which is a fact well known[4] to the public, all of which
circumstances make us the more anxious to have you come to
Nauvoo and investigate the whole matter.

Now Sir is it not an easy matter to distinguish between those
who have pledged themselves to exterminate innocent men,
women and children, and those who have only stood in their own
defence and in defence of their innocent families and that to‹o› in
accordance with the constitution & laws of the country as required
by their oaths and as good and law abiding citizens.

In regard to the destruction of the press the truth only needs to
be presented before your Excellency to satisfy you of the Justice of
the proceedings. The press was established by a set of men who had
already set themselves at defiance of the [p. 2] laws, ‹and›
authorities of the city and had threatened the lives of some of its
principle officers, and who also made in ‹it no› private matter that
the press was established for the express purpose of destroy=ing the
city and as will be shown by the affidavit of Joseph Jackson[5] and as
they stated to me in their threats.

Mr Babbit informs me that reports are in circulation that we
have taken property which belongs to ‹the› Mr Law‹s› and others.

There has been no property meddled with to my knowledge
belonging to any person, except property we have purchased of the
rightful owners, Mr Law turned over some property to a Mr Hicks
to pay a debt. This I purchased of Mr Hicks and I am responsible to
him for the amount. We have been especially careful to preserve
the property of those who are exciting the public against us
inasmuch as we knew ‹that› every means would be used which
could be invented to raise excitement and we have appointed the
police to watch this property and see that no harm was done to it
by any person as they had tried to fire their own building and was
detected in the act, the fire was extinguished by the policemen and
no property damaged.

There has ‹been› no prisoners been taken in this city neither
any persons held as hostage only some ‹who are› residents of this

place who had broke the laws, no stranger has been interfered with, nor detained in the city, under any circumstances.

In haste I have the honor to remain Dr Sir your most obedt. Sevt.

Joseph Smith
L Genl N L

To Emma Smith, June 23, 1844

To Maria and Sarah Lawrence, June 23, 1844

After reviewing the Mormon evidence and Joseph Smith's letter of June 22, Governor Ford answered at length later the same day, stating that at its center the existing excitement in Hancock County was due to the destruction of the *Expositor* "and the subsequent refusal of the individuals accused to be accountable" according to the laws of the state. After considering the facts in the case, the Governor expressed his opinion that Joseph's "conduct in the destruction of the press was a very gross outrage upon the laws and liberties of the people." He admitted that the sheet "may have been full of libels, but this did not authorize you to destroy it." He identified four violations of the Constitution in the destruction of the press and concluded that the only solution would be for the guilty parties to submit "implicitly to the process of the court." He added, "The whole country is now up in arms, and a vast number of people are ready to take the matter into their own hands. Such a state of things might force me to call out the militia to prevent a civil war. And such is the excitement of the country that I fear the militia, when assembled, would be beyond legal control." He warned, however, that if those accused did not submit, "I will be obliged to call out the militia; and if a few thousand will not be sufficient, many thousands will be." The Governor concluded by guaranteeing the safety of all persons brought to Carthage from Nauvoo either for trial or as witnesses.[1]

596

In response, also on June 22, Joseph defended the action of the city officials in destroying the *Expositor* on the ground that "the loss of character by libel and the loss of life by mobocratic prints" was a greater loss "than a little property." Joseph argued that his appeal to the municipal court on *habeas corpus* and his appearance before Justice Wells had been in accordance with the law as interpreted by "the ablest counsel," and if lawyers had belied their profession, "the evil be upon their heads." He insisted that his action was not an act of insolence but "a last resort to save us from being thrown into the power of the mob." To the governor's order that the guilty parties submit immediately to trial, Joseph wrote, "We would not hesitate to stand another trial . . . were it not that we are confident our lives would be in danger. We dare not come. . . . And although your Excellency might be well-disposed in the matter, the appearance of the mob forbids our coming. We dare not do it." He pointed out further that mass meetings in the county were urging the "utter extermination" of the Mormons. In the face of these threats, the Prophet concluded to "leave the city forthwith to lay the facts before the General Government."[2]

At daybreak on June 23, Joseph crossed the Mississippi River westward with his brother Hyrum and Willard Richards with the ultimate anticipation of heading east. The place of William Jordan in Montrose was evidently the "Safety" whence he wrote these letters to Emma and to Maria and Sarah Lawrence.

Safety June 23

Emma Smith

Brother Lewis has some money of mine—H.C. Kimball has $1000, in his hand of mine, Br [John] Neff, Lancaster Co, Pa.,— $400,

You may sell the Quincy Property.—or any property that

belongs to me you can find any thing about, for your support and children & mother. Do not dispair—If god ever opens a door that is possible for me I will see you again. I do not know where I shall go, or what I shall do, but shall if possible endeavor to get to the city of washington.

May God Almighty bless you & the children & mother & all my friends. My heart ble[e]ds, no more at present. If you conclude to go to Kirtland, Cincinnati, or any other place, I wish you would contrive to inform me, this evening.

Joseph Smith

P.S. If in your power I want you should help Dr Richards' family. [p. 1]

Mrs Emma Smith
Nauvoo [p. 2]

Montrose, June 23, 1844.
9 O Clock A.M.

Dear Maria & Sarah:[1]—I take opportunity this morning to communicate to you two some of the peepings of my heart; for you know my thoughts for you & for the City & fo people that I love. God bless & protect you all! Amen. I dare not linger in Nauvoo Our enimies shall not cease their infernal howling until they have drunk my lifes blood. I do not know what I shall do. or where I shall go, but if possi=ble I will try to interview with President Tyler.[2] Perhaps California or Austin [Texas] will be more sy[m]pethetic. Speak of this to no one I want you two to make arrangements with R. Cahoon for passage at your earliest conven=ience. I want for you to tarry in Cincinnati untill you hear from me. Keep all things treasured up in your breasts. burn this letter as you read it. I close in hast[e]. Do not dispare. Pray for me as I bleed my heart for you. I remain your loyal friend and companion,

Joseph Smith

Maria and Sarah Lawrence

To Thomas Ford,
June 23, 1844

From his place of "safety" across the Mississippi River at Montrose during the afternoon of June 23, Joseph Smith learned that a posse had come that morning from the governor to arrest him, but not finding him in the city had returned to Carthage, and that friends were urging that he return to Nauvoo and give himself up—that the governor had pledged to protect him while he underwent "a legal and fair trial." More disconcerting were reports that some Saints were "dreadfully tried in their faith to think that Joseph would leave them in the hour of danger." Consequently, after some consultation, the Prophet decided to return to Nauvoo that evening.[1] At 2:00 P.M. from the bank of the Mississippi River, he again addressed Governor Ford.

Bank of the River Missisippi
Sunday June 23d 1844. 2 P.M.

His Excellency
Thomas Ford
    Sir: I wrote you a long communication at 12 last night, expressive of my views of your Excellency's communication of yesterday. I thought your Letter rather severe, but one of my friends has just come to me with an explanation from the captain of your

599

possie which softened the subject matter of your communication, and gives us greater assur=ance of protection, and that your Excellency has succeeded in bringing in subjection the spirits, which surround your Excellency, to some extent. And I declare again the only objection I ever had or ever made to trial by my country at any time was what I have made in my last letter – on account of assassins, & [the] reason I have to fear deathly conse=quences from their hands. But from the Explanation I now offer to come to you at Carthage on the morrow as early as shall be convenient for your possie to escort us[2] in to Head Quarters, provided we can have a fair trial, ⟨which we⟩ not be abused, nor have my witnesses abused, and have all things done in due form of law, without partiality, and you may depend on my honour without the show of a great armed force to produce excitement in the minds of the timid.

We I will meet your possie ⟨if this letter is satisfactory if not inform me⟩ at or near the Mound at or about two oclock tomorrow afternoon, which [p. 1] will be as soon as we can get our witnesses & prepare for trial. We shall expect to take our witnesses with us and not have to wait a subpoena, or a part at least, so as not ⟨to⟩ detain the procedings, although we[3] may want time for counsel.

We remain most Respectfully your Excellencys Humble servants

Joseph Smith
Hyrum Smith

His Excellency Thomas Ford
Head Quarters Carthage

To Thomas Ford, June 24, 1844

Early on June 24, after returning to Nauvoo the previous evening, Joseph Smith and the seventeen others originally charged with riot in the *Expositor* case, set out for Carthage to comply with the Governor's request. At 10:00 A.M., four miles west of Carthage, the company met some sixty mounted militia under Captain Dunn with an order from the governor to obtain all state arms in possession of the Nauvoo Legion, whereupon Joseph wrote these lines to Governor Ford.[1]

Four miles west of Carthage
Mound Hancock Co. Ill.
Monday 10 oclock

His Excellency Gov Ford
    Dear Sir   on my way to Carthage to answer your Request, this morning, I have met Capt Dunn who has made known to me your order to surrender the state arms in possession of the Nauvoo Legion, which demand I shall most cheerfully comply with, and that the same may be done properly and without trouble to the state – I shall return with Capt Dunn to Nauvoo, see that the arms are put in his possession, and shall then return to head quarters in

his company, when I shall most cheerfully submit to any requisition of the Governor of our state

With all due respect to your Excellency I remain sir most Respectfully

your obt servant
Joseph Smith

To Emma Smith, June 25, 1844

After returning to Nauvoo to supervise the surrender of state arms in the possession of the Nauvoo Legion, it was midnight before Joseph Smith and those with him arrived in Carthage. The next morning, they surrendered themselves to the authorities of the state, and shortly thereafter, while awaiting developments on the riot charge, Joseph was confronted with an additional charge of treason based upon the declaration of martial law in Nauvoo on June 18. That same morning the ugliness of the situation manifested itself when a contingent of the hostile Carthage Greys mutinied as Governor Ford was introducing the Mormon prisoners to units of the state militia. A few hours later, from the confines of his hotel room, Joseph wrote this letter to Emma.[1]

Carthage June 25, 1844
2 1/2 O Clock P.M.

Dear Emma— I have had an interview with the Gov. Ford & he treats us honorably Myself & Hyrum have been again arrested for Treason because we called out the Nauvoo Legion but when the truth comes out we have nothing to fear. We all feel calm & composed.

This morning Gov. Ford introduced myself & Hyrum to The

malitia, in a very appropri=ate manner as Gen. *Joseph Smith* &
General Hyrum Smith. There was a little mutiny among the
"Carthage Greys"; but I think the Gov. has & will succeed in
enforcing the laws. I do hope the people of Nauvoo will continue
placid pacific & prayerful.

N.B. Governor Ford has just concluded to send some of his
malitia to Nauvoo to protect the citizens, & I wish that I they may
be kindly treated. They will co-ope=rate with the police to keep
the peace of the city The Governors orders will be read in hearing
of the police & officers of the Legion, as I suppose.

P.S. 3 O Clock The Governor has just agreed to march his
army to Nauvoo, & I shall come along with him. The prisoners, all
that can be will be admitted to bail

I am as ever
Joseph Smith

Emma Smith

*Carthage Jail, Carthage, Illinois, about 1865. Taken from a copy of an
unmarked photograph. (LDS Church Archives.)*

To Emma Smith, June 25, 1844. Handwriting of John Taylor. See text, pp. 603-4. (LDS Church Archives.)

To Thomas Ford,
June 26, 1844

To Judge Thomas,
June 26, 1844

In the afternoon of June 25, Joseph and Hyrum Smith and thirteen others were brought before Robert Smith, Carthage justice of the peace (who was also captain of the Carthage Greys), on the charge of riot in the *Expositor* case. During the course of the proceedings, bail was set at $500 for each of the defendants, which was promptly paid. At this point, the Smiths could have gone free, had it not been for the additional charge of treason. Since treason was a capital crime for which bail could be set only by a circuit judge, none of whom were in the vicinity, Justice Smith adjourned the hearing in the riot case without considering the charge of treason and issued an order stating that Joseph and Hyrum Smith had been examined before him on the treason charge and that trial had been postponed by reason of the absence of material witnesses. The order committed the prisoners to be held in the local jail until "discharged by due course of law." Joseph Smith remonstrated against the legality of the order and sought an audience with Governor Ford, but the governor refused to intervene.[1] Writing the next morning from the jail, Joseph again sought an interview with the governor. He also wrote to the circuit judge Jesse B. Thomas, who had advised the Prophet in the case ten days earlier.

Carthage Jail, June 26th 1844
10. mi past 8. A M.

His Excellency, Gov. Ford.
    Sir. I would again solicit your Excellency for an interview,
having been much disappointed the past evening. I hope you will
not deny me this privilige any longer than your public duties shall
absolutely require– We have been committed under a false
mittimus, and consequently the proceedings are illegal, & we
desire the time may be hastened when all things shall be made
right, and we relieved from this imprisonment, Your Servt.

                        Joseph Smith

P.S. Please send an answer per bearer.[2] [p. 1]

His Excelly Gov. Ford
Head Quarters Carthage [p. 2]

Carthage Jail. June 26. 1844

His Hon. Judge Thomas.
Dear Sir.
    You will perceive by my date that I am in prison.—Myself and
Brother Hyrum were arrested yesterday on charge of treason,
without bringing us before the magistrate. last evening we were
committed on a mittimus from Justice Robert F. Smith. stating that
we had been before the magistrate, *which is utterly false*, but, from
the appearance of the case at present, we can have no reasonable
prospect. of any thing but ~~mob~~ ‹partial decisions of› law.–and all
the prospect we have of Justice being done, is to get our case on
Habeus corpus before an impartial Judge.—the excitement &
prejudice is such in this place testimony is of little avail:
    Therefore, Sir, I earnestly request your Honor. to repair to
Nauvoo without delay. and make yourself at home at my house

until the papers can be in readiness for you to bring us an Hab[e]us.
Our witnesses are all at Nauvoo—& there you can easily
investigate the whole matter. And I will be responsible to you for
all trouble and expense.

Joseph Smith

Carthage Jail, June 26, 1844
10. min. past 8 A.M. —

His Excellency, Gov. Ford.

Sir, I would again solicit your Excellency for an interview, having been much disappointed the past evening. I hope you will not deny me this privilege any longer than your public duties shall absolutely require — We have been committed under a false Mittimus, and consequently the proceedings are illegal, & we desire the time may be hastened when all things shall be made right, and we relieved from this imprisonment;

Your Sev.
Joseph Smith

P S. please send an answer by bearer.

The interview will take place at my earliest leisure to day
Thomas Ford

To Thomas Ford, June 26, 1844. Handwriting of Willard Richards. Note Governor Ford's reply penned on the bottom of the letter. See text, p. 607. (LDS Church Archives.)

To Emma Smith, June 27, 1844

To Lawyer Browning, June 27, 1844

At twenty-seven minutes past nine on the morning of June 26, according to Willard Richards's precise designations, Governor Ford and his aide, Colonel Thomas Geddes, arrived at the Carthage jail in response to Joseph Smith's request, whereupon a lengthy interview took place in which Joseph reviewed his course of action in the *Expositor* affair and received assurances of a fair trial. The rest of the day was highlighted by legal maneuverings and ominous reports of impending violence. At twenty minutes past six that evening, Joseph began dictating a letter to Emma but got no further than the date: "Carthage Jail, June 26th 1844, 20 Past 6 P.M." The next morning, the date and time were written over to read "27th" at "20 Past 8 A.M.," and Joseph finished dictating the letter. He then took the pen himself, added a postscript, and, shortly before ten, having just learned that the governor was about to disband most of the troops and depart for Nauvoo, dictated a second postscript. At 12:20 the Prophet sent a request for the professional services of the Quincy lawyer Orville H. Browning.[1]

Carthage Jail Jun. 27th 1844,
20. Past 8. A M.

Dear Emma
    The Gov continues his courtesies, and permits us to see our
friends. We hear this morning that the Governor will not go down
with his troops to day‹(to Nauvoo)›as was anticipated last Evening
but, if he does come down with his troops you will be protected, &
I want you to tell Bro Dunham² to instruct the people to stay at
home and attend to their own business and let there be no groups
or gathering together unless by permission of the Gov– they are
called together to receive communications from the Gov– which
would please our people, but let the Gov. direct.—Bro Dunham of
course, will obey the orders of the Government officers, and render
them the assistance they require. There is no danger of any
"exterminating order" Should there be a mutiny among the troops,
(which we do not anticipate, excitement is abating,) a part will
remain loyal, and stand for the defence of the state & our rights;
There is one principle which is Eternal, it is the duty of all men to
protect their lives ~~from every~~ and the lives of their households
whenever ~~occasion~~ ‹necessity› requires. and no power has a right
to forbid~~id~~ it. ~~when w[...]st~~ should the last extreme arrive,– but *I
anticipate no such extreme,*–but caution is the parent of safety.—

Joseph Smith

PS Dear Emma,
    I am very much resigned to my lot knowing I am Justified and
have done the best that could be done give my love to the children
[p. 1] and all my Friends Mr Brower³ and all who ~~in after~~ inquire
after me and as for treason I know that I have not commited any
and they cannot prove one apearance of any thing of the kind So
you need not have any fears that any harme can happen to us on
that score may God ~~bll~~ bless you all Amen

Joseph Smith

P.S. 20 mi[n] to 10—I just learn that the Govrnor is about to disband his troops, all but a guard to protect us and the peace,–and come himself to Nauvoo and deliver a speech to the people. This is right as I suppose. [p. 2]

Mrs Emma Smith
Nauvoo.

per Mr Joel S. Miles [p. 3]

Carthage Jail, June 27th 1844

Lawyer Browning.[1]
Sir,
     Myself and brother Hyrum are in Jail on [a] charge of Treason, to come up for examination on Saturday morning 29th inst. and we request your professional services at that time, on our defence without fail,
                              Most Respectfully
                              Your Servt.
                              Joseph Smith

     P.S. There is no ~~ground~~ <cause> of action, for we have not been guilty of any crime; neither is there any just cause of suspicion against us ~~when facts are shown~~ but certain circumstances make your attendance very necessary.

J.S.

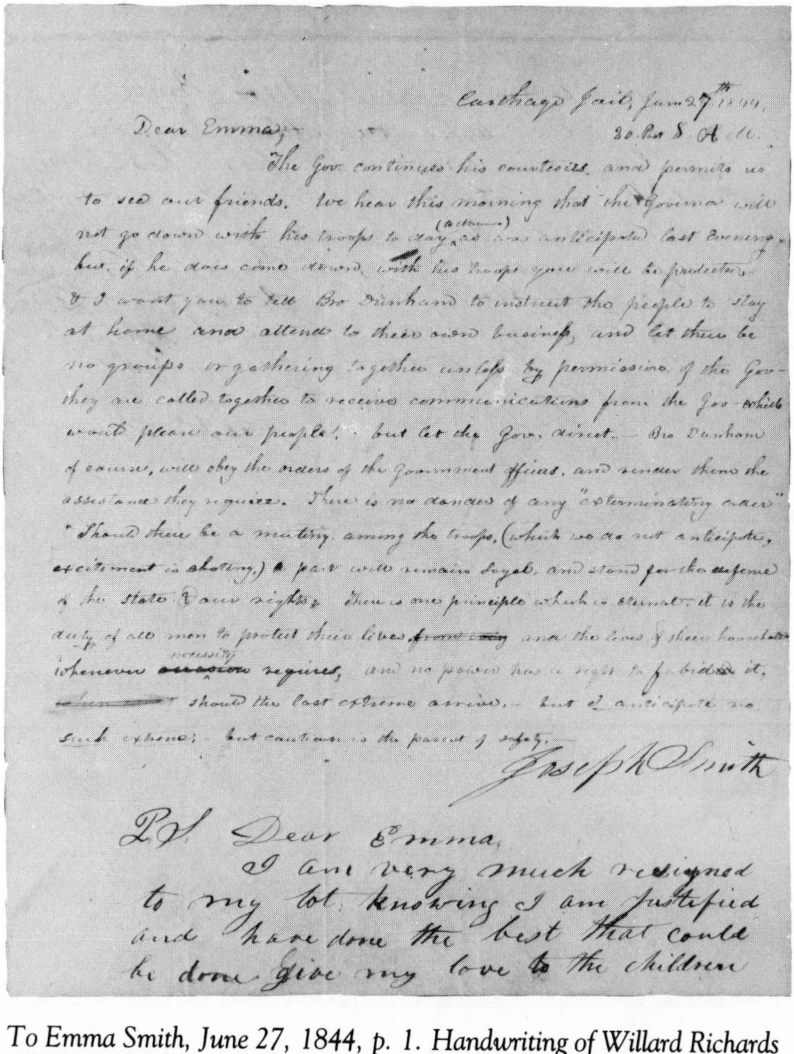

Carthage Jail, June 27th 1844,
20 past 8 A.M.

Dear Emma,—

The Gov. continues his courtesies, and permits us to see our friends. We hear this morning that the Governor will not go down with his troops to day (at Nauvoo) as was anticipated last Evening, but if he does come down with his troops you will be protected. & I want you to tell Bro Dunham to instruct the people to stay at home and attend to their own business, and let there be no groups or gathering together unless by permission of the Gov. they are called together to receive communications from the Gov. which would please our people. but let the Gov. direct.— Bro Dunham of course, will obey the orders of the Government officers, and render them the assistance they require. There is no danger of any "extermination order" Should there be a mutiny among the troops, (which we do not anticipate, excitement is abating,) a part will remain loyal, and stand for the defence of the state & our rights; There is one principle which is eternal. it is the duty of all men to protect their lives ~~from any~~ and the lives of their households whenever ~~occasion~~ necessity requires, and no power has a right to forbid it, ~~should~~ should the last extreme arrive,— but I anticipate no such extreme;— but caution is the parent of safety.—

Joseph Smith

P.S. Dear Emma,

I am very much resigned to my lot, knowing I am justified and have done the best that could be done give my love to the children

To Emma Smith, June 27, 1844, p. 1. Handwriting of Willard Richards and Joseph Smith. *See text, p. 611.* *(RLDS Church Archives.)*

and all my Friends, My Brower
and all who in after inquire
after me; and as for treason
I know that I have not committed
any, and they cannot prove one
appearance of any thing of the kind,
So you need not have any fears
that any harm can happen to
us on that score. may God
bless you all. Amen.
                              Joseph Smith

P.S. 20. mi; to 10. I Just hear'd that the Gov mor is about to disband
his troops all but a guard to protect us and the peace, and come
himself to Nauvoo and deliver a speech to the people. This is right,
as I suppose.

To Emma Smith, June 27, 1844, p. 2. Handwriting of Joseph Smith and
Willard Richards. See text, pp. 611-12. (RLDS Church Archives.)

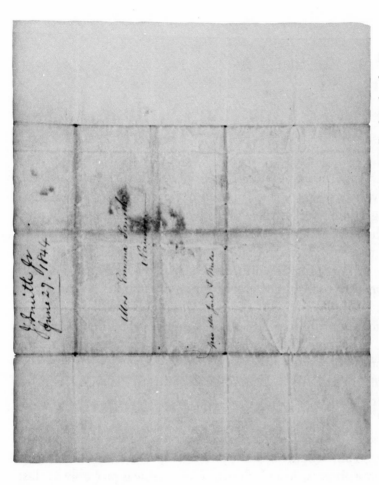

To Emma Smith, June 27, 1844, p. 3. Handwriting of Willard Richards.
See text, p. 612. (RLDS Church Archives.)

—A Mark Hofmann forgery.

To Jonathan Dunham,
June 27, 1844

During the excitement that followed the destruction of the Nauvoo *Expositor*, some thirteen hundred Illinois state militia had gathered at Carthage, and five hundred more at Warsaw, in Hancock County, anxious to vent their wrath against the Mormons at Nauvoo. A plan had been discussed for a show of force by marching the militia to Nauvoo; but fearing a collision between the troops and the Mormon community with its two-thousand-man Nauvoo Legion, Governor Ford had rejected the idea, opting instead to take a small force himself and address the people. Consequently, on the morning of June 27, the governor disbanded all of the state militia except for three companies, one that would accompany him to Nauvoo, and two others, made up of Carthage Greys, to remain as a guard at the jail.[1]

Some time after learning that the governor was going to Nauvoo and would leave the jail in the protection of inveterate Mormon-haters, Joseph Smith sent what was probably his last written communication, a letter to the Nauvoo Legion commander, Jonathan Dunham. A few hours later the Prophet was dead.

Carthage Jail June 27th 1844

Major General Dunham
    Dear Sir You are hereby ordered to resigne the defence of the City of Nauvoo to Captain Singlton[2] and proceed to this place

616

without delay with what ever numbers of the Nauvoo Ledgion as may safely and immediately come. Let this be done quietly and orderly but with great hast[e] we are in the hands of our sworn enemies.[3]

Joseph Smith

To Jonathan Dunham, June 27, 1844. Handwriting of Joseph Smith. See text, pp. 616-17. (Dr. Richard Marks, Phoenix, Arizona.)

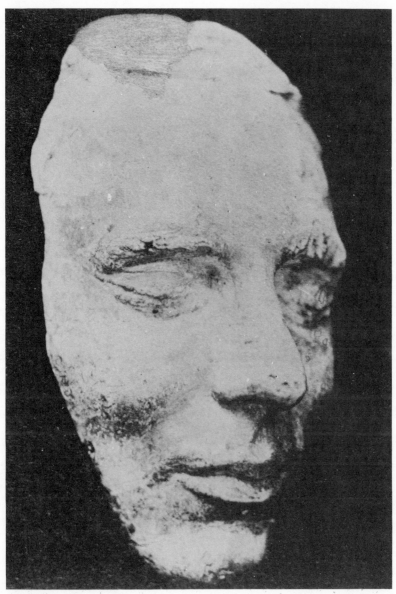

Original Joseph Smith death mask. (Charles W. Carter Collection, LDS Church Archives.)

Appendixes
Maps
Notes
Bibliography
Index

Appendix A:
Joseph Smith's Family

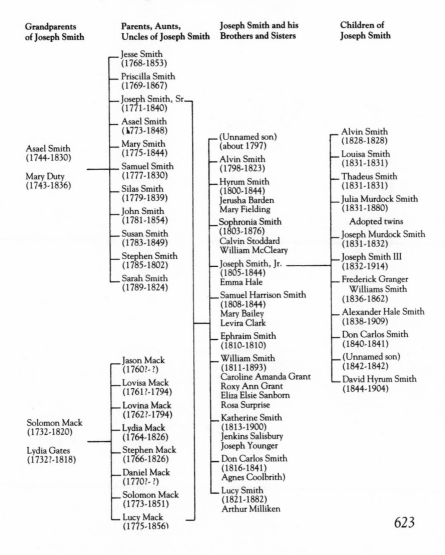

Grandparents of Joseph Smith	Parents, Aunts, Uncles of Joseph Smith	Joseph Smith and his Brothers and Sisters	Children of Joseph Smith
	Jesse Smith (1768-1853)		
	Priscilla Smith (1769-1867)		
	Joseph Smith, Sr. (1771-1840)		
	Asael Smith (1773-1848)	(Unnamed son) (about 1797)	Alvin Smith (1828-1828)
Asael Smith (1744-1830)	Mary Smith (1775-1844)		Louisa Smith (1831-1831)
	Samuel Smith (1777-1830)	Alvin Smith (1798-1823)	Thadeus Smith (1831-1831)
Mary Duty (1743-1836)	Silas Smith (1779-1839)	Hyrum Smith (1800-1844) Jerusha Barden Mary Fielding	Julia Murdock Smith (1831-1880)
	John Smith (1781-1854)	Sophronia Smith (1803-1876) Calvin Stoddard William McCleary	Adopted twins Joseph Murdock Smith (1831-1832)
	Susan Smith (1783-1849)		
	Stephen Smith (1785-1802)	Joseph Smith, Jr. (1805-1844) Emma Hale	Joseph Smith III (1832-1914)
	Sarah Smith (1789-1824)	Samuel Harrison Smith (1808-1844) Mary Bailey Levira Clark	Frederick Granger Williams Smith (1836-1862) Alexander Hale Smith (1838-1909)
		Ephraim Smith (1810-1810)	Don Carlos Smith (1840-1841)
	Jason Mack (1760?-?)	William Smith (1811-1893) Caroline Amanda Grant Roxy Ann Grant Eliza Elsie Sanborn Rosa Surprise	(Unnamed son) (1842-1842) David Hyrum Smith (1844-1904)
Solomon Mack (1732-1820)	Lovisa Mack (1761?-1794) Lovina Mack (1762?-1794)	Katherine Smith (1813-1900) Jenkins Salisbury Joseph Younger	
	Lydia Mack (1764-1826)		
Lydia Gates (1732?-1818)	Stephen Mack (1766-1826)	Don Carlos Smith (1816-1841) Agnes Coolbrith	
	Daniel Mack (1770?-?)		
	Solomon Mack (1773-1851)	Lucy Smith (1821-1882) Arthur Milliken	
	Lucy Mack (1775-1856)		

623

Appendix B:
Joseph Smith Chronology

1805	December 23	Born at Sharon, Windsor County, Vermont.
1811		Family moved to Lebanon, New Hampshire.
1813		Contracted typhus fever; leg operation.
1816		Family moved to Palmyra, New York.
1820	Spring	First Vision.
1823	September 21	First Moroni visitation.
	November 19	Death of brother Alvin.
1827	January 18	Married Emma Hale at Bainbridge, New York.
	September 22	Obtained Book of Mormon plates.
	December	Moved to Harmony, Pennsylvania.
1828		116 pages of Book of Mormon lost.
	June 15	Son Alvin born; died same day.
1829	May-June	Priesthood received.
	June	Finished Book of Mormon translation.
1830	March	Book of Mormon published.
	April 6	Church organized.
	June	Visions of Moses revealed.
	December	Writings of Moses revealed.
1831	January	Moved to Kirtland, Ohio.
	Spring	Commenced revision of the Bible.
	April 30	Twins (Thadeus, Louisa) born; lived only three hours.
	May 9	Adopted Murdock twins, Joseph and Julia.
	June 19	Started for Jackson County, Missouri.
	July	Revelation designating site for city of Zion (D&C 57).
	September 12	Moved to Hiram, Ohio.
	December	Preached in area of Kirtland-Ravenna, Ohio, to counteract effects of anti-Mormon *Ohio Star* articles.
1832	January 25	Sustained president of High Priesthood at Amherst, Ohio, conference.
	February 16	Revelation of postmortal state of mankind (D&C 76).
	March 24	Tarred and feathered by mob at Hiram, Ohio.
	March 29	Adopted son, Joseph M., died.
	April 1	Started for Missouri.
	June	Arrived back at Kirtland after delay at Greenville, Indiana.

	October	Traveled to Albany, New York City, and Boston, with Newel K. Whitney.
	November 6	Returned to Kirtland. Son, Joseph Smith III, born.
	December 25	Revelation on war (D&C 87).
1833	February 27	Revelation known as the Word of Wisdom (D&C 89).
	March 18	First Presidency organized.
	July 23	Cornerstones for Kirtland Temple laid.
	October 5	Left Kirtland on proselyting mission to Canada.
	November 4	Returned to Kirtland.
	November 22	News of expulsion of saints from Jackson County.
1834	February 17	High council organized at Kirtland.
	February 26	Left Kirtland to proselyte volunteers for Zion's Camp.
	March 28	Returned to Kirtland.
	April 1-3	Attended court at Chardon in Hurlbut case.
	April 12	Fishing on Lake Erie.
	April 22	Conference at Norton, Ohio.
	May 5	Left Kirtland for Missouri at head of Zion's Camp.
	June 19	Arrived in Clay County, Missouri.
	August 1	Returned to Kirtland.
	October	Visited Saints in Michigan.
	November	Participated in school of elders in Kirtland.
1835	February 14	Quorum of Twelve organized.
	February 28	Quorum of Seventy organized.
	March 28	Revelation on priesthood (D&C 107).
	July	Egyptian mummies and papyrus obtained.
	October 8-11	Attended father during illness.
	November	Studying Hebrew and Greek.
1836	March 27	Dedicated Kirtland Temple.
	April 3	Vision of Savior in Kirtland Temple.
	May 17	Met grandmother, Mary Duty, at Fairport and accompanied her to Kirtland.
	June 20	Son Frederick born.
	July 25	Left Kirtland for East.
	July 30	Visited part of New York City burned in 1835 fire.
	September	Returned to Kirtland.
	November 2	Kirtland Safety Society Bank established.
1837	April 6	Solemn assembly at Kirtland Temple.
	May	Denounced by dissenters at Kirtland.
	May 30	Acquitted in Grandison Newel case.
	June	Seriously ill.
	July 23	Revelation to the Twelve (D&C 112).
	August	Visited Saints in Canada.
	September 3	Conference in Kirtland; Three of Twelve rejected.
	September 27	Left Kirtland for Missouri.
	November 7	Conference at Far West, Missouri.
	December	Returned to Kirtland, dissension in Church.

1838	January 12	Left Kirtland to escape mob violence.
	March 14	Arrived with family at Far West, Missouri.
	April 30	Commenced writing history.
	May 14	Plowed garden.
	May 19	Selected site for new settlement, Adam-ondi-Ahman.
	June 2	Son Alexander born.
	August 6	Election-day fight at Gallatin, Missouri
	September 4	Commenced study of law.
	October 11	Led harrassed Saints from DeWitt to Far West.
	October 27	Extermination order issued by Governor Boggs.
	October 30	Haun's Mill massacre.
	October 31	Surrendered to Missouri militia at Far West; imprisoned.
	November 4	Arrived under guard at Independence.
	November	Hearing at Richmond.
	December 1	Confined at Liberty Jail to await trial.
1839	April 6	Taken from Liberty Jail to Gallatin for trial.
	April 15	Started for Boone County on change of venue; escaped.
	April 22	Reunited with family at Quincy, Illinois.
	May 10	Moved to Commerce, Illinois.
	June	Involved in resettlement of Saints at Nauvoo.
	July 21-22	Administered to sick.
	October 29	Left Nauvoo to present Mormon grievances to federal government.
	November 28	Arrived at Washington, D.C.
	November 29	Visited President Martin Van Buren.
	December	Visited Saints in Philadelphia and New Jersey.
1840	February	Left Washington, D.C., for home.
	March 4	Arrived at Nauvoo.
	September 14	Death of father, Joseph Smith, Sr.
1841	January 30	Elected Trustee-in-trust.
	February 1	Elected to Nauvoo city council.
	February 4	Elected lieutenant general of Nauvoo Legion.
	April 5	Sealed to Louisa Beaman.
	April 6	Laid cornerstone for Nauvoo Temple.
	May 2	Entertained Stephen A. Douglas.
	June 4	Arrested on old Missouri charges.
	June 9-10	Trial before Judge Douglas at Monmouth, Illinois; acquitted.
	July 3	Patriotic address to Nauvoo Legion.
	August 7	Brother, Don Carlos, died at age twenty-six.
	August 12	Spoke to visiting Sac and Fox Indians at Nauvoo.
	September 14	Attended military parade at Montrose, Iowa.
	November 8	Dedicated baptism font in Nauvoo temple.
1842	January 5	Commenced selling goods at new store in Nauvoo.
	January 15	Correcting proof for new edition of Book of Mormon.
	March 1	Commenced publication of Book of Abraham.
	March 15	Officiated at installation of Nauvoo masonic lodge; received first degree of masonry.

	March 15	Became editor of *Times and Seasons*.
	March 17	Organized Female Relief Society.
	March 27	Engaged in baptims for the dead in Mississippi River.
	April	Forced to apply for bankruptcy.
	May 4	Introduced temple endowment.
	May 7	Life endangered during review of Nauvoo Legion.
	May 14	Worked in garden after city council meeting.
	May 19	Elected Mayor of Nauvoo.
	August 8	Arrested for complicity in Boggs assassination attempt; forced into hiding.
	September 16	Sitting for portrait.
	December 13	Chopped and hauled wood.
	December 26	Second arrest in Boggs case.
1843	January 5	Acquitted of charges in Boggs case by Judge Nathaniel Pope.
	January 18	Enjoyed day with invited guests at dinner; fifteenth wedding anniversary.
	February 3	Studied German; read proof on Doctrine and Covenants.
	February 8	Went sliding on ice with son Frederick.
	February-March	Attended mother during illness.
	March 4	Sealed to Emily Partridge.
	March 13	Wrestled William Wall; blessed twenty-seven children in the evening.
	April 23	Took his children on pleasure ride in carriage.
	May 1	Sealed to Lucy Walker.
	May 16	Traveled to Ramus.
	May 28	Sealed to Emma for time and eternity.
	June 3	Pleasure trip to Quincy with family and friends on River.
	June 13	Left Nauvoo to visit relatives at Dixon, Illinois.
	June 23	Arrested at Dixon by officers disguised as missionaries.
	June 30	Arrived at Nauvoo.
	July 1	Discharged by Nauvoo court.
	July 12	Revelation on marriage recorded (D&C 132).
	August 31	Moving into Nauvoo Mansion.
	September 4	Attended circus with family.
	September 16	Reviewed Nauvoo Legion.
	September 28	Introduced fulness of priesthood ordinances.
	December 25	Entertained fifty couples on Christmas Day.
1844	January 29	Elected candidate for U.S. Presidency.
	February 20	Instructed Twelve to investigate location for Saints in California or Oregon.
	March 11	Council of Fifty organized.
	March 18	Studying German.
	April 3	Presided at municipal court hearing.
	April 5	Attended dedication of Nauvoo masonic temple.
	April 5-7	King Follett discourse.
	April 26	Life threatened by Higbees and Fosters.
	May 10	Prospectus of Nauvoo *Expositor* distributed by dissenters.

May 17	Nominated for U.S. presidential candidate at Nauvoo convention.
June 7	Nauvoo *Expositor* published.
June 10	Ordered destruction of Nauvoo *Expositor* press.
June 12	Arrested for destroying press.
June 18	Placed Nauvoo under martial law.
June 25	Surrendered at Carthage to face riot charge.
June 27	Shot by mob at Carthage jail.

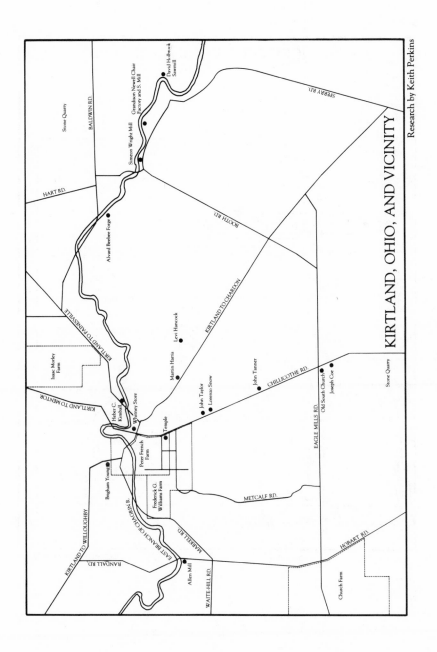

KIRTLAND, OHIO, AND VICINITY

Research by Keith Perkins

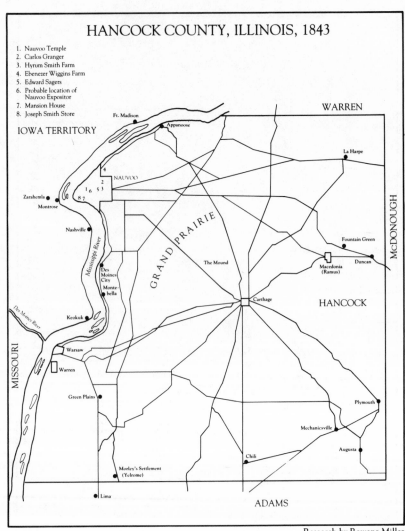

HANCOCK COUNTY, ILLINOIS, 1843

1. Nauvoo Temple
2. Carlos Granger
3. Hyrum Smith Farm
4. Ebenezer Wiggins Farm
5. Edward Sagers
6. Probable location of
   Nauvoo Expositor
7. Mansion House
8. Joseph Smith Store

IOWA TERRITORY

Ft. Madison

Appanoose

WARREN

La Harpe

4
2
NAUVOO
1 6 5 3
8 7

Zarahemla

Montrose

Nashville

Fountain Green

PRAIRIE

The Mound

GRAND

Macedonia
(Ramus)

Duncan

McDONOUGH

Des
Moines
City

Monte-
bella

Carthage

HANCOCK

Mississippi River

Des Moines River

Keokuk

Warsaw

Warren

MISSOURI

Green Plains

Plymouth

Mechanicsville

Chili

Augusta

Morley's Settlement
(Yelrome)

Lima

ADAMS

Research by Rowena Miller

KIRTLAND, OHIO, 1837

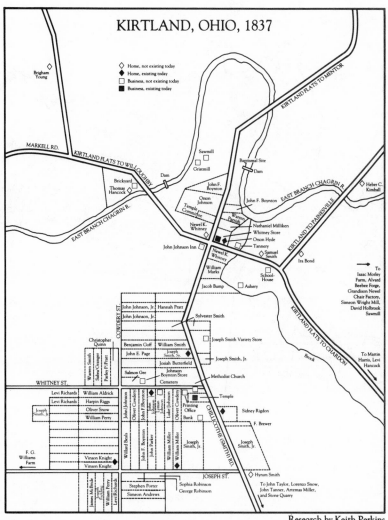

◇ Home, not existing today
◆ Home, existing today
☐ Business, not existing today
■ Business, existing today

Brigham Young

MARKELL RD.

KIRTLAND FLATS TO WILLOUGHBY

EAST BRANCH CHAGRIN R.

KIRTLAND FLATS TO MENTOR

Sawmill
Gristmill
Dam

Baptismal Site
Dam

Brickyard
Thomas Hancock

John F. Boynton

EAST BRANCH CHAGRIN R.

Heber C. Kimball

Orson Johnson

John F. Boynton

KIRTLAND TO PAINESVILLE

Temple Committee

Warren Parrish

Newel K. Whitney

Nathaniel Milliken
Whitney Store
Orson Hyde
Tannery

John Johnson Inn

Newel K. Whitney

Samuel Smith

Ira Bond

To Isaac Morley Farm, Alvard Beebee Forge, Grandison Newel Chair Factory, Simeon Wright Mill, David Holbrook Sawmill

William Marks

School-House

Jacob Bump

Aashery

COWDERY ST.

John Johnson, Jr.

Hannah Pratt

John Johnson, Jr.

Sylvester Smith

KIRTLAND FLATS TO CHARDON

Christopher Quinn

Benjamin Goff

William Smith

Joseph Smith Variety Store

Warren Smith
Sidna Granger
Parley P. Pratt

John E. Page

Joseph Smith, Sr.

Joseph Smith, Jr.

Brook

To Martin Harris, Levi Hancock

Josiah Butterfield

Salmon Gee

Johnson Boynton Store

Methodist Church

WHITNEY ST.

Cemetery

Levi Richards

William Aldrick

Levi Richards

Harpin Riggs

John Johnson
Oliver Cowdery
John F. Boynton
John Johnson
Lyman Johnson
Luke Johnson
Oliver Cowdery

Temple

Joseph Smith, Jr.

Oliver Snow

Printing Office

Sidney Rigdon

William Perry

Bank

CHILLICOTHE (SMITH) RD.

F. Brewer

Willard Bush
John F. Boynton
John Parker
William Miller
William Miller

Joseph Smith, Jr.

Joseph Smith, Jr.

F. G. Williams Farm

Vinson Knight

Vinson Knight

JOSEPH ST.

Hyrum Smith

James McBride
Joseph Fielding
William Perry
Levi Richards

Stephen Porter

Simeon Andrews

Sophia Robinson

George Robinson

To John Taylor, Lorenzo Snow, John Tanner, Artemas Millet, and Stone Quarry

Research by Keith Perkins

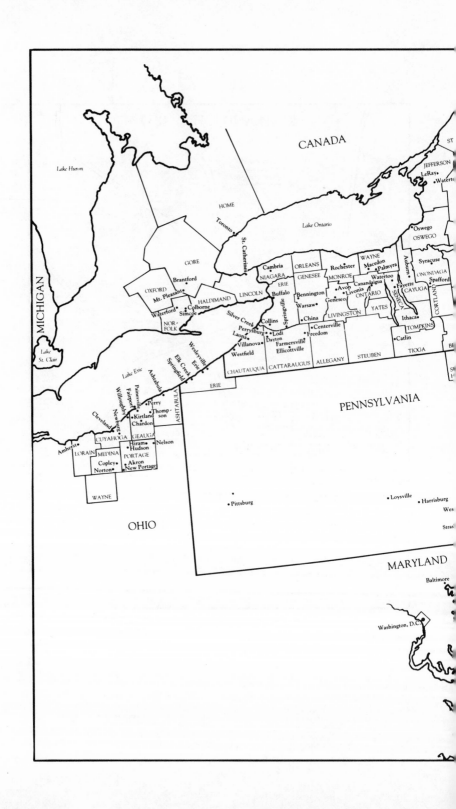

Lake Huron

CANADA

JEFFERSON
LeRay•
•Watert

HOME

Toronto•

St. Catharines

Lake Ontario

•Oswego

OSWEGO

GORE

MICHIGAN

OXFORD
Mt. Pleasant•

Brantford

Waterford•
Simcoe•
Colborne

HALDIMAND

NOR-
FOLK

LINCOLN

Silver Creek
Perrysburg•
Laona•

Villanova•
Westfield

CHAUTAUQUA

Cambria

NIAGARA
ERIE

Buffalo

Bennington

Warsaw•

Collins
•Lodi
Dayton

Ellicottville

CATTARAUGUS

ORLEANS

GENESEE

Springville

•China

Centerville
•Freedom

Farmersville

ALLEGANY

Rochester

MONROE

•Avon
•Livonia

Geneseo•

LIVINGSTON

WAYNE
Macedon
•Palmyra

Waterloo
Canandaigua•
ONTARIO

YATES

STEUBEN

Syracuse

ONONDAGA
•Spafford

Auburn•
•Fayette
SENECA
CAYUGA

Ithaca•

TOMPKINS

•Catlin

TIOGA

CORTLAND

Westfield
Laona•

Weslerville
Elk Creek
Springfield

Lake Erie

ERIE

Paincsville
Fairport•
Cleveland• Newburg•

Kirtland•
Chardon

•Perry
•Thomp-
son

Ashtabula

ASHTABULA

PENNSYLVANIA

Lake
St. Clair

Amherst•

LORAIN MEDINA

CUYAHOGA

Copley•
Norton•

GEAUGA
Hiram•
•Hudson Nelson

PORTAGE
•Akron
•New Portage

WAYNE

OHIO

•Pittsburg

•Loysville
•Harrisburg

Wes

Stras

MARYLAND

Baltimore

Washington, D.C.

ST

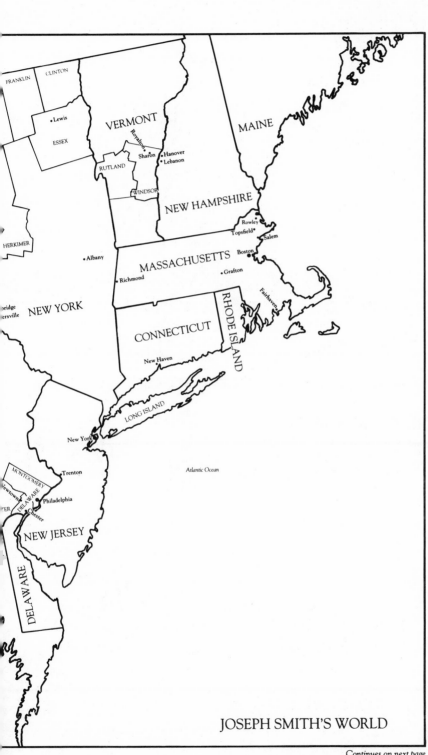

FRANKLIN

CLINTON

• Lewis

ESSEX

VERMONT

Royalton

Sharon• •Hanover
•Lebanon

RUTLAND

WINDSOR

NEW HAMPSHIRE

MAINE

HERKIMER

• Albany

Rowley•
Topsfield•
Salem

Boston

MASSACHUSETTS

• Grafton

• Richmond

Fairhaven

bridge
ersville

NEW YORK

CONNECTICUT

RHODE ISLAND

New Haven

LONG ISLAND

New York

MONTGOMERY

Trenton

Atlantic Ocean

ewtown
DELAWARE
•Philadelphia
•Chester

ER

NEW JERSEY

DELAWARE

JOSEPH SMITH'S WORLD

Continues on next page

Continued from preceding page

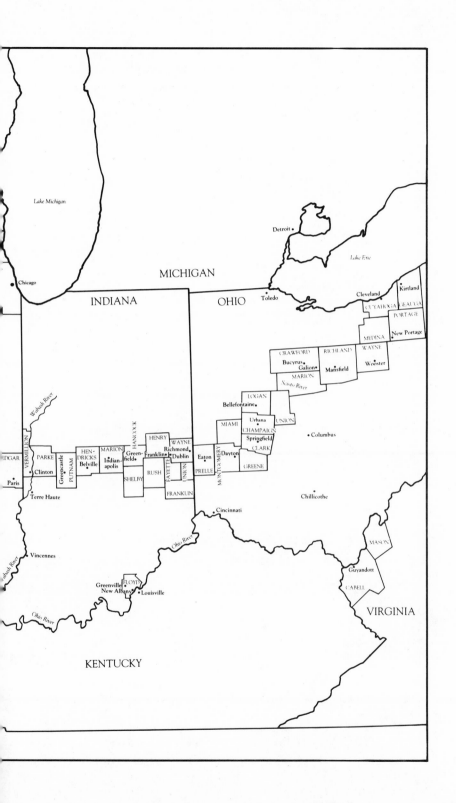

Lake Michigan

MICHIGAN

INDIANA

OHIO

Chicago

Detroit •

Lake Erie

Toledo

Cleveland • Kirtland

CUYAHOGA GEAUGA

PORTAGE

New Portage

MEDINA

CRAWFORD RICHLAND WAYNE

Bucyrus•
Galion•

Mansfield

Wooster

MARION

Scioto River

LOGAN

Bellefontaine•

MIAMI

Urbana•

UNION

CHAMPAIGN

Springfield•

CLARK

• Columbus

Wabash River

VERMILLION

PARKE

Clinton•

HEN-
DRICKS

MARION

HANCOCK

HENRY

WAYNE

Richmond•

Dublin

Eaton•

Dayton•

Greencastle•

PUTNAM

Belville•

Indian-
apolis

Green-
field•

Franklin•

FAYETTE

UNION

PRELLE

MONTGOMERY

GREENE

•Paris

EDGAR

SHELBY

RUSH

FRANKLIN

Terre Haute•

Chillicothe•

Cincinnati•

MASON

Ohio River

Vincennes•

Guyandott•

CABELL

Wabash River

Greenville•
New Albany•

FLOYD

•Louisville

VIRGINIA

Ohio River

KENTUCKY

Notes

Preface

1. Hockett, *Introduction to Research in American History*, p. 64.
2. May, "Ghost Writing and History," pp. 460-61.
3. Carr, *What Is History*, p. 27.
4. Cited in Wood, *Philip the Fair and Boniface VIII*, pp. 84-86.
5. Jessee, "Howard Coray's Recollections of Joseph Smith," p. 346.
6. See Joseph Smith's 1832 History, p. 4 of this work.
7. Smith to Phelps, November 27, 1832, p. 262 of this work; Smith, *History of the Church* 6:409.
8. Jessee, "The Reliability of Joseph Smith's History," pp. 23-46.
9. Smith to the Church of the Latter Day Saints, March 20, 1839, p. 396 of this work.
10. Smith to the saints in Nauvoo, September 1, 1842, p. 544 of this work.
11. Smith, *History of the Church* 5:336.

Introduction

1. For an analysis of Joseph Smith's writing style, see Elinore H. Partridge, "Characteristics of Joseph Smith's Style."
2. Michener, "My First 75 Years."
3. In Plimpton, "Interview with Ernest Hemingway," p. 222.

History, 1832

Ms. Joseph Smith Letterbook 1, pp. 1-6, Joseph Smith Papers, LDS Church Archives, Salt Lake City, Utah. The account was written on the first three leaves of what became Joseph Smith's first letterbook, and the leaves were afterward cut from the volume. The non-holograph portions of the document are in the handwriting of Frederick G. Williams. Published in part in Jessee, "The Early Accounts of Joseph Smith's First Vision," pp. 278-80.

1. D&C 21:1.
2. Oliver Cowdery (1806-1850), teacher, lawyer, and newspaper editor, was born in Wells, Rutland County, Vermont. He assisted Joseph Smith as a scribe during translation of the Book of Mormon and was a witness with Joseph to early Church foundation experiences. Manager of the Church printing office in Kirtland, Ohio, he was called as "assistant president" to Joseph Smith in 1836. He left the Church in 1838 but returned ten years later. (Jenson, *Biographical Encyclopedia* 1:246-51. R. L. Anderson, *Investigating the Book of Mormon Witnesses*, pp. 37-65.)

According to John Whitmer, Oliver Cowdery wrote a history covering the period
from the finding of the Book of Mormon plates to June 12, 1831. (John Whitmer, "The
Book of John Whitmer," ch. 6.)

3. D&C 47:1, 3. John Whitmer (1802-1878) was among the earliest to accept the message
of the Restoration. He assisted Joseph Smith in a clerical capacity and, after his appointment as historian, was called to preside over the Church in Missouri. (Jenson, *Biographical
Encyclopedia* 1:251-52.)

4. D&C 69:3.

5. Smith to Phelps, July 31, 1832, p. 250 of this work.

6. The dating of this manuscript between July 20 and November 27, 1832, follows from the
fact that Frederick G. Williams, in whose hand it is partly written, did not begin his clerical work for Joseph Smith until the former date, and it had to be completed prior to
November 27, when the volume in which it was written was converted to a letterbook.
(See Jessee, "The Early Accounts of Joseph Smith's First Vision," pp. 277-78.)

7. See appendix A.

8. Emma Hale (1804-1879) was born in Harmony, Susquehanna County, Pennsylvania.
(Family Group Records Collection.)

9. Isaac Hale (1763-1839) married Elizabeth Lewis on September 20, 1789.

10. Martin Harris (1783-1875), who assisted Joseph Smith monetarily and clerically during
the translation of the Book of Mormon, was born in Easttown, Saratoga County, New
York, and moved to Palmyra, Wayne County, New York in 1827. (Jenson, *Biographical
Encyclopedia* 1:271.)

11. Martin Harris's trip to New York City is detailed in Roberts, *Comprehensive History* 1:
99-109; Kimball, "The Anthon Transcript: People, Primary Sources, and Problems,"
pp. 325-52; and Bachman, "Sealed in a Book: Preliminary Observations on the Newly
Found 'Anthon Transcript,'" pp. 321-45. See also Bachman, "A Look at the Newly Discovered Joseph Smith Manuscript," pp. 69-73.

12. The nature of the chastisement is set forth in D&C 3 and 10.

13. Oliver Cowdery's clerical work on the Book of Mormon manuscript began on April 5, 1829. Most of
the extant original Book of Mormon manuscript is in his handwriting. (See Jessee, "The
Original Book of Mormon Manuscript," pp. 259-78.)

14. Neither the handwriting of Emma Hale Smith nor of Samuel H. Smith appears in the sur-
viving pages of the original Book of Mormon manuscript.

Diary, 1832-1834

Ms. Joseph Smith Papers, LDS Church Archives. Material from this diary was published in
Smith, *History of the Church*, beginning at 1:416.

1. First settled twenty years previous, Kirtland, Geauga County, became the Latter-day
Saint gathering place in Ohio in 1831. Joseph Smith arrived there from New York on
February 1, 1831. The Mormon experience in Ohio is reviewed in Allen and Leonard,
Story of the Latter-day Saints, pp. 53-101; and Parkin, *Conflict at Kirtland.*

2. Sophronia Smith Stoddard (1803-1876), born in Tunbridge, Vermont, was Joseph
Smith's elder sister. She married Calvin W. Stoddard at Palmyra, New York, on De-
cember 30, 1827. (*Utah Genealogical and Historical Magazine* 26:102, 151; Stoddard
Family Bible, in possession of Buddy Youngreen.)

3. Katherine Smith Salisbury (1813-1900), born in Lebanon, New Hampshire, was a
younger sister of Joseph Smith. She married Wilkins Jenkins Salisbury on January 8,
1831. (*Utah Genealogical and Historical Magazine* 26:102, 151-52.)

4. Frederick Granger Williams (1787-1842), a physician, was converted by Mormon missionaries who came through Kirtland, Ohio, in October 1830. He was appointed clerk to

Joseph Smith in July 1832 and became a counselor in the First Presidency in 1833. (Jenson, *Biographical Encyclopedia* 1:51-52.)

5. No one by the name of King is listed in the Kirtland census or tax lists; however, a David King owned property in Chester township bordering Kirtland on the south.

6. Although no Gilmores are listed in the Kirtland census or tax lists, three Gilmores (Samuel, James, and Ashbel) owned property in Chester township bordering Kirtland on the south.

7. Noah Packard (1796-1860), a member of the Kirtland high council, was born in New Hampshire but was living in Parkman, Geauga County, Ohio, when converted in 1832. (Jenson, *Biographical Encyclopedia* 2:684.)

8. Solomon Humphery (1775-1834), a native of New England, was a member of Zion's Camp in 1834. (Jenson, *Biographical Encyclopedia* 4:689-90.)

9. Lyman Johnson (1811-1856), a businessman and lawyer, was a member of the Council of the Twelve from 1835-1838. He was born in Pomfret, Vermont, and joined the Church in 1831. He was a missionary in the eastern states, New England, and Canada in 1832 and 1833 with Orson Pratt. In 1838 he was excommunicated from the Church. (Jenson, *Biographical Encyclopedia* 1:91-92.)

10. Orson Pratt (1811-1881), a member of the Council of the Twelve from 1835 to 1881, was born in Hartford, New York. A younger brother of Parley Pratt, he left Kirtland with Lyman Johnson in February 1832 for missionary work in the East; he returned in February 1833 after traveling four thousand miles, baptizing 104 people, and organizing several branches of the Church. (*Deseret News*, June 9, 1858.)

11. Probably Jesse Gause, born Jesse Goss (1784?-1836?), served as a counselor with Sidney Rigdon to Joseph Smith in the Church Presidency from March 8, 1832, until his disaffection later the same year. Born at East Marlborough, Chester County, Pennsylvania, Gause had been a member of the Society of Friends before joining the Latter-day Saints. He accompanied Joseph Smith to Missouri in 1832 and, upon his return to Kirtland, Ohio, joined Zebedee Coltrin on a proselyting mission to the East in August. At this point Gause fades from the annals of Mormon history. (Quinn, "Jesse Gause: Joseph Smith's Little-known Counselor.")

William E. McLellin (1806?-1883), a schoolteacher, joined the Church in Missouri in August 1831. He was a member of the Council of the Twelve from 1835 to 1838, when he left the Church. The cause of McLellin's 1832 excommunication is not known. McLellin spelled his name four different ways during his lifetime. The spelling used here is typical of the time period. (Jenson, *Biographical Encyclopedia* 1:82-83.)

12. D&C 86.

13. Freeman Nickerson (1778-1847) was baptized by Mormon missionaries at Perrysburg, Cattaraugus County, New York, in April 1833. It was probably at Nickerson's invitation that Joseph Smith traveled to Mt. Pleasant, Upper Canada, to proselyte in the area where some of Nickerson's married children were then living. (Jenson, *Biographical Encyclopedia* 4:690-91; Family Group Records Collection.)

14. David Elliott (1799-1852) was a member of the first quorum of the seventy. A native of Charleston, Montgomery County, New York, he joined the Church in January 1831. (Family Records Archive; Smith, *History of the Church* 2:203.)

15. Sidney Rigdon (1793-1876) was a popular Campbellite minister in Mentor, Ohio, when he accepted the message of the Restoration in the fall of 1830. Thereafter he was closely associated with Joseph Smith in a clerical capacity and in March 1832 became a counselor in the Church Presidency. Sidney Rigdon accompanied Joseph Smith and Freeman Nickerson to Upper Canada and helped Joseph keep his diary during the trip. (Jenson, *Biographical Encyclopedia* 1:31-34.)

16. Probably Cyprian Rudd, born in 1782 at Bennington, Bennington County, Vermont. The 1830 census lists Rudd (then in his forties), his wife, six children, and an older couple as living in Springfield, Erie County, Pennsylvania.

17. Handwriting of Sidney Rigdon.
18. Shadrach Roundy (1789-1872) was born in Rockingham, Windham County, Vermont. Family records show that he was living in Spafford, Onondaga County, New York, between 1815 and 1831, and in Willoughby, Ohio, between 1834 and 1838. He was converted in the winter of 1830-1831. (Family Group Records Collection.)
19. The 1830 Federal Census lists Job Lewis (in his fifties), his wife, and nine others in his family at Westfield, Chautauqua County, New York.
20. Census records identify Burl and Cotton Nash living in Portland, Chautauqua County, New York, a few miles east of Westfield.
21. At Perrysburg, Cattaraugus County, New York.
22. Joseph Smith's concern for his family was the subject of a revelation this day at Perrysburg, New York. (See D&C 100.) At this point in the diary, a later hand (Willard Richards) wrote, "See forward 20 pages 12 baptized," erroneously keying this entry to the list of those baptized at Mount Pleasant, Canada, on October 27 and 28. The error occurred when Richards took the recollection of the date of the baptism at face value, not realizing it was faulty.
23. Handwriting of Sidney Rigdon.
24. Friday fell on October 18, 1833.
25. Eleazer Freeman Nickerson (1806-1862) was born in Cavendish, Windsor County, Vermont. At the time of the visit of his father and Joseph Smith, Eleazer and other members of the family had located at Mt. Pleasant, Upper Canada. (Family Group Records Collection.)
26. Brantford, with an 1846 population of 2,000, was the predominant settlement in the Brantford Township, Gore District, Upper Canada. (W. H. Smith, *Smith's Canadian Gazetteer*, pp. 18-19.)
27. Mt. Pleasant is a small village in the south of Brantford Township, five miles from the town of Brantford on the Simcoe Road. Mt. Pleasant had a population of about 130 in the 1840s. (W. H. Smith, *Smith's Canadian Gazetteer*, p. 119.)
28. Colborne is a small village in Norfolk District, Upper Canada, one mile from Simcoe. Colborne had an 1881 population of 80. (Crossby, *Lovell's Gazetteer of British North America*, p. 214.)
29. Handwriting of Sidney Rigdon.
30. Handwriting of Oliver Cowdery.
31. A Marvin C. Davis is listed as a property holder in the 1836 Kirtland tax lists.
32. This phenomenon was widely observed. Exiled Latter-day Saints driven from Jackson County, Missouri, and encamped on the north bank of the Missouri River also reported the spectacular incident: "An unmeasurable shower of stars were dancing about in every direction, with the velocity of lightning," wrote one. Another wrote: "I witnessed the beautiful scene of the falling of the stars and went from house to house waking up the people to have them see it." (See Parkin, "History of the Latter-day Saints in Clay County, Missouri," pp. 44-47.)
33. Handwriting of Oliver Cowdery.
34. Handwriting of Frederick G. Williams.
35. The date of these baptisms is recorded incorrectly. On October 13 and 14 Joseph Smith was at Perrysburg, New York. The baptisms referred to here took place at Mt. Pleasant on October 27 and 28.
36. Moses C. Nickerson (1804-1871), born at Cavendish, Vermont, was a son of Freeman Nickerson and Huldah Chapman. (Family Group Records Collection.)
37. Andrew Rose (1782-1850), a native of Morris Plains, New Jersey, married Elizabeth Daniels; they were the parents of ten children. (Family Group Records Collection.)
38. Caroline Eliza Nickerson (1808-1889), born in Cavendish, Vermont, married Marshall M. Hubbard. (Family Group Records Collection.)

39. Probably the wife or daughter of Hiram Gates. She was born in 1802 at Brantford, Upper Canada. (Family Group Records Collection.)
40. Possibly Mary Birch (1783-1864), born at Brantford, Canada, to Charles Birch and Sarah Green; she married Henry Gates. (Temple Records Index Bureau.)
    An early plat showing land holdings at Mt. Pleasant indicates an alternate spelling of the name *Burtch*. (See "Plan of the Mount Pleasant and Phelps Tracts.")
41. Lydia Goldthwaite Bailey; see note 70, p. 655.
42. Possibly Elisabeth Gibbs (1819-1854), born in Canada to Joseph Gibbs and Elizabeth Strachan. (Temple Records Index Bureau.)
43. Early Mt. Pleasant land holdings list Abraham and Andrew Cook. ("Plan of the Mount Pleasant and Phelps Tracts.")
44. Orson Hyde (1805-1878), a member of the Council of the Twelve from 1835-1878, was a brother-in-law to Luke and Lyman Johnson. He was a Campbellite pastor in Ohio when he was converted by Mormon missionaries in 1831. He did extensive missionary work in the East and in New England in 1832. He was appointed with John Gould to deliver instructions to the Church in Missouri in 1833. His return is noted here bringing news of mob violence against the Saints in Jackson County, Missouri. (Jenson, *Biographical Encyclopedia* 1:80-82.)
45. John Gould (1808-1851), born in Ontario, Canada, was a member of the First Council of the Seventy in 1837. He was baptized prior to June 1833. (See Cook, *Revelations of the Prophet*, p. 204.)
46. After Independence, Missouri, was designated in an 1831 revelation as the center place of Zion, Latter-day Saints began moving there in large numbers. But political, social, and religious differences between the new settlers and the old brought open conflict. In July 1833, a mob destroyed Mormon property at Independence and committed violence upon some Church leaders. (Allen and Leonard, *Story of the Latter-day Saints*, pp. 81-90; see also p. 282-83 in this work.)
47. A council held in Kirtland on September 11, 1833, consisting of Frederick Williams, Sidney Rigdon, Newel Whitney, Joseph Smith, and Oliver Cowdery, resolved that a printing office be established there under the name of F. G. Williams & Co. to commence a new publication, the *Latter Day Saints' Messenger and Advocate*. The council also resolved to continue publication of *The Evening and the Morning Star*, printed at Independence, Missouri, prior to the destruction of the press there the previous July. The *Star* was to be published by Oliver Cowdery in Kirtland until it could be transferred to its former location in Missouri. The first Kirtland issue of the *Star* is dated December 1833. The *Messenger and Advocate* did not appear until the following October. (Smith, *History of the Church* 1:409.)
48. Don Carlos Smith (1816-1841), born in Norwich, Vermont, was a printer. President of the high priests quorum in Kirtland, he was the youngest brother of Joseph Smith. This marks the beginning of his printing career. He was editor of the *Elders' Journal* in Kirtland in 1837, and of the *Times and Seasons* in Nauvoo in 1839. (Smith, *History of the Church* 4:393-94; 398-99.)
49. Phineas Young (1799-1879), a brother of Brigham Young, joined the Church in April 1832 and was en route to Jackson County, Missouri, in 1833 when he received news of the driving of the Saints from that place. He returned to Kirtland and worked in the printing office. (*Deseret News*, February 3, 1858.)
50. Solomon Wilber Denton was employed in the Kirtland printing office until his disaffection in 1837. (Ebenezer Robinson, *The Return* 1 [August 1889].)
51. Hyrum Smith (1800-1844), born in Tunbridge, Vermont, was a witness to the Book of Mormon. A loyal supporter of his younger brother Joseph, he was a member of the committee to supervise transactions connected with building the Kirtland Temple. He later served as a counselor in the Church Presidency and as Church Patriarch. (Jenson, *Biographical Encyclopedia* 1:52.)

52. Samuel Harrison Smith (1808-1844), born in Tunbridge, Vermont, was a witness to the Book of Mormon. A farmer, he was one of the first converts to his brother's message, in 1829. He did early missionary work in New York and Ohio. He was a member of the Kirtland high council from 1834 to 1838. (Jenson, *Biographical Encyclopedia* 1:278-82.)

53. William Smith (1811-1893), born in Royalton, Vermont, was a brother of Joseph Smith and a member of the Council of the Twelve from 1835 to 1845. He was a participant in the march of Zion's Camp in 1834. Rebellious and headstrong, he was excommunicated in 1845. (Jenson, *Biographical Encyclopedia* 1:86-87.)

54. William Pratt (1802-1870), born in Wooster, New York, was a brother of Parley and Orson Pratt and a member of the first quorum of the seventy. He participated in the march of Zion's Camp in 1834. Geauga County tax records show that he owned sixty acres at Chester, just south of Kirtland, in 1834. (Pratt, *Autobiography*, p. 461; Smith, *History of the Church* 2:184, 204.)

55. David Patten (1800?-1838), a farmer, was a member of the Council of the Twelve from 1835 to 1838. He was born in Theresa, near Indian River Falls, New York. He joined the Church in Indiana in 1832 and served three proselyting missions prior to his departure for Missouri with William Pratt. He was killed in action against a mob near Crooked River, Missouri, in 1838. (Jenson, *Biographical Encyclopedia* 1:76-80; "History of David Patten," *Deseret News*, July 1858.)

56. Wilkins Jenkins Salisbury (1809-1853), a lawyer and blacksmith, was a member of the first quorum of the seventy. He married Joseph Smith's sister Katherine at Kirtland in 1831 and participated in the march of Zion's Camp in 1834. He was expelled from the Church for un-Christian conduct in 1836. (M. A. Anderson, *Ancestry and Posterity of Joseph Smith and Emma Hale*, p. 75; McGavin, *The Family of Joseph Smith*, pp. 95-108.)

57. Handwriting of Oliver Cowdery.

58. Newel K. Whitney (1795-1850), a merchant, was Church bishop from 1831 to 1850. He was a partner in the Gilbert & Whitney mercantile firm at Kirtland. He was baptized by Mormon missionaries in 1830 and was appointed bishop at Kirtland in 1831. (Jenson, *Biographical Encyclopedia* 1:222-27.)

59. John Johnson (1779-1843), a farmer, was born in Chesterfield, New Hampshire. He settled at Hiram, Ohio, in 1818 and joined the Church in 1831. He was a member of the Kirtland high council. Joseph Smith resided at his home in Hiram, Ohio, during work on the Bible revision. (*Deseret News*, May 26, 1858.)

60. As the social, religious, and ethical beliefs and practices of the Latter-day Saints came into conflict with those not of their faith, the Saints were plagued with agitation, distrust, and finally deliberate persecution. Antagonism against the Church in Ohio grew to such proportions, according to one witness, that "our enemies were raging and threatening destruction upon us, and we had to guard ourselves night after night, and for weeks were not permitted to take off our clothes, and were obliged to lay with our fire locks in our arms." (H. C. Kimball, "Extract from the Journal of Elder Heber C. Kimball," *Times and Seasons* 6:771; see also Parkin, *Conflict at Kirtland*, pp. 248-63.)

61. To consolidate and strengthen the business affairs of the Church for the benefit of the poor, the "United Order" or "United Firm" was established in March 1832, consisting of prominent Latter-day Saint merchants and landholders in Ohio and Missouri who united their holdings in a joint stewardship. The Firm, consisting of about a dozen Church leaders, was discontinued in April 1834. (See D&C 78 and 104; Arrington, Fox, and May, *Building the City of God*, p. 31; and Cook, *Revelations of the Prophet*, pp. 113-14, 167-68.)

62. Doctor Philastus Hurlbut (1809-1883) was born in Chittendon County, Vermont. (*Doctor* was his given name.) He joined the Church in 1833 but after a few months was excommunicated for immorality. He was subsequently employed by a Kirtland anti-Mormon committee to collect information disparaging to Joseph Smith and the Church.

Hurlbut was indicted for threatening to "wound, beat or kill" Joseph Smith. The preliminary hearing of his case was held at Painesville, Ohio, September 13-15, 1834, where it was ruled that Joseph "had reason to fear" Hurlbut, and the case was bound over for trial. (Parkin, *Conflict at Kirtland,* pp. 120-28; Maria S. Hurlbut statement, September 9, 1883.)

63. As originally written by Oliver Cowdery, the date was left blank. It was later supplied by Joseph Smith.

64. Handwriting of Frederick G. Williams.

65. According to Geauga County, Ohio, tax records, Elijah Smith owned 273 acres of land in Kirtland; Josiah Jones, 78 acres; Austin Loud, 2½ acres; Azariah Lyman, 8 acres; and Andrew Bardslee, 30 acres. In addition, Loud and Lyman jointly owned a sawmill, a gristmill, and 17 acres.

   Lyman was a pioneer settler of the area, having exchanged his farm in Massachusetts for land in the western wilderness in the early 1820s.

66. Handwriting of Frederick G. Williams.

67. On February 24, 1834, Joseph Smith presided at a council meeting in Kirtland to determine how best to restore fellow Church members to lands they had been driven from in Jackson County, Missouri. He departed with Parley Pratt on February 26 to visit branches of the Church in the East to solicit funds and volunteers to "assist in redeeming Zion." A revelation given that day named eight individuals traveling in pairs for this mission. (D&C 103:37-40; Smith, *History of the Church* 2:39-40. See also p. 313 of this work.)

68. Shadrach Roundy at Elk Creek, Erie County, Pennsylvania.

69. Job Lewis at Westfield, Chautauqua County, New York.

70. Parley Parker Pratt (1807-1857), born in Burlington, New York, was a member of the Council of the Twelve from 1835 to 1857. He was the elder brother of Orson Pratt. He became converted to the Church by reading the Book of Mormon in 1830. He was one of the four missionaries to Jackson County, Missouri, in 1830, and was among those driven from that county in 1833. In March 1834 he accompanied Joseph Smith into the settlements of western New York proselyting volunteers for Zion's Camp. (Jenson, *Biographical Encyclopedia* 1:83-85.)

71. This insertion by Parley P. Pratt.

72. Itinerary of Joseph Smith and Parley Pratt to obtain volunteers for the aid of Zion. Unidentified hand.

73. Handwriting of Parley Pratt.

74. Reuben McBride (1803-1891) was born in Chester, Washington County, New York. He was baptized March 4, 1834, and responded to the call for volunteers and participated later that year in the march of Zion's Camp. (Jenson, *Biographical Encyclopedia* 4:690.)

75. In Perrysburg, Cattaraugus County, New York.

76. The 1830 Federal Census lists a Hale Mathewson in Perrysburg, but no Mathews.

77. Possibly John McGown, who in 1830 was living at Olean to the south of Farmersville.

78. Probably Billings Walker, in his sixties, living with his wife and five children at Farmersville in 1830. (1830 Federal Census.)

79. Warren A. Cowdery (1788-1851), a physician and druggist, was born in Poultney, Vermont. An elder brother of Oliver Cowdery, Warren practiced medicine in Vermont and Freedom, New York. The 1830 census lists ten in his family besides himself. He moved to Freedom in 1815 and became postmaster. After his baptism he presided over the branch of the Church there beginning in 1834. He moved to Kirtland the next year and was involved in managing the book bindery and printing office. He was also editor of the *Messenger and Advocate* and was clerk to Joseph Smith. (Carl C. Curtis, Cowdery genealogical material.)

80. Heman Hyde (1788-1867) was born in Manchester, Vermont. Hyde and seven members of his family were living in Freedom, New York, in 1830.

Parley Pratt wrote, "We visited Freedom . . . tarried over Sunday, and preached several discourses, to which the people listened with great interest; we were kindly and hospitably entertained among them. We baptized a young man named Heman Hyde; his parents were Presbyterians, and his mother, on account of the strength of her traditions, thought that we were wrong, and told me afterwards that she would much rather have followed him to an earthly grave than to have seen him baptized. Soon afterwards, however, herself, her husband, and the rest of the family, with some thirty or forty others, were all baptized and organized into a branch of the Church." (Pratt, *Autobiography*, pp. 109-10.

81. Edmund Bosley (1776-1846) was born in Northumberland, Pennsylvania. In 1830 the Bosley family of nine was living in Livonia, Livingston County, New York.

82. In 1830 Alvah Beman (1775-1837) and his family of six, including four daughters, resided at Livonia, New York.

   Parley Pratt reported the visit to Beman's: "Among those whose hospitality we shared in that vicinity was old father Beeman and his amiable and interesting family. He was a good singer, and so were his three daughters; we were much edified and comforted in their society, and were deeply interested in hearing the old gentleman and brother Joseph converse on their early acquaintance and history. He had been intimate with Joseph long before the first organization of the Church; had assisted him to preserve the plates of the Book of Mormon from the enemy, and had at one time had them concealed under his own hearth." (Pratt, *Autobiography*, p. 110.)

83. Lyman Wight (1796-1858), born in Fairfield, New York, was a member of the Council of the Twelve from 1841 to 1848. A veteran of the War of 1812, he was affiliated with the Campbellites in Kirtland when converted to the Church in 1830. He was among those driven from Jackson County, Missouri, in 1833. The revelation that called missionaries to solicit volunteers for Zion's Camp listed Wight and Sidney Rigdon as companions. (D&C 103:38; Jenson, *Biographical Encyclopedia* 1:93.)

84. On March 17, 1834, a "conference of Elders" convened at the home of Alvah Beman. Among these elders were Joseph Smith, Sidney Rigdon, Parley Pratt, Lyman Wight, John Murdock, Orson Pratt, and Orson Hyde, high priests; and Roger Orton, Isaac McWithey, Joseph Young, Harvy Brown, Freeman Nickerson, and Henry Shibly, elders. The purpose of the meeting was "to obtain . . . men . . . to go and assist in the redemption of Zion" and to obtain funds for the purchase of land and for the relief of the Church at Kirtland. Joseph Smith, Edmund Bosley, Roger Orton, Freeman Nickerson, and Isaac McWithey were directed to unite their efforts to raise $2,000, which was felt "would deliver Kirtland from debt for the present." The conference also voted that Joseph, Sidney, and Lyman should soon return to Kirtland, and that Parley Pratt and Harvy Brown should visit the churches in the Black River country of New York to obtain money for the help of Zion. Orson Hyde, clerk of the conference, was instructed to remain in the area preaching until he could bring the collected moneys to Kirtland. This conference marked the end of Joseph and Parley's conjoint mission. (Kirtland Council Minutes, March 17, 1834.)

85. Isaac McWithey (ca. 1786-1851) and his family of four were living at Bennington, Genesee County, New York, in 1830.

86. Joseph Holbrook (1806-1885) joined the Church in 1833 and participated in the march of Zion's Camp in 1834. He worked on the Kirtland Temple and was a member of the first quorum of the seventy. (Esshom, *Pioneers and Prominent Men of Utah*, p. 938.)

87. The 1830 Federal Census lists Reuben Wilson (in his sixties) and his family of seven living in China, Genesee County, New York.

88. The 1830 Federal Census lists Joseph Starks (in his thirties) and his family of seven living at Sardinia, Erie County, about six miles east of Springville.

89. Vinson Knight (1804-1842), born in Norwich, Massachusetts, was appointed counselor

to Bishop Newel K. Whitney in Kirtland on January 13, 1836. Knight owned a farm at Perrysburg, New York. The 1830 Federal Census lists the Knight family of six. (Cook, *Revelations of the Prophet*, p. 265.)

90. At the Hurlbut trial, beginning April 2, 1834, it was ruled that Joseph Smith "had ground to fear that the said . . . Hurlbut would wound, beat or kill him, or destroy his property." Hurlbut was ordered to post a $200 bond "to keep the peace" for six months and to pay the court costs, which amounted to $112.59. (Geauga County, Ohio, Common Pleas Court, book M, April 9, 1834, p. 193.)

91. Possibly Samuel Rider, born in Massachusetts in 1805 and a property holder in Chardon in 1835.

92. Handwriting of Oliver Cowdery.

93. On April 5, 1834, John Johnson was granted a license to keep a tavern in Kirtland. Joseph Smith testified before the court on Johnson's qualifications. (Geauga County, Ohio, Common Pleas Court, book M, April 5, 1834, p. 184.)

94. Benjamin Bissell is one of a dozen attorneys listed in Geauga County tax records for the 1830s. He was a partner with Noah D. Matoon, a prominent Painesville lawyer. Bissell later served as presiding judge of the district court and was a member of the upper house of the state legislature. At the height of legal harassment against Joseph Smith in 1837, Bissell was the Prophet's attorney. (*History of Geauga and Lake Counties, Ohio*, p. 30.)

95. Handwriting of Frederick G. Williams.

96. Heber C. Kimball (1801-1868), born in Sheldon, Vermont, was a member of the Council of the Twelve from 1835 to 1847. He was a counselor in the First Presidency from 1847 to 1868. Engaged as a potter in Mendon, New York, when converted by Mormon missionaries in April 1832, he moved to Kirtland in 1833. He participated in the march of Zion's Camp in 1834. (Jenson, *Biographical Encyclopedia* 1:34-37.)

97. See note 61.

98. See note 90.

99. Algernon Sidney Gilbert (1789-1834), born in New Haven, Connecticut, was a merchant at Painesville, Ohio, and subsequently a partner with Newel K. Whitney in the firm Gilbert & Whitney in Kirtland. He joined the Church in 1830 and was among the Saints driven from Jackson County, Missouri, in 1833. He authored much correspondence between Church leaders and Missouri Governor Dunklin. He died during the march of Zion's Camp in 1834. (Smith, *History of the Church* 2:118-19.)

100. In the manuscript this sentence has been enclosed from the material around it by a pen line.

101. Handwriting of Oliver Cowdery.

102. Zebedee Coltrin (1804-1887), a member of the First Council of the Seventy from 1835 to 1837, was born at Ovid, Seneca County, New York. He joined the Church in 1830, was a member of the Kirtland high council, and participated in the march of Zion's Camp in 1834. (Jenson, *Biographical Encyclopedia* 1:190.)

103. William W. Williams (1790-1852) was born in Suffield, Connecticut. The 1830 Federal Census lists him and his family of ten at Newburg, Cayuga County, Ohio. (Temple Records Index Bureau.)

104. Joseph Bucklin Bosworth (1790-1850) was born in Scituate, Rhode Island. The 1830 Federal Census lists him and his family of eleven at Copley, Medina County, Ohio. (Early Church Information File.)

105. Jonathan Taylor, in his twenties, is listed in the 1830 Federal Census at Norton, Medina County, Ohio.

106. At the September 24, 1834, meeting of the Kirtland high council, Joseph Smith, Oliver Cowdery, Sidney Rigdon, and Frederick Williams were appointed a committee to "arrange the items of doctrine" of the Church and publish them as a "book of covenants."

107. The proceedings of the conference held at the residence of Richard Carpenter in Norton,

Medina County, Ohio, are summarized in the Kirtland Council Minutes, April 21, 1834, and in Smith, *History of the Church* 2:52-54. Seven high priests and thirteen elders were present. Carpenter, in his thirties, is listed at Norton in the 1830 Federal Census.

108. At this council, the revelation recorded in D&C 104 was given to the Church.

109. Jacob Myre (Meyer?), ordained an elder at New Portage, Ohio, June 6, 1835, was among those wounded during the attack at Haun's Mill, Missouri, in October 1839. (Smith, *History of the Church* 2:228; 3:326.)

110. Handwriting of Frederick G. Williams.

111. Milton Holmes (1794-1863), born in North Attleboro, Massachusetts, was living at Napoli, Cattaraugus County, New York, in 1830. He was called as a missionary to Canada with Lyman Johnson in February 1834, participated in the march of Zion's Camp, and was a member of the second quorum of the seventy. (Temple Records Index Bureau; Smith, *History of the Church* 2:35; 1830 Federal Census.)

112. Henry Herriman (1803-1891), born in Bradford, Essex County, Massachusetts, was a president of seventies from 1838 to 1891. He joined the Church in 1832 and moved to Kirtland in 1834. He was a missionary to Canada with Zebedee Coltrin in 1834 and was a Zion's Camp participant. (Cook, *Revelations of the Prophet*, p. 261.)

113. Sylvester Smith, born about 1805, was a member of the first quorum of the seventy from 1835 to 1837. A missionary to New England with Jared Carter in 1832, he was a member of the Kirtland high council from 1835 to 1836 and was a quarrelsome participant in Zion's Camp. He served as a temporary scribe to Joseph Smith in 1836 during an illness of Warren Parrish. He was excommunicated in December 1837. (Jenson, *Biographical Encyclopedia* 1:191; Cook, *Revelations of the Prophet*, p. 156.)

114. Harvey Stanley, born about 1811 in Kirtland, Ohio, was a member of the first quorum of the seventy. He was a Zion's Camp participant. (Temple Records Index Bureau.)

115. William F. Cahoon (1813-1893), a member of the first quorum of the seventy, was born in Harpersfield, Ashtabula County, Ohio. His parents moved to Kirtland in 1825, heard Mormon missionaries in 1830, and were baptized. He was a Zion's Camp participant. (Jenson, *Biographical Encyclopedia* 4:687-88.)

116. Unidentified writing.

117. Dexter Stillman (1804-1852), born in Colbrook, Connecticut, worked on the Kirtland Temple. (Temple Records Index Bureau; Smith, *History of the Church* 2:206.)

118. Lyman Eugene Johnson (1811-1856), a merchant and lawyer, was a member of the Council of the Twelve from 1835 to 1838. A son of John Johnson, he was born in Pomfret, Windsor County, Vermont, and was baptized in 1831. He was a missionary with Orson Pratt to the eastern states in 1832, was one of the eight men chosen in 1834 to solicit funds and volunteers for the assistance of the Saints driven from Jackson County, and was a participant in Zion's Camp. He was excommunicated in 1838. (Jenson, *Biographical Encyclopedia* 1:91-92.)

119. Handwriting of Oliver Cowdery. In the manuscript, half a page preceding this entry is blank.

120. Reference to the cholera epidemic that was sweeping the country at the time. (See note 10, p. 670.)

121. Jared Carter (1801-1850), born at Benson, Vermont, joined the Church and was ordained an elder in 1831. He was a missionary in Michigan in 1832 and was a member of the Kirtland high council. He was also one of the committee for transacting business connected with construction of the Kirtland Temple. (Smith, *History of the Church* 2:333, 277-80; Kirtland Council Minutes, September 19, 1835.)

122. Handwriting of Oliver Cowdery.

123. Oliver Cowdery retained this office through September 1837, when he was found in transgression, but continued as one of four assistant counselors to Joseph Smith. (Smith, *History of the Church* 2:511.)

124. Pages 94-102 of this diary have been numbered but are blank.
125. Handwriting unidentified.
126. The 1830 Federal Census lists Elisha Hubbard, in his fifties, at Perrysburg, Cattaraugus County, New York. "Perysburgh" has been added in pencil.
127. Samuel and James McBride are listed in the 1830 Federal Census at Villanova, Chautauqua County, New York.
128. The 1830 Federal Census lists Eleazer, Samuel, and Richard Nickerson at Yarmouth, Barnstable County, Massachusetts.
129. Handwriting of Oliver Cowdery.
130. This statement, written in light pencil in contrast to the ink generally used in the diary, probably refers to the conference held at Norton, Medina County, Ohio, on April 12, 1834.

Diary, 1835-1836

Ms. Joseph Smith Papers, LDS Church Archives. Material from this diary was published in Smith, *History of the Church,* beginning at 2:281.

1. Handwriting of Oliver Cowdery.
2. Ezra Thayre was a member of the committee to purchase land for Mormon settlement at Kirtland in 1833. He was a participant in Zion's Camp in 1834. (Smith, *History of the Church* 1:335; 2:185.)
3. A characteristic of Joseph Smith's holograph writing is his consistent lack of punctuation. However, occasionally he did take time to review what he had written and add this literary convenience. In the foregoing entry the punctuation is his own, and at the beginning of newly created sentences he has changed lowercase letters to uppercase ones.
4. On November 28, 1834, the Kirtland high council met to consider a letter presented to them by John and Joseph Tippets, members of the Church from Lewis, Essex County, New York, listing money and property totaling $848.40 being sent by the Church in Essex County to purchase land in Missouri. Desiring the counsel of the Church leadership on the matter, the two men were advised to remain in Kirtland during the winter and make part of their money available for use of the Church there, to be repaid with interest the following year. At a high council meeting on August 24, 1835, the Tippetses were appointed to go to Missouri the coming fall "to purchase land for the church in Essex, New York." Joseph Smith's September 23 entry marks the departure of these men. (See Kirtland Council Minutes, November 28, 1834; August 24, 1835.)
5. David Whitmer (1805-1888), a Book of Mormon witness, was born near Harrisburg, Pennsylvania. He first met Joseph Smith during a business trip to Palmyra, New York in 1828. He was baptized in June 1829 and was a member of the Missouri high council. (Jenson, *Biographical Encyclopedia* 1:263-71; R. L. Anderson, *Investigating the Book of Mormon Witnesses,* pp. 67-92.)
6. John Whitmer wrote of this meeting on September 24: "We met in counsel at the house of J. Smith, Jr., the seer, where we according to a previous commandment given, appointed David Whitmer captain of the Lord's Host, and Presidents F. G. Williams and Sidney Rigdon his assistants' and President W. W. Phelps, myself and John Corrill, as an assistant quorum, and Joseph Smith, Jr., the seer, to stand at the head and be assisted by Hyrum Smith and Oliver Cowdery. This much for the war department, by revelation." (Whitmer, "Book of John Whitmer," ch. 17.)
7. Handwriting of Oliver Cowdery.
8. On March 12, 1835, shortly after their appointment, the Council of the Twelve were called on a mission to the eastern states to "hold conferences in the vicinity of the several branches of the Church for the purpose of regulating all things necessary for their welfare." The Twelve left Kirtland on May 4 and returned September 26, 1835. ("A Record of the Transactions of the Twelve Apostles of the Church of Christ," p. 4.)

9. On this date the presidency, consisting of Joseph Smith, Sidney Rigdon, David Whitmer, William Phelps, John Whitmer, Hyrum Smith, and Oliver Cowdery, met to consider two charges against the Twelve: one from a Warren A. Cowdery letter containing reports "derogatory to the character and teaching" of the Twelve while on their mission to the East, and another from William McLellin and Orson Hyde expressing dissatisfaction with Sidney Rigdon. The charges growing out of the Cowdery letter were found to be false, and the McLellin and Hyde matter was satisfactorily resolved. (Kirtland Council Minutes, September 26, 1835. See also the Joseph Smith diary entry of January 16, 1836.)

10. Thomas B. Marsh (1799-1866), a member of the Council of the Twelve from 1835 to 1838, was born in Acton, Massachusetts. An early Church convert, he moved to Kirtland in 1831 and to Jackson County in 1832. He was among the Saints driven from Jackson County the following year. He was a member of the Clay County high council in Missouri in 1834 and was named President of the Quorum of the Twelve in 1835. (Jenson, *Biographical Encyclopedia* 1:74-76.)

11. Brigham Young (1801-1877) was a member of the Council of the Twelve from 1835 to 1847 and Church President from 1848 to 1877. Born in Whitingham, Vermont, he was a carpenter, painter, and glazier in Mendon, New York, when he joined the Church in 1832. He moved to Kirtland in 1833 and participated in Zion's Camp the following year. His Kirtland years were divided between missionary work and labor on the temple. (Jenson, *Biographical Encyclopedia* 1:8-14.)

12. Francis Gladden Bishop was born in 1809 at Greece, Monroe County, New York. An elder, he had been president of the branch at Westfield, New York. On this date he was charged with "advancing heretical doctrines . . . derogatory to the character of the Church." In 1842 he was excommunicated for purveying his own revelations as doctrine. (Kirtland Council Minutes, September 28, 1835; Smith, *History of the Church* 2:284-85.)

13. A charge was brought against Avery for rebelling against the decision of the elder's court that took away his license. However, Avery came forward, readily complied with the requisitions of the council, and was restored to his office. (Kirtland Council Minutes, September 29, 1835.)

14. Phineas Young was accused of "unchristian like conduct" in transactions involving the transfer of copies of the Book of Mormon during a recent proselyting journey, but the council found no cause for action, and he was acquitted. (Kirtland Council Minutes, September 29, 1835.)

15. Lorenzo Young (1807-1895), a nurseryman, born in Smyrna, New York, was a brother to Brigham Young, a participant in Zion's Camp, and a worker on the Kirtland Temple. A charge had been brought against Lorenzo by W. W. Phelps for teaching that "poor men ought not to raise up seed or children" but that marriage relations were nevertheless acceptable. The charge was dismissed. (Jenson, *Biographical Encyclopedia* 4:724-25; Kirtland Council Minutes, September 29, 1835.)

16. In July 1835 the Kirtland Saints purchased Egyptian records from one Michael Chandler, who had come to Kirtland after hearing of Joseph Smith's notoriety as a linguist. A "Grammar & Alphabet of the Egyptian Language" was the product of early study of these ancient materials. (Smith, *History of the Church* 2:235-36.)

17. William W. Phelps (1792-1872), a newspaper editor, was born in Hanover, New Jersey. After arriving in Kirtland in 1831, he was appointed to assist in the Church printing office. He was the editor of *The Evening and the Morning Star* and was a counselor to David Whitmer in the Missouri stake presidency. He assisted Joseph Smith in a clerical capacity. (Jenson, *Biographical Encyclopedia* 3:692-97.)

18. Commencing in the September issue of the *Latter Day Saints' Messenger and Advocate* published in Kirtland under the editorship of John Whitmer, Joseph Smith published three letters in successive issues with the intent "that perhaps the elders traveling

through the world . . . may be aided in a measure, in doctrine, and in the way of their duty." (See *Messenger and Advocate*, September–December 1835; also Smith, *History of the Church* 2:253-72.)

19. Handwriting of Frederick G. Williams.

20. Dean Gould was a non-Mormon member of Zion's Camp, but he was baptized upon his arrival in Missouri. (Smith, *History of the Church* 2:72, 95.)

21. The council considered charges against the two Goulds by Reynolds Cahoon—John for "making expressions . . . calculated to do injury to the . . . cause . . . and manifesting a very strong dissatisfaction against the teachings of the Presidency of the Church"; and Dean for "using wrong expressions and threatening the Elders of the Church," specifically Sidney Rigdon. At this meeting "the wound was healed." (Kirtland Council Minutes, October 3, 1835.)

22. John Corrill, an architect, was born in 1794 in Worcester County, Massachusetts. He was living in Harpersville, Ashtabula County, Ohio, when he was converted in 1830. He served as a second counselor to Bishop Edward Partridge from 1831 to 1837 and was prominent in Missouri Church affairs. He directed the later stages of the Kirtland Temple construction. He was appointed Church historian in 1838 but soon after left the Church. (See Cook, *Revelations of the Prophet*, p. 68.)

23. The calling of a "solemn assembly" in December 1832 (D&C 88:70), in which an "endowment" of spiritual power, a day of Pentecost, would be poured out upon the faithful "first laborers" in the kingdom in order that they might be "prepared and able to overcome all things," was to be preceded by a period of preparation consisting of study classes and participation in the ordinances of washing and anointing. (See Cook, *Revelations of the Prophet*, pp. 182-83.)

24. To better qualify the elders of the Church for the building of the kingdom and to prepare for the anticipated "solemn assembly," a school, known as the "school of the prophets" or "school of the elders," was organized in Kirtland. Beginning in 1833, instruction continued during four winter seasons. The 1835-1836 session of the school met between November 2 and March 29. An important part of the school, which generally convened in the printing office, was the study of Hebrew. (Cook, *Revelations of the Prophet*, pp. 185-91.)

Heber Kimball noted that four hundred attended the school in the winter of 1835. He wrote, "Some studied grammar and other branches. We also employed the celebrated Hebrew teacher Mr. Seixas, who gave us much insight in a short time, into that language. . . . The Elders and church had been previously commanded to seek learning and study the best books, and get a knowledge of countries, kingdoms, languages &c., which inspired us with an untiring thirst after knowledge." ("Journal and Record of Heber Chase Kimball," pp. 34-35.)

25. Possibly Jonathan Stevens, who, along with his two sons Uzziel and Lyman and his son-in-law John E. Page, was told by the Kirtland high council in August 1835 to settle his family in Kirtland and then go forth to preach the gospel. (Kirtland Council Minutes, August 24, 1835.)

26. The translation work referred to eventually produced the Book of Abraham, canonized as LDS scripture.

27. Handwriting of Warren Parrish to page 38 of the manuscript.

28. Ebenezer Robinson (1816-1891), a printer, was born in Floyd, Oneida County, New York. He learned the printing trade in Utica, New York, and Ravenna, Ohio. He came to Kirtland in May 1835 and began work in the printing office. He was appointed Church clerk and recorder, and as clerk of the high council in Missouri in 1838. He served as publisher and coeditor of the *Times and Seasons* from 1839 to 1840. (See Robinson, "Items of Personal History of the Editor," *The Return*, vols. 1-3.)

Of his baptism, Robinson wrote, "At dinner that day, (Oct. 16, 1835) Joseph Smith,

Jr. finished his meal a little before the others at the table, and went and stood in the door-
way (the door being open, it being a warm pleasant day,) with his back to the door jamb,
when we arose and went and stood before him, and looking him in the face said, 'do you
know what I want? when he replied, 'No, without it is to go into the waters of Jordan.'
We told him that was what we wanted, when he said he would attend to it that afternoon. We then went to the printing office together, he to his council room which ad-
joined the room where we worked, and we to our work in the printing office. We worked
until well on to the evening, feeling very anxious all the time, for it seemed that we could
not live over night without being baptized; after enduring it as long as we could, went to
the door of their room, and gently opened it, (a thing we had never presumed to do before.) As soon as Mr. Smith saw us he said, 'yes, yes, brethren, Brother Robinson wishes
to be baptized, we will adjourn and attend to that.' We repaired to the water, (the Chagrin river which flows through Kirtland,) and, after a season of prayer, Brother Joseph
Smith, jr., baptized us by immersion." (Robinson, *The Return*, 1:74.)
29. One of those confirmed on October 18 was Ebenezer Robinson.
30. For information on John F. Boynton, see note 41.
      John Whitmer adds this detail to the events of October 18: "This day assembled in
the House of the Lord as usual, and the Spirit of the Lord descended upon J. Smith, Jr.,
the seer, and he prophesied saying, the Lord has showed me this day by the Spirit of revelation that the distress and sickness that has heretofore prevailed among the children of
Zion will be mitigated from this time forth. And it came to pass that some of the first elders or presidents of the church received a prophetic blessing by revelation through the
means prepared in the last days to receive the word of the LORD, J. Smith, Jr. Therefore
Joseph dictated blessings for himself, Hyrum Smith, Sidney Rigdon, F. G. Williams,
Oliver Cowdery, David Whitmer, W. W. Phelps, and myself, as you will find recorded in
the Patriarchal blessing book in Kirtland, Ohio, Book A." (Whitmer, "Book of John
Whitmer," ch. 17.)
31. A prayer offered on this day was recorded following the November 27, 1835, diary entry
on pages 50-51 of the manuscript. (See p. 93 of this work.)
32. Probably Joseph B. Hawkes (1799-1862) born in Buxton, New York. Family records
show him in Pontiac, Oakland County, Michigan, in 1834, and in Far West, Missouri,
in 1836. (Family Group Records Collection.)
33. The William Perry family of four was among those who migrated to Missouri with the
Kirtland Camp in 1838. (Smith, *History of the Church* 3:92.)
34. Samuel H. Smith married Mary Bailey on August 13, 1834. A daughter, Susanna, the
first of four children, was born October 27, 1833. Mary Bailey died in 1841. (See the
entry of November 3, 1835, on p. 72 of this work.)
35. Warren Parrish, born about 1800, was a brother-in-law of David Patten. A member of
the first quorum of the seventy, he was baptized by Brigham Young in May 1833 and participated in Zion's Camp in 1834. He was secretary of the Kirtland bank in 1836. A year
later he renounced his membership and openly dissented against the Church. (Smith,
History of the Church 2:184, 203, 293, 484-86, 528.)
36. Edward Partridge (1793-1840), born in Pittsfield, Massachusetts, was a hatter, living in
Painesville, Ohio, when he was converted by Mormon missionaries in 1830. He was the
first bishop of the Church, in 1831, and was called to oversee the settlement of the Saints
in Zion (Jackson County, Missouri) in 1831. In 1833 he was a victim of mob violence. In
January 1835 he went on a proselyting mission in the eastern states and New England, returning to Kirtland on October 29, where he remained until the following spring. (Jenson, *Biographical Encyclopedia* 1:218-22.)
37. The "large journal" referred to here later became volume A-1 of the manuscript of Joseph
Smith's *History of the Church*. The involvement of Frederick Williams, Warren Parrish,
and Warren A. Cowdery in writing Joseph's "large Journal," its format and content, and

its discontinuance and later use for the Church history are outlined in Jessee, "The Writing of Joseph Smith's History," pp. 283-84.

38. A discussion of Joseph Smith's master plan for Kirtland is found in Parkin, *Conflict at Kirtland*, pp. 210-12.

    According to Wilford Woodruff, "Joseph presented us in some degree the plot of the city of Kirtland . . . as it was given him by vision. It was great, marvelous and glorious. The city extended to the east, west, north, and south. Steam boats will come puffing into the city. Our goods will be conveyed upon railroads from Kirtland to many places and probably to Zion. Houses of worship would be reared unto the most high. Beautiful streets was to be made for the saints to walk in, Kings of the earth would come to behold the glory thereof, and many glorious things not now to be named would be bestowed upon the saints." (Wilford Woodruff Diary, April 6, 1837.)

39. Samuel and Susanna Kimball Whitney from Marlborough, Vermont.

40. The high council met at Edmund Bosley's to consider a charge made by William Smith against David Elliott and his wife for "beating and whipping" their fifteen-year-old daughter. During the hearing Joseph testified he "was satisfied that the girl was at fault, and that the neighbors were trying to create a difficulty." The council ruled, however, that "the complaint was not without foundation," that Elliott had "acted injudiciously and brought a disgrace upon himself, upon his daughter & upon this Church, because he ought to have trained his child in a way that should not have required the rod at the age of 15 years." After confessing their wrongdoing and promising to improve, the accused were "restored to fellowship." (Kirtland Council Minutes, October 29, 1835.)

41. John F. Boynton (1811-1890), a merchant, lecturer, and inventor, was a member of the Council of the Twelve from 1835 to 1837. He was born in Bradford, Massachusetts, and joined the Church in 1832. He established a mercantile business in Kirtland with Lyman Johnson. He left the Church in 1837. (Jenson, *Biographical Encyclopedia* 1:91.)

42. Mary Elliott was confronted with the same charge previously brought against her husband, with the same result. See note 40.

43. The 1830 Federal Census lists Francis Porter (in his forties) and his family of eleven, at LeRoy, Jefferson County, New York.

44. See note 24.

45. Daniel Levy Madura Piexotto was a graduate of Columbia College and Medical School. As a medical lecturer and editor he had helped found the Academy of Medicine and from 1830 to 1832 was president of the New York County Medical Society. When Joseph Smith met him, Piexotto was Professor of Theory and Practice of Physics and Obstetrics at Willoughby Medical College. (Zucker, "Joseph Smith as a Student of Hebrew," p. 44; also *History of Geauga and Lake Counties, Ohio*, p. 40.)

46. George A. Smith (1817-1875), member of the Council of the Twelve from 1839 to 1875, was born in Potsdam, New York. He was a cousin of Joseph Smith. Baptized in 1832, he moved to Kirtland in 1833 and was a participant in Zion's Camp in 1834. He was called to the first quorum of the seventy. On June 5, 1835, he and a second cousin, Lyman Smith, were sent on a proselyting mission: "We traveled about two thousand miles on foot, without purse or scrip, through the eastern part of Ohio, the western part of Pennsylvania and New York; held about eighty meetings, baptized eight, and preached from house to house continually." The two missionaries arrived back in Kirtland on November 2, 1835. (*Deseret News*, August 18, 1858.)

47. King Follett (1788-1844), a native of Vermont, was living in Cayahoga County, Ohio, when he joined the Latter-day Saints in 1831. (Smith, *History of the Church* 6:248-49.)

48. Isaac Morley (1786-1865), a cooper, was born in Montague, Massachusetts. Among the first converts in Kirtland, Ohio, he was appointed counselor to Bishop Edward Partridge in 1831. He was among those driven from Jackson County, Missouri, in 1833, and he went east with Bishop Partridge on a proselyting mission in 1835; he arrived back in Kirtland on November 5, 1835. (Jenson, *Biographical Encyclopedia* 1:235-36.)

49. Thomas Burdick, born about 1795 at Canajoharie, Montgomery County, New York, was appointed Church clerk to record membership licenses in February 1836. The following year he was Kirtland justice of the peace and a member of the high council. (Smith, *History of the Church* 2:400, 522.)
50. See entry of November 3, 1835, on pp. 71-72 of this work.
51. James 5:17-18.
52. Zerubbabel Snow (1809-1888) was born in St. Johnsbury, Vermont, where he was converted in 1832. He was commissary of Zion's Camp in 1834. He became associate justice of Utah Territory in 1850. (Jenson, *Biographical Encyclopedia* 4:691.)
53. Joseph Young (1797-1881), one of the presidents of the seventy from 1835 to 1881, was born in Hopkinton, Massachusetts. Baptized by his brother Brigham in 1832, he participated in Zion's Camp in 1834 and engaged in missionary work in New York and Massachusetts in 1835. (Jenson, *Biographical Encyclopedia* 1:187-88.)
54. Isaac Hill (1806-1879) was born in Brighton, Beaver County, Pennsylvania. According to Geauga County tax lists, he owned two and a half acres in Kirtland in 1836. (Early Church Information File.)
55. John Smith (1781-1854), born in Derryfield, New Hampshire, was an uncle to Joseph Smith. He joined the Church in 1832 and moved to Kirtland the following year. He later became the Church's presiding Patriarch from 1849 to 1854. (Jenson, *Biographical Encyclopedia* 1:182-83.)
56. This insertion in the hand of William W. Phelps was probably added at a later date.
57. Robert Matthews, alias Robert Matthias, alias Joshua the Jewish minister, a joiner and merchant, was born in Cambridge, New York, in the decade after 1795. He resided at Albany in 1830 with his wife and family of five. He was a religious eccentric who claimed to be God the Father reincarnated in the body of Matthias the ancient apostle. In 1830 he prophesied the destruction of Albany. He taught that no man who shaved could be a true Christian. He left Albany and his family to embark on a grand apostolic preaching tour through the East and South. Upon his return to New York, he joined with kindred spirits—Pierson and Folger. He was described as "one of the most striking figures in the New York of the early Thirties." Committed to the hospital for the insane at Bellevue for a time, he was brought to trial in April 1835 at White Plains, New York, on murder charges following the death of Mr. Pierson after he ate blackberries prepared by Matthias. He was acquitted of the murder charge but was confined in jail three months for brutality. Little is known of Matthias after he left Kirtland. An 1839 newspaper reported that the people of Little Rock, Arkansas, had seized him, shaved his beard, and threatened him with a closer shave by "Dr. Lynch" if he did not leave town. (Seldes, *The Stammering Century*, pp. 118-31; *Alton Commercial Gazette*, February 19, 1839; Parkin, *Conflict at Kirtland*, pp. 244-47.)
58. Artemus Millet (1790-1874), born in Westmoreland, New Hampshire. (Early Church Information File.)
59. Jacob Bump, born in 1791 in Butternuts, Otsego County, New York. He was a participant in Zion's Camp but later joined dissenters at Kirtland to depose Joseph Smith. (*Deseret News*, February 10, 1858.)
60. Hezekiah Peck, born in 1782 in Windham County, Vermont, was living at Bainbridge, Chenango County, New York, in 1830 when he and his wife were converted. He was named as a counselor to Bishop John Corrill in Missouri in 1833. (Smith, *History of the Church* 1:88, 363; 1830 Federal Census.)
61. Harvey Whitlock, born in 1809 in Massachusetts, joined the Church and moved to Jackson County, Missouri, in 1831. He was among those expelled in 1833. He was excommunicated in 1835. (Cook, *Revelations of the Prophet*, p. 81.)
62. Possibly Elial Strong, one of the first converts from Rutland, Tioga County, Pennsylvania. He was baptized in 1831. Strong was among the missionaries that converted

Heber C. Kimball and Brigham Young at Mendon, New York, that same year. (Journal History, December 31, 1831; April 15, 1832.)

63. Handwriting of Frederick G. Williams.

64. Handwriting of Warren Parrish to page 87 of the manuscript.

65. Preserved Harris (1785-1867), born in Palmyra, New York, was the younger brother of Martin (born in 1783) and Emer Harris (born in 1781). Their father, Nathan, born March 23, 1758, at Providence, Rhode Island, died at Mentor, Lake County, Ohio, on November 11, 1835. (Family Group Records Collection.)

66. Lorenzo Lewis had been cut off from the Church by the Kirtland high council on September 28, 1835, for immorality. The case is recorded in the Kirtland Council Minutes.

67. Simeon Carter (1794-1869), born in Killingworth, Connecticut, was a member of the Missouri high council. (Smith, *History of the Church* 2:523.)

68. Andrew Jackson Squires, having been ordained an elder and "preached the gospel successfully," had joined the Methodists for a time but desired to return to fellowship in the Church. At this council, convened to hear his case, Joseph Smith spoke on the "impropriety of turning away from the truth," and Sidney Rigdon spoke on the "folly of fellowshipping any doctrine or spirit aside from that of Christ." After a repentant expression, Squires was again restored to fellowship and his office as elder. (Kirtland Council Minutes, November 22, 1835.)

69. Newell Knight (1800-1847), a miller, was born in Marlborough, Vermont. He was living in Colesville, New York, when converted by Joseph Smith. He moved to Ohio, then Missouri, in 1831. He was among those expelled from Jackson County in 1833. His first wife, Sally Coburn, died in Missouri in September 1834. Returning to Ohio, he worked on the Kirtland Temple and boarded at the Hyrum Smith home, where he met Lydia Bailey. (Jenson, *Biographical Encyclopedia* 2:773-75.)

70. Lydia Goldthwaite Knight (1812-1884), born in Sutton, Massachusetts, married Calvin Bailey in 1828 but was deserted by her husband three years later. While visiting friends or relatives in Mt. Pleasant, Ontario, Canada, in 1833, Lydia was converted by Joseph Smith. Returning to her parents in New York in 1834 and being derided for her religion, she gathered with the Saints at Kirtland in 1835. While working for Hyrum Smith, she met Newell Knight, who was boarding at Hyrum's home. (Jenson, *Biographical Encyclopedia* 2:775-76.)

71. Harvey Redfield (1788-1802), born in Killingworth, Massachusetts. (Family Group Records Collection.)

72. Jesse Hitchcock was born in 1801 in Ash County, North Carolina. He was a member of the Missouri high council from 1836 to 1837. (Smith, *History of the Church* 2:482.)

73. Robert Rathbone (1799-1874) was born in Lisbon, New London, Connecticut. He was a missionary with Luke Johnson in southern Ohio in 1831. (Family Group Records Collection; Jenson, *Biographical Encyclopedia* 1:85.)

74. George Morey, born in 1803 in Pittstown, New York, was living in Vermillion County, Indiana, in 1830. He was a member of the Missouri high council from 1837 to 1838. (Family Group Records Collection; Smith, *History of the Church* 2:504.)

75. Solon Foster (1811-1896), born in Danby, Tompkins County, New York, was baptized in 1833. He was a participant in Zion's Camp. (Early Church Information File.)

76. See *Messenger and Advocate*, December 1835, pp. 225-30.

77. In 1830 Henry Capron was living at Booneville, Oneida County, New York. (1830 Federal Census.)

78. Harriet Howe (1804-1879), born in Friendship, Allegheny County, New York, helped make clothing for the workmen on the Kirtland Temple. (Temple Records Index Bureau; Journal History, October 22, 1867.)

79. Probably Henry Kingsbury (1781-1841), born in Enfield, Connecticut. (Family Group Records Collection.)

80. David Dort (1793-1841), born in Surry, New Hampshire, moved to Michigan about 1822. He married Joseph Smith's cousin Mary and later her sister Fanny, daughters of Joseph's maternal uncle and aunt Stephen and Temperance Mack. (Sprague, "Progenitors.")

81. Almira Mack Scobey (1805-1886) was the youngest daughter of Joseph Smith's maternal uncle Steven Mack and his wife Temperance Bond. (Sprague, "Progenitors.")

82. Thomas Carrico, born in 1802 at Beverly, Essex County, Massachusetts, was baptized in 1834. He was appointed doorkeeper of the Kirtland Temple. See entries of January 13 and 15, 1836, pp. 129 and 135 of this work. (Record, Nauvoo Ninth Ward High Priests, p. 12.)

83. Thankful Halsey.

84. On this date, Joseph Smith inserted a notice in the *Messenger and Advocate* to inform his friends and all others "that whenever they wish to address me thro' the Post Office, they will be kind enough to pay the postage on the same. My friends will excuse me in this matter, as I am willing to pay postage on letters to hear from *them*; but am unwilling to pay for insults and menaces,—consequently, must refuse all, unpaid."

85. Gideon Carter (1798-1838), born in Benson, Vermont, was baptized in 1831. A missionary with Sylvester Smith in the eastern states and New England in 1832, he was killed at Crooked River, Missouri. (Jenson, *Biographical Encyclopedia* 3:615-16.)

86. William Draper (1774-1854), born in Wyoming, Susquehannah County, Pennsylvania. (Family Group Records Collection.)

87. See entry of December 4, pp. 96-97 of this work.

88. Levi Jackman (1797-1876), born in Orange County, Vermont, was living in Portage County, Ohio, when he joined the Church in 1831. A participant in the march of Zion's Camp and a member of the Missouri high council, he returned to Kirtland in July 1835 and worked on the Temple. (Jenson, *Biographical Encyclopedia* 2:769-70.)

89. Elijah Fordham (1798-1879) was born in New York City but lived in Pontiac, Michigan, from 1831 to 1833. He was a participant in Zion's Camp. (Family Group Records Collectipn; Smith, *History of the Church* 2:183.)

90. James Emmet (1803-1852), born in Boone County, Kentucky, joined the Church in 1831 in Illinois. (Family Group Records Collection.)

91. Truman Angell (1810-1887), a carpenter, joiner, and architect, was born in Providence, Rhode Island. He lived in China, New York, when he was converted in 1834. He moved to Kirtland in 1835 and worked on the Kirtland Temple. He was a member of the second quorum of the seventy and was the Church architect of the Nauvoo and Salt Lake temples. (Biography of Truman O. Angell.)

92. William Felshaw (1800-1866), born in Granville, Washington County, New York, lived for a time in Hoosick, Rensselaer County, New York, before moving to Kirtland about 1833. (Family Group Records Collection.)

93. Emer Harris (1781-1869), born in Cambridge, Washington County, New York, was the elder brother of Martin Harris. He joined the Latter-day Saints and moved to Kirtland in 1831. (Family Group Records Collection; Harris, "Reminiscences.")

94. Truman Jackson, living at Verona, Oneida County, New York, in 1830, was a member of the elders quorum in Kirtland in 1836 and was a seventy in 1837. (1830 Federal Census; Smith, *History of the Church* 2:400.)

95. Samuel Rolph (1793-1867), a joiner, was born in Concord, New Hampshire. He resided in Maine when he was converted. He moved to Kirtland in 1835 and worked on the temple. (Cook, *Revelations of the Prophet*, pp. 272-73.)

96. Elias Higbee (1795-1843), born in Galloway, Gloucester County, New Jersey, lived in Cincinnati, Ohio, when he was converted in 1832. He was among those driven from Jackson County, Missouri, and was a worker on the Kirtland Temple. (Jenson, *Biographical Encyclopedia* 1:253.)

97. Albert Brown (1807-1901), born in Windsor, Hartford County, Connecticut, lived in Hoosick, Rensselaer County, New York, in 1830. He was a participant in Zion's Camp. (1830 Federal Census; Smith, *History of the Church* 2:183.)

98. William F. Cahoon (1813-1893), born in Harpersfield, Ashtabula County, Ohio, was baptized at Kirtland in 1830. He was a missionary in Ohio, Pennsylvania, and New York from 1832 to 1833 and was a participant in Zion's Camp in 1834. He was a member of the first quorum of the seventy in 1835 and worked on the Kirtland Temple. (Jenson, *Biographical Encyclopedia* 1:192-93.)

99. Salmon Gee (1792-1845), born in Lyme, New London County, Connecticut, was a president of the seventy from 1837 to 1838. He was living in Geauga County, Ohio, when he joined the Church in 1832. He was a member of the Kirtland high council. (Jenson, *Biographical Encyclopedia* 1:192-93.)

100. Zemira Draper (1812-1876) was born in Crambe, Northumberland County, Upper Canada. He was a son of William Draper. (Family Group Records Collection.)

101. John Rudd was an 1830 resident of Erie County, Pennsylvania.

102. Alexander Badlam (1808-1894), born in Norfolk County, Massachusetts, was a member of the first quorum of the seventy and a participant in Zion's Camp. (Early Church Information File; Smith, *History of the Church* 2:183, 204.)

103. Probably John Tanner (1778-1850), born in Hopkinton, Rhode Island, and living in Warren County, New York, when converted after the miraculous healing of his leg in 1832. He gave substantial sums of money for the benefit of the Church in Kirtland. (Jenson, *Biographical Encyclopedia* 2:799-802.)

104. Leonard Rich (1818-1875) resided at Warsaw, Genessee County, New York, in 1830. He was one of the presidents of the seventy from 1835 to 1837 and participated in Zion's Camp. (Family Group Records Collection; Smith, *History of the Church* 2:184, 203.)

105. Angeline Eliza Works (1814-1880) was born in Aurelius, Cayuga County, New York. A sister to Brigham Young's first wife, Miriam, she married Ebenezer Robinson on December 13, 1835. (Family Group Records Collection.)

106. Probably Hiram E. Booth, an 1835 Kirtland property owner.

107. Orson Johnson, a native of Bath, New Hampshire, was a member of the Kirtland high council in 1834. (Smith, *History of the Church* 2:151.)

108. Peter Whitmer (1809-1836), a tailor born in Fayette, Seneca County, New York, was a witness to the Book of Mormon. One of the four Lamanite missionaries to western Missouri in the fall of 1830, he was a member of the Missouri high council. (Jenson, *Biographical Encyclopedia* 1:277.)

109. Ebenezer Jennings was living at Chester, Geauga County, Ohio, in 1830 and was a property owner at Kirtland in 1832. (1830 Federal Census; 1832 Geauga County, Ohio, tax list.)

110. Sylvester M. Smith died at the age of eleven weeks and four days. (Early Church Information File.)

111. The committee organized to oversee the building of the Kirtland Temple consisted of Hyrum Smith, Reynolds Cahoon, and Jared Carter. These men managed a store in Kirtland through which business pertaining to the construction of the temple was transacted. (Smith, *History of the Church* 2:333.)

112. See entry of November 3, 1835, pp. 71-72 of this work.

113. Half a page is left blank in the manuscript at this point.

114. Reynolds Cahoon (1790-1862), born in Cambridge, Washington County, New York, was among the first converts to the Church in Ohio in 1830. He was appointed counselor to Bishop Newel K. Whitney in Kirtland in 1832. A member of the committee in charge of building the Kirtland Temple, he was a manager of the Kirtland store through which business connected with temple construction was transacted. (See Cook, *Revelations of the Prophet*, p. 73.)

115. Handwriting of Frederick G. Williams.
116. Lyman R. Sherman (1804-1839), born in Monkton, Vermont, was one of the presidents of the seventy from 1835 to 1837. He moved to Kirtland in 1833 and was a member of the Kirtland high council in 1837. (Jenson, *Biographical Encyclopedia* 1:190; Cook, *Revelations of the Prophet*, p. 217.)
117. See D&C 108.
118. Handwriting of Warren Parrish to page 122 of the manuscript.
119. Almon Babbitt (1813-1856), an attorney, was born in Cheshire, Berkshire County, Massachusetts. He was baptized in 1833 and was a member of Zion's Camp. He was appointed to the first quorum of the seventy in 1835. (Cook, *Revelations of the Prophet*, pp. 251-52.)

     Babbitt was brought before the high council for traducing the character of Joseph Smith. His case was not completely resolved until January 2, 1836, when he reconciled his difficulty and was "restored to fellowship." (Kirtland Council Minutes, December 28, 1835; January 2, 1836.)
120. Oliver Olney (1800-1841) resided at Shalersville, Portage County, Ohio, in 1830. He was president of the teachers quorum in Kirtland from 1836 to 1838. (Smith, *History of the Church* 2:371.)
121. Among those who received blessings at this time were Lyman Wight, Ezra Hayes, and George Morey.
122. Calvin Stoddard (1801-1836) married Joseph Smith's sister Sophronia in Palmyra, New York, in 1827. He helped build the Kirtland Temple. (*Utah Genealogical and Historical Magazine* 26:102, 151; Stoddard family Bible; Smith, *History of the Church* 2:206.)
123. On December 29, 1835, Johnson had brought charges against William Smith of "unchristian like conduct in speaking disrespectfully of President Joseph Smith . . . and the revelations & commandments given through him" and for "attempting to inflict personal violence." (Kirtland Council Minutes, December 29, 1835.)
124. See entry of December 28, 1835, on p. 119 of this work.
125. The Western Reserve College at Hudson, Summit County, Ohio, about twenty-eight miles south of Kirtland, was founded in 1826. The curriculum of the college in the 1830s was theology, languages, philosophy, and mathematics. (Perrin, *History of Summit County, Ohio*, pp. 446-66.)
126. This marks the hiring of Joshua Seixas, a Jewish scholar who taught Hebrew in Kirtland between January 26 and March 29, 1836. Seixas was born prior to 1803 in either Cuba or Virginia and died in the 1870s. He taught Hebrew and other languages in Andover, Massachusetts, and at the Spanish and Portuguese Synagogue in New York City. The first edition of his Hebrew Grammar appeared in 1833, and in the fall of 1835 he was teaching at Oberlin College. Among his students was Lorenzo Snow, whose sister Eliza had joined the Latter-day Saints and was then living in the Joseph Smith household in Kirtland. Possibly from this source Joseph first heard of Seixas. After completing the course at Oberlin, Seixas was hired for a six-week term of instruction at the Western Reserve College in Hudson, beginning in December and ending January 23, 1836. Three days later he arrived in Kirtland. (Snow, "Who Was Professor Joshua Seixas?" pp. 67-71; Zucker, "Joseph Smith as a Student of Hebrew," pp. 41-55.)
127. Thomas Grover (1807-1886), a riverboat captain, was born in Whitehall, Washington County, New York. He was living in Freedom, New York, when he joined the Latter-day Saints in 1834. He moved to Kirtland in 1835 and was a member of the Kirtland high council in 1836. (Jenson, *Biographical Encyclopedia* 4:137-40; Cook, *Revelations of the Prophet*, p. 259.)
128. Hyram Dayton (1798-1881), a native of Herkimer, New York, was living in Parkman, Geauga County, Ohio in 1830. (Family Group Records Collection.)
129. Samuel James was a member of the Kirtland high council in 1836. (Smith, *History of the Church* 2:366.)

130. The 1830 Federal Census lists Russell Weaver, in his forties, living at Cambria, Niagara County, New York.
131. Joseph Rose, born in 1792 in Orange County, New York, was numbered with the second quorum of the seventy at Kirtland. (Early Church Information File.)
132. The presidency at Kirtland consisted of Joseph Smith, Sen., Sidney Rigdon, and Hyrum Smith, and at Zion (Jackson County, Missouri) of David Whitmer, John Whitmer, and William W. Phelps. (Smith, *History of the Church* 2:364.)
133. John P. Greene (1793-1844), a shoemaker, was born in Herkimer County, New York. He married Brigham Young's sister Rhoda and was living in Mendon, New York, when he joined the Church. He moved to Kirtland in 1832 and was among those who solicited money and volunteers for Zion's Camp in 1834. (Jenson, *Biographical Encyclopedia* 2: 633-36.)
134. Luke Johnson (1807-1861), a farmer, was a member of the Council of the Twelve from 1835 to 1837. Born in Pomfret, Vermont, he was living in Hiram, Ohio, when he was converted in 1831. A son of John Johnson and brother-in-law to Orson Hyde, he was a member of the Kirtland high council from 1834 to 1835 and a participant in the march of Zion's Camp. He left the Church in 1838 but returned in 1846. (Jenson, *Biographical Encyclopedia* 1:85-86.)
135. In the Kirtland high council.
136. John E. Page (1799-1867), a member of the Council of the Twelve from 1838 to 1846, was born in Trenton, Oneida County, New York. Converted in Ohio in 1833, he moved to Kirtland in the fall of 1835 and was a missionary to Canada in 1836 and 1837, traveling five thousand miles and baptizing six hundred people. He left the Church in 1846. (Jenson, *Biographical Encyclopedia* 1:92-93.)
137. Joseph C. Kingsbury (1812-1898), born in Enfield, Connecticut, was baptized in Kirtland in 1832. He became a member of the Kirtland high council in 1836. (Jenson, *Biographical Encyclopedia* 4:509.)
138. John Murdock (1792-1871), born in Kortright, New York, was living in Orange, Ohio, when he joined the Latter-day Saints in 1830. His wife died following the birth of twins on April 30, 1831. The twins, Joseph and Julia, were adopted by Joseph and Emma Smith. John Murdock participated in Zion's Camp in 1834. (Jenson, *Biographical Encyclopedia* 2:362-64.)
139. Solomon Hancock (1793-1847), born in Springfield, Massachusetts, was converted in 1830 and moved to Jackson County, Missouri, in 1832. He was a member of the Missouri high council from 1834 to 1838. (Cook, *Revelations of the Prophet*, pp. 77-78.)
140. See p. 124.
141. Oliver Cowdery had been elected by the Geauga County Democratic Convention on October 10, 1835, as a delegate to the state convention held at Columbus on January 8, 1836. He left Kirtland on January 3. (See Arrington, "Oliver Cowdery's Kirtland, Ohio, 'Sketch Book,'" pp. 414-15.)
142. William Cowdery (1765-1847), born at East Haddam, Connecticut, was the father of Oliver Cowdery. (Curtis, Cowdery Genealogy.)
143. Ira Bond (1798-1887) was born in Caldwell, New Jersey. After moving to Mendon, New York, he was among the first Mormon converts, in 1832. Bond owned 178 acres and a dwelling house valued at $465 at Kirtland in 1836. (Journal History, April 14, 1832.)
144. Amos R. Orton, in his thirties, was living in Olean, Cattaraugus County, New York, in 1830. He was a member of the seventies quorum and worked on the Kirtland Temple. (1830 Federal Census; Early Church Information File; Smith, *History of the Church* 2:206.)
145. Oliver Cowdery summarized the events of January 15 in his diary: "The several Quorums of the authorities of the Church met today, and transacted important business preparatory to the endowment. The Spirit of the Lord was in our midst." (Oliver Cowdery Diary, January 15, 1836.)

146. See entry of September 28, 1835, pp. 59-60 of this work.
147. Reference is made to the May 4 to September 26, 1835, mission of the Twelve, during which they traveled through the eastern states and New England holding conferences and regulating the affairs of the Church. (See note 8, p. 649.)
148. While the Twelve were on their mission to the east in 1835, they were censured by the Presidency for neglecting "to teach the Church in Freedom, New York the necessity of contributing of their earthly substance for the building of the House of the Lord" in Kirtland. The censure was based upon a letter sent them by Warren Cowdery. In a note of reconciliation, published in the February 1836 *Messenger and Advocate*, Cowdery apologized, stating that he had since learned that he was wrong in the matter.
149. Possibly the handwriting of Jesse Hitchcock.
150. Handwriting of Warren Parrish.
151. Possibly the handwriting of Jesse Hitchcock.
152. Handwriting of Warren Parrish.
153. William Farrington Cahoon (1813-1893), born in Harpersfield, Ashtabula County, Ohio, was the eldest son of Reynolds Cahoon. (Family Group Records Collection.)
154. Larona Cahoon (1817-1840) was born in Harpersfield, Ashtabula County, Ohio. She was the eldest daughter of Reynolds Cahoon. (Family Group Records Collection.)
155. Tunis Rappleye (1807-1883), born in Ovid, Seneca County, New York, was living at Bedford, Kings County, New York, in 1830. (Family Group Records Collection.)
156. Louisa Elizabeth Cutler (1816-1854), born in Lisle, Broome County, New York, was a daughter of Alpheus Cutler. (Family Group Records Collection.)
157. Possibly the handwriting of Jesse Hitchcock.
158. See note 45, p. 653.
159. Handwriting of Warren Parrish.
160. This paragraph was crossed out in the original since it repeats much that was written in the first paragraph under this entry.
161. A sanctifying ordinance in preparation for the endowment. (See Cook, *Revelations of the Prophet*, pp. 216-17.)
162. Alvin Smith (1793-1823), the eldest brother of Joseph Smith, who, according to his mother, died from an overdose of calomel administered by a doctor called in for the emergency of Alvin's illness. (L. Smith, *Biographical Sketches of Joseph Smith the Prophet*, p. 87.)
163. Oliver Cowdery also recorded the events of January 21: "At about three o'clock P.M. I assembled in our office garret, having all things prepared for the occasion, with presidents Joseph Smith, jr. F.G. Williams, Sidney Rigdon Hyrum Smith, David Whitmer, John Whitmer and elder John Corrill, and washed our bodies with pure water before the Lord, preparatory to the annointing with holy oil. After we were washed, our bodies were perfumed with a sweet smelling oderous wash. At evening the presidents of the Church, with the two bishop[s] and their counsellors, and elder Warren Parrish, met in the presidents' room, the high councils of Kirtland and Zion in their rooms. Those named in the first room were annointed with the same kind of oil and in the man[ner] that were Moses and Aaron, and those who stood before the Lord in ancient days, and those in the other rooms with annointing oil prepared for them. The glorious scene is too great to be described in this book, therefore, I only say, that the heavens were opened to many, and great and marvelous things were shown." (Oliver Cowdery Diary, January 21, 1836.)
164. Possibly the handwriting of Jesse Hitchcock.
165. Handwriting of Warren Parrish.
166. Handwriting of Sylvester Smith.
167. Of January 22, Oliver Cowdery wrote, "At evening met in the president's room where were the presidents, the twelve, the presidents of the 70, the high councils of Kirtland and Zion, and the bishops and their counsellors. The presidents proceeded and an-

nointed Thomas B. Marsh, the president of the twelve, and he annointed the other eleven. The Twelve then proceeded, president Marsh taking the lead, and annointed the presidents of the Seventy. Elder Don Carlos Smith was ordained and annointed president of the high priesthood of the Melchisedek priesthood, by the presidents of the Church. Near the close of the meeting, 2 o'clock in the morning, almost all present broke out in tongues and songs of Zion." (Oliver Cowdery Diary, January 22, 1836.)

168. According to Oliver Cowdery, "The quorums met today: we had a good season. At evening met the presidency in the upper room in the printing office, and conversed upon the time of, and preparation and sanctification for the endowment." (Oliver Cowdery Diary, January 24, 1836.)

169. Reuben Hedlock, born about 1805, was a carpenter living in Avon, Livingston County, New York, in 1830. (1830 Federal Census.)

170. John Morton (1790-1858), born in Portsmouth, New Hampshire, was living at Mendon, New York, in 1832, when he was converted to the Church. (Temple Records Index Bureau; Journal History, April 14, 1832.)

171. Marietta, Angeline, Joanna, and Nancy Carter were the daughters of John S. Carter, a member of the Kirtland high council who died of cholera during the march of Zion's Camp.

172. The elders quorum minutes provide this perspective: "Met to proceed with the anointing of the Elders of the Most High. Counselor Morton organized those who were anointed in order for supplications. President Beman finished the anointing. The first presidency came and sealed our anointing by prayer and shout of Hosanna. The first counselor organized those who had been anointed in order for supplication. They gave us some instructions and left us. President Beman spoke to the assembly. Sever[al] spoke and there seemed to be a cloud of darkness in the room. Pres. O. Cowdery & H. Smith came and gave some instructions and the cloud was broken and some shouted, Hosanna and others spake with tongues. The first president (J. Smith jr) returned and reprimanded us for our evil deeds which was the cause of our darkness. He prophesied saying this night the key is turned to the nations, and the angel John is about commencing his mission to prophesy before kings, and rulers, nations tongues and people. The assembly was dismissed with prayer." (A Record of the First Quorum of Elders, pp. 4-5.)

173. Handwriting of Warren Parrish.

174. Two pages of the manuscript are numbered 151.

175. See entry of January 25, 1836, pp. 149-50 and note 37 on pp. 652-53 of this work.

176. Possibly the handwriting of Jesse Hitchcock.

177. Probably Levi Jackman (1797-1876), born in Berkshire, Orange County, Vermont. (Early Church Information File.)

178. Joseph Coe (1784-1854), born in Genoa, Cayuga County, New York. He was living in Essex County, New Jersey, in 1830. He was a member of the Kirtland high council from 1834 to 1837. (See Cook, Revelations of the Prophet, pp. 86-87.)

179. Handwriting of Warren Parrish.

180. February 12 entry continues following entry of February 14.

181. Meeting on February 13, the Twelve accepted the first resolution but presented this amendment to the second: "That none be ordained to any office in the branches to which they belong to a general conference, appointed by those, or under the direction of those who are designated in the Book of Covenants as having authority to ordain and set in order all the Officers of the church abroad & from that conference receive their ordination." (Kirtland Council Minutes, February 13, 1836.)

182. According to Oliver Cowdery, Professor Seixas was still absent on February 15: "Att. Heb. School. The profess[or] being abscent, our class appointed myself to look over them for the time. After, assisted pres. Smith to overlook the 11 o'clock. In the afternoon met pres's. J. Smith, jr. S. Rigdon, W.W. Phelps John Whitmer and elder S. James in the

office study and united in prayer for Professor Seixas and his family, pres. Smith taking the lead: The items asked for were in substance as follows: That the Lord will have mercy upon the man whom we have employed to teach us the Hebrew language; that all evil prejudice may be taken from his heart, and that the Spirit of God may visit him continually by night and by day, that he may be lead to embrace the gospel and believe the book of Mormon; that he will give him the spirit of humility and meekness that we may become his teachers in the things of salvation, that he may come forth and be baptized into the Church of Christ, that we may be benefitted with the knowledge he has of languages: and that the Lord will have mercy upon his family, and visit them with his Holy Spirit and cause them to embrace the fulness of the gospel, that they may be saved with him. We do not ask to become his teachers only that he may become our brother in the faith of the gospel, that his soul may be saved: all of which are asked in the name of the Lord Jesus Christ. Amen." (Oliver Cowdery Diary, February 15, 1836.)

183. Oliver Cowdery was also present at the Seixas lodgings: "We found him weary with his labors in teaching the school." (Oliver Cowdery Diary, February 19, 1836.)

184. Elijah Fuller (1811-1879) was born in Windham, Greene County, New York. Still living in Windham, New York, at this time, Fuller did not join the Latter-day Saints until 1842. (Family Group Records Collection.)

185. Either John O. Waterman, born August 8, 1769, in Chatham, Portland County, Connecticut, or a son by the same name born in 1794. (Family Group Records Collection.)

186. Made of white canvas curtains that could be raised or lowered at pleasure, the veil of the Kirtland Temple was for the purpose of dividing the main meeting room into four sections, allowing four separate meetings to be held simultaneously. (E. R. Snow, *Autobiography of Lorenzo Snow*, p. 12.)

187. The temple.

188. At this meeting the names of several individuals were presented for ordination to priesthood offices in the Church: William Wightman, Charles Wightman, David Cluff, Truman Jackson, Reuben Barton, and Daniel Miles were received as elders, and Moses Daily as a high priest; nineteen others whose names were presented for ordination were rejected. (Kirtland Council Minutes, February 24, 1836.)

189. Oliver Cowdery writes, "In the evening met the quorums of the Church in the Lord's house, and heard the petitions of several brethren, who wished to be ordained. Was appointed by the council, in company with pres. Orson Hyde and Sylvester Smith, to draft resolutions to be adopted as a rule of Church, regulating the recording of licenses, and conference minutes." (Oliver Cowdery Diary, February 24, 1836.)

190. Oliver Cowdery adds the following detail: "Professor Seixas left this morning to visit his family at Hudson, Ohio. I was called to lay hands upon pres. T.B. Marsh, in company with pres. J. Smith, jr. and also upon my brother-in-law, Peter Whitmer, jr. the latter was very sick of a Typhus fever, and was immediately heald and arose from his bed. I heard the other was better. In the afternoon and evening met pres. Orson Hyde and Sylvester Smith in committee and dictated resolutions to be introduced Thursday evening for the consideration of the quorums." (Oliver Cowdery Diary, February 27, 1836.)

191. Edward Irving.

192. Possibly the handwriting of Jesse Hitchcock.

193. The authorities of the Church assembled at the temple were as follows: The Presidency, Quorum of Twelve, the high councils of Kirtland and Zion, the bishoprics of Kirtland and Zion, the seven presidents of the seventy, and the presidencies of the high priests, elders, priests, teachers, and deacons. The purpose of the assembly was to consider the work of the committee appointed February 24 to draft resolutions governing the licensing of official members of the Church. (See note 189.)

194. The resolutions, read by Oliver Cowdery, chairman of the committee, were as follows: "Whereas the records of the several conferences, held by the Elders of the church, and

the ordinations of many of the official members of the same, in many cases have been imperfectly kept since its organization, to avoid ever after, any inconvenience, difficulty or injury in consequence of such neglect your committee recommend. 1st. That all licenses hereafter granted by these authorities assembled as a quorum or by general conference held for the purpose of transacting the business of the church, be recorded at full length, by a clerk, appointed for that purpose in a book to be kept in this branch of the church until it shall be thought advisable by the heads of the church, to order other books and appoint other clerks to record licenses as above. And that said recording clerk be required to endorse a certificate under his own hand and signature on the back of said licenses, specifying the time when & place where such license was recorded, and also a reference to the letter and page of the Book containing the same.

2d. That this quorum appoint two persons to sign Licenses given as afore said, one as chairman, and the other as clerk of conference, and that it shall be the duty of said person appointed to sign licenses as clerk of conference immediately thereafter, to deliver the same into the hands of the recording Clerk.

3d. That all general conferences abroad give each individual, whom they ordained a certificate signed by the chairman & Clerk of said conference and stating the time and place of such conference, and the office to which the individual has been ordained, and that when such certificate has been forwarded to the person hereafter authorized to sign licences as clerk of conference, such person shall together with the chairman of conference, immediately sign a license, and said clerk of conference shall, after the same has been recorded forward it to the proper person.

4th. That all official members in good standing & fellowship in the various branches of this church, are requested to forward their present licenses accompanied by a certificate of their virtues & faithful walk before the Lord, signed by the chairman and clerk. of a general conference, or by the clerk of the branch of the church in which official member resides, by the advice & direction of such Church, to the clerk of conference whose duty it shall be to fill a new license as directed in the 3d article. And that all licenses signed recorded and endorsed, as specified in the first article shall be considered good and valid to all intents & purposes in the business, and spiritual affairs of this church as a religious society, or before any court of record of this or any other country wherein preachers of the Gospel are entitled to special privileges, answering in all respects as an original record without the necessity of refering to any other document.

5. That the recording clerk be required to publish quarterly in a paper published by some member or members of this church, a list of the names of the several persons for whom he has recorded licenses within the last quarter.

6. That this quorum appoint two persons to sign as chairman and clerk of conference, Pro. Tempre licenses for the standing chairman and clerk who shall be appointed as named in the 2d article and also to act in their absence in signing other licenses. as specified in the foregoing article

Kirtland Feb. 27. 1836   Oliver Cowdery
                           Orson Hyde   Committee
                           Sylvester Smith

(Kirtland Council Minutes, March 3, 1836.)

195. Handwriting of Warren Parrish.
196. All of the Twelve voted to recall their previous amendment to the resolution except John F. Boynton, Orson Pratt, and Lyman Johnson. (Kirtland Council Minutes, March 3, 1836.)
197. Oliver Cowdery summarized this day's activities: "Att. Heb. School. met the quorums in the evening in the Lord's house, and read the committee's report previously drawn, which was adopted without amendment, except a small addition in the last article, extending the power of certain conference[s] further, in signing licenses. I confess the hand

of God in this matter, in giving me his Holy Spirit, to indite this valuable article, as by it the elders will enjoy their privileges as citizens, and the churches be freed from imposition." (Oliver Cowdery Diary, March 3, 1836.)

198. In the evening of March 5, Joseph Smith met with Oliver Cowdery, Sidney Rigdon, the Twelve, and Warren Cowdery in the upper room of the printing office. According to Oliver Cowdery, "the Twelve had profered a charge against my brother for a letter he wrote last summer upon the subject of their teaching while at the Freedom conference. My brother confessed his mistake, upon the testimony of the Twelve, and said he was willing to publish that they were not in the fault, but that he was satisfied they delivered those instructions which he had supposed they had not." (Oliver Cowdery Diary, March 5, 1836.) The resolution of the matter was the publication of the Warren Cowdery statement in the *Messenger and Advocate* of February 1836. (See note 148.)

199. Joseph's absence from meetings may be explained from Oliver Cowdery's entry for the day: "Did not attend meeting in consequence of there not being sufficient room for so many in the small houses occupied for meetings." (Oliver Cowdery Diary, March 6, 1836.)

200. The low area of Kirtland lying north of the temple in the vicinity of the Newel K. Whitney store.

201. Solomon Hancock's wife, Alta Adams Hancock, died January 18, 1835, in Clay County, Missouri. (Temple Records Index Bureau.)

202. Erastus B. Wightman, Osmon M. Duel, Chapman Duncan, Joshua Bosley, and Heman Hyde were sustained for ordination; four others were rejected. (Kirtland Council Minutes, March 17, 1836.)

203. Ezekiel Johnson (1776-1848) was born at Uxbridge, Massachusetts. His twenty-one-year-old daughter, Susan Ellen, died at Kirtland on March 16, 1836. (Family Group Records Collection.)

204. Oliver Cowdery writes, "We prepared for the dedication of the Lord's house. I met in the president's room, pres. J. Smith, jr. S. Rigdon, my brother W.A. Cowdery & Elder W. Parrish, and assisted in writing a prayer for the dedication of the house." (Oliver Cowdery Diary, March 26, 1836.)

205. At this point in the manuscript, the following material was crossed out and a fresh start made: "President F G. Williams Presdt. Joseph Smith, Sen ~~father~~ and Presdt W W. Phelps occupied the first pulpit ‹in the west end of the house› for the Melchisedec priest=hood, Presdt. S. Rigdon, Myself, and Prest. Hyrum Smith the 2nd— Presdt D. Whitmer Presdt O. Cowdery and Presdt John Whitmer the 3d— The 4th was [p. 173] occupied by the president of the high priests and his counsellors, and 2 choiristers— The 12. apostles on the right, the high council of Kirtland on the left, The pulpits ‹in the east end of the house› for the Aaronic priesthood were occu=pied in the following manner— The Bishop of Kirtland and his counsellors in the first pulpit— the Bishop of Zion and his counsellors in the 2nd— the presdt. of the priest[s] and his counsellors in the 3d— the presdt. of ‹the Teachers and his counsellors in the 4th—› ~~the 7 presdt of the seventies~~ The high council of Zion on the right, the 7. presdt of the Seventies on the left."

206. "Recd by contribution $960.00" was written in the same hand sometime after the text that surrounds it. Ira Ames, who was in charge of the donations at the door during the temple dedication, noted, "There were three large tin pans full of gold & silver. . . . A great many strangers came from the country to see it [the temple] and all donated freely." (Ira Ames Journal, 1836.)

207. The two hymns referred to are "Ere Long the Veil Will Rend in Twain," by Parley P. Pratt and "O Happy Souls, Who Pray," by William W. Phelps.

208. "This Earth Was Once a Garden Place," by William W. Phelps. (*Hymns*, no. 389.)

209. Possibly the handwriting of Jesse Hitchcock.

210. "How Pleased and Blessed Was I to Hear the People Cry," by Watts.

211. See D&C 109.
212. Handwriting of Warren Parrish.
213. "The Spirit of God Like a Fire Is Burning," by William W. Phelps. (*Hymns*, no. 213.)
214. Oliver Cowdery's report of the Kirtland Temple dedication, which adds substantial detail, was published in *Messenger and Advocate* 3:274-81.
215. Possibly the handwriting of Jesse Hitchcock.
216. Handwriting of Warren Parrish.
217. Leman Copley, born in 1781 in Connecticut, owned 759 acres of land at Thompson, Ohio, in 1832. After his conversion in March 1831, he agreed to allow fellow Church members to settle on his land, but he afterward went back on his agreement. He testified against Joseph Smith at the 1834 Philastus Hurlbut trial and was subsequently disfellowshipped. (Geauga County, Ohio, tax lists; Cook, *Revelations of the Prophet*, p. 67.)
218. Handwriting of Warren A. Cowdery.
219. See D&C 110.

History, 1838

Ms. Joseph Smith, *History of the Church,* vol. A-1, pp. 1-10. Except where indicated, the portion of the history given here is in the handwriting of James Mulholland. Ms., LDS Church Archives.

1. Joseph Smith Journal entitled "The Scriptory Book of Joseph Smith Jr.," April 30–May 4, 1838, pp. 37-38.
2. James Mulholland (1804-1839) commenced writing for Joseph Smith September 3, 1838. (James Mulholland Diary.)
3. Joseph Smith Journal, 1839, kept by James Mulholland.
4. This insertion, in the handwriting of Willard Richards, was added in 1842 when Richards began assisting Joseph as a secretary. Since this information was added to the manuscript later in 1842, after the *History* began its serialized appearance in the *Times and Seasons*, it was not included in early publications of the *History*. The material that constitutes note A is found on pp. 131-32 of the History manuscript: "When I was 5 years old or thereabouts I was attacked with the Typhus Fever, and at one time, during my sickness, my father dispaired of my life. The Doctors broke the fever, after which it settled under my shoulder & the Dr. –‹Dr. Parker› caled it a sprained shoulder & anointed it with bone ointment, & freely applied the hot shovel, when it proved to be a swelling under the arm which was opened, & discharged freely, after which the disease removed & desended into my left Leg & ancle & terminated in a fever sore of the worst kind, and I endured the most acute suffering for a long time under the care of Drs. Smith, Stone & Perkins of Hanover. At one time eleven Doctors came from the ‹ Dartmouth › medical college at Hanover New Hampshire, for the purpose of amputation, but, young as I was, I utterly refused to give my assent to the operation; but I consented to their Trying an experiment by removing a ‹large portion› great of the bone from my left leg. which they did. & fourteen additional peices of bone afterwards worked out before my leg healed, during which time I was reduced so very low that my mother could carry me with ease, & after I began to get about I went on crutches till I started for the State of New York where In the mean time my father had gone to the State of New York for the purpose of preparing a place for the removal of his family, which he affected by sending a man after us by the name of Caleb Howard, who, after he had got started on the Journey with my mother & family spent the money he had rec[e]ived of my father in drinking & gambling &c. We fell in with a family by the name of Gates who were travelling west, & Howard drove me

from the waggon & made me travel in my weak state through the snow 40 miles per day
for several days, during which time I suffered the most excrutiating weariness & pain, &
all this that Mr Howard might enjoy the society of two of Mr Gates' Daughters which he
took on the waggon where I should have Rode, & thus he [p. 131] continued to do day
day after day through the Journey, & when my brothers remonstrated with Mr Howard
for his treatment to me.–he would knock them down with the butt of his whip.–When
we arrived at Utica, N. York Howard threw the goods out of the waggon into the street &
attempted to run away with the Horses & waggon, but my mother seized the horses by the
reign[s], & calling witnesses forbid his taking them away as they were her property. On
our way from Utica I was left to ride on the last ~~waggon~~ ‹sleigh› in the company, ‹(the
Gates family were in sleighs)› but when that came up I was knocked down by the driver,
one of Gate's sons, & left to wallow in my blood until a stranger came along, picked me
up, & carried me to the Town of Palmyra.– Howard having spent all our funds My
Mother was compelled to pay our landlords bills from Utica to Palmyra, in bits of cloth,
clothing &c the last payment being made with the drops [earrings] taken from Sister
Sophron[i]a's ears, for that purpose. Although the snow was generally deep through the
country during this Journey we performed the whole ‹on› ~~except~~ wheels, except the first
two days, when we were accompanied by my mothers mother, Grandmother, Lydia
Mack who was injured by the upsetting of the sleigh, & not wishing to accompany her
friends west, tarried by the way with her friends in Vermont, & we soon after heard of her
death supposing that she never recovered from the injury received by the overturn of the
sleigh."

5. Addenda, note E, page 2, following page 553 of the text of the Joseph Smith History, vol.
   A-1, contains this note on Joseph Smith's ancestry: "Joseph Smith ‹Sen.› was born July
   12th 1771, in Topsfield, Essex County, Massachusetts; his father, Asael Smith was born
   March 7th, 1744 Topsfield, Massachusetts; his father Samuel Smith was born Jan'y 26th
   1714 Topsfield Massachusetts; his father Samuel Smith was born Jan'y 26th 1666,
   Topsfield; his father Robert Smith came from England."
6. "Or thereabout" is in the hand of Willard Richards.
7. Insertion by Willard Richards.
8. Note B on pages 132-33 of the manuscript, vol. A-1, along with the insertion here, is in
   the hand of Willard Richards: "When the light had departed I had no strength, but soon
   recovering in some degree. I went home. & as I leaned up to the fire piece Mother enquired what the matter was. I replied never mind all is well. I am well enough off. I then
   told my mother I have learned for myself that Presbyterianism is not true.—It seems as
   though the adversary was aware at a very early period of my life that I was destined to
   prove a disturbur & [p. 132] annoyer of his kingdom, or else why should the powers of
   Darkness combine against me, why the oppression & persecution that arose against me,
   almost in my infancy?"
       According to Willard Richards's diary, note B was recorded on December 2, 1842,
   which explains why it does not appear in the publication of the History in the *Times and
   Seasons* beginning in March that year.
9. "Or thereabouts" is in the hand of Willard Richards.
10. "Foibles" is in the hand of Willard Richards.
11. Note C on page 133 of the manuscript, vol. A-1, is in the hand of Willard Richards: "In
    making this confession, no one need suppose me guilty of any great or malignant sins: a
    disposition to commit such was never in my nature; but I was guilty of Levity, & some-
    times associated with Jovial company &c, not consistent with that character which
    ought to be maintained by one who was called of God as I had been; but this will not seem
    very strange to any one who recollects my youth & is acquainted with my native cheery
    Temperament." Willard Richards recorded this material on December 2, 1842; hence,
    like notes A and B, it does not appear in the *Times and Seasons* publication of the *History*
    that commenced earlier that year.

12. When Brigham H. Roberts prepared the *History* for publication in its seven-volume format at the turn of the century, he wrote "Moroni" above the name of "Nephi" and keyed his insertion to the following reference at the bottom of the page: "Evidently a clerical error; see Book Doc & Cov., Sec 50, par 2; Sec 106, par 20; also Elders' Journal Vol. 1, page 43. Should read Moroni."

13. The asterisk inserted by James Mulholland is keyed to an attached note in the manuscript containing these words on the one side: "I mentioned to President Smith that I considered it necessary that an explanation of the location of the place where the box was deposited would be required in order that the history be satisfactory. J.M." On the back of the note, Mulholland wrote, "Convenient to the little village of Manchester, Ontario County, New York, stands a hill of considerable size, and the most elevated of any in the neighborhood. On the west side of this hill not far from the top."

14. Alvin's death occurred on November 19, 1823. (See Rich, "Where Were the Moroni Visits?" pp. 255-58.)

15. Josiah Stowell, born in Winchester, New Hampshire, on March 22, 1770, had extensive property holdings on the Susquehanna River near South Bainbridge, New York. The Stowells moved to the area from southeastern Vermont when their New York allegiance during the Revolutionary War forced them to leave that state.

16. See note 11, p. 640.

Historical Sketch, March 1, 1842

P. Joseph Smith, "Church History," *Times and Seasons* 3 (March 1, 1842): 706-10. Similarities between this text and Orson Pratt's *An Interesting Account of Several Remarkable Visions,* published in 1840, indicate that Joseph used the Pratt document as a guideline for his response to Wentworth.

1. Malone, *Dictionary of American Biography* 10:657-59; *The National Cyclopaedia of American Biography* 10:482-83.

2. George Barstow (1812-1883), an attorney, was born at Haverhill, New Hampshire, and studied at Dartmouth College in 1835. He was a practicing attorney in Boston, Massachusetts, and New Hampshire. In 1842 he published a history of New Hampshire that reached a second edition in 1851. About 1850 he moved to San Francisco, California, where he practiced law and was professor of medical jurisprudence at the University of the Pacific; he served in the California House of Representatives and was president of the Young Men's Christian Association. He died in San Francisco, leaving a wife but no children. (Bell, *Bench and Bar of New Hampshire,* p. 171.)

3. The last part of this letter was later published as the Articles of Faith of The Church of Jesus Christ of Latter-day Saints. See Pearl of Great Price.

Note on Anthon Transcript, February 1828

ADS. Joseph Smith Papers, LDS Church Archives. Although this document is undated, the similarity of ink color of the Joseph Smith statement with the characters on the reverse side argues for an 1828 writing date. Published in the *Ensign* 10 (July 1980), inside front and back covers.

1. For details of the events described here and of the discovery of the document itself, see Smith, *History of the Church* 1:11-12, 18-21; Joseph Smith 1832 History, pp. 7-8 of this

work; Roberts, *Comprehensive History* 1:99-109; Bachman, "Sealed in a Book: Preliminary Observations on the Newly Found 'Anthon Transcript,'" pp. 321-45.

To Oliver Cowdery, October 22, 1829

Rc. The earliest source of this letter is the copy by Frederick G. Williams in Joseph Smith's
Letterbook 1, p. 9, Joseph Smith Papers, LDS Church Archives.

1. For the setting in which this letter was written, see R. L. Anderson, "Gold Plates and
   Printer's Ink," pp. 71-76.
2. Joseph Smith applied for copyright of the Book of Mormon on June 11, 1829. Ibid.,
   p. 75.

To Hyrum Smith, March 3, 1831

ALS. Joseph Smith Papers, LDS Church Archives. At the time he received this letter,
Hyrum Smith was residing with Newel Knight in Colesville, New York. After Hyrum's departure, Knight found the letter and kept it. Following his death, his wife, Lydia, displayed it
as a valuable keepsake of the early Church until she gave it to Susa Young Gates after 1881
in payment for a literary favor. We know this because it was still in the possession of Mrs.
Knight in March 1881 when Daniel Tyler notified Wilford Woodruff of its existence and
content. It was evidently from Susa Young Gates that the letter came to the Church
Archives. (See "An Unpublished Letter of the Prophet Joseph," *Improvement Era* 9 (December 1905): 167-69. The letter of Daniel Tyler to Wilford Woodruff, March 3, 1881,
Ms., is in the Wilford Woodruff Papers, LDS Church Archives.)

1. D&C 32.
2. Atkinson, "The Winter of the Deep Snow," pp. 47-62. See also Pratt, *Autobiography*, p.
   52, for his description of the journey west.
3. Jennings, "The First Mormon Mission to the Indians," pp. 288-99.
4. D&C 37:3; 38:31. See also Porter, "A Study of the Origins of The Church of Jesus Christ
   of Latter-day Saints in the States of New York and Pennsylvania, 1816-1831," pp.
   286-98.
5. When Joseph arrived in Kirtland, he found that the Saints "were striving to do the will
   of God, so far as they knew it, though some strange notions and false spirits had crept
   in among them." (Smith, *History of the Church* 1:146.) John Whitmer elaborated: "The
   disciples had all things common and were going to destruction very fast as to temporal
   things, for they considered from reading the scripture that what belonged to one brother,
   belonged to any of the brethren, therefore they would take each other's clothes and other
   property and use it without leave, which brought confusion and disappointments."
   (Whitmer, "The Book of John Whitmer," ch. 2.)
6. The Delaware chief at this time was Kik-Tha-We-Nund (William Anderson), a half-
   breed. Parley Pratt's account of the meeting with the Delaware leader is in his *Autobiography*, pp. 53-56. See also Jennings, "The First Mormon Mission to the Indians," pp.
   288-99.
7. Shortly after Orson Pratt, a nineteen-year-old convert, first met Joseph Smith in
   November 1830, he was ordained an elder and went on his first proselyting mission to

Colesville, New York. In February 1831, Pratt and Samuel Harrison Smith, Joseph's brother, left the Colesville area and walked to Kirtland, Ohio, the new center of gathering. (Jenson, *Biographical Encyclopedia* 18:87-90.)

8. Probably David Strong Jackway or Jackways, whose father, William Jackway, a Revolutionary War veteran, came to Palmyra, New York, in 1787. William Jackway owned a 500-acre farm, and he and his son David were hatters by trade. (Jackway, "The Jackway Family.") A David Jackways, in his fifties, is listed in the 1840 Palmyra, New York, census.

To Emma Smith, June 6, 1832

ALS. Chicago Historical Society, Chicago, Illinois. Published in LaMar C. Berrett, "An Impressive Letter from the Pen of Joseph Smith," *BYU Studies* 11 (Summer 1971): 517-23.

1. D&C 57:1-4.
2. Roberts, *Comprehensive History* 1:282-84; Smith, *History of the Church* 1:266-70; D&C 78:9-10; Far West Record, April 26, 30, 1832.
3. Joseph Smith (*History of the Church* 1:271-72) states that Whitney broke his leg while attempting to jump from the speeding stagecoach. Whitney reported that the mishap came in consequence of "the upsetting of the stage." (Whitney, Ms. dictated to Willard Richards.)
4. Daniel D. Porter, one of the early settlers of Greenville, came to Indiana from New England some time before 1826. He was followed in a few years by his brothers, Julius R. and James. James, a doctor, was probably the one who attended Whitney. (See Smith, *History of the Church* 1:271.) Julius R., a tavern-keeper and merchant, took his brother Daniel's place in the tavern business. (*History of the Ohio Falls Cities and Their Counties* 2:295.)
5. Greenville, Floyd County, Indiana.
6. The name Chagrin was changed to Willoughby upon organization of that Cayahoga County, Ohio, township in 1834.
7. The stay of Joseph Smith and Newel K. Whitney at Greenville had a sinister side to it. Joseph wrote, "While at this place I frequently walked out in the woods, where I saw several fresh graves; and one day when I rose from the dinner table, I walked directly to the door and commenced vomiting most profusely. I raised large quantities of blood and poisonous matter, and so great were the muscular contortions of my system, that my jaw in a few moments was dislocated. . . . the effect of the poison was so powerful, as to cause much of the hair to become loosened from my head." (Smith, *History of the Church* 1:271.)
8. Mary, daughter of Hyrum and Jerusha Barden Smith, was born June 27, 1829, at Manchester, New York, and died May 29, 1832, at Kirtland, Ohio.
9. Elizabeth Ann, wife of Newel K. Whitney.
10. At a conference of the Church held at Amherst, Ohio, January 25, 1832, William McLellin (1806-1883) was called on a proselyting mission "into the south countries" with Luke Johnson. A month later he stopped in Middlebury, Ohio, due to ill health, and "kept store" for one Col. Sumner. In April he decided to permanently discontinue his mission and returned to Hiram, Ohio, "determined to seek a companion and come to Zion." On April 16, four days after meeting twenty-two-year-old Emeline Miller, the couple were married, and on May 2 he left for Independence, Missouri. (Jenson, *Biographical Encyclopedia* 1:82; also William McLellin letter to Samuel McLellin, August 4, 1832.)

To William W. Phelps, July 31, 1832

RC. In the hand of Frederick G. Williams, Joseph Smith Papers, LDS Church Archives.

1. See letter of November 27, 1832, pp. 259-62 of this work.
2. Joseph Smith moved his family from Kirtland thirty miles southeast to Hiram, Ohio, in September 1831 and took residence with the family of John Johnson. (See Smith, *History of the Church* 1:215.)
3. Frederick G. Williams's tenure as scribe for Joseph Smith began eleven days prior to the date of this letter, from which time he was "constantly" in the Prophet's employ. (Frederick G. Williams, undated manuscript.)
4. Consisting of about one hundred men, women, and children, this was the same company with which William McLellin traveled to Missouri. (See note 10, p. 669.) They left Portage County, Ohio, on May 2 and arrived at Independence on June 16, 1832. (William E. McLellin to Samuel McLellin, August 4, 1832.)
5. All who went to Zion (Jackson County, Missouri) were required to "lay all things before the bishop in Zion" and to take a certificate of recommendation from the bishop at their former place of residence. (D&C 72:15, 17, 25.)
6. See note 10, p. 669.
7. On March 24, 1832, a week prior to Joseph's departure for Missouri, Joseph and Sidney Rigdon had been set upon by a mob and violently beaten, tarred, and feathered. Joseph wrote that "the spirit of mobocracy was very prevalent through that whole region of country at the time," and that those who had beaten him continued to menace John Johnson for a long time, forcing Joseph and Sidney to move their families back to Kirtland. (Smith, *History of the Church* 1:261-66; Parkin, "Conflict at Kirtland," pp. 248ff.)
8. "The Vision" refers to section 76 of the Doctrine and Covenants.
9. During this time Joseph Smith was engaged in a revision of the King James Version of the Bible (See Matthews, *A Plainer Translation*, pp. 21-53.
10. Cholera, essentially a waterborne disease caused by sewage-contaminated food or water, is characterized by diarrhea, vomiting, muscular cramps, dehydration, and collapse. The disease raged violently in the nineteenth century along immigrant routes into the United States beginning in 1832. (Marks and Beatty, *Epidemics*, p. 191.)
11. Almira Scobey, a cousin of Joseph Smith.
12. "Detroit was an obvious target [for the disease], the more so because, ignoring an inexhaustible supply of fresh water flowing by in the Detroit River, most of the inhabitants used water from wells. Because the land was low and marshy and outhouses were placed with no regard to location, contamination of well water was the rule rather than the exception." (Marks and Beatty, *Epidemics*, p. 191.)
13. When the Sauk and Fox Indians, led by Chief Black Hawk, contested the cession of 50 million acres of their land in Illinois, Wisconsin, and Missouri to the United States, the result was the Black Hawk War. Early in 1832 Black Hawk crossed the Mississippi River with several hundred followers intent upon reoccupying some of the questioned land. When he refused to withdraw, fighting erupted as the Indians attacked and burned frontier settlements. The war ended on August 3 near the mouth of the Bad Axe River in southern Wisconsin when Black Hawk's forces were massacred as they attempted to retreat into Iowa.
14. At a conference in Amherst, Ohio, on January 25, 1832, Orson Pratt, Lyman Johnson, and others, were called on a proselyting mission to "the eastern countries." At the same time this letter was written, the two men were laboring in New England. When they returned to Kirtland in February 1833, they had traveled some four thousand miles, held 207 meetings, baptized 104 persons, and organized several branches of the Church. (D&C 75:14; "History of Orson Pratt," *Deseret News*, June 2 and 9, 1858.)

To Emma Smith, October 13, 1832

ALS. RLDS Church Archives, Independence, Missouri. Published in "Letters of Joseph Smith, the Martyr," *The Saints' Herald* 26 (December 1, 1879): 356.

1. D&C 57:1-3, 6-8.
2. On the subject of the United Firm, see Smith, *History of the Church* 1:270; Roberts, *Comprehensive History* 1:284-85; Far West Record, April 30, 1832; Arrington, Fox, and May, *Building the City of God*, pp. 31, 35; and Cook, *Revelations of the Prophet*, pp. 167-68.
3. Far West Record, April 30, 1832; D&C 84:112-14.
4. Benjamin T. Onderdonk (1791-1861) was consecrated bishop of the Protestant Episcopal Church's New York diocese on November 26, 1830. In 1845 he was suspended from his office on charges of immorality. (*Dictionary of American Biography* 7:38-39.)
5. Newel K. Whitney, undated manuscript dictated to Willard Richards, Ms., LDS Church Archives.
6. Pearl Street, the center of New York City commerce where the dry-goods merchants had their warehouses, was located near the southern end of Manhattan Island. One of the principle hotels of the city was the large male boarding house, the Pearl Street House, located at 88 Pearl Street. One traveler wrote, "To obtain some idea of the commerce of New York, a stranger should view the Broadway, where the stores of the jewellers and mercers are situated. In Wall Street the bankers have their offices—in South Street the wholesale merchants transact their business—in Pearl Street the dry-good merchants have their warehouses. . . . The conveyance of merchandise to the different warehouses employs two thousand carts. Their passing and repassing produces a continual noise." (Stokes, *The Iconography of Manhattan Island, 1498-1909* 3:1707-8, 1801.)
7. The population of New York City at this time was a little over 200,000.
8. Julia Murdock, one of twins born April 30, 1831, was Joseph Smith's adopted daughter.
9. The cholera epidemic that swept through New York City in the summer of 1832 left 1,520 dead out of 3,731 cases before July 31. It was reported that of a population of two hundred thousand, seventy thousand fled the city, carrying the disease to the interior. (Marks and Beatty, *Epidemics*, p. 201; Divett, "His Chastening Rod: Cholera Epidemics and the Mormons," p. 6-15; "The Cholera," *The Evening and the Morning Star*, August 1832, p. [1].)
10. At the time of the writing of this letter, Emma was expecting their fourth natural child.

To William W. Phelps, November 27, 1832

Dft. Joseph Smith Papers, LDS Church Archives. The original letter was evidently dictated by Joseph Smith to Frederick G. Williams and has not been found. The copy produced here is the first item in Joseph Smith's first letterbook and appears to be the original draft. The non-holograph portion of the letter is in the handwriting of Frederick G. Williams. A portion of the letter was published in January 1833 in *The Evening and the Morning Star* and in 1876 was canonized as section 85 of the Doctrine and Covenants. Nearly the entire letter is published in Smith, *History of the Church* 1:297-99.

1. D&C 58:56; 63:24, 27. On the Mormon experience in Missouri, see Allen and Leonard, *Story of the Latter-day Saints*, pp. 60-134, and Parkin, "Missouri's Impact on the Church," pp. 57-63.
2. D&C 72:15-18, 23, 25.
3. "Let Every Man Learn His Duty," *The Evening and the Morning Star*, January 1833.
4. Corrill, *Brief History of the Church of Jesus Christ of Latter Day Saints*, pp. 18-19.

5. Smith, *History of the Church* 1:319.
6. The 1830 Federal Census lists James McMahon, James White, and Adam Fisher in Mason County, bordering Cabell County, Virginia (now West Virginia), where Guandott is located, and Micajah Dillon and Abraham and Henry Kingrey in Franklin County. David Hough is listed at Wooster, Wayne County, Ohio.
7. Vienna Jacques. See p. 293.

To William W. Phelps, January 11, 1833

Rc. In the handwriting of Frederick G. Williams in Joseph Smith's Letterbook 1, pp. 18-20, Joseph Smith Papers, LDS Church Archives. Published in Smith, *History of the Church* 1:316-17.

1. Term used to designate the revelation that is now D&C 88.

To Mr. Editor, January 4, 1833

Rc. Copied by Frederick G. Williams in Joseph Smith's Letterbook 1, pp. 14-18, Joseph Smith Papers, LDS Church Archives. Published in part in *American Revivalist, and Rochester Observer,* February 1833; and in *History of the Church* 1:312-16. Although the retained copies of this letter and another to the same person on February 12 indicate some question as to the name of the recipient, the editor was N. C. Saxton, publisher of a religious paper at Rochester, New York, the *American Revivalist, and Rochester Observer,* which was "Dedicated to the Interests of Zion Generally, and Especially to Revivals of Religion." The paper was published weekly on Saturdays.

1. Smith, *History of the Church* 1:301.
2. D&C 87:1.

To N. C. Saxton, February 12, 1833

Rc. Copied by Frederick G. Williams in Joseph Smith's Letterbook 1, pp. 27-28, Joseph Smith Papers, LDS Church Archives. Published in Smith, *History of the Church* 1:326.

1. With slight editorial changes, the last paragraph of Joseph Smith's letter of January 4 had been published in the February 2, 1833, issue of the *American Revivalist, and Rochester Observer* under this heading: "Mormonism.—We have received a communication on this subject, from Mr. J. Smith Jr., who we suppose, is a principal leader of the sect that embraces Mormonism. It is written throughout with much good feeling and urbanity.

   "With our own views of truth, we do not feel that it would be consistent with our duty, or for the benefit of our readers to enter into a discussion on this subject, nor have we room for the whole letter. Still we think our readers may be gratified in learning something of the author's views, and therefore present them with the following extract, not holding ourselves responsible for its sentiments."

To Emma Smith, March 6, 1833

ALS. The original letter is in the possession of Brent F. Ashworth, Provo, Utah.

1. D&C 42:30-34; 78:3.

To Newel K. Whitney [1833-34]

ALS. University of Utah Library, Salt Lake City, Utah.

1. Howe, Statement, April 8, 1885; "To The Public," *Painesville* [Ohio] *Telegraph,* January 31, 1834.
2. E. D. Howe described Hurlbut as a "good sized, fine looking" fellow, "full of gab, but illiterate." Details on the life of Hurlbut are found in Smith, *History of the Church* 1:252, 354-55; Parkin, "Conflict at Kirtland," pp. 120-28; Hurlbut, Biographical Sketch of her Husband D. P. Hurlbut, April 15, 1855; Howe, Statement, April 8, 1885.
3. The letter would be dated after the excommunication of Hurlbut, June 23, 1833, and prior to the dissolution of the United Firm on April 10, 1834.
4. Possibly the Kirtland real estate known as the French Farm.

To William Phelps and others, August 10, 1833

Rc. The source of this letter is a copy by Edward Partridge, one of the recipients, in his family record, pp. 16-18, Edward Partridge Papers, LDS Church Archives.

1. Smith, *History of the Church* 1:390-94.

To William Phelps and others, August 18, 1833

ALS. Joseph Smith Papers, LDS Church Archives.

1. George A. Smith, who arrived in Kirtland, Ohio, in May 1833, wrote, "In consequence of the persecution which raged against the Prophet Joseph and the constant threats to do him violence it was found necessary to keep continual guard to prevent his being murdered by his enemies, who were headed by Joseph H. Wakefield and Dr. P. Hurlbut the latter of whom had been expelled from the Church for Adultery—during the fall and winter I took a part of this service going 2½ miles to guard at President Rigdon's." (Smith, "Memoirs of George A. Smith.")
2. After the destruction of the Church press in Independence, Missouri, in July 1833, another press was obtained and brought to Kirtland. *The Evening and the Morning Star* was published there until September 1834, when it was replaced by the *Messenger and Advocate,* edited by Oliver Cowdery.
3. Handwriting of Frederick G. Williams.

To Vienna Jacques, September 4, 1833

L[S]. In the handwriting of Frederick G. Williams, Joseph Smith Papers, LDS Church Archives. The fact that the signature was cut from the letter suggests that it was a holograph. A clerical note erroneously attributes the entire letter to Joseph's hand and states that the signature was cut off by President Brigham Young on March 4, 1859. The name of the addressee, "Viana Jaquish," in Joseph's hand (and spelling) next to the missing signature helps substantiate his personal signature. Published in Smith, *History of the Church* 1:407-9.

1. *Women's Exponent* 7:20-21; 8:12; 12:152. D&C 90:28-30.
2. Agnes Coolbrith and Mary Bailey were baptized in Boston, Massachusetts, by Samuel H. Smith and Orson Hyde during their 1832 proselyting activity in that city. Joining the

Saints in Kirtland in 1833, Agnes and Mary found lodging in the Joseph Smith, Sr., home and later married the Smith sons Don Carlos and Samuel Harrison. (Samuel H. Smith Diary, June 26 and July 30, 1832; *Times and Seasons* 2:325; R. Smith, *Mary Bailey.*)

3. David Patten was among missionaries sent east from Kirtland in March 1833. He traveled to the area of his birth in Jefferson County, New York, concentrating his efforts in Theresa, Orleans, and Henderson. ("History of David Patten," *Deseret News*, July 1858.)

4. Descriptions of the plans for the House of the Lord and the city plat are in Smith, *History of the Church* 1:357-62.

To Silas Smith, September 26, 1833

Tr. The earliest source of this letter is in Lucy Mack Smith's "The History of Lucy Smith Mother of the Prophet," pp. 228-32, Ms., LDS Church Archives. The portion of the manuscript containing the letter was written by Martha Jane Knowlton Coray, who, along with her husband Howard, wrote the Lucy Smith history from material dictated or obtained from the Prophet's mother about 1845. The statement of personal involvement in the first paragraph of the letter suggests that the original may have been a holograph. Published in Lucy Smith, *Biographical Sketches of Joseph Smith the Prophet*, pp. 205-8.

1. Joseph Smith, Sr., Patriarchal Blessing Book 1, p. 3.

2. George A. Smith, "Memoirs of George A. Smith," p. 2.

3. At this point in the manuscript, the following words have been inserted in the handwriting of Robert Campbell: "and by faith was translated. I may [believe] that Noah was a perfect man in his generation & also walked with God." (Lucy Smith, "The History of Lucy Smith Mother of the Prophet," p. 231.)

To Moses Nickerson, November 19, 1833

Rc. Written by Oliver Cowdery in Joseph Smith's Letterbook 1, pp. 62-65, Joseph Smith Papers, LDS Church Archives. Published in Smith, *History of the Church* 1:441-43.

1. For details of this missionary journey, see Joseph Smith's Diary between the dates indicated, pp. 17-20 of this work.

To Edward Partridge and others, December 10, 1833

Rc. Written by Frederick G. Williams in Joseph Smith's Letterbook 1, pp. 70-75, Joseph Smith Papers, LDS Church Archives. Published in Smith, *History of the Church* 1:453-56.

1. Details of the expulsion of the Saints from Jackson County are found in Lyon, "Independence, Missouri, and the Mormons, 1827-1833," pp. 10-19; Smith, *History of the Church* 1:426-40; Parkin, "A History of the Latter-day Saints in Clay County, Missouri, from 1833 to 1837."

2. The circumstances in which Andrew Barber was killed and Philo Dibble seriously wounded are found in Smith, *History of the Church* 1:430-31.

3. See, for example, D&C 58:52-56; 63:24-31.

4. D&C 58:4.

5. D&C 100:13.

To Edward Partridge and others, March 30, 1834

Rc. Written by Thomas Burdick in the Oliver Cowdery Letterbook, pp. 30-36, Huntington Library, San Marino, California. An accompanying letter from Oliver Cowdery to William Phelps indicates that Oliver Cowdery wrote the original at Joseph Smith's dictation.

1. Smith, History of the Church 1:445.
2. Ibid. 1:457.
3. John Corrill to Oliver Cowdery, December 1833, The Evening and the Morning Star, January 1834, p. 126.
4. D&C 101:43, 55-58; 103:1, 15-17, 21, 30-40; Smith, History of the Church 2:36-40; Crawley and Anderson, "The Political and Social Realities of Zion's Camp," pp. 406-20.
5. Called at a Missouri conference to contact the Church in Ohio to "take some measures for the relief or restoration of the people . . . plundered and driven from their homes" in Missouri. Parley Pratt and Lyman Wight left Clay County in February 1834 and arrived in Kirtland, Ohio, some time in March. (Pratt, Autobiography, pp. 107-8.)
6. See p. 285.

To Emma Smith, May 18, 1834

AL[S]. RLDS Church Archives, Independence, Missouri. Published in "Letters of Joseph Smith, the Martyr," The Saints' Herald 26 (December 1, 1879): 356-57.

1. Dunklin to Phelps, Morley, Whitmer, Partridge, Corrill, and Gilbert, February 4, 1834. Detailed treatment of the Zion's Camp march is found in Smith, History of the Church 2:61-134; also Crawley and Anderson, "The Political and Social Realities of Zion's Camp," pp. 406-20; and Parkin, "A History of the Latter-day Saints in Clay County, Missouri," pp. 135-87.
2. Frederick G. Williams was the Zion's Camp historian. According to George A. Smith, a participant in the camp, the Williams journal was lost. (Smith, "Memoirs of George A. Smith," p. 43.)
3. At the time of this writing, Oliver Cowdery was the Church printer in Kirtland and editor of The Evening and the Morning Star.
4. Relatives of Joseph Smith in Zion's Camp besides Jenkins Salisbury, the husband of Joseph's sister Catherine, were his brother William and his cousins Jesse J. and George A. Smith. Jesse J. died on July 1, 1834, after the arrival of the Camp in Missouri. (Smith, History of the Church 2:120, 185.)
5. Handwriting of Frederick G. Williams.

To Emma Smith, June 4, 1834

Rc. Copied by James Mulholland in Joseph Smith's Letterbook 2, pp. 56-58, Joseph Smith Papers, LDS Church Archives.

1. Zion's Camp crossed the Mississippi River at Louisiana, Missouri, on June 4 and 5, 1834. (See Smith, History of the Church 2:82-83; Heber C. Kimball Diary, June 4-5, 1834.)
2. The 1830 U.S. census lists Alden Childs at Connewango, Cattaraugus County, New York.
3. Solon or James Foster.
4. Harpin Riggs, born April 12, 1809, at Oxford, New Haven County, Connecticut. (Early Church Information File.)
5. Addison Wren is probably a corruption of Addison Green.
6. At this time Lyman Wight and Hyrum Smith were leading a contingent of Zion's Camp

volunteers from Michigan. They joined the main group at Salt River in Monroe County, Missouri, on June 8. (Smith, *History of the Church* 2:87-88.)

7. Appended to Joseph's letter to Emma was one of Frederick G. Williams to his wife Rebecca. (See Joseph Smith Letterbook 2, pp. 58-59.)

To Lyman Wight and others, August 16, 1834

Rc. Written by Frederick G. Williams in Joseph Smith's Letterbook 1, pp. 84-87, Joseph Smith Papers, LDS Church Archives. Published in Smith, *History of the Church* 2:144-46.

1. *The Evening and the Morning Star*, May 1834, p. 160.
2. Smith, *History of the Church* 2:88.
3. Pratt, *Autobiography*, p. 115.
4. Smith, *History of the Church* 2:123.
5. Ibid., p. 139.
6. Sylvester Smith's activities with Zion's Camp are noted in Smith, *History of the Church* 2:65-66, 68-69, 83, 100, 101.
7. See the editorial "The Progress of the Gospel," *The Evening and the Morning Star*, August 1834, p. 180.
8. About July 1, 1834, Joseph Smith met with other Church leaders at the home of Lyman Wight near Liberty and organized the high council in Missouri consisting of twelve high priests under the presidency of David Whitmer, William W. Phelps, and John Whitmer. This council was the governing Church authority in Missouri. (See Smith, *History of the Church* 2:122-25; and Parkin, "History of the Latter-day Saints in Clay County, Missouri," pp. 227-38.)
9. The suspension points are in the original. A marginal insertion by Frederick Williams reads, "The better it shall be for them and for Zion inasmuch as the indignation of the people Sleepeth for a while our time should be employed to the best advantage altho it is not the will of God that any one of their ambassadors should hold their peace after they have started upon their Journey."
10. A marginal note at this point, in the same hand as the rest of the text, adds, "for the church even that they shall be driven from City to City and but few shall remain to receive an inheritance if these things are not kept there remaineth a scorge."
11. On the cholera epidemic, see notes 10, 12, p. 670.

To Oliver Cowdery, September 24, 1834

P. *The Evening and the Morning Star* (Kirtland, Ohio), September 1834.

1. *The National Cyclopedia of American Biography* 4:161; *Dictionary of American Biography* 3:446-48.
2. Smith, *History of the Church* 1:120-21.

To Oliver Cowdery, December 1834

P. *Latter Day Saints' Messenger and Advocate* 1 (December 1834): 40.

1. Maria S. Hurlbut statement, June 19, 1883. Howe, *Mormonism Unvailed*, pp. 231-69. An analysis of the Hurlbut affidavits is found in R. L. Anderson, "Joseph Smith's New York Reputation Reappraised," pp. 283-314.
2. *Messenger and Advocate* 1 (December 1834): 41-42.

To Almira Scobey, June 2, 1835

ALS. William W. Phelps Papers, LDS Church Archives.

1. D&C 105:13-14, 18, 33; Far West Record, June 23, 1834; Smith, History of the Church 2:112-13.
2. Smith, History of the Church 2:122-25, 227. On William W. Phelps and his activities, see also Bowen, "The Versatile W. W. Phelps: Mormon Writer, Educator, and Pioneer."
3. Almira Mack Scobey (1805-1886) and her twin brother, Almon, were the youngest children of Joseph Smith's maternal uncle, Steven Mack, and his wife, Temperance Bond, pioneer settlers of Pontiac, Michigan. Almira was baptized in 1830 and married William Scobey on August 7, 1831. Scobey died in December 1833 and Almira lived for a time with a Curtis family in Liberty, Clay County, Missouri, before she married Benjamin Covey in Kirtland, Ohio, in 1836. (Sprague, "The Progenitors and Descendants of Col. Steven Mack and Temperance Bond Mack," Ms., LDS Genealogical Department, Salt Lake City, Utah.)

To Sally Phelps, July 20, 1835

ALS. The original of this letter has not been found. The source here is the facsimile publication in Leah Y. Phelps, "Letters of Faith from Kirtland," Improvement Era 45 (August 1942): 529. The Genealogical Department of the LDS Church has a microfilm of letters of William W. Phelps to his wife, Sally, which includes part of a letter dated July 20, 1835. This holograph may have been part of that letter, but it does not appear on the film.

To Brethren, June 15, 1835

LS. Photocopy of the original in the handwriting of William W. Phelps, Joseph Smith Papers, LDS Church Archives.

1. Kirtland Revelation Book, p. 102.

To Hezekiah Peck, August 31, 1835

Rc. The only known source of this letter is the copy by John Whitmer in chapter 16 of his Church history, "The Book of John Whitmer." Ms., RLDS Church Archives, Independence, Missouri. Published in F. Mark McKiernan and Roger D. Launius, eds., An Early Latter Day Saint History: The Book of John Whitmer (Independence, Mo.: Herald House, 1980), pp. 148-50.

1. D&C 47; 69. McKiernan and Launius, An Early Latter Day Saint History: The Book of John Whitmer, pp. 148-50.
2. Hezekiah Peck, born in 1782 in Windham County, Vermont, was baptized in June 1830 at Colesville, New York. He accompanied the Colesville Saints to Ohio and Missouri and in June 1833 was designated a counselor to newly appointed bishop John Corrill. (Smith, History of the Church 1:88, 363.)

To Emma Smith, August 19, 1836

P. The original of this letter evidently no longer exists. The copy here is from "Letters of Joseph Smith, The Martyr," *The Saints' Herald* 26 (1 December 1879): 357. A notation following the publication indicates that the letter bore no postmark but was addressed to Geauga County, Ohio, and presumably carried by Hyrum Smith.

1. D&C 111; Roberts, *Comprehensive History* 1:410-12; Robinson, "Items of Personal History," pp. 104ff; Proper, "Joseph Smith and Salem," pp. 88-97; Smith, *History of the Church* 2:463-66.

To John Corrill and the Church in Zion, September 4, 1837

Rc. Written by George W. Robinson in Joseph Smith's "Scriptory Book," pp. 18-22, Joseph Smith Papers, LDS Church Archives. Published in Smith, *History of the Church* 2:508-9.

1. Young, "History of Brigham Young," *Deseret News*, February 10, 1858, p. 386; "Memoirs of George A. Smith," p. 89; Hepzibah Richards to Willard Richards, January 18, 1838. For the development and causes of the difficulty in Kirtland in 1837, see Allen and Leonard, *Story of the Latter-day Saints*, pp. 110-16; and Parkin, *Conflict at Kirtland*, pp. 279-325.

Diary Entry, March 13, 1838

Ms. Written by George W. Robinson in Joseph Smith's "Scriptory Book," pp. 16-17, Joseph Smith Papers, LDS Church Archives. Published in Smith, *History of the Church* 3:8-9.

1. Smith, *History of the Church* 3:1.
2. Ibid. 2:513; 3:13-14.
3. George W. Harris, born in 1780 in Berkshire County, Massachusetts, was baptized by Orson Pratt at Terre Haute, Indiana, in November 1833. (Early Church Information File.)

To the Presidency of the Church in Kirtland, March 29, 1838

Rc. Written by George W. Robinson in Joseph Smith's Scriptory Book, pp. 23-26, Joseph Smith Papers, LDS Church Archives. Published in Smith, *History of the Church* 3:10-12.

1. The printing office was burned on January 16, 1838, shortly after Joseph Smith had left Kirtland. The cause of the fire is discussed in Parkin, *Conflict at Kirtland*, pp. 322-23.
2. The Parrishites consisted of about thirty dissenters dedicated to the destruction of the Church at Kirtland. Under the leadership of the Prophet's former secretary, Warren Parrish, the group undertook to seize Church property and challenge the leadership of Joseph Smith. (Parkin, *Conflict at Kirtland*, pp. 314-17.)
3. Phelps and Whitmer were dropped from the Church at Far West on March 10, 1838, on charges of misusing Church funds. (See Smith, *History of the Church* 3:7-8.)

4. Daniel Sanborn Miles (1772-1845), born in Sanbornton, New Hampshire, was baptized by Orson Pratt and Lyman Johnson in 1832. He arrived in Far West, Missouri, from Kirtland, on March 14, 1838. (Cook, *Revelations of the Prophet*, p. 267.)
5. Levi Richards (1799-1876), brother of Willard Richards, was born at Hopkinton, Massachusetts. Dr. Richards, a practitioner of Thompsonian medicine, was baptized at Kirtland in 1836. He left Kirtland for Missouri with Brigham Young in December 1837 to escape mob violence. Orson Whitney, *History of Utah* 4:445.
6. Daniel Carter (1803-1887), born in Benson, Vermont.

To Hyrum Smith, May 25, 1838

ADS. Joseph Smith Papers, LDS Church Archives.

1. Smith, *History of the Church* 3:34-37.
2. The location of "Plattisgrove" where Hyrum Smith received this note is not known. However, Hyrum had arrived in Far West in time to accompany his brother north again on May 28. Subsequently, Hyrum returned to Far West on May 30 and Joseph on June 1. The next day Emma Smith gave birth to a son, Alexander Hale Smith. Two days later, Joseph, Hyrum, and others returned to Daviess County, where they continued laying out the proposed city, Adam-ondi-Ahman. (Smith, *History of the Church* 3:37-38.)

To Emma Smith, November 4, 1838

AL[S]. RLDS Church Archives, Independence, Missouri. Published in *The History of the Reorganized Church of Jesus Christ of Latter Day Saints* 2:286-87.

1. Details of the conflict in northern Missouri are given in general treatments of Church history. See Smith, *History of the Church* 3:55-190; Roberts, *Comprehensive History* 1:447-93; Allen and Leonard, *The Story of the Latter-day Saints*, pp. 120-30. See also Gentry, "A History of the Latter-day Saints in Northern Missouri from 1836-1839;" Parkin, "A History of the Latter-day Saints in Clay County, Missouri, from 1833 to 1837."
2. Samuel D. Lucas was major-general in command of the fourth division of Missouri militia with headquarters at Independence, Jackson County. Lucas and David R. Atchison were commanding third- and fourth-division militia units in Caldwell County on October 30, when Atchison withdrew from his post, according to one source, because of the inhuman demands of the Boggs extermination order. This left Lucas as the senior officer. Apparently unaware that Major-general John B. Clark (at the time proceeding toward the scene of action from Howard County with militia of his first division) had been named supreme commander of the forces operating against the Saints, Lucas presided at the surrender of Far West. (*History of Caldwell and Livingston Counties, Missouri*, pp. 132-33; *Document Containing the Correspondence, Orders, &c.*, pp. 70-72.)
3. Pratt, *Autobiography*, pp. 228-29.
4. Parley P. Pratt to Mary Ann Pratt, November 4, 1838.
5. George M. Hinkle had been appointed to the Missouri High Council in January 1836 to fill the place of Orson Pratt, who had been called to the Council of the Twelve. At the time spoken of here, Hinkle was the commanding officer of the Mormon militia defending Far West. Under the guise of a truce, Hinkle had surrendered the Mormon leaders to the Missouri militia. (Pratt, *Autobiography*, p. 186; Smith, *History of the Church* 2:357.)
6. William Hull, who surrendered American forces to the British at Detroit in 1812.
7. John Corrill's disaffection culminated with his excommunication on March 17, 1839. (Smith, *History of the Church* 3:283-84.)

8. Moses G. Wilson, one of the justices of the Jackson County court, was an officer in the fourth division of the Missouri state militia under Samuel Lucas. Wilson's company of Jackson County troops escorted the Latter-day Saint prisoners to Independence. (*History of Jackson County*, p. 178.)

9. John B. Clark, born in 1802 in Kentucky, came with his father's family to Howard County, Missouri, in 1818. He was appointed clerk of the county court in 1823, colonel of militia in 1825, and major-general in 1836. He fought in the Black Hawk War. In 1849 Clark was elected to the state legislature and, beginning in 1854, served three terms in the U.S. Congress. He was a Confederate brigadier-general during the Civil War.

Clark was the recipient on October 27, 1838, of Governor Boggs's extermination order against the Mormons and was given supreme command of the militia forces, but he did not arrive at Far West until after the Chuch leaders were surrendered to General Lucas. (*History of Howard and Chariton Counties, Missouri*, pp. 252-53.)

10. Lucas wrote that when his men, guarding the Mormon prisoners to Independence, arrived at Williams's ferry on the Missouri River on November 3, he received General Clark's orders to return the prisoners to Richmond but refused because he had not yet learned that Clark had been designated his superior by Governor Boggs and "could not, under any circumstances, be commanded by a junior Major General." (Lucas to Boggs, November 5, 1838, in *Document Containing the Correspondence, Orders, &c*, pp. 70-72.)

To Emma Smith, November 12, 1838

ALS. RLDS Church Archives, Independence, Missouri. Published in *History of the Reorganized Church* 2:290-91.

1. Lyman Wight Journal, cited in *History of the Reorganized Church* 2:296-97.

2. Austin A. King (1801-1870) was governor of Missouri from 1848 to 1852. Born in Tennessee, he came to Richmond in 1837 from Columbia, Missouri, where he had previously practiced law. Between 1837 and 1848 King served as judge of Missouri's fifth judicial circuit, consisting of the counties of Clinton, Ray, Caldwell, Clay, Platte, and Buchanan. In 1862 he was elected to the U.S. Congress. (*History of Ray County, Missouri*, pp. 259-61; Conard, *Encyclopedia of the History of Missouri* 3:537.)

3. Amos Rees was Clay County prosecuting attorney from 1831 to 1834 and in 1835 was one of the county's five practicing lawyers. From 1831 to 1837 Rees was attorney for Missouri's fifth judicial circuit. He later moved to Platte City, Missouri, and after that, to Fort Leavenworth, Kansas, where he was a prominent lawyer. He played a key role in the founding of Leavenworth as one of three trustees of the Town Company that parceled the land for settlement following the treaty with the Delaware Indians.

Information furnished by Rees and Wiley Williams was an immediate cause for the issuance of the Boggs extermination order. At the time, Rees was a major in the Ray County Militia. (Woodson, *History of Clay County*, p. 330; Moore, *Early History of Leavenworth City and County*, pp. 23, 255.)

4. Alexander William Doniphan (1808-1887) was a prominent Clay County lawyer beginning in 1833. Three times he represented Clay County in the Missouri general assembly. During the Mormon difficulties in 1838, Doniphan commanded the first brigade of David Atchison's third division of Missouri militia. He later achieved distinction as an officer in the Mexican War. (*History of Ray County, Missouri*, pp. 498-502; Maynard, "Alexander William Doniphan: Man of Justice," pp. 462-72.

5. George W. Robinson was a son-in-law of Sidney Rigdon.

6. Lyman Wight.

7. Almon W. Babbitt (1813-1856) had been a member of Zion's Camp and was named to the first quorum of the seventy in 1835. At the conclusion of a proselyting mission to

Canada, he had led a company of immigrating Saints to Missouri in 1838. (Jenson, *Bio-graphical Encyclopedia* 1:284.)

8. Sterling Price (1809-1867), a native of Virginia, arrived in Missouri in 1831 and engaged in merchandising and farming. He was elected to the U.S. Congress in 1844 but resigned his seat to participate in the Mexican War, where his service brought him a commission of brigadier general. Beginning in 1852 he served a term as governor of Missouri and subsequently fought in the Civil War.

A contingent of Missouri militia under Price guarded the Latter-day Saint prisoners from Independence to Richmond and was involved in guard duty at the Richmond court. (Conard, *Encyclopedia of the History of Missouri* 5:229-31.)

To Emma Smith, December 1, 1838

ALS. Joseph Smith Papers, LDS Church Archives.

1. Pratt, *History of the Late Persecutions Inflicted by the State of Missouri upon the Mormons*, p. 52. It was during the Richmond hearing that the rebuke of the guard by Joseph Smith took place as described by Pratt in his *Autobiography*, pp. 210-11.

2. Sidney Rigdon stated that the charge of treason came in consequence of the Mormon militia in Caldwell County being under arms at the time General Lucas's army approached Far West: "This calling out of the militia, was what they founded the charge of treason upon." (*Times and Seasons* 6:277.) Joseph Smith noted, "Our treason consisted of having whipped the mob out of Daviess county and taking their cannon from them." (Smith, *History of the Church* 3:212.) General David R. Atchison, one of the Missouri militia commanders at the scene of the conflict in upper Missouri, wrote in a letter to the federal garrison at Fort Leavenworth that the citizens of the northern counties had raised "mob after mob . . . for the purpose of driving a community of fanatics, (called Mormons) from those counties and from the State. Those things have at length goaded the Mormons into a state of desperation that has now made them aggressors instead of acting on the defensive. This places the citizens of this whole community in the unpleasant attitude that the civil and decent part of the community now have to engage in war to arrest a torrent that has been let loose by a cowardly mob." (Atchison to Col. Mason, Commanding at Leavenworth, October 27, 1838.)

3. This charge grew out of the killing of Moses Rowland in the Crooked River battle in October 1838. (Roberts, *Comprehensive History* 1:474-76.)

4. Samuel Bogart was a Methodist minister and had been captain of Ray County "minute men" in the Crooked River fight. (*Document Containing the Correspondence, Orders, &c.*, p. 108.)

To the Church in Caldwell County, December 16, 1838

Ls. Written in an unknown hand, Joseph Smith Papers, LDS Church Archives. Another copy of this letter, in a different hand, was found in the papers of Wilford Woodruff in 1857. This latter copy has slight differences in the text and is not complete. Published in *Times and Seasons* 1 (April 1840): 82-86; and in Smith, *History of the Church* 3:226-33.

1. Esther, chapters 2-8.

2. By the time Joseph wrote this letter, a sizable number of people had become disaffected and left the Church, some of whose testimony at the Richmond hearing in November contributed significantly to the imprisonment of Joseph Smith and those with him.

Among these were Sampson Avard, John Corrill, John Cleminson, Reed Peck, William W. Phelps, Orson Hyde, George Hinkle, John Whitmer, David Whitmer, Oliver Cowdery, Lyman E. Johnson, William McLellin, Thomas Marsh, and Martin Harris. (See Roberts, *Comprehensive History* 1:428-44, 472-74, 500-508; Gentry, "The Danite Band of 1838," pp. 421-50; *Document Containing the Correspondence, Orders &c.*, pp. 97-163.)

3. Isaiah 29:21.
4. Numbers 16:1-3, 31-35; Jude 11.
5. Numbers 22; 31:8.
6. Numbers 16:1-3.
7. Under Sampson Avard, the Danite organization in Missouri became involved in retaliatory actions against those who had committed depredations against the Latter-day Saints, and attributed this action to the Church Presidency. (On Avard and the Danites, see Gentry, "The Danite Band of 1838," pp. 421-50.)

To Presendia Huntington Buell, March 15, 1839

Tr. The earliest known source of this letter is a copy in the handwriting of Thomas Bullock inserted at page 898 of volume C-1 in Joseph Smith's *History of the Church*, Ms., Joseph Smith Papers, LDS Church Archives. Thomas Bullock made this copy of the letter on December 16, 1854, from the original then still in the possession of Presendia Huntington. (Historian's Office Journal, December 16, 1854.) Published in Smith, *History of the Church* 3:285-86.

1. For the jail description, see Joseph and Eunice McRae, *The Liberty and Carthage Jails*, pp. 48-50. The experience of Joseph Smith and others in the Liberty Jail is considered in Arrington, "Church Leaders in Liberty Jail," pp. 20-26; also Jessee, "'Walls, Grates, and Screeking Iron Doors'; The Prison Experience of Mormon Leaders in Missouri—1838-39."
2. Presendia Huntington (1810-1892) was born in Watertown, Jefferson County, New York. She married Norman Buell in 1827, was baptized in Kirtland in 1836, and shortly thereafter moved to Clay County, Missouri, with her husband, where she was living at the time of Joseph Smith's incarceration at Liberty. Presendia described her first visit to the jail: "When we arrived we found a heavy guard outside and inside the door. We were watched very closely, lest we should have tools to help the prisoners escape. I took dinner with the brethren in prison; they were much pleased to see the faces of true friends; but I cannot describe my feelings on seeing that man of God there confined in such a trying time for the saints." (As quoted in Tullidge, *The Women of Mormondom*, p. 209.)
3. At the time of the writing of this letter, the Mormon population of Missouri had been mostly driven from the state and were clustered mainly around Quincy in western Illinois.
4. The words in brackets come from the published text. The manuscript is blank at this point.

To the Church of Latterday Saints at Quincy, Illinois, and Scattered Abroad and to Bishop Partridge in Particular, March 20, 1839

LS. In the handwriting of Alexander McRae, and Caleb Baldwin, with corrections by Joseph Smith, Joseph Smith Papers, LDS Church Archives. Published in Smith, *History of the Church* 3:289-305.

1. Emma Smith to Joseph Smith, March 7, 1839, in Joseph Smith Letterbook, 2, p. 37.
2. The letters of Edward Partridge, Don Carlos Smith, and William Smith are published in Smith, *History of the Church* 3:272-74.
3. Wight's diary in *History of the Reorganized Church* 2:323.
4. These sections first appeared in the 1876 edition of the Doctrine and Covenants.
5. D&C 121:1-6 was extracted from the letter beginning at this point.
6. Reference is made to the January hearing at Liberty in which Sidney Rigdon obtained his freedom.
7. Joseph refers to their second unsuccessful jailbreak attempt of March 4.
8. Haun's Mill, a tiny Latter-day Saint community on Shoal Creek in Caldwell County, was attacked on October 28, 1838, by a large number of Missouri state militia under the command of Colonel Thomas Jennings. The attack, which left seventeen members of the community dead, was marked by acts of vicious cruelty. (Roberts, *Comprehensive History* 1:480-83.)
9. David R. Atchison (1807-1886) was one of the legal counsel to the Mormon prisoners in the Liberty Jail. (Roberts, *Comprehensive History* 1:467.)
10. D&C 121:7-25 was extracted from the letter beginning at this point.
11. Except for this segment of the manuscript to the end of page 13, written by Caleb Baldwin, the entire March 20 letter, with its continuation, is in the handwriting of Alexander McRae.
12. D&C 121:33 was extracted from the letter beginning at this point.
13. In June 1833 Reynolds Cahoon was named first counselor and John Smith president of a stake organized at Adam-ondi-Ahman, Missouri. (Smith, *History of the Church* 3:38.)
14. See p. 415.
15. Robert Lucas, Governor of Iowa Territory.
16. D&C 121:34-46 is an extract beginning at this point.
17. D&C 122:1-9 is an extract from the letter beginning at this point.
18. "Fierce" written over "fearce."
19. Capital O written over small *o*.
20. D&C 123:1-17 is an extract from the letter beginning at this point.
21. A portion of page 11 has disintegrated. The restoration of the missing text comes from an extant copy of the second part (continuation) of the letter. The copy was written by Alexander McRae and signed by the five occupants of the jail.

To Emma Smith, March 21, 1839

ALS. Joseph Smith Papers, LDS Church Archives.

1. John Howe Cleveland was the husband of Sarah Marietta Kingsley Cleveland, one of the initial members of the Nauvoo Relief Society. A non-Mormon, Judge Cleveland moved his family to Nauvoo shortly after the Saints began to settle there, but because of poor business prospects, he returned to Quincy, Illinois, in 1843. (*Times and Seasons* 4 [May 1, 1843]: 187.)
2. Old Major was Joseph Smith's dog.

To Isaac Galland, March 22, 1839

P. *Times and Seasons* 1 (February 1840): 51-56.

1. A treatment of Isaac Galland and his relationship with the Latter-day Saints is in Cook, "Isaac Galland—Mormon Benefactor," pp. 261-84.

   Joseph Smith later wrote, "Isaac Galland, who is one of our benefactors, having under his control a large quantity of land, in the immediate vicinity of our city, and a considerable portion of the city plat, opened both his heart and his hands, and 'when we were strangers, took us in,' and bade us welcome to share with him in his abundance, leaving his dwelling house, the most splendid edifice in the vicinity, for our accommodation, and partook himself to a small, uncomfortable dwelling. He sold us his large estates on very reasonable terms, and on long credit, so that we might have an opportunity of paying for them without being distressed, and has since taken our lands in Missouri in payment for the whole amount, and has given us a clear and indisputable title for the same. And in addition to the first purchase, we have exchanged lands with him in Missouri to the amount of eighty thousand dollars. He is the honored instrument the Lord used to prepare a home for us, when we were driven from our inheritances, having given him control of vast bodies of land, and prepared his heart to make the use of it the Lord intended he should. Being a man of extensive information, great talents, and high literary fame, he devoted all his powers and influence to give us a standing." (Smith, *History of the Church* 4:270-71.)

2. Smith, *History of the Church* 3:260-61; 265-67.
3. At this point a footnote reads, "He was thus informed by the Missourians."
4. At this time the prisoners at the Richmond jail were Parley P. Pratt, Morris Phelps, Darwin Chase, Norman Shearer, King Follett, and Luman Gibbs.
5. Israel Barlow (1806-1883), a native of Granville, Massachusetts, was one of the leaders of the group of Saints who first met Galland in 1838. Not authorized to make decisions for the Church, Barlow had conveyed the information to Church authorities in Quincy, Illinois, upon his arrival there. (Early Church Information File; Smith, *History of the Church* 3:265.)

To Emma Smith, April 4, 1839

ALS. Beinecke Rare Book and Manuscript Library, Yale University, New Haven, Connecticut. After he was finished writing, Joseph went back over the letter and added punctuation and capitalization.

1. "State of Missouri vs. Joseph Smith Jr. et al.," Circuit Court, Daviess County, Missouri.
2. Probably Joanna Carter, living in the Smith household at the time.

Journal Extract, November 1839

P. "Extract From the Private Journal of Joseph Smith Jr.," *Times and Seasons* 1 (November 1839): 2-9.

1. Dean C. Jessee, "'Walls, Grates, and Screeking Iron Doors': The Prison Experience of Mormon Leaders in Missouri—1838-1839," Paper delivered at the Restoration History Lecture Series, Graceland College, February 25, 1980.
2. *Times and Seasons* 1:1.
3. On the difficulties encountered during this midwinter trip to Missouri, see Smith, *History of the Church* 3:1-3; 5:211.
4. Hiram G. Parks was commander of the second brigade of David Atchison's third division of Missouri militia. (*Document Containing the Correspondence, Orders, &c.*, p. 32.)
5. Moses G. Wilson.
6. Joel Turnham served as judge of the Clay County court from 1827 to 1830, 1838 to 1844, and 1854 to 1856. (Woodson, *History of Clay County*, pp. 331-32.)
7. Cornelius Gilliam was sheriff of Clay County from 1830 to 1834 and a state senator representing Platte County from 1838 to 1842. During the "Mormon war" of 1838, Gilliam commanded men from the Platte purchase who were painted, feathered, and dressed like

Indians. "Gilliam himself wore a full Indian costume, had his war paint on, and called himself 'the Delaware Chief,' and his men 'the Delaware amarujans.' They would whoop and yell, and otherwise comport themselves as savages." (*History of Caldwell and Livingston Counties, Missouri*, p. 134.)

To Henry G. Sherwood, November 7, 1839.

LS. Illinois State Historical Library, Springfield, Illinois. The part of this letter that is not a Joseph Smith holograph was written by Elias Higbee.

1. Smith, *History of the Church* 4:12-13.
2. Henry G. Sherwood (1785-1862) was a member of the high council at Kirtland and, later, Nauvoo. In February 1841 he was elected Nauvoo city marshal. (Early Church Information File; Smith, *History of the Church* 2:510-11; 4:12, 492.)
3. John A. Hicks was president of the elders at Nauvoo. He was excommunicated October 4, 1841. (Smith, *History of the Church* 4:341, 428.)
4. Jonathan Hampton (1811-1844), born in East Gwillimbury, York, Canada, was converted by Brigham Young in 1835. (Family Group Records Collection.)

To Emma Smith, November 9, 1839

AL[S]. RLDS Church Archives, Independence, Missouri. Published in "Letters of Joseph Smith," *The Saints' Herald* 26 (December 1, 1879): 357.

1. John Snyder (1800-1875) was born in New Brunswick, Nova Scotia. After moving to Upper Canada, he was converted at Toronto in 1836 and was engaged in missionary work in England in 1837. After the expulsion from Missouri in 1838, Snyder established his family at Springfield, Illinois. (Cook, *Revelations of the Prophet*, pp. 277-78.)

To Emma Smith, January 20, 1840

ALS. Chicago Historical Society, Chicago, Illinois. A June 12, 1885, letter to Albert Hager of the Chicago Historical Society from Joseph Smith III at Lamoni, Iowa, states that in a recent visit to his old home in Nauvoo he had found letters of his father to his mother and that he was enclosing one dated 1840 "which if of any value to the archives of your society, please accept." (Joseph Smith III to Albert Hager, June 12, 1885, Ms. Chicago Historical Society.)

1. Details of Joseph Smith's trip to Washington, D.C., are found in his *History of the Church* 4:19-92.
2. Among those who had passed away was James Mulholland, the Prophet's secretary, who died November 3, 1839, at thirty-five years of age. (Smith, *History of the Church* 4: 88-89.)

To Mr. Editor, Sir, January 22, 1840

LS. Written in an unknown hand, the original letter is in the possession of Dr. J. C. Hayward, Logan, Utah. It was published in the *Chester County Register and Examiner*, Chester County, Pennsylvania, February 11, 1840.

1. The sentiments set forth in the following thirteen articles are Joseph Smith's personal affirmation of a statement on law and Church government written by Oliver Cowdery in

1835 and published that same year in the *Messenger and Advocate* and the Doctrine and Covenants. (Compare D&C 134.)

To Robert D. Foster, March 11, 1840

Ls. In the handwriting of Orson Hyde. Joseph Smith Papers, LDS Church Archives.

1. Smith, *History of the Church* 4:19-89.
2. Higbee's letters from Washington, D.C., are published in Smith, *History of the Church* 4:81-88.

To the High Council, June 18, 1840

Ds. In the handwriting of Robert B. Thompson. Joseph Smith Papers, LDS Church Archives. Published in Smith, *History of the Church* 4:136-37.

1. Smith, *History of the Church* 4:16-17.
2. Alanson Ripley had been a member of the Committee on Removal designated to assist in the removal of the Saints during the expulsion from Missouri. (Smith, *History of the Church* 3:254.)
3. Smith, *History of the Church* 4:138, 141, 144-45.

To Newel K. Whitney, December 12, 1840

ALS. Joseph Smith Papers, LDS Church Archives.

Agreement, May 14, 1841

AD. Joseph Smith Papers, LDS Church Archives.

1. Ebenezer Fairchild Wiggins (1806-1873) was born in Scott County, Kentucky. Elender More Wiggins (1810-1871) was born in Wabash, Illinois. The couple had five children at the time of this transaction. The Wigginses had purchased the farm in 1835; it was located just outside the northeast boundary of Nauvoo. (Family Group Records Collection; Nauvoo Restoration Index.)

To William W. Phelps, July 22, 1840

Rc. Copied by Robert B. Thompson in Joseph Smith's Letterbook 2, pp. 157-58, Joseph Smith Papers, LDS Church Archives.

1. Smith, *History of the Church* 3:6-8. *Document Containing the Correspondence, Orders, &c.,* pp. 120-25.
2. Bowen, "The Versatile W. W. Phelps," pp. 84-101. Smith, *History of the Church* 4: 142-43.

To Oliver Granger, July 1840

Rc. Written by Robert B. Thompson in Joseph Smith's Letterbook 2, pp. 159-61. Joseph Smith Papers, LDS Church Archives. The copy of the letter is undated, but the July date is suggested by the fact that the letter was written to Granger in answer to his letter dated June 23, 1840. Published in Smith, *History of the Church* 4:164-67.

1. The subject of the Kirtland economy and Joseph Smith's indebtedness has been dealt with by Hill, Rooker, and Wimmer in "The Kirtland Economy Revisited: A Market Critique of Sectarian Economics," pp. 391-475. This study concludes that viewing the issue from the perspective of the time, there is reason to believe that sufficient Kirtland assets were available to manage the accumulated debt had not unforeseen circumstances prevented it.
2. Oliver Granger (1794-1841), born in Phelps, Ontario County, New York, had been a member of the Kirtland high council. (See Cook, *Revelations of the Prophet*, p. 230.)
3. Levi Richards.
4. Almon Babbitt had accused Joseph Smith and Sidney Rigdon of extravagance and boasting during their 1839-40 trip to Washington, D.C., and of holding secret councils in the Lord's House at Kirtland to the exclusion of "certain brethren." Charges brought by Joseph against Babbitt were subsequently withdrawn when the matter was aired before the Nauvoo high council on September 5, 1840. (See Smith, *History of the Church* 4: 187-88.)

To the Twelve, December 15, 1840

LS. In the handwriting of Robert B. Thompson. Joseph Smith Papers, LDS Church Archives. Published in Smith, *History of the Church* 4:226-32.

1. D&C 118:4.
2. The mission of the Twelve in England is treated in Allen and Thorp, "The Mission of the Twelve to England, 1840-41: Mormon Apostles and the Working Classes," pp. 499-526; and in Esplin, "The Emergence of Brigham Young and the Twelve to Mormon Leadership," ch. 10.
3. Richards and Young to the First Presidency, September 5, 1840; published in Walker, "The Willard Richards and Brigham Young 5 September 1840 Letter From England to Nauvoo," pp. 466-75.
4. Joseph Smith, Sr., died September 14, 1840.
5. The original letter was cross-written on four pages. When the first three pages were completed, the third page was turned sideways and the writing continued at right angles over the existing text. Pages numbered [p. 1a] [p. 2a], etc., indicate cross-written material and the page upon which it appears.
6. Theodore Turley (1801-1871) was captain of the company of Saints that left England aboard the ship *North America* on September 7, 1840. (Family Group Records Collection; Esshom, *Pioneers and Prominent Men*, p. 1218; Smith, *History of the Church* 4: 187-88.)
7. The letter, dated October 12, 1840, at Manchester, England, was sent to the editors of the *Times and Seasons* and was published in the December 15, 1840, issue of that paper.
8. Seymour Brunson, a member of the Nauvoo high council, died August 10, 1840; the funeral discourse on baptism for the dead was given August 15. (Jenson, *Biographical Encyclopedia* 3:331.)
9. At the April 8, 1840, Nauvoo conference, Orson Hyde and John E. Page were called to go on a mission to the Jews. Page subsequently withdrew from the assignment, but Hyde ultimately visited Jerusalem and dedicated Palestine for the return of the Jews on October 24, 1841. (Smith, *History of the Church* 4:109, 372-79, 454-59.)

To Oliver Granger, January 26, 1841

Ls. In the handwriting of Robert B. Thompson, Huntington Library, San Marino, California.

  1. Smith, *History of the Church* 4:204.

To Amos Keeler, March 16, 1841

Ls. In the handwriting of Robert B. Thompson, Pennsylvania Historical Society.

  1. Hill, Rooker, and Wimmer, "The Kirtland Economy Revisited," pp. 417, 424.

To Oliver Granger, May 4, 1841

Ls. In the handwriting of Robert B. Thompson, Joseph Smith Papers, LDS Church Archives.

  1. Smith, *History of the Church* 4:408-9.
  2. On Isaac Galland's errand in the East, see pp. 496-97.
  3. The reference here is to Joseph's brother, Don Carlos Smith, and to Don Carlos's wife, Agnes Coolbrith Smith.

To Smith Tuttle, October 9, 1841

Ls. In the handwriting of John S. Fullmer, Illinois State Historical Society. Published in Smith, *History of the Church* 4:430-33.

  1. Smith, *History of the Church* 4:170-72; Flanders, *Nauvoo: Kingdom on the Mississippi*, pp. 41-43; Miller and Miller, *Nauvoo: The City of Joseph*, pp. 27-35; Lyndon Cook, "Isaac Galland—Mormon Benefactor."
  2. Although Galland was eventually relieved of his power of attorney as Church agent, and became estranged from Church fellowship, there is no evidence of formal action against him for wrongdoing. (See Cook, "Isaac Galland—Mormon Benefactor," p. 281.)

To John Bernhisel, November 16, 1841

Ls. In the handwriting of John Taylor, Joseph Smith Papers, LDS Church Archives.

  1. Barrett, "John M. Bernhisel, Mormon Elder in Congress."
  2. Stevens, *Incidents of Travel in Central America, Chiapas, and Yucatan.*
  3. John Bernhisel to Joseph Smith, September 8, 1841.

To Browning and Bushnell, December 7, 1841

Rc. In the handwriting of John S. Fullmer, Joseph Smith Letterbook 2, p. 217, Joseph Smith Papers, LDS Church Archives. Published in Smith, *History of the Church* 4:468-69.

  1. Hill, Rooker, and Wimmer, "The Kirtland Economy Revisited," p. 463.

To Nancy Rigdon, 1842

P. The earliest known source of this letter is John C. Bennett's publication of it in the *Sangamo Journal* on August 19, 1842. Bennett claimed that the original letter was in his possession and was written by Willard Richards at Joseph Smith's dictation. (John C. Bennett, *The History of the Saints: An Exposé of Joe Smith and Mormonism* (Boston, 1842), pp. 243, 245.) In November 1855 the letter was copied into the manuscript of Joseph Smith's History under the date of August 27, 1842, by Thomas Bullock, a clerk in the Church Historian's Office. A manuscript copy of the letter in the Joseph Smith Papers places the date of the original writing "about January 1842" and designates it as "Joseph's Letter to Nancy Rigdon."

There are slight differences in the punctuation and word usage in Bennett's two publications of the letter in the *Sangamo Journal* and his *History of the Saints*. A comparison shows that the manuscript copy in the Smith papers and its publication in the Joseph Smith History follows the latter source. With the exception of frequent underlining and capitalization (certainly not a part of the original letter), the text used here is that of the *Sangamo Journal*.

1. On Bennett, see Cook, *Revelations of the Prophet*, p. 253; Hill, *Joseph Smith, the First Mormon*, ch. 4.
2. The beginning of plural marriage among the Latter-day Saints is discussed in Arrington and Bitton, *The Mormon Experience*, pp. 194-99; Roberts, *Comprehensive History* 2: 93-110; and Bachman, "A Study of the Mormon Practice of Plural Marriage Before the Death of Joseph Smith."
3. The Nancy Rigdon episode is reviewed in Bachman, "Plural Marriage," pp. 238-45, and Hale, "The Purported Letter of Joseph Smith to Nancy Rigdon." John W. Rigdon's statement is a deposition dated July 28, 1905. The Roberts statement is on page 134 of the Joseph Smith *History*.
4. "Secured" in *The History of the Saints* version.
5. "It is" in the *History* version.
6. "Lie" in the *History* version.
7. "More" in the *History* version.

To Edward Hunter, January 5, 1842

Ls. In the handwriting of Willard Richards, Joseph Smith Papers, LDS Church Archives. Published in Smith, *History of the Church* 4:491-92.

1. Jenson, *Biographical Encyclopedia* 1:227-32. Hunter, *Edward Hunter, Faithful Steward*, pp. 45-66.
2. On Joseph Smith's store, see Brown, "The Sacred Departments for Temple Work in Nauvoo: The Assembly Room and the Council Chamber," pp. 362-65; Flanders, *Nauvoo: Kingdom on the Mississippi*, pp. 161-63.
3. A later insertion indicates that the painting was done by Edward Martin.

Note of Authorization, February 24, 1842

ADS. Illinois State Historical Library, Springfield, Illinois.

1. "Items of Personal History of the Editor," pp. 257-62; Smith, *History of the Church* 4:239. Stocks, "The Book of Mormon, 1830-1879: A Publishing History," pp. 51-65.

To Edward Hunter, March 9, 11, 1842

LS. In the handwriting of William Law and Willard Richards, Joseph Smith Papers, LDS Church Archives. Published in Smith, *History of the Church* 4:548-49.

1. Edward Hunter to Joseph Smith, February 10, 1842.
2. Probably Jacob Weiler (1808-1896), born in Lancaster County, Pennsylvania. At age ten, he, with his family, moved to Brandywine, Chester County, Pennsylvania, where Jacob worked as a miller. After hearing Mormon missionaries preach in the West Nantmeal seminary, he joined the Latter-day Saints and moved to Nauvoo in July 1841. He later served nearly forty years as bishop of the Salt Lake City Third Ward. (Journal History, May 1, 1897, p. 2.)
3. The portion of the letter written March 9 is in the handwriting of William Law, and the March 11 segment by Willard Richards.

To Jennetta Richards, June 23, 1842

Ls. In the handwriting of William Clayton, Joseph Smith Papers, LDS Church Archives. Published in Smith, *History of the Church* 5:40-41.

1. Jenson, *Biographical Encyclopedia* 1:53-56.

To Emma Smith, August 16, 1842

Rc. The earliest known copy of this letter is in the hand of William Clayton, "The Book of the Law of the Lord," pp. 173-75, LDS Church Archives. Published in Smith, *History of the Church* 5:103-5.

1. Smith, *History of the Church* 5:86-98. On the Boggs assassination attempt see McLaws, "The Attempted Assassination of Missouri's Ex-Governor, Lilburn W. Boggs," pp. 50-62; and Jennings, "Two Iowa Postmasters View Nauvoo: Anti-Mormon Letters to the Governor of Missouri," pp. 275-92.
   The opinion of U.S. District Attorney Justin Butterfield on the legality of the Joseph Smith arrest attempt on the Boggs charge is found in a Butterfield letter to Sidney Rigdon dated October 20, 1842, Smith, *History of the Church* 5:173-79. The charge against Joseph Smith was dismissed by Illinois Supreme Court judge Nathanial Pope at a hearing on the case in Springfield, Illinois, in January 1843. (Smith, *History of the Church* 5:220-45.)
2. In September 1841 an expedition from Nauvoo established a sawmill near the falls of the Black River on Winnebago Indian lands in present-day Jackson County, Wisconsin, to provide lumber for Nauvoo building projects—notably the Nauvoo House and the Nauvoo Temple. As bishop, and one of the trustees of the Nauvoo House Association, George Miller played a leading role in the Wisconsin "pinery." (Flanders, *Nauvoo: Kingdom on the Mississippi*, pp. 182-85.)
3. Erastus H. Derby (1810-1890) was born at Hawley, Franklin County, Massachusetts. He married Ruhamah B. Knowlton in 1834. Four of their twelve children had been born at the time of the writing of this letter. On August 29, 1843, Derby was bound over to keep the peace for six months before the Nauvoo mayor's court, at which time he gave up his license as an elder in the Church. The birthplaces of subsequent children indicate that he was living in Cook County, Illinois, and Williams County, Ohio, between 1844 and 1860. (Smith, *History of the Church* 5:556; Family Group Records Collection.)
4. George Miller (1794-1856) was born in Virginia. He moved to Kentucky in 1806 and to

Illinois by 1834. Baptized by John Taylor in 1839, he was appointed in January 1841 to replace Edward Partridge as bishop and, in October, Don Carlos Smith as president of the high priests in Nauvoo. In 1842 he was designated brigadier-general of the first cohort of the Nauvoo Legion. After the death of Joseph Smith, he followed Lyman Wight to Texas and later joined with James J. Strang. (Cook, "A More Virtuous Man . . . ," pp. 402-7; Mills, "De Tal Palo Tal Astilla," pp. 86-112.)

5. William Law (1809-1892), born in northern Ireland. After coming to America, Law settled in Mercer County, Pennsylvania, and later moved to Churchville, Ontario, Canada, where he was converted in 1836. He moved to Nauvoo in 1839 and was appointed counselor in the First Presidency in 1841. He left the Church in 1844. (Cook, "'Brother Joseph is Truly a Wonderful Man . . . ,'" pp. 207-18.)

6. James H. Ralston, a Democrat, had served on the Illinois Supreme Court as fifth circuit justice, and on the state legislature. As a friend of the Latter-day Saints, Ralston's name had been substituted for that of the Whig presidential elector, Abraham Lincoln, in the 1840 election, although the Saints had generally voted Whig. (Oaks and Hill, *Carthage Conspiracy*, pp. 77-78, 92-93.)

7. Probably Lorin Walker.

8. William Clayton (1814-1879) was a convert from England who arrived in Nauvoo in 1840. He began secretarial work in Joseph Smith's office early in 1842, and when Willard Richards was absent from Nauvoo between June and October, the major clerical responsibility of the office was Clayton's. (Jenson, *Biographical Encyclopedia* 1:717-18.)

9. Lorenzo Wasson (ca. 1818-1857) was born at Amboy, Lee County, Illinois. A nephew of Emma Smith, he was the eldest son of Elizabeth Hale and Benjamin Wasson. (Family Group Records Collection.)

To Wilson Law, August 16, 1842

Rc. In the handwriting of William Clayton, Joseph Smith Papers, LDS Church Archives. Published in Smith, *History of the Church* 5:105-6.

1. Wilson Law (1807-1877), brother of William Law, was a charter member of the Nauvoo city council and was elected brigadier general of the Nauvoo Legion in 1841. (Smith, *History of the Church* 4:287, 296.)

2. In his letter of the previous day, Law had written affirming his devotion to "the glorious cause of liberty and truth," and his readiness "in a moment's warning to defend the rights of man, both civil and religious." (Law to Smith, August 15, 1842, in Smith, *History of the Church* 5:96.)

Reflections, August 16, 23, 1842

Ms. In the handwriting of William Clayton, "The Book of the Law of the Lord," pp. 135, 164-65, 179-81, LDS Church Archives. Published in Smith, *History of the Church* 5: 106-9, 124-28.

1. "The Book of the Law of the Lord" is a large leather-bound letterbook-diary-account book containing copies of letters, revelations, and other documents of historical importance intermixed with Joseph Smith's diary entries and a record of donations to the Church during the Prophet's Nauvoo years. It is the original source for portions of Joseph Smith's History of the Church.

2. Dimick B. Huntington (1808-1879) was born at Watertown, Jefferson County, New York. On March 8, 1841, he was appointed one of the Nauvoo city constables and on

May 23, 1842, coroner of the city. (Jenson, *Biographical Encyclopedia* 4:748; Smith, *History of the Church* 4:308; 5:18.)

3. John Davis Parker (1799-1891) was born at Saratoga, New York. A wagonwright and farmer, he married Almeda Roundy, daughter of Shadrach Roundy. He was a member of the first quorum of the seventy after participating in Zion's Camp. He guarded Joseph Smith during his 1842 exile. (Esshom, *Pioneers and Prominent Men,* p. 1086.)

4. Amasa Lyman (1813-1877) was born in Lyman, Grafton County, New Hampshire. He joined the Church in 1832 and moved to Kirtland, Ohio. After the expulsion from Missouri, Lyman settled in Lee County, Iowa, in 1840 but moved to Nauvoo in 1841. He was appointed to the Council of the Twelve in August 1842. (Cook, *Revelations of the Prophet,* pp. 266-67.)

5. Joseph Bates Noble (1810-1900) was born at Egremont, Berkshire County, Massachusetts. Converted by Brigham Young in 1832, he participated in Zion's Camp. In August 1841 he was named counselor to Elias Smith in the Iowa Stake. Later that year he moved to Nauvoo and was appointed bishop of the Fifth Ward. Noble had performed the marriage that joined his sister-in-law, Louisa Beman, to Joseph Smith in April 1841. (Jenson, *Historical Record* 6:237-40.)

6. Arthur Milliken (1817-1882) was born at Saco, Maine. In Nauvoo he was employed as scribe for William Smith in recording patriarchal blessings. Milliken married Joseph Smith's youngest sister, Lucy, in 1840. (*Utah Genealogical and Historical Magazine* 26:152.)

7. Jonathan Dunham (1800-1845) was captain of the Nauvoo police.

8. Joseph Knight (1772-1847), born at Oakham, Worcester County, Massachusetts, was one of the first converts to the Church. He was visiting in the Smith home when Joseph Smith obtained the Book of Mormon plates in September 1827. While working on the translation at Harmony, Pennsylvania, Joseph was occasionally employed by Knight, then living at Colesville, New York. (*Utah Genealogical and Historical Magazine* 26:108; Smith, *History of the Church* 1:47.)

9. Joseph Knight, Jr., (1808-1866) was born at Halifax, Vermont. (*Utah Genealogical and Historical Magazine* 26:146.)

10. Orrin Porter Rockwell (1813-1879) was one of the Church's early converts. He was born at Belcher, Massachusetts. (*Utah Genealogical and Historical Magazine* 26:154.)

To the Whitneys, August 18, 1842

ALS. Photocopy in Joseph Smith Papers, LDS Church Archives.

1. Jenson, *Biographical Encyclopedia* 1:222-27.

2. Ibid., p. 226; J. F. Smith, *Blood Atonement and the Origin of Plural Marriage,* pp. 73-74. Revelation of July 27, 1842.

"Sealings" were ordinances whereby righteous husbands and wives, including plural wives, were joined under priesthood authority for time and eternity. Not all sealings involved connubial relationships.

To All the Saints, September 1, 1842

Ls. In the handwriting of William Clayton, Joseph Smith Papers, LDS Church Archives. Although the letter was written by William Clayton and also addressed to him, it contains a broken wax seal as if it had been carried and then opened. Published in Smith, *History of the Church* 5:142-44.

1. Smith, *History of the Church* 5:136-38, 141-53.

To James A. Bennet, September 8, 1842

RC. In the hand of William Clayton, Joseph Smith Papers, LDS Church Archives. Published in Smith, *History of the Church* 5:156-59.

1. Lyndon Cook notes that Bennet became associated with Joseph Smith through John C. Bennett about 1841, and that he was an "apparent unscrupulous opportunist" who "had fantasies which included fame as an author, governor of Illinois, general of the Nauvoo Legion, and successor to Joseph Smith." Bennet was baptized by Brigham Young but regarded the ordinance as "a mere 'frolic in the clear blue ocean.'" (Cook, "James Arlington Bennet and the Mormons," pp. 247-49.) Also Newell and Avery, "New Light on the Sun: Emma Smith and the *New York Sun* Letter," pp. 23-25.
2. Willard Richards to Joseph Smith, August 9, 1842.
3. At a conference of the Church held in New York City, April 15, 1841, Lucien R. Foster was elected president of the branch, and John Bernhisel, bishop. (Smith, *History of the Church* 4:344.)
4. James Gordon Bennett was editor of the *New York Herald*. In December 1841 Bennett's favorable treatment of the Saints in the *Herald* brought a resolution from Joseph Smith before the Nauvoo city council urging the citizens to subscribe to the *Herald* "and thus be found patronizing true merit, industry, and enterprise." (Smith, *History of the Church* 4:477-78.)

To Sidney Rigdon, March 27, 1843

Rc. In the handwriting of Willard Richards, Joseph Smith Papers, LDS Church Archives. Published in Smith, *History of the Church* 5:312-14.

1. Joseph Smith to Horace Hotchkiss, November 26, 1842, in Smith, *History of the Church* 5:195-96.
2. Joseph Smith to Richard M. Young, February 9, 1843, in Smith, *History of the Church* 5:266-67.
3. The letter was delivered by Willard Richards the same day Joseph wrote it, and Sidney Rigdon immediately penned an answer. Rigdon wrote in a very conciliatory tone, disclaiming any connection with Bennett or wrongdoing as postmaster. With respect to Jared Carter, Rigdon wrote, "If there is anything in his mind unfavorably disposed to you, he has, as far as I know, kept it to himself; for he never said anything to me, nor in my hearing, from which I could draw even an inference of that kind." (Smith, *History of the Church* 5:314-16.) At the 1842 October conference Joseph proposed to dismiss Sidney Rigdon as his counselor, but Hyrum Smith and others urged leniency, and the proposition was defeated.

To Lucien Adams, October 2, 1843

ALS. Location of the original not known. The text here is from a photocopy in the Joseph Smith Papers, LDS Church Archives.

1. James Adams (1783-1843) was born at Limsbury, Hartford County, Connecticut. After marrying Harriet Denton, also of Hartford, in 1809, Adams moved to Oswego, New York, where their five children were born. Moving to Springfield, Illinois, in 1821, Adams practiced law and served as justice of the peace for many years beginning about 1823. He fought in the Winnebago and Black Hawk Indian wars in 1827 and 1831-32. He was one of the founders of the Springfield Masonic Lodge in 1839 and was elected

Sangamon County Probate Judge in 1843, which office he held until his death. After his conversion, Adams was one of the first recipients of the endowment in May 1842 and was an early participant in the practice of plural marriage. (*History of the Early Settlers of Sangamon County, Illinois*, p. 76; Smith, *History of the Church* 5:1-2, 433, 527-28; Walgren, "James Adams: Early Springfield Mormon and Freemason," pp. 121-36.)

2. Enders, "The Steamboat Maid of Iowa: Mormon Mistress of the Mississippi," pp. 321-35; Oaks and Bentley, "Joseph Smith and Legal Process: In the Wake of the Steamboat Nauvoo," p. 780.

3. Lucien Adams was born December 10, 1816, at Oswego, New York, the eldest son of James and Harriet Denton Adams. (Power, *History of the Early Settlers of Sangamon County*, p. 76.)

To William Clayton, December 9, 1843

ADS. Joseph Smith Papers, LDS Church Archives.

1. Smith, *History of the Church* 6:7-8.
2. Ibid. 6:108.

To Thomas Ford, January 1, 1844

Rc. In the handwriting of William W. Phelps, Joseph Smith Papers, LDS Church Archives.

1. Roberts, *Comprehensive History* 2:196-98; Smith, *History of the Church* 6:100-101.
2. Thomas Ford to Joseph Smith, December 12, 1844.
3. Levi Williams was the Warsaw citizen accused of having kidnapped the Averys. (Roberts, *Comprehensive History* 2:198.)
4. Accused in the assassination attempt on ex-Governor Lilburn Boggs, Rockwell was apprehended at St. Louis in March 1843, taken to Jackson County, imprisoned, mistreated, and eventually, on December 13, acquitted. Emaciated, he arrived back in Nauvoo on Christmas Day, 1843. (Smith, *History of the Church* 5:135-42; Schindler, *Orrin Porter Rockwell*, ch. 5.)

Joseph Smith III Blessing, January 17, 1844

Ms. In the handwriting of Thomas Bullock, but the filing notation on the reverse side, except for the date, is Joseph Smith's. RLDS Church Archives, Independence, Missouri. The document was acquired in February 1981 by Mark Hofmann from a descendant of Thomas Bullock. Published in *LDS Church News*, March 21, 1981.

1. See Esplin, "Joseph, Brigham and the Twelve: A Succession of Continuity," pp. 301-41; Quinn, "Joseph Smith III's 1844 Blessing and the Mormons of Utah," pp. 69-90; Hinckley, "The Joseph Smith III Document and the Keys of the Kingdom," pp. 20-22.

To Reuben McBride, January 18, 1844

Rc. In the handwriting of Thomas Bullock, Joseph Smith Papers, LDS Church Archives.

1. Reuben McBride was born at Chester, Washington County, New York, June 16, 1803. Immediately following his baptism at Villanova, Chautauqua County, New York, in

March 1834, he left with Zion's Camp. When the body of the Saints left Kirtland in 1838, McBride remained as custodian of the temple and other property. He came to Utah in 1850 but went back the following year to lead a remnant of the Kirtland Saints to Utah. (*Deseret Evening News*, March 9, 1891.)
2. Statement of Reuben McBride, December 12, 1853; also, Joseph Coe to Joseph Smith, January 1, 1844.
3. Reuben McBride to Joseph Smith, January 1, 1844.

To Joseph Coe, January 18, 1844

Rc. In the handwriting of Thomas Bullock, Joseph Smith Papers, LDS Church Archives.

To Joseph L. Heywood, February 13, 1844

Rc. In the handwriting of William Clayton, Joseph Smith Papers, LDS Church Archives.
Published in Smith, *History of the Church* 6:213-14.

1. Jenson, *Biographical Encyclopedia* 1:646-48; *Deseret Evening News*, November 5, 1910, p. 8.

To Barbara Matilda Neff, May 1844

ADS. Papers of Barbara Matilda Neff Moses, LDS Church Archives.

1. Jenson, *Biographical Encyclopedia* 2:785-86.
2. The Phelps and Smith entries in the autograph book are dated by the other Nauvoo writings in the book, written between May 8 and 13, 1844.

To Joel Hamilton Walker, June 1, 1844

Rc. In the handwriting of William W. Phelps, Joseph Smith Papers, LDS Church Archives.
Published in Smith, *History of the Church* 6:425.

1. Smith, *History of the Church* 6:275-77, 424-25.

To Mr. Tewksbury, June 4, 1844

Rc. In the handwriting of William W. Phelps, Joseph Smith Papers, LDS Church Archives.
Published in Smith, *History of the Church* 6:427.

1. Freeman Nickerson to the editor of the *Daily Ledger*, April 11, 1842, in *Times and Seasons* 3 (May 16, 1842), pp. 797-98. Journal History, September 11, 1842. Both the 1830 and 1840 Federal Census lists Abijah R. Tewksbury. In 1840 he was evidently in his forties and had a family of eight; his occupation was commerce.

To Washington Tucker, June 12, 1844

Rc. In the handwriting of John McEwan, Joseph Smith Papers, LDS Church Archives.
Published in Smith, *History of the Church* 6:459.

1. See pp. 585-86.
2. Smith, *History of the Church* 6:458-59.

To Thomas Ford, June 14, 1844

LS. In the handwriting of John McEwan, Joseph Smith Papers, LDS Church Archives. Published in Smith, *History of the Church* 6:466-67. A note on the address side of the letter indicates that it was delivered to the governor by the "politeness of S. James Special Messenger." After Governor Ford read the letter, the original was evidently returned to Joseph Smith.

1. Smith, *History of the Church* 6:430-58; Oaks and Hill, *Carthage Conspiracy*, pp. 14-16. The legal question of the destruction of the *Expositor* is dealt with in Oaks, "The Suppression of the Nauvoo Expositor," pp. 862-903.

To Thomas Ford, June 16, 1844

LS. In the handwriting of Thomas Bullock, Joseph Smith Papers, LDS Church Archives. Published in Smith, *History of the Church* 6:480. As indicated in the body of the letter and a note on the address side, the document was delivered by special messenger; the original was evidently returned to Joseph Smith.

1. Smith, *History of the Church* 6:479, 487-91, 582.
2. Smith, *History of the Church* 6:480-82.

To Isaac Morley, June 16, 1844

Rc. In the handwriting of Willard Richards, Joseph Smith Papers, LDS Church Archives. Published in Smith, *History of the Church* 6:482-83.

To John Smith, June 17, 1844

LS. In the handwriting of William Clayton, Joseph Smith Papers, LDS Church Archives. Published in Smith, *History of the Church* 6:485-86.

To Thomas Ford, June 22, 1844

Dft. In the handwriting of John McEwan, Joseph Smith Papers, LDS Church Archives. There are two drafts of this letter, the other being in the hand of William Clayton. Published in Smith, *History of the Church* 6:525-27.

1. Smith, *History of the Church* 6:497; Thomas Ford to Joseph Smith, June 21, 1844.
2. All insertions and other textual alterations in the letter are penciled in a different hand than McEwan's.
3. The earlier draft of the letter designates Colonel Woodworth and Dr. Lyons as the bearers of the letter. The McEwan draft retained the plural "bearers" and "men," although Lyons's name was left out.
4. "Fact well known" has been designated for transposition to "well known fact."
5. The Joseph Jackson affidavits are in Smith, *History of the Church* 6:524.

To Emma Smith, June 23, 1844

LS. In the handwriting of Willard Richards, RLDS Church Archives, Independence, Missouri. Published in *History of the Reorganized Church* 2:770.

1. Thomas Ford to Joseph Smith, June 22, 1844. In Smith, *History of the Church* 6:533-37.
2. Joseph Smith to Thomas Ford, June 22, 1844, 12:00 P.M., in Smith, *History of the Church* 6:538-41.

To Maria and Sarah Lawrence, June 23, 1844

Tr. In an unknown hand, Joseph Smith Papers, LDS Church Archives. Handwriting characteristics suggest that the letter is probably a copy made at a later time.

1. Maria Lawrence was born at Pickering, Upper Canada, on December 18, 1823, and her sister, Sarah, at the same place, on May 13, 1826. They were daughters of Edward and Margaret Lawrence. Following Edward's death, Margaret married Josiah Butterfield in Nauvoo. Maria and Sarah were sealed to Joseph Smith in 1843. After the death of the Prophet, Maria married Almon W. Babbitt in 1846, but she and their only child died the next year. After marrying Heber C. Kimball in 1846 and divorcing him in 1851, Sarah married Joseph Mount and went with him to California. She died at San Francisco in 1872. (*Deseret News*, August 6, 1897, p. 5; Cook, "Brother Joseph Is Truly a Wonderful Man . . . ," p. 211; Kimball, *Heber C. Kimball*, p. 310.)
2. John Tyler (1790-1862) became tenth President of the U.S. on the death of William Henry Harrison in 1841.

To Thomas Ford, June 23, 1844

Rc. In the handwriting of Willard Richards, Joseph Smith Papers, LDS Church Archives. Published in Smith, *History of the Church* 6:550.

1. Smith, *History of the Church* 6:548-50; Oaks and Hill, *Carthage Conspiracy*, p. 17.
2. "Us" written over "Me."
3. "We" written over "I."

To Thomas Ford, June 24, 1844

Rc. In the handwriting of Willard Richards, Joseph Smith Papers, LDS Church Archives. Published in Smith, *History of the Church* 6:556.

1. Smith, *History of the Church* 6:553-56.

To Emma Smith, June 25, 1844

Rc. In the handwriting of John Taylor, Joseph Smith Papers, LDS Church Archives. Published in Smith, *History of the Church* 6:565.

1. Smith, *History of the Church* 6:559-65; Oaks and Hill, *Carthage Conspiracy*, p. 17.

To Thomas Ford, June 26, 1844

Ls. In the handwriting of Willard Richards, Joseph Smith Papers, LDS Church Archives. Published in Smith, *History of the Church* 6:575-76.

1. Oaks, "The Suppression of the Nauvoo Expositor," pp. 866-67; Oaks and Hill, *Carthage Conspiracy*, pp. 18-19; Smith, *History of the Church* 6:567-76.
2. The Governor's reply, appended to Joseph's letter, was received back at the jail at twelve minutes before 9:00 A.M. on June 26: "The interview will take place at my earliest leisure to day. Thomas Ford".

To Judge Thomas, June 26, 1844

Rc. In the handwriting of Willard Richards, Joseph Smith Papers, LDS Church Archives. Published in Smith, *History of the Church* 6:590-91.

To Emma Smith, June 27, 1844

ALS. RLDS Church Archives, Independence, Missouri. The nonholograph portions of the letter were written by Willard Richards. Published in *History of the Reorganized Church* 2:771.

1. Joseph Smith Diary (kept by Willard Richards), June 27, 1844; Smith, *History of the Church* 6:576-613; Oaks and Hill, *Carthage Conspiracy*, pp. 19-20.
2. With the demise of John C. Bennett, Jonathan Dunham had become acting major general of the Nauvoo Legion.
3. Probably Colonel J. Brewer, the U.S. Army officer who arrived with his wife at the Mansion House about 9:00 P.M. on June 22 and on June 26 was among the witnesses listed for the Joseph Smith trial. (Smith, *History of the Church* 6:525, 576.)

To Lawyer Browning, June 27, 1844

Rc. In the handwriting of Willard Richards, Joseph Smith Papers, LDS Church Archives. Published in Smith, *History of the Church* 6:613.

1. The thirty-nine-year-old Quincy lawyer Orville H. Browning was regarded as the most able speaker in the state. He had eloquently defended Joseph Smith before Stephen A. Douglas at Monmouth when the Prophet was arrested in an 1841 Missouri extradition attempt. (Smith, *History of the Church* 4:367-70; Oaks and Hill, *Carthage Conspiracy*, pp. 80-81.)

To Jonathan Dunham, June 27, 1844

ALS. Original in private hands.

1. Ford, *History of Illinois*, pp. 339-42.
2. James W. Singleton (1811-1892) was born in Virginia. He practiced law at Mount Sterling and later served in the U.S. House of Representatives from 1879 to 1883. Captain Singleton and his contingent of Brown County, Illinois, militia were sent on June 25, according to Governor Ford, to "guard" Nauvoo and "take command of the Legion." (Clayton, *Illinois Fact Book*, p. 118; Ford, *History*, p. 555.)

3. According to Allen Stout, an officer in the Nauvoo Legion, "Dunham did not let a single man or mortal know that he had received such orders and we were kept in the City under arms not knowing but all was well, till the mob came and forced the prison and slew Joseph and Hyrum Smith." (Allen Stout, Autobiography and Diary, p. 21.) According to Stenhouse, Dunham "put the Prophet's communication into his pocket and gave no heed to the call for help. No one was acquainted with the contents of the paper, and the officer was, therefore, he presumed, safe in disregarding it." Stenhouse added, "After the Prophet's death, by some accident or other, this communication was lost and was picked up on the street and read. The intelligence that Joseph had called for aid and none had been rendered him was soon bruited among the Saints, and excited their deepest indignation, as they were not only ready to march at a moment's notice, but were eager for the opportunity." (Stenhouse, *Rocky Mountain Saints,* p. 164.)

   Considering Joseph Smith's letter to Emma (written the same day as the Dunham letter) urging her to "tell Bro Dunham to instruct the people to stay at home and attend to their own business and let there be no groups or gathering together unless by permission of the Governor" and emphasizing, "Bro Dunham of course, will obey the orders of the Government officers, and render them the assistance they require"; and not knowing the sequence in which Dunham received the two sets of June 27 instructions from Joseph; and considering the order given by Governor Ford on June 25 to Captain Singleton; and not knowing the extent of Singleton's jurisdiction over the Nauvoo Legion; it is difficult to substantiate the Stout-Stenhouse scenario regarding Dunham's June 27 actions or to know why the Prophet's call for the Nauvoo Legion went unheeded.

Bibliography

Allen, James B., and Malcom R. Thorp. "The Mission of the Twelve to England, 1840-41: Mormon Apostles and the Working Classes." *BYU Studies* 15 (Summer 1975): 499-526.

Allen, James B., and Glen Leonard. *Story of the Latter-day Saints.* Salt Lake City: Deseret Book Co., 1976.

Alton Commercial Gazette, Alton, Illinois, February 19, 1839.

The American Revivalist and Rochester Observer. Rochester, New York. 1832.

Ames, Ira. Autobiography and Journal, 1836. Ms. LDS Church Archives, Salt Lake City, Utah.

Anderson, Mary Audentia. *Ancestry and Posterity of Joseph Smith and Emma Hale.* Independence, Missouri: Herald Publishing House, 1929.

Anderson, Richard L. "Gold Plates and Printer's Ink." *Ensign* (September 1976): 71-76.

————. *Investigating the Book of Mormon Witnesses.* Salt Lake City: Deseret Book Co., 1981.

————. "Joseph Smith's New York Reputation Reappraised." *BYU Studies* 10 (Spring 1970): 283-314.

Angell, Truman O. Autobiographical Sketches. 1875, 1884. Ms. LDS Church Archives, Salt Lake City, Utah.

Arrington, Leonard J. "Church Leaders in Liberty Jail." *BYU Studies* 13 (Autumn 1972): 20-26.

————. "Oliver Cowdery's Kirtland, Ohio, 'Sketch Book.'" *BYU Studies* 12 (Summer 1972): 414-15.

Arrington, Leonard J., Feramorz Y. Fox, and Dean L. May. *Building the City of God: Community and Cooperation Among the Mormons.* Salt Lake City: Deseret Book Co., 1976.

Arrington, Leonard J., and Davis Bitton. *The Mormon Experience.* New York: Alfred A. Knopf and Company, 1979.

Asher and Adams New Topographical Atlas and Gazetteer of New York. New York, 1870.

Atchison, David R., and A. W. Doniphan. Letter to Colonel Mason, October 27, 1838. Ms. LDS Church Archives, Salt Lake City, Utah. Photocopy.

Atkinson, Eleanor. "The Winter of the Deep Snow." *Illinois State Historical Society Occasional Publications (Transactions)*: 47:62. 1901.

Atlas of Chautauqa Co., N.Y., 1881.

Bachman, Danel. "A Look at the Newly Discovered Joseph Smith Manuscript." *Ensign* 10 (July 1980): pp. 69-73.

———. "A Study of the Mormon Practice of Plural Marriage Before the Death of Joseph Smith." Master's thesis, Purdue University, 1975.

———. "Sealed in a Book: Preliminary Observations on the Newly Found 'Anthon Transcript.'" *BYU Studies* 20 (Summer 1980): 321-45.

Barber, John W., and Henry Howe. *Historical Collections of the State of New York*. New York, 1841.

Barrett, Gwynn W. "John M. Bernhisel, Mormon Elder in Congress." Ph.D. diss., Brigham Young University, 1968.

Bell, Charles H. *Bench and Bar of New Hampshire*. New York, 1894.

Bennett, John C. *The History of the Saints: An Exposé of Joe Smith and Mormonism*. Boston, 1842.

Berrett, LaMar C. "An Impressive Letter from the Pen of Joseph Smith." *BYU Studies* 11 (Summer 1971): 517-23.

Bowen, Walter D. "The Versatile W. W. Phelps: Mormon Writer, Educator, and Pioneer." Master's thesis, Brigham Young University, 1957.

Brown, Lisle G. "The Sacred Departments for Temple Work in Nauvoo: The Assembly Room and the Council Chamber." *BYU Studies* 19 (Spring 1979): 362-65.

Carr, Edward H. *What Is History?* New York: Alfred A. Knopf & Company, 1961.

Chester County Register and Examiner. Chester County, Pennsylvania.

Colton's General Atlas. New York, 1874.

Conard, Howard, ed. *Encyclopedia of the History of Missouri*. St. Louis, Missouri, 1901. 6 vols.

Cook, Lyndon W. "A More Virtuous Man. . . ." *BYU Studies* 19 (Spring 1979): 402-7.

———. "'Brother Joseph is Truly a Wonderful Man. He Is All We Could Wish a Prophet to Be': Pre-1844 Letters of William Law." *BYU Studies* 20 (Winter 1980): 207-18.

———. "Isaac Galland—Mormon Benefactor." *BYU Studies* 19 (Spring 1979): 261-84.

———. "James Arlington Bennet and the Mormons." *BYU Studies* 19 (Winter 1979): 247-49.

———. *The Revelations of the Prophet Joseph Smith*. Provo, Utah: Seventy's Mission Bookstore, 1981.

Corrill, John. *Brief History of the Church of Jesus Christ of Latter Day Saints*. St. Louis, Missouri, 1839.

Cowdery, Oliver. Diary. 1836. Ms. LDS Church Archives, Salt Lake City, Utah.

Crawley, Peter, and Richard L. Anderson. "The Political and Social Realities of Zion's Camp." *BYU Studies* 14 (Summer 1974): 406-20.

Crossby, P. A., ed. *Lovell's Gazetter of British North America.* Montreal, 1881.

Curtis, Carl C. Cowdery Genealogical Material. Ms. LDS Genealogical Department, Salt Lake City, Utah.

Deseret News. February 3, 1858; May 26, 1858; June 9, 1858; March 9, 1891; November 5, 1910.

Divett, Robert T. "His Chastening Rod: Cholera Epidemics and the Mormons." *Dialogue: A Journal of Mormon Thought* 12 (Autumn 1979): 6-15.

Doctrine and Covenants, rev. ed. Salt Lake City: The Church of Jesus Christ of Latter-day Saints, 1981.

Dunham, Jonathan. Autobiography and Diary. Ms. LDS Church Archives, Salt Lake City,Utah.

Dunklin, Daniel to Wm. W. Phelps, Isaac Morley, John Whitmer, Edward Partridge, John Corrill, and A. S. Gilbert, February 4, 1834. Ms. LDS Church Archives, Salt Lake City, Utah.

Early Church Information File. LDS Genealogical Department, Salt Lake City, Utah.

Edwards, F. Henry, ed. *History of the Reorganized Church of Jesus Christ of Latter Day Saints.* Independence, Missouri: Herald Publishing House, 1967.

Elders' Journal of the Church of Latter Day Saints, 1837-1838. Kirtland, Ohio [Far West, Missouri].

Enders, Donald L. "The Steamboat Maid of Iowa: Mormon Mistress of the Mississippi." *BYU Studies* 19 (Spring 1979): 321-35.

Esplin, Ronald K. "The Emergence of Brigham Young and the Twelve to Mormon Leadership." Ph.D. diss., Brigham Young University, 1981.

————. "Joseph, Brigham and the Twelve: A Succession of Continuity." *BYU Studies* 21 (Summer 1981): 301-341.

Esshom, Frank. *Pioneers and Prominent Men of Utah.* Salt Lake City: Utah Pioneers Book Publishing Co., 1913.

The Evening and the Morning Star. Independence, Missouri, and Kirtland, Ohio, 1832-1834.

Family Group Records Collection. LDS Genealogical Department, Salt Lake City, Utah.

Far West Record, April 26, 30, 1832. Ms. LDS Church Archives, Salt Lake City, Utah. Also *Far West Record.* Edited by Donald Q. Cannon and Lyndon W. Cook. Salt Lake City: Deseret Book Co., 1983.

Flanders, Robert. *Nauvoo: Kingdom on the Mississippi.* Urbana: University of Illinois Press, 1965.

Ford, Thomas. *A History of Illinois.* Chicago, 1854.

Geauga County, Ohio, Common Pleas Court, book M, April 9, 1834; book P, September 13-15, 1834. Chicago Historical Society, Chicago, Illinois.

Gentry, Leland H. "A History of the Latter-day Saints in Northern Missouri from 1836-1839." Ph.D. diss., Brigham Young University, 1965.

————. "The Danite Band of 1838." *BYU Studies* 14 (Summer 1974): 421-50.

Hale, Van. "The Purported Letter of Joseph Smith to Nancy Rigdon." Paper presented at the sixteenth Annual Meeting of the Mormon History Association, 1981.

Harris, Martin H. Reminiscences and Journal. Ms. LDS Church Archives, Salt Lake City, Utah.

Hill, Donna. *Joseph Smith, the First Mormon.* Garden City, New York: Doubleday, 1977.

Hill, Marvin C., Keith Rooker, and Larry T. Wimmer. "The Kirtland Economy Revisited: A Market Critique of Sectarian Economics." *BYU Studies* 17 (Summer 1977): 391-475.

Hinckley, Gordon B. "The Joseph Smith III Document and the Keys of the Kingdom." *Ensign* 11 (May 1981): 20-22.

Historian's Office Journal. Ms. LDS Church Archives, Salt Lake City, Utah.

History of Caldwell and Livingston Counties, Missouri. St. Louis: National Historical Co., 1886.

History of Geauga and Lake Counties, Ohio. Philadelphia: Williams Brothers, 1878.

History of Howard and Chariton Counties, Missouri. St. Louis: National Historical Co., 1883.

History of Jackson County, Missouri. Cape Girardeau, Mo., 1966.

History of the Ohio Falls Cities and Their Counties. Cleveland, Ohio: L. A. Williams Co., 1882.

History of Ray County, Missouri. St. Louis: Missouri Historical Co., 1881.

Hockett, Homer C. *Introduction to Research in American History.* New York: Macmillan, 1931.

Howe, E. D. *Mormonism Unvailed.* Painesville, Ohio, 1834.

————. Statement, April 8, 1885. Ms. Chicago Historical Society, Chicago, Illinois.

Hunter, William E. *Edward Hunter, Faithful Steward.* Salt Lake City: Mrs. William E. Hunter, 1970.

Hurlbut, Maria S. Biographical Sketch of Her Husband D. P. Hurlbut, April 15, 1855. Ms. Chicago Historical Society, Chicago, Illinois.

Hymns. Rev. and enl. Salt Lake City: The Church of Jesus Christ of Latter-day Saints, 1948.

"Items of Personal History of the Editor." *The Return* 2 (Davis City, Iowa, May 1890): 257-62.

Jackway, David V. "The Jackway Family." Ms. Kings Daughter's Library, Palmyra, New York.

Jennings, Warren A. "The First Mormon Mission to the Indians." *The Kansas Historical Quarterly* 37 (Autumn 1971): 288-99.

————. "Two Iowa Postmasters View Nauvoo: Anti-Mormon Letter to the Governor of Missouri." *BYU Studies* 11 (Spring 1971): 275-92.

Jenson, Andrew. *Encyclopedic History of the Church of Jesus Christ of Latter-day Saints.* Salt Lake City, Utah, 1941.

————. *Latter-day Saint Biographical Encyclopedia,* 4 vols. Salt Lake City: Andrew Jenson History Co., 1901.

Jessee, Dean C. "The Early Accounts of Joseph Smith's First Vision." *BYU Studies* 9 (Spring 1969): 275-94.

————. "Howard Coray's Recollection of Joseph Smith." *BYU Studies* 17 (Spring 1977): 346.

————. "The Original Book of Mormon Manuscript." *BYU Studies* 10 (Spring 1970): 259-78.

————. "The Reliability of Joseph Smith's History." *Journal of Mormon History* 3 (1976): 23-46.

———. "'Walls, Grates, and Screeking Iron Doors': The Prison Experience of Mormon Leaders in Missouri—1838-1839." Paper presented at the Restoration History Lecture Series, Graceland College, Lamoni, Iowa, February 25, 1980.

———. "The Writing of Joseph Smith's History." *BYU Studies* 11 (Spring 1971): 439-73.

Journal History of the Church of Jesus Christ of Latter-day Saints, 1830—. Ms. LDS Church Archives, Salt Lake City, Utah.

Kimball, Heber C. "The Journal and Record of Heber Chase Kimball." Ms. LDS Church Archives, Salt Lake City, Utah.

Kimball, Stanley B. "The Anthon Transcript: People, Primary Sources, and Problems." *BYU Studies* 10 (Spring 1970): 325-52.

———. *Heber C. Kimball.* Urbana: University of Illinois Press, 1981.

Kirtland Council Minutes. Ms. LDS Church Archives, Salt Lake City, Utah.

Kirtland Revelation Book. Ms. LDS Church Archives, Salt Lake City, Utah.

Latter Day Saints' Messenger and Advocate. Kirtland, Ohio 1834-1837.

Longworth's American Almanac, New York Register, and City Directory. (New York). 1822-1848.

Lyon, T. Edgar. "Independence, Missouri, and the Mormons, 1827-1833." *BYU Studies* 13 (Autumn 1962): 10-19.

Malone, Dumas. *Dictionary of American Biography.* New York: Charles Scribner's Sons, 1962.

Marks, Geoffrey, and William K. Beatty. *Epidemics.* New York: Charles Scribner's Sons, 1976.

Matthews, Robert. *A Plainer Translation: Joseph Smith's Translation of the Bible.* Provo, Utah: Brigham Young University Press, 1975.

May, Ernest R. "Ghost Writing and History." *American Scholar* 22 (Autumn 1953): 460-61.

Maynard, Gregory. "Alexander William Doniphan: Man of Justice." *BYU Studies* 13 (Summer 1973): 462-72.

McGavin, Cecil E. *The Family of Joseph Smith.* Salt Lake City: Bookcraft, 1963.

McLaws, Monte B. "Attempted Assassination of Missouri's Ex-Governor, Lilburn W. Boggs." *Missouri Historical Review* 60 (October 1965): 50-62.

McRae, Joseph, and Eunice McRae. *Historical Facts Regarding the Liberty and Carthage Jails.* Salt Lake City: Utah Printing, 1954.

Michener, James A. "My First 75 Years." *Family Weekly,* October 10, 1982.

Miller, David, and Della Miller. *Nauvoo: the City of Joseph.* Santa Barbara: Peregrine Smith, 1974.

Mills, H. W. "De Tal Palo Tal Astilla." *Annual Publications of the Historical Society of Southern California* 10 (1917): 86-112.

Moore, H. Miles. *Early History of Leavenworth City and County.* Leavenworth, Kansas, 1906.

Moses, Matilda Neff. Papers. LDS Church Archives, Salt Lake City, Utah.

Mulholland, James. Diary. Ms. LDS Church Archives, Salt Lake City, Utah.

Nauvoo Restoration Index. Ms. Nauvoo Restoration. LDS Church Archives, Salt Lake City, Utah.

Newell, Linda K., and Valeen T. Avery. "New Light on the Sun: Emma Smith and the *New York Sun* Letter." *Journal of Mormon History* 6 (1979): 23-25.

Oaks, Dallin H. "The Suppression of the Nauvoo Expositor." *Utah Law Review* 9 (Winter 1965): 862-903.

Oaks, Dallin H., and Joseph I. Bentley. "Joseph Smith and Legal Process: In the Wake of the Steamboat Nauvoo." *BYU Law Review* 3 (1976): 735-82.

Oaks, Dallin H., and Marvin S. Hill. *Carthage Conspiracy: The Trial of the Accused Assassins of Joseph Smith.* Urbana: University of Illinois Press, 1975.

Painesville [Ohio] *Telegraph.* "To the Public." January 31, 1834.

Parkin, Max. *Conflict at Kirtland: A Study of the Nature and Causes of External and Internal Conflict of the Mormons in Ohio between 1830 and 1838.* Salt Lake City: Max H. Parkin, 1966.

———. "A History of the Latter-day Saints in Clay County, Missouri, from 1833 to 1837." Ph.D. diss., Brigham Young University, 1976.

———. "Missouri's Impact on the Church." *Ensign* 9 (April 1979): 57-63.

Partridge, Elinore H., "Characteristics of Joseph Smith's Style and Notes on the Authorship of the Lectures on Faith." Task Papers in LDS History. No. 14. 1976.

Perrin, William H., ed. *History of Summit County Ohio.* Chicago, 1881.

Phelps, Leah Y. "Letters of Faith from Kirtland." *Improvement Era* 45 (August 1942): 529.

Phelps, William W. Letters. LDS Genealogical Library, Salt Lake City, Utah.

———. Papers. LDS Church Archives, Salt Lake City, Utah.

"Plan of Mount Pleasant and Phelps Tracts." Ms. LDS Church Archives, Salt Lake City, Utah.

Plimpton, George. "Interview with Ernest Hemingway." *Writers at Work: The Paris Review Interviews, Second Series.* New York: Viking Press, 1963.

Porter, Larry. "A Study of the Origins of The Church of Jesus Christ of Latter-day Saints in the States of New York and Pennsylvania, 1816-1831." Ph.D. diss., Brigham Young University, 1971.

Power, John C. *History of the Early Settlers of Sangamon County.* Springfield, Illinois, 1876.

Pratt, Orson. *An Interesting Account of Several Remarkable Visions.* Edinburgh, Scotland, 1840.

Pratt, Parley P. *Autobiography of Parley Parker Pratt.* Salt Lake City: Deseret Book Co., 1938.

———. *History of the Late Persecution Inflicted by the State of Missouri upon the Mormons.* Detroit, 1839.

Proper, David R. "Joseph Smith and Salem." *Essex Institute Historical Collection* 100 (April 1964): 88-97.

Quinn, D. Michael. "Jesse Gause: Joseph Smith's Little-known Counselor." Forthcoming in *BYU Studies.*

———. "Joseph Smith III's 1844 Blessing and the Mormons of Utah." *Dialogue* 15 (Summer 1982): 69-90.

A Record of the First Quorum of Elders Belonging to the Church of Christ: in Kirtland Geauga Co. Ohio." Ms. RLDS Church Archives.

"A Record of the High Priests of the Ninth Ward of the City of Nauvoo," November 22, 1844-February 19, 1845. Ms. LDS Church Archives, Salt Lake City, Utah.

"A Record of the Transactions of the Twelve Apostles of the Church of Christ . . . " 1835. Ms. LDS Church Archives, Salt Lake City, Utah.

Rich, Russell R. "Where Were the Moroni Visits?" *BYU Studies* 10 (Spring 1970): 255-58.

Roberts, Brigham H. *A Comprehensive History of The Church of Jesus Christ of Latter-day Saints, Century One.* 6 vols. Salt Lake City: The Church of Jesus Christ of Latter-day Saints, 1930. Also 2nd ed. rev. 1964.

Robinson, Ebenezer. "Items of Personal History of the Editor." *The Return.* Davis City, Iowa: Church of Christ. 1889-1890.

The Saints' Herald. (January 1860) Reorganized Church of Jesus Christ of Latter Day Saints. Lamoni, Iowa.

Sangamon Journal. 1831-1850. Springfield, Illinois.

Seldes, Gilbert. *The Stammering Century.* New York: Peter Smith, 1928.

Schindler, Harold. *Orrin Porter Rockwell: Man of God, Son of Thunder.* Salt Lake City: University of Utah Press, 1966.

Smith, George A. "Memoirs of George Albert Smith." Ms. LDS Church Archives, Salt Lake City, Utah.

Smith, Joseph. Diary. Ms. LDS Church Archives, Salt Lake City, Utah.

———. History of the Church. 6 vols. Ms. LDS Church Archives, Salt Lake City, Utah.

———. *History of the Church of Jesus Christ of Latter-day Saints.* B. H. Roberts, ed. 7 vols., 2nd ed. rev. Salt Lake City, Utah, 1964.

———. Papers. Beinecke Rare Book and Manuscript Library, Yale University, New Haven, Connecticut; Chicago Historical Society, Chicago, Illinois; Huntington Library, San Marino, California; Illinois State Historical Library, Springfield, Illinois; LDS Church Archives, Salt Lake City, Utah; Pennsylvania Historical Society, Philadelphia, Pennsylvania; RLDS Church Archives, Independence, Missouri; University of Utah Library, Salt Lake City, Utah.

———. "The Book of the Law of the Lord." Ms. LDS Church Archives, Salt Lake City, Utah.

Smith, Joseph, III. Letter to Albert Hager. June 12, 1885. Ms. Chicago Historical Society.

Smith, Joseph F., Jr. *Blood Atonement and the Origin of Plural Marriage.* Salt Lake City: Deseret News Press, 1905.

Smith, Lucy Mack. *Biographical Sketches of Joseph Smith the Prophet and His Progenitors for Many Generations.* Liverpool, England: 1853.

———. "The History of Lucy Smith Mother of the Prophet." Ms. LDS Church Archives, Salt Lake City, Utah.

Smith, Ruby K. *Mary Bailey.* Salt Lake City: Deseret Book Co., 1954.

Smith, Samuel H. Diary. LDS Church Archives, Salt Lake City, Utah.

Smith, William H. *Smiths' Canadian Gazetteer.* Toronto, 1846.

Snow, Eliza R. *Biography and Family Record of Lorenzo Snow.* Salt Lake City, Utah, 1884.

Snow, Leroi C. "Who Was Professor Joshua Seixas?" *Improvement Era* 39 (February 1936): 67-71.

Sprague, Locke A. "The Progenitors and Descendants of Col. Steven Mack and Temperance Bond Mack as Related to the David Cooper and Rollin Sprague Families." Ms. LDS Genealogical Department, Salt Lake City, Utah.

"State of Missouri vs. Joseph Smith Jr. et al." Circuit Court, Daviess County, Missouri. Ms. State Historical Society of Missouri, Columbia, Missouri.

Stenhouse, Thomas B. H. *The Rocky Mountain Saints.* New York, 1873.

Stevens, John Lloyd. *Incidents of Travel in Central America, Chiapas, and Yucatan.* New York: Harper Brothers, 1841.

Stocks, Hugh C. "The Book of Mormon, 1830-1879: A Publishing History." MLA thesis, UCLA, 1979.

Stokes, I. N. Phelps. *The Iconography of Manhattan Island, 1498-1909.* New York: Robert H. Dodd, 1916.

Temple Records Index Bureau. LDS Genealogical Department, Salt Lake City, Utah.

Times and Seasons 1839-1846. Nauvoo, Illinois.

Tullidge, Edward. *The Women of Mormondom.* New York: Tullidge & Crandall, 1877.

Tyler, Daniel. Letter to Wilford Woodruff, March 3, 1881. Ms. Wilford Woodruff Papers, LDS Church Archives, Salt Lake City, Utah.

Utah Genealogical and Historical Magazine 26 (1935).

Walgren, Kent L. "James Adams: Early Springfield Mormon and Freemason." *Journal of the Illinois State Historical Society* 75 (Summer 1982): 121-36.

Walker, Ronald K. "The Willard Richards and Brigham Young 5 September 1840 Letter from England to Nauvoo." *BYU Studies* 18 (Spring 1978): 466-75.

Whitney, Orson F. *History of Utah.* 4 vols. Salt Lake City: George Q. Cannon and Sons Co., 1904.

Whitmer, John. "The Book of John Whitmer." Ms. RLDS Church Archives, Independence, Missouri. Published in *An Early Latter-day Saint History: The Book of John Whitmer.* F. Mark McKiernan and Roger D. Launius, ed. Independence, Missouri: Herald House, 1980.

Wilcox, David F., ed. *Quincy and Adams County History and Representative Men.* 2 vols. Chicago, Illinois, 1919.

Woman's Exponent 7 (July 1, 1878); 8 (June 15, 1879); 12 (March 1, 1884).

Wood, Charles T., ed. *Philip the Fair and Boniface VIII.* New York: Holt, Rinehart and Winston, 1967.

Woodruff, Wilford. Diary. LDS Church Archives, Salt Lake City, Utah.

Woodson, W. H. *History of Clay County, Missouri.* Topeka, Kansas, 1920.

Zucker, Louis C. "Joseph Smith as a Student of Hebrew." *Dialogue* 2 (Summer 1968): 41-55.

Index

Aaron called by revelation, 421
Abiram, 377
Abraham, 284, 298-300, 395
Accountability, 298
Acts, chapter three, 204
Adam-ondi-Ahman, 358, 679
Adams, James, 557, 693-94
Adams, Lucien, 557, 694
Administering to the sick: Frederick G.
   Williams to go to Cleveland for, 36; to
   Joseph Smith, Sr., 63; to JS and Warren
   Parrish, 93; to Josiah Clark, 94; to
   Angeline Works, 101-3; to Samuel
   Brannan, 104; to Sidney Rigdon, 129-30;
   to Sidney Rigdon's wife, 163; to cripples,
   296; to Thomas Marsh, 662; to Peter
   Whitmer, Jr., 662
Adultery, 379-80
Affidavit on kidnappings, 562-63
Affliction, bearing, 284-85
Agreement (May 14, 1841), 468, 686
Aldrich, James, 98
Alphabet, Egyptian. See Egyptian
Ambition, 401-2
America, 214-15. See also United States
American Revivalist, and Rochester Observer,
   269-70, 275, 672
Ames, Ira, 664
Ancestry and family of Joseph Smith, 623,
   666
Anderson, William, 230, 668
Andrew, Hazard, 38
Angell, Truman, 98-99, 656
Angels: JS sees and converses with, 75-77;
   seen in visions, 147, 151; presence of,
   during ordinance, 149; at dedication of
   temple, 180; after washing of feet, 184;
   mindful of martyred, 400-401. See also
   Moroni
Anointing, washing and: of presidencies,
   145-48; on second day, 148-49; of apostles
   and seventies, 149-50; of quorums,

150-52, 661; Oliver Cowdery describes,
   660
Anthon, Charles, 7-8, 209, 223-24, 667
Apostasy, 271-72, 351-53
Apostles. See Twelve, Council of
Ark of God, man who steadies, 261
Armor of God, 347
Arms, state, surrendering, 601-3
Arrest of Church leaders, 360-62, 585-86,
   599-603, 679-80, 690
Articles of Faith, 219-20, 667
Ashtabula, Ohio, 17
Aspirations, unrighteous, 396, 476
Assistant President of Church, 37-38, 648
Atchison, David R., 393, 417, 679, 681, 683
Australia, elders sent to, 484-85
Authority, 137, 401-2, 476, 561
Authorization, Note of (February 24, 1842),
   515, 689
Autographs, 575-76, 695
Avard, Sampson, 380-81, 405, 681-82
Avery, Allen, 60, 650
Avery, Daniel, 559, 562, 564
Avery, Philander, 559, 562

Babbitt, Almon W: accuses JS and Sidney
   Rigdon, 119, 658, 687; confession of,
   123; to deliver letter, 368; conduct of,
   475-77; fellowship withdrawn from, 477;
   to preside over Kirtland Stake, 489-90; to
   have control of plates, 494; supervises
   disposal of Church property, 572; reports
   rumor of confiscated property, 594;
   background of, 658, 680-81; marries
   Maria Lawrence, 697
Babylon, 78
Badlam, Alexander, 98-99, 657
Bail for Smiths, 606
Bailey, Calvin, 655
Bailey, Lydia, 22, 304
Bailey, Mary (sister-in-law of JS), 295, 652,
   673-74

709

Church Service (after 1830)

Revelation, Visions, Blessings

THE PERSONAL WRITINGS
OF JOSEPH SMITH
Designed by Ralph Reynolds
Jacket lettering by Warren Luch
Maps by Ralph Reynolds and Karen Morales
Composed by Easy Type
in Goudy Old Style
Printed by Fairfield Graphics
on Warren's 1854 Cream Medium, text stock
Bound by Fairfield Graphics
in Joanna Devon and stamped in white
with Multicolor Antique, Olive endsheets

19.95

9-15-92

Joseph Smith